TOUCHSTONE

BOOKS BY BARBARA GRIZZUTI HARRISON

Visions of Glory:
A History and a Memory of Jehovah's Witnesses
Unlearning the Lie:
Sexism in School

Visions of Glory

A History and a Memory
of Jehovah's Witnesses

BARBARA GRIZZUTI HARRISON

A Touchstone Book
Published by Simon and Schuster

Designed by Irving Perkins
Manufactured in the United States of America

1   2   3   4   5   6   7   8   9   10

Library of Congress Cataloging in Publication Data

Harrison, Barbara Grizzuti.
Visions of glory.

Bibliography: p.
Includes index.
1. Jehovah's Witnesses—History. 2. Harrison,
Barbara Grizzuti. 3. Converts, Catholic—Biography.
4. Jehovah's Witnesses—United States—Biography.
I. Title
BX8525.7.H37   289.9   77-29024

ISBN 0-671-22530-8
ISBN 0-671-25101-5 Pbk.

The author gratefully acknowledges permission to reprint excerpts from the following:

Statement by Dr. Walter Martin in an interview on "The 700 Club" television program broadcast June 11, 1976, Christian Broadcasting Network.

Faith on the March, by A. H. Macmillan, copyright © 1957 by A. H. Macmillan. Reprinted by permission of the publishers, Prentice Hall, Inc.

Religious Movements in Contemporary America, edited by Irving I. Zaretsky and Mark P. Leone, copyright © 1974 by Princeton University Press. Selections from E. Mansell Pattison, Lee R. Cooper, Lep Pfeffer and Nathan Adler. Reprinted by permission of the publisher, Princeton University Press.

ACKNOWLEDGMENTS

Without the support and generosity of friends and colleagues, and without the gift of time and space provided by the MacDowell Colony, I could not have written this book.

For trusting me enough to share intimate details of their lives, I thank David Maslanka, Walter Szykitka—and others who are unnamed, but not unloved. My debt to them is very great.

For the invaluable information and advice they gave so freely, I thank Bernard and Charlotte Atkins, Leon Friedman, Ralph deGia, Father Robert Kennedy, Jim Peck.

For their creative research and editorial assistance, I thank Tonia Foster and Paul Kelly—and the librarians at the Brooklyn Public Library, who eased their task.

For their perceptive insights and criticism, which helped me to understand not only my subject, but myself and my past, I thank Sheila Lehman, Tom Wilson, Sol Yurick, L. L. Zeiger, and David Zeiger.

No words can express my gratitude to the members of my family who always listened, even when their patience was sorely tried, and who were emotional bulwarks when I was sorely tried: Carol Grizzuti, Dominick Grizzuti, Richard Grizzuti; and my children (who managed, with grace, to live with my obsessions), Anna and Joshua Harrison.

For Father Michael Crimmins, Alice Hagen, and Rose Moss, who gave me a very special kind of encouragement at a very crucial time, I have love and regard.

And finally, I thank and esteem my editor, Alice E. Mayhew, for her good counsel and her good work.

(Throughout this book, I have changed names and identities to protect the privacy of those concerned.)

This book is for Arnold Horowitz

Contents

I. *Personal Beginnings: 1944*

JEHOVAH'S WITNESSES are believers in a fundamentalist, apocalyptic, prophetic religion which has been proclaiming, since the 1930s, that "Millions Now Living Will Never Die." The world will end, they say, with the destruction of the wicked at Armageddon, in our lifetime. Only the chosen will survive. They intensify their preaching efforts in order to increase the number of survivors (there are now more than two million Jehovah's Witnesses in 210 countries). They are also increasing their property holdings. [*Yearbook*, 1977,* p. 30]

The Witnesses are a widely varied group of individuals who subject themselves to total conformity in practice, outlook, and belief. To the extent to which they are known—their notoriety follows from their refusal to receive blood transfusions, salute the flag, or serve in the army of any country, as well as from their aggressive proselytizing—they are perceived as rather drab, somewhat eccentric people and dismissed as an irrelevant joke. Little is known of their motives, their anguish, their glorious surges of communal happiness, and little thought is given to the comment their existence makes on the larger society.

In February, 1944, the Supreme Court of the United States affirmed the conviction of Mrs. Sarah Prince of Brockton, Massachusetts, who had been fined for allowing her 9-year-old niece Betty Simmons to distribute the literature of Jehovah's Witnesses on the streets. The Court, by a 5–4 decision, upheld the Massachusetts Child Labor Law under which no girl under 18 (and no boy under 12) could sell magazines or newspapers in a public place; the law could be validly enforced, the Court ruled, against those who allow young children under their care to sell religious literature on the streets.

Hayden C. Covington, legal counsel for the Witnesses, who had, since 1939, come before the Court with sixteen major constitutional issues involving religious liberty, freedom of speech, and freedom of the press, contended that the Massachusetts law was in violation of both the constitutional guarantee of religious freedom and the basic rights of parenthood.

On the basis of past decisions, Covington might reasonably have expected to win his case. The Witnesses' bitterly controversial cases had produced twenty-seven Court opinions [See *American Political Science Review*,

---

* Abbreviated codes for sources frequently cited are listed on page 395.

1944, 1945], almost all of them ultimately favorable to the Witnesses and many of them strengthening the First and Fourteenth Amendments (and, therefore, the cause of civil liberties in the United States).

In the Prince case, however, Covington's arguments did not prevail. Justice Wiley Rutledge voiced the majority opinion that "neither rights of religion nor rights of parenthood are beyond limitation." "Parents may be free to become martyrs themselves," he said, "but it does not follow that they are free . . . to make martyrs of their children before they have reached the age . . . when they can make that choice for themselves."

Ironically, the Witnesses, bitter foes of the Catholic Church—which they refer to now, as they did then, as "the scarlet whore of Babylon"—found support from the only Catholic on the bench, Justice Frank Murphy. In a separate dissent, Justice Murphy insisted that the sidewalk "as well as the cathedral or the evangelist's tent is a proper place, under the Constitution, to worship." [*Prince v. Commonwealth of Massachusetts*, 351 U.S. 158 (1944)]

In 1944, in a small town in the Southwest, a jury returned a verdict of not guilty in the trial of Mary Lou Smith, a 15-year-old girl who had pumped seventeen bullets into her father and brother, killing them both. She had had, defense counsel said, periodic vivid dreams since the onset of menstruation; she was adjudged temporarily not responsible for her acts because she had committed her murders while hallucinating.

These events are unrelated, except in my mind. I have never met Betty Simmons or Mary Lou Smith, nor do I know what has become of them. But I feel, somehow, as if we are siblings. They wander, like ghosts, in the baggage of my mind.

In 1944, when I, like Betty Simmons, was 9 years old, I became one of Jehovah's Witnesses. Whatever effects the Supreme Court's ruling may have had on children of Jehovah's Witnesses in Brockton, Massachusetts, it is certain that nobody thought to enforce the Court's ruling in Brooklyn, New York. After my baptism at a national convention of 25,000 Witnesses in Buffalo, New York, in the summer of 1944, I became an ardent proselytizer, distributing *The Watchtower* and *Awake!* magazines on street corners and from door to door, spending as much as 150 hours a month in the service of my newly found God—under the directives of the Watchtower Bible and Tract Society, the legal and corporate arm of Jehovah's Witnesses.

As I had been immersed in water to symbolize my "dedication to do God's will," I became, also, drenched in the dark blood-poetry of a religion whose adherents drew joy from the prospect of the imminent end of the world. I preached sweet doom; I believed that Armageddon would come in my lifetime, with a great shaking and rending and tearing of unbelieving flesh, with unsanctified babies swimming in blood, torrents of blood. I believed also that after the slaughter Jehovah had arranged for His enemies at

Armageddon, this quintessentially masculine God—vengeful in battle and benevolent to survivors—would turn the earth into an Eden for true believers.

Coincidentally with my conversion, I got my first period. We used to sing this hymn: "Here is He who comes from Eden/ All His raiments stained with blood." My raiments were stained with blood too. But the blood of the Son of Man was purifying, redemptive, cleansing, sacrificial. Mine was proof of my having inherited the curse placed upon the seductress Eve. Mine was filthy. I examined my discharges with horror and fascination, as if the secret of life—or a harbinger of death—were to be found in that dull, mysterious effluence.

I was, in equal measure, guilt-ridden and—supposing myself to be in on the secrets of the cosmos—self-righteous and smug. I grew up awaiting the final, orgasmic burst of violence after which all things would come together in a cosmic ecstasy of joy—this in a religion that was totally antierotic, that expressed disgust and contempt for the world.

My ignorance of sexual matters was so profound that it frequently led to comedies of error. Nothing I've ever read has inclined me to believe that Jehovah has a sense of humor; and I must say that I consider it a strike against Him that He wouldn't find this story funny:

One night shortly after my conversion, a visiting elder of the congregation, as he was avuncularly tucking me into bed, asked me if I was guilty of performing evil practices with my hands under the covers at night. I was puzzled. He was persistent. Finally, I thought I understood. And I burst into wild tears of self-recrimination. Under the covers at night, I bit my cuticles—a practice which, in fact, did afford me a kind of sensual pleasure. (I didn't learn about masturbation—which the Witnesses call "idolatry," because "the masturbator's affection is diverted away from the Creator and is bestowed upon a coveted object" [*TW*, Sept. 15, 1973, p. 568], until much later.)

So, having confessed to a sin I hadn't known existed, I was advised of the necessity for keeping one's body pure from sin; cold baths were recommended. I couldn't see the connection, but one never questioned the imperatives of an elder, so I subjected my impure body to so many icy baths in midwinter that I began to look like a bleached prune. My mother thought I was demented. But I couldn't tell *her* that I'd been biting my cuticles, because to have incurred God's wrath—and to see the beady eye of the elder steadfastly upon me at every religious meeting I went to—was torment enough.

I used to preach, from door to door, that an increase in the number of rapes was one of the signs heralding the end of the world; but I didn't know what rape was. I knew that good Christians didn't commit "unnatural acts"; but I didn't know what "unnatural acts" were. (And I couldn't ask anybody, because all the Witnesses I knew began immediately to resemble Edith Sitwell eating an unripe persimmon when these abominations were spoken of.) Consequently, I spent a lot of time praying that I was not committing unnatural acts or rape.

Once, having heard that Hitler had a mistress, I asked my mother what a mistress was. (I had an inkling that it might be some kind of sinister super-housekeeper, like Judith Anderson in *Rebecca*.) I knew from my mother's silence, and from her cold, hard, and frightened face, that the question was somehow a grievous offense. I knew that I had done something wrong, but as usual, I didn't know what.

The fact was that I never knew how to buy God's—or my mother's—approval. There were sins I consciously and knowingly committed. That was bad, but it was bearable. I could always pray to God to forgive me, say, for reading the Bible for its "dirty parts"; for preferring the Song of Solomon to all the *begats* of Genesis. But the offenses that made me most horribly guilty were those I had committed unconsciously; as an imperfect being descended from the wretched Eve, I was bound, so I had been taught, to offend Jehovah seventy-seven times a day without my even knowing what I was doing wrong.

There was guilt, and there was glory: I walked a spiritual tightrope.

I feel now that for the twelve years I spent as one of Jehovah's Witnesses, three of them as a member of the Watchtower Society's headquarters staff, I was living out a vivid dream, hallucinating within the closed system of logic and private reality of a religion that relished disaster; rejoiced in the evil of human nature; lusted for certitude; ordered its members to disdain the painful present in exchange for the glorious future; corrupted ritual, ethics, and doctrine into ritualism, legalism, and dogmatism.

I was convinced that 1914 marked "the beginning of the times of the end." So firmly did Jehovah's Witnesses believe this to be true that there were those who, in 1944, refused to get their teeth filled, postponing all care of their bodies until God saw to their regeneration in His New World. (One zealous Witness I knew carried a supply of cloves to alleviate the pain of an aching molar which she did not wish to have treated by her dentist, since the time was so short till Jehovah would provide a new and perfect one. To this day, I associate the fragrance of cloves with the imminence of disaster.)

More than thirty years have passed, but though their hopes have not been fulfilled, the Witnesses have persevered with increased fervor and conviction. Their attitude toward the world remains the same: because all their longing is for the future, they are bound to hate the present—the material, the sexual, the fleshly. It's impossible to savor and enjoy the present, or to bend one's energies to shape and mold the world into the form of goodness, if you are waiting only for it to be smashed by God. There is a kind of ruthless glee in the way Jehovah's Witnesses point to earthquakes, race riots, heroin addiction, the failure of the United Nations, divorce, famine (and liberalized abortion laws) as proof of the nearness of Armageddon.

The God I worshiped was not the God before whom one swoons in ecstasy, or with whom one contends: He was an awesome and awful judge, whom one approached through his "channel," the "divinely appointed Theocratic organization"—the Watchtower Bible and Tract Society. The Christ in whose name I prayed was not a social reformer, nor was he God incarnate, the embodiment of the world's most thrilling mystery, God-made-man. He was, rather, merely a legal instrument (albeit the most important one) in God's wrangles with the Devil. All the history of the world is seen, by Jehovah's Witnesses, as a contest between Jehovah and Satan:

> God's primary purpose is the vindication of [His] supremacy. In carrying out this purpose, God sent Jesus to earth. . . . The beginning of the end for Satan came when Christ took power in heaven as King. This happened in 1914. Christ's first act was casting Satan out of heaven, and this was followed by great troubles on earth. This will be climaxed in God's battle, Armageddon: the complete destruction of the Devil and his system of things, his world. . . . Christ is now in his second presence. He will always remain invisible to humans, but his presence is proved by world events since 1914. [*Who Are Jehovah's Witnesses?* by Milton G. Henschel, Secretary to Nathan H. Knorr, third President of the Watchtower Bible and Tract Society]

Hayden Covington once described the beginnings of the world in the Garden of Eden: "It was a legal matter. The [forbidden] tree served as a legal sign, a guidepost between the God-King and man in their governmental dealings with each other. Adam and Eve failed to fulfill their contract." It is a contractual, not an ecstatic, religion.

I rehearse, I jealously preserve preconversion memories; they flash before my mind like magical slides. I treasure a series of intense, isolated moments. I hoard happy images that are pure, unsullied by values assigned to them by others. Afterward, there was nothing in the world to which I was permitted to give my own meaning; afterward, when the world began to turn for me on the axis of God's displeasure, I was obliged to regard all events as part of God's plan for the universe as understood only by Jehovah's Witnesses. Afterward, meanings were assigned to all things. The world was flattened out into right and wrong; all experience was sealed into compartments marked Good and Evil. Before my conversion, each beloved object and event had the luminosity and purity of a thing complete in itself, a thing to which no significance is attributed other than that which it chooses to reveal.

Images of innocence: dark, cool, sweet rooms and a mulberry bush; fevers, delirium and clean sheets and chicken soup and mustard plasters; summer dusk and hide-and-seek; Hershey Kisses in cut-glass bowls; Brooklyn stoops; sunlight in a large kitchen, the Sunday gravy cooking; the Andrews Sisters singing "I'll Be with You in Apple Blossom Time."

Saturdays I played with the beautiful twins Barbara and Violet, who mirrored each other's loveliness, like Snow White and Rose Red. I thought it was impossible that they should ever be lonely or frightened. I wanted the half of me that had escaped to come back, so that I could be whole, like Barbara-and-Violet.

Sunday afternoons I went to my father's mother's house. I sat at Grandma's vanity table—pink-and-white, muslined and taffetaed, skirted and ribboned—and played with antique Italian jewelry in velvet-lined leather boxes and held small bottles of perfume with mysterious amber residues. From the trellised grape arbor of the roof garden Grandpa had built I imagined I saw Coney Island and the parachute ride. One day, in an attic cupboard, I found a pearl-handled revolver; it belonged, they said, to the distant cousin who smelled of herbs and spices and soap—the old lady who cried when Little Augie Stefano was shot in a barber's chair.

The house of my mother's family, near the Brooklyn Navy Yard, always smelled of fermenting wine and of incense to the saints; its walls and tin ceilings were poverty-brown and -green; but there was always a store-bought chocolate cake waiting in the icebox for my visit. And my grandfather sang me the Italian Fascist Youth Anthem as he hoed his Victory Garden: Mussolini had made the trains run on time, but the good soil of Brooklyn yielded better tomatoes than the harsh soil of Calabria.

These are the fragments I jealously preserve like the crèche from Italy (sweet Mary, humble Joseph, and tiny Jesus—always perfect and new) that adorned each Christmas morning.

After my conversion, I began immediately to have a dream, which recurred until I released myself from bondage to that religion twelve years later, when I was 21. In the dream, I am standing in my grandmother's walled garden. At the far corner of the garden, where the climbing red roses shine like bright blood against the whitewashed wall, stands a creature icy, resplendent, of indeterminate sex. The creature calls to me. In my dream its voice is tactile; I feel it flow through my veins like molten silver. I am rendered bloodless, will-less; the creature extends its arms in a gesture that is at once magisterial and maternal, entreating and commanding. I walk toward its embrace, fearful but glad, unable not to abandon myself to a splendid doom. The creature seizes me in its arms and I am hurled out of the garden, a ravaged Humpty-Dumpty flying through dark and hostile space, alone.

I understand that dream to have been telling me my truest feelings, which my conscious, waking mind censored for long hard years: I under-

stand it to be my soul's perception that my religion had isolated and alienated me from the world, which it perceived as evil and menacing, and
which I regarded, at the bedrock level of my being, as imperfect but not
un-good; my religion savaged those to whom it offered salvation. For twelve
years I lived in fear.

In 1944, the world was at war. Patton had landed with the Fifth Army at
Salerno. The covers of news magazines were decorated with Bombs for
Hitler. Places named Mindanao and Madang briefly stained the American
consciousness. A novel called *Two Jills in a Jeep* appeared on the best-seller
lists. Gandhi was in jail. The West Coast having been designated by Executive Order 9066 as a military area, all persons of Japanese ancestry, aliens
and citizens, had been evacuated and were confined to camps. The War
Production Board had promised civilians that more hairpins would soon be
available, but announced regretfully that the shortage of "mechanical refrig-
erators" was likely to continue. Six million Jews were dead or dying.

Of all these events I had an almost perfect innocence. I perceived the war
in terms of daily realities: sand in a regulation red bucket outside the vesti
bule door; dark-green air-raid curtains; rubber bands and tinfoil balls and
old newspapers competitively offered to my fourth-grade teacher for the
war effort. Uncle Tony was Somewhere-in-Burma and would send me the
ear of a Jap. Dick Tracy and Uncle Don told us how to recognize Japanese
secret agents; but Hirohito was less real than The Shadow (who *knew*), the
threat of enemy missiles less to be feared than the creaking door of the
Inner Sanctum, and the conflict between the Allies and the Axis of less
moment than the continuing debate between me and my friend Lorraine
over whether real beauties had auburn hair and blue eyes or blond hair and
gray eyes.

When I became a Witness, I began to take the war seriously. The Witnesses certainly took it seriously. For one thing hundreds of Witnesses—
who regard national emblems as "graven images"—were imprisoned for not
saluting the American flag. Over 4,000 male Witnesses spent the duration
in federal penitentiaries for refusal to join the armed services.

In the midst of wartime fervor, the Supreme Court, in an unpopular
decision, found a state regulation requiring schoolchildren, under penalty of
expulsion, to salute the flag invalid. [*West Virginia Board of Education v. Barnette,* 1943] An earlier decision of the Court [*Minersville District v. Gobitas,*
1940] which had resulted in the mass expulsion of Witness children from
schools all over America, was thus reversed. The Court ruled that the *Gobitas* case had been "wrongly decided" and that to oblige children to salute the
flag was an infringement of the Fourteenth Amendment. Also, in 1943, in
the case of *Taylor v. Mississippi,* the Court unanimously set aside the conviction of three of Jehovah's Witnesses under a statute that made it a felony "to

teach or preach orally any principles, or distribute any printed matter, calculated to incite violence, sabotage, or disloyalty to state or nation." The
Court, refusing to uphold the claim that the Witnesses had created "an
attitude of stubborn refusal to salute, honor, or respect the flag or government of the United States and the State of Mississippi," ruled that the
Witnesses were not guilty of "evil or sinister purpose," that they were not
shown "to have advocated or incited subversive action against the nation or
state."

Unfortunately, the news that the Witnesses were not subversive had not
filtered down to P.S. 86 in Bensonhurst. Having to remain seated, in my
blue-and-white middy, during flag salute at school assembly was an act of
defiance from which I inwardly recoiled. I wanted desperately to be liked—
despite the fact that the Witnesses took pleasure in anything that could be
construed as "persecution," viewing any opposition as proof of their being
God's chosen. Not saluting the flag, being the only child in my school who
did not contribute to the Red Cross (the Witnesses consider preaching the
gospel the only act of charity worth performing), and not bringing in tinfoil
balls for the War Drive did not endear me to my classmates. I wanted to
please everybody—my teachers, my spiritual overseers, my mother (above
all my mother); and of course, I could not.

I had learned as a very small child that it was my primary duty in life to
"make nice." (Even now, when I hear Italian mothers exhorting their small
girls to "make nice"—which means not so much to be good as to maintain
the appearance of goodness—I cringe.) When I was little, I was required to
respond to inquiries about my health in this manner: "Fine and dandy, just
like sugar candy, thank you." And to curtsy. If that sounds as if it were
from a Shirley Temple movie, it is. Brought up to be the Italian working-
class Shirley Temple from Bensonhurst, I did not find it terribly difficult to
learn to "make nice" for God and His earthly representatives. Behaving
well was relatively easy and a passionate desire to win approval guaranteed
that I conformed. But behaving well never made me feel *good*—in part, no
doubt, because I couldn't have two sets of good behavior: one for the Witnesses, and one for my teachers at P.S. 86. I armed myself against the
criticism of teachers and peers by telling myself that they were wicked and
anyway scheduled for destruction. That didn't work either. I felt as if I
were the bad person, unworthy to live forever, yet superior to those who
wouldn't consent to listen to my preaching about living-forever-on-a-per-
fect-earth. Very messy indeed.

I believed that I had The Truth. One of the things I had The Truth
about was the war. In 1944, if one read, as I did, only the literature of
Jehovah's Witnesses, one was given to believe that World War II was a plot
hatched by Satan and the Vatican to stop the Witnesses from preaching the
gospel. And the Witnesses' neutrality often led to their being arrested, and

sometimes to their being victims of mob violence. The Witnesses' view of the global conflict was, in its own way, as narrow and parochial as my little-girl's view had been. The war was perceived in terms of *their* realities. (In 1945, a group of Witnesses of whom I was one was surrounded by a hostile and threatening group in Coney Island. Coney Island was then populated almost entirely by Jews, and we had come to preach the second coming of Christ on a High Holy Day, at a time when the papers were full of news of Nazi atrocities. We were delighted with our day's measure of "persecution"—never stopping to think about the people to whom we were preaching, and never supposing that there might be anything undesirable in our timing.)

All history, as seen by the Witnesses, revolves around them. They are guilty of what theologian Charles Davis calls "pride of history": they "reject temporality as man's mode of existence or else close that temporality against the transcendent; either history has no meaning at all or it means everything." [Davis, *Temptations of Religion* (New York: Harper and Row, 1974)]

The Witnesses were able, without irony, to remark in their 1945 *Yearbook*, "Today men and women are living in marvellous times . . . a most joyful time." Convinced of the *meaning* of the war (it was one of the signs given by Jesus as proof of the impending end of all evil and all suffering at Armageddon), they were able to disengage themselves from the bloody *facts* of the war. Between themselves and terror stood their interpretation of Bible prophecy—and numbers: numbers pulled from the Bible books of Matthew, Daniel, and Revelation and contorted into the shape of a chronology to prove that we were living in the last days; to prove that that all was part of a divine scheme.

On September 14, my birthday, all over the world—in Dresden, London, Hiroshima—Witnesses opened their day with this obligatory daily text from the 1945 *Yearbook:*

> It is a marvelous day. Though it appears partly dark because of persecutions and oppression by enemies, yet Jehovah's clear light of truth is shining and his blessings upon his people help to brighten the situation and prevent it from being altogether dark. It is a day by itself, for it precedes the 1000-year reign of his beloved Son. It is a particular day that Jehovah God has reserved for himself for vindicating his name. . . . At the evening of his day he will rise up and go forth by his King to give his own testimony to his supremacy and universal sovereignty. Then the day will be light. It will be lightened with the blaze of his glory by his complete victory over all Satan's organization.

In the 1945 *Yearbook*, an account of the Witnesses' worldwide preaching activities for that year, one looks in vain for a mention of the genocide against the Jews—although there is no shortage of detail of the "persecution" of the Witnesses. Witnesses are "haled before magistrates and judges"; but except for one brief mention of one "publisher [preacher] zealously proclaiming the message" in Palestine [p. 90], the reality of the Jews is disregarded. The *Yearbook* informs us that a ban imposed on the work of the Witnesses by the Government of South Africa was removed in 1943, and the Witnesses rejoice; but apartheid is not mentioned. Social and political realities are ignored except to demonstrate the fulfillment of Bible prophecy. There are complaints that the Witnesses' literature is banned in India under Defence of India rules; but Gandhi is not mentioned, nor is the struggle for Indian independence seen to be of any significance.

Even Hitler is dismissed, or seen through their rabid anti-Catholicism as a lackey of the Roman Catholic Church. Vatican City is blamed for the rise of fascism not only in Italy and Germany, but in Argentina as well. The bombing of Britain:

> At times there have been attacks from the air that have made regular Kingdom service extremely difficult. . . . The Lord's protecting care has been marvelously demonstrated, for none [of the Witnesses] have lost their lives although in the midst of destruction on every hand. . . . On several occasions home Bible-study meetings have been in progress when bombs have struck either the home or nearby dwellings and both the brethren and the newly interested in whose homes the studies were being held have had marvelous escapes.

For those who did not respond to the "preaching of the good news of the Kingdom," there is no pity [pp. 110–11]. And the Witnesses, who court persecution as proof that they are God's chosen, also expound upon their "marvelous escapes" as proof that they are God's chosen, and see no contradiction in offering up these mutually exclusive claims. "While the demons are carrying out the policy of the Devil through their agents on the earth . . . the horrors brought by the robot bomb, day and night, did not retard the witnesses, because the servants of the Lord in the British Isles were determined to reach as many people of goodwill as possible."

Bombs exist only as obstacles in the path of the monomaniacal preachers of "good news." "At this time it is very difficult to reach some nations, because of the raging war. . . . Every nation under the sun is affected by the war, but God's message concerning the end of this 'present evil world' and the establishment of the New World cannot wait until men get done fighting. . . . This sort of thing has been carried on for generations and ages." Human suffering is understood as "this sort of thing."

In the 1945 *Yearbook* (distributed only among Witnesses, and not among "outsiders" in an "alien world") they hold the mirror to themselves, fascinated by their objectified image. "Why is it," they ask, "that Jehovah's witnesses are so different from everybody else? It is not because of the way they walk or talk or how they dress or how they act in general. The only thing that makes them different is the way they worship."

And indeed, the way in which they worship *is* different. All of Jehovah's Witnesses are proselytizers. All preach from door to door . . . and fill out, for their local congregations, little yellow slips on which they write the number of hours spent each week at work in the fields of the Lord, and the number of books and booklets "placed" with householders for a "contribution," and the number of return visits. For the Witnesses there is salvation, and comfort, in numbers.

In 1944, according to the 1945 *Yearbook* [p. 56], there were fewer than 65,000 "publishers of the Kingdom news"—that is, Witnesses—in the United States. These publishers distributed 15,298,997 books and booklets, and 7,448,325 copies of the society's magazines—one of them to my father. They made 4,803,084 "back-calls" upon interested persons; one of these interested persons, or "people of goodwill," as they would have it, was my father.

My father was a potential "sheep"; he had not, when a Witness first approached him, demonstrated a "goatlike disposition."

I should explain about "sheep" and "goats": Like any closed society, Witnesses have their own peculiar terminology. They talk to one another in a code that is impenetrable to outsiders. (The year of our conversion, my brother, who was then 4 years old, told a notoriously quick-tempered uncle that one of our cousins was not "In The Truth" but was "of goodwill." My uncle, unused to being diminished by 4-year-olds, slapped him in the face. My brother, reporting to my mother, said he would keep his "integrity" in spite of my uncle's hearty slap.) The Witnesses are able to identify outsiders, or defectors, or hangers-on, by the slightest misuse of code language. (Years later, when, after leaving the Witnesses, I had a love affair with a black jazz musician, I saw again how language could be used to distinguish those really "in the life" from those on the periphery. If, in 1956, for example, somebody had had the misfortune to say *hep* instead of *hip* in front of a jazz musician, he would instantly have been shunned as an alien.)

The Witnesses, who disdain metaphysical inquiry and allow for no doctrinal embroidery or fancywork among their members, play with words to keep the illusion that there is something new under their sun. Over the years, they have made small but, to them, important changes in terminology: What used to be called the New World was later described as the New System and is now uniformly referred to as the New Order. Such changes keep the Witnesses alert to potential apostates in their ranks and help preserve them as a cohesive, homogeneous whole. A Witness in Pago-Pago can immediately claim as brother a Witness from Kalamazoo. Any departure from the universal language they use to enforce their feeling of solidarity

and brotherhood and their containment within a holy sphere, any verbal
eccentricity, starts alarm bells ringing in the heads of Witnesses. (In their
publications, Jehovah's Witnesses use a lower-case *w* for witnesses: Jehovah's witnesses. To say *I am one of Jehovah's witnesses*, therefore, is to say not,
I am a member of a strange cult with an esoteric name, but I am someone
whom Jehovah has chosen to bear witness to His name.)

In their work of dividing the "sheep" from the "goats," Jehovah's Witnesses are often met with resistance they deem goatlike.

When I was 9, I rang doorbells all over Brooklyn. I was almost always
alone. Occasionally I rang doorbells with companions of my own age; and
we did daft little bits of business to punctuate our high seriousness. Sometimes, sitting on the stairs of apartment buildings with booklets like "Religion Reaps the Whirlwind!" heaped around us, the girls would "practice"
kissing. What a gorgeous dodge! We couldn't kiss the boys—that would
have been too frankly sexual, and scary. We kissed each other, clinically; it
was science (we thought), not sex. One hot summer day, my friend Lena
and I preached in an apartment house where each door was graced with a
mezzuzah; afterward, not one door having been opened to us, we peed on
the floor of the bright-red gilded elevator, giggling, not exchanging a word.
We kept our hot secrets to ourselves. We had no confessors. If, after one of
our escapades, we felt guilty, we dealt with our guilt alone—usually by the
expedient of ignoring one another, or deliberately fracturing our friendships. We told the adults as little as possible.

Meanwhile, the adults were busy at their own games. Sometimes I was
assigned to preach with Crazy Sally as my companion—Crazy Sally, who
wore her craziness *à la mode:* peroxided hair glopped on top of her head,
shedding hairpins as Ophelia strewed flowers; high heels and white anklets;
twin shopping bags; rolling, hyperthyroidic eyes. The grown-ups thought
The Truth would save Crazy Sally (35, a virgin whose father, a cop, had
shot himself in her bed); they, like Sally, thought the psychiatrists in whose
care she'd been were the "instruments of Satan." But they were (I felt)
ashamed to be seen with her. So they "gave" her to a child. Me. Once my
assigned door-to-door companion was a middle-aged Italian woman with
vacant eyes and a wet smile from whom all the adults drew back in repug-
nance, or contempt. In a flat, weary monotone, she told me that she'd been
in Kings County Hospital for electric-shock treatment. "It was for my
sins," she said. "I wanted to go to the convention at Niagara Falls and my
husband said he'd give me forty dollars if I did to him what prostitutes did,
and I did it, and the Lord's spirit left me, and I went crazy. Jehovah," she
added, "doesn't let people go crazy unless they break his laws." And she
trudged from door to door after me, to expiate her sins.

I rang doorbells in tenements that smelled of chicken fat; in walk-ups (in
one dark hallway a black baby vomited on my shoulder as its mother, who

could not have been more than five years older than I, vomited in the sink of her beer-bottle-littered kitchen—I remember marveling that her breasts were smaller than mine); in the vestibules of neat two-story brick and stucco houses with garish plaster madonnas in the bay windows (in one vestibule a man who smelled stale with age whispered an invitation for me to suck his cock). I rang the bells of large, quiet houses in Flatbush with wraparound porches and Henry James lawns. Once, a handsome Jesuit— "a wicked representative of *the Vatican*" whom I was obliged to despise, and whose ascetic face and gentle manner I immediately loved—served me iced tea and as we swung together on a porch swing told me, "Saint Augustine says, 'Only love God, and do as you will.' "

Most of the doors were slammed in my face. So many rejections! I told myself they were rejecting Jehovah, not me. (But even now, I feel naked in front of a closed door.)

Well, no wonder doors were slammed in our faces. Who, opening the door at 9 o'clock on Sunday morning to the importunings of a stranger bearing ragged pronouncements of redemption/doom, is likely to be charming, or charitable, or kind?

The Witnesses, gaining access to an ear, or to a door cracked slightly open, assault the householder in a manner both gentle and persistent, with remarkable opening statements like these:

"Good morning. I have come to bring you good news about a perfect new world without crime. Wouldn't you like to live in a world where you didn't have to lock your doors, and where all citizens lived under the law and order of a perfect ruler?"

"I am bringing all your neighbors a message of comfort and hope from the Bible. I see that you have a little child. Wouldn't you like him to grow up in a world where there was no sickness and no death?" (I said that once to a woman with a child in her arms. She said, "My baby is dying of leukemia.")

"Hello. Isn't the weather beautiful today? Wouldn't you like to live in a world where the weather was always perfect? I see that you've been reading a newspaper. Doesn't racial unrest disturb you? Wouldn't you like to live in a world where all races live in peace and harmony together?"

"I've come with a message from the Lord." (I said *that* once, and a disembodied voice from behind a peephole said, "Tell the Lord to send it Western Union.")

Given any kind of opening, the Witnesses then recite a tidy little sermon, flipping their New World Translation of the Bible to well-worn passages; offer their literature; and depart—to record the reactions of the householder on a House-to-House record slip. They mark *I* for Interested; *NI* for Not Interested; *GW* for Goodwill; *O* for Opposed; *NH* for Not Home. These scrupulously kept records form the basis for return visits. (In 1956, the year

I left the Witnesses—or, according to them, the year the Holy Spirit left *me*—it was estimated that each New York city block was "worked" by the Witnesses in this fashion three times a year.)

On December 24, 1943, my father bought, for 5 cents, a copy of *The Watchtower* magazine from a mild-eyed man standing on a street corner selling *The Watchtower* and *Consolation* magazines and calling out slogans to the oblivious Christmas Eve shoppers. Jehovah's Witnesses had inaugurated the "magazine street-corner work" in 1940. They had become familiar street-corner fixtures, canvas "magazine bags" slung from their shoulders holding the few copies of their journals they might reasonably expect to sell. In the early '40s, when Witnesses were likely to call out inflammatory slogans like "Religion Is a Snare and a Racket," they were sometimes arrested and often verbally abused. Looking back at those days when a Witness stood a fair chance of being noticed, a recent Watchtower publication comments, almost nostalgically (persecution and derision are sweet to those whom the world scorns), "The witnesses called aloud their arresting announcements . . . of the theocratic government. . . . This street work was to provide a striking target for those bent on framing mischief by law and violently opposing these peaceful messengers of good will." [*JWDP*, p. 186] By 1944, however, most passersby did nothing more violent than avert their eyes from street-corner Witnesses. Stationary Witnesses calling out slogans that touched few nerves were—although they conceived of themselves as actively and aggressively proselytizing—islands of eccentricity. The seller meekly endured the indifference of passersby. His certitude that he dwelt in the absolute allowed him to enjoy his singularity from the undifferentiated masses who casually disregarded him. It was really more aggressive an act to buy a *Watchtower* magazine than to sell one.

Here is Mario, standing on the street corner, exuding earnestness and the sadness of the isolated whose singularity is a blessing and a burden:

"Read *The Watchtower* and learn about God's Kingdom!"

"*The Watchtower*—announcing God's Theocratic Government."

"Read all about God's purposes for man."

"Read *Consolation*—a journal of fact, hope, and courage."

My father, impulsive and kind, was never oblivious to sadness, and he savored any evidence of eccentricity as he would a good red table wine. He loved the odd fact; he regarded with affection the quirks of human behavior. ("Did you know," he told me, when I was too little to understand why this should be interesting, "that the man who wrote the lyrics to 'I Did Not Raise My Boy to Be a Soldier' in 1913 wrote the lyrics to 'America, I Give My Son to Thee' in 1914?") Connoisseur of Union Square soapbox orators, mischievous, he loved good-natured contention. He was stubborn in argument and, uneducated and ill informed, frequently irritating; but it was never his intention to draw blood. He relished good talk, lively verbal jousting. Also, he had a heart of custard. So the sight of the lone magazine seller standing like an obdurate island among the masses of Christmas revelers moved him to pity and inspired his curiosity. He bought, from mild-eyed Mario, a copy of *The Watchtower*. And, because he would have considered it an abuse of hospitality not to, he gave Mario our address so that Mario might, as he put it, "Call back to further explain God's purposes."

Several weeks later, we received a visit from Mario, accompanied by his daughter Annie, whose inertia was dazzling. A 17-year-old Frank Sinatra freak, a bubble-gum-snapping bobby-soxer, she followed her intense father with obvious reluctance and remorseless listlessness. She had a crush on a young male Witness and did everything she could to cultivate his interest in her. I, of course, thought 17 was a magical age, a formed, sophisticated age. How slyly she regarded me as I drank in every exotic word of her father's salvation pitch! Annie's condescension to me lent to the evening a *frisson* of special tension.

My mother and father agreed to participate in a "home Bible study." Every Monday night we sat down—Mario; Annie; my 4-year-old brother, Rickie; my father; my mother; and I—to a study of the Witnesses' latest textbook, *The Truth Shall Make You Free.* We took turns reading paragraphs from "the *Truth* book." After each paragraph was read, Mario propounded a question from a glossy question booklet, and one of us volunteered to answer—that is, to summarize the paragraph. Then Mario would read the Scriptures cited in the text to corroborate the Witnesses' exposition, and one of us would undertake to comment on them.

My father found this approach to knowledge antithetical to all his instincts. His casual curiosity had been quickly sated. He had a restless, irritable intelligence that could not be satisfied by rote learning. He had left Catholicism—he had never been a visceral Catholic—because he found the Catholicism of his immigrant parents gloomy, pedantic, dogma-ridden, and womanish. He had briefly embraced Presbyterianism because the Presbyterian minister was a "regular guy," the Presbyterian church was right around the corner, and Presbyterian hot dog picnics satisfied his gregarious nature. When we moved away from the Presbyterian church on the corner, he left Presbyterianism; the local betting parlor did just as well as a social club, which was all he had really had in mind; and he retreated into his own real nature—cynical, doubting, agnostic, playful, and kind.

He liked to tease God. He soon understood that he could not tease the Witnesses. He argued mischievously; and then, as he understood that his wife and daughter were devouring whole what Mario taught, and were growing swollen with fanaticism that was bound to separate us from him, he argued fiercely; and then, as we became lost to him, he argued wearily. From the beginning, my father understood that the Witnesses were not people with whom he could exchange the quick, slighting, bantering, argumentative blows that had formed the whole of his intellectual exchange. They were not, like his Calabrian *paesani*, people who could argue ritualistically, with the appearance of ferocity, and then disengage and, exhilarated and worn from the excitement of debate, exchange pleasantries and share a pitcher of wine. He understood that these were people with whom he was locked in mortal combat.

When, not two months after Mario's first visit, my mother accepted an invitation to attend a meeting of the Witnesses at the local "Kingdom Hall," my father behaved in a way that allowed us to report excitedly to Mario that he had become "an opposer of The Truth."

Every Sunday morning my mother, who was beautiful, baked muffins. Three months after Mario's first visit, she declared her intention to go preaching, Sunday morning, from door to door. Attaching all the fervor of her passionate nature to her newfound, consuming religion, she—who had always been outwardly submissive to my father—declined to bake the muffins. No one else has fought so passionately over muffins in the history of the world. My father—who pronounced himself fed up with all this female nonsense—packed his suitcases to leave home. He didn't leave. He never could bring himself to leave. But we became a bitterly divided household. (We never had muffins again.)

My brother tagged along with my mother and me, going to meetings, trailing behind her skirt as she went from door to door. His boredom at meetings occasionally found boorish expression, and he was reprimanded by the elders. He seemed not to care what the elders, or anybody else, said to him. Soon he allied himself with my father, who had been driven to noisy, militant atheism by the presence of two female religious fanatics in his previously patriarchal household. (When your wife and daughter are in love with God, it's hard to compete—particularly since God is good enough to be physically remote and thrillingly elusive.) By the time my brother was 8—and sleeping in my father's double bed, while I shared "the children's bedroom" with my mother—he had become so totally immersed in street life that he was a stranger to us all.

What made my mother such an easy mark for conversion? I can only guess, from what I subsequently came to understand about the appeal the Witnesses have for women. For women whose experience has taught them that all human relationships are treacherous and capricious and frighteningly volatile, an escape from the confusions of the world into the certainties of a fundamentalist religion provides the illusion of safety, and of rest. Female Witnesses outnumber male Witnesses 3 to 2. As a child, I observed that it was not extraordinary for women who became Jehovah's Witnesses to remove themselves from their husbands' bedrooms as a first step to getting closer to God. Many unhappily married and sexually embittered women fall in love with Jehovah.

My mother's mother had been a renowned village beauty in her native Abruzzi. Vain, stupid, courted for her beauty, she made a miserable marriage with a man who was her equal in looks and much her superior in intelligence. My maternal grandfather was the last of three male children to arrive at Ellis Island. A patron in the Abruzzi had paid the steerage passage for the older boys—and kept my grandfather as a kind of indentured servant in return. Grandpa—whose fierce temper was legend—worked for five years as a shepherd; he lived a life of involuntary solitude in a hut. By the time he reached America, his ability to express himself in speech had practically atrophied, so seldom had he had occasion to talk to another human being during the five years of his servitude. Having married my grandmother for her beauty, he noisily lamented his error to the day of her death. Unlike his brothers, he was never more than a laborer, and he railed against his fate with all the strength of a large but thwarted intelligence. My grandmother, a compulsive eater and a diabetic, grew fat; she stunned herself into insensibility with food, and surrounded herself with saints and incense and an army of black-robed churchy friends. Grandpa's rage found expression in violent fits of anger directed against his five children—not one of whom survived childhood without a nose broken by him. My mother's nose was broken when he slammed an iron into her face in a senseless, voiceless seizure of unprovoked rage. Her mother never protected her.

My mother left this house, over which the threat of violence always hung (a house that smelled richly—and claustrophobically—of fermenting wine and incense and all the stale, dark-brown smells of poverty) when she was 19, to marry my father. Whether she loved my father I do not know. After she became a Witness, my mother destroyed every letter they had ever exchanged, every photograph she had ever had taken with him. She no longer wore her wedding band. My aunts say she used to write my father poetry; if she did, it was burned with the rest of her preconversion past. In my father's sisters' house, there are pictures of my mother as a bride. She looks vulnerable, soft, eager; perhaps it was a trick of lighting, photographer's magic: she looks like a girl in love.

My mother was 20 when I was born. I never knew the tender girl of the studio portraits. I knew a woman hotly involved in family intrigues, a woman who entered my bedroom at night to weep.

I have two vivid images preserved from the days before our conversion (clues, not evidence): I remember awakening one night and seeing, from my bedroom, my mother's ripe, full-breasted naked body (which I had never seen before), masses of unrestrained chestnut hair soft on her shoulders, and hearing my father's voice saying, "Connie, don't walk around like that. It isn't nice." And I remember walking in on her when she was nursing my baby brother behind a closed door and her begging me not to tell my father I had seen her naked breasts. I remember those moments of her nakedness; but I know her in the armor of her zeal.

Like most second-generation Southern Italians, my mother grew up insu-

lar and clannish; in the teeth of the sorry evidence, she was instructed to
believe that only the family could ever shelter, embrace, nourish. The rest
of the world was hostile, menacing, exploitive, threatening, incomprehensible, and not deserving of comprehension. *They* were always out to get you.
In fact, the family was the smell of incense, beatings, and swollen, angry
voices. The Church was no refuge; the Church was her mother's and, she
thought, an old ladies' home. It could never be hers. She looked for Family
in my father's family—and found jealousies and rivalries, and there too she
was an alien. She could not (this is conjecture) love either her family or the
world. She chose a religion; she chose "spiritual brothers and sisters"—who
told her, as her family had, that the world was *other* and evil, alien, and
cruel. She found shelter. She waited for God to smash the wicked world.
All her longing was for the future; all her love was for a jealous, devouring
God who promised her rest.

    What predisposed me toward my conversion? In recent years, when el-
ders of Jehovah's Witnesses have come to call on me, they have usually
asked—out of their zeal to assign spiritual cause and effect to all mysterious
acts of the spirit, to tame experience by defining it, and to render apostasy
less threatening by subjecting apostates to the rigors of private logic—
whether, when I was 9, I'd made a conscious decision to serve Jehovah;
whether from true knowledge and absolute belief I chose to "dedicate myself to God." (If they can believe that my water baptism was the act of a
dutiful daughter, an aberration of youth rather than an independent act of
choice and mature will, they can dispose of me in their minds, categorize
and forget me.) Of course I can't answer their question. I choose to believe
in free will; but the motives of that little girl who pledged her life to God
are necessarily obscure to me. My childhood has been fed into the devouring maw of psychoanalysis, but the leap into belief (or into fancy) is still
unsusceptible of analysis, still mysterious.
    Sometimes, in an effort to understand my own past, I try to "read" my
own daughter. Could she, I wonder, an ardent preadolescent girl whose
temperament tends toward the ecstatic, lend herself to religious conversion?
    Anna, my 12-year-old daughter, is as familiar to me as my own skin and,
in her breezy unselfconsciousness and tidy self-possession, as mysterious to
me as a being from another planet. Her luminous and determined curiosity
about the world, while it is often outrageous, is never cold or casual or
predatory; her passionate prodding and seeking is a form of reverence and
of love. Anna reads the classified columns of *New York Review* for the
breathtaking pleasure of learning about the varieties of human folly. She
once called up a famous personage—getting his phone number through a
combination of incredible industry, imagination, and luck—to tell him that
he was a "bad person." (She didn't like the views he held on having chil-

dren; in her opinion—Anna has an opinion about practically everything—he was a "child hater.") She is currently reading *Death Notebooks* and *The Happy Hooker*. She regularly fires off letters to magazines, heads of state, and boards of education to tell them where they have gone wrong. She just as frequently fires off letters to her girlfriends to tell them where she has gone wrong. (She insists upon clarity.) One Easter Sunday, when Anna was 9, she took herself off to the black Baptist church on our corner to attend services, and when that was over, she visited the local Irish Catholic church to see what they were up to. She also occasionally visits the Hare Krishnas; also, synagogues. She hasn't decided whether to believe in God or not. She is fierce, dramatic, vulnerable, sophisticated, innocent, and moral. She is, as I once explained drunkenly to someone who thought she might be the better for a little vigorous repression, a teleological child. That is, she is concerned with final causes, with ends and purposes and means; she would like to see evidence of design and purpose in the world. All her adventures are means to that end.

But Anna cannot conceive of a life in which one is not free to move around, explore, argue, flirt with ideas and dismiss them, form passionate alliances and friendships according to no imperative but one's own nature and volition. She regards love as unconditional; she expects nurturance as her birthright. She feels sorry for me because I did not have a "normal childhood." "Poor Mom," she says. To have spent one's childhood in love with/tyrannized by a vengeful Jehovah is not Anna's idea of a good time—nor is it her idea of goodness. It fills her with terror and pity that anyone—especially her mother—could have grown up in a religion in which love was conditional upon rigid adherence to dogma and established practice; in which approval had to be bought from authoritarian external sources; in which people did not fight openly and love fiercely and forgive generously and make decisions of their own and mistakes of their own and have adventures of their own.

The person Anna is cannot help me to understand the person I was.

Nor can the person my brother became help me to understand the person I became. I ask myself how my brother escaped the religion that threw its meshes so tightly over me. Why was he not hounded for years by the obsessive guilt and the desperate desire for approval that informed all my postconversion actions? Partly, I suppose, luck, and an accident of temperament; but also, I think, because of the peculiarly guilt-inspiring double messages girls received as Jehovah's Witnesses. Girls were taught that it was their nature to be spiritual but, paradoxically, that they were more prone to depravity than were boys. In my religion, everything beautiful and noble and spiritual and good was represented by a woman; and everything evil and depraved and monstrous was represented by a woman. I learned that "God's organization"—the "bride of Christ," or His 144,000 heavenly co-rulers—was represented by a chaste virgin. I also learned that "Babylon the Great," or "false religion," was "The mother of the abominations or the 'disgusting things of the earth.' . . . She likes to get drunk on human blood. . . . Babylon the Great is . . . pictured as a woman, an international harlot." [*Babylon*, pp. 576–83]

Young girls were thought not to have the "urges" boys had. They were not only caretakers of their own sleepy sexuality, but protectors of boys' vital male animal impulses as well. They were thus doubly responsible and, if they fell, doubly damned.

To be female, I learned, was to be Temptation; nothing short of death— the transformation of your atoms into a lilac bush—could change that. (I used to dream deliciously of dying, of being as inert, and as unaccountable, as the dust I came from.) If, then, a woman were to fall from grace, her fall would be mighty indeed—and her willful nature would lead her into that awful abyss where she would be deprived of the redemptive love of God and the validating love of man. But if a man were to fall, he would merely be stumbling over his own feet of clay.

I spent my childhood walking a religious tightrope, maintaining a difficult and dizzying balance. I was expected to perform well at schoolwork so that glory would accrue to Jehovah and "his organization"; but I was also continually made aware of the perils of falling prey to "the wisdom of this world which is foolishness to God." I had constantly to defend myself against the danger of trusting my own judgment. To question or to criticize God's "earthly representatives" was a sure sign of "demonic influence"; to express doubt openly was to risk being treated as a spiritual leper. I was always an honor student at school; but this was hardly an occasion for unqualified joy. I felt, rather, as if I were courting spiritual disaster: while I was congratulated for having "given a witness" by virtue of my academic excellence, I was, in the next breath, warned against the danger of supposing that my intelligence could function independently of God's. The effect of all this was to convince me that my intelligence was like some kind of tricky, predatory animal which, if it was not kept firmly reined, would surely spring on and destroy me.

But sexual guilt and the carefully nurtured fear of intellectual pride, while they may have acted as glues to adhere me to my religion for many dry years, do not (I think) explain my conversion to that religion.

I look for clues; I find very few. I had read precociously and voraciously from the time I was seven. *War and Peace*, *Gone with the Wind*, and *Little Women* were my favorite books. When my mother learned that I knew what Kotex was, she destroyed all my books, including *Heidi*, because it made me "cry too much." (Books were messengers from the bad world.) I envied the small brides of the Catholic Church, solemn young girls receiving First Communion (sprigs of lily of the valley, white leather catechisms, lace veils). I loved the way Catholic churches smelled. When, during my father's brief flirtation with the Presbyterian Church, I attended Sunday school, I was sure that I had incurred God's disfavor: "Be quiet and you'll hear a pin drop," the Sunday-school teacher said before each lesson. I never heard the pin—which I assumed God Himself was dropping from the clouds—drop. I thought everybody else did. I thought the Presbyterian God did not love me. I do know that when Mario came with his books and his message, I drank in his words as if I were parched. I remember the way the book we studied—*The Truth Shall Make You Free*—looked and felt in my hand. It smelled wonderfully of new glue. Embossed in gold on its azure-blue cover was a circle which embraced a line of smiling people in varied headgear—all with straight, nondescript Anglo-Saxon features; all clasping textbooks in their hands. These, Mario explained, were "people of goodwill from all lands worshiping Jehovah." The *Truth* book (published in 1943, printed in the Watchtower Society's own factory, with a first printing of 2½ million copies), like all publications of Jehovah's Witnesses written and published after 1942, was "written" by the Watchtower Bible and Tract Society. Since, as Mario explained, God's organization was not democratic but "theocratic," no single person could claim authorship. That would have been too idiosyncratic, allowing honor to accrue to one person, rather than to "Jehovah's visible instrument on earth, the Watchtower Bible and Tract Society." No author, then; but, on the dedication page, "Dedicated to Jehovah and to Jesus Christ." I did like that. As a child, I perceived this not as arrogance, but as evidence of a familiar, familial relationship with the Deity that was both cozy and exhilarating.

The romance of that book, its garish color plates! Illustrations of Jesus being stoned by the "Jewish religionists" out of the temple; spectacularly un-Darwinian pictures of dinosaurs and lambs roaming the Edenic earth—which resembled the pictures in my school geography book of the Panama Canal Zone; scenes of "free men" (Witnesses) in Nazi concentration camps, their hollow-cheeked faces radiant with the nobility of suffering; illustrations of Jephthah's daughter, girdled in gold, dancing with tambourines in pseudo-Arabian splendor, her father dressed exactly like the Roman warriors in the Metropolitan Museum of Art; representations of a beastlike Nebuchadnezzar (who looked like the Wolf Man), crouched on all fours eating weeds in front of a crumbling Corinthian temple; illustrations of a pompadoured Eve with an Elizabethan forehead and high, sharp breasts, offering a miniature pineapple to an Adam modeled after Tyrone Power, glistening green foliage and arum lilies with thrusting tendrils covering the important parts of her naked perfection.

"Worldly and religious scientists," I read, "worshiping their own brains and other men, pass by the very source of truthful information, God's word." How, indeed, could "worldly scientists" vie with the wonderful imagery of the *Truth* book—images of creation and destruction; images of water and blood:

> As the earth rotated on its axis . . . thrown-off matter gradually formed into great rings about the earth at its equator, where the centrifugal force of the spinning earth was most powerful. . . . According to the density and specific gravity of the materials thrown off from the molten earth, they formed into rings of water mixed with mineral substance, the densest and heaviest being nearest the earthcore, the next heavy being immediately next out beyond it, and so on, the lightest being thrown out farthest and being almost wholly a water ring. Thus an annular or ring system existed, and the appearance to the eye of God was like that of a great wheel, with wheels within wheels, and with the molten earth itself as the spherical hub of them. [*Truth*, chapter on earth's creation, pp. 50–70]

(Actually, the Witnesses do rely upon the evidence of worldly scientists when it suits them: the water-ring theory derives from Isaac Vail's book *The Earth's Annular System*, published in 1886.)

> Adam's descendants, now multiplied over the earth, were out of the water, being on dry land. At the same time they were in the water, being within the water canopy which had been there since before Adam's creation. . . . The movement of the waters of the great canopy far overhead was toward the poles; . . . as a result the thickness of the canopy out above the earth's equator was becoming very thin, almost admitting direct sunlight through, . . . the edges of the canopy nearing the poles were growing dangerously weak, rotating with growing slowness to the point of having little centrifugal force to resist the downward pull of earth's gravity. The fall of the canopy was imminent, awaiting God's removal of his restraining power. [*Truth*, p. 135]

God "removed his restraining power" 1,656 years after the day of Adam's creation, say the Witnesses (who dismiss the evidence of the radiocarbon clock, as they dismiss the theory of evolution); and so, 1,656 years after Adam's creation, the Great Flood—survived by Noah (who was, according to their reckoning, 500 years old)—covered the entire earth.

According to the *Truth* book, Noah "typified" Christ; Noah's wife "pictured" the bride of Christ (the 144,000 Jehovah's Witnesses who will share Christ's heavenly reign); and Noah's three sons and three daughters-in-law "pictured" the "great crowd of other sheep," Jehovah's Witnesses who will live forever on an Edenic, cleansed earth; the ark "pictured" the new world. (Theologians have accused the Witnesses of "absurd typology." I thought it was marvelous magic—like those Chinese ivory balls one opens to find another ivory ball within, and within that another ball, and within that, another—secrets within secrets.)

Most important, the Flood "foreshadowed" the destruction of the ungodly in our day. "Reckoning each of the six creative days of Genesis to have been of 7,000 years' duration," the Witnesses concluded, in 1944, that "From Adam's creation to the end of 1943 A.D. is 5,971 years. We are therefore near the end of 6,000 years of human history with tremendous events [Armageddon, and the 1,000-year reign of Christ] upon us." [p. 152]

The Witnesses do not distinguish among the lyrical, poetic, mystical, historical, prophetic, and epistological books of the Bible; so from the *Truth* book I learned this hop-skip-and-jump chronology (which German theologian Kurt Hutten has called the result of "knight-jump exegesis") [see Hoekema]; I zigzagged my way through the Pentateuch to Revelation to Daniel, marveling at the wondrous way in which this divine jigsaw fitted together:

In 1914 Christ's Kingdom was established in the heavens. (Satan, who had had access to the heavens, presumably to play in the fields of the Lord and have his way with renegade angels, was shortly thereafter restricted to "the realms of the earth"—which accounts for World War I.) This was how the Witnesses (in 1944) arrived at the year 1914: From Luke 21:24 we learned that Jerusalem would be trampled upon by the nations until the "times of the Gentiles" were fulfilled. Now skip to Daniel 7:14, which, according to the Witnesses' reading, proves that Christ was to receive a kingdom that would never be destroyed. When was Christ to receive his kingdom? At the end of the Gentile times—the period in which there was no representative government of Jehovah (such as Israel had been) upon the earth. When had the Gentile times begun? In 607 B.C., when Israel, a theocracy, lost her sovereignty and became enslaved to Babylon.

To prove this, we switch to Daniel 3, which contains the account of Nebuchadnezzar's dream of a hewn-down tree, its stump in the earth banded with iron and brass, and of Nebuchadnezzar's seven subsequent years of madness, during which he lived like a beast of the field. (I always thought of the escarole my mother forced me to eat when I thought of Nebuchadnezzar gobbling weeds; it was an "untheocratic" parallel, which I immediately censored.) Nebuchadnezzar was told that "seven times" would pass over him, after which his sanity, and his kingdom—waiting for him like the banded tree—would be restored:

> In the miniature fulfillment of the dream . . . Nebuchadnezzar . . . became like a beast, without human understanding, for seven years, after which he regained sanity and exercised his lordship over the empire. This makes it clear that the "seven times" began with Nebuchadnezzar's overturning of Jehovah's typical theocracy in Jerusalem in 606 B.C. . . . The Gentile powers or governments were not exclusive in the field. [pp. 236–38]

In Nebuchadnezzar's case, seven times meant seven literal years. In the *major* fulfillment of the prophecy, however, these "seven times" symbolize the Gentile times.

When would the Gentile times end and Christ take power in heaven? Skip to Revelation 12:6 and 12:14. There we learn that "a time, and times, and half a time" are equivalent to 1,260 days. A time, and times, and half a time are three and a half times. Three and a half times constitute half of seven times; hence seven times equals twice 1,260 days, or 2,520 days. But 2,520 days is equivalent only to 7 years. So skip to Ezekiel 4:6: "I have appointed thee every day for a year." Apply this rule, and 2,520 days means 2,520 years: Since Jerusalem was destroyed

> in the summer of 606 B.C. that year had its beginning in the fall of 607 B.C. and its ending in the fall of 606 B.C. Inasmuch as the count of the Gentile "seven times" began its first year at the fall of 607 B.C., it is simple to calculate when they end. From the fall of 607 B.C. to the fall of B.C. 1 is exactly 606 years. From the fall of B.C. 1 to the fall of A.D. 1 is one year, do not forget. Hence, from the fall of B.C. 1 to the fall of A.D. 1914 is 1,914 years. Add now 606 years and 1,914 years, and the sum total is 2,520 years, ending in the fall of 1914. [p. 239]

It was rather tortuous, one might suppose, for a 9-year-old to work her way through that labyrinthine logic; but though I was never able to understand algebra and never able to grasp the first thing about geometry, I learned my way through that maze. (God was in the heart of the maze.) I did not know that since 1873 the Witnesses had arranged and rearranged pieces of the jigsaw puzzle—which had yielded several different, earlier dates for the apocalypse; nor did I know that there was never any basis in secular history for assuming 607 to be the year of Jerusalem's destruction. I knew only what I was told, and I believed it. I can only imagine how insufferable that sure belief made me appear to others—to those who saw only my certainty and knew nothing about my guilt.

It was even jolly to think how, soon, we were all going to be persecuted. Jolly, perhaps, isn't the word: It was thrilling. It made us glad. It was our burden to "beat back those religious-political enemies of freedom of worship and victoriously carry on declaring the day of God's vengeance against Babylon and comforting [sic] all that mourn." We knew that we would be "viciously persecuted" by "Satan's offspring . . . 'organized religion,' " which preached all manner of pagan doctrines—hellfire, the Trinity, the immortality of the soul. We alone knew that "babylonish religion under the Vatican's leadership" would act as a "supranational power for the postwar confederation of nations" (the United Nations, pictured in the Bible as "the abomination of desolation"). We alone knew also that the "hitherto docile political and commercial powers" would awake to realize how organized religion—and in particular, the "Roman Catholic Hierarchy," which would act as the "spiritual police force" of the entire postwar earth—had "befooled" them. And the nations of the world would turn against religion, that "great whore," that "blood-drunk woman" who rides the back of the abominable scarlet-colored beast. [pp. 348–52] And Jehovah would step in to protect His people; and that would be the beginning of Armageddon.

In the meantime, we could expect to be persecuted. (It was a "privilege" to be persecuted.) My mother, I remember, would wonder how she could remove her moustache in the concentration camp she was prepared to be assigned to by the Vatican. (No depilatories in concentration camps.) I would wonder, I remember, whether we would have bowel movements in Jehovah's clean New World, or whether the Lord would find a less odoriferous way of dealing with waste; and I would wonder whether, in the New World, we would be allowed to choose our own mates. It was very real to us.

It was *all* real. The words I savored that felt new and good on my tongue: *nephesh*, the Hebrew word for soul (what 9-year-old knew *that*, and knew that it implied mortality?); *Nephilim*, the hybrid offspring of angels breeding with women (bigger, better, richer than a fairy tale—and true). I knew that Christ had died not on a cross—I threw my gold crucifix with its beautifully tendoned Jesus away, wrapping it in toilet tissue first, so as not to handle the Devilish thing—but on a stake. I knew that Christmas and Easter were pagan holidays and that I must never allow myself to be seduced by their glitter.

And I knew that if I didn't believe, I would "fall into deeper darkness" . . . "and the old world falls a terrible end."

Had Armageddon come exactly on schedule, it would have arrived in 1972. ("From Adam's creation to the end of 1943 A.D. is 5,971 years.") In 1944, we were 29 years away from the seven-thousandth year of human history, according to the Witnesses' reckoning. In later years, the Witnesses juggled figures a little and came up with 1975 as the date of the apocalypse: "Six thousand years from man's creation will end in 1975, and the seventh period of a thousand years of human history will begin in the fall of 1975 C.E. [Common Era]. . . . It would not be by mere chance or accident . . . for the reign of Jesus Christ to run parallel with the seventh millennium of man's existence." [*Life*] The Witnesses are now in the process of slithering away from 1975 as they have in the past slithered from other dates. In spite of their modest claim that they do not know "the day and the hour," they have nevertheless led their followers to believe in at least five apocalyptic dates.

In 1966, *Life Everlasting in Freedom of the Sons of God* identified 1975 as "the end of the sixth 1,000 year day of man's existence (in early autumn)." When 1975 came along, the Watchtower Society's vice-president, F. W. Franz, was asked if in that year Armageddon would be finished and Satan bound. He agreed that it could happen, but hedged, warning the Witnesses not to make specific predictions, but to be awake and alert, for "no question, time is running out."

According to *The Watchtower* magazine of May 1, 1975, Franz (who would appear to be the Witnesses' spiritual timekeeper) said, speaking before a group of missionaries, that

> according to dependable Bible chronology, 6,000 years of human his-
> tory will end this coming September [1975] according to the lunar
> calendar. This coincides with a time when "the human species is
> about to starve itself to death," as well as its being faced with poison-
> ing by pollution and destruction by nuclear weapons. Franz added:
> "There's no basis for believing that mankind, faced with what it now
> faces, can exist for the seventh thousand-year period" under the pres-
> ent system of things. Does this mean that we know exactly when God
> will destroy this old system and establish a new one? Franz showed
> that we do not, for we do not know how short was the time interval
> between Adam's creation and the creation of Eve, at which point
> God's rest day of seven thousand years began. But, he pointed out,
> "we should not think that this year of 1975 is of no significance to us,"
> for the Bible proves that Jehovah is "the greatest chronologist" and
> "we have the anchor date, 1914, marking the end of the Gentile
> Times." So, he continued, "we are filled with anticipation for the near
> future, for our generation."

Whenever the Witnesses appear to be at the end of their singularly long tether, they add a new wrinkle to the tissue stretched thin over the 100 years of their existence. *The time interval between Adam's creation and the creation of Eve* is just such a new wrinkle, allowing them, once again, to justify the nonappearance of Armageddon. Faced with the postponement of their hopes, the Witnesses are instructed to believe that the Watchtower Society is "fallible." God's word, however, is not—and the Watchtower Society is the "sole visible channel" through which God reveals the true meaning of prophecy "in his due time," as the "light grows clearer and clearer." [*Faith*] They are not infallible; they are merely the instrument God uses to make clear His purposes. This would seem to be a distinction without a difference.

The Witnesses continue to grow in number and in strength, even as their chronology continues to falter. Sociologists who have examined the phenomenon of apocalyptic religions have found that almost no religion survives three false dates. [Festinger, Leon, Henry W. Riecken, and Stanley Schachter, *When Prophecy Fails* (New York: Harper Torchbooks, 1955)] The Witnesses are a striking exception. What accounts for their staying power? "Hope deferred," says the Psalmist, "maketh the heart sad." One might reasonably expect the Witnesses to grow weary with waiting. Still they wait.

Why this tenacity of belief? What needs does this religion gratify? Why do people choose abandonment of personality, a harsh, disciplinary, self-negating religion? Why do women, in particular, choose an all-consuming religion; why, in particular, do they choose suffering—renunciation of sexual and family ties in exchange for a love affair with a vengeful God?

Jehovah's Witnesses are enjoined to "hate" the "world"; that hatred can express itself in a visceral loathing for "worldings," in contemptuous disdain for the strivings of others. Hatred for the world is combined with an insistence that the flesh is intrinsically evil, to be feared, doomed. Sexuality is blunted and repressed; "persecution" is courted as evidence of God's favor. Does the fear and loathing of the physical world spring from deformed psyches? Or is it explainable in terms of a leap into a belief so rigorous and rigid that a world view has been imposed, through external discipline, upon passive personalities?

Is abdication of will attainable; and at what cost? What happens when antithetical instincts (for example, the recognition that one can "love that which God hates") collide with programmed belief?

What are the consequences for one who, after years of total dedication and belief, finds himself no longer able to believe and leaves not only a religion, but a world view, behind? How do precepts of good and evil color one's view of the world and affect one's emotional and political choices? How does one make new connections with the world, learn to see and to feel independently, learn to redefine the world? How do old religious patterns—fanaticism, total immersion, moral strictures—assert and repeat themselves in secular life?

I can answer some of these questions by reflecting on my experience. And some of the answers may be ascertained through the testimony of others who have left what used to be their spiritual home; what these survivors have to say is more eloquent than abstract analysis.

But it is necessary also to look at the history and the doctrinal and organizational evolution of this sect.

To examine one prophetic, apocalyptic cult is to explore the existential experience to which human society is bound at any given moment. (Is it an accident that Jehovah's Witnesses, followers of the Maharishi, and greening-of-America counterculturists have all pointed to 1975 as the time of mystical transformation?) Jehovah's Witnesses may be regarded as people seeking religious renewal and liberation in order to heal deep personal psychic wounds—people who contain and channel their craziness in a "crazy" religion; but the *form* their religion takes may also be seen as a response to social and cultural realities. To look closely at the psychology of a single all-consuming religion is necessarily to examine human nature, while to understand its ideology and to trace its historical genesis and development is to gain insight into the contradictions, necessities, and turmoil of

Visions of Glory

the society and culture that gave it life. [See Lanternari, Vittorio, *The Religions of the Oppressed* (New York: Mentor Books), pp. v-viii]

Jehovah's Witnesses willfully place themselves outside the mainstream and relish their role as outcasts; nonetheless, they borrow from the worst of mass culture and, it will be seen, tend to reinforce the status quo. Terrified of dissolution and real-life change, sedate, orderly, law-abiding, they despise flamboyant manifestations of rebellion; they are, in fact, a reactionary force, tending to blunt not only revolution, but social reform. They proclaim the destruction of the Establishment and yet play a role that is socially static and conservative.

Demonstrably racist and sexist, they nevertheless draw most of their members from the ranks of the oppressed: oppressed people respond to the assurance that the day of the Lord is at hand, when all manner of blessings shall be their reward and the evil oppressors shall be blotted out. In search of an ultimate solution, they give themselves over to a dull submission to a tyrannical force.

Jehovah's Witnesses are a microcosm of mankind trying desperately, often pitifully, to find possibility, hope, and grace in a moral wilderness. This is their story (and mine).

II. *Organizational Beginnings:*
(1873–1912) Charles Taze Russell

Since 1873 we have been living in the seventh millennium . . . the lease of Gentile dominion. "The Times of the Gentiles" will expire with the year 1914; and . . . the advent of him whose right it is to take the dominion was due in 1874. . . . 1874 is the exact date of Our Lord's return. . . . Only twenty-four years of the harvest period remain, the close of which will witness the end of the reign of evil and the ushering in of the glorious Millennial day; and within this period the dark night of the world's greatest tribulation must find place.—Charles Taze Russell, *Studies in the Scriptures*, Volume III, *Thy Kingdom Come* (1891), pp. 211, 305–06

SCIENCE AND SECULARISM, industrialism and invention flourished.

Everyone believed in progress.

In the period of Jacksonian democracy, worship of the aristocratic Calvinist God did not flourish. The masses—farmers and workers—were exalted. The doctrine of a favored few was irreconcilable with the mythologizing of the masses. The 1840s, '50s, and '60s in America were

> an age of mass movements—an age of lectures, public schools, circuses, museums, penny newspapers, varied propaganda, political caucuses, woman suffrage conventions, temperance reform, proletarian unrest, labor organization, Mormonism, Millerism, . . . mesmerism, phrenology . . . Madmen and women, men with beards, Dunkers, Muggletonians, Come-outers, Groaners, Agrarians, Seventh-Day Baptists, Quakers, Abolitionists, Unitarians. . . .
>
> At every corner critical thought and economic change were eating away the foundations of the traditional family system . . . the factory system and the rise of public schools were offering women wider opportunities; easier divorce laws were giving them a new sense of independence. . . . girls [were] more defiant of parental authority and more determined to exercise their own pleasure both in the choice of work and of husbands. . . .
>
> The revolution in technology, the reconstruction of the social order under the impact of the machine industry, the advance of science into the domain of cosmogony, the economic independence brought to the

nation by increased wealth, the ferment of political equality, the
changing status of women, the clash of parties over domestic issues,
and the new contacts with foreign countries reset the intellectual stage
for speculation about life and for all forms of imaginative literature.
[Beard, Charles A. and Mary R., *The Rise of American Civilization*,
Vol. I, pp. 728, 757, 761, (New York: Macmillan, 1927)]

In 1859, Darwin, disregarding accepted biblical chronology, asserted the
antiquity of man and the earth. Rejecting the belief that each species was
the result of an original divine act, he proclaimed the mutability of the
species and the survival of the fittest. Cornerstones of Christian faith—original sin, the Virgin Birth, salvation by faith, the resurrection of the dead—
were challenged by the new rationalism. The intellectual life of America
was stirred by fresh currents of inquiry and criticism. [See Beard, p. 733.]

"Higher criticism" threatened the established churches. Established Protestant sects were thrown into turmoil. As the frontier expanded, new sects
proliferated. Enthusiastic evangelical revival meetings became boisterously
expressive of strange dreams and wondrous portents. Two-Seed-in-the-
Spirit Predestinarian Baptists fought with Free-Will Baptists. Schisms tore
the churches apart. Presbyterians split into four or five divisions.

In 1843, William Miller had confidently announced the second coming of
Christ, and his followers earnestly awaited their salvation and the end of
the world. The world did not end; but second-adventists continued to
flourish. American adventist evangelists took their message as far as Korea.
Apocalyptic adventist sects (such as those founded and led by Elliott and
Cummings in 1866, Brewer and Decker in 1867, Seiss in 1870, and the
Russian Mennonites, in 1889) proliferated.

Protestantism was splintering, becoming free-wheeling, effervescent,
drunk on the wine of individualism. Only in the industrial cities, among
new immigrants, did the center hold: Roman Catholics continued to acknowledge the ecclesiastical authority of their Church.

In 1860, the U.S. census reported that one-third of the population was
sustained by "manufacturing industry." Workers had left the soil for the
cities (villages had become cities; cities had become railway and industrial
centers). By the middle of the 19th century, the old planting aristocracy
had been replaced by Abbots, Laurences, Astors, and Vanderbilts. The
1860s saw the rise of labor unions. During the 1870s, the Rockefellers assumed command of their oil empire. The immense concentration of wealth
and power, the consolidation of industry and railways, and the shift of
economic power of financiers led to bloody fights between labor and employers.

In 1872 a million American voters approved a Populist platform which
declared that America was ruled by a plutocracy, that impoverished labor
was tyrannized by "a hireling army," that the ballot box was rendered

worthless by corruption, "that the fruits of the toil of millions are boldly stolen to build up colossal fortunes for a few unprecedented in the history of mankind; and the possessors of these in turn despise the republic and endanger liberty."

In 1873, as the post–Civil War inflationary boom went bust, a devastating panic hit the United States, leaving unemployment and poverty in its wake; the country sank into an industrial depression which lasted for five years.

In 1874, the anthracite regions of Pennsylvania—including Allegheny (now a part of Pittsburgh), the home of Charles Taze Russell—were terrorized by violence that threatened the social order. A secret society known as the Molly Maguires, fierce avengers of cruelty in the mines, beat and murdered mine owners and foremen, and they, in turn, sent their goons to beat and murder the Molly Maguires.

Fear of anarchists and anarchism was widespread; and social utopians preached a dispensation of human grace.

> The "Time of the End," a period of one hundred and fifteen years, from A.D. 1799 to A.D. 1914, is particularly marked in the Scriptures. . . . discoveries, inventions,.etc., pave the way to the coming Millennium of favor, making ready the mechanical devices which will economize labor, and provide the world in general with time and conveniences . . . the increase of knowledge among the masses [will give] to all a taste of liberty and luxury, before Christ's rule is established . . . class-power . . . will result in the uprising of the masses and the overthrow of corporative Trusts, etc., with which will fall also all the present dominions of earth, civil, and ecclesiastical. . . . All the discoveries, inventions and advantages which make our day the superior of every other day are but so many elements working together in this day of preparation for the incoming millennial age, when true and healthful reform, and actual progress in every direction, will be the order, to all and for all. [*SS*, Vol. III, *Thy Kingdom Come*, pp. 23, 59]

Charles Taze Russell, founder and first president of the Watchtower Bible and Tract Society, was a child of his time. He believed in progress. He looked around him, saw class warfare on the horizon, and declared that "the old order of things must pass away, and the new must supersede it . . . the change," he predicted, "will be violently opposed by those advantaged by the present order." In his second volume of *Studies in the Scriptures* (consisting of seven volumes, which achieved a circulation of 10 million copies in thirty-four languages), Russell wrote that "revolution world-wide [would] be the outcome, resulting in the final destruction of the old order and the introduction and establishment of the new." His feeling that a wonderful new world order was at hand was reinforced by what he perceived to be the fulfillment of Daniel 12:4: "But thou, O Daniel, shut up the words, and seal the book, even to the time of the end: many shall run to and fro, and knowledge shall be increased."

Impassioned as a child contemplating his first toy railroad, Russell wrote: "The predicted running to and fro—much rapid travelling—also confirms it. [The] steamboat, steam-car, telegraph . . . all belong to the Time of the End. . . . Today thousands of mammoth cars and steamships are carrying multitudes hither and thither, 'to and fro.' " [p. 63]

A fevered visionary who would not allow the world to confound him, who wished above all to have everything cohere, and who sought to impose logic and a pattern on the disparate elements of his time, Russell looked at class conflict and steam cars; fertilized what he saw with the rich products of his imaginings, an idiosyncratic reading of Bible chronology that was inventive and convoluted, a gorgeously eccentric interpretation of history, and some borrowings from Madame Blavatsky's heady mystical theories on the "inner meaning" of the Great Pyramid of Egypt—and came up with a fancy new religion.

Russell was to become notorious for various lurid scandals in which he was accused, in and out of court, of being money-mad, power-mad, and sex-mad. He is still regarded by Jehovah's Witnesses as a modern-day "Elias," perhaps the first true Christian since "apostasy came to full bloom . . . during the centuries of spiritual darkness" that began "in the fourth century." [*Yearbook*, 1975, p. 33]

The Witnesses say they are "the most ancient religious group of worshipers of the true God . . . Abel was . . . the first." Abel sacrificed the firstlings of his flock to Jehovah; Russell sacrificed a haberdashery business.

Charles Taze Russell—later known as "Pastor" Russell—was born on February 16, 1852. The second son of Scotch-Irish parents, Joseph L. Russell and Ann Eliza Birney Russell, he was raised a Presbyterian; at an unspecified later date he joined the Congregational Church because of its "more liberal views." His mother died when he was 9, the year the Civil War began.

In 1863, the year of the Emancipation Proclamation, 11-year-old Russell, according to Watchtower sources, entered a business partnership with his father, for which he himself drew up the contract under which the business was brought into being and managed. By the time he was 15, he and his father had succeeded in establishing a chain of men's-clothing stores radiating out from Pittsburgh. According to the Witnesses, Russell eventually closed out his business for a quarter of a million dollars. [*JWDP*] According to the *American Encyclopedia of Biography*, 1968, Russell "sold shirts to make a living until he got his first congregation."

It is said that Ann Russell dedicated Charles Taze to God when he was born. (Of Mrs. Russell's firstborn, nothing is known.) It is also said that Pastor Russell's father frequently found his son, when Charles was as young as 12, poring over a Bible concordance in the family store in the early hours of the morning.

It is a strange picture: young Russell keeping the business books by day and reading The Book by gaslight in the small hours of the morning—but not so strange, after all, when one considers the Mellons, Carnegies, and Rockefellers of Russell's time, millionaires who regarded the Deity as the Great Paymaster who kept all His good children (good equaling rich) on His dole.

As a youth Russell seems to have been obsessed with hellfire and torment; he also apparently saw himself as the instrument of men's salvation. An early associate of Russell's tells us that 14-year-old Charles Taze would go out Saturday nights "to where men gathered . . . to loaf, and would write Bible texts on the sidewalk with colored chalk. . . . He hoped to attract their attention, so that they might accept Christ and avoid being lost and going to eternal torment." [*Faith*, p. 17]

I find this image of an adolescent God-obsessed fanatic both irritating and touching. It was a time when men were given over to wild hyperbole and extravagant behavior; nevertheless, there is something disquieting about it. Most men and women had other things on their minds: the nation was entering the Reconstruction period; the Ku Klux Klan was formed; the Suffrage Movement, which was to culminate in 1869 with Wyoming's giving women the vote, was going strong; slavery had been abolished. Abraham Lincoln had delivered the Gettysburg Address not more that 120 miles from Allegheny. These events seem not to have interested Russell at all; nothing interested Russell more than his own spiritual seesawing between certainty and despair. He was firmly planted in the center of his own universe.

When Russell was 17, he suffered a revulsion against the concept of eternal punishment and against the doctrine of predestination. He deserted the sidewalks and immersed himself in a study of Oriental religions (his later infatuation with the Pyramids may have been a holdover from this time). But Eastern religion did not satisfy him. Never a man to do things by halves, he renounced religion at the age of 17. One detects more than a hint of megalomania in his renunciation, which, as he saw it, would necessarily affect not only himself, but all of "suffering humanity": "I'm just going to forget the whole thing and give all my attention to business. If I make some money I can use that to help suffering humanity, even though I cannot help do them any good spiritually." [*Yearbook*, 1975, p. 35]

Russell's crisis of faith lasted a year. In 1870, when he was 18, "shaken in faith regarding many long-accepted doctrines . . . a ready prey to the logic of infidelity" [*Ibid.*], Russell entered a dim meeting hall in Allegheny where Second Adventists congregated to find out what this small group believed that would be more convincing than the teachings of the established churches. The sermon he heard was enough to bring him around to a belief that Jehovah had truly inspired the Scriptures and to prove to him the link between the Apostles and Prophets.

From 1870 to 1875, Russell, together with six young men of his acquaintance, studied the Bible. Russell's small schismatic band was soon convinced that Jehovah had blessed them with increasing light and truth. [*Yearbook*, 1975, p. 36] They had come to believe that the second coming of Christ would be invisible; Russell pronounced himself deeply disappointed in the teaching of the Second Adventists, who believed in the visible return of Christ and the destruction of the earth and its inhabitants in 1873 or 1874. To Russell these predictions seemed naive, not to say crude, and he felt they could only bring scorn on the faithful who awaited the Kingdom. Russell—who seems always to have regarded himself as the cynosure of all eyes and never to have doubted that his spiritual odyssey was of compelling significance to all of mankind—promptly acted to remove the reflected reproach he felt contaminated him and to set the record straight. In 1873, when he was 21, Russell wrote a booklet called "The Object and Manner of the Lord's Return"; he published 50,000 copies at his own expense.

This was the year of the great industrial panic, the year Carnegie embarked on his steel mergers in Russell's native Allegheny. In 1870, Rockefeller founded his dynasty with Standard Oil. In 1872, Victoria Woodhull ran for President as the candidate of the People's Party.

None of these events is alluded to in the Witnesses' biographical references to Russell. (The Civil War might not have taken place.) As far as the Witnesses are concerned, all of these events are the detritus of human history. What was significant about the last half of the 19th century is that "as the conclusion of the system of things approached, the Most High God, Jehovah, acted to identify the 'wheat' [the sons of God—*them*] in a pronounced way." [*Ibid.*, p. 33]

In January, 1876, Russell came across a periodical called *The Herald of the Morning*, published by N. H. Barbour of Rochester, New York. Barbour, like Russell, believed that the object of Christ's return was not to destroy the physical earth, but to "bless all families of the earth." [*Ibid.*, p. 36] Barbour and Russell shared the belief that Christ would come invisibly, like "a thief in the night," and that Adventists erred when they expected to see the Lord in the flesh. When he found this kindred soul, Russell affiliated his Pittsburgh Bible Class—which by this time had grown to 30 members— with Barbour's slightly larger Rochester group. He contributed money to the *Herald* and became its coeditor. In 1877, when he was 25, Russell sold out his business interests and began to travel from city to city, delivering sermons. (The same year, eleven leaders of the Molly Maguires were hanged in Pennsylvania. This put an end to the secret society, but not to violence in the mines.) Charles Taze Russell was thereafter known as Pastor Russell.

Pastor Russell prohibited collections at his meetings and depended, according to the Witnesses, on unsolicited contributions after all his money was exhausted. How Russell managed to "exhaust" a quarter of a million dollars—if indeed he did, or if he'd had it in the first place—was to become a matter of fierce contention between him and the woman he later married and a subject for speculation during the lawsuits and counterlawsuits that kept him in the public eye during the last quarter of the 19th century.

In 1877, Russell and Barbour jointly wrote and published *Three Worlds, and the Harvest of This World.* The Biblical chronology set forth in that volume, and in Russell's subsequent books, is labyrinthine. One despairs of making it explicable. Indeed, I feel justified in conjecturing that many of Russell's followers must have accepted his sanguine conclusions without comprehending his premises.

Russell preached that the 6,000 years of man's existence on earth had ended in 1872—Victoria Woodhull also foresaw an end to "man's" rule in 1872, but she meant by that something quite different—and that the seventh millennium had begun in 1873. The glorified Christ became invisibly present in 1874. Shortly after 1874 had begun the "antitypical Jubilee," an event "foreshadowed" by the ancient jubilees observed under the Mosaic Law. For forty years, the "saints," God's consecrated ones, would be "harvested," until, on October 1, 1914, the Gentile Times would end. On October 1, 1914, the evil worldly system would collapse, God would have His everlasting day, and there would be a general "Restitution" for all mankind—but not before the "living saints" (Russell and his followers) would be suddenly and miraculously caught away bodily to be with their Lord, in 1878.

In October, 1914, of course, the world was three months into the bloodiest war of its history—and Russell, not having been "caught away," was very much alive and in the flesh. As a recent publication of Jehovah's Witnesses remarks, somewhat laconically, "Something must have been miscalculated." [*God's Kingdom of a Thousand Years Has Approached,* 1973, p. 188]

It is interesting that Russell himself wrote [*SS,* Vol. III, *The Time Is at Hand,* 1905, p. 243]: "For it be distinctly noticed that if the Chronology, or any of these time-periods, be changed but one year, the beauty and force of this parallelism [with the Jewish Jubilee cycles] are destroyed. . . . If the Chronology be altered but one year, more or less—it would spoil the parallelism."

As we have seen, the parallelism has been destroyed with a vengeance. Russell, playing with exactly the same Scriptures (Daniel, Ezekiel, Matthew, Luke, Revelation) as current Witnesses, came up with totally different dates. Only 1914 remains a fixed date, and it has been assigned a different meaning.

The established churches of Russell's day called his calculations ridiculous, as, in the event, they proved to be. The Witnesses, however, do not

hesitate to complain that the clergy, who dismissed Russell as a fringe lunatic, "were really being used by Satan." [*JWDP*] That the major sects of his
day were right and Russell wrong does not, in so brazen a tautology, count
for anything. And the Witnesses continue to juggle Scripture with the
abandon of those who are able to brush away empirical evidence as if it
were a gnat on the countenance of their Lord.

Russell's calculations are not easy to unravel; they are, however, not
without a certain quaint interest. (New dates, previously unmentioned,
spring up like weeds in Russell's writings, which defy synopsis. How that
man loved numbers and charts! It is fruitless to speculate, perhaps, but
what if he hadn't been a child-whiz bookkeeper?) Russell wasn't the first, or
the last, man to snow people with numbers.

In *Thy Kingdom Come* (Volume III of *Studies in the Scriptures*, 1891), Russell calls attention to the 2,300 days of Daniel's prophecy and, by legerde-
main, comes up with 1846 as

> the time when God's sanctuary would be cleansed of the defiling er-
> rors and principles of Papacy. . . . We have noted the fulfillment of
> the 1,260 days, or the time, times, and half a time of Papacy's power
> to persecute, and the beginning, in 1799, of the Time of the End. We
> have seen how 1,290 days marked the beginning of an understanding
> of the mysteries of prophecy in the year 1829, culminating in the
> great movement of 1844 known as the Second-Advent movement
> when . . . the wise Virgins went forth to meet the Bridegroom, thirty
> years prior to his actual coming. . . . We have remarked, with special
> delight, the 1,335 days, pointing . . . to 1874 as the exact date of our
> Lord's return. [pp. 305–06]

Eighteen forty-six . . . 1799 . . . 1829 . . . 1844 . . . 1874; 1,260 days
. . . 1,290 days . . . 1,335 days . . . No wonder the Witnesses won't allow
"outsiders" access to the *Studies in the Scriptures* (which are very hard indeed
to come by). Even they, who justify all past error on the ground that Biblical dates are "ingeniously hidden" and cannot be ascertained until God sees
fit to shed His light on the "mathematically precise" meaning of prophecy—
which is usually after their prophecy has failed—must prefer not to have to
expose to ridicule all of Russell's peculiar reckonings. They certainly prefer
to forget that their founder dragged Napoleon Bonaparte into his calculations:

> . . . the exact date of the beginning of the "Time of the End" . . .
> is shown to be Napoleon's invasion of Egypt, which covered a period
> of a year and five months. He sailed May, 1798, and, returning,
> landed in France October 9, 1799. . . . Napoleon's work, together
> with the French Revolution, broke the spell of religious superstition,
> . . . awakened the world to a fuller sense of the powers and preroga-
> tives of manhood and broke the Papal dominion. . . . The era closing

with A.D. 1799, marked by Napoleon's Egyptian campaign, sealed and defined the limit of Papal dominion over the nations. . . . The time appointed [1,260 years of power] having expired, the predicted judgment against the system began, which must finally "consume and destroy all into the end." . . . Napoleon took away the Papacy's civil jurisdiction in the city of Rome, which was recognized nominally from the promulgation of Justinian's decree, A.D. 533, but actually from the overthrow of the Ostrogoth monarchy, A.D. 539—just 1,260 years before 1799. [pp. 44–58]

This idiosyncratic reading of history would be greeted with incredulity by most scholars. (But since "worldly scientists" are engaged in a conspiracy with Satan the Devil to deceive mankind, this is an obstacle Witnesses take in stride.) Russell was eclectic. Having convinced himself that Napoleon was clearly portrayed in prophecy as "the man of destiny," he revised history to bend it to his theological will. (One must be forgiven for wondering if Russell did not see himself as just such another man as Napoleon—a man of destiny who dealt the Papacy mortal wounds. Speaking of himself in the third person, Russell once wrote, only "the author, and, so far as he knows, no one else, had noticed . . . the opportunity for restitution of human perfection and all that was lost in Adam, due at the close of the Gospel high-calling." *Only the author* . . . If one were inclined to indulge in a bit of psychohistorical speculation, one might easily conclude that Pastor Russell was suffering from an Elias-Napoleon complex.)

The Witnesses today no longer read the French Revolution into the Book of Revelation; and the meaning of the Book of Daniel, into which Russell read the fanciful interpretation that the King of the North pictured "the Roman Empire's representative," and the King of the South pictured "a representative of Egypt's kingdom," has been amended. In current Witness theology, the King of the North "pictures" "the Communist bloc of nations," and the King of the South is "manifestly the Anglo-American World Power." [*TW*, Feb. 1, 1976, p. 94]

But the Witnesses still hold that Russell's writings were the vehicle God used to reveal His divine will and to separate the peoples of the earth into the sheep and the goats.

Russell, according to his successor, J. F. Rutherford, "made no claim of a special revelation from God, but held that it was God's due time for the Bible to be understood; and that, being fully consecrated to the Lord and to his service, he was permitted to understand it." There was no special revelation granted from God, but he was permitted to understand what nobody else understood. [*JWDP*]

Some things have not changed. The Witnesses are still ferociously anti-Papist, and the appeal to the disenfranchised that characterized Russell's work (Russell believed that there would be a conflict between "the classes and the masses") underlines the work of his successors, although it has taken different form; and the peculiarly American flavor of this religion, which translated American technology and class struggle into quasi-mystical terms, remains.

"The revolution and independence of the American colonies—the successful establishment of a prosperous Republic, a government by the people and for the people, without interference of either royalty or priestcraft," Russell wrote, "set a new lesson before the now-awakening people, who for so many centuries had slumbered in ignorance." [*SS*, Vol. III, pp. 51–52]

America gave birth to this religion; and it remains in essence American. The law-and-order God of the Witnesses is Middle American. The Witnesses are international and claim not to be chauvinistic; the American Revolution is now dismissed, as is the French Revolution, as irrelevant to God's purposes. Still, one wonders. Witness workers in British headquarters were forbidden, in the 1950s, to take their ritual morning tea break on the grounds that it was "untheocratic" and counterproductive; I can't help feeling that what was being objected to was that it was un-American. "My God," a friend once said to me, "I've just seen fifty thousand Witnesses at a convention—and they all look alike!" They do all like alike; they all look Midwestern. Even when they are clad in saris and loincloths, muu-muus and kimonos, there is something ineffably missionary-Midwestern about the aura they project. And Paradise restored, if the illustrations in Watchtower publications are to be taken literally, will look exactly like an endless Kansas picnic—or a Texas barbecue. Most of the survivors of Armageddon will be attired in clothes from Montgomery Ward; and they will have crew cuts and bouffant hairdos, and skirts decorously short. (Innocence, to the Witnesses, suggests a shirt and tie.) The Witness dream of Eden is a dream of American suburbia—with a few people in exotic foreign dress to lend exoticism to the proceedings.

Russell fortified his chronology with cranky evidence from "God's Stone Witness—the Pyramid." "The Great Pyramid [is] a part of [God's] instrumentality for convincing the world of his wisdom, foreknowledge and grace. . . . located in the geographical center of the land surface of the world, the measurements of the Great Pyramid represent the earth and God's plan for the earth's salvation. . . . in it are contained prophetical and chronological teachings." Can Russell have believed the earth was flat? There can be no center of the surface of a sphere. [*SS*, Vol. III, pp. 317, 326]

Russell believed that the measurements of the Pyramid proved that 1914 would be the end of the world order. He read more things into the Entrance Passage of the Pyramid than an art critic might read into an Abstract Expressionist painting. The Entrance Passage, he believed, validated his view that "the Day of the Lord induces the spirit of liberty; and the spirit of liberty, coming in contact with the pride, wealth and power of those still in control, will be the cause of the trouble which the Scriptures assure us will be very great. . . . Capitalists, and all men, see it coming, and 'men's hearts are failing them for fear, and for looking after the things coming.' " The "Pit" of the Pyramid, he believed, symbolized that "the evil systems—civil, social and religious—of the 'present evil world' will there sink into oblivion, into destruction." [*SS*, Vol. VI, *The New Creation*, p. 343]

"The Great Pyramid witnesses, not only the downward course of man in sin, but also the various steps in the divine plan by which preparation is made for his full recovery from the fall, through the way of life, opened up by the death and resurrection of our Lord Jesus." [*Ibid.*, p. 356]

Among the more extravagant claims Russell made for the Great Pyramid were that the Pit of the Pyramid symbolized the descent of the nations into anarchism and that the ventilating tubes or air passages of the Queen's Chambers suggested that "the condition of human perfection, when reached [after the Restitution], may be made an everlasting state." [*Ibid.*, p. 370] (The Witnesses had not yet fixed on the doctrine of everlasting life on earth; Russell's followers believed that they would be lifted up to heaven. The everlasting-life-on-a-perfect-earth doctrine grew as they grew in numbers.) How ventilating tubes and air passages suggested an everlasting state of perfection is unclear. The Pyramid, Russell further asserted, was absolute proof that the theory of evolution was untrue.

Pittsburgh newspapers reported that on the night of the Memorial of Christ's death in 1878, Russell was found on the Sixth Street Bridge dressed in a white robe, waiting to be wafted to heaven.

Russell told reporters that on that night of glory-be that was not to be, he was home in bed. "However, some of the more radical ones might have been there," he said, "but I was not." [*Faith*, p. 27]

(Parenthetically, it's worth noting that the only holiday Witnesses celebrate is the Memorial of Christ's death—and they "celebrate" it by listening to a speech. Neither Christ's birth nor His resurrection is marked on their gloomy calendars.)

Many of the "saints," who had been instructed to believe that Russell's interpretation of Biblical chronology was impeccable, were disappointed when the expected miracle did not come off. Russell, we are told, did not for a moment feel cast down; he "realized that what God so plainly declared must some time have a fulfillment," and he "wanted to have it just in God's time and way." [*Ibid.*, pp. 26–27]

After the saints were stranded on the Sixth Street Bridge, Russell "reexamined" Scripture and decided that the true significance of the year 1878 was that from that time on, none of the saints would "sleep in death," [*Ibid.*, p. 27] but would, upon death, immediately be resurrected, to life in heaven with Christ.

Russell's colleague Barbour was not satisfied. In a bitter article written for *Herald of the Morning*, Barbour argued that "Christ's death was no more a settlement of the penalty of man's sins than would the sticking of a pin through the body of a fly and causing it suffering and death be considered by an earthly parent as a just settlement for misdemeanor in his child." [*Ibid.*, p. 28] So, Barbour and Russell split. This was to be the first of many schisms. None of the schismatic sects has flourished.

Russell, who saw the Lord's hand in everything that pertained to him, including his finances, withdrew financial support from *Herald of the Morning*, understanding it to be the Lord's will for him to start another journal. In 1879, together with five other contributors, he funded *Zion's Watch Tower and Herald of Christ's Presence*. Russell was editor and publisher of the *Watch Tower*, which had a first-issue printing of 6,000 copies. [*Ibid.*, p. 28]

(In 1976, over 279 million magazines were distributed by the Watchtower Society worldwide. [*Yearbook*, 1977, pp. 30–31])

Between 1879 and 1880, Russell and his associates founded thirty congregations—called "ecclesias"—in Pennsylvania, New Jersey, Massachusetts, Delaware, Ohio, and Michigan.

Today, the 40,155 congregations of Jehovah's Witnesses are governed from the Brooklyn headquarters of the Watchtower Bible and Tract Society. [*Ibid.*] The Witnesses describe their structure as "theocratic"; it is more accurate to call it totalitarian. During the 1880s, ecclesias of Russellite Bible Students voted congregationally on some matters and elected a board of elders who were responsible for directing congregational matters. Today elders of congregations are appointed by the eighteen-man governing body in Brooklyn (an all-white, all-male group with a median age of 60); elders and governors form a self-perpetuating elite. Early ecclesias were "linked together by accepting the pattern of activity in Pittsburgh, where Charles Taze Russell and other Watchtower writers were elders." [*Yearbook*, 1975, p. 39]

There were, in 1976, 2,248,390 Jehovah's Witnesses, all active proselytizers, in 210 countries. [*Yearbook*, 1977, pp. 30–31] In 1881, when Zion's Watch Tower Tract Society was established as an unincorporated body with Russell as its manager, there were 100 proselytizing Russellites, known as "colporteurs." By 1885, the number had grown to 300 colporteurs. [*Yearbook*, 1975, pp. 39–40] By 1914, there were 1,200 congregations of Russellites.

The unincorporated Zion's Watch Tower Tract Society, the printing organization to which Russell ("with others") is supposed to have contributed $35,000 of his fortune, was incorporated as Zion's Watch Tower Tract Society in 1884. [*Yearbook*, 1975, p. 40]

Russell was the president of the organization that is today known as the Watch Tower Bible and Tract Society of Pennsylvania. Mrs. Russell was a director of the Society and served as its secretary and treasurer for some years. [*Yearbook*, 1975, p. 66] According to its charter, "The purpose for which the corporation is formed is, the dissemination of Bible Truths in various languages by means of the publication of tracts, pamphlets, papers and other religious documents and by the use of all other lawful means which its Board of Directors, duly constituted, shall deem expedient for the furtherance of the purpose stated." [*JWDP*, p. 27]

By 1889, the Watch Tower Society had begun to amass property. A four-story brick building in Allegheny, known as the Bible House, was built and legally held in title by the Tower Publishing Company. [*Yearbook*, 1975, p. 42] A holding company for his private interests, the Tower Publishing Company (which Russell used, at one time, to publish literature for the Watch Tower Society at a price agreed upon by the board of directors—of which he was president), built the Bible House "at a cost of $34,000." [*JWDP*, p. 27; *Yearbook*, 1975, p. 42] In 1898, ownership of the Tower Publishing plant and real estate was transferred by donation to the Watch Tower Society. The board of the Watch Tower Society evaluated the Allegheny property and equipment at $164,033.65. [*Yearbook*, 1975, p. 42] (There were at this time 400 preachers associated with the Watch Tower Society.) The Allegheny building remained the Society's headquarters for twenty years.

Russell's critics charged him with financial flimflammery, arguing, on circumstantial evidence, that he was manipulating publishing houses and property to assure himself of an outlet for his prolific writings for his personal enrichment. The Pastor was beset with troubles, assailed from within and without his organization. His wife became his bitterest and most outspoken enemy. Lawsuits and civil investigations brought him notoriety—welcome notoriety; he wore it like a mantle of righteousness. The more trouble, the more he was able to insist that the Devil was out to crush him; his scandalous behavior was transformed, by his followers, into proof of his holiness. Every time new litigation was brought against him, each time he was reviled, each time something horrible befell him as a result of his own conduct—things humiliating enough to send most men fleeing to obscurity—he puffed himself up and offered it as proof that, like Jesus, he was persecuted as a Messenger of Truth.

Russell's associate Hugh Macmillan writes, in *Faith on the March*, of the Pastor's flamboyant behavior, "Even Jesus was called a 'devil,' 'gluttonous,' and a 'winebibber.' And [Jesus] said they would treat his followers in the same way."

I can show you a thousand women that would be glad to be in your place and that would know my wishes and do them. . . . I can show you a thousand women that if I would say, "I want sweet potatoes," sweet potatoes would be there. If I wanted pumpkin pie, pumpkin pie would be there.—Attributed to Charles Taze Russell by Mrs. Maria Frances Ackley Russell [Court transcript, Superior Court of Pennsylvania]

I am like a jellyfish; I float around here and there. I touch this one and that one, and if she responds I take her to me, and if not I float on to others.—Attributed to Charles Taze Russell by Mrs. Russell [Court transcript, Court of Common Pleas, Pittsburgh, Pennsylvania]

In 1894 Maria Frances Russell was—as far as the world could see—her beleaguered husband's staunchest ally. In 1897, Mrs. Russell fled from her husband, later declaring, "Even a dog has more rights than I had." For years the Russells' marital difficulties were grist for the mills of the tabloids, providing entertainment for the masses and ammunition for Russell's religious antagonists. Mrs. Russell was not amused.

In the early 1890s, some of Russell's associates attempted to wrest control of the Watch Tower Society from him. They charged him with financial dishonesty and with aberrant, autocratic behavior. The Pastor, they asserted, not content to lay down doctrinal law for his followers, was so greatly intruding upon the private lives of the Bible Students as to tell them whom they might or might not marry. Russell, it was stated, was "in a deplorably sinful state—dishonest, a traitor, a liar." [*ZWT*, June 11, 1894]

Russell issued a countercharge that there was a "conspiracy" in his own office and in his own household—a "special and cunning attack made by the great enemy"—"to shatter the body of Christ." [*Ibid.*]

Matters came to a head in 1894. There were rumors of marital discord between the Pastor and his wife, who was a regular contributor to *Zion's Watch Tower* and an associate editor of that magazine. Mrs. Russell, it was stated, together with all of Russell's household and office workers, was under compulsion to lie for him. According to one of Russell's closest associates, a Mr. Rogers, Mrs. Russell was often observed "weeping bitter tears over Brother Russell's sins." [*Ibid.*]

Maria Russell undertook to speak in her husband's behalf. For eighteen days she visited congregations in ten cities to stanch the flow of rumors and to defend her husband. She represented her husband as a just, noble, and generous man, maligned by "false teachers" of "damnable heresies," wolves in sheep's clothing.

This is a partial account of her vindication of the man she was later to charge with extreme cruelty:

> [A Bible Student] told that my husband forbids people to marry, and as proof of this related how he once sent Mr. Bryan a three day's journey into the country at an expense of twelve dollars, in order to prevent a wedding. I answered . . . that Mr. Russell never forbade anyone to marry, and that not a living being could truthfully say that he or she had been forbidden; but that I knew that when his opinion

was *specially asked* he gave the Apostle Paul's advice (I Cor. 7:25–35).
. . . It was to my husband's credit that he spared neither trouble nor
expense in order to let a sister in Christ know something of what he
knew of the *character* of the man she was about to marry; that, thus
informed, she might the better judge for herself whether or not he
would make a desirable husband. [*Ibid.*]

This ambiguous statement, which might just as easily have led Bible Students to conclude that Russell did indeed seek to influence the personal
decisions of the "sisters," served to convince the majority of Russell's followers that he was acting in the best interests of his flock. (One wonders
just how much prompting Russell needed to offer the Apostle Paul's advice:
"Concerning virgins . . . I say that it is good for a man so to be./Art thou
loosed from a wife? seek not a wife/But if thou marry, thou hast not sinned;
and if a virgin marry, she hath not sinned. Nevertheless such shall have
trouble in the flesh./ But this I say, brethren, the time is short; it remain-
eth, that both they that have wives be as though they had none;/I would
have you without carefulness. He that is unmarried careth for the things
that belong to the Lord,/But he that is married careth for the things that are
of the world, how he may please his wife./There is a difference also between a wife and a virgin. The unmarried woman careth for the things of
the Lord, that she may be holy both in body and in spirit: but she that is
married careth for the things of the world, how she may please her hus-
band/ . . . attend upon the Lord without distraction.")

Mrs. Russell had also to contend with the charge that her husband had
written a Mr. Adamson, shortly after Adamson married, to "make his Will
so as to give what money he had to the Tract Fund, and to be sure not to
let Mrs. Adamson see that letter." What the Pastor had in fact written,
Mrs. Russell steadfastly maintained, was that Mrs. Adamson deserved consideration "on general principles . . . even if [she was] out of harmony on
religious subjects. . . . [Pastor Russell] advised that if Mr. Adamson decided to will *any portion* of his effects to the *Tract Fund*, it would be wise,
under the circumstances, . . . and to the interest of his domestic happiness,
not to inform Mrs. Adamson respecting it." [*Ibid.*]

Maria Russell's arguments in defense of her beleaguered husband may
have been impassioned; they were hardly conclusive. They were, however,
successful. Women in Russell's ecclesias all over the country reported having dreams in which their beloved Pastor Russell was scourged and flagel-
lated, but shielded by a protecting angel. Female Russellites seemed to be
in the grip of hysteria: one Bible Student reported that she had had a
"prophetic" dream in which "someone in the congregation hurled a stone at
the head of the preacher, which struck him in the mouth, from whence the
blood flowed profusely." In her dream, she "ran to his aid and tried to wipe
away the blood, which only flowed the more."

It is doubtful that Mrs. Russell's rebuttals of the charges brought against her husband were, in themselves, enough to persuade anyone that the Pastor was blameless. It would seem, rather, that *anything* Mrs. Russell said in Russell's defense would suffice for those whose investment in their religion was so great that to leave it would cause a gaping hole in the fabric of their lives. The "persecution" the faithful endured served to reinforce their conviction that they were a tiny band of comradely brothers and sisters united in a common cause against the wolves howling at the gates of their belief.

Those who continued to follow Russell—and they were in the majority—could conclude, self-importantly, that they were the focus of Satan's ire; they regarded their "fiery ordeal" as evidence that Jehovah had allowed a "sifting" to take place in his organization, in order to cleanse it of those whose "jealousy, envy and malice had eaten as doth a canker into their hearts." It was proof, furthermore, that they were living in the time of the end, when " 'dogs' of quarrelsome, snappish dispositions, always seeking their own advance," would engender contention among the Lord's people. [*Ibid.*]

Mrs. Russell, implicitly acknowledging that her husband was not entirely without fault, wrote that the truth was contained "in imperfect earthen vessells; but . . . the very frailness of the vessels only manifests the more clearly that the excellency of power is of God and not of us." She adamantly denied, however, that Russell, that frail vessel whose honor she preserved, had enlisted her "enforced cooperation" as had been rumored; she fiercely denied that she was "in absolute opposition to [her] husband's course." [*Ibid.*; see *Yearbook*, 1975]

Three years later, in 1897, after eighteen years of marriage, Maria Frances Ackley Russell made a public about-face. She left her "imperfect earthen vessel," fleeing to relatives in Chicago to gain protection from the man who she claimed was committing gross improprieties with other women and who, furthermore, was trying to have her incarcerated in a lunatic asylum.

In 1903, Mrs. Russell filed for legal separation in the Court of Common Pleas at Pittsburgh, Pennsylvania. The case came up for trial in 1906 before Justice Collier and a jury; it was a sensational case—a Victorian gothic, with intimations of perversions, imprisonments, madness; and it was resolved in Mrs. Russell's favor. Pastor Russell fought Mrs. Russell's demands for separation and alimony for five years, initiating libel suits against newspapers and a minister along the way. On March 4, 1908, Mrs. Russell was granted a divorce. In 1909, she appealed for an increase in alimony, and Russell moved out of the jurisdiction of the Pittsburgh courts, transferred all his assets to the Watch Tower Society so that he could declare himself penniless, and moved his staff and his operations to Brooklyn, New York, to avoid being jailed for failure to pay alimony. Finally, in 1911, the courts, on appeal, ruled conclusively in behalf of Mrs. Russell, Justice Orlady of the Superior Court of Pennsylvania stating, with barely concealed anger, that Pastor Russell's "course of conduct toward his wife evidenced such insistent egotism and extravagant self-praise that it would be manifest to the jury that his conduct toward her was one of continual arrogant domination that would necessarily render the life of any sensitive Christian woman a burden and make her life intolerable."

The Witnesses contend, in order to protect Russell's claim that he was never sullied by divorce, that the decree—styled "In Divorce"—was "a partial or qualified divorce," in effect a legal separation. In 1913, Mrs. Russell, appearing before the (New York) Board of Tax Commissioners, which was investigating Russell's financial affairs, agreed that she had secured a "limited divorce" from the Commonwealth of Pennsylvania: "I asked for a limited divorce because it carries with it support, while absolute divorce does not, though I could have secured an absolute divorce on the same evidence."

The Witnesses have in recent years published an expurgated version of Pastor and Mrs. Russell's difficulties—a story which for many years they kept scrupulously shrouded. (In all my years as a Witness—including the three years I spent at Watchtower headquarters—no one ever mentioned the Russells, least of all the old-timers, who, when past presidents of the Watchtower Society were mentioned, discoursed on the fact that they didn't follow "personalities" or "any man," but only God's organization.) It pleases the Witnesses now—perhaps we have the resurgence of feminism to thank for it—to hold up Maria Frances Ackley Russell as an object lesson: Vanity, thy name is woman. Their interpretation of events [*Yearbook*, 1975; pp. 65–75; see also *WT*, June 15, 1972, and *JWDP*, p. 45] is that shortly after her tour in defense of her husband, Mrs. Russell, "an educated, intelligent woman" (the adjectives are pejorative), attempted to usurp the Pastor's rightful place and asserted herself concerning the material intended for publication in *The Watch Tower*. For this she was compared to Moses's sister Miriam, who tried to usurp her brother's place as the leader of the Israelites but who was prevented because of Jehovah's displeasure.

In a letter to a friend written on December 27, 1899, less than five years after his wife had acted to preserve his reputation, Russell added Mrs. Russell to his Enemies List: "Our dear Sister Russell became afflicted with the same malady which has smitten others—ambition." For thirteen years "a noble, true helpmate," Mrs. Russell allowed her "ambitious spirit" to be "fanned" when she received warm receptions at congregations. She "seemed to forget that she was received, not merely for herself, but . . . as the representative of her husband." She began to "strike for the gratification of her own ambition," insisting upon her liberty to use her talents to write and speak what she pleased. "I told her, kindly but plainly," Russell wrote, "that I could not think it to be the Lord's will to encourage her to take any part of the work so long as she manifested so ambitious a spirit." Complaining of a "female conspiracy" against the Lord's organization, Russell wrote, "The result was a considerable slander and misrepresentation, for of course it would not suit [the women's] purposes to tell the plain unvarnished truth, that Sister Russell was ambitious. . . . When she desired to come back, I totally refused, except upon a promise that she should make reasonable acknowledgement of the wrong course she had been pursuing." [*TW*, June 15, 1972]

The man whose financial treatment of Mrs. Russell Justice Orlady characterized as "radically different from the standard imposed upon him by the law, and recognized by all the courts of this country" wrote in 1906,

> I was not aware of it at the time, but learned subsequently that the conspirators [of 1894] endeavored to sow seeds of discord in my wife's heart by flattery, "woman's rights" arguments, etc. However, . . . I was spared the humiliation of seeing my wife amongst those conspirators. . . . As matters began to setttle down, the "woman's rights" ideas and personal ambition began again to come to the top, and I perceived that Mrs. Russell's active campaign in my defense, and the very cordial reception given her by the dear friends at that time . . . had done her injury by increasing her self-appreciation. . . . I was continually harassed with suggestions of alterations of my writings. I was pained to note this growing disposition so foreign to the humble mind which characterized her for the first thirteen happy years.

For the past three years you have been gradually forcing upon me the evidence that we both erred in judgment when we married—that we are not adaptable to each other. . . . I conclude that no one is adapted to me—except the Lord. I am glad that He and I understand each other and have confidence in each other." Letter of July 8, 1896, from Pastor Russell to his wife, Exhibit No. 3, Court Transcript, Superior Court of Pennsylvania

In an undated letter, Pastor Russell wrote her of his pleasure in the memory of her devotion—her inability to live without him, her longing to die first. And, indeed, he tells her, he feels the same, but it is her "fall," her "everlasting loss," that gives him the greatest pain rather than the thought of his own lonely future.

Pastor Russell was determined to brand his wife as a blazing "suffragette." In *People's Pulpit*, the Pastor wrote: "She came under the influence of what is popularly known as 'Women's Rights,' and, because she could not have her own way and write what she chose for the columns of my journal [of which, it is to be remembered, Mrs. Russell was associate editor], she endeavored to coerce me and took one step after another, apparently determined that if she could not coerce, she would crush and destroy my life and influence." [See *Brooklyn Eagle*, Oct. 31, 1911.]

The official Watchtower version has it that Mrs. Russell became ill in 1897, and her husband gave her much cheerful and kind attention to "touch her heart and restore it to its former loving and tender condition." [*Yearbook*, 1975] Having thus applied balm to her wayward spirit, Russell, in the presence of an official Bible Students Committee, gained his wife's agreement not to interfere in his management of *Zion's Watch Tower:* "I then asked her in their presence if she would shake hands. She hesitated, but finally gave me her hand. I then said, 'Now, will you kiss me, dear, as a token of the degree of change of mind which you have indicated?' Again she hesitated, but finally did kiss me and otherwise manifested a renewal of affection in the presence of the Committee." Russell was so good as to allow his wife to lead a weekly meeting of the "Sisters of the Allegheny Church." His amplitude of spirit was to no avail. Mrs. Russell left her long-suffering husband in 1897, after her illness; and he dutifully made arrangements for her financial support, providing her with a separate home and all that a reasonable woman could ask.

The court transcripts (as published by the *Brooklyn Eagle*) tell a different story.

The court records tell the story of a woman sick and afraid, abandoned in an empty four-story mansion, bewildered, agitated, cut off from help. It is a penny-dreadful story, full of Victorian vapors and horrors; but the pain of a woman being pushed into insanity, tormented by vindictive messages sent to her in the guise of husbandly love through her husband's intimate, is undisguised in the purple prose of her defense lawyer and the majestic prose of a judge splendid in his wrath. There is something impressive about the peculiar genius of a man who could inspire adoration and worship—particularly among women—while judges and courts threatened him with jail sentences and exposed him as a sophist and a fraud.

Pastor Russell stood ready to take on the whole world; he loved to be hated equally as he loved to be loved. He always had to stand stage center, whether the audience threw eggs or roses. Only indifference was terrible to him.

From the brief by Congressman Stephen Porter, attorney for Mrs. Russell, which Justice Orlady of the Superior Court reviewed after Pastor Russell appealed the separation verdict handed down by the Court of Common Pleas, we read of the "kind and loving attention" Russell tendered his wife during her illness:

> The apartments in which the Russells lived were on the fourth floor of a business house on Arch Street, Allegheny, Pa. There was no neighbor within calling distance at night, and although for a number of years the building had been occupied by the employees of the Watch Tower at night; yet shortly after respondent had started . . . reports about his wife's sanity, all of the employees were removed

from the building, leaving Mrs. Russell, in case her husband was absent, alone.

The conditions were those of utter desolation with respect to her. What must have been the feelings of this woman after . . . years of indignities? She, no doubt, was crushed, humiliated, and brokenhearted, and would naturally have apprehensions of the absence of her husband to take some sort of proceedings founded upon his alleged pretense of her mental unsoundness, and there is no doubt that her husband at this time was seriously considering the advisability of inquiring into his wife's mental condition by an expert examination, and notwithstanding the fact that when asked the question on the witness stand he denied [it], his letter to Judge Breedon (Exhibit No. 15) contains this statement:

"Indeed, had it not been for my dislike of publicity on the lady's account as well as my own, I would have felt it only a reasonable duty to have asked the court to appoint a competent expert examination respecting the lady's mental condition."

While living alone with his wife in this large building, he prepares a cunningly worded letter to the effect that they have reconciled their differences, and then on Friday evening of that week he presents it to his wife for her signature, and all night long he follows her about from room to room, urging, coaxing, pleading and threatening until her head is in a whirl of doubts and fears, and thus forces her to sign the letter under protest. This is undenied by the respondent, and although the defense was based on the fact that a reconciliation had occured between the libellant and respondent, the remarkable fact exists that this letter, which was in possession of the respondent, was never even offered in evidence.

The insulting letters to her relatives and friends, warning them not to harbor the libellant or communicate with her were repeated on November 8, 1897, and a copy given to the libellant (Exhibit No. 11). A few days after this the respondent telephoned a message to his wife that he was going out of the city, he did not say where or what for.

The wife drew her own conclusions about his intentions. He then wittily circulated false reports of her mental derangement, and all this maneuvering to completely isolate her from all society and that of her own family, the withdrawal at night of all employees of the Watch Tower from the building in which she lived, and the utter desolation of her home and the withdrawal of all support, to her mind pointed to one conclusion, namely, that he proposed to deal with her upon the pretext of insanity, and that his unrevealed errand that night might be for such purpose. The libellant left the building and took a train for Chicago to seek the protection and counsel of her brother, who is a member of the bar in that city.

Mrs. Russell's testimony on cross-examination by Attorney Porter (Court of Common Pleas):

Q. Did [Mr. Russell] say anything to you . . . while you were sick, as to what was the nature of your sickness?

A. He said it was a judgment on me from God.

Q. For what?

A. I wasn't in harmony with him.

Pastor Russell's testimony under cross-examination by Attorney Porter:

Q. Did you or did you not tell her that her sickness was the judgment of God on her for her failure to obey you?

A. I did not.

Q. You didn't do that?

A. No.

Q. Nothing of that kind?

A. No, sir. I did say some things like that.

Q. What did you say?

A. Miss. Ball, who was her special friend, and who I knew would tell her, I told her in my opinion, this was a judgment from the Lord on her.

Q. And you intended Miss. Ball to tell her that?

A. Yes, sir. I wished her to. I thought she ought to know it.

Q. (By the Court): Was that the time she had erysipelas?

A. Yes, sir.

Q. Did you believe that was the judgment of the Almighty?

A. I think so.

Q. Where did you get that authority?

A. Well, whether my judgment is good or not—

Mrs. Russell testified that the Pastor frequently "kissed and fondled" Rose Ball, the "special friend" who was used to convey her husband's messages to her sickroom. She testified that being informed, in this way, and by this messenger, that her sickness was "a judgment" caused her to have a serious relapse.

Q. (By the Court): That is your idea of good treatment?

A. That was my idea. I was treating the lady the very best, there couldn't have been a kinder treatment given to anybody in the world, and I know I couldn't say this to herself, she wouldn't take it from me, and I thought that it might prove beneficial to her, and I prayed at the time that this sickness might result to her advantage, and I hoped it would.

> Finally, however, [Mrs. Russell] did recover after about nine weeks' illness. She was again about the duties of her home in the spring and summer of 1897, when one day, in the presence of this same Rose Ball, he demands of his wife an itemized statement of her outlays.

Something he had never required before, probably because he realized
that she had more of his money than he did. Such a demand at any
time would be inexpressibly humiliating to her, and when made in the
presence of Rose Ball would be inexcusably and utterly intolerable.
[Attorney Porter's brief, Court of Common Pleas, reviewed by Justice
Orlady of the Superior Court of Pennsylvania]

The Witnesses today use the same defense that Pastor Russell proffered
and Justice Orlady discredited, that the Russells kissed and made up in the
presence of a committee convened to witness Mrs. Russell's capitulation to
her husband's demands that she cease "interfering" in his management of
Zion's Watch Tower.

The court records tell a different story:

[Pastor Russell] called an assembly of his followers to this city for a
secret meeting at the so-called Tabernacle; and another similar meeting on Sabbath evening, the fifth instance. These meetings were attended by about sixty people, a number of whom were from a distance. The respondent confesses that at the meeting he stated that his
wife was weak-minded and under the spell of a Satanic influence
which proceeded from her sisters. This statement was nothing more
or less than a genteel way of stating that his wife's mind was unbalanced, and notwithstanding the fact that Mrs. Russell was within the
building at the time this meeting was held, she was locked out under
the direction of the respondent.

In addition to this statement, which he made to this assembly, Mrs.
Helen Brace testified, and it was not denied, that his wife was suffering from mental aberration. We find also in a letter to Mr. Brown
(Exhibit No. 5), just three days after that meeting of September 5,
1897, a similar statement, as in his letter he tells Mr. Brown that his
wife's mind is poisoned and that she is semi-hypnotized by his sister.
"Weak-minded," "mind-poisoned," under "Satanic hypnotic influence," "mind unbalanced" were the expressions that he used to many
people concerning his wife. The only charitable excuse he could find
for her is that she was passing through a critical time of life, which
was not true, but which, had it been true, would have made his conduct toward her only the more brutal. Bear in mind the fact that those
people of the Russell organization knew Mrs. Russell through her
writings and hearing these reports from the lips of her husband, of
course would think that he was putting it in the mildest possible language, owing to the fact that he was her husband and wanted to shield
her, and would naturally conclude that she was insane.

But this is not all, the very next day after that meeting of September 5, 1897, respondent sent insulting and threatening letters to libellant's relatives and intimate friends, warning them under threats of
legal proceedings and suits for damage, not to harbor libellant or have
any communications whatever with her. He had already turned his

whole congregation against her by the meetings of September 4 and 5, 1897, from which she was excluded, and now, September 6, 1897, is endeavoring to cut her off from the last natural ties, her own relatives and a few loyal friends, among them the respondent's own father and his wife, who is the sister of the libellant. The conduct of the respondent in proclaiming in the little world in which he and his wife lived that his wife was mentally unbalanced was, as was well said by the Court [of Common Pleas] in its charge to the jury, a great indignity, in fact, it would be almost impossible to conceive of one which would be greater: and surely was such an indignity, as when coupled with other matters heretofore referred to as "to render the condition of any woman of ordinary sensibility and delicacy of feeling intolerable and her life a burden."

It is painful to imagine Maria Russell before that Committee—obliged to kiss the smiling, smarmy man who held her up to shame. Furthermore, as in any witch trial, there are strange sexual overtones in Charles Taze Russell's behavior. An intriguing Freudian puzzle is contained in Attorney Porter's brief:

> Pastor Russell "went about among her associates and told them *she was under the hypnotic influence of Satan in the form of her sister, who was his father's second wife*." [Italics mine.]

Russell had married his stepmother's sister and then accused his father's second wife of being a manifestation of the Devil.

Whatever the pathology that led Russell to such stunning abuse of Mrs. Russell, his contention (which is perpetuated by the Watchtower Society today) that their difficulties stemmed from her militant desire to take over his publications was given little credence by the Court:

> It will be noted [said Congressman Porter] . . . that Mr. Russell in [his] letter of July 8, 1896, [stated] his conviction that they made a mistake in getting married, and that that conviction had been growing on him for three years, which would make it begin in 1893 [one year before Mrs. Russell's defense tour—which she had sworn, before the "Church," she had not been under external compulsion to undertake]. *The dispute about the editorship of the paper began in 1896; therefore it could not have been the dispute about the same that forced the conviction upon Mrs. Russell that their marriage was a mistake, and which conviction he says had been growing on him for three years.* [Italics mine.]

There seems no doubt that Pastor Russell would brook no interference with his management of religious affairs. There is little doubt in my mind that the Russells' disagreements over editorial policies were not the cause of their breakup, but a symptom of Pastor Russell's spiritual malaise. In the letter of July 8, 1896, which was crucial to the divorce case, Russell stated his antiwoman views, which repelled Justice Orlady and which would have condemned strong women to spinsterhood: "I am convinced that our difficulty is a growing one generally; that it is a great mistake for strong-minded men and women to marry. If they will marry, the strong-minded had far better marry such as are not too intellectual and high-spirited, for there never can, in the nature of things, be peace under present-time conditions where the two are on an equality."

Mrs. Russell, according to testimony not contradicted by her husband, was so far removed from a status of equality that she complained, "Even a dog has more rights than I have." "You have no rights at all that I am bound to respect," replied Mr. Russell.

Another part of the testimony which Russell did not trouble to contradict makes it very hard indeed to think of Maria Russell as a Castrating Suffragette.

> When leaving home for the far West, she helped him get ready, and then putting her hand on his arm, she said: "Husband, you are going far away. There are lots of railroad accidents, and we might never meet again. Surely, you don't want to leave your wife in this cold, indifferent way."

But he did. He pushed her away, slammed the door in her face, and departed.

Perhaps Mrs. Russell's extravagant fear of losing her mate to a railway accident was, in reality, a repressed desire never to see the man again. She can scarcely be blamed for wishing to be rid of the man who dismissed those who were indifferent to his message as "swinish, quarrelsome . . . selfish and wicked." [*ZWT*, 1914, p. 5980]

> In the Watch Tower office, . . . [Russell] took [Mrs. Russell] by the arm and forcibly ejected her, with the statement, "Get out of here, you blasphemer."
> "You are my wife only in a legal sense."
> "A wife has no rights which a husband is bound to respect."

So did the "kindest of husbands" rail against his "suffragette" wife. Nor, as Porter pointed out, did he deny that he did so; "in fact," Porter wrote, "it might be said that the case is somewhat remarkable for the great number of failures to contradict the libellant by respondent when he had ample opportunity to do so."

Outside the courtroom, Russell exercised himself in frenzies of self-justification; inside the courtroom, he assumed a pose of Olympian disdain.

Russell, the evidence shows, refused to extend to his wife even the minimal courtesies. It was to the ultimate good fortune of Maria Russell that her husband was a ceaseless letter writer: maintaining a stony silence in person, the man who had once written on sidewalks to inform unbelievers of God's wrath fired off letters to the poor woman to whom he would not deign to speak. Fortunately for Mrs. Russell, she was not so gaga as to destroy the evidence.

In a letter of July 9, 1896, Russell wrote: "To avoid misunderstanding, let me say, under the circumstances it properly devolves upon you to make the advances on the line of social amenities between us. It would be improper for me to take the initiative in the matter of amenities such as, 'good morning,' 'good night,' etc." (Exhibit 2, Superior Court)

In view of the evidence, Congressman Porter's summary is remarkably restrained:

> The atmosphere of this home from July, 1896, to the time when she withdrew from it in November, 1897, was filled with unbearable silence and utter neglect. This, of itself, was an indignity of such a character as to render the condition of a woman of Mrs. Russell's delicacy of feeling intolerable and her life burdensome.

Reviewing the evidence, Justice Orlady ruled in Mrs. Russell's favor with barely concealed anger:

> The indignities offered to [Mrs. Russell] in treating her as a menial in the presence of servants, intimating that she was of unsound mind and that she was under the influence of wicked and designing persons, fully warranted her withdrawal from his house, and fully justified her fear that he intended to further humiliate her, by a threat to resort to legal proceedings to test her sanity. There is not a syllable in the testimony to justify his repeated aspersions on her character and her mental condition, nor does he intimate in any way that there was any difference between them other than that she did not agree with him in his views of life and methods of conducting business. He says himself that she is a woman of high intellectual qualities and perfect moral character. While he denied in a general way that he attempted to belittle his wife as she claimed, the general effect of his own testimony is a strong confirmation of her allegations.
>
> In an analysis of the testimony it is quite difficult to understand the view of the respondent in regard to his duty as a husband to his wife. From his standpoint he doubtless felt that his rights as a husband were radically different from the standard imposed upon him by the law, and recognized by all the courts of this country. . . . His course of conduct toward his wife evidenced such insistent egotism and extravagant self-praise that it would be manifest to the jury that his conduct toward her was one of continual arrogant domination that would necessarily render the life of any sensitive Christian woman a burden and make her conditions intolerable.

No charge of adultery was brought against Charles Taze Russell by his wife. In the trial of 1906 before the Court of Common Pleas, Maria Russell testified that Rose Ball—the bearer of messages to Mrs. Russell's sickroom—had once told her that Pastor Russell said: "I am like a jellyfish. I float around here and there. I touch this one and that one, and if she responds I take her to me, and if not, I float on to others." Russell denied the story. Judge Collier charged the jury: "This little incident about this girl that was in the family, that is beyond the ground of the libel and has nothing to do with the case because not being put in it or allowed to pass."

The press did not allow the jellyfish story—or Russell's relationship with "this girl that was in the family," Miss Ball—to pass. Russell brought suit against *The Washington Post* and the Chicago *Mission Friend* for promoting the jellyfish story and for charging him with promiscuity and immorality; he won both cases.

Much has been made of the fact that the jellyfish story was discredited. As did the Pastor then, so do the Witnesses now try to discredit totally all of Mrs. Russell's evidence. It is true that although Maria Russell knew where Rose Ball was living, she made no attempt to procure her as a witness in order to substantiate the jellyfish story. It is also true that Rose Ball would surely have been a hostile witness; she married a director of the Watch Tower Society and may thus be presumed to have been firmly in Pastor Russell's pocket. If she was not in his pocket, she was quite often (literally) on his knee; this Russell did not deny.

Maria Russell alleged that she had discovered proof of "improprieties" between her husband and Rose Ball. Pastor Russell testified that he had gone into Miss Ball's room at night "to minister to the sick." He admitted that he had kissed Miss Ball, but only to administer "spiritual tonic." He admitted that he fondled Miss Ball and dandled her on his knee, but only because his wife had asked him to display affection to the poor little orphan girl the Russells had taken into their home in 1888. Mrs. Russell, he said, used to kiss her too; and Rose was, after all, as he told a reporter from the *Toledo Blade*, "an adopted child of the family in short dresses."

No mention at all is made, in current Watchtower accounts, of Miss Ball's message-bearing excursions into Maria Russell's sickroom, visitations which terrified the Pastor's wife and which Justice Orlady admitted as pertinent, persuasive evidence in Mrs. Russell's behalf.

Russell attributed accounts of his improprieties with women to "the jealousy of the clergy." Given as he was to prodigious bouts of self-justification, popping into and out of law courts and entertaining reporters as if he were royalty, it is interesting that he did not choose to dispute the *Brooklyn Eagle*'s account that

> trouble arose in Pastor Russell's congregation in Allegheny relative to allegations that Pastor Russell was in the habit of locking himself into a room with female members of his congregation. Following an understanding between himself and his congregation, Pastor Russell took a vow, of which the following is one of seven paragraphs: "So far as

reasonably possible, I will avoid being in the same room with any of the opposite sex alone, unless the door to the room stands wide open." [*Brooklyn Eagle*, Oct. 28, 1911]

His followers, it would seem, didn't entirely trust him; but they adored him just the same. Their piety was not affronted by his peccadilloes; they relished, it would seem, the mingled odors of sanctimony and spice.

A dispatch received this morning from Pittsburgh stated that the announcement of the removal of headquarters of the Watch Tower Society to Brooklyn was coincident with the hearing before Judges Brown and Ford of that city to have the preacher jailed, but Mr. Russell denied this morning that the action in court in any way influenced the removal.—Brooklyn Eagle

When Mrs. Russell applied for an increase of alimony in 1900 in the Pennsylvania courts, Russell divested himself of his personal assets and re-moved himself and his headquarters staff to Hicks Street in Brooklyn, New York. He purchased Plymouth Church, which had been completed in 1868 for the Plymouth Congregation of which Henry Ward Beecher was pastor. The Watch Tower Society also bought Beecher's four-story brownstone parsonage at 124 Columbia Heights, a building that overlooked what has been called the most glorious urban view in the world—the New York skyline and the Brooklyn Bridge. The Beecher residence became the home of the headquarters staff of 30-odd Russellites; the remodeled Hicks Street building became known as the Brooklyn Tabernacle:

> Russell prepared and began to execute an all-out campaign of world-wide proportion as a final testimony to the nations that these few remaining years prior to 1914 would be their last opportunity to make peace with God before he came to execute his judgments. . . . Russell immediately realized that the four-story Bible house in Alle-gheny-Pittsburgh . . . was now too small to serve as a suitable center for the international work developing throughout the world.
>
> In order to hold title to this property in New York state it was thought advisable for the witnesses to form a new corporation. The Watch Tower Bible Society of Pennsylvania was subject to certain legal restrictions. So, . . . on February 23, 1909, the People's Pulpit Association was given legal identity as decreed by New York Su-preme Court Justice Isaac N. Miller. [*JWDP*] *

---

* The charter of the People's Pulpit Association reads, in part, as follows: "Its corporate purposes are, charitable, benevolent, scientific, historical, literary and religious purposes; the moral and mental improvement of men and women, the dissemination of Bible Truths in various languages by means of the publication of tracts, pamphlets, papers and other religious documents, and for religious missionary work."

In 1914, the International Bible Students Association—a British corporation—was formed; it had a Brooklyn, New York, address. The Watch Tower Bible and Tract Society of Pennsyl-vania, as parent organization,

represents all the activities . . . with which THE WATCH TOWER and its Editor are

When the Pennsylvania courts ordered Russell to pay alimony to his wife, he filed a plea that he had nothing with which to pay, as he had transferred all his property, evaluated at $317,000, to the Watch Tower Bible and Tract Society. The courts had answered that the transaction was a fraud upon his wife and that Russell still controlled the Pittsburgh property, inasmuch as he still controlled the Society. (He had, upon transferring his assets, required the issuance to him of one voting share for every $10 contribution. Russell thus acquired enough voting shares to give him control of the annual elections.) Referring to one transaction involving a sheriff's sale of property worth $20,000 for less than $200, the Court of Common Pleas said, "The purpose of this whole transaction was to deprive the wife of her dower interest and was a fraud on her." Evidence was produced in the alimony case to show that Russell had accumulated a fortune through stock speculation and donations from his followers. His substantial properties, it was alleged, were carried in the name of various holding companies which he controlled. Maria Russell's attorneys, who spent many months investigating Russell's finances, alleged that the United States Investment Company, a holding corporation, had become the owner of Russell properties. The company's charter showed that its capital stock was divided among Russell and two associates—one of whom was Ernest C. Hennings, a director of the Watch Tower Society and the husband of Rose Ball.

Russell remained unruffled throughout these disclosures. For one thing, his loyal followers, who remained convinced that their Pastor was the Messenger of the Millennium and not a Prophet of Mammon, greeted him,

---

associated. All of the work done through the INTERNATIONAL BIBLE STUDENTS ASSOCIATION and PEOPLE'S PULPIT ASSOCIATION, directly and indirectly, is the work of the WATCH TOWER BIBLE AND TRACT SOCIETY [of Pennsylvania]. . . . The Editor of THE WATCH TOWER is the President of all three of these Societies. All financial responsibility connected with the work proceeds from the WATCH TOWER BIBLE AND TRACT SOCIETY [of Pennsylvania]. From it the other Societies and all the branches of the work receive their financial support. . . . The parent society Charter by the State of Pennsylvania is not by law permitted to hold property in New York State; hence the necessity for organizing a subsidiary society to hold any real estate in New York. Similarly the laws of Great Britain prevent any foreign society from holding title to real estate there. This necessitated the organization of the INTERNATIONAL BIBLE STUDENTS ASSOCIATION with a British charter. Thus it comes that we use sometimes the one name and sometimes the other in various parts of our work—yet they all in the end mean the WATCH TOWER BIBLE AND TRACT SOCIETY [the Pennsylvania corporation]—to which all donations should be made. [*TWT*, 1914, p. 371]
All of the corporations formed by the Society work under the direction of the Pennsylvania corporation.
The certificate of corporation for the People's Pulpit Society was filed and recorded March 4, 1909; the corporation's name was legally changed to Watchtower Bible and Tract Society, Inc. on February 6, 1939; and on January 16, 1956, it was changed to its present name, Watchtower Bible and Tract Society of New York, Inc.

upon his return from a European trip, with a gift of $9,000 to pay back alimony. For another, Russell had small entertainments to distract him.

If Russell did not drift from woman to woman, they certainly seemed to be drawn to him. One woman was Sophie Hassan, whose infatuation with the Pastor led her, on more than one occasion, to crouch humbly in the vestibule of the Pastor's headquarters in Brooklyn, always removing her shoes so as not to besmirch the ground upon which Russell—her "bridegroom"—had trodden. Sixteen-year-old Sophie made a pest of herself; Russell called the cops, and Sophie was carted off to the Kings Park Asylum for observation. Later Russell mused, in the columns of *The Watch Tower*, that "fallen angels" have a nasty habit of materializing on earth, assuming the form of some living person, and committing "licentious acts." [*TWT*, January 1, 1911]

If Russell, who is depicted as a kind of latter-day Job by his successors, ever trembled, ever lost his incredible self-assurance, there is little evidence. He had certainly not on the morning of April 3, 1909, when he granted an interview to a reporter from the *Brooklyn Eagle* in his office at Bethel:

> "All men are more or less influenced by a pretty woman's charms," he said, spreading out his hands in a deprecatory gesture. "Although I do not say this was the reason the court granted my former wife's application for an increase in alimony. I had been paying her $40 a month, and the new order was that it be made $100 a month. I told the court I could not pay it and so they are now trying to put me in jail for contempt. Well, I am not afraid. If they want me back in Pittsburgh, I will go. But I do not intend to pay more than the $40 a month."
>
> Pastor Russell admitted that his wife had secured a decree of separation from him on the ground of cruelty. He said that he had refused to open the columns of a semi-monthly of which he is the editor to the women's suffrage campaign, of which she was and is a disciple. Then, also, he had refused to kiss her face at a railway station.
>
> "The decree was granted in her favor not so much because I was cruel," the preacher explained with a smile. "It was only that the jury believed that we could not live together happily any more anyway. Since then she has been persecuting me in every possible way. . . . Ah, it is really too bad. Because before she became a suffragist she was an ideal wife. I might say she was as perfect as it is possible for anyone to be. . . .
>
> "I did not leave [Pittsburgh] because I was afraid to be put in jail."

Russell contended, as do the Witnesses today, that the move from Pittsburgh to New York (which Judge MacFarlane called "in bad taste, at the very least") was planned some time before Mrs. Russell's request for increased alimony, as was his transfer of $20,000 to the Watch Tower Society: "We are all working in the interest of the Lord," he told the *Eagle*'s reporter. He declared that it was easier to sell books and pamphlets from Brooklyn than from Pittsburgh, because there were "hundreds of thousands of very very intelligent people in Brooklyn. . . . Believe me, we are doing it all for the Lord."

Brooklyn, so often the butt of bad jokes, has seldom received such oily praise. When I told a resident of Brooklyn Heights, the elegant, moneyed section of Brooklyn where the Watch Tower Society holds property tax-assessed in 1971 for $14 million, of Russell's panegyric to the very very intelligent people of Brooklyn, he said: "Tell the Witnesses for me that we're at least intelligent enough to know that any religion that puts plastic flowers in its windows can't possibly be the true religion. . . . Can't the Lord provide fresh flowers?" *Only the Dead Know Brooklyn*, wrote Thomas Wolfe, a neighbor of the Witnesses. Walt Whitman's *Leaves of Grass* was written a few blocks away from Watchtower headquarters, too—Brooklyn has always been fertile literary country. But the Witnesses don't respect the brilliant dead: As they have erected building after building, they have knocked down some of the landmarks most revered by the very very intelligent people of Brooklyn Heights. Prior to a Landmarks Commission ruling which militates against that sort of thing, they destroyed, among other landmarks, the house John Roebling lived in when, incapacitated by the bends but with his telescope at the window, he supervised the engineering of the Brooklyn Bridge. The brownstone Roebling used to live in, at 110 Columbia Heights, is now the Watchtower Bible School of Gilead, a missionary school and residence; the architecture can most kindly be described as undistinguished.

If I were to die tomorrow, I think my former wife would soon follow me, for she could not live unless she had me to nag.—Charles Taze Russell [*Brooklyn Eagle*, May 4, 1909]

This is a ghoulish, syrupy chocolate bonbon, *Who-Is-the-Mysterious-Veiled-Lady-Who-Brings-Roses-to-Rudolph-Valentino's-Grave?* anecdote told, deadpan, in the Witnesses' 1975 *Yearbook:*

> At C. T. Russell's funeral at Pittsburgh in 1916 . . . "an incident occurred just before the services . . . that refuted lies told in the paper about Brother Russell. The hall was filled long before the time for the services to begin and it was very quiet, and then a veiled figure was seen to walk up the aisle to the casket and to lay something on it. Up front one could see what it was—a bunch of lilies of the valley, Brother Russell's favorite flower. There was a ribbon attached, saying, 'To My Beloved Husband.' It was Mrs. Russell. They had never been divorced and this was a public acknowledgment."

If the Veiled Lady was indeed Maria Frances Russell, she'd had a sudden and complete change of heart. In 1913, Mrs. Russell testified against her former husband at a public meeting of the (New York) Board of Tax Commissioners investigating Russell's finances; she testified against him once again in a libel suit he initiated (and lost, on procedural grounds) against a Canadian minister, J. J. Ross; and in 1914—two years before Russell's death in a railway car near Pampa, Texas—she issued a detailed denial that any reconciliation between her and Russell was in process. In a letter addressed to the Rev. DeWitt Cobb of the Second M. E. Church of Asbury Park, New Jersey, Maria Russell wrote:

> For sixteen years we have walked far apart in every sense of the word, and paths so divergent give no assurance of coming together. If Mr. R.'s followers are circulating such a report, they have manufactured it out of their imaginings.

Maria wrote that one of Russell's female followers, "an entire stranger" to her, represented Russell as sick in body and penitent in soul. Maria said that her intention all along had been to oppose unrighteousness, and that she would consider it her Christian duty to save Russell's soul from sin and the consequences of sin; she would go to the dying man, she said, with forgiveness, and with her prayers.

> That would be, however, only at his express request and acknowledgment of the wrongs he had done, for the time was (when I was with him) that he did not want my prayers, and said so. [*Brooklyn Eagle*, July 6, 1914]

III. *Waiting for the World to Die*

Woman is merely a lowly creature whom God created for man as man's helper.—*Let God Be True* (Watchtower Bible and Tract Society, 1946), p. 24

I was a fashion designer and I traveled all over Europe and I had a fabulous career, but it's nothing compared with knowing the joy of Jehovah. I gave it all up, so you *have* to know this is the Truth. . . . You're a career girl—you know what it all means; I had glamour, prestige, salary, everything. But I knew I wasn't pleasing to God. Now instead of having a career where I'm making my name known, I'm making Jehovah's name known. *My* name isn't worth anything. I'm *nothing* without Him.—Remark made by a female Witness at the "Divine Purpose District Convention," August 10, 1974

Woman is habituated to living on her knees; ordinarily she expects her salvation to come down from heaven where the males sit enthroned. . . . This dream of annihilation is in fact an avid will to exist.—Simone de Beauvoir, *The Second Sex*, pp. 600–06

I SLEPT fitfully the night of the day I read the account of Maria Russell's court testimony. I understood how strong a hold that woman—consigned, by the Witnesses, to an eternity of lovelessness—had on my imagination. Once I thought I heard her voice. "Don't leave me," she said. "Help me." I don't believe in "voices" (words like Yin, Yang, Zen, astral projection, and What-is-your-astrological-sign? send me fleeing from a room as quick as you can say UFO); I put it down to overtiredness.

My brain flashed an unwelcome signal to me. I resurrected the warnings I'd read, over and over, for years and years, in *The Watchtower* and *Awake!* magazines. Make mock of Jehovah's Witnesses, the warnings said, and demons will take over your mind. (I even remembered—I hadn't thought of it for years—how, when I was 10 years old, I flew in the face of my elders' strict admonitions and played the Ouija Board—a sure way to invite the demons into your life.) I reminded myself that it would be extraordinary if I didn't, occasionally, get nightmarish nudges from a programmed past (as one might experience pain in an amputated limb), dismissed all thoughts of "demon influence," felt maudlin pity for the bludgeoned little girl I'd been, and fell into a troubled sleep.

I dreamed of God as the last link in the food chain, the Ultimate Predator, the Final Devourer. I dreamed He swallowed women up alive. I saw an endless procession of Pastor Russells offering up women as sacrifices, and I saw the women greet their bloody consummation with a smile.

The official stance of the Witnesses toward women has been consistent. It derives from Paul; "The head of every man is Christ; and the head of the woman is the man; and the head of Christ is God." [I Corinthians 11:3] Sometimes, in their zeal, they achieve black-comedic effects: In *Aid to Bible Understanding*, a 1971 Watchtower publication, we are told that a female zebra—whose "characteristic or quality [is that she craves] sexual satisfaction from any quarter"—symbolizes "Israel unfaithfully seeking after pagan nations and their gods." [p. 202]

Russell set the tone. In *Studies in the Scriptures*, Volume VI, *The New Creation*, published in 1911, after his divorce, he professed to see sex as an evil necessity, a messy marital obligation that was part of the marriage contract rather than a pleasure and a joy. "Sexual appetites," he said, "war against the spirit of the New Creation." (He writes in the spirit of the injunction issued to dutiful, nonorgasmic Victorian wives: "Lie back and think of England.")

"Strength of mind and body," Russell asserted, "by divine arrangement abides with, and constitutes man the head of the family . . . it is for the husband to weigh, to consider, to balance, to decide."

A woman with strength of mind was more to be despised than one who had the good sense to remain as passive, humble—silly—as God, in His wisdom, had made her:

> Depraved and selfish [women], disposed not only to rebel against an unreasonable and improper headship, but even to dispute any and every proposition, and to haggle and quarrel over it . . . while not claiming to be the provider for the family, nevertheless [attempt] directly or indirectly, to usurp the authority of the head of the home, to take and to hold the control of the purse and of the family. . . . Should . . . a wife gifted with superior talent, judgment and abilities . . . be regarded as the head of the family, and the husband as the helpmate? . . . No. . . . No woman should marry a man beneath her in character and talents—one whom she would not properly look up to as her "head." And no man should marry a woman his superior. [A man married to a] superior woman . . . would gradually lose what little manhood he possessed, gradually drop everything into the hands of his wife, and become merely her tool, her slave, to provide the living and keep her commandments. [This would be] a degradation of his flesh. [If a superior woman cannot] reverence [her husband, she

> must cultivate humility and submission,] hide her light under a
> bushel. [*Ibid.*]

It may be that Charles Russell had Maria in mind, and he probably had
himself in mind when he wrote that a husband was "thoroughly justified in
considering himself deserted, and in taking up a separate home to which he
could take such of the children as had not been thoroughly poisoned by the
mother's wrong course" if his wife exercised "petty tyrannies" to make his
home "a veritable purgatory." [*Ibid.*]

Russell professed that he had received so many letters from "the matri-
monial furnace of affliction" as to convince him that the single state was
better than the married state, Our Lord being the noblest example of those
who chose not to marry.

When I became a Witness, in 1944, marriage was frowned upon. In
1941, at a convention in St. Louis, Missouri, J. F. Rutherford, Russell's
successor, combining evangelistic fervor with vaudevillean flair, said that a
woman was nothing more than (as Kipling had put it) "a rag and a bone and
a hank of hair." (The women in the convention audience, I am told, applauded fervently.) Marriage, it was implied, was "selfish"; it kept one from
entering the full-time service of the Lord, afflicted one with "tribulations of
the flesh." (We were, on the other hand, told that "forbidding to marry"
was one of the signs of the end of the world, and that the celibacy imposed
on priests and nuns by the Catholic Church was wicked and Satanish;
voluntary celibacy, however, among *us*, was proof of total commitment to
Jehovah.)

I remember a family of Greek Witnesses: an imposing matriarch; a pale,
insignificant father; two daughters, Olivia and Thea—one beautiful, the
other plain. (Plain Thea played the opening and closing hymns on the upright piano at meetings in the Kingdom Hall; everyone felt sorry for her—
and liked her better, and treated her more kindly than they did Olivia.)
People gossiped about Sister L., the mother: She'd been overheard telling
her beautiful daughter, as they watched a bridal party pass by, "See that
bride? That's what I want for *you.*" Olivia, it was rumored, whenever a
male Witness from headquarters was invited to her family's private house
for supper, would plant herself in front of a window with an open Bible in
her hand, so that she could be found enchanting—a picture of spiritual and
physical beauty to entice men.

The fact that the L.'s lived in a private house was not insignificant: In our
largely working-class South Brooklyn congregation, very few people lived
in private houses. Class animosity was never allowed to rise to the surface—
brothers and sisters, we all "loved" one another—but class animosity would
find expression in backbiting, in whispered conversations about somebody
or other's not being sufficiently "theocratic," or dedicated to Jehovah. It

was remarkable how many people who lived in private houses were "untheocratic."

My own family had a kind of Depression mentality. My father, a printer, and a member of the very strong Typographers Union, made a decent-enough living, but he tended to be somewhat profligate (he liked to play the horses). There was never enough money for frills. We went to a "poor people's dentist"—the kind who charges $2 for every visit and keeps you coming back forever, so that in the end, you wind up paying thousands of dollars. We had a 25-cents-a-week insurance policy. My mother spent hours of her days comparison-shopping—finding the market where the broccoli was 3 cents cheaper. We bought cheap clothes. My underpants were, to my intense humiliation, always falling off—in the subways; once in school when I was reading a paper on the auditorium stage—because we bought the cheap kind, the kind whose elastic turned into a gluey, stretchy mess when you washed them.

My mother and her friends judged other Witnesses (in spite of the constant exhortations to be nonjudgmental) on the basis of their profligacy. If you used heavy cream or Kleenex, you were self-indulgent, a Bad Person. We were both suspicious and envious of anyone who had more money than we had. We asked God to forgive us our failures of love. We maintained our do-gooder, passive mentality, behaving "nice" in front of the people we mistrusted, suppressing our genuine emotions; anger and hostility—even when appropriate, provoked by petty meannesses, or by the controlling wrath of an elder who was attempting to buttress his own sense of worth—merely evoked a Christian smile. Aggressive behavior was not allowed us. We never fought it out like gentlemen. We needed to believe we belonged to a sacred society—even though the people inside it frequently behaved like horses' asses. Inside, we seethed, we burned. We turned our hostility against the alien world.

We all knew men and women who'd "given each other up" in order to serve Jehovah. We regarded them with a kind of awe. People known to be in love but determined to deny their love never sat in the same row of hard-backed chairs at meetings; the air around them, as they studiously avoided each other, was charged with electric tension. We all knew, and honored, men and women who set off for missionary work in foreign countries to put oceans between them and their temptations. They pledged their troth to wait for the New World to marry. For us younger Witnesses, they were the soul of romance.

Our South Brooklyn congregation was not far from Bethel, Watchtower headquarters. We felt about young male "Bethelites," whose characteristics we lovingly rehearsed, as other young girls might feel about glamorous, unattainable movie stars. They moved through our lives, and in our fantasies, like gods. They were not permitted to marry if they wished to remain at Bethel. Often they dated girls from local congregations—took them to a roller-skating rink, danced the tango after dinner in parents' homes. Those dates were like being courted by a handsome slave in the service of a jealous king, or a sailor in a foreign port. Cinderella was always left on her doorstep; Prince Charming never returned to reclaim her. When I was 13, a beautiful young man with a Southern accent that turned me to jelly took me to see Jane Wyman and Lew Ayres in *Johnny Belinda* at the Brooklyn Paramount, and then we walked across the Brooklyn Bridge, holding hands and talking about God. *He* talked; I, practiced in the art of humility and not knowing how to combine humility with something called "personality," which the Witness girls endlessly discussed, listened, occasionally uttering a monosyllabic response. He never took me out again: there were other girls who knew better than I how to combine "submissiveness" with charming artifice. But even for those popular girls who had "personality," there was always an underlying sadness. The Bethelites took them out (kissed them sometimes, usually chastely, sometimes scandalously); the young women groomed themselves, as young women do, for romance, but nothing, they knew, was likely to come of it. Young women charmed; but their charms could not seduce. They had a powerful rival—God.

When two Witnesses did marry—usually after months of clandestine meetings and hot, claustrophobic secrecy—we spoke of them wonderingly, critically. We were jealous, and couldn't admit it. They had violated an ethic that was all the stronger because it was not an absolute imperative; they had broken an unwritten law. ("Martha's getting married," we would say, in tones one might use to say, "Martha's having an abortion!") Once I saw my uncle kiss a woman from the congregation in a dark parked car. I felt fear and excitement and guilt—their guilt, my guilt for having seen them. My mother told me, reluctantly, her back turned, her rigid spine expressing infinite displeasure, that my uncle and the woman were to be married. Both families kept the news secret.

When two Witnesses got married, we watched to see how great the evidence of their "selfishness" would be: Would they pioneer (work as full-time proselytizers) together? Would they have children right away? If they did pioneer, their having married would be—with more or less charity—more or less forgiven (although, of course, we knew they were doing *it*. No one, then, talked much about *it*). If they had children immediately, they gained a reputation for foolishness or "immaturity"; how could one, selfishly, have children in a world so close to dying? If they neither pioneered nor had children, it was clear that they had married for "selfish purposes"—to do *it*. Some Witnesses, marrying, felt compelled to say they were marrying "for companionship"—the implication being that they were not doing *it*, or at least not doing *it* a lot. Whether or not a newly married couple had a double bed was a subject of consuming interest. Young Witness girls weaseled their way into a lot of bedrooms—we were like a roving Hays

Office—to see if the marital bed was twin or double; if a bed was double, it thrilled and alarmed us.

As the years passed, the Witnesses' attitude toward marriage slowly changed. By the time I was at Watchtower headquarters, in the early 1950s, missionaries were drifting back across the seas, reuniting, marrying without stigma. Male Bethelites were permitted to marry provided that they, and their prospective mates, had served at Bethel headquarters for ten years. (The first beneficiary of this change of regulations was the man who amended the regulations—Nathan H. Knorr, third president of the Watchtower Society.) Young men and women are now warned against the dangers of premarital intimacy. They are encouraged to keep themselves pure for Christian matrimony. They may now marry with impunity. (It is still regarded as somewhat foolhardy to bring children into a dying world. Children are, after all, unpredictable, potential rebels; they divert emotional and financial resources away from God—and from "his organization.")

The Witnesses' response to changing sexual mores in the sexually permissive 1960s and '70s has guaranteed that they will not lose all their young people to whimsy or willfullness or spontaneity—that is, to depravity: to the evil world where all sexual appetites are indiscriminately gratified. Better to marry—within the organization—than to burn with worldly sexual libertines.

The Witnesses tend now, as they move toward the mainstream, to reinforce the nuclear family and traditional family roles:

> In the Christian congregation the family is recognized as the basic unit of Christian society. . . . Children are commanded to obey their parents, and fathers particularly are charged with the responsibility of bringing them up in the discipline and authoritative advice of Jehovah.
>
> The man used as an overseer in the Christian congregation, if married, must exhibit high standards as a family head, presiding properly and having his children in subjection. . . . Wives are exhorted to love their husbands and children, to be workers at home, and to subject themselves to their own husbands.
>
> The apostle Paul strongly admonished against breaking up the family relationship, appealing to the unbeliever on the basis of the welfare of the unbelieving mate as well as of the children. He stressed the great value of the family relationship when he pointed out that God views the young children as holy, even though the unbelieving mate has not been cleansed from his sins by faith in Christ. . . .
>
> The inspired Scriptures have foretold a vicious attack on the family institution with a consequent breaking down of morality and of human society outside the Christian congregation.—*Aid*, pp. 564–65

Still, Paul's saturnine attitude toward marriage—"It is better to marry than to burn" [I Corinthians 7:9]—informs their views. *The Watchtower* suggests that while sexual desire "can seem quite compelling" in a young adult, "time might show that the Christian could make a success of singleness without being tormented by desire." [*TW*, Nov. 15, 1974] *The Watchtower* advises its readers to wait till they are "past the period of primary surge of desire . . . to evaluate" the decision to marry or not to marry. Singleness is still thought to be the better course.

(When I was at Bethel, the "Factory Servant"—the overseer in charge of all printing operations—summoned all 400 factory workers to announce his decision to marry one of the Bethel housekeepers. He apologized to us for "not maintaining the honored state of singleness" and assured us, with his wife-to-be at his side, that neither his own regrettable personal necessities, nor his wife, nor their marriage would ever supplant or take precedence over his first priority, which was to serve Jehovah as our overseer. His wife-to-be applauded with the rest of us.)

Responding to external realities, the Witnesses choose now to emphasize the horrors attendant upon premarital intimacy, the vileness of "unnatural acts." And their language is no less stringent than one would expect from people who look upon the Sistine Chapel and see, in that unrivaled magnificence, "pornography . . . rampant." [*Aw*, Jan. 8, 1975]

Masturbation is "unnatural." Mentally deranged people are notorious masturbators. *The Watchtower* can't resist a jibe at the Catholic Church: "Many mentally disturbed priests and nuns are chronic masturbators." Unemployed persons and prisoners masturbate. If a Witness masturbates in a "state of semi-conscious sleep," Jehovah will no doubt forgive him or her; but for added insurance, it would be wise to speak to an elder or (if you are a woman) to a mature sister. [*TW*, Sept. 13, 1973]

(The sense of guilt nourished by such injunctions is so debilitating that many young men and women do voluntarily turn to their elders for spiritual advice, willingly subjecting themselves to an inquisition and disapprobation. I was a closet masturbator—literally: a closet was the only private place I could find; and although I did not ask for help to redeem me from this evil practice, I was convinced, every time I saw an elder with a scowl, that he had seen through the walls to the heart of my evil.)

It is wrong to look at somebody passionately, or to touch anybody passionately. (When I was at Bethel, men and women were instructed not to hold hands unless they planned to marry. "Holding hands can be a clean expression of affection between persons contemplating marriage. True, it does have a stimulating effect, but this is natural and not necessarily bad." [*TW*, Jan. 1, 1974] Kissing is acceptable as long as it is a "clean expression of affection" and not passionate.) It is a serious violation of God's will to "excite each other sexually by putting . . . hands on each other's private parts." Fornication refers not just to sexual union between unmarried persons, but "to lewd conduct such as one might find in places of prostitution."

[*TW*, Oct. 1, 1973] Avoid the occasions of sin: "Ice-skate, play tennis, have a restaurant meal together, visit some museum or local point of interest and beauty." Surround yourself with people.

Oral and anal sex—within marriage, and performed by consenting adults—are perversions: male and female homosexuals indulge in these practices. You don't have to perform a homosexual act to qualify as a homosexual: if you have homosexual fantasies, you are a homosexual in your heart—and God sees your heart.

This is an example of how self-hatred leads to self-abnegation:

> I had been a homosexual since the age of eight. . . . I was a pervert. I can still recall at least 150 males with whom I *repeatedly* engaged in *every* kind of sexual perversion. . . . Actually, by the gay world's standards, I might have been considered only a moderate homosexual since I engaged in immorality with less than three different men each day. Secretly, I knew that my homosexuality was wrong. . . . I was invited to a meeting of Jehovah's witnesses. . . . The idea of living forever in a paradise earth really appealed to me. . . . It was a question of either serving Jehovah and living or staying "gay" and dying. . . . I resigned from all acting engagements, even though it meant giving up many material comforts and much public exposure as an actor. I realized that the atmosphere in the field of acting is simply not conducive to practicing true Christianity or any decent morality. . . . I have married a fine Christian woman. [*TW*, Aug. 15, 1974, pp. 487–88]

I couldn't have been more than 12 when my friend Milly, a Witness who was two years my senior—and light-years ahead of me in sophistication and daring—invited me to her house after a morning of proselytizing and proposed that we "talk dirty." I acquiesced—partly because it was fun to talk dirty, but mostly because I was regarded by most Witness girls as a smart-ass goody-goody snot, and I was inclined to purchase popularity at any price.

Talking dirty led inevitably to bed, where Milly showed me "how babies nurse," "how grown-ups do it." Milly slid her finger along my vagina—a favor I was too scared, to rigid, to return. I told her I was scared; I said we shouldn't do it. "Dumb," Milly said. "You don't get pregnant from a girl on top of you." Too scared to protest that that wasn't what I was scared of— Jehovah's wrath was what I was scared of—I allowed myself to be seduced. I didn't enjoy it.

Later, as I was walking home, a man called to me from a parked car. "Do you know where Suzie lives?" he asked. "I'm sorry, no," I said. "That's too bad," he said, "I wanted to suck her pussy." Hearing him but not hearing him, I repeated, "No, I'm sorry." "Have you ever been laid in a car?" he asked. I *did* hear that, and I ran, convinced that this was a punishment, that

I was a dirty, wicked girl who invited lewd comments. I was tortured by the certainty that *they*—God, the elders, my mother—all *knew* and were allowing me to suffer the agonies of waiting before they revealed my wickedness to the world.

I overheard my chiropractor tell a patient that he had to report all cases of VD to the Board of Health. I fled from his office, knowing that he was talking about me; I waited for men in a white truck from the Board of Health to haul me away. Baby-sitting one night, I read the symptoms of gonorrhea in *Dr. Fishbein's Medical Home Examiner.* A bone spur on the heel was one of the symptoms. I looked at my heels—what was that protuberance?

I couldn't understand why they all waited so long to punish me. I wanted to be exposed; it was better than this endless watching and waiting. In sixth grade, a girl passed me a note: "Do you want to fuck?" it said. *Everybody* knew! No wonder my mother didn't love me. Even Milly didn't like me. I had thought to buy her approval. Milly refused to talk to me. "I wouldn't study *The Watchtower* with *her,*" she told her friends. "She's a know-it-all. Thinks she's too good for everybody." Her malice was transparent to me; I was too *bad* for everybody. I never told. All that summer, none of Milly's crowd ever invited me to go to Coney Island with them. I spent all my time preaching.

Not all Witnesses are successful in their struggles against their sexual nature. When I was interviewing Witnesses at a district convention at Aqueduct Race Track in 1974, I found that while few women were willing to admit that sex, or the Women's Movement, posed any kind of problem for them at all, male Witnesses frequently acknowledged that the prohibition against premarital sex might conceivably create conflicts. Not all Witnesses have become their personae; occasionally, at Aqueduct, most often with men, a hint of jocularity and frivolity entered conversations. It was almost immediately aborted, as they remembered that I was not one of them.

At the convention at Aqueduct, I did find, in the midst of certainty, among 25,000 pain-evaders and happiness-proclaimers, two men who stood out like birds of paradise: Bo Jacks, dressed in poison-green silk, pimp straw hat, platform shoes; and Ron Bookers, resplendent in a white ruffled, sequined shirt. On their partially exposed black-is-beautiful 18-year-old chests hung gold chains and medallions surrounded by sparkling stones. They admitted to being in trouble. Their confusion was refreshing; it felt like something precious. They were trying hard to be Jehovah's Witnesses; their mothers had raised them to be Witnesses, but, "Yeah, sometimes it's hard. It's hard to be a Jehovah's Witness; it's hard, like the Witnesses can't . . . you don't suppose' to like . . . you gotta be good, you can't party, you gotta go to all the meetings, field service and stuff. For a young lady, it's kind of easy. There's nothing to do, you know, she could stay home, she could do her mother chores. But how're *we* gonna kill time? . . .

"Sex? That's the hardest thing in the life. It's hard. You know, I'm not gonna say I never had sex, 'cause you know I do, but I try, you know, to keep it to a certain extent where I can stop. I really want to get married. Therefore it would be legal, I wouldn't have to do it behind doors. You know, you can get kicked out of the Witnesses for having sex. If you're not baptized, you get public reproof. I had public reproof. They find out 'cause somebody tell on you or you tell on yourself; it's suppose' to be you tell on yourself. But like myself, since I'm not baptized, I can't help myself, I gotta have sex. See, the sisters won't have nothin' to do with me, 'cause their parents told them, don't mess with a brother 'less he dressed up in a suit and tie. Well, that's not my thing. Who I have sex with, they call them 'worldly people.' But I wouldn't marry one of them. You find the Witness sisters, they don't lie, they don't cheat, they was brought up like a human being. . . .

"I'm trying. I'm really trying."

As Middle American as apple pie (but not quite so Middle American as to enshrine Mom on her kitchen-pedestal), the Watchtower Society reacts to "New Wedding" ceremonies with irritation. Witnesses exchange vows in the Kingdom Hall meeting place, after an elder of the congregation gives an "upbuilding talk" on the appropriate behavior of husbands and wives.

> *The groom:* "I ——— take you ——— to be my wedded wife, to love and to cherish in accordance with the divine law as set forth in the Holy Scriptures for Christian husbands, for as long as we both shall live together on earth according to God's marital arrangement."
> *The bride:* "I ——— take you ——— to be my wedded husband, to love and to cherish and deeply respect, in accordance with the divine law as set forth in the Holy Scriptures for Christian wives, for as long as we both shall live together on earth according to God's marital arrangement." [*TW*, May 15, 1974, p. 275]

The Witnesses' attitude toward women is consistent with Russell's misogynistic tone. (It is not really an anomaly that Russell's will specified women as his executors. He could trust them, of course, to execute his will without a murmur: they were his trustworthy servants.)

Although women bear the brunt of door-to-door proselytizing, there are no female elders in congregations of Jehovah's Witnesses (who learned from the example of Maria Russell that it is impossible to give a woman a crumb without her wanting to be invited to the banquet). There are no women in the governing body of the Witnesses, or on the board of directors of the Watch Tower Bible and Tract Society or its sister corporations.

When there are no qualified male members present in a congregation, a woman may perform duties otherwise reserved for men; she must, however, in that event, and if she is teaching others in the presence of her husband or another male, "wear some form of head covering besides her hair, which she normally always has." [*Aid*, p. 725] Besides her hair, which she normally always has. Unintentional humor is attendant upon bad grammar.

A Christian husband is instructed to be mindful of the "limitations and vicissitudes" of his wife and to "consider the opinions, likes, and dislikes of his wife, *even giving her the preference when there is no issue at stake.*" [*Aw*, April 22, 1972, p. 11; italics mine] *The Watchtower* fosters womanly dependence with Talmudic specificity: "a married woman who favors having her ears pierced should rightly consult her husbandly head." [*TW*, May 15, 1974, p. 319] A zealous husband expresses love for his wife by trying to please her in little ways "without sacrificing his headship or the best interests of his family." A woman's qualities are "an expression of the man's honor and dignity." [*Aw*, May 22, 1972, p. 13] (She is nothing without a male "head," as men are nothing without Christ.) The Christian woman should be happy to acknowledge her subordinate position by the modesty and submissiveness she displays.

Are the women happy?

If women had complete equality with men, governments would draft women to fight in the fields, jungles, and trenches. . . . Would you really want equality with men in digging coal out of a mine thousands of feet underground if men did their share of the housework? Would you really want to spend equal time plowing fields and shoveling manure with your husband if he agreed to help you cook and clean at home?—Awake!, May 22, 1972, p. 7

They profess to be happy.

Irving I. Zaretsky and Mark P. Leone *(Religious Movements in Contemporary America)* believe that women in evangelical religions gain a position of their own in the community without reference to their husbands. (A female Witness who has an unbelieving mate is told to "accept his headship" *except* in regard to worship. She is to defer to him in all other matters, but not to permit his indifference or opposition to deter her from going to religious meetings, proselytizing, or instructing her children in the faith.) Religion, Zaretsky and Leone suggest, becomes an acceptable form of activity for women who cannot operate in the secular world because they lack the necessary education or certification. Their religion becomes the "avenue that short-circuits a whole set of life-problems."

For disaffected women whose experience has taught them that all human relationships are threateningly volatile, capricious, and unreliable, the Witnesses provide an answer. Relate to God. God is a safe lover, a constant lover, a consuming lover. For women who are mired in oppressive poverty—and for a smaller number of guilt-ridden affluent women—the Witnesses provide an answer: Jehovah's New World will eradicate poverty; He will redistribute the wealth. Explicitly antifeminist, the Witnesses nevertheless provide a vehicle for downtrodden women—their religion allows their voices, drowned by the voices of the menacing world, to emerge. As female Witnesses preach from door to door, instructing people in their homes, they experience a multiplication of their personalities. People *listen* to them; they are valuable, bearers of a life-giving message. Even the indifference with which they are most often greeted adds to their self-esteem, their self-importance: if the world is indifferent to them, the world is indifferent to Jehovah. For women who are afraid of choice, afraid of the responsibility of freedom, the Witnesses offer this solution: Choose God, and all your choices, all your decisions will be forever made for you. For women who long for a sense of community, "God's visible organization" becomes a family. Sometimes the brothers and sisters squabble, but they are always *there*, a buffer between the Witnesses and the senseless world, a bulwark against a bewildering and hostile world. The parent-God is always there. Women whose self-hatred is pathological find a congenial home among the Witnesses; they are told that it is desirable to be persecuted, Godly to be hated, proof of goodness to be considered worthless by the world. Women who fear and hate the world are secure in the knowledge that God will smash the evil world for them. They find hope in a world without hope.

Here are some of their voices (these are the voices in which they speak to nonbelievers):

"I had searched for years to find answers, and the Witnesses are the only people who have answers for the world situation. I think I would have been the kind that would be on the soapbox complaining about my taxes if it were not for the Witnesses; now I understand that *I* can't do it—God will. Women's liberation? Everlasting life is what *I'm* concerned about. If Libbers were truly living according to the Scriptures, they wouldn't need to be liberated, because Christian women have all the freedom they need. I can see why a career girl like *you* would rebel. I'm fortunate. My husband supports me. . . . He's an unbeliever, but he gives me money for transportation to conventions. . . . I'm not oppressed. None of Jehovah's people are oppressed. *We* have a hope for the future."

"I used to be involved in lots of different organizations and clubs, but not anymore. Now I stay home and study the Bible with my children."

"My liberation came when I realized there was no future in higher education because this whole system is dying. I wasn't involved in drugs like a lot of the people who are in The Truth now. The opposite of dropping out— being popular—is just as dangerous: I was the captain of twirlers, vice-president of the art club, on the senior-class board, on the community-action committee—you name it. Now I know that I was just calling attention to myself. And I was surrounded by temptations to immorality. . . . I did volunteer work in orphanages and I worked with retarded children because

I loved people. But when I got The Truth, I left college and I stopped all those worldly activities to preach full time; because now I know the real way to serve people who are suffering physically and mentally is to serve Jehovah. . . . My classmates jeered at me. But we're told we're going to be hated by this world, and it's better to be persecuted than to be popular."

A 40-year-old woman, her green eyes shining with the rich gleam of lunacy, all ruffles and bows and corkscrew curls, a neat approximation of an Ivory Snow queen: "I'll wait for God's kingdom to get married. Men in our organization have headship. It works nicely; families keep together. . . . Dating? It's been such a long time. I won't go out with worldly men. But I keep busy and occupied. I preach. I work for a doctor; I like to read books about cancer. I don't watch R-rated movies or read dirty books. I never think of sex. . . . Do you think of it a lot? Probably you do. I don't judge people, though."

A 70-year-old woman with a halting, singsong voice: "I had a very unhappy marriage. My husband would do things that weren't proper, and I was always miserable and I prayed to God that nothing should happen to my husband but that he should go away; so my prayers were answered and he did plumbing work out of town. . . . I used to try so hard to be nice to people, but I was always 'done.' Now that I've found the fountain of living waters, I'm not 'done' anymore. . . . I'm not oppressed. I don't need women's liberation because I'm in harmony with righteousness, and I'm with those who are inclined toward righteousness, and I'm not oppressed, and I'm not 'done.' "

A 20-year-old woman who believes herself to be dying of leukemia invites me radiantly to join her "in finding real peace and security by becoming one with Jehovah's people. I'm dying," she says, sweetly smiling, "but I will be resurrected on a perfect earth. Live with me!"

These are the voices the outside world hears. In the daily realities of the women's lives, one hears a murmur of different voices.

They have fun together. They sing together; they dance together (they may be the only people left, outside of Roseland, who dance the cha-cha-cha). They tell each other mildly risqué jokes (never in the presence of men). Sometimes they hold hands when they preach together. They read and underline *The Watchtower* together, as a form of communion. Drawing courage from one another, they are subtly subversive of its text—particularly when the text refers to their relationships with believing or unbelieving mates: they giggle together about how they can avoid sex without giving the appearance of being delinquent in "rendering their marriage dues." If their husbands oppose their religious will, they huddle together for warmth. They gossip together like girls about the men they'll marry in the New World. If, as I frequently heard women complain when I was a Witness, their husbands were lax in "assuming headship," if their husbands would not "take the lead"—placing in their hands the real power in the family while their husbands wore the face of authority—they would talk about ways of subverting their own strength; or they would heave sighs together, in a sisterhood of tea and sympathy and soon-to-be-alleviated grief. They commiserated with one another; they swapped fantasies of truly dominant men, dreaming together of the transformation of their men in the Edenic paradise for which they long. They take crank cures together—grape-and-garlic cures for cancer, mutual toe massages for everything from arthritis to migraines; they flock to the same chiropractors, the same miracle doctors.

I have never known, really, whether the Darby-and-Joan marriages I saw among the Witnesses were truly happy. Many couples had the appearance of happiness, setting off together with their book bags and their satchels to preach together; speaking—like two-headed animals—in one voice; alluding, sometimes, to shared nocturnal pleasures. I assume—inasmuch as some of the Witnesses I knew were mischievous neurotics, some thwarted ecstatics, some decent good people, some as healthily vulgar as others were prudishly, prudently upright and uptight, some profoundly bitter and others temperamentally sanguine—that their marriages were as diverse as their personalities, though outwardly they all conformed.

I have asked Witness women why, if women are not inferior to men, they are not elders, ministers, shepherds of the flock. I have been answered, "I don't know. I believe in the inherent wisdom of the Bible. We don't have to justify our position with biology or anthropology. God is our Creator and our Regulator; He knows what's best. Our responsibilities are worked out by God; we don't make decisions." Mary Brady, an unpaid clerical worker married to an administrator at Bethel, said (and I think she was telling her truth): "My subordinate role gratifies me. I'm happy to lean on my husband, happy for him to provide my living. He offers me a home; I take care of his home. I get financial and spiritual support. He honors me. I'm not a sex object or a nursemaid. He's stronger, I'm weaker. A relationship of equals is something I do not desire. I have a right to my opinions. But if I had a burning insight, I'd tell it to my husband. Why would I need to share it with anybody else? When men abuse their wives, it's a perversion of headship. Chafing comes from the abuses of God's arrangements. I'm happy. Like," she said, "you can't compare bananas and onions." "Which are women?" I asked, liking her, sensing vulnerability under her steel-gray poise. "Bananas, of course," she answered . . . and then, as she saw the raised eyebrow of the male elder to whom she kept looking for approval, she—surprised and threatened by her own levity—improvised nervously: "Well, Jehovah created all fruits and vegetables to serve their purpose, and we need bananas and we need onions; eating would be pretty dull without onions." Then she asked me if I was a lesbian. "We don't approve of lesbians," she said.

The Witnesses encourage women to exercise a degree of autonomy over their own bodies. Contraceptives are acceptable. Women are encouraged to breast-feed babies (and made to feel slightly guilty if they do not); recent Watchtower publications have endorsed giving birth in one's home.

Abortion, however, is, under any circumstances, murder—even when birth might jeopardize the pregnant woman's life. Diabetes, hypertension, or other grave cardiovascular diseases are not reasons to abort, nor does the danger of giving birth to a defective or deformed child constitute justification for abortion: Jehovah can always undo the damage in His coming New Order. [See *TW*, March 15, 1975, p. 191–92.]

Artificial insemination by an anonymous donor is regarded as a form of adultery; both the wife and her consenting mate will be penalized by expulsion from the congregation. In cases in which a husband's sperm is introduced artificially to impregnate his wife, "They would have to resolve any personal questions of propriety as to the manner of acquiring the semen." [*Aw*, Aug. 8, 1974, p. 22]

The Witnesses' feelings about rape can be summed up in the familiar: She got no more than she deserved. Virtuous women don't *get* raped. They might get killed, but they don't get raped. And if it isn't the rapist's victim's fault, it's the rapist's *mother's* fault. Rape is on the increase because "Satan the Devil together with his demons is influencing the minds of mankind" as we approach the end of the world. However, "Womankind must share the blame." Not only do they invite rape by advertising their wares in immodest dress and being arrogant enough to think they can walk alone after 10 o'clock with impunity, but

> to begin with, until the age of five or six years . . . little boys have their personalities molded largely by women, their mothers. . . . It is usually the mother that has the most opportunities to inculcate in her son respect for womankind, both by word and by example. But far too many mothers have come short in this regard. Especially and specifically blameworthy are those female relatives, such as an aunt or even a mother, who have used boys as sexual playthings, thereby starting them on a road that leads to their having aggressive feelings toward women. [*Aw*, March 8, 1974, p. 15]

Women are discouraged from learning to defend themselves; they must scream. Indeed, their only recourse is to scream—if they do not scream, and the rapist has his way with them, *they are guilty of fornication or adultery*. If they do scream and get raped anyway, they're in the clear. If they scream and get killed, God will resurrect them. Watchtower publications have testimonials of women who screamed and got off safely; one woman screamed first—and then told her would-be rapist the story of Noah and the Flood. The rapist and she disagreed about how many years Noah had preached before the flood: he said two hundred, she said forty.

Witness women's determination to rejoice in their subjugation may be attributed to a passion for the absolute. Louis Aragon has said that a passion for the absolute is the same as a passion for unhappiness. I think that is simplistic: I think masochistic and self-rejecting women choose an identification with God or with Christ (and withdraw from the world); this identification fosters narcissism, feelings of superiority and omnipotence—which, in a horrible circularity, lead back, through guilt, to masochistic, self-deprecatory behavior. On the one hand, Witness women are narcissistic and enjoy feelings of omnipotence; on the other, they experience guilt, inadequacy, inferiority, and self-hatred. This schizoid personality formation is ultimately self-defeating; but it springs from an avid will to exist: in a world where "marginal" people are expendable, a world dehumanized by technology and bureaucracy, Witness women feel that they *count*. Even their pain is valuable to them: their pains are the arrows of God. Their blood suffering belongs to Him. Their religion enables them to make sense of the world—the world where people don't "behave right," where people do one another wrong. ("I was 'done,'" one Witness woman kept repeating to me. "Before I found The Truth I was always 'done.'") It is a way for personally and socially dislocated persons—women, blacks, freaks, junkies, the disenfranchised poor—to improve themselves and their lives, to gain status otherwise denied them. Women who despise themselves project their evil image onto others—onto "evil worldlings" who will (they so frantically hope) persecute them. ("Any one who does not conform to God's standard of moral excellence is wicked, bad, evil, or worthless."—*Aid*, p. 1653)

A Witness woman believes she is special, different; she "maintains her integrity in an alien world." She needs the society of "the friends" to validate her existence; and each deprivation she endures draws her closer to "God's organization": when the Watchtower Society forbade Witnesses to celebrate Christmas, or birthdays, the response of one elderly woman was "We felt we were privileged to know things others were ignorant about." When I told my Bethel roommate that I was leaving religion, she said, with anguish, "But where will you *go?*" Her anguish was for me; it was also for herself—my defection terrified her, it threatened her security. The only way Witnesses can deal with defectors is to abort their love for them immediately. We are carriers of a dread disease—doubt, and disaffection. My roommate, a generous, loving woman, pleaded with me not to leave the only light in the darkness of the cold and brutal world. A month later, when she knew I would not turn back from my decision, she told me I was like a dog going back to its own vomit. When I told her I could not countenance the idea of a God who would kill babies at Armageddon, she said, "You are presuming to be more compassionate than Jehovah." And she refused ever to speak to me again.

Talented women frequently throw away their talents—which serve the Devil and gratify the flesh; or they subordinate their talents to the relentless demands of their religion. Happiness has not come from economic and social rewards, so they seek ultimate happiness, the crown of happiness only the Lover-God can bestow. Wordly success is dust and ashes without the revivifying flame of God's love.

The Witnesses have a stunning ambivalence toward worldly success. On the one hand, they profess to despise it, as they profess to despise materialism and the acquisition of wealth. On the other hand, its glitter fascinates and enthralls them. They have never neglected to try to impress me with the successes of people I knew when I was a Witness: "Remember Johnny D. who was at Bethel when you were there? He makes seventy-five thousand dollars a year, and he has four color television sets." . . . "Remember Peter and Clara, whom you studied with? Peter has a million-dollar business now." (Peter used to play the trombone with the Detroit Symphony Orchestra; he gave that up—self-indulgence, he said it was—and, I am expected to believe, made a million by accident. There is always the subtle implication that Jehovah had a hand in the manufacture of that million, the very kind of success for which successful "worldlings" will be destroyed.) When I was a Witness, I heard dozens of stories of famous people who were, if not actually Witnesses, "people of goodwill": Bing Crosby's first wife, Dixie Lee, was rumored to have studied the Bible with the Witnesses—Crosby, according to the Witnesses, was "opposed"; Nelson Eddy had, it was said, once contributed money to the Watchtower Society; Eisenhower's mother, the Witnesses go to great lengths to prove, was a Witness; Gorgeous George's wife was a Witness, they said; and (this is true) Mickey Spillane was a Witness.

Teresa Graves, the television actress who used, in her preconversion days, to wriggle onto *Laugh-In* with words like RING MY CHIMES and WHITE SALE painted on her beautiful black body, became one of Jehovah's Witnesses. Her job, she said, came second. She found it difficult to reconcile herself to her affluence. Unlike most of the never-never-land people in Beverly Hills, she remembered there was a Watts down there beneath the plateaued swimming pools and the smog; and her social consciousness, combined with a sense of impotence, led her straight to an ultimate solution: She spent as much as 100 hours a month proselytizing, the only door-to-door television star. Graves played a cop in the television series *Get Christie Love!* She would not, however, as a Witness, act in a role that required nudity, or "cleavage." She acknowledged with distaste having once, in her unenlightened past, played a bosomy Countess Dracula in a film called

Vampira. But she did not recoil from playing a law-and-order enforcement-type person protecting the moneyed classes. "Render unto Caesar" . . .

Watchtower and *Awake!* magazines frequently have articles contributed by actors, artists, and musicians (always anonymous) who gave it all up for Jehovah (they are usually women); or by Witnesses whose worldly successes left them, unaccountably, fragmented and depressed.

A highly placed television network executive, a former member of New York Media Women, a feminist consciousness-raising and political-activist group [*TW*, July 1, 1974, pp. 387–93], transferred "the feeling of solidarity, of trust, of love . . . 'sisterhood,' " from the Women's Movement to Jehovah's Witnesses when it became apparent to her that Women's Liberation "did not have the answers." "Confused, disillusioned, and saddened" by ideological quarrels within the Movement, depressed that "many of the women I had admired and who were taking over the leadership were lesbians," discouraged because many men walked out on feminist women to find more "feminine" women, disturbed because women were deserting their families and putting down motherhood and child-rearing as atavistic and bourgeois, she opted for a movement that would tolerate no ideological dissension, that answered all her questions definitively, and that delivered her from her terror of sexual differences, of sexual and personal choice. She instructed her lawyers to drop the $2-million lawsuit she had filed against the network after she was fired in 1971, allegedly because she had refused to date her boss, and rested her case with the Judge who will resolve all injustices.

(*Age quod agis*, said St. Wilfrid of Whitby: Do what you do. *Laborare est orare*, said St. Benedict: To work is to pray.)

Remember those dreadful Walter Keane paintings of wistful children with enormous sad eyes? They were paintings that appealed to custard-hearts and uninformed aesthetic tastes; and each tug on the melting heartstrings of an undiscriminating public enriched the coffers of the painter of those sentimental assembly-line vulgarities. An anonymous article in *Awake!* [July 8, 1975, pp. 12–15], written as if it were by Mrs. Keane, tells the story of the writer's struggle with alcoholism and despair, her flirtation with the occult and assorted Eastern-inspired fads, her three broken marriages, and her subsequent conversion to a God who will wipe away tears from all eyes. The writer describes a legal fracas and a televised paint-in to establish whether she or the man who was once her husband was the maker of those teary paintings. She speculates as to why her "art" gave her so little satisfaction, why her financial good fortune satisfied her not at all; and she concludes that what was missing in her moneyed life was Jehovah. Now that she is one of Jehovah's Witnesses, she says, "the sad, lost look of the eyes is giving way . . . to a happier look. My husband even named one of my recent happy big-eyed children 'The Eye Witness'!" And, she says, she'll paint them in half the time she used to require—because Jehovah has given her creative propulsion; she'll spend the rest of her time preaching.

Secular work is only a means to support their preaching. Art does not nourish or sustain or ennoble. Everything must be utilitarian, practical—at the most, decorative. Michelangelo was a pornographer. The Cathedral at Chartres is a Devil place. Their God will destroy all man's art at Armageddon; not a poem or a song man has made will survive that burning day.

A friend of mine who was a Witness for three troubled years tells me that she quit going to Witness meetings because "They made me pinch my Joey. . . . They scolded him from the podium when he was only three years old to make him quiet," Sara says, "and they said he couldn't play with his crayons, he had to keep still and listen to the *Watchtower* discussion or he wouldn't live forever in the New World . . . so I was humiliated, and I pinched him to shut him up; and then I felt guilty—because how could a good mother pinch her son for God?"

When it is assumed that human nature is basically evil, that a child inherits the sinful nature of his first parents, Adam and Eve, the expression of idiosyncratic views, self-assertion, and rebellion are perceived as a smack in the face of a wrathful God. It falls to the parents—God's surrogates—to bring the evil impulses of the child under holy control. If a 2-year-old doesn't eat his carrots, it is not his parents he is offending, it is God. His instincts must be squashed, because they are evil; his spirit must be broken, because pride leads to a Lucifer-fall. The child is controlled and dominated—in the name of a God of love. The child is disciplined in the name of a judgmental God, from Whom all rewards and punishments flow.

Poor Sara. She was convinced that at a convention of 50,000 people, her Joey was the only unruly child. She may well have been right: meetings and conventions of Jehovah's Witnesses are remarkable for the stillness—the unnatural stillness, the lobotomized good behavior—of Witness children. Their voices are not heard.

The Witnesses are the best child-squashers and -controllers I know. (I don't know how many Witness children get God and their mothers mixed up as I did, but I suspect that I was not the only one who suffered that primal disorientation: how is one to know, if sanctions are said to issue from a remote, invisible Deity but are in fact administered by parents who speak in the voice of that Deity, who is *Who?*)

The instructions Charles Taze Russell issued for raising children [*SS*, Vol. VI] are as saccharine as the lace valentines of his day; but Russell's flowery language disguises an iron determination to repress all the child's true feelings: "Is my little boy feeling happy this morning? Does he love papa and mama and sister and brother and doggie?" [p. 552] (I once knew a little boy who put his doggie in the washing machine to see how he'd come out of the wringer—and I can't say I blame him. The Witnesses may quote "Train up a child in the way he must go and when he is old he will not depart from it" all they like; I have a feeling that it is of such stuff ax murderers are made.) No verbal or physical aggression is permitted the child; aggression is interpreted as hostility toward God.

Russell instructed parents to "apply suggestion" to their children. There was nothing to be gained and everything to be lost, in Russell's view, by allowing a child to relate directly and individualistically to his environment. The child must relate only to God (and to His representatives); the material world exists only to provide moral lessons. The world is thus stripped of its poetry and its mystery; the child is taught how to *see* as well as how to feel.

A mud puddle becomes the occasion for a sermon: While dressing a child, Russell advised, "talk about the pretty wee birdies and about the big sun looking in at the window and calling all to get up and be good and happy, and learn more lessons about God." On a rainy day, call the child's attention to "the beautiful rain which God has provided for giving the flowers and trees and grass a drink and a bath to refresh them . . . and for cattle and for us to bathe in and be clean" and happy and praise Him and love Him and serve Him: "This will be an opportunity for wearing storm cloaks and heavy boots, and how thankful we should be that we have these and a rain-proof home and school." [pp. 550–51]

The reverse coin of Russell's cheery optimism was the admonition to withdraw affection if the child flouted God's or his parents' imperatives: "I know you didn't mean to be bad, but you will get no good-night kiss tonight. You have failed to please us again. I am so sorry my little daughter failed again, I do not doubt your good intentions, dear." [p. 553] (Russell practiced this sinister-sweetness behavioral therapy with his wife, whom he refused to embrace or kiss when she acted in contravention of his will, which he equated with God's will; it failed with headstrong Maria, but he never lost faith in its efficacy.)

To play, in Russell's view, was to be immoral: a "desire to be amused" led, in due time, to a craving for "the theater and the nonsense of the clown." [pp. 556–57] Idleness was a sin and a shame. If the mind and the imagination were kept a blank slate, Russell believed, the child's handwriting would cover it soon—with "unclean thoughts, the contemplation of obscene pictures." [p. 542] Of course Russell was afraid of leisure: it is true that only in leisure can vice flourish; it is also true that only in leisure can art flourish. "[The child] should be encouraged to read such books as would give information and not novels . . . weedy, trashy, dreamy literature, that will do him harm and leave him unprepared for the duties of life." [p. 541]

Not only do we find that people cannot see the divine plan in studying the Bible by

*itself, but we see, also, that if anyone lays the [Watchtower] "Scripture Studies"
aside, even after he has . . . read them for ten years—if he then lays them aside and
ignores them and goes to the Bible alone, though he has understood his Bible for ten
years, our experience shows that within two years he goes into darkness. On the other
hand, if he had merely read the "Scripture Studies" with their references and had not
read a page of the Bible as such, he would be in the light at the end of two years,
because he would have the light of the Scriptures.—TWT, Sept. 15, 1910* [quoted
in Hoekema]

*It may be that you disagree with the way matters have been handled in connection
with the remodeling or building of a Kingdom Hall. Perhaps you feel that you would
have selected a different design, another type of floor covering or a different color of
drapes. But are there not many possible designs, many types of floor coverings and
numerous colors of drapes? Will a different interior decoration affect our relationship
with Jehovah?—TW, July 15, 1974, p. 437*

The greatest danger for a Witness child, as for an adult, is to think auton-
omously. To reason independently is an affront to the God whose ways are
higher than our ways, the God one may never question. Fortunately, say
the Witnesses, they have been provided with "a visible instrument or
agency on earth" through which Christ provides "spiritual food" to his
"slaves." [LGBT] *Jehovah has graciously provided "an instrument or channel to
teach his people on earth."* [Qualified] That channel is the Watchtower Bible
and Tract Society, which, though it makes no claim of infallibility, nevertheless excommunicates anyone who comes to conclusions independent of
its own. Everything falls within the province of this "Channel"—draperies
or the divine plan, it's all the same: the explanation for everything belongs
to them.

(I knew that I was intractable, that I was "hardhearted" and had probably
caused God's holy spirit to abandon me, when I found, to my sorrow, that
"God's organization" could not explain God to me. When I was a girl, I
thought—and the guilt and shame attendant upon this aberrant thought
shriveled my soul—that Jehovah was like Mr. Rochester or the absent father in *The Turn of the Screw:* a felt presence that moved darkly through my
life, His motives often inexplicable, His word law, His love mysteriously
withheld.)

When everything is given (by "God's organization"), nothing more is required. It was thought to be worse than redundant—it was thought to be a
mark of contempt for God's "channel"—for a young Witness to go to a
college or university:

"In sending [a child to college] at the present time," Russell wrote, parents "should feel a great trepidation, a great fear, lest this outward polish in
the wisdom of the world should efface all the polish of faith and character
and heart which they as the parents and proper instructors of the child had
been bestowing upon it from infancy and before." Russell believed that the

danger of "rationalistic teachings called Higher Criticism, Evolution, etc." was so great that one should be "content with such education as could be obtained in the public schools and high schools or preparatory schools." With typical American entrepreneurial mentality, Russell pontificated: "By the time [the youngster] has had six years schooling in practical business, the probabilities are that he will be much better able to cope with present conditions than the youth who has spent the same number of years under college training." And with smug Philistinism, he added: "We write with full consciousness that to the worldly minded this advice is foolishness or worse." [*SS*, Vol. VI]

Since Russell's time, nothing has changed. Parents are still reminded that they must render an account to God, Who has placed in their hands the responsibility to convey His desires to children. They are God-appointed guardians and God-appointed moral censors; and their homes reek with the stale small of religiosity—religion by rote, dogma uninformed by the energy of spiritual passion.

Fathers, for example, are admonished to work with their sons in keeping the family car in good shape. How is this related to the Bible? How indeed? Well, since everything connected with producing the car is in harmony with God's law, keeping it in working order also fulfills that law. A father should point this out as he and his son work together.

Mothers, too, ought to sit down and make a dress with their daughters, for this gives a woman the opportunity to impress upon her child the biblical principle of "doing all things for the glory of God." She can learn economy; she can learn modesty. It is tedious and wearisome and unrelenting. A mother and daughter, a father and son can take no natural joy in each other's presence unless they form a trinity with God.

Parents are instructed to "have such a fine program outlined for their children that little or no time remains for *outside* associations." [*TW*, Feb. 1, 1974, pp. 84–86] They are also told to determine with whom *inside* the congregation their children may appropriately associate. This advice seems to be at odds with the Witnesses' obligation to love all their brothers and to eschew judging others; but the rationale for forbidding children to associate with Witnesses who are "strongly influenced by the world in attitude, speech, and actions" is that a parent, in enforcing such sanctions, is not making a personal assessment of an individual's worth, but applying *God's standards*. This fosters a feeling of omnipotence in parents; and it enables them, unwittingly, to use children as a vehicle for hostilities and antagonisms they feel toward other adults but are not permitted to acknowledge: adults who "have it in" for other adult Witnesses may simply forbid their own kids to play with the kids of parents they dislike. Antipathies and animosities that are rigorously repressed thus surface, disguised by a veneer of sanctimony and spirituality: the parents tell themselves they are acting

on a mandate from God; they do not allow themselves—they *cannot* allow
themselves—to understand that they are inflicting gratuitous cruelty, that
they are guilty of a failure of love. The suffering that accrues to the outlaw/
outcaste child who is a pawn in this duplicitous game (a victim of his parents' unconscious) is fathomless. The child perceives his rejection to be a
judgment from God: God, not the kid next door, has rejected and abandoned him. Forbidden to have worldly associates, rejected within the congregation as unsuitable, "untheocratic," he is bereft.

David Maslanka, a young composer who was raised as a Witness, tells me
that his childhood "was like a dark, airless chamber illuminated by rain-
bow-colored fantasies. My mother was a 'suspect' Witness," he says; "the
other Witnesses thought she was off center, flirting with spiritualism. So
they wouldn't allow their kids to play with me. I blamed my mother and I
pitied her; and I felt that evil forces were working within me, too. I lived in
almost absolute isolation. I used to pray someone would invite me to sit
next to him at meetings; no one ever did. I felt despised. When I was 11,
my mother was excommunicated because of dabbling with the occult; and,
since I had burned my bridges by refusing to have worldly friends, there
was nobody at all I could talk to, nobody at all." David still finds it hard, so
scarring was that brief and bitter experience, to talk freely: in his intensely
passionate music, great blocks of glorious colored sound alternate with great
blocks of dark, Rousseauvian silence. His music reminds me of ruined
Mayan temples thrusting out of the jungle density and stillness, stone upon
stone rising from dark decay, sheer will conquering a ripe darkness illuminated with rainbow flashes of blinding light.

Many Witness kids were forbidden to play with me because I was judged
to be too smart for my own good—for *their* own good (and, I suspect,
because my mother's beauty and her highly effectual proselytizing evoked
jealousies that could not be expressed). I remember once, feeling sophisticated and daring, using a bobby-soxer word—*devastating* ("This fudge sun-
dae is devastating"); and a Witness mother pounced—she had been waiting.
"Only Jehovah can *devastate*," she said fiercely, the fire of the Inquisition
burning in her eyes. And she forbade her daughter, my best friend, to play
with me. I was 10 years old. I have never forgiven her cruelty, the tears I
shed on her account. She was old and sour; her railroad flat smelled as if a
hundred years of poverty had been ground into the walls; she pounded the
pavements with her message of life-everlasting, hope-and-joy, her legs bulg-
ing with varicose veins, her face perpetually distorted in a grimace of pain;
and her husband was deaf—her life was a hollow shout; but I have never
forgiven her. Both David and I are unforgiving; David and I also share the
same reaction when people like us: We find it difficult to believe. People
think we're *nice!* We are enormously, outrageously grateful for small kindnesses; every kindness comes as a surprise.

The Witnesses have not seen fit to change their views on education. Why bother with Devil-knowledge? Why imperil your standing with the all-knowing God? To what practical uses can a college education possibly be put? For the Witnesses, all knowledge must be practical, utilitarian: At the Watchtower Bible Missionary School of Gilead, established in 1942 for full-time preachers, no humanities are taught, and no creative arts. The Gilead School was built on an 800-acre farm that the Society had owned and operated since 1935 to provide food for Brooklyn Bethel; "Kingdom Farm" was located 255 miles northwest of New York City in South Lansing, in the Finger Lakes district of New York, adjacent to Cornell. Witnesses enrolled in the five-month course were also assigned farm chores "to relieve nervous tension." (Gilead means "heap of witness." The property was later sold, and the school moved to a new building constructed for that purpose on Columbia Heights in 1968.) Future missionaries are taught "a course in college arithmetic; instructions on shipping and use of Society's forms and reports; manner of dealing with government officials; the required international law; a course in English and grammar . . . the essentials of the needed foreign language." No academic credentials are necessary for enrollment; the principal training given to the tuition-free students is "Bible research and public Bible speaking, and the understanding of Theocratic organization instructions." [*JWDP*, p. 204] Confrontation with metaphysical, philosophical, theological, or moral problems is avoided, as are sociology and psychology ("Inferiority complexes and superiority complexes," an elder once said to me, "are just different terms for selfishness"); Freud and Marx might never have lived. (Emotional problems are the result of "demon influence.") When morality is legislated, there is no reason to discuss its nuances—there are no nuances. (One reference work, *Aid to Bible Understanding*, a concordance published by the Watchtower Society, devotes as much space to "grayheadedness" as to "goodness.")

I have, as a consequence of this attitude toward "worldly wisdom," known Witnesses who have not read a single book or magazine not published by the Watchtower Bible and Tract Society for twenty years. I am still amazed at my own youthful temerity: defiantly, when I was at Bethel headquarters, I smuggled *New Yorker*s into the building, locking myself into an unused guest room to read them. *Raise High the Roof Beam, Carpenters!* Salinger, I then thought, would know me, would understand me; and I loved (love) him for that.

Of course I did what I was told and did not go to college. In high school, I took a commercial and then a "cooperative" course—going to school and working in the office of a tool-and-die factory on alternate weeks. I was the despair of my teachers, who pleaded with me to take college-preparatory courses. I protested, rebutted, denied; but in the unredeemed, unredeemable part of my God-possessed heart—that tiny corner which denied Him access—I longed to do what I explained I could not, in good conscience, do. If anyone had picked me up bodily, bound and shackled, and deposited me on any campus in the Western world, I would have considered it a deliverance; Mephistopheles could have had my soul for the price of a course in Freshman English. I ached—wanting so much to be one of them, despising my own longings—when I saw book-laden college students. I seldom allowed my mind to know what my heart was doing. Vice was the Flatbush Avenue bus. I rode the Flatbush Avenue bus, pretending to be on my way to Brooklyn College, hoping that someone would mistake me for one of those privileged people free to learn and to explore. And all this time, I believed that I still believed; I preached with fervor and conviction.

My life was a crazy-quilt of conflicted desires. College was the Tower of Babel; I harbored secret longings to go to college. I was gratified when my intelligence was respected by my teachers; I was even more gratified when a schoolmate mistook me for a cheerleader. I loved touching people, soul to soul, when I preached; I longed to rub souls with the world. My infatuation with Academia informed most of my adult life. Two of my favorite places in the world are Harvard's Widener Library and Radcliffe garden. Scholars are like alchemists to me; entering a locked room at the Widener is for me, still, like entering the Holy of Holies. I romanticize. Once, sitting in the Radcliffe garden with my daughter, I tried to force my bewildered child to enter my pleasure. She, of course, had no reason to think she was on hallowed ground; she saw no angels guarding the gates of my heaven with flaming swords. "Mommy," she said, "it's just a small garden—with weeds."

The Witnesses tied up the whole history of the human race in one knot. My friend Walter Szykitka, who was a Witness for twenty-eight years, explains:

> I was kicked out of the sixth grade for not saluting the flag. Thirty Witness kids from New Jersey, all expelled, went to school in an old hotel in Lakewood, a one-teacher schoolhouse. The teacher was a Witness who'd been to a "normal school" somewhere around 1912. It was terrible. I'd been a good student up to then, and those two years screwed me up. I didn't learn anything. I felt freaky, really bad, ashamed. But I thought that the error was in me. The Witnesses tied up the whole history of the world in one knot. They explained everything.
>
> I didn't allow internal conflicts to surface till I went to Bethel. Then I felt a certain . . . *restlessness*. I'd go into bookstores and look for clues, for books that might tell me something, satisfy this undefined longing; I wanted something to calm the restlessness. I told myself I was haunting bookstores for "corroborative evidence." That was bullshit. But it wasn't till I was in my twenties that I could seriously question whether I was prepared to reject a whole world-view that governed every part of my life. I was like somebody that grew up in a

fake *Our Town*, like somebody who has to believe all the American images and myths because those are the only givens; I was like somebody who lived in a version of America that never really existed. I lived a version of my life that never really existed. It took years to absorb the consequences of my thinking and reading.

I had lived my life until the age of twenty-five or -six believing that I was never going to die, or that if I did die in a car crash or something, God would resurrect me and I'd live forever in the New World. I can remember the exact moment when I realized I was not going to live forever. The physical moment: I was working in my office at Bethel and I got up from my desk to go into the file cabinet; I was bending down to get a file, and—it came out of nowhere—I said, Hey, you're going to die one day. And in that one second the knot unraveled.

The Watchtower [April 1, 1975, p. 217] quotes the Australian *Journal of Personality*, March 1973: "A disproportionately large number of highly creative children were Jehovah's Witnesses. Four children from the total sample of 394 were members of this sect, and all four showed high creative ability. The girl who gained the highest total score on the Torrance [creativity] tests, and the girl who was the only child, male or female, to be included in the top 20 percent of all five performance measures, were both Jehovah's Witnesses." On the face of it, this seems difficult to reconcile with the fact that college students from authoritarian fundamentalist religions have been found, in psychological testing, to have "constricted and rigid cognitive and perceptual functioning on projective and intelligence tests, lower scholastic achievement, lack of creative responsivity with conventional routine aesthetic attitudes, . . . and generally poorer overall adjustment and achievement in comparison with students in matched groups." [E. Mansell Pattison, Z&L, p. 424] On reflection, however, the Australian statistics yield to another interpretation. The children tested were 12 years old. Sexuality rigorously repressed in puberty conduces to a strongly colored fantasy life. The imagination of very young Witnesses is fueled and fired by the rich imagery of destruction and creation with which they live. It is not surprising that the tension produced by the clash between force-fed dogmatic certainty and inner confusion, and the friction created by the rub of the socially isolated against the world, may be, for a time, *creative* tension. The tragedy is that creative young Witnesses will not be permitted to explore or fulfill their potential—unless, for them, the knot unravels.

God told Noah that every living creature should be meat unto him; but that he must not eat the blood, because the life is in the blood.—Leviticus 17:10, New World Translation

On April 18, 1951, the State of Illinois went to court to take temporary custody of a child of Witness parents in order to administer a blood transfusion to the dying infant. Six-day-old Cheryl Labrenz was the victim of a rare medical syndrome that was destroying her red blood cells. The doctors' consensus was that the baby would die without blood transfusions. Cheryl's parents, Darrell and Rhoda Labrenz, paid no heed; they were concerned, they said, with their infant's eternal welfare. They were prepared to see her die, knowing that Jehovah would resurrect her and give her everlasting life—and that they would be consigned to everlasting death if they did not adhere to God's laws prohibiting the ingesting of blood. Cheryl became a ward of the Court for the time necessary to administer the lifesaving transfusions.

The Labrenz case was the first of many in which minor children became wards of the Court so that blood transfusions, prohibited by the governing body of Jehovah's Witnesses since 1944, could be administered. (If a hospital administers blood transfusions without parental consent, the hospital and its doctors are liable to charges of assault, or of manslaughter if a minor child dies.) *

An absurdly literal reading of the Mosaic injunction not to "eat blood," together with Paul's instructions (Acts 21:25) for Christians to "keep themselves from things offered to idols, and from blood, and from strangled, and from fornication," is bolstered by the Witnesses with the declaration that blood transfusion dates back to the ancient Egyptians (anything pagan is sinful) and by the seemingly contradictory fact that "the earliest reported case was a futile attempt to save the life of Pope Innocent VIII in 1492." [*Yearbook*, 1975, p. 222] (If the Church—whose genius it is to absorb and assimilate pagan practices so as to make Christ accessible to all people— does it, according to Witness logic, it can't possibly be right.)

It cannot be said that the Witnesses are not willing to endure grave discomfort, or to die for their beliefs. I have known Witnesses who scurried

---

* *People ex rel. Wallace v. Labrenz*, 411 Ill. 618 (1952). When the situation involved a minor child, decision to overrule the parents' convictions has prevailed. (See *State v. Perricone*, 181 A. 2d 751 [1962]; *Raleigh Fitkin Hospital v. Anderson*, 201 A. 2d 537 [1964]; all cases appealed but denied *certiorari* by the U.S. Supreme Court.) The majority of cases have been decided in favor of court authorization of blood transfusion, even for unwilling recipients, on grounds of the State's right to uphold life (*United States v. George*, 239 F. Supp. 752 [1965]). The courts have had to decide whether to restrict religious liberty against an individual's will in order to save his life. In a case heard before the Illinois Supreme Court, it was ruled that religious practices can be infringed only when they threaten *public* health, welfare, or morals. In dealing with "a competent adult who "has steadfastly maintained her belief that acceptance of a blood transfusion is a violation of the law of God," even though the Court may consider her beliefs "unwise, foolish, or ridiculous, in the absence of an overriding danger to society we may not permit interference" (*In re Brooks*, 205 N.E. 2d 435 [1965]). The courts have quoted Brandeis: "The makers of our Constitution . . . conferred, as against the government, the right to be let alone—the most comprehensive of rights and the most valued of civilized man" (*Olmstead v. U.S.* 277 U.S. 438 [1928]). In the case of *John F. Kennedy Memorial Hospital v. Heston* (1971), a court ordered, against the will of her parents, that a minor Witness receive a blood transfusion (which resulted in her recovery). In a decision that was later to be quoted in the celebrated Karen Anne Quinlan case, the court ruled that "there is no constitutional right to choose to die. . . . The State's interest in sustaining life . . . is hardly different than its interest in the case of suicide."

frantically from doctor to doctor, postponing vital operations in an often futile attempt to find a practitioner who would agree to operate without transfusing blood. (I have also been told, in confidence, by doctors that they did at the last moment—when it was apparent that the patient's life was at stake—administer blood transfusions unbeknownst to the Witness, in default of the agreement not to do so.) On the other hand, Watchtower publications are full of testimonials of people who were told that they would die without transfusions—and who, refusing transfusions, nevertheless lived. The 1975 *Yearbook* [pp. 224–25] cites the case of a woman with an aneurysm in a main artery leading to her spleen; she lost 70 percent of her blood, but survived without a transfusion. The Witnesses, she told her doctors, do not believe in divine healing. However, "because we obeyed Jehovah's command concerning blood, all of us have been blessed." This is a wonderful example of having it every which way: If you are a Witness and die because of refusing transfusions, you will live forever after your Paradise resurrection; the chances are, however—and the Witnesses bolster this with pseudoscientific evidence as to the efficacy of saline transfusions—that Jehovah will "bless" you and you will survive without a transfusion.

During World War II, male Witnesses imprisoned under Selective Service draft laws went so far as to refuse to be vaccinated, regarding vaccination, not illogically, as being no different from blood transfusion. Hugh Macmillan [*Faith*, pp. 188–90], the elder assigned to visit and counsel imprisoned Witnesses, set them straight. He told the young men in solitary confinement that "All of us who visit our foreign branches are vaccinated or we stay at home. Now, vaccination," he said, with dubious logic, "is not anything like blood transfusion. No blood is used in the vaccine. It is a scrum." He advised the jailed Witnesses to act as the prophet Jeremiah had. Jeremiah had told the governmental authorities of his time, "I am in your hands; do with me as you wish; if you put me to death, innocent blood will be on your hands." "They have you where they could vaccinate an elephant," Macmillan said, "and they will vaccinate you all" whether you agree to it or not. "If evil resulted," he told the prisoners "the government would be held responsible" by God. The blood of the innocent would be on Caesar's hands. The Witnesses agreed not only to accept transfusions, but to write a letter of apology to prison officials "for the trouble they had caused." (As one draft resister said to me about Witnesses in prison, "They were the good niggers.") My sympathy is with the Witnesses who were willing to endure solitary confinement and withdrawal of all jail privileges and who listened to the voice of their conscience. Individual conscience, however, was overruled by the voice of authority. The jailed Witnesses were forced to violate their consciences, which told them that vaccine would pollute the bloodstream they had been taught to regard as sacred.

I grudgingly admire the brave silliness of adult Witnesses who are willing to risk the consequence of death by refusing to receive blood. They are analogous, in my mind, to would-be assassins of bad men—who are just as brave, just as silly, just as futile, and whose orientation is similarly futuristic. But how can one admire an adult who makes that life-or-death decision for a child? It is apparently a monstrous, unnatural act. But one must remember the brainwashing to which the Witnesses are constantly subjected; they are not monstrous child-haters; they are sad men and women with a mission and an obsession that overrules natural necessities and concerns.

They are surgically prepared by their overseers even to amputate their grief: "Because of the wonderful hope of the resurrection, a Christian is not overwhelmed with tears and grief. His sorrow is not as great or as deep as that upon those who have no knowledge of the hope the Bible gives." [*Aw*, May 8, 1975, p. 23]

To suppress natural grief is to invite disaster. The Witnesses are psyched up to deny their grief. But I have seen Witnesses give way to an excess of grief that was terrifying. I knew a young mother who lost two small children in one year—one was run over by a car; the other died of pneumonia. The child who was struck by a car might have been saved by blood transfusions. In her fear and terror, his mother—who had been taught to make sense of the world, and who could not make sense of this senseless slaughter—held him dying in her arms while she argued with doctors about blood transfusions. When her daughter died, six months later, she entered an unnatural calm, a false and dreadful stillness. She began to tell fellow Witnesses that she was sure her children were in heaven, that they visited her comfortingly in her dreams. The Witnesses, frightened by her apostasy— she could reasonably expect, according to their dogma, only to see her children resurrected to an earthly life, heaven being reserved for 144,000 older Witnesses—chided her for expressing heretical views. They scolded; they did not comfort. And yet many of them, many of the people who withheld comfort from a woman driven mad by grief, weren't monsters either. They were afraid of her because her grief threatened the security of their belief. She wasn't *supposed* to abandon herself to grief. So they chose to see her grief as Devil-inspired apostasy.

At Witness meetings, skits (called "demonstrations") are put on offering role models for emulation, exemplifying appropriate behavior. This is one of them, verbatim, written by a man who later repudiated his belief. He is one of the kindest men I know; I have never known him to do a mean thing; and he wrote and produced this happy-ending bloody call to arms:

BLOOD TRANSFUSION

Cast of Characters

FRANK MILLER—One of Jehovah's witnesses and the father.
DOROTHY MILLER—The mother.

SHARON MILLER—The daughter who needs a blood transfusion.

BILLY MILLER—The son.

DOCTOR GORDON—The doctor treating Sharon.

FATHER O'BRIEN—The Catholic priest who tries to disprove the fact that God's Word is against blood transfusion.

REPORTER—From the local newspaper, looking for a sensational story.

Part I

SETTING: *Desk on stage at right, facing left. Two chairs facing audience at left of desk. Off stage at right is cot with blanket. On doctor's desk is telephone and a few papers. As scene opens doctor is seated at desk.*

VOICE FROM THE SIDE: The faith of Jehovah's witnesses has been tested in many different ways in times past and is being tested in many ways today. Recently many of Jehovah's servants have been faced with a new test—blood transfusion. Blood transfusion is the practice of transferring blood from the veins of one person to another. As in intravenous feeding, it is a feeding upon blood and is an unscriptural practice. The way Jehovah's servants find themselves faced with this issue often happens as it did with Brother and Sister Miller.

(Music)

One day, suddenly, their young daughter complained of extreme pains in her chest. They rushed their crying daughter, Sharon, to the office of Doctor Gordon for help.

(Brother Miller enters from left carrying his daughter, Sharon, who is crying. Also entering are Sister Miller and son, Billy.)

(The voice continues, with characters making appropriate actions)·

Doctor Gordon directed that immediately the ailing child be taken into his inner office for examination. As Sister Miller quieted her daughter, the doctor began his examination. Shortly he asked Brother and Sister Miller to go to his outer office while he made a more extensive examination to see what could be done to help little Sharon. Once in the outer office Brother and Sister Miller waited anxiously—minutes seemed like hours—and the next half hour seemed like an eternity. Finally, the examination was completed. The doctor entered and sat at his desk.

(Music—crescendo)

DOCTOR GORDON: Mr. and Mrs. Miller, I'm afraid your little daughter has a lung congestion. She'll have to have an immediate operation.

SISTER MILLER: Oh, no!

DOCTOR GORDON: It's usually not a serious operation but we've run into some difficulty. Your daughter'll undoubtedly need a blood transfusion. But we've checked her blood and it's a rare type. We don't have any on hand here.

SISTER MILLER: *(To Brother Miller)* Oh, Frank, what're we going to do?

BROTHER MILLER: There's only one thing we can do, Dorothy.

DOCTOR GORDON: Now look, I didn't mean to worry you. We'll be able to get the blood we need all right. The Red Cross will have it. *(Dials phone)*

BROTHER MILLER: But, Doctor . . .

DOCTOR GORDON: *(Interrupting)* Now don't worry, Mr. Miller. We'll get the blood all right. *(To telephone)* Hello? Is this the Red Cross? This is Doctor Gordon. I need two pints of type XX blood for an emergency operation right away. Can you get it to me? . . . All right. . . . *(To Millers)* They're checking now. *(To phone)* You have none? . . . Are you sure? . . . All right. I'll call the Central Blood Bank. *(To Millers)* They didn't have any, but don't worry. They'll have it at the Central Blood Bank.

BROTHER MILLER: But, Doctor . . .

DOCTOR GORDON: *(To telephone, jiggling receiver)* Operator! This is an emergency. Connect me with the Central Blood Bank . . . and please hurry. *(To Millers)* The operator is putting the call through now.

BROTHER MILLER: But, Doctor Gordon, I'm afraid you don't understand. We can't let Sharon have a blood transfusion.

DOCTOR GORDON: *(Astonished)* You can't what?

BROTHER MILLER: We can't let Sharon have a blood transfusion.

DOCTOR GORDON: *(Slowly to telephone)* Operator, never mind that call. *(To Brother and Sister Miller)* You can't let your daughter have a blood transfusion? Suppose you tell me what you mean by that?

BROTHER MILLER: Well, you see, it's against our religion.

DOCTOR GORDON: Against your religion? What kind of religion is that?

BROTHER MILLER: It's based on the Bible, Doctor. You see, we're Jehovah's witnesses.

DOCTOR GORDON: You mean to tell me that your not letting Sharon have a blood transfusion is based on the Bible?

BROTHER MILLER: That's right. You see, in the Bible it says that right after the flood God said no one should eat blood. In Genesis, the 9th chapter and the third verse, he said: "But flesh with the life . . ."

DOCTOR GORDON: *(Interrupting angrily)* God said! God said! I don't care what God said. All I know is that your little daughter is in there dying, Mr. Miller. We have to operate immediately. And she's going to need a blood transfusion. If she doesn't get it, she doesn't stand a chance. . . . *(Pleadingly)* Mrs. Miller, don't you understand what this means? Won't you tell your husband . . .

SISTER MILLER: *(Interrupting)* I'm sorry, Doctor, but if God commands that we're not supposed to . . .

DOCTOR GORDON: *(Interrupting)* What kind of a God is this? I thought God is love. But this isn't love. This is murder!

BROTHER MILLER: Doctor, if you'll only let us explain.

DOCTOR GORDON: *(Sharply)* I won't let you explain anything. If we

give your daughter a shot of Adrenalin Chloride now we can post-
pone the operation until tomorrow. I want you to go home and
think this over and then come back to my office here in the
morning.

BROTHER MILLER: I'm certain our answer will still be the same,
Doctor.

BILLY: Daddy, Sharon isn't going to die, is she?

BROTHER MILLER: We hope not, Billy. *(To Doctor Gordon)* We'll see
you in the morning, Doctor Gordon.

(Brother and Sister Miller and Billy exit left.)

(Doctor Gordon picks up telephone and dials number.)

DOCTOR GORDON: *(To telephone)* Hello, Father O'Brien? . . . This is
Doctor Gordon. I have a problem and I need your help. . . . I'll
have to perform an operation tomorrow morning on a lovely little
girl. But she's going to need a blood transfusion and her parents
won't permit it. They're Jehovah's witnesses and say it's against the
Bible or something. . . . No, I didn't discuss it with them very
much. He started to recite a Bible verse but I just couldn't stand to
hear talk of the girl not getting the blood she'll need to keep her
alive. So I sent them home and told them to think it over and come
back tomorrow. But I know they won't change their minds. That's
why I called you, Father. They'll be here at 10 o'clock in the morning and if you could come over here and talk to them I'm sure you
could convince them that God doesn't mind if their daughter gets a
blood transfusion. If you come, I'm sure you'll be instrumental in
saving a life. . . . Thank you, Father. I'll look for you in the
morning.

Part II

VOICE FROM THE SIDE: Morning came and as 10 o'clock approached the
priest arrived. Another visitor arrived, too. A local newspaper reporter came in search of a sensational news story. Then, shortly
after 10 o'clock, Brother and Sister Miller arrived.

DOCTOR GORDON: Mrs. and Mr. Miller, I'd like to have you meet
Father O'Brien. He's the priest from the local parish. I told him
about your religious beliefs and he offered to help if he could. *(Exchange greetings)* Now, tell me, do you feel any differently today
than you did yesterday?

BROTHER MILLER: No, we don't, Doctor Gordon. We still feel the
same.

DOCTOR GORDON: Just as I expected, Father.

FATHER O'BRIEN: Doctor Gordon told me what a lovely daughter you
have, Mr. and Mrs. Miller, and it disturbed me to think that possibly because of some misunderstanding she might lose her life. Now
I'm sure there's nothing in the Bible that says God wants us to let
little Sharon die instead of saving her life.

BROTHER MILLER: There is if you try to use a blood transfusion, Mr.
O'Brien. I tried to show Doctor Gordon yesterday that after the

flood God commanded that no one should eat blood. Here, I have
my Bible with me and I can read it for you. It's in Genesis 9:3,4:
"Every moving thing that liveth shall be meat for you; even as the
green herb have I given you all things. But flesh with the life
thereof, which is the blood thereof, shall ye not eat."

FATHER O'BRIEN: Yes, but that was a long time ago, my friend.
Surely today, when the life of your child is in danger, you can't go
back to an ancient law . . .

BROTHER MILLER: But this command was part of a covenant with man
that God says is everlasting. Why, 850 years later, when he gave
the Law covenant to the nation of Israel, he gave the same command, at Leviticus 17:14.

FATHER O'BRIEN: But Christians don't have to abide by those laws,
Mr. Miller. Christ did away with that when he died on the cross.
The Christian principle is love and certainly nothing could be more
loving than for a person to give some of his own precious blood to
save another person's life.

DOCTOR GORDON: And this is your own child, Mr. Miller. Surely
your love for your child is great enough to permit you to overlook . . .

BROTHER MILLER: It's true, the Christian principle is love and the
Scripture I just read is from the old Law covenant given to the
Jews. But Christians, too, are commanded not to eat blood, at Acts
21:25.

DOCTOR GORDON: Well, I don't think you would be violating that
command anyway. You're not really eating blood. You're taking it
into your veins.

BROTHER MILLER: You know as well as I do, Doctor, that people are
fed through the veins. That's eating, because you call it intravenous
feeding.

DOCTOR GORDON: But these Bible verses mention animal blood. This
is something different. This is human blood.

BROTHER MILLER: At Leviticus 7:26 it says "Ye shall eat no manner of
blood."

REPORTER: Mr. Miller, I'm no authority on religion, but doesn't it
seem that the life of your child is important? After all, she's so
young and you're making an important decision for her. Do you
think you have that right?

BROTHER MILLER: As her father, it's not only my right, it's my obligation.

REPORTER: I don't think it is, Mr. Miller. Not when it means her life.
We have laws in this country, and I'm going to do all I can to see
that the courts of this land use those laws to save your daughter's
life. And I know my paper'll back me up to the limit. This is something I think the people ought to know about. I think a religion like
yours is dangerous to the people and it ought to be stopped. Where
are your principles?

BROTHER MILLER: Now before you fly off the handle, I'd like to tell you what I think about that. When my wife and I try our best to live our faith in the face of such difficulties and you say, "We have laws in this country," it makes us wonder what country you're thinking of. What you need is a history lesson, to learn that this country was founded by people who placed God's law above man's and were willing to die and lose their loved ones to obey God's laws. Your paper has probably written articles and editorials praising those people, and then when persons like you are faced with the same kind of decisions you fail miserably yourselves and condemn others who try to keep their faith in God—and just to sell a few newspapers. Now, I ask you, where are *your* principles?

And then to have this gentleman (*gesturing toward priest*) come along, dressed so everyone will know that he claims to be a Christian, and to try to convince us with sweet talk and eloquent expressions of love that we should break Christian laws.

You called us murderers, Doctor Gordon, but this man is a traitor—against God—and with no good reason not even an excuse.

You people seem to think that we haven't given a single thought to our daughter's life. I want you to know that we have. This has been the most trying decision of our lives. If you have children you know what I mean. It's out of love for our child that we've made the decision we have. You see, we love our child so much that we're willing to live without her for a few years, now in this corrupt old world, so we'll be able to live with her forever in God's new world.

DOCTOR GORDON: Forever? In a new world?

BROTHER MILLER: That's right. That's our faith, based on the Bible, and by God's grace we're going to keep that faith—regardless of what you, or Mr. O'Brien, or our newspaper friend—or the whole world—says or thinks about it.

DOCTOR GORDON: Mr. Miller, I respect your faith and I'm going to operate on your daughter and do the best I can without a blood transfusion. With extreme care during the operation and the use of blood substitutes there is a slim possibility that she may get along without it.

MRS. MILLER: (*going to Gordon to shake his hand*) Oh, thank you, Doctor Gordon.

VOICE FROM THE SIDE: And so Dr. Gordon operated. And now you wonder how the operation turned out. Well, this story ended happily. The operation was a success and the blood substitutes provided little Sharon with the strength necessary to recover. (*Music*) As weeks and months passed, Sharon got stronger and stronger, until that day when Brother and Sister Miller, and little Billy, stopped by to see Doctor Gordon—and there was little Sharon, as cute and pretty as ever, waiting for them as though nothing had ever happened.

(Sharon rushes up to her mother and hugs her.)
SHARON: Mommy!
(Then she turns toward her father and hugs him.)
SHARON: Daddy!
BILLY: *(pulling at her dress)* Hello, Sharon.
SHARON: Hello, Billy.
(Mr. Miller lowers her to kiss Billy on the cheek.)
MRS. MILLER: Thank you, so much, for everything, Doctor Gordon.
DOCTOR GORDON: I was very happy to do all I could, Mrs. Miller.
MR. MILLER: I want to thank you too, Doctor.
DOCTOR GORDON: Mr. Miller, I want you to know how much I ad-
    mire you. I admire you and your fine family and your faith in God
    (shaking hands). God bless you.
(All go to leave.)
DOCTOR GORDON: Bye, Sharon.
SHARON: Bye, Doctor Gordon. *(Throws him a kiss.)*
(Music crescendo)

                          The End.

One of the graphic artists who illustrates *The Watchtower* and *Awake!*
magazines used to work for Walt Disney; and the happy-family scenes with
which those magazines are illustrated resemble a Disney dream of American G-rated life: Daddy (a Ronald Reagan look-alike) sits in slippered comfort in a fat armchair, Bible—or Watchtower publication—in his manicured
but virile hand; Mommy (a lacquered Sandra Dee) perches in a Mommy
chair in her spotless suburban-tract living room, her impeccably Peck and
Peck body inclined in graceful submission toward her mate; and at the feet
of this glowing pair sit two fresh-faced Mouseketeer children. They might
all have been designed as blueprints for First Families—on spiritual guard
even while taking their homey ease.

People believe their own myths; unfortunately, they can't always live
them. The Father Knows Best ideal toward which the Witnesses reach—
happy families sitting down to a prebreakfast Bible discussion, working together in the door-to-door field ministry, sitting together in scrubbed and
pleasant rows at meetings—is a soothing invention.

It is true that conversion to "The Truth" may result in major behavioral
changes that can equip marginal people for life in the real world—the world
that has bruised and defeated them: alcoholics stop drinking; addicts get off
junk; men who are unemployed find work—with a little help from "the
friends" (the Witnesses tend to use *lazy* and *unemployed* as if they were syn-
onyms); women who were sloppy housekeepers, once taught that cleanliness is part of Godliness, become living advertisements for *Küche, Kirche,
Kinder;* and children, rigorously controlled, do not (as long as they remain
Witnesses) smoke, dope, litter, fornicate, or rebel.

These accommodations appear, on the surface, to improve family life; mechanistically, they do. But changing the outer man (or woman) does not—although change does sometimes work from the outside in—annul or change the inner personality configuration that made them Witnesses in the first place. They are dependent for approval and sense of worth on external authority; their sights are fixed on a future that will dispel the pain of the present and make up for the deprivations of the past. They are, in an expression borrowed from the 1950s (in which decade they seem permanently mired), outer-directed.

At conventions, where there is indeed great communal tenderness, they radiate happiness. They look like picture-book families, kindergarten-primer families. But the maggots of their frustrations and discontents—their fear and distrust of the material world, of the present—often eat into their apple-pie lives. Depression among Witnesses is widespread, as are tight-lipped repressed familial animosities for which there is no appropriate outlet. ("Children have emotions. They are not to be shown in fits of anger or pouting. Direct their emotions to useful ends such as singing or playing a musical instrument or dancing. These things also give glory to the Creator. . . . Husbands must rebuke their wives in a spirit of love; and wives must never nag or be aggressively demanding."—From a speech given at a local congregation of Jehovah's Witnesses)

They seek, by their busy-ness—each family is instructed to have one full-time preacher—to lock up their discontents in an attic of their minds. Frequently their discontents flare up in odd ways. I have observed families quarreling over such how-many-angels-can-dance-on-the-head-of-a-pin issues as "Will our cats live through Armageddon and live forever in the New World?" (I'm not making that up. One woman who insisted that her cats would live forever was threatened by her husband with public reproof from an elder.) You might wonder who would seek to ask such a question. Someone who has only the future. That people do ask one another such questions, and have bitter fallings-out over them, is proved by this depressing exercise in unreality, a speech at a recent convention of Jehovah's Witnesses in New York: "Brothers, do not ask, 'Will some form of money be used in the New System? What about machinery, such as cars, TV, computers? Will we have them after Armageddon, in God's New Order? Shall I save up money now to buy them? Shall I buy a new car and a new TV so I can start off on the right foot in the New System?" Such speculations are food and drink—and fuel for contentious arguments—among people who have no more questions to ask, since all their questions have been answered.

If thy brother, the son of thy mother, or thy son, or thy daughter, or the wife of thy bosom, or thy friend, which is as thine own soul, entice thee secretly, saying, Let us go and serve other gods, which thou hast not known, thou, nor thy fathers; . . . Thou shalt not consent unto him, nor hearken unto him; neither shall thine eye pity

*him, neither shalt thou spare, neither shalt thou conceal him: But thou shalt surely
kill him; thine hand shall be first upon him to put him to death, and afterwards the
hand of all the people. And thou shalt stone him with stones, that he die.* . . .
—*Deuteronomy 13:6–10*

The Watchtower, while it does not go so far as to advocate the execution of
idolators, does assure its readers that to testify against a family member
whose behavior is antithetical to its instructions is a viable way of protecting the "moral fiber" of God's organization. "Yielding to the influence of a
close family member . . . to disregard God's law can only spell disaster.
. . . Relatives . . . could cause one to fail in giving God exclusive devotion.
. . . Anyone . . . taking on undue importance in our lives can lead to our
not being exclusively devoted to God. . . . because the object of a person's
craving diverts affection from God and in this way becomes an idol." [*TW,*
June 15, 1975, pp. 381–82] Every member of one's household is a potential
enemy, a potential threat.

Witnesses are instructed to be "examples" to one another in godly conduct. To objectify oneself, and others, as "examples," to be obliged to regard oneself and others as the personification of a doctrinaire idea rather
than as complex, complicated human beings is a reduction of humanity that
may lead—has led—to schizophrenia, and certainly to depressive behavior.

These are excerpts from a five-minute play ("demonstration") written to
be performed at congregations of Jehovah's Witnesses:

> Because the God of this world is not Jehovah, this is not a happy
> world. It is a miserable world, reeking with disillusionment and bit-
> terness, permeated with hatred and jealousy, saturated with disap-
> pointment and heartache. But, true to his promise, Jehovah has taken
> a people out of this wretched world—a people for his name—
> Jehovah's witnesses. And because they have accepted Jehovah as their
> God, these people are happy—truly happy. They enjoy peace of
> mind, receive rich blessings continually from the hand of their God
> and look to the future with anticipation.
>
> We would like you to meet the Spencer family—a happy, theocratic
> family.
>
> First, there's Brother Spencer. Bill Spencer. Bill is a friendly fel-
> low, and he knows the importance of there always being a warm,
> friendly atmosphere around the home. "After all," he says, "what's a
> home, if it isn't friendly?" Bill has enthusiasm too. Especially when it
> comes to Kingdom activity. In fact, it's his enthusiasm that helps keep
> the family so active and alive. He knows this is his Scriptural obliga-
> tion.
>
> Next, we'd like to have you meet Gladys, his wife. Nice woman,
> Gladys. Works hard, like a theocratic wife should. Bill takes the lead;
> she follows. The more you get to know these two and the way they
> work together so beautifully, the better you like them. Gladys is one

who has always had dreams about the future. You know how most women are: A home in the country, a little garden, two or three children running around the place and all that. Funny thing about those dreams, though. Since coming into the truth, all of a sudden they're not important any more. Oh, she thinks about the new world all right. Guess we all do. But she realizes she has a job to do now, and she enjoys every minute of it.

And one of her big jobs is helping train their son, Jimmy. There he is now. He causes them a few anxieties now and then, but generally speaking, he's a good boy.

They have overcome their problems—by following the advice of the Scriptures and Jehovah's organization.

[Scene I of the play has Bill and Jimmy and Gladys sitting at the breakfast table, discussing a Bible text (Jimmy: "We speak the truth to the people. The religious leaders tell lies to the people in church") and reviewing, from the *Yearbook*, the work of the Witnesses in the Philippine Islands. In Scene II they all go out preaching from door to door together; and before they go together to a meeting at the Kingdom Hall, Jimmy sets the table for the meal his mother has cooked, in a "spirit of joyful cooperation," and they discuss their morning's preaching activities. There then follows a monologue by Bill Spencer, discussing the nature of his happiness.]

The holy God expresses his purpose for good toward his servants by providing them with opportunities to experience progressive states of happiness from one period of joyful existence to another.

How true that is. Since knowing Jehovah it has been just one progressive state of happiness after another.

Before knowing Jehovah our happiness depended on things that might not last until tomorrow. *And we never were really happy.* We were always hoping for something better. And if we found that what we hoped in wasn't going to come, everything seemed so useless.

[Bill explains that before his conversion, he had looked forward to "getting a job as a doctor at the Glenwood Hospital out on Long Island." There were no openings at Glenwood. So, showing, it would seem to the ungodly eye, a remarkable lack of enterprise and imagination, Gladys and Bill did office work ("And I had worked so hard to learn the medical profession!") while the bills piled up and they quarreled, and little Jimmy, a fifth-grader, threw his clothes on the floor and neglected to learn how to read, and they were altogether miserable. Then a Witness came to call. Bill studied the Bible with him. Gladys wasn't having any. Jimmy continued to throw his clothes on the floor and to forget how to spell his name. In Scene III, Bill offers his woes to his Bible instructor. The Witness tells him how to deal with the recalcitrant Gladys and the delinquent Jimmy.]

Well, I wouldn't try to force her into anything, Bill. If you see that
you're getting nowhere by trying to reason with her, then don't try.
There have been many cases like yours. The Apostle Paul even wrote
about split families like that. But he advised that you should just continue to fulfill your marriage obligations and that perhaps in time,
with love and consideration and tact, you may win over your mate to
the truth. So I'd say, just be a good husband to her and let her see
that this message has done something for you, has given you a hope,
something to live for, and she may wonder about it in time and want
to know more about it.

Show love for your son; instead of hitting him or hollering at him,
take him aside and kindly explain to him what he should do and why;
there should be some improvement. And also bring God into the picture and tell him what God requires of little boys and what they will
receive if they are good.

[Bill decides to give up his career—"my doctor's profession"—because
"there are higher principles in life." He begins "to exercise Christian principles in the home, . . . Christian love toward Gladys" (who has not been
consulted about his "doctor's profession") "and Jimmy. After a while they
began to notice this and it began to have its effects." Bill is happy. Jimmy
wants to live in the New World, so he learns to read and picks his clothes
up off the floor. Bill buys his wife a mixer, and his kindness inspires her to
ask him about his newfound religion. She likes what she hears and decides
she wants to live in the New World too. Jimmy sets the table instead of
sassing.]

Bill: So Jehovah provided me with another source of happiness.
Then it was like learning the truth all over again. But this time it was
even more thrilling than before. I was giving to someone else—
Gladys. My wife. It made me happier than words can express. We
studied hard. The more Gladys learned, the more she wanted to
learn. Then we began teaching Jimmy, too. We began attending
meetings together. All three of us. This was real progress. And then
we even began going out in the service together. In only a few months
we developed into a real happy, theocratic family.

We were serving Jehovah. We even got rid of all our bills, without
the doctor's profession. . . . I never knew that one person could experience so much happiness. . . . "Happy is the people whose god is
Jehovah."

And we never were really happy. The man, no longer a Witness, who wrote
this idyll was married to a Witness for three years before he could tell his
wife that he was gravely troubled by profound doubts. When he admitted
to doubt (he felt he was putting his life in her hands), her response, unantic-
ipated, incredible to him, was that she herself had not believed for two of

the three years they had lived together; her faith was a dry husk. During those years of doubt—of torment (the fact that the pap they listened to was corny, tacky, does not lessen the authenticity of their suffering)—they had been in the full-time ministry, living a Gladys/Bill exemplary life; and they were unable to share their core feelings with each other. They divorced their feelings from their actions, and their marriage was a charade. They were strangers afraid of damaging each other. They were each other's "examples." Sex was lousy. They spent their honeymoon playing checkers, and things never progressed much beyond that point. Each assumed the other to be frigid.

When I preached to Irv, he'd say I was full of shit, and I'd say, Well, when you throw pearls to swine . . . *and he got so mad:* You call me a swine? *and he broke tables and lamps.* . . .

Pain is multiplied when one member of a marriage is not a Witness. Because women outnumber men among the Witnesses, the likelihood is that the unbelieving mate will be the husband. The believing woman is told that she may be the instrument of her husband's salvation. This places an intolerable burden upon her: She cannot but feel superior to the man who is scheduled for destruction, while at the same time she must act as if the man who despises or is indifferent to her beloved Jehovah is, by Divine arrangement, the head of her household. She is constrained from leaving her mate, even if he is abusive; she is, in effect, the caretaker of his soul. She may seek divorce only on the ground of adultery. The Witnesses used not to regard homosexuality as a scriptural ground for divorce; they have in recent years enlarged their definition of adultery to encompass homosexual infidelity. At one time, bestiality was a ground for divorce. (Women were victims of doctrinaire semantics: "Bestiality is not the same as adultery or fornication."—*Aid*, p. 217)

A woman asking whether she might justifiably secure a legal separation from a husband who beat her was told, in the columns of *The Watchtower* (May 1, 1975), of another Witness whose alcoholic husband abused her—beat her, slapped her, kicked and punched her—for twenty years: "The Bible's truth enabled her to endure and to be a happy Christian." This happy Christian had frequently to barricade the entrance of her barn, cowering with her eleven children, when her husband arrived with blood lust in an alcoholic rage. After twenty years of this, her husband, according to *The Watchtower*, quit drinking, "improved in controlling his temper," and began to accompany her to meetings. "Marriage mates should strive to remain together despite marital problems resulting from human imperfection." *The Watchtower* pointed out that in addition to being derelict in her spiritual duties to an unbelieving mate, a woman who chose to leave him might also find herself having to work to support herself; her secular work might "consume time now used in spiritual activities." *The Watchtower* did not neglect to suggest that the abused woman might be responsible for her victimization: "Do you nag or provoke him? 'A leaking roof . . . and a contentious wife are comparable.' " [*TW*, May 1, 1975, pp. 286–87]

Can a woman live like this with any degree of self-respect? Women live with men they hate. Because there is no comfort for them anywhere else—so they have been told, by their mentors, whom they do respect—they become increasingly dependent upon the Watchtower Society. They are God's foundlings, turning to "His organization" for the warmth and support the Watchtower Society has assured them is available nowhere else.

Opposition from their mates allows women to feel martyred and to gain status within the organization. Their increased worth within the organization compensates for their domestic suffering.

I think of the years I spent feeling contemptuous of my dear father, of his impotence in the face of the contempt of his wife and daughter. He was our head, our master, we were told, in all things but worship. But our whole life was worship! His nominal "headship" was as empty as our treacly declarations of submission. My beautifully gregarious father could have no friends of his own in our house: they drank and made dirty talk and defiled. *Our* friends were always there, at his table, in his living room, preaching at him or indifferent toward him, glaring at him when he helped himself to food, a small revenge, as we were saying Grace. His presence was tolerated.

He argued pugnaciously with the Witnesses, who provoked him to impotent rage by fielding all his questions with rote reiteration of Bible texts; his rage increased geometrically as they refused to be provoked to answering rage, never sacrificing their studied demeanor to the urgency of passion or of anger. My father thought that was inhuman; "Stone-wall Jehovahs," he called them. "Your God is no better than Hitler," he said. "The whole world is a concentration camp—everybody's going to the ovens but you." "We love you," they replied. "We want to help you." But their love was for my mother; she grew sleek and beautiful with it, while my father raged.

He packed his bags frequently to leave. My mother did not want him to leave; he was the means of her financial support—and she was preaching one hundred hours a month. He threatened so often to leave that my brother, when he was 7, packed his suitcases for him, snot and tears all over his face, and dared him to leave us. He did not. (I never saw my brother cry again.) My mother and I would go out to preach on Christmas mornings, leaving my father alone, bereft and windily angry. We told ourselves we were doing God's will; his very opposition was proof of it.

My father wanted once to take me to the country for a weekend; and I—wretched child that I was—refused to go unless I could take my Watchtower study books with me. We were both adamant; neither of us would yield. My brother tells me how my father spent that weekend: driving wildly, blindly along mountain roads, courting his own destruction. I had won.

One Christmas Eve, when I was alone with my father, who was drinking dully, steadily, there was a poltergeist phenomenon in our kitchen—cups and saucers and plates and pots spun wildly around and settled with a thunderous crash while he went on drinking. It was as if the universe had wheeled drunkenly in protest and settled at his feet. (I do not think I am imagining this. I think I had an awful hunger for my father's love.)

My mother was my "sister" in the faith—and God's surrogate. How she wanted and needed a perfect, "theocratic" child. So often I displeased her. Days of heavy silence were her reproach. In her silence and mine she wrote letters to me, when we lived together, and posted them, and handed them to me when the mailman came, her face averted from my gaze. They were the words she could not say. (Now we have no more words.) And we were rivals for the love of God, and allies against my father. And rivals for the love of men. Every man who came to see me was seduced by my mother's lofty spirituality, by the faint fragrance of suffering and martyrdom that accompanied her. I was imperfect, available flesh; she, removed from the arena of sexuality, was pure, untouchable spirituality. It was never any contest. (All this my father watched.) I admired her, I envied her, I was jealous of her—my mother, my sister (we are each other's failures). I have wanted so often to tell her I love her; the words are locked in my throat. I lack charity. I have wanted to hear her say she is sorry (for our loss, our defeat, for failing me). I have wanted to tell her I am sorry (for our loss, our defeat, for failing her). But we have no more words.

I was over 30 before I felt I had any right to my father's love. He gave it freely when I asked; I had only to ask. When my father lay dying, we thought, of a massive coronary, I said, reaching down to touch his wired chest, "Daddy, I'm so glad the last years have made us friends." "We were always friends, Bobbie," he said. "It was just that we didn't always know it." I felt as if I had entered my childhood at last, reclaimed what I had wantonly thrown away. I had sacrificed him for God, stolen from him and from myself the best love I had to offer and to receive. My friendship with my father has been healing, redemptive; it has made me whole. He has forgiven me those sorry years. That amplitude of spirit humbles me.

At a convention of Witnesses, I watched a Bible "drama" that was meant to illustrate the danger of rebellion against Jehovah. The highlight of the production came when a small child, whose mother and father had been among 14,700 Israelites destroyed by Jehovah for insurrection against Moses, sobbed wildly for his dead parents: "Oh, Mommy, oh, Daddy, why did you do it? Why did you sin against Jehovah?" A voice from the wings thundered: "Don't cry, my dear, though your heart is breaking. . . . We must not mourn for those who are punished. We must not cry for those Jehovah kills." That drew ecstatic applause.

As I left the convention grounds, feeling pity and anger, and remorse (there was a time when I had been able to tolerate the idea of a vengeful Jehovah's destroying my own father), I ran into a free-lance photographer whose extraordinarily beautiful and gentle face invited confidence. "They're telling people to rejoice in the destruction of their own families!" I said to him. But it turned out that he, a former acid-head from a poor Cuban family, was, although "not a baptized Christian," studying the Bible with the Witnesses. "I don't know," he said. "The world is so bad. . . . If I didn't have this, what's my purpose in life? What am I doing with my life? The world is full of such bad things. Corruption and all. People aren't kind. . . . The Witnesses made me give up my beard. I liked my beard, but the elders told me it was wrong, and I figured, Christ gave his life up for people he didn't even know, so what's a beard?"

"But how do you feel when you know old friends of yours, maybe even members of your family, are going to be destroyed at Armageddon?" I asked this sweet, shy man. In a dead voice, he gave me the history of the world—Adam and Eve, the ransom, the signs foretelling the end of the world. His face had nothing to do with his words. His face was creased and earnest with suffering. "No," I said. "Please tell me what you *feel*." "Well," he said, "I try not to think about it too much. Well, really . . . sometimes I think . . . other people are human beings too. I guess I feel some pain. I'm struggling to accept it. . . . It'll be nice when the earth is clean, when there isn't any more death and suffering. Jesus was kind. . . . I try to think that even though certain people I love are going to perish, I have to be happy because God says I should be. Though sometimes, like when we have family gatherings, and I have so much fun, you know . . . I think . . . well, it hurts. I think about it a lot. Like, my mother . . ." And he began to cry.

IV. *Accumulating Wealth While the World Refuses to Die*

I sought a prophet and I found a businessman! Instead of a humble seeker after truth, I found the cleverest propagandist of the age, a man before whom Mary Baker Eddy, Madame Blavatsky, . . . and Joseph Smith pale into puerile ineffectiveness. . . . I found not a blazing zealot . . . but a shrewd old man . . . When it comes to raising money, most pastors, board secretaries and financial representatives of benevolent causes can sit at Russell's feet. Russell may know nothing theoretically about the science of psychology, but he is a past master of the thing itself. He might say, if he were utterly candid, The longest way round is often the shortest way home: It is better to put an idea into people's heads that will constrain them to give of what they suppose is their own volition, than to extract money by urgency.— William T. Ellis, *The Continent* (National Presbyterian weekly), week of Sept. 30, 1912

We have no church organization in the ordinary sense of the word, no bondage of any kind, no obligation to pay, either to the parent society or anybody else, either ten per cent or any other sum. . . . No solicitations for money in any way are authorized by this Society; . . . every amount, therefore, that has come into our hands, and been used, has been a voluntary donation from a willing heart. . . . It is true of the Lord's people in general . . . that among them are not many rich, not many wise, not many learned, not many noble, but chiefly the poor of this world. . . . One million dollars have been spent in the service of present truth this year.—Charles Taze Russell, 1914 Annual Report, *The Watch Tower*, December 1, 1914, Vol. XXXV, No. 24, p. 5591 (371–72)

It is not uncommon to find a charismatic leader being sued for sexual, financial, or legal breaches which he feels are his due right as a superior being.—E. Mansell Pattison, "Faith Healing and Glossalia," Z&L, p. 432

IN 1911, the market price for wheat was 59 cents to $1 a bushel. In Charles Taze Russell's Hicks Street Tabernacle, "miracle wheat" was being sold for $60 a bushel, or $1 a pound.

In 1904, K. B. Stoner, a 70-year-old veteran of the Confederate Army, farming in Fincastle, Virginia, discovered an unusual strain of wheat growing in a little garden patch in back of his house. Stoner's experimentations led him to the conclusion that the uncommonly heavy wheat, when planted thinly, in Virginia soil, yielded as much as 1½ to 2 times as much grain as ordinary wheat. It was bruited about that the "miracle wheat" had appeared in Stoner's garden as a result of Stoner's asking the Lord for a miracle. Stoner later laconically denied that he and the Lord were in collusion to increase the yield of grain.

Stoner sold his wheat for $5 a bushel—five times the market price of regular wheat.

Russell's Tabernacle sold "miracle wheat" for $55 more a bushel than Stoner.

The "miracle wheat" came into the hands of the Watch Tower Society when the president of the United Cemeteries Corporation of Pittsburgh gave J. A. Bohnet, a director of the Watch Tower Bible and Tract Society, "permission" to plant the Stoner wheat on his land and expressed his willingness to donate the crop to the Watch Tower Society. Inasmuch as the United Cemeteries Corporation—of which Russell was a trustee—was later found to be a dummy corporation for Watch Tower assets, this was hardly an act of disinterested charity. It was a very carefully nurtured "miracle" indeed.

The *Brooklyn Eagle* charged Russell with exploitation, taking raucous delight in his "bunco game." The *Eagle*'s investigative reporters' diligence led to an examination of the $60-a-bushel wheat by the Department of Postal Inspection, the Polytechnic Institute, and the Department of Agriculture. The consensus of chemical analysts was that the Stoner-brand "miracle wheat" was better than some and not so good as others. An official of the Department of Agriculture, in a letter published by the *Rural New Yorker*, declared that the "miracle wheat" did not merit the extravagant claims made for it:

> This variety . . . is closely related to the soft winter wheats of the Atlantic Coast, of which Fultz, Fulcaster, etc., are leading types. From our experiments with Mr. Stoner's variety we have found it to be satisfactory, but particularly for the region where it was first grown: It does not merit the extravagant claims made for it. It is a little better, perhaps, than the varieties grown in Virginia and vicinity only because it was a carefully selected strain.

Tests showed, in fact, that Fultz wheat—which was selling for $1 a bushel—yielded, under ordinary circumstances, twice as much as the $60 miracle wheat: Fultz seed yielded 66 bushels to Stoner's 33.

Russell once again sang his persecution song: The pastors of the city are jealous of me, he said. "Other people than my own," said Russell, "wouldn't believe that this wheat contains extraordinary qualities. It is too much of a miracle for them to comprehend." Russell cited the prophet Ezekiel—"I will call for corn and increase it"—and delivered himself of the opinion that the "miracle wheat" was "a sign" that the Lord was fulfilling the prophecy that the desert would bloom like a rose. Directors of the Watch Tower Society, possibly with a view to litigious trouble ahead, sought to temper Russell's extravagant claims. The original advertisement in *The Watch Tower* had stated that the yield of "miracle wheat" ought to be from 10 to 15 times that of ordinary wheat; but one "Brother" Dockey informed an *Eagle* reporter that "no guarantee is offered that 'miracle wheat' possesses powers of extraordinary yield." As things heated up and the *Eagle* continued, scarcely containing its glee, to deride Russell (who very carefully allowed his fellow directors to act as agents for the sale of the wheat, promoting the picture of himself as an objective, non-profit-making observer of God's bounty), Watch Tower spokesmen issued slithery disclaimers: "The advertisement in *The Watch Tower* does not say that miracle wheat is worth $1 a pound," said the general counsel for the Watch Tower Society. "It says simply that Brother Bohnet is willing to sell it at that price. It is purely a donation sale, for the benefit of the society, and those who buy at the price quoted do so with the understanding and the idea that they are voluntarily giving aid to the society. I might place high value upon worthless furniture if I wished to, and if people wanted to buy at the price I named they could do so, if they wished, though I made no claims that the furniture had any real value beyond that of ordinary furniture."

Clearly, two sets of messages were being communicated—one to the "worldly" and one to the believers.

Russell offered to return money to anyone who was dissatisfied.

But the damage had been done. Russell knew how to sell wheat to credulous believers; the *Eagle* knew how to sell newspapers to people eager for diversion.

On September 23, 1912, the *Eagle* ran a cartoon called "Easy Money Puzzle." It showed a fat gilded banker standing on the steps of the "Onion Bank" calling to a sinister, sloppy old peddler with a top hat and a scraggly beard sneakily carrying off a parcel of loot. "You're wasting your time," the banker said. "Come on in here!" The cartoon's caption read, "If Pastor Russell can get a dollar a pound for Miracle Wheat, what could he get for Miracle stocks and bonds in the old Union Bank?" (The Union—"Onion"—bank was liquidated in 1912; the bank was unable to pay more than half of what it had held in trust for its depositors. The *Eagle* had been in large measure responsible for the exposure of "ill-smelling" securities which led to the bank's downfall.)

Russell sued the *Eagle* for libel, demanding $100,000 in damages for "injury to his reputation, good name, fame and standing." The complaint alleged that Russell—who was on holiday in Europe when suit was brought on his behalf against the *Eagle*—had been "brought into scandal and reproach and has been held up to odium, scandal, disgrace and contempt among his neighbors, friends, and the readers of his journal, books and other writings and among parishioners and members of his congregation."

The *Eagle*'s defense was that the sale of "miracle wheat" was a scheme intended to benefit the Watch Tower Bible and Tract Society, of which Pastor Russell had complete control, and that its articles and cartoons were justified by the facts: "This plaintiff has held himself out to be a teacher of other people, a public leader, and the public press has a right to criticize him or his doctrines."

The case was brought before Justice Charles H. Kelby and a jury in the Kings County Supreme Court.

Several farmers testified—their testimony avidly received by Russell's followers, who jammed the courtroom—that "miracle wheat" produced up to twice the yield of ordinary wheat when planted thin.

It was thin testimony, and skimpy cause for rejoicing. The *Eagle*, in its defense, called a government agronomist, who testified that the Department of Agriculture had tested "miracle wheat" under carefully checked conditions and found it to be a good-yielding wheat, but no better than other varieties. In competitive testing, he said—bolstering his testimony with certified copies of the public records of the Department of Agriculture—it had ranked eighteenth in one test, tenth in another, and third in a test when it was thinly sown.

There were several bizarre aspects to the trial. One amusing grace note was that Russell's vanity prompted him to have his attorney protest that Russell's beard was not, as in the cartoon, scraggly at all, but kempt. Russell's doctrines—held, by the Court, to be relevant to the libel—were held up for ridicule. One dogma, in particular, brought delight to the pastor's antagonists. This was the Pastor's conceit that "old worthies" such as King David, Moses, Solomon, et al., were due for resurrection before 1914 to rule as princes in the earth. One of the juicier allegations made against the Watch Tower Society was that it had coerced an insane man, Hope Hay, into contributing $10,000 to its funds. William E. Van Amburgh (the newspapers frequently misspelled his name *Van Amberg*), secretary-treasurer of the Watch Tower Society, acknowledged that Mr. Hay was in an "insane asylum" and that the Watch Tower Society was footing his bills, but denied that Mr. Hay had not given his money of his own free will.

Russell did not take the stand; he conveyed all his messages through attorney J. F. Rutherford (who was to become the second president of the Watch Tower Bible and Tract Society, after Russell's death). "What the character of the plaintiff is," the *Eagle*'s attorney told the jury, "you can infer from the fact that he did not take the witness stand and let you look in his eyes as he told of his past life. He did not give you and me the chance to question him as to . . . why he left Pittsburgh, why he came here, and what he intends to do when he leaves here."

The burden of Justice Kelby's charge to the jury was that as a matter of law, the cartoon was libelous in itself unless justified by the evidence. The burden of proof, Kelby charged, was upon the *Eagle*: "Truth is always a defense in a libel suit, but the defendant must prove the truth is as broad as the charge."

The jury of twelve men was out for less than forty-five minutes before it returned a verdict of not guilty in the *Eagle*'s favor.

The evidence that weighed most heavily with the jury was that of Mr. Van Amburgh.

Van Amburgh was an ingenuous, unresponsive witness; he acted more like a junior bookkeeper than like the financial officer of a corporation that had spent millions of dollars in a decade. He was, however, rigorously cross-examined; his grudging testimony, together with the subpoenaed financial records of the Society, gave weight to the *Eagle*'s claim that the Watch Tower Society, under Russell's control, had flourished financially in spite of the newspaper's exposés and could therefore lay no claim to having been "damaged":

"How much in donations did the Watch Tower Society get in 1912?"

"$202,000," Van Amburgh replied.

"How much in 1911?"

"$169,000."

"How much in 1910?"

$139,000."

"So that since this alleged libel was published your income has increased?"

"Yes, the work of the society is growing very fast, but it might have grown faster if it had not been for the libel."

"But your annual report of the Watch Tower does not show that your society gets anything from its affiliated corporations?"

"No, sir. It is not a detailed report."

Persistent prodding by the *Eagle*'s attorneys revealed the existence of two dummy corporations, the United States Investment Co., Ltd., and the United Cemeteries Corporation. (The president of the Cemeteries Corp. was a doctor—a nice little incongruity that tickled the fancy of the unbelievers in the courtroom.)

"And you say you do not know who the stockholders of the Investment Company are?"

"No, sir," said the secretary-treasurer. "I could not say."

"Did you ever hear any complaints from the directors of the Investment Company that they did not get . . . interest?"

"No, sir."

"Are not the owners of the companies the same persons?"

"I do not know as an absolute certainty."

"And did you not take title to property as a dummy for the Watch Tower Society?"

"Yes, sir. I took title to a farm near Pittsburgh some years ago. The money was that of the Watch Tower Society. I deeded it to the United States Society, which, in turn, signed it over to the United Cemetaries Company."

. . .

"Why do you not do all your business in the name of the Watch Tower Society; that is, why do you need the dummy corporations?"

"Some people seem to think that a religious corporation should do no so-called secular business whatever," said Van Amburgh, who had compounded his troubles by saying that the reason *he* held the title to substantial properties used by the Watch Tower Society was that the Investment Company did not deal in mortgages. "They do not see the propriety of it—No, let me change that answer—I mean that the United States Investment Company and the United Cemeteries were in existence before I ever came to Pittsburgh, and we have continued to use those companies for their convenience ever since."

The Watch Tower Society has, from time to time, advised "children of light" to act as cunningly as serpents when they deal with "children of darkness." Van Amburgh was a singularly unwily serpent; every time he opened his mouth, the *Eagle*'s attorneys milked him of information that destroyed the credibility of Russell's organization. Every word he said contributed to the jury's impression that the Watch Tower Society was a sophisticated financial corporation masquerading as primitive Christianity on a non-profit-making crusade.

Russell, for example, had not just "growed," like Topsy, into a "latter-day Elias." He had a press agent and a public relations man, to enhance his image and to act as an advance man on his world tours. (The man whose dying words were "Bring me a toga" may have believed that Jehovah had chosen him among the earth's billions; but he wasn't taking any chances that Jehovah's choice would go unnoticed.) Van Amburgh's testimony further revealed that while any donor contributing $10 to the Watch Tower Society was entitled to a voting share, in fact only 50,000 voting certificates had been issued; 47,000 of those had been issued to Charles Taze Russell, whose yearly reelection was thus secure. Four hundred to five hundred thousand donors might have availed themselves of voting shares; only fifty or sixty donors did so. Clearly, this was a tribute to Russell's manipulative genius and to the intensity of his followers' belief. It was at this time that Russell was pleading financial impoverishment as justification for not paying Maria Russell increased alimony.

It is not surprising that although Russell's attorneys pleaded that a finding in favor of the *Eagle* would be tantamount to calling a simple man of God "a crook," the finding went against Russell. Once out of the courtroom, true to form, Russell flung his reticence away as if it were a cloak of rags and tried, once again, to cover himself with glory. He had been "smitten," he said, like Our Lord and like St. Paul. "I, like them," he proclaimed, "have been refused the law's protection. I murmur not."

Indeed he did not murmur. He bellowed and bawled and contrived to turn his disgrace to his advantage. Maintaining the pose of injured innocence, he said, flatly, that he had had "nothing whatever to do" with "miracle wheat." It seems unbelievable that his followers should have swallowed that; but Russell took care to frost his bald statement with the anticlerical declarations they loved: The *Eagle*, he said, had in reality been "the champion of certain clerical enemies of mine." "All manner of evil" had been spoken against him "for the sake of the doctrines of Christ." Anyone who turned against him, therefore, would be repudiating not a crooked old man, but Christ Himself.

Once again, Russell cried *wolf;* and once again the hungry wolf in his elaborate fairy tale was the Catholic Church, against which the Watch Tower Bible and Tract Society was the only protection.

"Presumably because there were seven Catholics on the jury," Russell said, "the *Eagle*'s attorney was prompted to refer to the Sisters of Charity and their noble work as nurses without referring to the fact that those nurses are well paid and that the hospitals, in large measure, are supported by state taxation." Russell's organization was pure, according to his arguments—which also took into consideration the Church's wealth—precisely because it did *not* engage in acts of charity; the Church, he implied, used charity as a cover for sneaky thievery:

> The Watch Tower Bible and Tract Society was held up to scorn because it did not have any hospital work, nor draw any revenue from taxations, and because the female members of the Society do not visit the workshops of the land weekly or monthly on pay day and exact donations to its work. Our society was held up to scorn because we do not send a wagon around the city collecting groceries and provisions for the upkeep of our work; because we do not take up collections, even on Sunday; because we have never solicited a penny or a dollar from anybody; and because we never have fairs, grab-bags, "chances," or "raffles." Our society was held up to ridicule because it offers its literature free to the poor while other similar societies charge both rich and poor alike for their tracts and other publications.

Nor did the Protestants escape: For defending the *Eagle*, he said, "the Protestants on the jury were led to hope for escape from eternal torment through the 'pearly gates of heaven,' welcomed with the words, 'Well done,' for giving the *Eagle* the verdict. Neither I nor my attorneys could offer such inducements conscientiously."

> Our home, "Bethel," where some of our society's workers reside, was held up to scorn—likened to a harem, etc. This surely did cut me deeply to the heart. I am quite willing to suffer if need be, for my faithfulness to the Lord and His Word; but it gave me great pain that the arrows intended for me did not all center upon myself—that the more than a hundred saintly earnest men, women, and children, co-laborers with me in the Lord's work, should thus be made to unjustly suffer. I can only urge upon them to apply to themselves the words of the apostle: "Cast not away, therefore, your confidence, which hath great recompense of reward; . . . Ye shall receive the promise; ye endured a great fight of afflictions; partly, whilst ye were made a gazing stock and partly whilst ye became companions of them that were so used."

"I am the more encouraged," said the man who implied that Protestants on the jury had voted against him because of the *Eagle*'s attorneys' enticing them with the promise of entry into the "pearly gates of heaven," "because I realize that the great Day of Blessing, the great Thousand Year of Messiah's Kingdom, is near at hand, is dawning now. Soon Satan, the 'Prince of Darkness,' will be bound. . . . No longer will darkness be permitted to masquerade as light, and the light be slandered as darkness."

Ministry to the poor, visitation of the sick, care for the orphaned, these are outside of the pale of Russellite activities. The limit of his benevolence is to send his literature free to "the Lord's poor."—William T. Ellis, *The Continent* [*op. cit.* 1913]

Likely you have noted that Jehovah's witnesses try to maintain exemplary conduct and show love for one another. But you may feel that they should be more concerned about the problems people are facing now—hunger, sickness, poverty and the like. You may feel that they should undertake extensive charity drives. . . . Jehovah's witnesses do not solicit money and other material things from people and then take credit for the good deeds such contributions make possible. As was true of Jesus Christ, their main concern is to give spiritual aid to all whom they possibly can. . . . While material giving may bring temporary relief, spiritual giving can aid people to enjoy the . . . permanent solution to man's problems that only God's kingdom . . . can provide. [*Aw*, April 8, 1975, p. 18]

The Witnesses view organized charity as a scheme to draw men's attention away from the salvation that lies only in the coming Kingdom of God; they are self-congratulatory because they are not engaged in charity as normally (but not necessarily legally) defined. (They excoriate those whose consciences "become sensitive in an exaggerated or unbalanced way"—those, that is, who refuse to pay war taxes; they honor Caesar by paying their taxes, "leaving with the government the responsibility of how money is used." [*TW*, April 1, 1975] Witnesses are taught to believe that all forms of charity are corrupt (charities line the pockets of bureaucrats or the clergy) and redundant (God, not the American Cancer Society, will cure cancer).

The Watchtower Society comes to the aid of congregations that have been struck by natural calamities—earthquakes, hurricanes, floods; it is not, however, in favor or "promiscuous charity." *

The Witnesses pride themselves on not gathering in "rice Christians." To be a relief recipient one must have impeccable credentials as a Witness. In the United States and overseas, the Watchtower Society has no funds for hospitals, shelters, clinics, or rehabilitation services. The deserving poor get fed. Years after I ceased being a Witness, I lived, for eight years, in India and in Guatemala. I was overwhelmed by the beauty and generosity of Mother Teresa in Calcutta—to her, all the dying belong to God—and by the untiring efforts of Maryknoll priests and nuns to keep babies from dying of roundworms; I was in awe of priests and missionaries, who, un-heralded, in isolated poverty holes, kept people alive, regardless of their religious beliefs. (I had had an incredibly parochial view of the Church, and of churches, still: I believed what I had been taught to believe—that all religious emissaries were venal.)

I have a clear memory (which, unfortunately, I cannot document) of the excommunication of two Witness missionaries, in the late 1940s, who had taken it upon themselves, without a directive from the Watchtower Society, to introduce to starving agrarian workers in Southeast Asia better ways of growing rice. Their actions were construed as a dereliction of duty—their duty was to preach the gospel. The Witnesses have consistently taken the position that the greatest act of charity is the preaching of the gospel; they have no mandate to engage in "social reform."

I have a copy of a speech delivered by a Witness twenty years ago that might just as well have been given yesterday. In it, he quotes a *New York Times* article of 1951 which reports that women in parts of India "were feeding their children cakes of soft mud to keep them from starving. Thou-

* After World War II, Witnesses in America, Canada, Switzerland, and Sweden contributed clothing and money to Witnesses in Austria, Belgium, Bulgaria, China, Czechoslovakia, Denmark, England, Finland, France, Germany, Greece, Hungary, Italy, the Netherlands, Norway, the Philippine Republic, Poland, and Rumania. Clothing shipments amounted to 1,056,247 pounds; food shipments totaled 718,873 pounds; the monetary value of the shipments was estimated by the Watchtower Society at $1,322,406. The Society has no regular, ongoing funds set aside for relief; these were individual contributions. [*Yearbook*, 1975, p. 209] American Witnesses gave out of pocket $140,000 to supply CARE packages to Germany alone, and contributed 220 tons of clothing to their German counterparts. [*Yearbook*, 1974, p. 217] [I remember sorting out clothing with dozens of other young girls and women in an old ware-house near the Watchtower printing plant. (Proximity to Bethel—and to Bethelites—was al-ways desirable.) We all skimmed off the best of the lot for ourselves. This is not to denigrate the volunteer work of the Witnesses, who really did see this work as an act of solidarity and love (enlivened by mild flirtations with male Bethelites). The beneficiaries of this largesse were not those who were interested only in obtaining a CARE package, but those who had been active in the field for at least six months.] [*Yearbook*, 1974, p. 217]

sands of persons too poor even to buy the scanty Government grain rations are keeping themselves alive by eating grass, snails, lotus roots and herbs." The man who gave this speech cited the famine as an analogy for spiritual famine: "There was plenty of mud," he said, "but this is not life-giving, and therefore is a famine. The same is true of spiritual food." The horrible fact of starvation is used, but he did not say how he felt. Compassion is derailed. Television and the papers bombard all of us with others' pain—Bangladesh, the South Bronx insinuate themselves into the cocktail hour with the 6-o'clock news. Unless we cauterize our senses, it is too much for our minds to encompass. The Witnesses, reacting, perhaps as do many of us, to this saturation, sanitize pain.

Through individual acts of charity, Witnesses sometimes proffer assistance to members of the congregation who are in financial need. Because the Watchtower Society itself sets aside no funds for charity, giving is spontaneous and always the responsibility of the individual. It is truly impressive to watch the Witnesses come to the aid of a member of "the family" who is in need. Sick or elderly Witnesses get their shopping and cooking done for them. The Witnesses put themselves at one another's service (and place themselves in one another's debt). Whatever skills they have, they use to one another's advantage.

But some people get more help than others. A subtle caste system obtains. It is human to wish to select one's own company. But, taught to love one another diffusely, the Witnesses cannot consciously admit that they find some of their brothers and sisters more attractive than others. So they judge people on the basis of how "theocratic"—how active and effective in the field ministry—they are. And they tend to exclude those who seem slightly "off."

One disaffected ex-Witness describes the mechanism of this rejection and discrimination:

> There was an old lady with horrible garlic breath and a retarded son. The Witnesses avoided her. But since they were taught that we are all equal in God's sight, and equally lovable, they couldn't take the responsibility for disliking her. They'd say, "What will people of goodwill think about her? She'll turn people away from The Truth." So they felt justified in ignoring her. She was poor and unattractive, and she had an even more grossly unattractive son. She had a dogged determination to be a Witness, but an imperfect grasp of Witness theology. It was a deadly combination.
>
> No one, to my knowledge, ever suggested to her ways in which she could better her condition or alleviate her burdens. The Witnesses had no facilities to help her son, and for her to have solicited help from other sources would have been interpreted as a defection.
>
> You'd keep running into this bind: The Witnesses had no support

facilities; but if you turned elsewhere, you were denying God's organization. My own son, for example, really suffered, because I was always fighting with my husband, who was not a believer. I thought, one summer, I'd send him to camp, to get him away from all the tension. The Witnesses didn't have camps; they told me that to send him to a worldly camp would damage his chances for everlasting life. And an elder told me that if I had managed my domestic life right, the tension wouldn't have arisen.

Neither my sister—who was also a Witness—nor I ever felt really embraced by the Witnesses. Both of us were shy; we couldn't participate in meetings, and we were scared and nervous about going from door to door. There was one kind woman who'd take me from door to door and do all the talking; she really loved me, I think; and she'd plead with me, for my soul's sake, to do the talking. I couldn't. I remember her with great affection. We'd sneak cigarettes together—Witnesses aren't allowed to smoke—and play Scrabble and do frivolous things. But she was the only one who could tolerate my weaknesses. The others excluded me. . . . I think the fact that I was Jewish made me suspect too. We were always hearing about how "stiff-necked" and proud and mercenary the Jews were—and that Jehovah chose them precisely because they were such unpromising material—so how could there not be residual anti-Semitism?

All my doubts came home to roost when my sister had major surgery. All the Witnesses called me. Not to ask how she was, but to inquire about whether she'd taken a blood transfusion. When I got angry—I said, "Where's your love? Don't you care how she is?"—they said I was behaving badly because of course they loved my sister: they wanted her to live in the New World; that was why they were asking. They kept hectoring me, and her, about whether she had had a blood transfusion and about when she was going to go from door to door again. The first time she tried to go from door to door, she sat on a stoop and cried. She didn't stop crying for three months. Then (this may seem like too small a thing to break the back of a religious commitment, but that's how it was) my sister's surgeon—she wouldn't, of course, go to a psychiatrist for help—told her to take dance classes for therapy. She went to the Jewish Community House on the corner where free classes were given; and the Witnesses said that if she were "spiritually healthy" she wouldn't need to do that. And they construed her turning to the JCH as a turning away from them. But what did they have to offer?

The Witnesses come to one another's aid, I'm saying, if you pass their tests. I'm not denying that they are capable of being incredibly helpful to one another; I'm saying that some people—like my sister and me—fall through the cracks. The more you need help, the more you're regarded as being undeserving of help. I don't know which is cause and which is effect: are their no-charity financial policies a result of their theology, or vice versa? I do know that since the organization doesn't believe in "promiscuous charity," the burden falls on individuals to be charitable—and charity comes to those who are acceptable, to those who are deemed worthy. We were not.

When I lived at Bethel, I saw, or heard of, these failures of charity.

A young woman who had been a full-time field worker (a "pioneer") came to Bethel headquarters after her husband had died of a sudden heart attack and her son had, accidentally it was supposed, hanged himself. She was put to work in the laundry room, operating a giant press. She was a perpetually smiling, sweet, singularly unassertive woman who seemed to have put her personal tragedies behind her. One day, her glasses slipped off and were smashed in the press. She began to howl and scream and cry that immemorial cry—"Why *me?*" Her roommate reported that she cried ("Why me?") in her sleep. She was judged unstable. She was given a Greyhound ticket to her parents' home in the Northwest. (I do not know what has become of her.)

An old man, who had been at Bethel for thirty years, grew senile. His senility took the form of his muttering obscenities at the dining-room table. He was given two "warnings," which his hardened arteries obviously couldn't assimilate, and then ordered to leave. He had no resources, financial or emotional. He was last seen begging in downtown Brooklyn.

In both these cases two factors are at work: The Watchtower Society has no charitable institutions to handle emotionally disturbed or mentally ill persons; and disturbance and illness are seen as evidence of the Lord's displeasure. There is no place for people in terrible trouble to go.

Fred Franz, at that time the Society's vice-president, told me once that he had been on board ship with a young Japanese missionary who was manifestly disturbed—babbling and incoherent. "I thought," Franz said, "I could cast the demons out of her, but Jesus said that his apostles should not practice that gift after His death; so I didn't presume." The missionary jumped overboard and died.

Needless to say, Jehovah's Witnesses have no lock on arbitrariness, arrogance, or unkindness. Every religious order has its horror stories. But because there is no institutionalized charity among the Witnesses, giving is individual, and not giving may be justified on theological grounds. (I am blurring definitions purposefully: I mean *giving* in the sense of spontaneous goodness, Christian love; and I mean *giving* financially. The two are not unrelated.) Misfits, the unattractive, the aberrant can be regarded as waste products of the Devil's world, not as fellow sufferers.

The publishing endeavors of the Jehovah [sic] Witnesses seem to be the most prosperous among . . . religious organizations in the U.S. . . . A spokesman for the Society would not reveal the revenues generated through publishing nor what the Society spends on its publishing activity. He would as soon give praise to the Prince of

Darkness as reveal such intimate details.—Media Industry Newsletter, November 23, 1973

The final smash had not come, as predicted, in 1914.

In 1890, there were, according to the Witnesses' current estimates, 400 "Bible Students." By 1914, according to an estimate of the *National Cyclopaedia of American Biography*, there were 50,000 Russellites. In 1976, according to the Witnesses' *Yearbook*, there were 2,248,390 Witnesses in 210 countries. In 1976 alone, 196,656 new Witnesses symbolized their dedication by water baptism. [*Yearbook*, 1977, pp. 30–31] In addition to growing in number, the Witnesses have managed, in the intervening years, to amass millions of dollars' worth of real estate.

Russell's early world tours served to convince him that there was no market for his message in the "Papal countries." He expressed most hope for Nordic and/or WASP countries like Norway, Switzerland, England, Ireland, Scotland. Perhaps he was seeing with the eye of the tourist who is drawn to the "clean," nonexotic lands. Because later, on the eve of what he assumed to be "the end of the time which God set apart for gathering," he voiced the opinion that the "heathen will probably fall in line more readily." [*TW*, #5980, 1914, pp. 326–27] As it happens, there are now, by latest count, 102,044 active Witnesses in West Germany and over 114,029 in Nigeria. [*Yearbook*, 1977, pp. 26, 28: Figures for 1976 Peak Publishers]

The Watchtower Society, as of November, 1975, had thirty-seven printeries—in Australia, Brazil, Canada, England, Finland, France, Germany, Ghana, Japan, Nigeria, the Philippines, South Africa, Sweden, Switzerland, the United States. . . .

Every two weeks, an average printing of 8,700,000 copies of *The Watchtower* magazine (in 79 languages) rolls off the 64 rotary presses contained in all those factories—an abundance that Russell, whose first edition of *Zion's Watch Tower* had a printing of 6,000 copies, could hardly have foreseen. From these factories comes the book the Watchtower Society claims has outsold all other books written in the 20th century. *The Truth That Leads to Everlasting Life* (1968), a 190-page hardbound book that sells for 25 cents a copy, has sold 74,000,000 copies in 91 languages—exceeding Dr. Spock's baby book by 50,000,000 copies. [*Yearbook*, 1975, p. 240] In Brooklyn alone, where the bulk of Watchtower property is located, 100,000 books and 800,000 magazines are printed daily. From these presses also comes *Awake!* (a kind of spiritually flavored *Reader's Digest*), a 32-page semimonthly published in 39 languages, with an average printing of 7,500,000. Until very recently, the publishers of *Awake!* blurbed it as a magazine with "no fetters . . . It features penetrating articles on social conditions. . . . *Awake!* pledges itself to . . . exposing hidden foes and subtle dangers." Featured articles in 1973 issues of the magazine that "recognizes facts, faces facts, is free to publish facts" were "Snail Fever—Slow Death for Millions"; "My Life as a Gypsy"; "Bamboo—Asia's Towering Grass"; "Twilight Years Can Be Useful Years" ("The aged [may] make bags, repair shoes and raise rabbits").

In the United States, in addition to an office building in Pittsburgh, Pennsylvania, the Society owns factory buildings, interconnected by bridges spanning the streets, covering four city blocks in Brooklyn, at the foot of the Brooklyn Bridge—close to 1,265,000 square feet of highly desirable urban property.

(In 1927, the Society moved into 117 Adams Street, Brooklyn, which contained 70,000 square feet of floor space. By 1950, additions to the original factory covered the entire city block. In 1956, a new factory, containing 192,000 square feet of floor space, was constructed at 77 Sands Street and linked by over-street bridge to the Adams Street buildings. In 1958, the Society purchased a nine-story factory on an adjoining block. In 1968 it completed an eleven-story structure which added 226,000 square feet of floor space to the complex. In 1969, the Squibb Pharmaceutical plant in Brooklyn was purchased by the Society, adding 632,792 square feet of floor space.) [*Yearbook*, 1975, pp. 242–43]

The spanking-clean, beige-and-green Watchtower factories dominate the urban landscape at the foot of the Brooklyn and Manhattan bridges. The flashing electric signs that used to advertise Squibb pharmaceutical products now ask us to READ THE BIBLE GOD'S HOLY WORD DAILY. READ THE WATCHTOWER ANNOUNCING GOD'S KINGDOM.

In 1974, when I last visited the No. 1 Factory Building at 117 Adams Street—announcing myself, not untruthfully, as a reporter from *More*, the media magazine—I was tempted, as I waited in the lobby for my host and tour guide, to scrawl graffiti on the spotless walls of what is surely the cleanest lav this side of the New World. I restrained myself, however, and concentrated on the three diesel generators that provide DC power for most of the factory's presses and machinery. The generators, the largest of which produces 550 horsepower, are framed by a squeaky-clean plate-glass window in the lobby, looking rather like the Ark of the Covenant in their splendid isolation, and eliciting a commensurate amount of awe from visiting Witnesses, to whom the place is a kind of Mecca. (I used, as a child, crossing the Manhattan Bridge by train, to announce, "There is the most important building in the world." To say things like that loudly enough for everyone to hear is known as "giving a witness.") I was intrigued by a flagged map in the lobby—like a battle map—that indicated the locations of Jehovah's Witnesses in 90 foreign countries. It was out of date, still showing the Belgian Congo. My tour guide, who did not then know that I had once worked as a proofreader in that factory, explained, "We have our eyes fixed on the New World of God's Kingdom. We are not interested in the things of this world." He had never heard of *More*: "We don't digest secular litera-ture. *The Watchtower* and *Awake!* are our spiritual food."

(It may be of interest to fact-lovers—and to those who doubt that the Watchtower Society is as self-contained as it purports to be—that the glue and ink used in the Brooklyn plants are manufactured there; 16 Watch-tower-owned freight-car loads of paper are used each week; 32 Linotype machines and 39 rotary presses are manned, as are flatbed and job presses and magazine-wrapping machines.* There are Graphotype and Addresso-graph machines too; for the most part, these are run by women. (My tour guide told me that women, being "weaker vessells," were "assigned un-strenuous work. If any sister has expressed a desire to work presses, I'm not aware of it." I am, however, aware of the fact that women work heavy, steam shirt-and-sheet presses and operate industrial floor-waxing machines in the Watchtower residence laundry.)

Many factory operations are technologically sophisticated; many others, which in commercial plants might be mechanized or computerized, are de-signed to require manual labor. This makes economic sense, because Wit-ness labor is so cheap. All members of the Bethel headquarters "family"—editorial and administrative staff as well as factory workers—receive the same small monthly stipend.

The Watchtower Society operates a small fruit farm in Washington, New Jersey, and a grain farm in South Lansing, New York.

A 1,698-acre farm near Newburgh, New York, provides food for the 1,400 headquarters workers.

Wheat, corn, oats, lettuce, tomatoes, squash, potatoes, onions, turnips, spinach, beets, kale, beans, carrots, apples, peaches, pears, strawberries, blackberries grow on this mini-conglomerate. And there are herds of beef cattle—about 800 head of Hereford, Angus, and Charolais—and dairy cat-tle; and hogs; and thousands of chickens bred for eating and thousands of Leghorns that lay close to 3,000 eggs a day. Beef is dressed here, bacon smoked, hog jowls are steamed in enormous kettles to be used as liverwurst. Fruit is frozen, canned, preserved; relishes, sauerkraut and horseradish are prepared; from the 420 gallons of milk produced each day, the Watchtower Society manufactures butter, ice cream, cheese—Swiss, Cheddar, Monte-rey, and Limburger. Everything the self-sustaining headquarters workers consume comes from Watchtower Farm, according to George Couch, the manager—with the exception of fish, condiments, spices, and some flour. The farm, one observer commented, "Exemplifies communal agriculture refined by technological sophistication . . . with the aid of machines, 92 cows are milked in two hours, but pears are still peeled by hand." [*The New York Times*, Jan. 2, 1973]

* These statistics are as of June 1973.

Couch estimates the cost of operating the Farm at $430,000 per year. From this cornucopia come approximately 2 million meals a year for headquarters workers. Each meal, Couch estimated in 1973, costs 30 cents. Depression prices; but also, depression wages: farm workers, like Brooklyn factory and office workers (who are not, officially, wage earners, but minister-volunteers), receive $20 a month for expenses such as transportation, and a modest allowance for clothing and other expenses, never exceeding $360, each year. (This is what makes it possible to sell books such as *The Truth That Leads to Everlasting Life* for "a contribution" of 25 cents.)

It takes, Couch told a *Times* reporter, 1,000 pounds of beef for a rib-roast meal, 60 hogs for a pork-chop meal. The meals are hearty, nutritionally balanced, and, on the whole, better than one would expect institutional food to be.

Five hundred workers live in dormitory residences on Watchtower Farm, which also accommodates two factories that provide 400,000 square feet of floor space.

These are the arterial properties. The heart of the religious body is in Brooklyn Heights—a lovely residential area not unlike Washington's Georgetown and Boston's Beacon Hill. The Watchtower Society's headquarters staff has grown from 355 men and women in 1950, to 607 in 1960, to 1,449 (approximately 200 of whom are women) in 1970, and its property holdings have grown commensurately. The Society has bought and built to provide offices and residences for factory workers and editorial and administrative staff and to accommodate the missionary school of Gilead, which, as part of a thrust toward centralization, was shifted, in the 1960s, from South Lansing, New York. The Watchtower community (or commune) in Brooklyn Heights is served by its own carpentry shop, laundry, tailor shop, and bakery (approximately 25 chefs and assistants labor to prepare three meals a day for headquarters workers).

Since the "miracle wheat" scandal, the Watchtower Society has maintained a discreetly low financial profile. Federal courts have ruled that the Watchtower Bible and Tract Society, Inc. (New York corporation), and the Watch Tower Bible and Tract Society (Pennsylvania corporation) are entitled to exemption from the filing of income-tax returns under the Federal Internal Revenue Act because the Societies are charitable corporations engaged in religious activity. Similar rulings have been made in Britain and in Canada. The Watchtower Society has not, however, succeeded in silencing speculation about its method of acquiring properties and about the extent of its holdings. Financial reports are never published. Calls from reporters, researchers, state senators inquiring into the finances of the Society go unanswered. Outsiders would need a guided tour through the property holdings of the Society, and the Society provides no tour guides. The Society's attorneys—Koozman and Hartman of New York City—refuse to answer requests for information.* The Society's bank of record, Chase Manhattan, likewise gives away no secrets. Rank-and-file Witnesses believe absolutely that the Society's stewardship is beyond reproach; they ask no questions. To question the Lord's "governing body," they are told, is to doubt the Lord Himself. These explanations are offered to them:

> The Society has reached its present world-wide extent, owning property worth millions of dollars paid for and maintained completely by voluntary contributions. . . . For years now, the Society has put a notice in *The Watchtower* once a year requesting each one who wishes to contribute during the year to state how much he wants to contribute and how the contributions would be sent, whether all at once or a certain amount at a time . . . in order that we might know how to lay out the work for the year to come; and the work is planned or expanded on the basis of what is indicated by these expressions. This would indicate the leading of the Lord in spreading the work. . . . The work progresses only to the extent of voluntary contributions. . . . [The Witnesses] have managed to pay as they go. [*Faith*, pp. 205, 207–08]

---

* On July 6, 1975, in a certified letter, I asked the following questions of Jerry Molohan, public relations officer of the Watch Tower Bible and Tract Society, and of George Hartman of Koozman and Hartman (1133 Avenue of the Americas, New York):

In order to make [a book about Jehovah's Witnesses] as objective as possible, and not to rely merely on rumor or conjecture, I should like, from primary and internal sources, information that is available from you.

Repeated calls to Mr. George Hartman . . . have proved unavailing. As you must know, when a journalist is denied access to information, the assumption he or she must make is that there is something to be hidden. I should like, therefore, to allow you to speak for yourselves; and I request, therefore, the following information:

. . . Are financial records of the Watchtower Bible and Tract Society (Pennsylvania and New York corporations) available? If so, to whom are they made available? May I have a record of your finances for the year 1974?

. . . Are meetings of the Pittsburgh (Penna.) corporation open to the public; and are financial reports there made public?

. . . Are moneys contributed to you invested in corporations other than your own?

. . . Who owns extranational branch buildings and properties? . . .

. . . How is the . . . governing body chosen? How are the members of the boards of directors of your corporations chosen? What is the difference between the governing body and the boards of directors?

. . . How are new buildings financed?

. . . May I know what architect and what construction firm you have employed for your buildings on Columbia Heights?

. . . Does money contributed to the U.S. corporations get funneled to other countries in which you operate? What is the vehicle for the transfer of funds? . . .

This letter went unanswered. Other writers have encountered the same indifference: Lee R. Cooper, who has written a brilliant paper on black Witnesses' adaptation in the ghetto, reports that "The Society's suspicion of outside investigators was a problem to consider in my approach to the West View [Philadelphia] congregation. . . . I made no effort to contact supervisory personnel or the Society's headquarters because past experiences indicated that requests for information would be unanswered and might have adverse repercussions for research." [Z&L, p. 706]

Financing of Watchtower properties in 1926, 1946, and 1955 is explained:

> Instead of borrowing money from a bank, we had borrowed it from
> our own people and the Society gave them a note at the regular rate of
> interest. It was understood by those receiving notes that they could
> request their money in full at any time if they might unexpectedly
> have need for it. These received their money at once and the rest were
> paid off as the regular voluntary contributions made it possible. Be-
> fore the notes had matured, all had been settled. [*Ibid.*, p. 210]

In order to arrive at some idea of the financial base of the Society's publishing operation, Cooper [Z&L, p. 717] made some calculations from a
Society statistical report for November, 1968.

In November, 1968 (according to *Kingdom Ministry*, the Watchtower Society's monthly newsletter), 817,776 copies of *The Truth That Leads to Everlasting Life* were sold at 25 cents per copy. This "would amount," Cooper
calculates, "to over two hundred thousand dollars ($204,444). Added to this
would be the income from six million *weekly* copies of the bi-monthly magazines *Awake!* and *The Watchtower*, a monthly sum approximating one million two hundred thousand dollars, an equal amount resting in the hands of
the 338,663 'publishers' who had 'placed' the magazines for ten cents a
copy. On these two published items alone, the Society would well have
grossed one million four hundred thousand dollars in one month."

Cooper was working with 1968 statistics for the United States alone. If
we look at worldwide statistics for 1974, the suggested gross is larger: in
1974, according to the 1975 *Yearbook*, 27,581,852 bound books were distributed, and 273,238,018 magazines, in addition to 12,409,287 booklets.

Most of these publications were sold for a nominal amount; some were
distributed free. The Society gives a 10- to 20-percent rebate on all literature sold by local congregations; Witnesses buy the literature they distribute for less than the "contribution" they solicit. They keep, on the average,
10 cents out of every $1 contribution they receive.

A spokesperson for the Society explains the process: "Today, much of
the money that is used to carry on the work is spent out of the pocket of the
individual minister of Jehovah's witnesses as he engages in the work himself. . . . They pay the printing cost of books they receive from the Society
and contributions they receive for them are used to obtain more. If they
give literature away, this money is out of their own pocket. . . . The contribution is figured to cover little more than printing cost." [*Faith*, p. 206,
207]

No money is ever solicited at meetings of Jehovah's Witnesses; there is,
however, a "Contribution Box" in every Kingdom Hall. Local congregations buy, rent, renovate, or erect their meeting places, "Kingdom Halls,"
with their own funds; often free labor is provided by the Witnesses, who

are proud that they do not have to borrow from worldly commercial organizations, but are able to use the funds set aside for the benefit of the chosen of Jehovah.

An idea of the magnitude of Watchtower operations is suggested by the fact that in 1971, according to the 1972 *Yearbook* (p. 255), $7,042,020.01 was contributed toward "expansion" and toward the care and feeding of foreign missionaries (who are now provided with room and board and $40 a month).

The public financial facts have not been sufficient to still conjectures in Brooklyn Heights, where the bulk of Watchtower property holdings is concentrated. The Society has been tangling with Heights residents since 1913.

In that year, angry residents of Brooklyn Heights hired a lawyer and brought Russell's financial officers before the City's Board of Tax Commissioners, demanding to know why properties held by the People's Pulpit Association and the Watch Tower Society should be tax-exempt. Treasurer Van Amburgh steered a course through the labyrinth of interlocking corporations and private individuals who held mortgages on property used by the Watch Tower Society, arguing that the properties were used solely and wholly for religious purposes. The Heights residents contended that all Watch Tower premises were used and occupied solely for business purposes and that the Watch Tower Society should be obliged to pay taxes on the property at 122-124 Columbia Heights (assessed, then, at $100,000) and on the Tabernacle at Hicks Street (assessed, in 1912, for $20,000). The ruling went against Russell (who was vacationing in Bermuda) and against the Watch Tower Society. The ruling, however, was overturned by the New York Supreme Court; and tax exemption was again affirmed in a 1915 ruling of the Appellate Division of the Supreme Court.

In 1971, real estate held in the name of the Watch Tower Bible and Tract Society in New York City was valued by the City Tax Commission at $14 million. The city ended the tax exemption the Society had enjoyed for most of its history under a 1971 law that permitted taxation of nonprofit organizations that were "not organized or conducted exclusively for religious" purposes. The State Legislature had permitted cities to restore to tax rolls all property except that "used exclusively for religious, charitable, hospital, educational, moral or mental improvement of men, women and children." Under protest, the Society paid $2 million to the city.

On July 11, 1974, in a unanimous opinion written by Associate Judge Hugh Jones, the Court of Appeals ruled that the Witnesses were "organized and conducted exclusively for religious purposes within the meaning of the statute." Tax exemption was ordered restored. "Administration of the religious organization of Jehovah's Witnesses," the Court ruled, "stems from the governing body at the international headquarters in Brooklyn, New York. The doctrines and beliefs of Jehovah's Witnesses are first promulgated by this governing body and then published either in *The Watchtower* or some of the other official publications of the society."

In a previous decision, in May, 1973, the Court of Appeals, New York State's highest court, had ruled against continuing tax exemption for the Association of the Bar of the City of New York and the Explorers Club, holding unanimously that neither was primarily charitable or educational. The Court said that tax-exempt property had increased to a third of the city's assessed valuation and 30 percent throughout the state. It pointed, in its decision, to estimates that half of all properties would be exempt by 1985 unless trends were reversed.

Early on the morning of Monday, November 18, 1974, a pipe-bomb explosion ripped open an iron gate and shattered windows in the Watchtower Society's printing complex. The police could suggest no motive for the crime. No one was willing to believe the bombing was a reaction to the Court's ruling; but the Heights' usually civic-minded residents, while deploring the violent act, exhibited no surge of neighborly goodwill. A community leader expressed the majority sentiment:

"While they're smiling and peddling sweet salvation, they're acting like Godzilla, gobbling up property, evicting people as if we were squatters on land which will eventually belong to them anyhow—when Jehovah gets rid of us. They don't mug anybody, they maintain their property well . . . but they don't pay taxes, and they don't contribute to communal life. How can you preach everlasting life and at the same time not care about people who have lived here all their lives? There are 1500 Witnesses living among us in their headquarters buildings, but they might as well be surrounded by a moat. It's as if we were living with a medieval commune in our midst."

In the aftermath of the explosion, Jerry Molohan, the Society's public relations officer, said that the Witnesses did not work with community groups because "Witnesses stay out of political affairs. . . . They don't get involved in our activities, and we don't get involved in theirs." [*New York Post*, Nov. 19, 1974]

But the Witnesses are not seen as passive. Dealing in some of the most lucrative urban property in the world has social consequences which involve them—no matter how they protest—in the affairs of the community as landlords. They are, calculatedly or not, involved.

In 1965, Brooklyn Heights, with its early-19th-century frame houses, its Gothic Revival structures, its imposing churches and Federal buildings and Victorian brownstones and carriage houses, was designated a National Landmark Area. The 50-block National Landmark boasted 663 pre–Civil War structures. But the Heights was more than a chaste and classical aesthetic oasis in the decaying city. Within its confines lived not only the genteel, elegant rich, but a large number of middle-class families in rent-controlled apartments, and working-class Irish and Italian families. The Heights managed to be both stuffy and flamboyant: Young Junior League matrons dressed in bright yellow coats from Bergdorf's watched their toddlers play in sandboxes, and homosexuals strolled hand in hand along the Heights Promenade. It was a community that was justly proud of its tolerant diversity.

In July, 1968, the Watchtower Bible and Tract Society went before the City's Landmarks Preservation Commission to obtain a "certificate of appropriateness" for a proposed $1-million dormitory and classroom building—a terraced structure with overhanging gardens and a slender, graceful stair tower—at Pineapple Street and Columbia Heights. The Society had at first proposed a twelve-story building; Heights residents, who tend to avert their eyes from the tall Watchtower dormitory and office buildings that are a jarring interruption to the generally uniform cornice line of Columbia Heights (the neighborhood's most noble and elegant street), protested ardently. The Brooklyn Heights Association threw itself passionately into a course of action designed to forestall the erection of what one architect called another "dead-and-stranded ocean-liner-type building." Acceding to community pressure, the Society scaled its building down to six stories and agreed to wrap its new structure around the front of three existing town houses. The capitulation did not silence the critics.

(The late Nathan Homer Knorr, the Society's third president—a steak-and-potatoes man who was as small-town-American as rhubarb pie—once, in a private talk to members of the Bethel family, described the whole of Europe as a junk shop fit to be leveled by a wrecker's ball. Knorr had no affection for classical architecture—it collects dirt and one gets lost in it. He was proud of the pastel sprays of flowers on each bedroom wall of the 122 Columbia Heights residence, painted, he said, by a lady who used to "decorate for Hollywood stars," and of the Cecil B. De Mille Biblical murals the lady executed for the headquarters meeting hall. There are no paintings in the public quarters of that building. It isn't surprising that the "terraced gardens" of the 1968 blueprint now have an abundance of plastic philodendron.)

In 1969, according to deeds and tax-exemption records, the Watchtower Society owned, in addition to its printing complex, three prime residential blocks, from Orange Street to Clark Street, on Columbia Heights. According to a *Daily News* reporter, Sylvia Carter, "Residents suspect . . . that the Society has, in fact, bought up adjoining property in private names. [Max] Larson [overseer in charge of printing operations] says individual names are listed on property records so officials have someone to contact about a building. All buildings are legal Witnesses property, they insist. Property questioned by tenants could not be traced, through deeds and tax-exemption records, to the Watchtower Society. But several owner corporations for buildings in the area could not be located at addresses listed on city records." [*Daily News*, March 9, 1969]

Heights merchant and realtor Bernard Atkins, who papers the windows of his florist shop on Montague Street, the main shopping artery for Brooklyn Heights, with Magic Marker manifestoes about the state of the nation and of the world, said, in one of his weekly position papers, "The Jehovah's Witnessess . . . embark upon a program of using their tax-free millions to swallow up building after building until they own a major portion of the Heights, a portion on which they pay almost no taxes and contribute nothing to the life of the community except for destroying lovely old brownstone houses and erecting ugly, modern structures." His wife, Charlotte Atkins, well known in the Heights for her support of community causes, was less formal and considerably more bitter. She suggests that the Watchtower Society "hits people with offers of cold cash . . . they're blockbusting, buying buildings for more than they're worth, making offers that can't be refused. They're eating us up in a silent, deathly way." Her wrath is compounded by the fact that a Watchtower proselytizer once told her husband, Bernard, "I see only death in your eyes." Charlotte Atkins, the kind of noisy busybody no neighborhood can survive without, says, "Next to the Witnesses, Burger King and McDonald's and Kentucky Fried are aesthetic geniuses and angels of light." Charlotte's charge of blockbusting pressure tactics cannot be supported by the known facts, but her bitterness is shared by many merchants.

In local Irish bars, working-class men (who have an imperfect knowledge of the way the Witnesses train their own people to be sophisticated mechanics, craftsmen, and artisans in the Watchtower printery) excoriate the Witnesses for using nonunion labor. They circulate ugly, unproved rumors to the effect that licensed plumbers and electricians have been approached and asked to say they have done jobs in fact done by nonlicensed Witness workers, in contravention of city building codes.

Former State Senator (now City Council President) Carol Bellamy, who, along with Assemblyman Mike Pesce, has worked with tenant groups threatened with eviction by the Watchtower Society, says, "We had a sense of dubious property holdings; we couldn't prove it." Bellamy also says, with no little amazement, that during all the time she has been in office she has never been called on for help by the Society: "Every other religious group, every other corporate entity has had occasion to call on me. . . . And every time my office has called them, on behalf of tenants, they yielded nothing. They have made themselves totally inaccessible. They were acting within their legal rights; what we construed to be the social and human rights of our constituents was of no concern to them."

In recent years, most of the community's animosity has focused on the Watchtower Society's ownership of two properties: a rent-controlled apartment house at One Clark Street and the once-fashionable Towers Hotel at 25 Clark Street.

The Society bought One Clark Street in 1967. Proceeding under the

1969 rent regulations which permitted landlords to evict tenants when apartments were required for the landlord's use, the Society served eviction notices on the building's 42 middle-class families, many of whom were paying a monthly rent of only $150. The Society offered to pay relocation expenses required under law; but the tenants' response was "Where are we going to move *to?*" Many of the tenants—some of whom had children enrolled in local public schools—felt that they were being pushed out of reasonable city housing into the suburbs by a vast, impersonal force. They grouped together to form the One Clark Street Tenants Association. At one point, three hundred residents of the Heights, most of them elderly women, staged a "flower promenade" protest against the evictions. They carried daffodils.

Flower power proved unavailing. By 1971 only 12 of the original tenants remained—the rest had departed because of constant harassment, according to the testimony of one resident before the Brooklyn Supreme Court. Dr. Harlow Fischman, a biologist, testified that he had complained to city agencies and the Watchtower Society about loud noises, filth, and lack of services.

As tenants moved out, young male headquarters workers moved in, converting apartments into dorms. Doors of apartments undergoing conversion remained open, according to the tenants; the halls were liberally coated with plaster dust. From time to time there were electricity blackouts, the tenants alleged, and no heat or hot water. One young mother remarked, as she departed for the suburbs, "These are the people who are going to transform the earth into a paradise, right? So far they've succeeded in turning a lot of people—some of them old and sick—out of their apartments. They've transformed city families into suburban families."

To such charges, the Watchtower spokesmen replied that the Witnesses too were really one large family. "How many families," retorted one householder, "do you find who don't have the gas turned on or use a stove, who take ten baths at once so the ceiling leaks, who have their beds made and laundry done each day by a sort of central housekeeping service, or who conduct wrestling matches at midnight?" Most tenants of One Clark Street recited a ritualistic liberal litany: "The Witnesses are good people, they're dedicated to their faith, we don't oppose their religious views. We just don't think they're considering the moral rights of the tenants of the buildings they buy." The Witnesses did not publicly interpret the resistance to their actions as an act of Satanic opposition to the message of the children of light, as they have sometimes done in the past. Heights community leaders have complained about title-abstract companies, insurance firms, trade associations, and other nonresidential users for converting brownstones into offices in the face of a citywide housing emergency. It was the Witnesses' role as businessmen that was being objected to, not their vocation as preachers.

The remaining tenants won what community leaders regard as a pyrrhic victory: they secured in the courts the right to stay in their apartments until they chose to move of their own accord. Nothing in law obliged the Watchtower Society to keep the building on the rental market. "I feel as if I'm living on a movie set in my own apartment," one tenant said. "All these earnest young men with briefcases and crew cuts and white socks marching in and out of the halls. . . . My son said to me, 'Daddy, when are we going to live in a real house again?' "

Still smarting from what one tenant called "an invasion of people who think *we're* aliens," the residents of the Heights began again to organize when, in 1974—five years after a Watchtower spokesman assured the press that further expansion plans were not under "current consideration"—rumors began to circulate that the Witnesses were about to buy the sixteen-story Towers Hotel. On August 10, 1974, 100 tenants of the 480-room hotel at 25 Clark Street, most of them middle-aged and elderly working people, were served eviction notices so that the owner-operator of the residential hotel could rent five additional floors to the Watchtower Society, which already occupied five floors of the shabby but still elegant hotel. Some of the tenants uneasily speculated that the management of the hotel wanted them out so that the property could be sold to the Watchtower Society. Bellamy and Assemblyman Pesce exhorted the tenants not to panic. The Watchtower Society would not respond to Carol Bellamy's phone calls. The Society's spokesman, Jerry Molohan, denied that the Witnesses were planning to buy the Towers. On November 19, 1974, he said, "I know of no plans to do so. What the future holds I don't know. At the moment it's the hotel's problem, not ours."

Early in 1975, the Watchtower Society bought the Towers Hotel.

(There is now speculation, among those who are close to the inner workings of the Watchtower Society, that the Towers has been bought as a residence for those of the Witnesses who expect, after Armageddon, to be part of the 144,000-member ruling class that will oversee the earthly paradise from thrones approximate to Jesus' in the heavens. If this seems too quaint to credit, it is to be remembered that, in 1929 the Witnesses built a palatial home in San Diego, California, in order to accommodate David, Moses, Isaac, Abraham, and the Hebrew prophets, whom they expected, then, to make a pre-Armageddon appearance in order to prepare earthlings for the apocalypse. Beth-Saarim, the California property, was used "in fact" as the residence of J. F. Rutherford, second president of the Watchtower Society. Claiming ill health, "Judge" Rutherford occupied the twenty-room Spanish mansion, valued at $1 million, as a "caretaker." The 1975 *Yearbook of Jehovah's Witnesses* states that this watering place cum resurrection waiting room was financed by "a direct contribution, . . . not at the expense of the Watchtower Society." [p. 194] One wonders why this disclaimer is necessary if indeed it was believed that this home was intended not as a kind of miniature San Simeon for Rutherford, but as a dormitory for "ancient worthies." [p. 146] According to *Current Biography, 1940*, "to avoid legal trouble the deed [to Beth-Saarim was] drawn in the prophets' name." The Witnesses' combination of acute business acumen and eccentric, picturesque doctrine is mind-boggling. While the Witnesses prepare to inherit the earth, their leaders are not prepared to accept second-class accommodations under the existing order. (If the meek are going to inherit the earth, they might as well start off in good neighborhoods.)

It is a sign of the frightened times that contrapuntal voices are now being raised against the chorus of bitterness in Brooklyn Heights. It is still safe to say that most Heights residents deplore the Watchtower Society's tactics. Preservationists for whom the architectural integrity of the Heights is a passion react with snobbish venom to the Witnesses' version of architecture. Small merchants are resentful of a financially self-contained community in their midst. Workers deplore the Witnesses' use of nonunion labor. People who are concerned with the flight of the middle class from the city—and those who are concerned with the old, sick, and socially dislocated—are enraged. However, there are those who are now inclined to tolerate their massive presence. The Witnesses may wake them up on Sunday mornings with their less-than-glad tidings; but they are safe neighbors. The Witnesses are now seen, among many Heights residents, as "a buffer against decay."

An insurance-trade newspaper called *The Search*, noting that hotels have become havens for addicts and "derelicts," praises the new ownership of the Towers: It has "infused a new quality. . . . Premises have been . . . repaired and maintained by expert workmen, with cleanliness, order and dignity." The new residents, Witnesses, have "added a new dimension to the safety and well-being of the community. The public press and other spokesmen have commented upon the presence of 'these clean-cut, decent, moral, high-value persons' as a buffer to the negative changing conditions in the neighborhood. Elderly people, as well, have indicated a feeling of safe-being because of their presence." [See *TW*, Oct. 15, 1975.]

(Each time the Watchtower Society annexes more Heights property, however, the residents of the Heights revert to a siege mentality—as they did when it was rumored that the Consolidated Edison Company was planning "to sell or give [as a tax write-off] the Empire Stores warehouse and nine acres of prime Fulton Ferry waterfront land" to the Witnesses. [*Phoenix*, Brooklyn, March 24, 1977] Con Ed—which has fought Landmark status for this property—advertised the sale of the land and property in *The New York Times* (March 20 and 27, 1977); minimum asking price was $1 million. The Witnesses have been "renting" a part of the property as a parking lot. According to one official of Con Ed, however, "no money has changed hands between us—and the Witnesses have improved the property, installing fences and lighting." New York Landmarks Commission Chairperson Beverly Moss, who insists that the property "belongs in the public domain," said she was "confused and upset" by Con Ed's move to dispose of the property, which has been called one of the most important historical areas in Brooklyn, if not the most important. Watchtower representative Robert Jankowski told one reporter, "It's Con Ed's property. You can draw any conclusions you wish, but there won't be anything said about it." It's remarks like that which make Heights residents nervous.)

The Witnesses are a bastion of law and order in Brooklyn Heights; they irritate people, but they are beginning less and less to frighten them. They commend themselves to the bewildered, terrified elderly residents of the Heights, and to large segments of the middle class, which is convinced of its impotence.

As I was writing this, a friend told me this story: In a fit of absentmindedness, she had left her Gucci handbag (credit cards, keys, money, airline tickets) on a crosstown bus. An hour later, she received a phone call from a young black man who said that he'd found her handbag and would be glad to go out of his way to deliver it to her. As she waited, she received another phone call, this one from the man's mother: "I want you to know," the woman said, "that the reason my son is returning your pocketbook is that we are Jehovah's Witnesses. We don't steal. We are honest people." *The Watchtower* and *Awake!* magazines are full of such testmonials to the Witnesses' personal honesty; they are true.

Testimony of Maria Russell, questioned by the Chairman of the City Board of Tax Commissioners, 1913:

> CHAIRMAN: *Does your husband get any return from the corporation beyond his expenses and a fair compensation for his work?*
> MRS. R: *I don't know that he gets any money, but he seems to get everything that a man of wealth could desire. He travels in the best style whenever he wants to; goes round the world, to California or Europe, on occasions, and all his expenses are paid out of the funds of the Watch Tower Society.*
> CHAIRMAN: *Does he hold any property in his own name?*
> MRS. R.: *No, I don't think so. He wouldn't dare do that, because then I might have a claim on it though my dower rights.*

There is nothing to support a notion that any official of the Watchtower Bible and Tract Society is amassing personal wealth. Some officials of the Society have lived and do live *as if* they were wealthy.

Control of the total organization is concentrated in a self-perpetuating group of officers, who appoint all supervisors and local congregational leaders; they "make reproofs and corrections and direct the conduct of the organization." [*JWDP*] All decisions and appointments handed down from the Society's headquarters are thought to have Jehovah's imprimatur.

Under Russell's presidency each $10 contribution to the Watch Tower Bible and Tract Society of Pennsylvania (parent organization of New York's Watchtower Bible and Tract Society and the International Bible Students Association) represented one voting share. In 1917, the Society's second president, J. F. Rutherford, moved to democratize the organization—or at least to provide the "Bible Students" with some feeling that they had a voice in corporate proceedings. He wished, inasmuch as "many of the Lord's dear children are poor in . . . worldly goods," to avoid the suggestion that "lucre" was "speaking for the Lord"; he proposed that every ecclesia (congregation) hold a general meeting to "vote upon their choice for members of the Board of Directors and Officers of the Society." The vote would not constitute a legal election, but would be "advisory, or in the nature of instructions to the Shareholders as to what is the will of the church at large." [*The Watch Tower*, Nov. 1, 1917, pp. 330–32]

During the 1920s and '30s, it became apparent to Rutherford that organizational survival and expansion depended on centralization of all powers in the governing body. In 1932, "elective elders" were replaced in the congregations "by a group of mature brothers called a 'service committee,' who were elected by the congregation to assist the local service director appointed by the Society." [*Yearbook*, 1975, p. 165] Elections, however, led to divisiveness at a time when it was crucial, in view of external pressures, for the Society to maintain a united front. In 1938 voting powers were removed from local congregations; the power to appoint overseers and their assistants was delivered to the Society. This was an arrangement, according to A. H. MacMillan, that would "continue into the new world and for a thousand years of Christ's reign." [*Faith*, p. 159] The arrangement was also viewed as analogous to Solomon's building of "the temple, the king's palace, and the house of the forest of Lebanon for judgment." [*Ibid.*]

The Witnesses reckon that their organization began to be "strengthened in 1918." It took Solomon twenty years to build his empire, and it took them twenty years to build theirs: The " 'twentieth year' ends with the beginning of the spring of 1938, and hence corresponds with the (lunar) year 1937 which ends in the spring of 1938. . . ." [*JWDP*, pp. 127–49] Some Witnesses were unable to swallow the analogy; in 1932 and in 1938 there were mass defections: "Those who opposed or resisted the theocratic arrangement," it was explained, "were not opposing or resisting men; they were striving against the spirit of God." [*Faith*, pp. 157; see also *Yearbook*, 1975, pp. 164–249.]

Under the leadership of Nathan H. Knorr, the organization was further "theocratized"—which is to say, centralized in a self-perpetuating rule.

There are no longer any stockholders in the Watch Tower Bible and Tract Society. In 1944, the Charter of the Society was amended; fixed membership was no longer contingent upon monetary contributions. Membership was limited to no more than 500 men, "all chosen on the basis of their active service to God." Each corporation has a Board of Directors.* In addition to these men, there is a central 18-man religious "governing body." The governing body, which meets weekly in Brooklyn, makes secular and religious decisions (the Witnesses, of course, would not recognize the distinction—the work of the governing body is, to them, by nature all spiritual), which are then implemented by the Boards of Directors. Membership in these bodies frequently overlaps.

In 1976, a further change was made in the structure of the governing body: "To facilitate its works, six committees of the Governing Body have been formed. Each will have its Chairman, who will serve for a period of one year. These Committees are supervisory in nature and it is not intended that they will handle all the details and routine work. The various corporations that have been serving the Kingdom interests so well until now will, of course, continue to fulfill their important role as legal agencies of Jehovah's witnesses, their Governing Body and its committees.

"These six committees, which began functioning on January 1, 1976, are as follows: Service Committee; Writing Committee; Publishing Committee; Teaching Committee; Personnel Committee; Chairman's Committee." [*TW*, Feb. 1, 1976]

This splintering of responsibility gave rise to the conjecture that Knorr—who was then 71 and reputed to be in failing health—had lost his grip on the Society's affairs.

Nathan Homer Knorr, who was born in Bethlehem, Pennsylvania, on April 23, 1905, died of a cancerous tumor on June 8, 1977. He was 72; he had been president of the Watchtower Bible and Tract Society since January 13, 1942. His wife, Audrey Mock Knorr, once a Bethel housekeeper, survives him.

As a youngster, Knorr attended the Dutch Reformed Church. When he was 16, he read some Watchtower publications, and he later joined a local Bible Study group. When he graduated from high school in Allentown, Pennsylvania, Knorr became a full-time preacher, and he joined the headquarters staff soon thereafter. He rose from a job in the shipping department to become coordinator of all printing operations. In 1932 he was named general manager of the publishing-office plant. Knorr became vice-president of the Watchtower Society in 1935; seven years later, when he was 37 years old, he became the Society's president.

---

* "The [Pennsylvania] Society has a board of seven directors, for the management of the Society's affairs. According to the Society's charter, at each annual meeting members of the Board of Directors are elected by all the incumbent members of the Society. After such annual election [held in Pittsburgh, Pennsylvania] the Board of Directors elects its own officers, such as president of the Society, etc. According to the terms of the Charter the Society acts as the 'administrative agency' for all of Jehovah's Christian witnesses earthwide."—*TW*, Jan. 15, 1976

Upon Knorr's death, Frederick W. Franz, who was 83 years old, became president of the Watchtower Society by unanimous vote of the Board of Directors.

Franz was born in Covington, Kentucky, in 1893 and terminated his studies at the University of Cincinnati to become a full-time preacher in 1914. A member of the headquarters staff since June 2, 1920, he became a director of the Pennsylvania corporation in 1943 and vice-president of the Watch Tower Bible and Tract Society of Pennsylvania in 1945; he became a director of the New York corporation in 1949.

Franz is a bachelor. He has taught himself several languages, including Hebrew and Greek, and is regarded by the Witnesses as their foremost Bible scholar:

> In regard to doctrinal material, for many years Rutherford [Knorr's predecessor] had leaned heavily on the keen Bible brain of Fred Franz. Nathan Knorr had managed the business of the legal corporations for so long that by unanimous quiet consent he automatically slipped into the presidency. [Cole, p. 107]

I remember Franz as an ascetic, kindly man, with an engaging sense of humor and a gift for self-mockery. Much loved by the Witnesses, he is as unworldly as Knorr was businesslike. When I knew him, he was adorably sweet-spirited (though, from my point of view, maddeningly earnest when it came to dogma). A flamboyant orator, he was personally reticent, though not inaccessible. He seemed to have scant regard for his personal appearance; still slim and handsome in his 60s, he was as likely as not to be found shuffling around headquarters in bedroom slippers and mismatched socks. His minor, unselfconscious eccentricities of dress and demeanor, and a nature that was by turns reclusive and gregarious, endeared him to all of the headquarters staff. I have never met a Witness who did not like Franz. He seemed never to have incurred the animosity that Russell, Rutherford, and Knorr, all in their turn, did. It was regarded as an honor to be invited to his spartan room.

(I think he liked me very much; when I left Bethel, at a time when Franz was secluding himself in one of the Society's country properties, he was reported to have said, "She would never have left if I had been there to help her." I still have a lingering affection for him—and choose to read that remark as one of loving concern rather than of arrogance.)

Franz's great age has necessitated further changes in the Society's structure: each corporation now has not one but, for the first time in Watchtower history, two vice-presidents. Society spokesman Robert Janowski reports "no basic change" in the Society, in spite of death and new appointments. "The organization will continue to be run by a committee arrangement," he said. "Brother Franz was elected president to satisfy legal requirements; spiritual matters will not be affected."

On the next rung of the hierarchical ladder, beneath the Society's officers, are supervisory officials known as district- and circuit-overseers.
These men, frequently accompanied by their wives, visit each congregation
twice a year, instructing congregational elders and accompanying Witnesses
from door to door to help perfect their proselytizing techniques. They in-
spect and audit local finances, and they file with headquarters confidential
progress reports on each congregation as well as a "Personal Qualifications
Report" on elders and potential leaders.

Each congregation has a self-perpetuating, nonelected committee that
makes recommendations to the Society for appointing overseers and "ministerial servants." All baptized men over 20 are considered for these positions.
Meetings of the committee are characterized by a kind of Maoist self-criti-
cism (in the interest of "honesty and humility"—*Yearbook*, 1975). Each year
congregational elders rotate positions; no one enjoys the position of presiding overseer for an entire year. (Loyalty is thus given to the governing
body, rather than to an individual, and power is concentrated in the Society.)

No one—from the Society's president to a presiding overseer in Absalom
County, Missouri—is paid for his services.

The question of whether anyone is amassing personal wealth does not
arise at the congregational level, where elders and overseers may be full-
time preachers or have full- or part-time secular work, but receive no remu-
neration from the Society.

It doesn't arise at the circuit- or district-overseer level either. These men
are given modest monthly allowances by the Society, which barely cover
transportation costs. Within the Watchtower hierarchy, they come closest
to being *servi servorum Dei*—servants of the servants of God. (The Witnesses
refuse to apply the word *hierarchy* to themselves, reserving it as a pejorative
term for the Catholic Church. They are all *brothers*.) The peripatetic life of
these circuit and district emissaries is sometimes grueling, and almost always destructive of marital privacy. They have no homes of their own; they
are transients, living out of suitcases in homes of the local congregations
they serve. Depending on the affluence of the territory assigned them, their
accommodations may vary from a poolside villa in Southern California to a
curtained-off alcove in an Appalachian shack with no plumbing. They are
honored guests wherever they stay; but in their role as spiritual exemplars,
their public lives and their private lives meld, their private lives subsumed
into their public lives.

It is only at the highest echelons of the Society that the question of
money and life-style becomes interesting. Nathan Knorr received the same
$20 monthly allowance as does the humblest shipping clerk at the Bethel
factory, and as F. W. Franz does now.

Leaders of charismatic sects, splashy showmen like the Reverend Ike and the Guru Maharaj-ji, advertise and have fancy rationales for their lavish life-style—a life-style that tends to make the followers of such men feel rich by association. Knorr neither mortified the flesh nor surrounded himself with pomp, purple, and majesty. He lived like a moneyed business executive. He kept a distinctly low profile in a penthouse apartment at 122 Columbia Heights.

Knorr lived, as do a handful of other high officials (and their wives), in a suite of rooms overlooking the East River. (Franz lives rather simply.) Other Bethelites—including married couples—live two to a pleasant room and share communal toilets and baths. Knorr, in a self-contained apartment, had a valet and ate meals prepared for him in his own kitchen. Certainly no more than one would expect for the leader of a 2-million-member sect, this was remarkable only in the face of his protestations that he enjoyed no extraordinary privileges, and the fact that the Witnesses chose to take him at his word.

It is not easy to support leisure, and difficult to support vice, on $20 a month. Fortunate Bethelites occasionally get gifts of money or clothing from family or friends, so that they can live in some degree of comfort. Those who don't sharpen their razor blades on glass to make them last, or darn nylon stockings. Knorr, who regarded such minor deprivations as salutary, accepted the gift of a television set at a time when he was advising the rest of us at Bethel that to buy or watch television was to sell our time to the Devil.

Watchtower-owned cars are used for more than just official purposes. This is standard business procedure; it's just that the Watchtower Society purports to be different.

For a time, the Watchtower Society owned a yacht, which was used to carry missionaries to places inaccessible by land. I know that the yacht was used for pleasure purposes, because I've been on it: one night, when the ship was docked in New York Harbor, one of Knorr's aides invited a group of young men and women on board to drink and dance. I remember how carelessly we threw our beer cans overboard. (The destruction of the environment was not then used as one of the indications that we are living in the "last days." The Society, just like you and me, learned about the ecological crisis from the media and the scientists it despises, not through divine inspiration, and then turned around and triumphantly said, We told you so.)

We at Bethel used to point with pride to the fact that while missionaries of "false religion" traveled in first-class comfort to their assignments, our missionaries were sent third class and, like a religious Peace Corps, lived like the people among whom they served. It never occurred to us to worry that Knorr traveled first class. We were an adaptive group.

The phenomenon of denying the evidence, and making no connections or faulty connnections, is common to all people whose need to believe over-comes their rational judgment. Faced with the fact that some of their lead-ers have been suspected of hitting the bottle with a passion, confronted with the rumors that a small brothel was once maintained on Willow Street in Columbia Heights for the entertainment of Bethelites around mid-cen-tury, Witnesses' eyes glaze, and they will either refuse to countenance the charges or stoutly maintain that God's servants are "imperfect vessels."

Time speaks softly of the dead. In the case of the Witnesses, it is often mute. The Witnesses have notoriously short and selective memories. The Society smothers unsavory parts of its past under the blanket of its current preoccupations. During the 1940s and early '50s, when I was a Witness and a member of the headquarters staff, it was as if Charles Taze Russell had never existed. This vivid, controversial personality had at best a shadow life; he was seldom, if ever, spoken of. Any discussion of him was likely to be aborted with the phrase "We are not followers of any man." The Society does not talk unkindly of its dead; it doesn't talk of them. It was not until the mid and late '50s that edited accounts of Russell's life and activities began to appear in Watchtower histories. Merciful time (with help from revisionist historians) has blurred Russell's difficulties. In Watchtower his-tories, the man who died on October 31, 1916, with $200 in a personal bank account—having invested his money in the Society in return for vot-ing shares that gave him complete financial control—goes down as a simple, homey man.

Though I became a Witness in 1944, two years after the death of Judge Joseph F. Rutherford, Russell's successor, I never heard of the scandal that had attached to him. When I was at Bethel, I heard murmurings, from those who had known him, that Rutherford had been a stern and intimidat-ing man. But there was a general silence and lack of specificity. I never learned what longtime residents meant when they alluded to Rutherford's abrasiveness—or to traitors in their midst who had made devilish capital of it. What they had in mind, I now know, was the Moyle case—which has not yet been cosmeticized like the "miracle wheat" and the Jellyfish epi-sodes. The Moyle Case has no place in the Society's official histories.

In 1943, Olin R. Moyle, who had been general counsel under Ruther-ford, brought a $100,000 libel suit against eleven leaders of the Society and against the Watchtower corporations. The Appellate Division upheld the verdict of the Brooklyn Supreme Court, modifying it to reduce damages from $30,000 to $15,000.

In 1934, Moyle had divested himself of his material possessions and given up a lucrative law practice to live at Bethel with his wife and son and to serve as the Society's general counsel, receiving, like all his fellow volun-teers then, $10 a month for his services. Five years later, he wrote a private letter (dated July 21, 1939) to Judge Rutherford in which he charged Rutherford with encouraging lewdness and drunkenness; with being extraordinarily harsh to members of the Bethel staff who incurred his displeasure; and with living like a man of wealth:

"Shortly after our coming to Bethel," Moyle wrote, "we were shocked to witness the spectacle of our brethren receiving a trimming from you. C. J. Woodworth got a tongue lashing and was humiliated and called a jackass for saying that it served the devil to continue the present-day calendar. Knorr and others were similarly treated. Unfair reproaches have been given and your action violated freedom of speech. [You] called the . . . ushers who were at the Madison Square Garden convention sissies."

Earlier in 1939, rowdies who were presumed to be followers of Father Charles Coughlin, a dissident and anti-Semitic Catholic priest who was subsequently silenced, disrupted a rally in Madison Square Garden; Witnesses acting as ushers, armed with canes for the purpose of quelling interference, were arrested and charged with assault. Moyle defended the ushers, who were subsequently acquitted, in court.

> We publish that all in the Lord's organization are alike [Moyle wrote]. You know that this is not the case. Take for instance the difference between the accommodations furnished to you and your personal attendants compared to those furnished to some of the brethren. You have many homes—Bethel, Staten Island, California—and even at Kingdom Farm. I am informed one house has been kept for your sole use during the short periods you spend there. And what do the brethren at the farm receive? Small rooms, unheated through the bitter cold Winter; they live in their trunks, like campers.
>
> On the question of marriage of those who live at Bethel there is unequal and discriminatory treatment. One brother who left Bethel to get married was refused the privilege of pioneering [preaching full time] in New York as disapproval of his leaving Bethel. On the other hand, when Bonnie Boyd [J.F.R.'s confidential secretary] married she didn't leave Bethel and was permitted to bring in her husband in spite of the rule. . . .
>
> The Biblical injunctions against unclean, filthy speaking and jesting have never been abrogated. It is shocking and nauseating to hear vulgar speaking and smut at Bethel and it is stated by a sister that the loudest laughter at table arises when a filthy joke goes through; and your skirts are not clean.
>
> Under your tutelage there has grown up a glorification of alcohol. . . . There appears to be a definite policy of breaking in newcomers in the use of liquor, and resentment is shown against those who do not join them. . . . Teetotalers are looked on as weaklings.

With the letter of July 21, which he signed "Your brother in the King's service," Moyle tendered his resignation, to take effect September 1. Rutherford read the letter to the Bethel Family; he denounced Moyle when the

100-member staff was assembled for a meal in the Bethel dining room and ordered the Moyles to leave Bethel immediately. Moyle moved to Wisconsin. Following hard on his heels was one of Rutherford's "troubleshooters," Malcolm A. Howlett, a director of the Society. Howlett organized meetings for the purpose of telling Wisconsin Witnesses that Moyle had been excommunicated for "unfaithfulness to the organization." As a result, Moyle's attorney argued in court, Moyle was shunned by friends and clients and fellow Witnesses, and obliged to forsake his law practice. Subsequently, two articles in *The Watchtower* described Moyle as a "manpleaser," a "murmurer and complainer"; *Watchtower* articles accused him of not properly defending ushers who had been charged with assault at Madison Square Garden, and called him "a servant of the Evil One," a "Judas."

Moyle's attorney, Walter Bruchhausen, told Supreme Court Justice Henry L. Ughetta and a jury that Moyle had been "hounded, . . . libeled and pursued because he dared to disagreee with the ruthless Rutherford. . . . Rutherford became so obsessed with his power that he rode it ruthlessly, and would not tolerate those who dared to disagree with [him]."

Moyle testified that Judge Rutherford shouted angrily at members of the Bethel Family who disagreed with him or did things he disapproved of: "I was in court as attorney for some of Jehovah's Witnesses and with opposing counsel held a conference. Someone told a story. Everyone laughed and Judge Rutherford heard about it and said I was a manpleaser."

One of the witnesses for the defense was William J. Heath, a director of the Society and the husband of Bonnie Boyd, a man who traveled extensively with Rutherford and was on close personal terms with him. Heath, who had gotten punched in the eye in the Madison Square Garden fracas, testified that he had been surprised when Moyle, acting as his attorney, fraternized amiably with the lawyer who was representing his assailant. Later, he said, he complained to Rutherford of Moyle's "strange conduct," and Rutherford put Heath's case in the hands of another lawyer. Rutherford, Heath said, was "always gracious and kindly."

Malcolm Howlett's wife, Helen, testifying for the defense, said that Moyle was "in wrong" with Rutherford, who was a man of "some emotion"; she acknowledged that when Rutherford reprimanded at mealtime, he talked loudly into the amplifier and "expressed himself forcibly."

Two witnesses for the defense, G. Paulos and C. Hilton Ellison, testified that they had turned against Moyle, their longtime friend, because of having read in *The Watchtower* that Moyle was unfaithful, "unscriptural." That their faith in *The Watchtower* was total was demonstrated when Moyle's attorney called Paulos' attention to two of its past issues. One, in 1938, had expounded the dogma that Christ died to save all mankind, and the second, in 1941, had declared that Christ had died to save "the obedient ones"— Jehovah's Witnesses. Paulos said he believed that Jehovah's Witnesses were the only earthly organization carrying on God's work, and that Rutherford was "God's representative": "I first learned in *The Watchtower* that certain people will not be benefited by Christ's sacrifice. I accepted the modern version." Paulos, who evidently regarded *The Watchtower* as incapable of error, said he had chosen not to investigate the truth of Moyle's charges. Ellison, whose testimony was crucial because he was taken to be representative of all of the Witnesses, testified that he accepted *The Watchtower* articles and Howlett's statements as undeniable truth. He testified that "evil servants" were those who, like Moyle, "with knowledge of the Truth leave the Society."

Hayden C. Covington, chief defense counsel, replied:

> This libel suit is brought against a religious group which covenanted to wholeheartedly serve God and go from house to house and preach the gospel, as Jesus Christ did. Judge Rutherford was not ruthless. He was a kindly man. . . . Mr. Moyle agreed, as do all others, to abide in Bethel forever or until death or the Lord removed him.
>
> He made vicious, scurrilous charges as a cover for his resignation, but there is no voluntary resignation in our organization. A resolution was properly adopted dismissing him. He criticized the family of God at Bethel, and it is true, as we have stated in *The Watchtower*, that he became a servant of the Evil One. He acted as Judas, and this $100,000 lawsuit is worth 30 pieces of silver. He has already been well paid by the Evil One.

Judge Ughetta, less metaphysically inclined than Covington, awarded Moyle $30,000 in damages.

(Covington, an undisputably brilliant Constitutional lawyer who took First and Fourteenth Amendment cases to the United States Supreme Court for the Witnesses and won, and thus immeasurably protected us all, was later to leave Bethel himself. During the 1960s he acted, for a time, as Muhammad Ali's defense attorney in the fighter's draft case. Covington based his defense of Ali on the fact that Ali was a minister and therefore not subject to the draft—the same defense he had used successfully for thousands of draft-aged Witnesses. A spokesman in the Legal Department of the Watchtower Society, for whom he labored for so many years as a "volunteer," answered me evasively when I asked for information about Covington. I conjecture that Covington chose, for a time at least, not to employ his talents for the organization he had defended with so much passion and energy and brilliance.)

Moyle appears to have made an abortive attempt to set himself up as leader of a rival sect—the Pastoral Bible Institute, to which he hoped to draw straying Witnesses. This enterprise did not prosper. (No spin-off sects have prospered.)

V. *God Can't Kill Arnold*

I asked to be disfellowshipped July 19, 1974. When the new ruling for disfellowshipping smoking-offenders came in, two dear women friends got the ax. I took up smoking again purposely to get the ax, and smoked in front of any Witness who came into my home. I was interested to see who in their elaborate spy system would turn me in. It took about four weeks until the committee called me informing me that they knew. In a letter to headquarters, I told them I wanted to be disfellowshipped:

"I no longer consider you my brothers. I have lost respect for a society of people who want to sit in judgment of my conduct—who want to take the splinter out of my eye when their own has a rafter in it. I have lost respect for a society of people who do not understand that it's not what goes into a man's mouth that defiles him, but what comes out.

"Why have you never answered my letters? . . . Hypocritical Phariseeism is rampant. Love of the brothers has become a meaningless word. Meeting attendance has taken precedence over a brother in need. Not celebrating a birthday is a guarantee of spiritual maturity. . . . Does 'coming in The Truth' contribute to a person's sense of well-being and respect? Or are you imposing heavier burdens upon people than those they had in the world ? I bear the scars of my distress: I have twice tried to slash my wrists.

"Where will it stop? Will overeating be a disfellowshipping offense next? The Watchtower *and* Awake! *tell us it is 'a sin' to worry. Is worrying a disfellowshipping offense?*

"The Witnesses have lost their joy; they are their own Armageddon, and their own great tribulation." —From a letter sent to me by an excommunicated Witness.

"Disfellowshipping" is the Watchtower Society's term for excommunication.

The Society's governing body appoints, through its branch offices, "judicial committees" which act on behalf of the entire congregation in hearing cases of "sinful conduct" (such as fornication, adultery, apostasy, smoking) and render decisions that are known as resolutions of expulsion. Trial proceedings are confidential; members of the congregation are not permitted to question the decision of the committee and must comply with the committee's judgment. If they act in contravention of the committee's ruling, they become candidates for disfellowshipping on the ground of "rebelliousness."

Yet congregation members are often ignorant of the charges that have been brought against a disfellowshipped member and are not allowed to share the testimony that formed the basis of the committee's decision, are not told who it was that instigated the accusations, and further, have no information as to the accused's defense.

It appears now that many Witnesses are disaffected or at least greatly agitated by the Society's procedures for "disfellowshipping." From Manitoba, Canada, thousands of circulars have been sent to Witnesses in Britain, Europe, the Americas, Australia, and New Zealand complaining of alleged injustices by the governing body.

Until 1974, [*TW*, Aug. 1, 1974] Witnesses were not permitted to exchange a word of greeting with disfellowshipped persons. Obliged to present hard, unyielding faces to sinners, they could not smile at "antiChrists." A mother whose daughter was disfellowshipped and did not live under her roof could not, under pain of expulsion, speak to her child, unless dire emergency made it necessary. She might be permitted, for example, to inform her daughter of a death in the family, but not to share her grief. Perhaps because the Society has been publicly charged with "spiritual murders" for cutting these people off so brutally, it has softened its policy. Witnesses are now permitted to speak with those disfellowshipped, but not, unless they are elders, on "spiritual matters." Witnesses who have disfellowshipped minor children are told to "use God's word or other publications that discuss the Bible . . . in a corrective manner, not as though having a spiritual 'good time' with such a one in the way they could with the other children." [*Ibid.*]

While *The Watchtower* [March 15, 1959] admits that occasional injustices have been perpetrated as a result of prejudicial envy or dislike of the accused, or because of "an incorrect interpretation of Scriptural principles," it does not permit open discussion of disfellowshipping. Nor has it ever publicly apologized to people so victimized. The committee's decision must remain unchallenged; and the disfellowshipped person may not be given any spiritual comfort. Tens of thousands of Witnesses have been disfellowshipped since 1959. A disfellowshipped person must confess publicly, and announce and demonstrate to the satisfaction of the elders his intention to change his ways. (From 1963 to 1973, 36,671 persons were disfellowshipped in the United States. In the same time period, 14,508 persons were reinstated. [*TW*, Aug. 1, 1974]) In the majority of cases the severity of treatment militates against confession and repentance, and the humiliated disfellowshipped Witness enters despair—or, if he is lucky, freedom.

Indeed, despair is often the mirror image of the Witnesses' certainty.

I have often thought that many Witnesses were ambulatory schizophrenics, that their religion provided them with a vehicle for their craziness, a way to accommodate their fear and loathing of the menacing world. A study published in the *British Journal of Psychiatry* [June, 1975] tends to confirm this view: John Spencer, writing on "The Mental Health of Jehovah's Witnesses," reports that a study of Witnesses admitted to the Mental Health Services facilities of Western Australia "suggests that members of this section of the community are more likely to be admitted to a psychiatric hospital than the general population. Furthermore, followers of the sect are three times more likely to be diagnosed as suffering from schizophrenia and four times more likely from paranoid schizophrenia than the rest of the population."

Spencer says that the principal problem for a researcher "seems to be to decide whether extreme religiosity such as is seen in the so-called 'neurotic sects' is a symptom of an overt psychiatric disorder, or whether it is a complex defense mechanism against an underlying disorder." His study does not resolve the issue. It "suggests," he says, "that either the Jehovah's Witnesses sect tends to attract an excess of pre-psychotic individuals who may then break down, or else being a Jehovah's Witness is itself a stress which may precipitate a psychosis. Possibly both of these factors may operate together."

Religiosity, as Jung said, is an extremely varied phenomenon about which it is impossible to generalize. It may, as Jung believed, be a creative expression of man's natural urge to worship; it may be, as Erich Fromm writes, a means of self-preservation, a way of silencing anxiety, a symbolic means of communication. Spencer notes that there is clinical evidence to demonstrate that "even bizarre types of religiosity can be converted into constructive channels when such an intense religious experience is related to unmet psychological needs." He quotes previous studies that indicate that "when an individual's normal devices fail or the integration is threatened," he or she tends to move "towards the more enthusiastic, irrational, fundamental and emotive sects where the psychotic patient may well be supported, protected, and hidden from society."

What happens when a person whose psychological needs have been met by Jehovah's Witnesses is deemed unworthy of association with them and is expelled from the congregation? My own observations tell me that the "survival rate" among ex-Witnesses (both those who are disfellowshipped and those who leave of their own accord) is relatively low. (And the turnover rate, according to one ex-Witness who had access to headquarters records, is extraordinarily high.)

The Witnesses' explanation for deviant behavior after leaving the community is that "the demons have taken over the minds" of the defectors. It might be closer to the mark to say that the need for certainty and community that led certain people to become Witnesses in the first place drives them to find community and certainty and surcease from pain elsewhere. Ex-Witnesses who are functioning in the world still express anxiety, distress, and at best a lingering sadness:

I am a former Witness. Both parents baptized in 1951, when I was 7. I was 11 when I was baptized. Pioneered throughout my teens. Honor student. Married an unbaptized Witness at 21. (Didn't feel worthy enough to marry a full-fledged Brother!) Four children by caesarian and three miscarriages. Alcoholism and sleeping pills. Knew one more Seconal or pregnancy would probably end my life.

Because of my "evil" thoughts which I used alcohol to drown, and because of that alcoholism, I was certain I was to be destroyed. When I got to that point, I felt I had nothing to lose anyway, so I left. Everything! House, car, air conditioning, husband, natural family (all Witnesses), job, religion, and children.

It's been four years now. I have never been happier or healthier in my entire life. I am in charge of an outdoor labor crew. Taking a college course. Have a male partner of two years who loves me. No more asthma, no more inability to get to sleep. No more feeling of hopeless inadequacy, no fear of the future. Have worked in community projects.

I still feel sad. . . .   Sundiana G., New Orleans, Louisiana

I find myself often muddled and confused, and always struggling. I am almost 27 and stopped going to "the meetings" when I was 17. My main reason (I guess) for leaving then was the opposition I got for wanting to go to college—that and the lack of intelligent persons to converse with left me feeling very uncomfortable. I finally moved to my own apartment at 22 when I couldn't stand it anymore. I will never be able to rid myself of all of the gut fears and confusion that I now feel whenever I think about religion. I try to ignore the entire issue. I was never allowed to mingle socially or to date. I am now unable to function socially in groups of more than four people.— D.A.R., Philadelphia, Pennsylvania

I have been unable to tell psychiatrists what my life was as a Jehovah's Witness. No friend or lover has ever shared these experiences. My life was oppressed from two forces which combined to narrow my options to just about nothing. The religion forbade all but necessary contact with the outside world. My family still maintained the old Sicilian isolationism, sexual Puritanism, and sheltering of girls, primacy of the family, mistrust of strangers. . . .

I wrote in a journal throughout high school. Pages and pages of torment. All my friends were Witnesses. The world was in turmoil, frightening, inaccessible. I had never experienced it. All I wanted was one taste—a chance to make my own decision. Else what good was my faith, untested? Around and around. As I grew older my friendships dwindled. I was too aloof and intellectual for the Witnesses.

During all these years I changed from a person who could not fall asleep unless I prayed to one who could not remember the words. As I stood up to sing at meetings I felt a great weariness. I was practicing the worst deception. I was deceiving myself. At last, one day out in service with a friend, I simply could not open my mouth to speak.

After ringing the doorbell, I knew I would be unable to say a word, and I called to her for help. We looked at each other and all the doubt and fear and humiliation underlying our activity was in our eyes. She took me home. Later she married a Catholic and was disfellowshipped.

After this I hung on to my double life for a few more years, vacillating. I finally knew that I had to choose a life in one camp or the other, and I chose the world.

Now I suffer from freedom like everyone else who turns her back on authority.—E.Z., Moorestown, New Jersey

There is no voluntary resignation in our organization, Covington told a jury in the Moyle case.

For years after I left Bethel, I dreamed that I was back in the antiseptic halls of the Watchtower residence, fighting to find a way out. At each NO EXIT sign a Witness stood, smiling, barring my way: "There is no way out." The dream was trite; my fear was fresh and vivid and palpable.

Since my departure, I have had a series of strange encounters with Watchtower elders, each one puzzling, each one a walking version of the stale nightmare.

On Christmas Day, 1968, a member of the Watchtower headquarters staff rang my doorbell and asked, "Are you Connie Grizzuti's daughter who used to be associated with the Lord's sheep?" I leaped at once to the conclusion that something had happened to my mother. I had thought that I was "killing" my mother by leaving her religion; the appearance of that man on Christmas—the holiday we had regarded as devilish and abominable, the holiday that had drawn my mother and me together in sisterly mutual defiance of the world—triggered the guilt I had never been able to expiate. My mother is dead, I thought; I really have killed her.

The reality, less awful, was quite odd enough: "It has come to our attention," the man said, "that in 1963 you were observed making obeisance in the Shiva temple in Warangal, India. You are also known to have made the sign of the cross while passing a Roman Catholic Church in Guatemala City. These are grounds for disfellowshipping. If you can prove, before a group of elders, that you are innocent of the charges, disfellowshipping charges will be halted. If we remain convinced of your guilt, you may be reinstated in the Lord's organization if you beg forgiveness. If we judge you guilty and you do not confess, you will be disfellowshipped. If you refuse to appear before the elders, you will be automatically disfellowshipped."

Odd indeed. There was this silly, but somehow sinister, man underneath my Christmas tree (in itself proof of perfidy), and there were my children, looking no less startled than if Santa Claus himself had popped out of the chimney. And there was I, feeling menaced, understanding the absurdity of such feelings, but nonetheless frightened.

I said, "Wouldn't it be redundant to disfellowship me? After all, I left ten years ago of my own accord." He said, "But you can't leave. You can never leave us. We can expel you. But you, having been baptized into The Truth, are one of us until we say you're not."

I declined—I did not have the reporter's avarice for collecting facts or experience then—to appear before the elders. And I was frightened. (I did rather mischievously offer him some Christmas punch, which he waved away with a shudder of distaste.)

They did not disfellowship me; I don't know why. A friend who once worked in the "Service Department" of Bethel, which handles disfellowshipping procedures, suggests that some technicality may have gotten in the way. Perhaps somewhere along the line, a technical procedure had been violated. In any case, I was left to wonder if they had spies who followed former Witnesses around the world to collect evidence.

It was not until 1974 that I was paid another official visit.

Years before, I had converted a young Brooklyn girl who had later married a Bethelite. They had been assigned to circuit-overseer work in Alabama. Lee and Donald, having returned from their assignment, came to pay me a "friendly visit." I had fond memories of them both. I remembered Lee as a spunky, sweet, feisty kid, not overly serious, given to easy laughter. Donald, twenty years her senior, had had impressive reserve and movie-star-perfect good looks. He was serious about everything. We'd had, before he met Lee, a couple of dates. He was courteous, contained, formal. We went roller-skating; he was austere even in a roller-skating rink. (I liked him.) He did nothing casually; I should not have been surprised when he said, in firm, measured tones—spacing each word to give it weight—"I'd like this relationship to deepen beyond friendship." But I was taken aback by what seemed, even for a repressed Bethelite, to be an overly calculated approach to romance. I made one of those hopelessly inadequate, awkward speeches that begins, "I like you too much to encourage you. . . ." Still, I had been flattered, and I could not but regard him with affection.

I had not seen either of them for close to twenty years. The years had added dignity to Donald's almost-too-regular features; he was, if anything, more handsome than ever. Tomboy Lee had taken on some of her husband's coloration; she too now spoke in firm, measured tones, and I missed her careless spontaneity. She was dressed in what is called a matron's "ensemble," everything matching. She took in my cluttered living room with a swift, practiced glance and said, "It looks like a writer's house." (I took that as a reproach.) There was prefunctory conversation.

The first thing Donald said was that he hadn't come to "blackmail" or to "spank" me. He spoke of the "rife immorality" in the world today and requested my 11-year-old daughter, who was finding all of this fascinating, to leave the room so that he could discuss rife immorality. I replied that there was not much that could surprise my daughter (who had meanwhile kicked me in the shins to signal her unwillingness to depart) and that I felt perfectly free to speak in front of her.

Donald: "Do you consider yourself one of Jehovah's Witnesses?"

B.H.: "Of course not."

Donald: "What would you like the congregations to think of you?"

B.H.: "What they think of me is up to them, surely."

Donald: "When you were baptized into the New World Society you took out citizenship in a new order. Are you renouncing your citizenship?"

To that question I had no ready answer; it seemed preposterous that anyone should ask it.

Donald: "There are several reasons for leaving The Truth. One, you reject doctrine. Two, you have had personal conflicts with individual Witnesses or with the organization. Three, you have committed immoral acts, and your shame keeps you away. Which of these reasons applies to you?"

I shrank from the inquisition. I had looked forward to seeing Lee and Donald—partly out of curiosity; partly out of a notion that, once friends, we could find common ground; and partly, I guess, out of arrogance: Perhaps if I explained myself, I might be able to dent their certainty. I *did* want to explain myself. My tentative efforts were impatiently received by Donald. He parried everything I said with Scripture. Donald seemed genuinely to believe that people's motives were always clear to them.

"Did you know what you were doing when you were baptized?"

"But I was nine years old!"

"But did you *know* what you were doing?"

(My daughter, Anna, said later that it was like a TV game show: Donald was the moderator—with all the answers *and* all the questions—and I was the contestant.)

Donald grew clearly weary (my answers tended to be long). "Let's concentrate on immorality," he said.

My daughter settled herself in with a pleased anticipatory sigh. She had spent much of the previous week airing her opinions on abortion (pro) and open marriage (con), and she was eager, I could see, to engage herself in what she assumed would be a freewheeling discussion of morality and mores.

Donald said to his wife, the tone of his voice straightening Anna's spine, "Lee, I'd like you and Anna to leave the room. I'm sure Anna would like to show you her bedroom."

Anna, a dutiful hostess, departed as gracefully as thwarted curiosity would allow.

"I have asked the girls to leave so that if you wish to confide your immorality to me, you can do so privately. I will pray over you, if you like, so that the Lord's spirit may return to you."

When Anna returned, having stayed away for what she judged a decent interval, Donald was still discussing "rife immorality." Anna, grabbing her chance, offered, "Well, I kind of agree with you about immorality. I don't think anybody should fuck unless they really love each other."

Donald and Lee stood up to leave. Donald advised me that if I persisted in my course of action, I stood the risk of being disfellowshipped—like my friend Walter—"And then none of the Lord's people will ever be able to speak to you again."

Anna demanded, "You don't talk to *Walter*? But he's a good person. He's *nice.* That's not religion!"

Later she said, "They act pleasant. But they're not nice."

"Well, they're nice if you're one of them," I said.

"That's not nice," Anna said.

As Donald and Lee marched down the stairs, Donald called back over his shoulder, "Remember, we came here because we love you. We didn't come to spank you. We won't put in an official report on this. This was a friend-ship visit."

Three days later, Donald phoned. He proposed to visit with a committee of elders from the congregation to administer "spiritual discipline." I ac-quiesced almost hungrily. I had found my anger. And I wanted to know, What next?

I was convinced that this time they would inaugurate disfellowshipping procedures against me. I also felt that I needed protection, though I didn't know quite from what. I asked my brother if he would be with me when they came. My brother, though he wishes that I didn't feel compelled to write about the Witnesses, for our mother's sake, is absolutely decent and could not, furthermore, resist this "call upon the blood." He came and sat waiting, stern-faced, for whoever was to dare insult his sister. Donald came not with a committee of three, but with a single member of the headquar-ters staff. The agenda had been changed: no spiritual discipline, he said, just a talk. (Their motives and their actions were, and are, entirely obscure to me.) Donald asked my brother to leave the room. "Why do you need protection?" he asked. "What are you afraid of?"

My brother prevented me from having to answer. "I'm my sister's brother," he said, "and I'm not going anywhere. Anything my sister says, she says it to me too. Nothing she says could make me love her less. She's honest, she won't lie whether I'm here or not, and the two of you came together like two nuns, so I'm staying. Now what's your story?"

Donald offered a repeat of his previous performance. There were veiled hints of dire consequences if I did not "turn around and confess"; there was explicit spiritual blackmail: I would die at Armageddon. But Donald and his friend seemed to run out of energy; they began to talk about me in the third person, as if I weren't there. They started to preach to my brother.

He said, "Hey. You can't get my sister. So now you're hitting on me? Have some respect. You're in my sister's house."

They left. My brother and I looked at each other. "What was that all about?" he said. I said I had no idea.

The rules—games—are often obscure. A young friend of mine left the Witnesses and made absolutely clear to them her determination not to return. She sent a letter announcing her determination to the Watchtower Society—which didn't deign to reply—and another to her local congregation. She did receive a certified letter from the local congregation, regretting that she no longer wished to join with them in christian worship and indicating that they would respect her decision. The letter went on, however, to state that the congregation had been informed that she had indulged in certain indiscreet actions of an unchristian nature (and that they had witnesses), and wished to meet with her to discuss the matter, giving a date and place for the meeting and urging her to reply.

J. F. Rutherford, according to the records of the testimony in the Moyle case, thundered. Nathan H. Knorr's voice was rather thin, but pleasantly modulated, with an affecting timbre. He spoke with the practiced and prim voice of the headmaster who metes out reward and punishment dispassionately. It was a voice I learned, at Bethel, to dread, full of warm if fuzzy paternal concern one day, cold and razor-sharp the next, always rectitudinous. His rebukes were scathing. They came, as had Rutherford's, at mealtimes.

The morning bells woke us at 6:30. At 6:55, showered and dressed, we ran down the stairs to the basement dining hall. We sat at tables of ten. Our day began with tension and bustle. Breakfast, served briskly and efficiently by white-coated waiters, lasted ten minutes and was preceded by a discussion of the Bible text for the day. Knorr or, in his absence, a director of the Society called upon members of the "family" for comments on the text. Being late was a Bad Thing: four hundred sets of eyes turned upon you if you attempted to slide invisibly into your place. Absenting oneself from breakfast altogether was a Very Bad Thing. If you were not there when Knorr called upon you, it was a Terrible Thing. (I can remember "sleeping over"—a rare self-indulgence—no more than five times in three and a half years. On those occasions, I had breakfast at a cheap drugstore counter in the Heights; no other meals ever tasted as good. I drank coffee and ate sugary, doughy apple turnovers and looked around and thought wonderingly that this was the way other people lived all the time. I savored those few moments of anonymity.)

Sometimes, in addition to the discussion of the text, there was a harangue. (I remember the aroma of coffee brewing in the kitchen, the effort to look alert and intelligent when one was dopey with sleep and to arrange one's face muscles into an unrevealing mask.) We never, afterward, discussed among ourselves the justice of Knorr's attack; we avoided each other's eyes; there was no redress for the victim, no acquittal in a court of popular opinion.

The attack that stands out most vividly in my mind was one that was wrapped in an anti-Semitism that has infected the Watchtower Society since its beginning. In the Watchtower printery, and at the Bethel residence, we worked eight hours and forty minutes a day, five and a half days a week. We filled out time sheets daily at the factory, and there was no time allotted for coffee or rest breaks. An elderly Bethelite on my floor of the factory kept a small supply of chocolates and candies, which he sold to hungry workers at candy-store cost on an honor system; we dropped our nickels and dimes into a box while he was busy at his menial work. I suppose he made a few pennies' profit each day; and I suppose also that he was one of those who received no financial help from the outside, so that those pennies were important. I can't remember ever having heard him speak.

Knorr heard about the little enterprise and read the old man out, at great length, in public. He tied his attack to the fact that the man was a Jew. The Jews, Knorr asserted, had always been willful, penny-grubbing ingrates. Jehovah had chosen them precisely to show that such unappetizing raw material could be redeemed if they adhered to His laws. The candy seller was, Knorr said, demonstrating all the abysmal qualities that had led the Jews to kill Christ. And so on, for an hour, while I cringed. Part of the horror was in knowing that there was no one I could share it with, no one to whom I would or could protest; part of the horror was my guilt. My silence was complicitous.

We see the beginnings of the return of divine favor to fleshly Israel already manifested in the beginning of a turning away of their blindness and their prejudice against Christ Jesus, in the opening up of the land of promise and their expulsion from other lands, and also in the returning fruitfulness of Palestine itself. . . . Fleshly Israel, recovered from blindness, shall be used as a medium through whom the streams of salvation, issuing from the glorified, spiritual Israel, shall flow to all the families of the earth.—SS, Vol. III (1891), pp. 293, 307

Nothing in the return of the Jews to Palestine and the setting up of the Israeli republic corresponds with Bible prophecies concerning the restoration of Jehovah's name-people to his favor and organization.—LGBT, rev. ed., 1952, pp. 213–18

In 1911, Charles Taze Russell returned from a trip around the world to a great ovation in the New York Hippodrome, where he was acclaimed by thousands of New York Jews. Russell supported the Jews' return to Palestine. He saw the Jews as God's instruments. But even as he proclaimed that Israel would be the medium of salvation, he commented on the "unchanged physiognomy of Jews," their hooked noses, and talked with scarcely con-

cealed contempt of their supposed predilections: "Among the relics of antiquity that have come down to our day, there is no other object of so great
interest as the Jewish people. . . . The national characteristics of many centuries ago are still prominent, even to their fondness for the leeks and onions and garlic of Egypt, and their stiff-necked obstinacy." [*SS* III, pp. 243–
44]

Russell believed that the pogroms and the persecution of the Jews were
inspired by God (for their own good and for the ultimate glory of mankind);
and he believed also that a disproportionate number of Jews are blessed
with the ability to score worldly and financial success. [*Ibid.*, pp. 270–71]

Russell had proclaimed that "the deliverance of fleshly Israel" was due to
take place before 1914: "The re-establishment of Israel in the land of Palestine is one of the events to be expected in this day of the Lord." [*Ibid.*, p.
244] The year 1881, he believed, marked the time for "the turning back of
special light upon the long-blinded Jews." [p. 278] "Restitution," he wrote,
would begin in Palestine: "Abraham, Isaac, and Jacob, with Daniel and all
the holy prophets, will be made perfect—awakened from death to perfect
manhood, after the Gospel Church has been glorified; and they will constitute the 'princes in all the earth,' the earthly and visible representatives of
the Christ." [p. 265] He claimed to have it on the authority of missionaries
that since 1878, unprecedented "showers and dews in summer" had blessed
the Holy Land, preparing it for the influx of Jews, who were "buying land,
planting and building, and getting possession of the trade of the city . . .
many of them . . . rising to distinction far beyond their Gentile neighbors."
[pp. 265–66] Jews had been propelled to Palestine by persecution in Russia
and Germany, which had been "permitted" by God: "God has permitted
. . . afflictions and persecutions to come as a penalty for their national
crime of rejection of the gospel and crucifixion of the Redeemer. He will
. . . in due time reward the constancy of their faith in his promises. . . .
God foreknew their pride and hardness of heart. . . . Within the present
century a sifting and separating process is manifest among them, dividing
them into two classes, the Orthodox and the Non-orthodox Jews." The
Non-orthodox Jews, Russell declaimed, were "losing faith in a personal
God . . . drifting toward liberalism, rationalism, infidelity. The Orthodox
include most of the poor, oppressed Jews, as well as some of the wealthy
and learned, and are vastly more numerous than the Non-orthodox; though
the latter are by far the more influential and respected, often bankers, merchants, editors, etc." [p. 248]

Horrified equally by rich Jews and the specters of socialism and anarchism, that triple threat, as he saw it, could be eradicated by a simple
expedient: "Not until further persecutions shall have driven more of the
poorer Jews to Palestine, and modern civilization shall be still further advanced there, will the wealthier classes of Jews be attracted thither; and

then it will be in great measure from selfish motives—when the general and great time of trouble shall render property less secure in other lands than it is now. Then Palestine, far away from socialism and anarchism, will appear to be a haven of safety to the wealthy Jews." A singularly nasty vision, nor did it come to pass quite as Russell foretold. The Jews did not accept Christ as their Savior; and so, once again, the Watchtower Society had to modify its theology to accommodate external realities: By 1952, the Witnesses had changed their opinions, and Russell's fantasies had been put to rest: "Many Jewish leaders believe the Bible supports their being regathered a second time to their 'Holy Land of Palestine,' " the Witnesses were told (they were not told that Russell had shared and promulgated that belief). "Failing to see that spiritual Israel has become the heir to God's promises, they do not appreciate that the . . . fulfillment [of prophecy] applies to the 'Israel of God,' made up of those Jews, inwardly spiritual Israelites, who came out from captivity to this Babylonish world. . . . Israel's applying for admission into the United Nations and her accepting membership in that worldly body which assumes to take the place of Messiah's rule is a flat rejection of God's kingdom of the heavens." [*LGBT*, pp. 213–18]

It's an old and wicked story. The oppressed are blamed for their oppression: "To this day the natural circumcised Jews are suffering the sad consequences from the works of darkness that were done within their nation nineteen hundred years ago. This illustrates what can happen to a whole nation that comes under the influence of that unseen superhuman intelligence, Satan the Devil." [*TW*, Nov. 1, 1975, p. 654]

I had grown up in the gross and painful experience of casual anti-Semitism. By the time I was 15, I could no longer countenance it. I fell in love with a Jew. Arnold was my teacher—English 31J, New Utrecht High School. I occasionally visit that place just to look at it—a prisonlike building so bleak and unlikely that miraculously provided me with the essential person, the person who taught me how to love, and how to doubt.

If, before I met and loved Arnold, I felt that life was a tightrope, I felt afterward that my life was lived perpetually on a high wire with no safety net. I was obliged, by every tenet, to despise him. To be "yoked with an unbeliever," an atheist, and an intellectual . . . the pain was exquisite.

Arnold became interested in me because I was smart; he loved me because he thought I was good. He nourished and nurtured me. He paid me the irresistible compliment of totally comprehending me. He hated my religion, but he loved *me*. I had never before been loved unconditionally. He came, unbidden, to sit with me at every school assembly and hold my hand while everyone else stood to salute the flag. We were highly visible, and I was very much comforted. And this was during the McCarthy era. Arnold had a great deal to lose, and he risked it for me. Nobody had ever risked anything for me before. How could I believe he was wicked?

We drank malteds on his porch and read T. S. Eliot and listened to Mozart. We walked for hours, talking of God and goodness and happiness and death. We met surreptitiously. (My mother so feared and hated the man who was leading me into apostasy that she once threw a loaf of Arnold's Bread out the window; his very name was loathsome to her.) Arnold treated me with infinite tenderness; he was the least alarming man I had ever known. His fierce concentration on me, his solicitous care uncoupled with sexual aggression, was the gentlest and most thrilling love I had ever known. He made me feel what I had never felt before—valuable and good.

It was very hard. All my dreams centered around Arnold, who was becoming more important, certainly more real, to me than God. All my dreams were blood-colored. I fantasized that Arnold was converted and survived Armageddon to live forever with me in the New World, or that I would die with Arnold, in fire and flames, at Armageddon. I would try to make bargains with God—my life for his. When I entered Bethel, I confessed my terrors to Nathan H. Knorr. I said that I knew I could not rejoice in the destruction of "the wicked" at Armageddon (Arnold would be among them). I was told that being a woman, and therefore weak and sentimental, I would have to go against my sinful nature and obey God's superior wisdom—which meant never seeing Arnold again.

I did see him again. I had no choice. We never exchanged more than a chaste and solemn kiss; but he claimed me. (I never told him I loved him—I thought the words would set the world off its axis—but of course he knew. He said to me once, "You are so terribly unpossessive." I never knew what he meant.) When I was with him, I felt as if I were in a state of grace.

To say that our relationship was ambiguous is to belittle it; I know now that he loved many men and women, and all of them thought of Arnold as singularly their own. (It has not happened, as it often does, that his death clarified his life. For all of us who loved him, he moves still, mysteriously, enigmatically, through our imaginations, never defined, grieved for still, always loved.) I tell myself that he loved no one more than he loved me.

When I left religion, Arnold alone wept.

When I walked out the door of Bethel for the last time, one of my fellow workers said, "But *why?*"

"Because God can't kill Arnold," I said.

VI. *In Transition*

Some day this man Russell will die, his corruption will be discovered, and his followers will be without a church, without a leader; they will have confidence in no man, and in the end will be a thousand times worse off than had they never heard the name Russell.—Sermon, Rev. J. J. Ross, Hamilton, Toronto, Canada, April 7, 1917

"Your dying and this work going on. Why, when you die we will all complacently fold our arms and wait to go to heaven with you. We will quit then."—A. H. Macmillan to C. T. Russell [*Faith*, p. 69]

On october 31, 1916, Charles Taze Russell died in a railway car outside Pampa, Texas. He was 64. Almost nothing he had foreseen had come to pass.

It is doubtful that the Witnesses could have survived the debacle of their dreams had not World War I come along to deliver them. The Great War, which saw the imprisonment of their leaders, and which temporarily put a halt to their work, was the instrument of their salvation. It allowed them to reinterpret Bible prophecy and to reassemble their chronological complexities; and it provided them with an external focus at a time when internal dissension threatened to decimate their ranks.

In 1912, the Watch Tower Society launched what was to have been a final effort to get people out of the established churches. Debates were frequently held with rival Protestant churches. (One opposition speaker said his opponent's methods reminded him of a sign over a blacksmith shop: "All kinds of twisting and turning here.") Traveling ministers called "colporteurs" were equipped with "Eureka Drama" outfits (recorded lectures and music); and special representatives rented halls and theaters to show a four-part "Photo-Drama Creation": stereopticon slides and primitive motion pictures, prepared at a cost of $300,000, were synchronized with recorded lectures and music to provide potential converts with a panoramic view of human history, past and future, starting with Creation and ending with the 1,000-year reign of Christ. "The unfolding of a flower and hatching of a chick were among the memorable features . . . there was an accompaniment of very fine music, such gems as Narcissus and Humoresque." [*Yearbook*, 1975, pp. 59–60]

The Watchtower Society is now highly bureaucratized, but "C. T. Russell," according to A. H. Macmillan, "had no idea of building a strongly knit organization. . . . We saw no need for it. We expected 1914 would mark the end of this system of things on earth. Our big concern . . . was to preach as effectively and extensively as possible before that date arrived. In the meantime, we thought, we must prepare ourselves individually to go to heaven." [*Faith*, p. 44]

The hysteria induced by these expectations was released at "love feasts" at the conventions for which railway cars were hired to transport the Bible Students. Leaders lined up in front of the speakers' platform as Russellites filed along, shaking hands, partaking of diced communion bread, singing "Blest Be the Tie That Binds Our Hearts in Christian Love." They wept tears of joy. Such minor raptures no longer take place among the disciplined and regimented Witnesses, but they were commonplace then. They expected, then, to be united in a perpetual love feast in heaven; and they thought their reward was imminent.

On September 30, 1914, Elder Macmillan told an ecstatic convention audience in California: "This is probably the last public address I shall ever deliver, because we shall be going home soon." [*Ibid.*, p. 47]

On October 2, 1914, Charles Taze Russell entered the Bethel dining room. "The Gentile Times have ended, their kings have had their day," he rumbled. "Anyone disappointed? I'm not. Everything is moving right on schedule." [*Yearbook*, 1975, p. 73]

Thirty-six years previously, in 1878, a small band of Russellites had had to explain why they had not *then* been taken to heaven, since 1874 had marked the beginning of Christ's invisible presence in the spiritual "Temple of Jerusalem" and the economic panic of 1873 had been the first death spasm of a dying world. Once again, in 1914, they found themselves having to account for failure. In 1879, Russell had predicted that an international nihilist-Communist-anarchist uprising would begin early in 1914 and that this period of turbulence would be followed, on October 2, 1914, by the establishment of God's kingdom on earth and the calling of the "living saints" to glory.

When this did not happen, many of Russell's followers, according to his apologists, "grew sour" and left the organization. Those who remained explained: "The mistake C. T. Russell had made . . . was not as to the time, 1914, but his error was only as to *where* the Kingdom had been established—in heaven instead of on earth." [*Faith*, p. 60] World War I was the sign of the Devil's displeasure, and his death throes. He had been booted out of the heavens, where hitherto he had had free access to the angels in the courts of the Lord, and he was now stalking the earth: "We learned that Jesus, enthroned in heaven [in 1914], had immediately begun his war on Satan and his demon associates in heaven. Satan and his demons, those rebel spirit creatures associated with him, had been whipped and hurled to the earth, never to return to heaven. The Scriptures stated this event was to mark the beginning of a time of unparalleled trouble in the earth." [*Ibid.*, p. 59]

That the final collapse, and the final glory, had not occurred in 1914 was proof of God's beneficence: "Had Jehovah's great warrior, the Lord Jesus, continued the assault against Satan and his angels after that first skirmish which dusted those rebels from heaven, . . . no flesh would have been saved. So, for the sake of God's own people, and to fulfill his purpose, Jehovah 'cut short' those days of tribulation against the invisible rebel spirits by stopping his war for a period before . . . Armageddon," so that Jesus' prophecy—" 'This good news of the Kingdom will be preached in all the inhabited earth for the purpose of a witness to all the nations, and then the accomplished end will come' "—might be fulfilled. [*Ibid.*, pp. 59–60]

This new interpretation paved the way for an intensive proselytizing campaign, which obliged the Witnesses to begin work on a new theology: Before 1914, they had been concerned only with their heavenly destiny, the "harvesting of the saints." Now there began the evolution of a new idea, determined by altered circumstances. A handful of living saints would be called to heaven immediately upon their death; but a great number of as-yet-unredeemed worldlings would be given the opportunity to live forever on a cleansed and perfect earth.

And they scourged themselves for "independent thinking and private interpretation": "While we were all looking forward to 1914 and the end of wickedness and sorrow on the earth, many of us were thinking more of our own personal, individual 'change' than anything else. Perhaps some of us had been a bit too hasty in thinking that we were going to heaven right away, and the thing for us to do would be to keep busy in the Lord's service until he determined when any of his approved servants would be taken home to heaven." [*Ibid.*, pp. 47–48] But this did not preclude their complaining about nonbelievers. "As 1914 passed, then 1915 and 1916, the reproach heaped upon us increased. In our effort to discern the meaning of Bible prophecy before the expected events had actually occurred . . . some partially inaccurate public expressions were made. When these minor details did not develop, the more important major fulfillment that actually did occur was entirely overlooked by those lacking full faith in God's word." (They were also overlooked by weary thousands who ceased, after 1914, to associate themselves with an organization they believed had betrayed their trust.) "Instead of viewing the increasing number of facts, actual events, piling up world-wide from day to day since 1914 as undeniable proof of the correctness of the marked date publicized by the Watch Tower from 1879, scoffers seized upon some minor point of Russell's writings to ridicule and mock." [*Ibid.*, pp. 55–56]

Governments were reproached for not "surrendering their power" to the invisible Kingdom of God and for vesting their hopes instead in "the beast with seven heads"—the League of Nations.

The following exchange of letters is interesting for what it reveals about Witnesses who begin to ask hard questions and receive evasive answers.

> The inference is made . . . that the leaders of all nations should have "hailed and accepted" the kingdom, and that if they did so they would "hand over the imperial sovereignty to Jesus Christ." It is a serious matter for a national sovereign . . . to turn over that sovereignty to someone else. Was there sufficient information known in 1914 and was it absolutely clear enough to cast every shadow of a doubt from the minds of world leaders that Christ would begin his reign then so that they could take the heavy responsibility, without even having a plebiscite among their subjects, of turning over their sovereignty to some other ruler? And if this was known, definitely and without doubt of any kind (which is the kind of information a responsible ruler would have to have in order to take such a drastic step), what specific steps would the rulers have taken in order to do so? Would a king just drop everything and go to his home in the country? Would the legislature adjourn? Would the men in the treasury work no more and walk off the job?—Letter from Walter Szykitka, former headquarters worker, to Watchtower Bible and Tract Society, March 1, 1962

In answer to Szykitka's letter, the Society pointed out that in 1914 the rule of the Kingdom and the "end of Gentile Times" had been proclaimed throughout the world, but the Christian churches and heads of state had ignored the message. Since they did not follow the biblical rules for pure Christianity in getting their affairs in order, they found themselves embroiled in the First World War, a war in which the goal was domination rather than bringing about the rule of the Kingdom of God.

While governments refused to permit the King to take over their functions, Russell moved to conciliate. He had prepared the way for the failure of his prophecies:

> There surely is room for slight differences of opinion . . . and it behooves us to grant each other the widest latitude. The lease of power to the Gentiles may end in October 1914 or in October 1915. And the period of intense strife and anarchy . . . may be the final ending of the Gentile Times or the beginning of Messiah's reign.
>
> But we remind all our readers again, that we have not prophesied anything about the Times of the Gentiles closing in a time of trouble nor about the glorious epoch which will shortly follow that catastrophe. We have merely pointed out what the Scriptures say, giving our views respecting their meaning and asking our readers to judge, each for himself, what they signify. *These prophecies still read the same to us.*

. . . However *some* may make positive statements of what they know, and of what they do not know, *we never indulge in this;* but we merely state that we believe thus and so, for such and such reasons. [*TWT*, 1912, p. 377; quoted in *JWDP*, p. 53]

In November, 1914, a month after the Russellites' dreams of glory had been dashed:

Just how long after the Gentile Times close will be the revealment in "flaming fire" we do not know. . . . How long would this period be, in which present institutions will be ousted, and the present order of things be condemned and done away with, to make way for the Reign of Righteousness? We answer that . . . we might expect a transition to run on a good many years. [*TWT*, 1914, p. 327]

He left the time of "transition" open-ended; and this gave his followers the out they so desperately required. (And the war came along fortuitously, so that the Witnesses are able to point to 1914 as a marked date and to attach their prophecies to it, never mind that they were wrong in all particulars.)

In December, 1914, Russell wrote, with a mixture of pathos and bravado: "Even if the time of our change should not come within ten years, what more should we ask? Are we not a blessed, happy people? Is not our God faithful? If anyone knows anything better, let him take it. If any of you ever find anything better, we hope you will tell us." [*Ibid.*, p. 377]

If anyone knows better, let him take it. That, of course, is one of the keys to the survival of the organization Russell founded on soft mysticism, glorious visions, and worldly disaffection. The Witnesses had nowhere else to go. Their investment in their religion was total; to leave it would have meant spiritual and emotional bankruptcy. They were not equipped to function in a world without certainty. It was their life. To leave it would be a death.

(There was, when I was at Bethel, an old man, Brother Thorn, well into his 80s. He had lived through these times of promise and defeat, and his response to the vagaries of prophesying was, "Whenever I get to thinking a great deal of myself, I take myself into the corner, so to speak, and say, 'You little speck of dust. What have you got to be proud of?' " By the time I knew Thorn, who had been a colporteur in Russell's day, he was in advanced senility. One of my jobs was to clean the bathtub for the thirty men who lived on the first floor of the Bethel residence. Not infrequently, I would walk into the bathroom, having knocked to make sure none of the men was using the facilities, and find Thorn sitting on the toilet, his trousers draped around his ankles, nodding and beaming like a Buddha and welcoming me as if to a revival meeting: "Good morning, sister. God bless you." What a sad and inglorious end for a man who had expected to be raised to glory in 1914. But he was happy, and sweet—this "speck of dust" who was nothing without his God and his dreams.)

Russellites had endured scandal, the disapprobation of the world; they had cut themselves off from the world. They had been delivered from the staleness of the world to visions of glory; and they could not desert one another, or that vision of hope.

It is not to be supposed, however, that grumblings had not been heard among Russellites before the Pastor's death. Some Bible Students were growing weary. Russell had reproved potential rivals, who might have been forgiven for feeling that they could do at least as well as he at dates, and dampened individual inquiry as early as 1909: "From various quarters, the word came to us that the leaders of the [Bible] classes were protesting that Watch Tower publications should not be referred to in the meetings, but merely the Bible. This sounded loyal to God's word; but it was not so. It was merely the effort of these teachers to come between the people of God and the *Divinely provided light*." [*TWT*, 1909, p. 371 (italics original); quoted in *JWDP*, p. 46]

There is some evidence to suggest that Russell's control of his organization was eroding during the last three years of his life. Up to 1913, as majority shareholder of the Watch Tower Bible and Tract Society of Pennsylvania, he was able to control elections, having bought, by varied estimates, $250,000 to $300,000 of voting shares at $10 apiece. After 1913, the number of votes smaller shareholders had bought outnumbered Russell's. [Cole, pp. 60–69; *JWDP*, p. 64] Russell, by the time of his death, had less than one-fifth of the voting shares. The work of the Society, A. H. Macmillan told the *Brooklyn Eagle* [Nov. 28, 1916], had been for several years "largely in the hands of his lieutenants."

Russell's will bequeathed "merely love and Christian good wishes" to his flock and $200 to Maria Russell. He had made no provision for a successor, and the Society's vice-president, A. I. Ritchie, did not automatically succeed to the presidency, although Macmillan told *Eagle* reporters that he had little doubt Ritchie would be elected; Macmillan denied that J. F. Rutherford, then the Society's legal counsel, had a shot at the presidency. Under the provisions of the Society's charter, the board of directors was to handle its affairs until the next election, which was scheduled to be held in Pittsburgh on January 6, 1917. From October 31, 1916, to January 6, 1917, a board-appointed executive committee (composed of Rutherford, secretary-treasurer Van Amburgh, and Ritchie) directed the affairs of the Society; Macmillan, who was not a member of the Pennsylvania board, served as administrative aide.

It was a time of intense politicking, electioneering, maneuvering, manipulation, conspiracies, and dissension.

One of the bones of contention in the power struggle was A. H. Macmillan. Macmillan claims that shortly before Russell left on his final tour, he "wrote letters to . . . the heads of different departments, . . . informing them that 'A. H. Macmillan is to be in full charge of the office and the Bethel Home during my absence. Anything he says for you to do you must do; it doesn't make any difference whether you agree or not. If he tells you incorrectly, I'll attend to him when I get home.' " [*Faith*, p. 70]

Russell never got home. A majority of the members of the board was opposed to Macmillan's stewardship, and they were left to fight it out among themselves. Macmillan lost no time exercising his prerogatives. His story is that "a few ambitious ones at headquarters were holding caucuses here and there, doing a little electioneering to get their men in. However, Van Amburgh and I held a large number of votes. Many shareholders, knowing of our long association with Russell, sent their proxies to us to be cast for the one whom we thought best fitted for office"— J. F. Rutherford. [*op. cit.*, p. 68] Four members of the seven-man board of directors vigorously opposed Rutherford's presidency.

In this they were supported by P. S. L. Johnson, a traveling minister whom Russell had sent to England to preach to the troops. Johnson, who arrived in England in November, 1916, and immediately contrived to seize control of the Society's London bank account, is described as "a Jew who had forsaken Judaism to become a Lutheran minister before he came to a knowledge of the truth" and as a man whose "brilliance led to his downfall." [*JWDP*, p. 69] He is clearly seen as a kind of Lucifer. After his dismissal from headquarters, Johnson attempted unsuccessfully to form a sect of his own. He believed until his death that he was the world's high priest and Russell's legitimate successor. (If Bible Students needed any further evidence that Jews and intellectuals were tricksters to be abhorred, Johnson provided them with it.)

On January 6, 1917, Joseph Franklin Rutherford was elected second president of the Watch Tower Bible and Tract Society. The Lord, it was said, had chosen the right man for the job, though many of the headquarters staff evinced an intense antipathy for Rutherford, a wintry-bleak man whose personality could not have been more unlike that of the passionate Pastor, whose fires burned hot, and warmed when they did not scald.

In the spring of 1917, simmering opposition to Rutherford erupted when four directors of the Pennsylvania Society, at an extended session of the annual meeting, attempted to present a resolution amending the bylaws to place administrative powers in the hands of the board. Rutherford won this skirmish effortlessly—he simply ruled the motion out of order. Opposition stiffened, but did not prevail. The four dissenting directors were disposed of handily: as they were attempting to gather a five-man quorum in the Society's Brooklyn Hicks Street office, Macmillan called the cops to evict them. According to his folksy account, "an old Irishman, a typical old fellow . . . came in twirling a long nightstick around in his hand. 'Gentlemen,' he said to the four directors, 'it's after being serious for you now. Faith, and I know . . . Macmillan, but you fellows I don't know. Now you better be after going for fear there'll be trouble.' " After the friendly policeman's performance, the men thus warned, Macmillan says, grabbed their hats, tripped down the stairs, and fled to Borough Hall to get a lawyer. [*Faith*, pp. 79–80]

They could have saved themselves the bother. Through no fault of their own, they were not legally members of the board of directors. Russell had appointed them directors for life; but the law stipulated that they had to be elected by vote of the shareholders each year. Rutherford, having been elected to office, was by law a director, as were his two allies on the board, who had been elected vice-president and secretary-treasurer. Rutherford simply booted his enemies out, and took it upon himself to appoint sympathetic directors to fill the vacancies until the next corporation election in 1918.

Russell's autocratic heedlessness of the law had paid off handsomely for his successor. A legal lapse had altered the history of the Watch Tower Society.

Members of the headquarters staff who supported the dissident directors were more difficult to subdue. Their simmering resentment of Rutherford's and Macmillan's highhandedness erupted in the summer of 1917, when Rutherford, at a midday Bethel meal, presented each member of "the family" with a book called *The Finished Mystery*. This seventh volume of *Studies in the Scriptures*, which consisted of commentaries on Revelation, the Song of Solomon, and Ezekiel, was termed "the posthumous work of Pastor Russell." Headquarters workers fiercely challenged Rutherford's assertion that the volume had been assembled from notes prepared by Russell. For four or five hours they rioted in the dining hall, loudly denouncing Rutherford, shaking their fists at him, and using hard rolls as missiles.

The dissidents were eventually forced out of Bethel; some of them embarked on extensive speaking and letter-writing campaigns throughout the United States, Canada, and Europe. As a result, congregations of Bible Students were split into opposing factions, those loyal to Rutherford and those who thought he had desecrated the memory of their beloved Pastor and refused to accept his authority. There were bitter divisions among families: Bible Students who remained faithful to Rutherford were able to harden their hearts against their families by meditating on the fact that if Jesus deemed their fathers or their mothers or their sisters and brothers worthy of "the second death" it would be unbecoming of them to mourn; Christ had come to bring not peace, but a sword.

It is estimated by Watchtower sources that one-fifth of the Bible Students defected from the Society between 1917 and 1919. [*Yearbook*, 1975, pp. 93–94]

When I was a young member, Witnesses who had lived through their civil war still spoke of these turncoats with horror and fascination. They scratched away at their sores with a passion that bespoke animal fear—as if somehow those "disobedient ones" could reach down through the years and drag them into the terrible abyss of separation from their God.

The Watchtower Society is, in its strength, not loath now to publicize the internal problems that beset it during the World War. The Society is able, after all, to point to its continued existence; it has prospered, while opposition has foundered. To an unbelieving eye, it might seem apparent that craftiness and wheeling-dealing had won the day, and that legal loopholes and disappointed hopes determined the course of the Watch Tower Society from 1914 to 1918. As far as the Witnesses are concerned, however, this chapter in their history is, once more, a fulfillment of Bible prophecy: Christ had come to the Temple to judge his people in 1918. This was, they say, "a weeding out, a time of judgment, a cleansing of the entire organization" [*Faith*], a "sifting" that was inevitable in view of Jesus' having told his disciples that he would cast the "evil servant" out, and in view of Malachi's having said that God would "purify the sons of Levi."

"The man was not important. The message was." That became a popular catchphrase after Russell's death. During Rutherford's incumbency, a subtle but calculated shift took place to ensure that the Society would never again founder on the shoals of personal loyalties, nor would overwhelming admiration attach to "personalities." Russell had been regarded—had, indeed, regarded himself—as Ezekiel's "man with the inkhorn, marking the foreheads of people"; it is said that when he was asked, "Who is 'the faithful and wise servant' to whom Jesus gave stewardship of his spiritual wealth?" he replied, "Some say I am; while others say the Society is." [*Ibid.*, p. 126] His answer was Jesuitical, evasive: for all practical purposes, Russell had been the Society. Few men have believed so entirely in their own manifest destiny. Rutherford lost no time reinterpreting Matthew 24:45–47: "The faithful and wise servant," he said, was not a man, but a *class*, a "composite servant"—the Watch Tower Bible and Tract Society. No matter what its vicissitudes, it was this organization God had chosen; no man's personal peccadilloes or eccentricities or errors of judgment could alter that. The organization would, in perpetuity, be the "channel" for God's light. Russell had emphasized "character development," which meant, in effect, the careful cultivation of individual style and the enlargement of individual personality; Rutherford was to emphasize organizational and legal development, which led to the subduing of individual personalities and resulted in the development of a vast army of organization men and women. Collectively, Bible Students conducted themselves in ways that outraged the sensibilities of the conservative religious community—Rutherford's slogan "Religion Is a Snare and a Racket" was not designed to appease—but individually they reined in their personalities. This is a process that reached its completion under the presidency of Nathan H. Knorr, a consummate organization man. Witnesses are now virtually indistinguishable one from another (to the outsider, that is); and the spice of differences is thought to be as deadly as the sting of the asp.

Rutherford—six feet tall, hazel-eyed, portly and senatorial in appearance—permitted himself affectations in dress and demeanor. In the 1940s, he wore old-fashioned stand-up collars and a little black antebellum string tie, he sported a long black ribbon from which dangled a monocle, and he frequently carried a cane. But under his leadership, the organization became monolithic, and proselytizing techniques became uniform and highly structured. The days of fiery individualism were over. (Russell was fire; Rutherford was acid and ice; Knorr was rock, and gray.)

Joseph Franklin Rutherford was born on November 8, 1869, to James and Lenore Strickland Rutherford on their farm in Morgan County, Missouri. Little is known of his early life; Watchtower historians, in an effort to explain away what they call his "blunt" manner—his tattered humanity and his notorious insensitivity to other people's feelings—say that "his father was a strict disciplinarian, which deprived young Rutherford of any emotional life." [*Ibid.*, p. 73] When he was 20, he became official reporter for the courts of the Fourteenth Judicial District in Missouri; at 22, he was admitted to the bar. He practiced trial law in Boonville, Missouri, for fifteen years, campaigning briefly for William Jennings Bryan. His enemies, among them Father Coughlin, frequently ridiculed him for appropriating the title "Judge" to himself. His followers, leaping to his defense, protested that he had sat as a substitute judge in Missouri's Fourteenth Judicial District "on more than one occasion." It is probably safe to assume that the title was one of those Southern honorifics conferred upon anyone of any distinction at all (in Boonville, a very small pond, it cannot have been too hard to be a big fish).

The "judge" was introduced to the teachings of the Bible Students when a traveling colporteur brought him a copy of *Millennial Dawn*. Thereafter he and his wife, Mary, began to hold Bible classes in their home. He was baptized in 1906. In 1907, he became the Watch Tower Society's legal counsel in Pittsburgh; in 1909, he moved to the Society's new headquarters in Brooklyn and was admitted to the New York Bar; on May 24, 1909, he was admitted to practice before the U.S. Supreme Court.

Rutherford is said to have been skeptical of his ability to preach until one day he chanced upon a group of "colored men" in a field and, exercising Southern *droit de seigneur*, proceeded to lecture the field hands on Life, Death, and the Hereafter. His captive audience gratified him with choruses of "Praise the Lord, Judge!" A Missouri epiphany: From that moment, Rutherford never looked back.

Little is known of Rutherford's wife, Mary, and his son Malcolm. The

Judge seems to have lived a compartmentalized life, the private person and the public person never merging, as they did so spectacularly in the person of Charles Taze Russell.

Rutherford was 48 when he was elected president of the Watch Tower Society, a position he was to hold for twenty-four years, until his death in 1942.

Hostile encounters have not infrequently been experienced by marginal religious movements, whether with the law or with public opinion, or, most often, with both simultaneously. . . . A study of these encounters . . . reveals that in every case the tension is a function not of the group's theological beliefs, no matter how alien they appear to be, but of positions or practices which threaten or entrench upon strongly held national secular values. When, by reason of change either in the group's position or in national secular norms, the threat disappears or becomes manageable, the legitimization of the group and its acceptance by the general community are practically automatic and generally simultaneous. —Leo Pfeffer, "The Limitation of Marginal Religions in the United States," Z&L, pp. 14–15

In June, 1917, six months after Rutherford became Watch Tower president, Congress passed the Espionage Act, laying heavy penalties on all persons who interfered with mobilization of military forces. The Sedition Act of 1918 was an even more severe measure to suppress war criticism. Dissenters were often arrested without warrants, hauled off to jail, and held incommunicado without bail. Prejudicial courts sentenced war critics to extraordinarily long prison terms: one adolescent girl was given twenty years. There were government listeners and informers everywhere. Intelligence agencies of the departments of War, Navy, and State employed amateur as well as professional detectives to collect information on citizens.

The Witnesses' accounts of their travails during World War I reflect a parochialism. They view Rutherford's conviction on the charge of espionage and his nine-month imprisonment in the Atlanta penitentiary as proof of a special relationship with God; they ignore the fact that clergymen of all denominations were sent to prison—sometimes for doing nothing more than reading the Sermon on the Mount.

Although Watchtower publications now lambaste the rest of the clergy for their chauvinism during the Great War, Bible Students were themselves divided on the question of neutrality. Russell's personal representative delivered words of comfort to troops before they went off to the trenches. Many Bible Students, in the absence of a clear directive from the Society, fought at the front; others served in the Army Medical Corps.

Rutherford disclaimed any responsibility for those of his followers who resisted conscription; defending himself against the charge of sedition, he said that his advice had been simply to suggest that if they could not, in conscience, take part in war, the Draft Act allowed them to apply for exemption. He insisted that he had always advised the Bible Students to conform with the law of the State provided it did not conflict with a higher law.

In order to curb the excesses of wartime hysteria, members of the Congress had introduced the "France Amendment" to the Espionage Law. The amendment provided exemption from prosecution for any person who uttered "what is true, with good motives, and for justifiable ends." In a successful effort to defeat the France Amendment, the Attorney General said:

> Experience teaches that such an amendment would to a large degree nullify the value of the law and turn every trial into an academic debate on insoluble riddles as to what is true. Human motives are too complicated to be discussed, and the word "justifiable" is too elastic for practical use. . . .
>
> One of the most dangerous examples of . . . propaganda is the book called *The Finished Mystery*, a work written in extremely religious language and distributed in enormous numbers. The only effect of it is to lead soldiers to discredit our cause and to inspire a feeling at home of resistance to the draft. . . .
>
> The International Bible Students' Association pretends to the most religious motives, yet we have found that its headquarters have long been reported as the resort of German agents. . . .
>
> The passage of this amendment would greatly weaken American efficiency and help none but the enemy.—*Congressional Record*, May 4, 1918

Passage of the Espionage Act was a disastrous blow to civil liberties, and the Watch Tower Society was caught, as were so many others, in its net. Intelligence agents were disabused of the idea that dismantled radio equipment found in the Society's Brooklyn headquarters had been used to transmit broadcasts to the enemy; nevertheless, warrants for the arrest of Rutherford, Secretary-Treasurer Van Amburgh, A. H. Macmillan, and five members of the *Watch Tower* editorial committee were issued by the U.S. District Court for the Eastern District of New York on May 7, 1918. They were arraigned in Federal Court. A grand jury returned an indictment charging them with "unlawfully, feloniously and wilfully causing and attempting to cause insubordination, disloyalty and refusal of military duty in the military and naval forces of the United States of America, in, through and by personal solicitations, letters, public speeches, distribution and public circulation throughout the United States of America of a certain book called 'Volume Seven—*Scripture Studies—The Finished Mystery*'; and . . . obstructing the recruiting and enlistment service of the United States when the United States was at war." Rutherford, Van Amburgh, Macmillan, and R. J. Martin (one of the compilers of *The Finished Mystery*) were also charged with trading with the enemy. (Funds deposited in the Society's

Zurich bank account were alleged to have been earmarked for Germany.) The defendants were released on bail; on May 15, 1918, appearing before Judge Harland B. Howe, they pleaded not guilty to all charges. [*Yearbook*, 1975, pp. 104–05]

The trial lasted fifteen days. Outside, soldiers marched and clergymen stood on corners reading the Lord's Prayer. The defendants testified that they had never conspired to affect the draft or to interfere with the Government's prosecution of the war; that they had never had any intention of interfering in any manner with the war; that their work was wholly religious and not political; that they had never advised or encouraged anyone to resist the draft, but merely offered advice to conscientious objectors; that they were not opposed to the nation's going to war but that, as dedicated Christians, they could not themselves engage in mortal combat.

On June 20, 1918, after deliberating for four and a half hours, a jury returned a verdict of guilty. Seven defendants were sentenced to eighty years in the penitentiary (twenty years each on four counts, to run concurrently), and one defendant, Giovanni DeCecca, was sentenced to forty years (ten years on each of the same four counts). Friends and families of the convicted men sang "Blessed Be the Tie That Binds" in the Marshal's Office of the Brooklyn Federal Court. Rutherford proclaimed, "This is the happiest day of my life. To serve earthly punishment for the sake of one's religious belief is one of the greatest privileges a man could have." [*Ibid.*, p. 108. Reported in New York *Tribune*, June 22, 1918]

He had, however, gone to great lengths to avoid the "privileges" of earthly punishment. The Society had seriously compromised itself. The Bible Students wished to receive accolades for their neutrality as they also declared their unswerving loyalty to the United States Government: "We are not against the Government in any sense of the word. We recognize the Government of the United States as the best government on earth. We recognize that governments, being political and economic institutions, have the power and authority, under the fundamental law, to declare war and to draft their citizens." [*TWT*, 1917, p. 6221] Watch Tower leaders had conferred with government authorities and agreed to delete objectionable portions of *The Finished Mystery*. They took the further step of advising colporteurs to halt distribution of the volume.

When none of this served to keep their leaders out of prison, the Bible Students, at a convention in Pittsburgh on January 2–5, 1919, unanimously passed a resolution attesting to "their loyalty to the government and people of these United States." They protested that their leaders had "technically violated" a "law they did not understand." [Souvenir Report of the Bible Students Convention, Pittsburgh, Pennsylvania, January 2–5, 1919, p. 37; see also *JWDP*, p. 85]

The Watch Tower instructed its readers to honor President Wilson's designation of May 30, 1918, as a day of national prayer and supplication for the success of the American war effort. [*TWT*, June 1, 1918] The Bible Students did not then, nor do the Witnesses now, call themselves pacifists.

About one thing, however, the Bible Students were unequivocal and absolutely certain: "Without a doubt, the prosecution . . . had been initiated by some nominal ecclesiastical adherents. The Bible's terrible arraignment of the Papacy . . . is quite probably the cause of . . . action against them." They saw themselves as victims of a conspiracy of clergymen. [*TWT*, 1917]

Without question some of the orthodox clergy were glad of an excuse to be rid of the Bible Students. (Upton Sinclair was extremely censorious of the clergy for not leaping to Rutherford's defense.) But with the end of the war, and a change in the national temper, opposition to the Bible Students ebbed. In February, 1919, liberal newspapers began to agitate for the release of the Society's president and his associates. More than 700,000 names were secured on a petition for their release. On March 2, 1919, the judge who had convicted them recommended "immediate commutation" of their sentences. In a letter to Attorney General Thomas W. Gregory, he said, "My principal purpose was to make an example, as a warning to others, and I believed that the President would relieve them after the war was over. . . . They did much damage and it may well be claimed they ought not to be set at liberty so soon, but as they cannot do any more harm now, I am in favor of being as lenient as I was severe in imposing sentence." [See *JWDP*, p. 86; *Yearbook*, 1975, p. 116]

On March 25, federal authorities, acting on the instruction of Supreme Court Justice Louis Brandeis, released the Society's leaders from the penitentiary on bail of $10,000 each, pending further trial. On April 14, 1919, in a hearing before the Federal Second Circuit Court of Appeals in New York, their convictions were reversed, and they were remanded for retrial: "The defendants in this case," Judge Ward ruled, "did not have the temperate and impartial trial to which they were entitled." [*Rutherford v. U.S.*, 258 F855, 863] The indictments were later dismissed, the government entering a motion of *nolle prosequi*. [See *JWDP*, p. 86]

Jehovah's Witnesses now acknowledge that they "did not," during World War I, "display the proper neutrality of the Christian." [*JWDP*, p. 92] This admission does not prevent them from railing against the clergy for behaving as they did. That the clergy were not pure means that they were the instrument of the Devil; the fact that the *Witnesses* were not pure is, they say, proof that God was using them to fulfill the prophecy of Revelation 11:2, 7: "And I will give power unto my two witnesses, and they shall prophesy a thousand two hundred and threescore days, clothed in sackcloth. And when they shall have finished their testimony, the beast that ascendeth out of the bottomless pit shall make war against them, and shall overcome them, and kill them." The period of "witnessing," or prophesying in sackcloth and ashes, they say, began during the first month of November, 1917; and the Devil's beastly political system warred against the symbolic "two witnesses" of God, eventually "killing" them—or killing their work of prophesying. In 1919, they became "spiritually alive" again, in fulfillment of the prophecy that the two witnesses should be resurrected.

The Witnesses claim on the one hand that they were victims of a devilish religious-political conspiracy and, on the other, that they were exiled from God's favor during the War, their own period of "spiritual bondage" having been "typified" by the Jews' languishment in captivity in Babylon.

Their spiritual error, as they later saw it, was to misread Romans 13:1: "Let every soul be subject unto the higher powers. For there is no power but of God: the powers that be are ordained of God." They, like the orthodox churches, had understood the Apostle Paul's words to apply to governmental authorities. Their error, they say, was in not recognizing that the "higher powers" were in fact Jehovah God and Christ Jesus (a construction difficult to make in the context of Paul's injunction to the Romans).

From 1929, up until the politically volatile '60s, the "higher powers," in contradistinction to the World War I interpretation, were stated to be God, Jesus, and the "theocratic organization" through which the Father and Son worked: "When [Paul] says, 'The Powers that be are ordained of God,' does he have any reference whatsoever to the Gentile nations of the earth? Is it not more reasonable that he directs his words exclusively to the powers possessed and exercised in God's organization, and not to those that are exercised in Satan's organization?" [*TWT*, 1929, p. 164] This reading of Paul's words prepared the way for their principled stand of absolute neutrality during World War II—by which time the organization, free of internal problems, had grown so strong it could withstand external pressures, indeed thrive on them. The Witnesses remained faithful to this interpretation until the early '60s, when it became necessary to differentiate themselves from war protestors and civil-rights agitators and to be regarded as bastions of "normalcy" in a world that trembled on the brink of massive social change.

As the Witnesses became less and less a threat to the established order and the status quo in America, they performed another 180-degree turn: in the 1960s, without apology or embarrassment and with their customary aplomb, they once again reversed themselves and pronounced human governmental authorities as the "higher powers."

> Jehovah God, though not originating them, has allowed man's governmental authorities to come into existence, and they continue to exist by his permission. . . . There being no reason for Christians to set themselves in opposition to an arrangement that God has permitted they have good reason to be in subjection to the superior authorities. Governmental rulers, though they may be corrupt personally, would not normally punish others for doing good.—*Aid*, p. 1560
> Every soul must "be in subjection to the superior authorities," for

> these constitute an arrangement of God and are an object of fear, not
> to the law-abiding, but to those who do bad deeds. Christians are to
> be in law-abiding subjection, not only on account of the fear of pun-
> ishment, but on account of Christian conscience, therefore paying
> their taxes, rendering their dues.—*All Scrip*, p. 207

And so they readopted the reading of Romans 13—the reading for which
they had once calumnized the clergy.

It is no accident that during the '60s, when war protestors sprang up like
dandelions and law-and-order was a rallying cry for the middle class, the
expansion-minded Witnesses, who were perceived by the establishment as
less of a threat than "hippies" or political radicals, received preferential
treatment from draft boards. (See Chapter VII.) They are an example of
social Darwinism: they have evolved; and they have survived.

*The year of 1925 is the year clearly set in the Bible for the judgment on the
Satanic order that now rules the world. The offer to live forever is made to you and
you need not die unless you repudiate it. The perfect food will make you eternal. You
men who are bald will be bald no longer. Your teeth will be restored to you. You
will be as beautiful as you were in your youth. The whole world will be as beautiful
as Prospect Park in Spring.*—Judge Rutherford, 1921

*The kingdom of heaven is at hand; the King reigns; Satan's empire is falling;
millions now living will never die. . . . This is the day of all days. Behold, the King
reigns! You are his publicity agents. Therefore advertise, advertise, advertise, the
King and his kingdom!*—Judge Rutherford, Cedar Point, Ohio, 1922 [*TWT*,
1922, pp. 335–37]

In the calm that followed the storms of war, the Bible Students—the
release of their leaders had acted on them like a shot of adrenaline—were
mobilized by Rutherford to form an army of "Kingdom advertisers." Canvassers fanned out across the nation; sound trucks jarred the Sunday peace
in towns and in the country, blasting Rutherford's denunciations of the
churches. The "pastoral work" Russell had initiated was unorganized and
low-keyed in comparison with the highly organized proselytizing techniques perfected during the 1920s and '30s. Cities were divided into territo-
rial districts; female Bible Students went from door to door distributing
tracts, delivering memorized "testimonies" issued from headquarters, and
inviting householders to public lectures delivered by male Bible Students.

The Bible Students were less concerned now with "harvesting the saints"
than with aggressive attacks on the clergy: Watchtower publications ran
full-page pictures of a preacher walking down the aisle of a church with a
gun in one hand and a collection plate in the other. The Roman Catholic
Church was branded with "the number of the beast"—666—and was pictured as a semiclad harlot reeling drunkenly into fire and brimstone.

Millions of dollars were poured into radio broadcasts. Network facilities
were used weekly. In 1922, twenty-four acres of land was purchased in

Woodrow, Staten Island, New York, and the Society built its own radio station, WBBR, with a 25,000-watt directional antenna; it functioned until the Staten Island property was sold in 1957. During these Depression decades it began to develop its own printing plants, and to amass more property.

However harsh Pastor Russell's public messages might have been, there was a kind of starry-eyed gentleness, a sweet dreaminess about the Bible Students when they gathered together in his time. Rutherford put an end to that. There were no more "prayer, praise, and testimony" meetings, no more convention "love feasts." Now congregation meetings centered around readings of *The Watch Tower*, and Bible Students were required to answer catechistic questions by summarizing each paragraph of that journal. Their conventions, which had been otherworldly, self-congratulatory affairs of men and women who thought they were soon to reconvene in heaven, became occasions for scathing denunciations of the clergy. At a postwar convention, Rutherford, casting the first stone, "exposed the clergy's disloyalty by participating in the war" [*JWDP*, p. 105] (though the Pope, appalled by the carnage of the war, had called for a negotiated peace after the second battle of the Somme, at a time when the Bible Students were saying their prayers for the success of the American war effort). A series of "Resolutions" was presented at the conventions of the 1920s; all inveighed against the established churches; many castigated the clergy for their support of the League of Nations. (These resolutions are now said to have been fulfillments of the apocalyptic prophecies of Revelation, Chapter 8: each time Rutherford delivered a resolution, an angel "blew his trumpet.")

The Watch Tower Society was, in fact, pursuing a vigorous course of isolationism: London was branded "the seat of the beast"; "Let Britain withdraw from [the League—the seven-headed beast] tomorrow," Rutherford said in 1926, "and it will go down immediately." [*Ibid.*, p. 111]

During the Depression years—when Watch Tower literature was bartered—Russell's notion that the great war of Armageddon was to be essentially a fight between capital and labor, with Jehovah expropriating the spoils for the unpropertied meek, was dispensed with: Armageddon was now seen as God's fight against "Satan's organization," represented on earth by Religion, Politics, and Commerce; and the function of Jehovah's people was to warn of its arrival and, in the meantime, to abstain from taking any part in the political system.

Underneath was a bedrock conservatism: the Bible Students talked about the destruction of the status quo but abhorred attempts to change it. The failure of the clergy to fall prostrate before the invisible Christ, and its acceptance of the League, was seen as a major factor in "the rise of radical, revolutionary elements, pictured by the restless 'sea' of Revelation." [*Yearbook*, 1975, p. 136]

As they expanded, the Bible Students became more and more central-

ized, more and more uniform. The right to appoint congregational overseers was taken away from individual congregations and placed in the hands
of the Society. Rutherford, unlike Russell—who had allowed a certain
amount of latitude among his traveling representatives and derived some
pleasure from the eccentricities and foibles of others, when they did not
threaten to eclipse his own—insisted that each public speaker conform absolutely to headquarters material. There were to be no colorful embellish-
ments or departures from the prepared word.

Having grown up under Russell, who prized individualism, many Bible
Students chafed under Rutherford's authoritarian ("theocratic") dicta: "A
few spent their time studying—looking up ideas that were not published or
printed in the *Watchtower*. Their intention was to attract attention to themselves by telling something new. . . . Those who refused to swallow their
pride and follow the example of Jesus and his disciples in door-to-door ministry soon found themselves out of the organization entirely." [*Faith*, p. 158]
The regimentation imposed upon them, detested by so many, would serve
the Society well during the late 1930s when they tested the laws and the
patience of the land and were the object of vigorous opposition.

By 1927, the pressure for all Bible Students—male and female, elders
and laypersons—to become door-to-door preachers and to turn in weekly
activity reports to headquarters had become so intense that many of Rutherford's followers dropped away. (There is a very high turnover among the
Witnesses. One sees disproportionately few elderly people at Watchtower
conventions.) The departure of many Bible Students in 1927 was no doubt
hastened by the fact that Rutherford, who was as mathematically adroit as
his predecessor, had led the Bible Students to believe that 1925 marked the
time for Christ's anointed followers to go to heaven and for "the faithful
men of old" to be resurrected to rule as princes on the earth. Some Bible
Students made preparations for the resurrection of their loved ones in that
year—getting spare rooms ready, airing out old clothes from attic trunks.

I wonder about those imaginations: Did they *visualize* the ancient prophets rising from their graves? Were they brushed by a dream, or set on fire
by an imagined reality? When I was a child Witness, I used to ask, What
will the prophets wear when they're resurrected? Will they take planes
from Palestine to Brooklyn? How will they pay their carfare? Will they
speak English? Will we understand Hebrew? I wondered if we'd have
David and Jonathan to dinner, and whether they'd like Italian food. I tried
to imagine Noah riding a subway. My elders, I soon learned, were greatly
disquieted by my questions and my conjectures; I learned rapidly to quash
my curiosity, when instead of answers I met baleful, dismissive glances.
And my feeling, consequently, is that the Witnesses who believed these
stories were anesthetized, as if in a morphine dream, sleepwalking through
fantasies.

(In 1950, I ceased to wonder whether Prince David would find me attractive. At a convention that year in Yankee Stadium, Fred Franz, then the Society's vice-president, announced, "The princes are here in our midst, among us tonight!" A fearful hush came over that stadium. I was sitting, I remember, next to a Bethelite from Texas, of whom I was mildly enamored, woolgathering after seven hours of speeches, wondering whether he would take me home and, if so, whether he would kiss me good night. When Franz dropped his bombshell I felt a quick stab of disbelief, followed immediately by flutters of guilt, and then by overwhelming anxiety. Franz paused for maximum effect, as thousands gathered in the dusk shifted restlessly in their seats, craning to see—what? Did any of us believe that Solomon would step before the lectern? *"You,"* Franz cried anticlimactically, "are the princes"; and he explained that Jehovah had shed greater light on his word, and the princes were not, as we had for so many years believed, the "faithful men of old," but congregational overseers, whom God was grooming for positions of authority in his New World. There was great and fervent applause, as if a dream had been fulfilled, and not mercilessly deflated. I was very angry.)

What in the world did I suggest an international convention for when I have no special speech or message for them? Why bring them all here?—J. F. Rutherford to A. H. Macmillan, 1931 [*Yearbook,* 1975]

It is Scripturally and factually clear that only Almighty God Jehovah himself founded or ordains and continues to ordain his witnesses, and in proof of this he gives them his name.—Let God Be True, p. 222

In 1928 Rutherford had dazzled the Bible Students with further proof of their singularity by "revealing" to them the pagan origins of Christmas and birthday celebrations and abjuring them from celebrating those holidays. By 1931, having already framed eight resolutions "indicting ecclesiastics," he had run out of suitably impressive material with which to energize his followers. According to Macmillan, "he began to think about" what he would say to Bible Students that was new and of any consequence at an international convention scheduled for July 24–31 in Cleveland, Ohio. (The realities of dust bowls and Depression and war clouds over Europe seem not to have exercised his imagination.) "Isaiah 43 came to his mind": "But now thus saith the Lord that created thee, O Jacob, and he that formed thee, O Israel, Fear not: for I have redeemed thee, I have called thee by thy name; thou art mine. . . . Ye are my witnesses, saith the Lord, and my servant whom I have chosen."—Isaiah 43:1, 10, King James Version. (The American Standard Version, which the Witnesses preferred—at least until they produced their own New World Translation of the Bible—uses *Jehovah* in place of *the Lord.*) Rutherford "got up at two o'clock in the morning . . . and the Lord guided him." [*Yearbook,* 1975, p. 151] What Rutherford had come up with at 2 o'clock in the morning was a new name for Bible Students: Jehovah's witnesses. It was forever after a proof that Jehovah had chosen the Witnesses to be His people: who else was called by His name? The Lord, it is said, "guided" Rutherford; none of the Society's leaders has ever laid claim to direct inspiration—but that is surely a distinction without a difference.

Conventions of Witnesses are like catered weddings: you have to come home with party favors. The illusion that something new and fresh has come down from headquarters is essential to the ongoing work of the Society. This was something new; their batteries recharged, the newly christened Jehovah's Witnesses applied greater energy to the search for "the other sheep"—the "great multitude," who, they now saw clearly, would inherit the earth.

They began to deemphasize the glories of heaven and to focus on those "people of goodwill" who would ally themselves with the "heavenly class" and to whom, as a result, God's Kingdom-Blessings would come on earth. (The new emphasis proceeded in part, perhaps, from their failure to be gathered to heaven in 1925, and also from having to justify amassing property and accelerating their proselytizing in the face of the imminent destruction of the world.) Their God, who before was going to revivify and shower beneficence upon all the disinherited of the earth, had become more discriminating: the "other sheep" would live forever on earth; the "goats" of Jesus' parable would be destroyed. Those who did not heed the Witnesses' message were "goats."

At a convention in Washington, D.C., in 1935, Rutherford asked, "Will all those who have the hope of living forever on earth please stand?" And it became apparent that this was the moment thousands were waiting for—those thousands who did not entertain heavenly hopes (in Russell's day, they *all* had). Over half the audience stood. Rutherford cried, "Behold! The Great Multitude!" Everybody cheered. Now their preaching work had greater purpose, and greater intensity: millions now living would never die.

There are 144,000 places reserved in heaven, and most of these, it is assumed, have been taken up by first-century Christians and Russellites and Rutherfordites. The call is now to earthly life. (Vacancies may occur when one of the heavenly class sins against the Holy Spirit.) Attendance at the yearly Memorial of Christ's death—when those who expect to go to heaven to serve as Christ's coregents partake of bread and wine—reflect the changing expectations of the majority of Witnesses. In 1935, 35,000 Witnesses celebrated "the Lord's evening meal" in the United States; 71 percent of these partook of the Memorial emblems. In 1955, U.S. Memorial attendance was 878,303, and 1.9 percent ate the bread and drank the wine. One subject of painful, though romantic, conjecture for the Witnesses of the

1940s was what would happen if one marriage partner were of the heavenly class and the other of the earthly class. Their ultimate separation was assured, and as Jehovah was going to renew His mandate to multiply and replenish the earth to "other sheep" who survived Armageddon, they were forced to imagine the heavenly partner gazing down benevolently while the earthly partner was busy being fruitful and multiplying with a mate chosen for him or her by God for this purpose.

The commission to separate the sheep from the goats took some extravagant forms. In 1938, in London, a thousand-man, six-mile-long parade of Witnesses bore signs reading RELIGION IS A SNARE AND A RACKET. When they were heckled—observers took them for Communists—Rutherford neutralized the signs by adding SERVE GOD AND CHRIST THE KING. It must have been confusing to anyone who didn't know the Witnesses' definition of *religion*, which was that it came from the Latin, *to bind back*, and that it applied to all "false systems" of worship. (In 1951, the Witnesses began to make a distinction between "true religion" [them] and "false religion" [everybody else].)

The Witnesses no longer carry signs or banners, and the hand of God is seen in this, as it is seen in everything else: Grant Suiter, the Society's current secretary, has said that in view of the many public demonstrations of protest taking place, it must be clearly understood that the Witnesses have no part in these and that this form of their activity has come to an end, showing Jehovah's direction for them.

The hand of God was also seen in the introduction of the "magazine work"—hawking magazines on street corners—in 1940, when the Witnesses took up this new activity as another means of promoting their work, proving their loyalty and service to God as well as their wholehearted commitment to advancing the Kingdom.

They are always having to prove themselves, set themselves tests, always investing events with enormous significance; they are naked and afraid in the face of ordinary life and must substitute for the excitement of an inner life the scent of danger—Daniel in the lions' den. If ever a religion promised serenity, this is not it. The more trouble the outside world gave them, the more they made themselves the butt of opposition, the more secure they became in their beliefs. To be buffeted and racked by worldly forces, to choose martyrdom, to excite the animosity of a crowd satisfied some hunger in them, gave them rest of a kind, rest from self-doubt. What was important was that something should always be happening. As we shall see, during the 1930s and '40s, a great deal did happen: They were the victims of mob violence; they were jailed, molested, tarred and feathered; and it is not extravagant to say that they altered the history of civil liberties in the United States. There is reason to believe that they were complicit in their own victimization—manipulating national fears, milking national traumas to invite opposition, in order to enhance their self-esteem. In their persecution, they found a kind of peace.

Joseph Franklin Rutherford died on January 8, 1942, in San Diego, California. He was 72 years old. The nine months he had spent in the Atlanta Penitentiary had damaged his lungs, the Witnesses say; he had spent most of his presidency in the salubrious climate of San Diego, in Beth-Saarim, the mansion constructed for him and for "the ancient worthies."

His lieutenants, squabbling with local authorities who refused permission to bury Rutherford in a crypt at Beth-Saarim, did not disclose his death to his followers. The news was released by a local mortician. [*The New York Times*, Jan. 10, 1942] He was buried, three months after his death, on April 26, in Woodrow Cemetery, next to what was then the Watchtower radio station, WBBR.

I worked, the summer of 1953, at the Watchtower cannery in Woodrow, and I never knew Rutherford's grave was there. For all his public exposure, the private man remained mysterious, remote, inaccessible. His grave is unvisited.

VII. *Catholics, Mob Violence, Civil Liberties, and the Draft*

The psychological nub of their appeal, I believe, is their conviction that all members of the sect must constantly and fully participate in spreading the gospel of the sect, thus supplying to drab and commonplace lives a wonderfully consoling unity of action and purpose. . . . We constantly forget how deep the appeal of a communal life lived for a high purpose and involving sacrifice and even martyrdom is. And this appeal operates impartially whether the common purpose be good or bad, rational or unreasoned. Especially is it strong when it combines with its own intrinsic purpose a sanction for rebellion against constituted authority, moral and civil. . . . When we fail to realize this, when we subject the Witnesses to mob violence or to prison, we play directly into their hands and cease ourselves to be Christian.— Harry Lorin Binsse, *Commonweal*, Jan. 10, 1947, p. 318

DURING the 1930s and '40s, hundreds of Jehovah's Witnesses were arrested for selling without a license, disturbing the peace, violating Sunday Sabbath laws, refusing to salute the flag; 4,500 were jailed during World War II for violation of the Selective Service Act. Their houses were stoned and raided; their meeting halls were sacked; they were stricken from relief rolls.

The Witnesses were seen as a threat to national security and to interfaith harmony; they were heartily despised by conservative elements of the Roman Catholic Church, which they had insistently and aggressively calumnized. Both their message and the media they employed to promulgate it aroused ire. The Witnesses defied logic, made public nuisances of themselves, merrily invaded privacy and imposed noise pollution on unwitting victims, engaged in Know-Nothing Catholic-baiting, refused to participate in a war that was generally perceived to be a good and righteous war, and gravely offended the sensibilities of people of every class. In the opinion of the American Civil Liberties Union's Leon Friedman, they "deliberately, calculatedly tested the law"—and we must all be pleased that they did: they won 150 State Supreme Court cases and more than 30 precedent-setting Supreme Court cases, forcing the Court to broaden the meaning of the First and Fourteenth Amendments. It is impossible to speak of the history of civil liberties in this country without speaking of them. Whatever their motives, we are very much in their debt.

In the early part of the century, most of the religious opposition to the Witnesses originated with the Protestant churches, who saw them as wayward children. The Catholic Church, unthreatened, maintained a calm and silent dignity. As the Society expanded, and its fulminations against the Vatican grew louder and more abrasive, it became locked in bitter antagonism with the Catholic Church. With exceptions—all on the side of the Church—nobody behaved scrupulously or well.

Nineteen-forty-four: Our hatred for the Church was an invigorating elixir. It drove us to heights of inspired lunacy.

I had been baptized Catholic; I had never been confirmed or taken the Sacrament of the Eucharist. Shortly before my conversion, I went with a friend to Sunday Mass. In my working-class neighborhood, everybody was Catholic or Jewish except our family; we were No Religion. And I didn't much like being No Religion, feeling disinherited and rootless. A priest made some astringent remarks about the antireligious pests who went from door to door badgering people with lies about the Church, and he told his parishioners to slam their doors when Jehovah's Witnesses called. There was something oily and hateful in his voice from which I recoiled; I felt a surge of sympathy for those poor people—whoever they were—who were obliged to go from door to slammed door. The Church was magnificent, I thought, and magnificence ought not to condescend to abuse insignificant pests. (I also recoiled when Japanese were called Japs. I thought they should be afforded the courtesy of their full name, enemies or not. Very refined sensibilities for a 9-year-old—or an obstinate determination to cast in my lot with the maligned.) Later I wallowed in the Witnesses' vilification of the Church and the state.

I found the Witnesses, when they came, congenial. At first shocked, I slipped easily into listening without being offended to off-color jokes about the virginity of Mary; I began to be as derisive as my elders about "dog-collared" priests; I believed absolutely that nuns were forcibly imprisoned (or, alternatively, holding wild orgies within their cloisters); I crossed the street, afraid of contamination, when I passed the local convent, convinced that the shards of glass on top of the high walls that surrounded their green and lovely park were placed there to keep them from escaping (I dreamed of their black habits flying over walls, of bloodied hands and knees, of beseeching faces); I knew that young girls were corrupted in confessionals— and I censored wicked fantasies of fat-priest hands slipping up my legs. (I wonder how many other Witnesses derived quasi-sexual pleasure from the Watchtower's anti-Church tirades.) The wickedness of the Church was tangible; it was evidenced in its idols, its purple trappings. (When my brother was 4, he blubbered, tears all over his unhappy face, "They're ugly, the Christmas trees, they're ugly." It was the first Christmas we had not had a tree: he thought they were beautiful. When we learned that the Crucifix was a "pagan symbol"—Jesus, we were told, had died on a stake—my brother wrapped my gold cross, with its little agonized Jesus, its tiny crown of thorns, in toilet tissue and dropped it from his bedroom window. I wouldn't even retrieve the gold chain from which it hung; I was afraid to touch it.)

During World War II, the Witnesses—who were themselves being arrested as Fifth Columnists—gave voice to the idea, shared by many non-Catholics, that the Church was an elaborate political organization whose piety was a cloak for Machiavellian schemes of world power; they charged the Church with being the American Fifth Column. Rutherford had made himself highly unpopular by declaring that "religion has always been the chief instrument employed by the Devil to reproach the name of Almighty God . . . all liars and murderers are religionists . . . Eve desired religion, and the Devil saw to it that her desire was fulfilled." Not content with impugning the Church's relationship to the Almighty, Rutherford also attributed the growth of Communism and Nazism to the Church: "Communism has been encouraged by the Jesuits, the secret order of the Roman Catholic Hierarchy, and then used as a camouflage, or a scarecrow, to frighten the people. . . . In this manner, the Nazis of Germany were organized."

I believed, as did all Witnesses, that guns and ammunition were stored in the cellars and crypts of Catholic churches (and that these weapons were smuggled into churches in piano boxes—a picturesque detail which somehow gave weight to these wild charges). We believed that the Vatican had a standing army waiting for a command to take over America. (Inasmuch as America was at that time five-sixths Protestant, it is wonderful how the Church managed to horrify and fascinate us so.) Another picturesque conceit of Rutherford's was that when Armageddon came, all priests and nuns would disguise themselves in overalls in a futile attempt to hide their clerical robes from the Lord. (After World War II, we were absolutely sure that Hitler was hidden in the cellars of the Vatican.)

It is the Witnesses' contention that the Church initiated and engineered attacks against the Witnesses. The Witnesses' verbal abuse of the Church did elicit retaliatory attacks; ruffians and hoodlums often interpreted their priests' indictments of the Witnesses as a mandate to abuse the Witnesses physically.

Class prejudice and fear of foreigners and immigrants played a part in this two-way thrashing. The Witnesses, not troubling to substantiate their claim, said that the Ku Klux Klan was a Catholic terrorist organization, and

Watchtower Society representatives railed against Catholic mine workers of "foreign extraction" who objected to the Witnesses' blasting the peace with sound-car invectives against the Church. Catholics, calling Jehovah's Witnesses "a wart on the spirit of national advancement," said contrapuntally that the Witnesses were direct spiritual descendants of the American (Know-Nothing) Party of 1835 and spiritual siblings of the KKK, and that the Watchtower Society secured its attention from "the poorer classes of the South's farm tenants; from the hill-billies of the Southwest; from the Okies who, dejected and rejected, wander about hopelessly; from the ignorant, superstitious, and illiterate of large city slums." While the Society issued broadsides against the Church for creating the conditions that allowed Communism to flourish, lay Catholics regarded the Witnesses as "a most pernicious menace to the American way of life" and saw "a shocking parallel between their preachments and Communism." The Jesuit magazine *America*, while full of ripe invective, showed flashes of insight and pity: " 'Pastor' Russell answered their anguish"—the anguish of the chronically unemployed and the victims of social injustice—"by organizing the Russellites," who "continued to rant against and hate everyone and everything not of themselves." [H. C. McGinnis, *America*, Feb. 8, 15, 1941; March 22, 1941]

The Witnesses retorted that the doctrines of the Trinity and the immortality of the soul were "devilish" and that the Church was politically and spiritually corrupt; but the threat they posed to the religious establishment was probably not the determining factor in their persecution during the 1930s and '40s. It is more likely that the threat they posed to secular authorities was what landed them in jail. The American Legion and the Ku Klux Klan vociferated against the Witnesses because they were not patriotic at a time when national security was in jeopardy. What was really at issue was the American flag.

National unity is the basis of national security. . . . The ultimate foundation of a free society is the binding tie of cohesive sentiment. Such a sentiment is fostered by all those agencies of the mind and spirit which may serve to gather up the traditions of a people, transmit them from generation to generation, and thereby create that continuity of a treasured common life which constitutes a civilization. "We live by symbols." The flag is the symbol of our national unity, transcending all internal differences, however large, within the framework of the Constitution.—Justice Felix Frankfurter, June 3, 1940 (*Minersville School District v. Gobitis*, 310 U.S. 586, 60 S.Ct. 1010, 87 L.Ed., 1375)

On October 6, 1935, Judge Rutherford spoke on a coast-to-coast chain radio broadcast on "Saluting the Flag." In his scratchy, thin, wobbly but impassioned tenor, he told his listeners that Scriptural obligations and their relationship to God made it impossible for Jehovah's Witnesses to salute any "image or representation," including the American flag; Rutherford interpreted the second of the Ten Commandments—"Thou shalt not make unto thee any graven image, or any likeness . . . Thou shalt not bow down thyself to them, nor serve them"—to mean that saluting the flag constituted "idolatry." His lecture was published in a booklet called *Loyalty,* and the Witnesses distributed millions of copies of what appeared to be an inflammatory attack on a cherished institution.

The Witnesses accepted Rutherford's premises, though inconsistent with the rest of their beliefs—according to them, Christians are under no obligation to obey the letter of the Mosaic Law—with a fanaticism that was generally felt to be unlovely. That they were able to do so with slender Scriptural support could lead one to think that on some level they deliberately placed themselves in a position to invite persecution. Hayden C. Covington, then the Society's legal counsel, and a brilliant Constitutional lawyer, has said that lawmakers on municipal and state levels "deliberately laid every legal snare they could think of to foil" the Witnesses. But while the State protected its interest of national security, the Witnesses had something to gain by initiating lawsuits. They had no material emblems to suggest or to represent the singular glory they felt reposed in them. Their meetings, like their lives, were dull and oppressive. They had to look elsewhere, outside themselves, for the mark of God. He had chosen them, but how could they prove it? Not with magnificent edifices, not with a rich and varied history. They were young, comparatively weak, foolish and insignificant in the eyes of the world; they had no glorious music, no poetry, no formal ritual, no liturgy, and no martyrs. Their first leader had been a haberdasher and, by common view, a scoundrel; their second leader was an intemperate lawyer with a reputation for slick business transactions. However much they suspended disbelief, that must have rankled. Power and glory and all the world and the kingdoms of the world were soon to be theirs, but their leaders were not kings or shepherds or poets or sages. They were wilier, certainly, than most men, and vain, but they were not, by any standards, glorious. Ordinariness was the stale bread of the world from which the Witnesses had fled. To sustain their image of themselves, perhaps they needed to have something immense and extraordinary occur, something that would raise them above themselves, justify and exalt them. Rutherford had one weapon, the law. He used it. He made things happen.

A year and a month after Rutherford's broadcast about flag saluting, something that was to prove to be immense did happen.

On November 6, 1935, two elementary-school children in the coal-mining district of Pennsylvania refused to salute the flag. Their father, Walter Gobitis, was arrested, and the children were expelled from school. Gobitis initiated a suit against the Board of Education, Minersville School District. In 1936, 1,149 Witnesses were arrested for refusal to salute the flag and for violating a variety of state and municipal ordinances. [*Yearbook*, 1975, pp. 169–72]

The Supreme Court, having declined several times to review the expulsion of the Gobitis children for not participating in the flag-salute ceremony, accepted jurisdiction in 1940. With one dissenting voice, that of Justice Harlan Fiske Stone, the Court ruled to uphold the Gobitis children's expulsion and decided that school boards had the right to choose to require children to salute the American flag. The Court's majority decision, written by Justice Felix Frankfurter, was based on its opinion that religiously motivated refusal to salute the flag represented a threat to nationalism and security.

(Journalist Sydney Zion, who wrote Justice Black's obituary for *The New York Times*, provides an interesting personal dimension to the Court's decision. According to Zion, Mr. Justice Hugo Black confided that he had voted with the majority because "Felix [Frankfurter] mesmerized us. Felix was an immigrant, passionate about the flag and what it meant to him. We were so moved by his appeal that we went for it. Justice Stone wrote his dissent at the very last moment—and it was so brilliant, it showed us all up." Black remembered sitting beside a swimming pool with Justices William O. Douglas and Frank Murphy, and saying, " 'What are we going to do? Stone is right.' But we were wiped out by Felix's emotional appeal. . . . We decided to redress the wrong the next time around.")

The Court handed down its decision on June 3, 1940. Between June 12 and June 20, hundreds of physical attacks upon Witnesses were reported to the United States Department of Justice. (They are spoken of now in almost affectionate terms by the Witnesses; they are their stigmata, and they bind the Witnesses together in purpose.) In Kennebunk, Maine, a Kingdom Hall was burned. In Rockville, Maryland, police came to the assistance of a mob that was dispersing a Witness meeting. In Litchfield, Illinois, 60 Witness canvassers were set upon by practically every man and woman in the town. In Connersville, Indiana, a Witness was charged with riotous conspiracy, his attorney was mobbed, and he was beaten and driven out of town. In Nebraska, a Witness was lured from his house, abducted, and castrated. In West Virginia, the chief of police and deputy sheriff forced Witnesses to drink castor oil and paraded them through the streets tied together with police department rope. [Z&L] From 1940 to 1944, 2,500 incidences of mob violence were recorded.

The nation was threatened by war. An editorial in *The Saturday Evening Post* said:

> It seems likely that the United States harbors no other out-of-step and out-of-sympathy minority of anything like [the Witnesses'] size and militancy. In the event of war, they are sure to furnish the largest quota of conscientious objectors, and, perhaps, the most troublesome. In this near-war period, no other group so boldly condemns not only the current patriotic trend but patriotism, specifically and in general.

No other, for good measure, condemns so many other things by which Americans lay store.

The government did not sanction the fury of the mob. On June 16, 1940, U.S. Solicitor General Francis Biddle told an NBC radio audience: "Jehovah's Witnesses have been repeatedly set upon and beaten. . . . The Attorney General has ordered an immediate investigation of these charges. The people must be alert and watchful, and above all cool and sane. Since mob violence will make the government's task infinitely more difficult, it will not be tolerated. We shall not defeat the Nazi evil by emulating its methods."

In 1940, the ACLU defended 1,300 Witnesses in 200 legal cases.

Nor were the churches monolithically arrayed against the Witnesses; after the first wave of war hysteria had passed, liberal voices were raised in their defense and in reaction against mob terror. An editorial in the October 7, 1942, issue of *Christian Century*, which calls reports of mob violence in Springfield, Illinois, Klamath Falls, Oregon, and Little Rock, Arkansas, "physically nauseating," reflects the growing revulsion against mob violence among civil libertarians who were beginning to understand that their own First and Fourteenth Amendment rights were put in jeopardy when those of Jehovah's Witnesses were threatened:

> More than 100 workers on the War Emergency Pipeline which the government is laying stormed the grounds of a former hospital which the Witnesses had taken over for their meeting. These pipeline workers, according to the *Arkansas Gazette*, were "armed with guns, sticks, blackjacks and pipe." The attack was made after dark. Two men were shot, five others so severely beaten that they were taken to a Little Rock hospital. . . . "Occasionally another automobile would turn into the grounds. A dozen or more pipeliners pounced on each car and asked, 'Are you a Witness?' The usual answer came back in a firm voice: 'Yes, I am a Witness.' The driver and other male occupants were then ordered out. Some hesitated. They were dragged out and the pummeling began. Many used their fists, but others wielded clubs, long heavy screwdrivers and blackjacks. The beating usually continued until the victim fell." Remember, the ruffians who engaged in this sort of thing were workers on a government job. They were building a pipeline for Mr. Ickes' department. Mr. Ickes is supposed to be a champion of civil liberties. . . . If civil liberties have any meaning, if religious liberty is more than an empty phrase in this country, the national authorities must put a stop to such mob actions. If no one in the halls of government will speak out to demand that the members of this sect be protected in their constitutional rights, then the churches should do so.

The Witnesses fought their legal battles with skill. Hayden C. Covington earned a reputation for arguing brilliantly before the Court; but all Witnesses learned to equip themselves to deal with police and judges. At weekly "service meetings" during the war years, they received paralegal training. They held mock trials, some of them lasting for weeks, with overseers role-playing the parts of prosecution and defense attorneys. They were coached in how to respond to arresting officers, and how to behave procedurally in order to establish the basis for appellate review of convictions.

For eight years, the Witnesses maintained their own "Kingdom Schools" for children who had been expelled from public schools. The schools were communes. The children were, for the most part, boarders, since gasoline rationing made it impossible for them to return more than once or twice a month to their homes. Instructed by Witness teachers, they began each day with a discussion of a Bible text; one half-hour of Bible study daily was part of the curriculum. They performed kitchen chores and, regardless of age, spent most of Saturday and Sunday mornings proselytizing. It cannot be said to have been a carefree childhood.

Compulsory unification of opinion achieves only the unanimity of the graveyard. — *West Virginia State Board of Education v. Barnette,* 319 U.S. 624 (1943)

In 1943, the Witness children went back to their public-school classrooms. Mob violence had abated; America had changed. It had become silly to regard these children as a clear and present danger to the national security; and in fact, most Americans, obsessed with the idea that Japanese-Americans threatened their security, had transferred their fear and hatred to the "slant-eyed devils" in their midst. In 1943, the Supreme Court reversed the Gobitis decision by a vote of 6 to 3.

The way had been prepared for the Court's historic reversal in *West Virginia v. Barnette*:

In an earlier decision, the Court had voted 5 to 4 to uphold the validity of an ordinance requiring the licensing of colporteurs (proselytizers) in cities of Alabama, Arkansas, and Arizona *(Jones v. Opelika, 316, U.S. 584, 1942)*. In a vigorous dissenting opinion, Chief Justice Stone declared that in the decision a way had been found "for the effective suppression of speech and religion despite Constitutional guarantees." The liberal trio, Justices Black, Murphy, and Douglas, in their own dissenting opinion, took the unprecedented step of acknowledging that they had been wrong on the Gobitis flag-salute case.

Jones v. Opelika had roused part of the press to the threat to its own freedom. "As a result," according to an editorial in *Christian Century* (Jan. 13, 1943, p. 38),

> newspapers which undoubtedly regard Jehovah's witnesses as a collection of religious crackpots are now giving powerful support to the effort to obtain a reversal of the court's decision. By keeping the issue before the public and by providing eminent legal counsel they

have done much to reinstate it on the docket of the highest tribunal. It is a pity that church bodies, whose interests are equally at stake, have done nothing to parallel the efforts of the press to obtain a new hearing.

There may be a tendency in some quarters to minimize the importance of these cases because it is the rights of Jehovah's witnesses which are immediately involved. Do not the Witnesses stand for a hodgepodge of peculiar millennial ideas, and do they not seek to propagate these ideas in ways which sometimes make them a nuisance to the communities in which they are operating? They do. Then why worry about the means which may be taken to force them to conform to community norms or to keep their provocative tracts out of circulation? Because civil liberty under the Constitution means nothing unless it protects the rights of every citizen. Because it is only the attempt of the non-conformist to assert his rights which can test the extent and reality of our civil liberties. And because failure to uphold such civil liberties within the United States will render meaningless such talk as we may indulge in about extending the Four Freedoms to the rest of mankind.

The Court later reexamined the Constitutional issue upon which it had divided in *Jones v. Opelika*. The issue was whether religious liberty is violated by the imposition of a nondiscriminatory license tax on the sale of religious books and tracts. The Court ruled in *Murdock v. Pennsylvania* (319 U.S. 105, 1943) that a tax laid on the free exercise of religion, as protected by the First and Fourteenth Amendments, is unconstitutional. Jehovah's Witnesses were, in the opinion of Justice Douglas, engaged in an exercise of religion, equivalent to that of more conventional churches, and not in a commercial enterprise: "The hand distribution of religious tracts . . . occupies the same high estate under the First Amendment as do worship in the churches and preaching from the pulpits. It has the same claim to protection as the more orthodox and conventional exercises of religion."

Ruling that "an itinerant evangelist, however misguided or intolerant he may be, does not become a mere book agent by selling the Bible or religious tracts to help defray his expenses or to sustain him," the Court thus began to legitimize "marginal" religions and to recognize what has been called the minority concept of religion. Street solicitation was accepted as required religious activity and not as commercial peddling; similarly, the right of the Witnesses to regard flag saluting as idolatry, rather than as a patriotic ceremony, was recognized in the *Barnette* case. The right of minority groups to protection under the Bill of Rights was seen as essential to the preservation of the rights of the majority:

A curb upon the propagandist activity of the most odious sect—unless it can be shown to be a definite peril to society—is a potential attack upon the liberties of all citizens. Jehovah's Witnesses are, in our judgment, a particularly odious and fanatical sect, but the truth or falsity of their teaching is not at issue. . . . The license regulations which the Court validated applied to the vendors of all books and pamphlets, thereby including religious publications and, incidentally, those of this particular sect.

In the minds of the municipalities which passed the ordinances, the inclusion of Jehovah's Witnesses may well have been more than incidental. It may have furnished the motive for the whole project, the idea being to catch them by making a net that could be used to catch anybody; but there was no evidence to this effect before the Court, and that possibility need not enter into the argument. The point is that this *is* a net that may be used to catch anybody. No antipathy toward Jehovah's Witnesses, no belief that they are thinkers of dangerous thoughts and propagandists of anarchy, should be permitted to conceal this basic fact. They are the first victims, but any other locally unpopular group may be the next. They clashed with the law when they refused to apply for a license. Any other group may clash with it by being refused a license upon application, or by having the license refused or withdrawn.—*Christian Century*, June 24, 1942, p. 798

Clearly, their defenders did not find Jehovah's Witnesses acceptable; far from it. They found the threat to their own liberties—civil and religious—more odious and pernicious than the sect they were loath to endorse but obliged to defend:

It is unfortunate that the spearhead in the legal fight for religious liberty has to be a group which makes such poor use of it. "Hard cases make bad law," and a good deal of bad law has previously been made in the effort to restrict the activities or modify the mores of this eccentric sect.—*Christian Century*, May 12, 1943, p. 565

It is significant that the Witnesses, who filed appeals regularly on the basis of freedom of religion during the mid-1930s, did not get very far until they changed their tactics and grounded their appeals on freedom of the press in 1938. In that year, the Court struck down an ordinance against literature distribution (*Lovell v. Griffin, 303 U.S. 444*). Subsequent cases, based on a broad concept of multiple First Amendment rights of speech and advocacy, established new rights for the use of public places, door-to-door solicitation, and "freedom to promulgate."

The Court edged into the question of religious freedom to act, as opposed to freedom to believe, by way of freedom of the press. In 1940, the Court, overturning a conviction for breach of the peace by a Witness proselytizer, ruled that the First Amendment "embraces two concepts—freedom to believe and freedom to act. The first is absolute, but the second remains subject to regulation for the protection of society." Because the proselytizer "raised no such clear and present menace to public peace and order as to render him liable to conviction," his conviction was set aside. *(Cantwell v. Conn., 310 U.S. 296 [1940])*

The clear-and-present-danger argument was first advanced by Oliver Wendell Holmes and Louis Brandeis. The ambiguous maxim that freedom of speech or of conscience, or any other freedom, is to be upheld except where the actions constitute "a clear and present danger" to the nation was at issue in the Court's review of the Gobitis flag-salute case.

Civil libertarians asked, Who is to judge when any danger becomes "clear and present"?

> There have begun to sprout suggestions that a new rule needs to be adopted—a rule which would guarantee the preservation of civil liberties to those who are dedicated to their preservation for others, and would deny those liberties to those who would (if they had power) deny them to others. It is in the direction of some such rule as this that the four members of the highest court who will probably rule against Jehovah's Witnesses—Justices Frankfurter, Roberts, Reed, and Jackson—appear to be tending. But any such rule is also open to all the abuses of arbitrary application. The issue as to who is to be guaranteed civil liberty is the very center of the struggle for the preservation of the essential democratic freedoms today. And the return of these Jehovah's Witnesses to the Supreme Court will furnish a decisive test as to the degree of American loyalty to the ideals which inspired the Bill of Rights.—*Christian Century*, Jan. 13, 1943, p. 39

In the event, however, Justice Robert H. Jackson ruled that First Amendment freedoms "are susceptible of restriction only to prevent clear and immediate danger to interests which the state may lawfully protect." When *West Virginia v. Barnette* came before the Court, Justice James F. Byrnes, a liberal Roosevelt appointee, had replaced Justice Wiley Rutledge, a strict constructionist; three members of the Court had changed their minds since *Gobitis;* and two other members of the Court unexpectedly ruled with Justice Jackson that "to compel conscientiously scrupulous children to salute deprives them of the freedom of religion guaranteed by the Fourteenth Amendment." The Court ruled that refusal to salute the flag did not involve any

> collision with the rights asserted by any other individual, nor was it accompanied by any conduct which was not peaceable and orderly. . . . Censorship or suppression of expression of opinion is tolerated by our Constitution only when the expression presents a clear and present danger of action of a kind the State is empowered to prevent and punish. . . . Ultimate futility of . . . attempts to compel coherence is the lesson of every such effort from the Roman drive to stamp out Christianity, as a disturber of its pagan unity, the Inquisition, as a

means to religious and dynastic unity, the Siberian exiles, as a means to Russian unity, down to the fast-failing efforts of our present totalitarian enemies. Those who begin coercive elimination of dissent soon find themselves exterminating dissenters. . . . We apply the limitations of the Constitution with no fear that freedom to be intelligently and spiritually diverse or even contrary will disintegrate the social organization. . . . When they are so harmless to others or to the State as those we deal with here, the price is not too great. But freedom to differ is not limited to things that do not matter much. That would be a mere shadow of freedom. The test of its substance is the right to differ as to things that touch the heart of the existing order. . . . If there is any fixed star in our constitutional constellation, it is that no official, high or petty, can prescribe what shall be orthodox in politics, nationalism, religion, or other matters of opinion or force citizens to confess by word or act their faith therein. . . . We think the action of the local authorities in compelling the flag salute and pledge transcends constitutional limitations on their power and invades the sphere of intellect and spirit which it is the purpose of the First Amendment to our Constitution to preserve from all official control.

The claim, widely asserted, that Jehovah's Witnesses through boundless courage and unending perseverance have won more United States Supreme Court victories for the Bill of Rights than any other single group seems to have ample support.—A. L. Wirin, ACLU, *The Open Forum*, Aug. 21, 1943, p. 1

By the end of World War II, Jehovah's Witnesses had made 190 appeals to higher courts; they had won over 125 State Supreme Court cases, and most of 40 Supreme Court decisions.

The Witnesses established that distribution of literature "calculated to encourage disloyalty to the state and national governments" could not be made the basis for conviction under a sedition statute forbidding that which "tends to create disloyalty and causes an attitude of stubborn refusal to salute the flag":

> If the state cannot constrain one to violate his conscientious religious conviction by saluting the national emblem, then it cannot punish him for imparting his views on the subject to his followers and exhorting them to accept those views. . . . The statute as construed in these cases makes it a criminal offense to communicate to others views and opinions respecting governmental policies, and prophecies concerning the future of our own and other nations. As applied to the appellants it punishes them although what they communicated is not claimed or shown to have been done with an evil or a sinister purpose, to have advocated or incited subversive action against the nation or state, or to have threatened any clear and present danger to our institutions or our government. What these appellants communicated were their beliefs and opinions concerning domestic measures and trends in national and world affairs. . . . Under our decisions criminal sanctions cannot be

imposed for such communications.—*Taylor v. Miss.*, 319 U.S. 583, 1943

The Witnesses secured the right to preach in privately-owned or government-owned towns, and in apartments without the permission of landlords; the right to use sound amplifiers "at reasonable volume"; the right of parents to retain custody of children reared in their faith; the right to advertise meetings by placards; the right not to serve on juries.

Nineteen-forty-four: The Court had ruled, in *Barnette v. West Virginia*, that the Witnesses' "spiritual arbitrariness" would not "disintegrate the social order." Unhappily for me, this enlightened view was not shared by public-school children. At the time I was converted, the threat of mob violence had receded, and the days of communal suffering were an occasion for nostalgia; there was never any question of my being expelled from school or arrested. But I did spend a lot of time in the offices of principals, assistant principals, and deans explaining why I didn't salute the flag; and the Witnesses' admonition not to "make friends with the world" was, for me, almost entirely gratuitous: very few children wanted to make friends with me.

Teachers frequently singled me out for attention. The nicest regarded me with a mixture of admiration and pity; the coarsest treated me with frank and meddlesome curiosity; they all tried to change me. I was a challenge—intelligent, earnest, serious, aloof, passionate, and perverse, living a mysterious inner life that vexed or titillated them depending on their temperaments. This, while it fed but did not satisfy my hunger for approval, did not endear me to my peers.

I was almost always alone. I always had to be assigned a partner for school activities. In high school, walking down the corridor between classes was an agony repeated every forty-five minutes because nobody ever walked with me. I don't think anyone knew I suffered; I appeared remote and self-contained. But while I had created my isolation, and the other children reacted self-preservatively by scorning my difference and my alien behavior, I hated it. Everything commonplace enthralled me: girls' linking pinkies with other girls in easy friendship, sharing sodas and cupcakes in the lunchroom; it all seemed remarkable and unattainable. Other girls were famous for playing Chopin Polonaises, or being good at volleyball, or knowing about sex; I was notorious for not saluting the flag. I had a seventh-grade teacher who cultivated me as if I were an exotic flower; but when I became friendly with another girl in her class, she put an end to the friendship by telling the girl's mother that I was trying to convert her (I was) and that I was a pernicious influence. I learned to fear betrayal.

The simple act of going to a theater or to a ball game was filled with dread expectation, because the national anthem might be played, the flag saluted. . . . I could never expect not to be different from other people. (I had crushes on at least three of the Brooklyn Dodgers, and I haunted a car dealer from whom they bought their cars—but I was afraid to go to their games.) I never, in all those years, did less than was required of me; I never even tried to purchase the normality I wanted so desperately by relaxing my vigil. (The trouble was, of course, that while I wanted to be just like everybody else, I also enjoyed being extraordinary and unique—I must have wanted that more.)

During World War II, over 8,000 draft-age Witnesses registered with their draft boards as ministers. Roughly half were granted the ministerial classification, 4-D. Approximately 4,000 were imprisoned. It has been estimated that 60 to 70 percent of all federal offenders convicted for draft violations during World War II were Witnesses. There were more Witnesses in prison for refusing induction than there were Quakers. (Quakers accepted alternative civilian service—hospital work, work in charitable institutions— in lieu of induction in the armed forces; the Witnesses did not.)

When World War II ended, the Witnesses imprisoned for draft violations came home like conquering heroes. Denied the ministerial status they sought, they had spent the war years in federal penitentiaries, while at the local congregations myths grew up around them. Although I had never met them, I felt as if I had complete information about each of the four or five men whose triumphant return to my local South Brooklyn congregation was eagerly awaited. When they returned, it was as if bas-reliefs representing virtue, allegiance, and integrity had sprung to life and moved. Having been in prison lent them an aura of moral authority. We expected that their deprivations had increased their wisdom and spirituality; their suffering had made them glamorous. And sexy. Young girls who had grown up romancing about them were prepared to adore them.

We saw the returning convicts as whole of soul, adorable martyrs. Fellow prisoners had tended to see them as enigmatic nuisances.

Jim Peck and Ralph diGia, pacifists who are on the staff of the War Resisters League, were imprisoned conscientious objectors in Danbury Federal Penitentiary, where the Witnesses represented one-third to one-half the draft violators, from 1942 to 1945. They express no small amazement (and irritation) at the Witnesses' homogeneity and their determined aloofness from other prisoners, their lack of spontaneity, warmth and passion:

> PECK: If you were unlucky enough to land at a table with them in the
> mess hall, either they were silent or they tried to push their religion
> at you. I never saw them kid around, and I never saw them get
> worked up about anything; they were monomaniacal. When the

rest of us complained—we had a three-month strike against racial segregation, and naturally we griped about the food a lot—they remained completely indifferent and aloof. When some of us pulled "tough time," they unbent to the extent of telling us not to worry because *The Watchtower* said the war would be over on such-and-such a date and we'd be out of jail. The funny thing was, when the date came and went and the war still wasn't over, they never had any rationalization or excuse; they simply never mentioned it again.

DiGia: You couldn't have a real conversation with them. No hope. I never could understand their language. One of the Witnesses tried to convert me, and I said, "Look, we're all human beings." And he said, "No, only God is a Being; we're human creatures." How can you talk to somebody who makes distinctions like that? What does that even mean? . . . The Witnesses all spouted the same things. Most of them at Danbury were working-class Irish and Italian from poor Catholic families. Some were sophisticated urban types, and some were farm boys. Some were personable and some were mean. But it didn't matter which of them you talked to, you got the same language. . . . When enough of them arrived in Danbury, they were lodged together in one dorm; they were allowed to have meetings and run their own affairs. They *chose* segregation. They had their own authoritarian leadership; everyone learned the same thing at the same time. They were all strongly anti-Catholic. The main villain was "the Pope of Rome," the Vatican—not Hitler, not the warden, not the U.S. for putting them in jail. Somehow or other, "the Vatican," we were made to feel, was responsible for the whole war, and for our being in prison.

PECK: I never really got to know any of them. And I tried. All the other COs were really friendly. JWs never made a friend. They were quite distinct—they never saw themselves as a community of resisters.

DiGia: You talk a lot on work gangs; you become close. They didn't talk. After work, they'd go off and study the Bible. They had nothing to do with us.

PECK: They didn't consider themselves COs; they said they weren't conscientiously opposed to wars because they would fight at Armageddon—the final war of good versus evil—if God required them to. They resented being called COs.

DiGia: You could sense a lot of suppressed violence in them. They never actually fought with anyone, but you felt an underlying hostility and resentment. They seemed to resent our not accepting them as the Chosen. They reacted badly to being confronted or challenged. They got especially uneasy if you talked about race; most of them came out of racist, anti-Semitic backgrounds, and they still practiced a subtle racism. There were no blacks among the Witnesses in Danbury while I was there, so because the Witnesses were housed separately, they wound up being the only prisoners who weren't integrated with blacks. They'd say, "This government is run by man; man is not perfect; God will change things at Armageddon; we won't try to change things."

PECK: Their relationship with the guards was very different from that of the COs. The rest of us spoke up about injustice. They were strictly correct. They obeyed all the rules. They knew what to do for their own survival. Once I was asked to make up some red-white-and-blue victory-garden signs. I said, "If I'd wanted to do that, I wouldn't be here in the first place." I got ten days in the hole. I can't imagine a Witness making that kind of protest—because he wouldn't be able to find a Scripture saying you weren't allowed to make a red-white-and-blue victory-garden sign.

DIGIA: But if they'd been denied narrowly conceived religious rights, they'd have spoken up.

PECK: They never seemed to pull "tough time." They never got restless.

DIGIA: Well, they were always together, constantly reinforcing their belief that they had the truth and that they were superior. They nourished one another. They had a high survival rate in concentration camps, I understand, probably for the same reason. The rest of us—well, our outside lives impinged; not them. They were much more together than the other COs. The COs never acted as a homogeneous unit; they did. They were a *We*, doing it for God. We used to debate what was good, what was bad, what was moral, what was immoral; they had all the answers before they asked any of the questions. Their imperatives all came from the outside. From Covington. They didn't get the idea to be sheltered together; that came from the organization; but once the Society told them to live together, I think they would have died rather than live apart, with the rest of us. You got the feeling that nothing came from an individual, that they were—I don't know—*absent*.

PECK: Their attitude toward us was that of the religious toward the heathen.

DIGIA: The enlightened to the unenlightened, the washed to the unwashed.

PECK: Yes. They had no interest in us, no curiosity about us, no fellow feeling—unless we showed signs of accepting their belief.

DIGIA: They had no conception of our struggle.

PECK: A lot of jail is just waiting around. You stand and wait and wait and wait. They'd wait around in clumps. At one call-out when we were waiting and waiting, they made a formal attempt to preach to us. Otherwise they ignored us. They didn't think we were in any way different from murderers or bootleggers; the fact that we were there for conscience's sake didn't matter to them at all. I don't think they made a distinction between Gandhi and Hitler. The idea was, if you're not doing God's will—as expressed in *The Watchtower*—you could be planting daisies or shooting babies—it's all the same.

As a matter of fact, I think they tried harder to convert *non*-COs, people who didn't have a developed consciousness.

DiGia: During the Vietnam War, a JW came to my door, and he started his rap by saying how the world was in bad trouble, using Vietnam as evidence. So I said I'd been in prison with JWs during the Second World War, and that I thought it was a good thing that they didn't fight. He went right on talking as if I hadn't said anything. It all came back to me: how much like robots they were, disregarding anything anybody else said, not making any compassionate connection. He had no commonality of interest, no feeling that friendship had just been offered—he just continued his pitch. He couldn't have cared less. I remembered that the JWs had been told by their superiors that we COs were not "correctly motivated." It's strange—they don't have the strength to make independent decisions, or the courage to find out about other people; but they had the strength to go to concentration camps in Germany. A strange kind of courage. One year the WRL got a list from Spain, from Amnesty International, and I saw that the Spanish jails were full of JWs. But they didn't welcome any support from us. When I got out of prison, I was involved in the amnesty campaign, and of course we tried to enlist the Witnesses' support. Not available.

Peck: Their love, if it was there, didn't reach out to other people. Even among the Witnesses, I never felt real comradeship. They never kidded each other—and you kid one another in prison to stay sane; they didn't. No warmth, nothing playful. Just earnest one-track agreement. They never seemed to relax. We used to wonder if they were like that when they were alone together. Did they think they had to be superhuman in front of the rest of us? Did they talk about sex when the lights went out in their dorm? Prisoners obsess about sex. We never heard them mention it.

DiGia: I can't think what they were interested in except their theology. I can't remember anything that passed for what you'd call a conversation. You know, I have so little sense of them as individuals, I can't remember one singular thing about one single Witness. There was one guy who seemed awfully nice; I had the feeling that he was trying to reach out to us but that he was also afraid to get to know us, because it would scare him if he discovered we weren't bad people. How could any one who liked us believe God was going to savage us?

Peck: I really don't think of them as resisters. I think of them as capitulators. There are times I actually forget that the Witnesses ever went to jail.

Peck and diGia remark that the Witnesses did not think of themselves, nor did they wish to be thought of, as conscientious objectors. Very few Witnesses applied for CO status; those who did were regarded, by the rest of us, as compromisers. The only honorable course—directed by the

Watchtower Society—was to apply for ministerial exemption. Even fewer Witnesses agreed to perform alternative civilian service; those who did were treated like outcasts by the rest of us. During the Vietnam War, the Society issued new imperatives: many Witnesses applied for CO status, and when ordered by the courts, they did perform alternative (civilian) service.

Under the 1940 Selective Service Act (Sec. 5d, Par. 360), "regular or duly ordained mininsters of religion" and divinity students were exempted from the draft (but not from registering for the draft). A "regular minister of religion" was defined as "a man who customarily preaches and teaches the principles of religion of a recognized church, religious cult, or religious organization of which he is a member, without having been formally ordained as a minister of religion; and who is recognized by such church, sect, or organization as a minister." Under the Act, the Witnesses were "considered to constitute a recognized religious sect."

Hayden C. Covington and General Lewis B. Hershey, Deputy Director of Selective Service, arranged for the exemption of "full-time" ministers (called "pioneers") and members of the Bethel Family. (It would have been unthinkable, during the First World War, when leaders of the Society were imprisoned under the Sedition and Espionage Acts, for such an agreement to be made.)

Those who were once persecuted were now privileged. But while "pioneers" appointed by the Society, and members of the Bethel family, had no trouble getting ministerial exemptions, such was not the case for Witnesses who spent most of their time in secular employment.

The local boards were empowered to use their own discretion with respect to those Witnesses who were not clearly granted exemption by the Act. As Major Edward S. Shattuck, Chief of the Legal Division of Selective Service, wrote, "In the last analysis, it is the function of the local selective service board to review the facts in each case and make the proper classification decision." (File Ref. III—Ministers; Sec. 5d; Par. 360b; Jan. 25, 1941)

Covington contends that many boards acted in an "arbitrary and capricious" manner by denying Witnesses ministerial status. [pp. 9, 13, U.S.A. v. Ray Robert Hartman (Brief for appellant by Covington) Oct. 1953] But it can't be denied that the boards, given wide discretionary powers and with popular sentiment to contend with, had a tough time. "Each of Jehovah's witnesses is a minister. If he is not a preacher he is not one of Jehovah's witnesses," Covington argued. If the boards had followed that criterion, they would have been obliged to classify as a minister every Witness who registered for the draft. Theoretically, one could be converted in June, baptized in July, spend seven hours preaching in August, and be granted ministerial exemption. World War II was a popular war; it is easy to see why local boards did not grant across-the-board exemptions where the case for exemption looked at all thin. The Witnesses' argument, which is difficult to controvert, is that if they are a recognized religion, they do have the right to establish the criteria as to who is a minister of that religion. [Cole, pp. 201–203]

Congress had made no provision for a judicial review of a registrant's classification. Witnesses who were sentenced in district courts for violation of the Selective Service Act were denied the right to plead their cases. The decisions of the local boards made in conformity with regulations were final, even though they may have been erroneous. But, after the war in Europe was over, the Supreme Court, reversing a prior decision (*Falbo v. U.S.*, 320 U.S 549, Jan. 3, 1944), condemned the practice of denying registrants the right to defend themselves against indictments brought against them. William Murray Estep, one of Jehovah's Witnesses, was classified 1-A and ordered to report for induction; he refused to be inducted, claiming he was exempt from service because he was a minister. He was indicted for violation of the Act. At the trial he sought to attack the classification given him by the local board. The court ruled that no such defense could be tendered; he was sentenced to three and one-half years. The judgment of conviction was affirmed on appeal. (*Estep v. U.S.*, 326, U.S. 114, Feb. 4, 1946)

The Supreme Court ruled that Estep's conviction "reduced criminal trials under the Act to proceedings . . . barren of the customary safeguards which the law has designed for the protection of the accused." Mr. Justice Murphy, concurring with the majority opinion of Mr. Justice Douglas, wrote:

> To sustain the convictions . . . would require adherence to the proposition that a person may be criminally punished without ever being accorded the opportunity to prove that the prosecution is based upon an invalid administrative order. That is a proposition to which I cannot subscribe. It violates the most elementary and fundamental concepts of due process of law. [p. 9 (Oct. Term 1945. Nos. 292 and 66 on Writ of Certiorari to U.S. Circuit Court of Appeals for the Third Circuit)]

Also concurring, Mr. Justice Rutledge wrote:

> I do not think Congress can make it a crime punishable by the federal judicial power to violate an administrative order without affording an adequate opportunity to show its constitutional invalidity. [p. 15 *(Ibid.)*]

The *Estep* ruling that courts must allow draft registrants to prove that local boards acted without jurisdiction meant that the boards were no longer the final arbiters of registrants' fate—a significant addition to the literature of civil liberties, because it prevented local boards from the unchecked exercise of local prejudices. The *Estep* case is an important one in the annals of civil liberties. The Court did not rule on the merits of Estep's claim that he was a minister; it simply ruled that the appeals court had acted in violation of due process by not allowing him to make a defense. *Estep* set an important precedent: due process of law could not be eroded, even during a national emergency.

At the beginning of the war, district judges, according to Covington, were almost "totally antagonistic. They were against any defense being made by Jehovah's Witnesses at their trials." [*Faith*, p. 187] They were, he says, greatly prejudiced. "After a large number of cases continued to flow through their courts," Covington says, "many of the judges began to change and mellow. They afterward took a more restrained attitude in presiding at the trial of cases involving Jehovah's Witnesses." [*Ibid.*, p. 186]

The *Estep* case had something to do with their "mellowing," of course, as did victory in the European theater of war. As the threat to national security diminished, both courts and draft boards exerted less pressure on dissenters. Unorthodox religions were beginning, in a less repressive climate, to enjoy the full protection of the courts.

A decision of the United States Court of Appeals reflects this trend:

> Whatever a draft board or a court, or anybody else for that matter, may think of [Jehovah's Witnesses] is of little consequence. . . . They . . . are entitled to the same treatment as the members of any other religious organization. . . .
>
> One may preach or teach from the pulpit, from the curbstone, in the fields, or at the residential fronts. . . . To be a "regular minister" of religion the translation of religious principles into the lives of his fellows must be the dominating factor in his own life, and must have that continuity of purpose and action that renders other purposes and actions relatively unimportant.—*Hull v. Stalter*, 151 F. 2d 633 (1945)

The courts treated draft-age Witnesses with increasing leniency as time went on, accelerating the process of legitimizing a marginal religion.

Dickinson v. U.S. is a case in point: George Lewis Dickinson claimed a 4-D exemption in 1948; he was at that time working forty hours a week as a radio repairman, devoting "an uncertain number of hours a week" leading two Bible study groups and "several hours a week" proselytizing. The board classified him 1-A. After 1950, he requested reclassification, because he had, in the spring of 1949, quit his job and begun to work as a "pioneer," devoting 150 hours each month to proselytizing. He continued to work five hours a week as a radio repairman. The local board refused to change his classification. The Supreme Court ruled, Mr. Justice Tom Clark delivering the opinion, that

> Dickinson made out a case which meets the statutory criteria. He was ordained in accordance with the ritual of his sect and . . . he meets

the vital test of regularly, as a vocation, teaching and preaching the principles of his sect and conducting public worship in the tradition of his religion. That the ordination, doctrines, or manner of preaching that this sect employs diverge from the orthodox and traditional is no concern of ours; of course the statute does not purport to impose a test of orthodoxy. . . .

The statutory definition of a "regular or duly ordained minister" does not preclude all secular employment. . . . A statutory ban on all secular work would mete out draft exemptions with an uneven hand, to the detriment of those who minister to the poor and thus need some secular work in order to survive. . . .

Dismissal of the claim solely on the basis of suspicion and speculation is both contrary to the spirit of the Act and foreign to our concepts of justice.—*Dickinson v. United States*, 346 U.S. 389

"Suspicion and speculation" had in fact arisen that Dickinson and many like him had quit their secular jobs precisely in order to evade the draft. From 1939 to 1945 the number of "pioneer" Witnesses doubled. Early during World War II, the government charged that the Society's publications were urging more Witnesses into the full-time work in order to evade the draft. The government's interpretation of the Society's instructions was challenged successfully by Covington, who said that from the beginning of its history, the Society had urged Witnesses into full-time preaching. (He was right.)

Arguing the case of Dickinson, Covington posed as an ecumenicist and a defender of democracy. Raising the specter of "godless communism," he argued passionately—though perhaps somewhat disingenuously—that

the preaching activities of ministers of religion and evangelists bear burdens that ordinarily fall on the Government. They do work of an eleemosynary comforting nature. The Government would be required to do this if there were no religions. The Government would be required to impose additional taxes. . . . It may have to draft people to do the work of charity. Christian preaching to the people of this land does what the Government could not possibly do.

The value of the moral restraints placed upon the people by the work of ministers and evangelists cannot be limited. An invaluable sense of personal duty to principles of justice and righteousness results from the work of ministers of all religions. It is not confined to the general populace. Politicians, officials of government and all public officers are constantly reminded of this sense of responsibility to these principles that comes from preaching.

If democracy is to last, ministers must be kept free from compulsory military service. The dry-rot of internal corruption has destroyed some of the greatest nations on earth because of lack of Christian principles. Preaching and proselytizing the people through the word of God is an insurance against barbarism and the disintegration of the nation.

This brief is a victory of pragmatism over literalism. The Watchtower Society, of which Covington was an officer, certainly did not believe that "an invaluable sense of personal duty to principles of justice and righteousness results from the work of ministers of all religions." Covington's eloquent pleading for democracy scarcely jibes with the Witnesses' refusal to vote. The "disintegration of the nation" was faced, by the Witnesses, with jubilation, not remorse: they prayed daily for the disintegration of all nations in a bloody God-designed catastrophe. But Covington was not above using Cold War rhetoric, any more than he was above citing St. Francis and St. Dominic as precedents for lay preaching. Covington brilliantly utilized anything that worked, and the Court was being asked to adjudicate legal, not theological, matters. Covington's brief for Dickinson was an example of what the Witnesses call using the Devil's weapons against the children of darkness; it reminds me of the many times I heard the Society's officers brag about securing victory by being "wily as serpents, and harmless as doves."

By the time of the Korean War, which was, if not entirely unpopular, certainly fairly incomprehensible to most Americans, the concept of minority religion was so deeply ingrained in the legal fabric that by Covington's own admission [Cole, pp. 121–22, 200–06], the Witnesses were winning many more draft cases than they had in World War II: "The federal courts," he said, "have borne down hard on local boards and appeal boards for capricious and arbitrary refusal to permit registrants who are Witnesses a fair opportunity to state their case, or denial of their exempt status, as ministers."

The Korean war saw a further improvement in the Witnesses' status: convicted draft violators were paroled earlier and, by all accounts, treated better than other COs. And during the war in Vietnam, draft-age Witnesses received discriminatory preferential treatment from boards and courts.

Bureau of Prisons statistics show that 75 percent of the men serving time in jail for draft violations during the Vietnamese war were Jehovah's Witnesses. As of June, 1968, 574 out of 739 Selective Service violators in federal penitentiaries were Jehovah's Witnesses. (The reason the number of total draft violators is surprisingly low is [in addition to the fact that Canada harbored many COs] that there were built-in loopholes in the law which many resisters—or evaders—took advantage of; the New York City Board of Education, for example, received 20,000 more applications for teachers' licenses in 1969 than it had in 1968. [Jehovah's Witnesses could not, for the most part, have leaped into that draft-exempt profession: most have no college degree.]) It is generally conceded that the Witnesses were accorded more courtesy of belief and trust than any other class of objector.

(The above statistics, and the following quotations, come from Dr. Willard Gaylin's book *In the Service of Their Country: War Resisters in Prison* (New York: Viking, 1970).)

Voices from Federal Penitentiaries:

> One of the fellows did an informal check and found out that the average Muslim received one and a half more years than the JWs.—a black civil-rights worker [p. 91]

> There is that whole silly hypocrisy of talking about rehabilitation. In actuality it is quite clear that what they want to do is punish us. It's so obvious. You merely have to study the difference in the attitudes of the Parole Board toward the JWs and the rest of us. The JWs are granted paroles—some after twelve or fifteen months. None of us gets out then.—an Irish-Catholic poverty worker [p. 136]

> I can't even get in an argument with [one of the JWs] over religion, which is the only thing he seems to know, because . . . it's a snobbish thing for me to say, but that son-of-a-bitch is as ignorant a person as I have ever met. Yet his attitudes constantly reflect an enormous, unwarranted conceit. . . . He refers to the other prisoners as dumb cons.
> It's a combination of his personal habits, his lumpishness, and his unwarranted conceit that simply repulses me. He never does anything. He sits like a log for hours on end, and I sense that in his mind he's knocking me and I can't stand it. This is the thing that gets me . . . this supercilious attitude of his. . . . I doubt that he has the intelligence to be supercilious, but I can't stand that attitude. It's totally unjustified and gratuitous in every respect, and it's that which bugs me. . . . His attitude that he's a Christian, in particular, drives me crazy, because I know he couldn't possibly be a Christian. I'm not a Christian but I like to think I know what a Christian should be, and there aren't that many of them around.
> At times when he's got his back toward me for a small second a huge compassionate feeling will seize me and I will say, "He's just a human being. He isn't as fortunate as you are and he has as much right . . . he has to be what he is."—a WASP college graduate [pp. 203–04]

During the Indochinese conflict the Witnesses were less intransigent (and perhaps wilier) than they had been during World War II. Their strategy changed: a large number applied for CO status—and those who asked for a CO, rather than a ministerial, exemption invariably got it.

Covington argued that the fact that the Witnesses were not pacifists did not militate against their being COs.

The issue of pacifism arose in 1950, when 10,000 foreign delegates to a convention in Yankee Stadium had difficulty clearing immigration because they were charged with being pacifists. Pragmatic as always, the Watchtower Society declared that they were "neutral"—but not pacifists. In a petition adopted by the U.S. delegates (which Covington incorporated in one of his legal briefs—*U.S. v. Ray Robert Hartman*), it was declared that the definition of *pacifism* found in Webster's "does not fit a true Christian. Jehovah's witnesses began with Abel. A long list of witnesses for Jehovah have records in theocratic warfare showing they were not pacifists. The exploits of Abraham, Moses, Joshua, Barak, Gideon, Jephthah, Samson, Samuel and David demonstrate this. . . . The military exploits of all of these famous witnesses for Jehovah were part of theocratic warfare. However, such witnesses did not fight for Babylon, the Medes or the Persians. They fought under the direction of God for the theocratic nation of Israel. Since the fall of the Jewish nation and the advent of Christianity the warfare of his Christians has not extended to military weapons. . . . Modern-day Christians, Jehovah's witnesses, follow the rule of love of God and love of neighbor. . . . There is no retaliation by Jehovah's witnesses. Killing of a burglar who breaks in at night is justified. Killing a thief who breaks in by day is condemned." It was probably the first time a judge of the appellate courts was asked to decide a case on the basis of what Jephtha and Barak had done, and the first time anybody was asked to make a moral distinction between killing by night and killing by day.

Witnesses who were instructed by their local boards to report for alternative civilian work refused to obey that injunction. They were then prosecuted for failure to report for service. They did perform alternative service when ordered to do so by a judge of the courts, apparently justifying this about-face by contending that the courts, as opposed to the draft boards, constituted part of the "higher powers" they were commanded by the Apostle Paul to obey. The Witnesses evidently considered compliance with draft-board orders to be tantamount to collaboration with military authorities; they accepted court orders to perform alternative civilian work as a form of "punishment" by duly constituted civilian authorities.

> Judges have been suspending sentence in order to place the defendant on probation, subject to his actual performance of the identical conscientious objector work which he had refused to perform on the order of the Selective Service Board. We take judicial notice that Jehovah's Witnesses are responding to court orders to perform the identical conscientious objector work which they will not perform in response to a Selective Service Board order.—*United States v. Daniels*, 429 F.2d 1273, 1274, 6th Cir., 1970
>
> The great majority [of defendants placed on probation] are Jehovah's Witnesses who were classified as conscientious objectors. They refused to report for alternative service because they regard the Selective Service System as an arm of the military. To perform work directed by the military would compromise their religious convictions.

A few years ago, I stumbled onto the idea that Jehovah's Witnesses would do alternative service if I ordered it because I am not in the military. Romans XIII teaches that the orders of those in civil authority are equivalent to the orders of God.

I know that Selective Service is happy about this solution, and a number of courts throughout the country are using the same technique.—Gus. J. Solomon, Chief Judge, U.S. District Court in Oregon (50 F.R.D. 481, 487, 1970)

It may be conjectured that the Witnesses were considerably less threatening to established authority than radical longhairs. They were not making whoopee or revolution on college campuses (and they were *clean* and quiet; and they didn't "off the pigs"; it's unlikely that many of them had ever even heard of Ho Chi Minh). In a climate of protest and rage, among 1960s freaks and moral anarchists, the Witnesses seemed like a breath of '40s small-town air.

In any case, it is a matter of record that the Witnesses were given preferential treatment by the courts. According to attorney Leon Friedman,

a strategy developed throughout the Federal judiciary as judge talked to judge; when a judge refused exemption to a Witness, the case would go to appeals. Although the general rule is that a sentence within the statutory maximum will not be disturbed by an appeal court, courts would in fact frequently vacate or reduce sentences. Appeal courts modified sentences imposed by trial courts, sentences which, in the ordinary way, would not be reviewable. In other words, an extraordinary situation arose in which lower courts were allowed to interpret statutes, in spite of the axiom that "a sentence imposed by a Federal district judge, if within the statutory limits, is generally not subject to review."

And draft lawyers loved it: "If you treat the Witnesses that way," we argued, "you have to treat our clients equally well."

Civil libertarians loved it because it permitted them to argue that "the importance of fair sentencing overrides the reluctance of appellate courts to interfere with the sentencing procedures." (Appellant's Brief, U.S. Court of Appeals, Second Circuit [Docket No. 71-2187], *McCord v. United States; United States v. McCord*, 466 F.2d 17 [1972]) The treatment of the Witnesses by appeals courts established the proposition that the sentencing judge's discretion, while broad, is not absolute.

The preferential treatment of the Witnesses had become paradigmatic. Draft lawyers used them to say to the courts, Why aren't you giving *our* conscientious clients equally good treatment?

Friedman and Chester Mirsky, attorneys for Michael Witt McCord, claimed, in their brief, that had McCord, a conscientious objector who had been sentenced to a one-year imprisonment by a lower court, been a Witness, he would never have been sentenced.

McCord had served one year of his civilian-work alternative—he worked for the American Friends Service Committee and for the Legal Aid Society—before he quit for conscientious reasons. He was, at the time of his appeal, a student at the Harvard Divinity School, and he was working to provide housing for the urban poor at the Boston Housing Authority. A man of tender conscience, McCord wrote to Selective Service Board:

> I oppose this system . . . because it is unfair in its operation and unfair in the sense that it accords the state a measure of power over its citizens to which it holds no legitimate claim. Each man has a right to his own life and no other man, nor any group of men, however idealistic their motives, possesses the moral authority to [force others] to forfeit this claim. . . .
>
> I am very deeply concerned about love and about how I can most honestly and generously manifest love for my brothers and sisters of this world—*all* of them (American, North Vietnamese, South Vietnamese, Russian—ALL). Of one thing I am absolutely certain: My notion of love is incompatible with war and with those activities and attitudes which make wars possible. . . . I am opposed to the activities of the Defense Department and of Selective Service, and . . . I reject . . . racism and chauvinism, and those philosophies like capitalism and communism which divide human beings and which relegate love and tenderness and nonviolence to inferior positions on the hierarchy of human values. . . .
>
> I am not an anarchist, but neither do I feel that my first moral and intellectual obligation is to the principle of majoritarian rule. Life, perhaps, would be a lot simpler if one knew that "the will of the people" was somehow infallible, but it's not, and life is not simple. There are times when a man must obey his conscience. I heard recently the story of a young Huguenot girl who was imprisoned for her Protestant beliefs in Southern France in the seventeenth century. She spent 39 years in prison, from the time she was fourteen. All she had to do to gain her release was speak two words, "J'abjure" ("I recant"). She refused; instead, in the stone wall she scratched another word— "Resistez."

McCord's attorneys said that their client "was, at all times, and is, prepared to continue [civilian alternative work] if ordered to do so by a court. Such a sentence is ordinarily imposed in similar cases involving Jehovah's Witnesses but was denied" McCord.

Attorney Mirsky told the court [Appellant's Brief, *op. cit.*]:

> The defendant's position is . . . very similar to many of the positions described today by Jehovah's Witnesses, although he is not one; he has arrived at his ideals and beliefs independently, but he presents the same picture to your Honor, it seems to me, as the philosophy of that of Jehovah's Witnesses. . . .

Many Courts . . . for years have given Jehovah's Witnesses who refused to comply with an order from the Selective Service System the right to comply in substance with that order from the Department of Probation, and have always continuously granted probation in cases like that. . . .

McCord . . . is exactly like a Jehovah's Witness. He states to your Honor he is willing to perform alternate service work. Not as a participant of Selective Service obligation, as a contingency obligation. . . .

The Jehovah's Witnesses have stated to the Court for years, we have taken the position that this is basically contradictory to our beliefs to accept an order from Selective Service. We are ready and willing and able in substance to perform alternative service work to anyone who wishes to order us. . . .

We feel that [McCord's] sentence . . . as imposed is itself basically a denial of the man's due process. . . . We feel that the man is placed in a position which is categorically a denial of his legal protection in relation to Jehovah's Witnesses. He stands as a CO, found to be a CO as your Honor knows, by the local board. He meets the requirements. Just as the Jehovah's Witnesses—one is a religious objector, one is a philosophical objector. He goes to jail, and one does not.

I think it is a denial of equal protection.

The position of the United States Assistant Attorney was that McCord had no right to "lump himself with the Jehovah's Witnesses. It's quite obvious," he argued,

that the Jehovah's Witnesses are an unusual problem, and the practice has been in this District, not exclusively, to allow them to complete their work. Their objection is based on religious grounds, very deep religious grounds. A Jehovah's Witness would rather be flogged and tortured to death, rather than obey the order of a sector of authority to serve. They serve only if it is imposed as a punishment of the Court.

But McCord's attorneys argued that "to grant such requests [to vacate sentence] to Jehovah's Witnesses while denying it to others in the same position is a violation of the equal protection tenets of the Fifth Amendment."

In the earlier draft case of Joel Simon Meyers against the United States of America (U.S. Court of Appeals for the Second Circuit, on appeal from the U.S. District Court for the Eastern District of New York; *Meyers v. United States*, 446 F.2d 37 [1971]), New York Civil Liberties attorney Alan H. Levine cited statistics from the Eastern District of New York which demonstrated that, from 1967 to 1970, 88.5 percent of all Jehovah's Witnesses who came before the courts for that district were offered probation; only 36.5 percent of the COs appearing before the courts were offered probation.

McCord's attorneys used these statistics to argue that Jehovah's Witnesses were being treated in a privileged manner that discriminated against other COs:

> If a federal statute prescribed a different mode of punishment for Jehovah's Witnesses and non–Jehovah's Witnesses, it would violate the equal protection clause. . . .
>
> The fact that special treatment of the Jehovah's Witnesses emerges out of informal judicial policy instead of being required by an explicit federal statute does not affect the reach of the equal protection guarantees. Any distinct governmental entity that engages in discriminatory treatment of one class is bound by the equal protection clause. Indeed discriminatory treatment by the judiciary is even more dangerous than that embodied in a statute since the courts can oversee explicit legislative discrimination. But who is to judge the judges?

The Assistant U.S. Attorney, however, took the position that

> There is absolutely no reason whatsoever whereby persons who are conscientious objectors who refuse to perform work should be equated in any way at all with the Jehovah's Witnesses.

Circuit Judge Waterman ruled against McCord, although he agreed that

> The appellant's statistical research does, in fact, tend to show that many federal district judges acting with their broad discretionary powers have been increasingly lenient in the sentences they have handed down in Selective Service cases. The statistics also show the Jehovah's Witness violators have regularly been included in the group toward whom an increasing number of judges have shown a growing lenience.

Dissenting Judge Feinberg said:

> I do not for a moment even intimate that the treatment of Jehovah's Witnesses, if it is as alleged, is not sensible. But in those circumstances I would think that considerations of fair play would suggest that appellant's sentence be no harsher than those given to Jehovah's Witnesses.—*United States v. McCord*, 466 F.2d 17 (1972)

Leon Friedman, one of McCord's attorneys, says that Judge Waterman said, off the record, "Jehovah's Witnesses are different from other people . . . I have a gardener who is a JW, and he's different . . . they're different, they think differently from the rest of us. . . . Maybe I should disqualify myself from cases they're involved in." Friedman says, "I'll never forget that."

VIII. *The Lure of Certainty*

Is it possible that there are people who say "God" and mean that this is something one can have in common? . . . Is it possible to believe that one can have a god without using him?—Rilke, *The Notebooks of Malte Laurids Brigge* (New York: W. W. Norton, pp. 29–30)

THE WORLD perceives them as different; and they feel themselves to be different. And that is the magic of a religion that fears magic, mystery, poetry—a religion that treats ecstasy as an aberration and flees from passion with a passion that is thoroughly small and dry.

I felt bad for sinning that day and asked the Lord to punish me with a pain. Also desiring to know the pains of labor. He gave me the pain right away, a period-pain, but different—spasms, like contractions! It was beautiful, and I was praising the Lord. Until the Devil said, "But you should take a pill, the pain is bad." I shunned his words, but then the pain became worse, and I took a pill; and the pain got even worse. At 3 A.M. it stopped. I slept and slept.

How wonderful it is to live a pure and simple life! It's really good to sit around a table and share thoughts with simple folk. . . .

I'm nervous and frenzied. I think of going to Russia to do missionary work with André. (I don't love him! And he loves Jehovah so much! Why don't I love him?) And I can't help smoking another cigarette. Bad. If I were a man people would leave me alone so much more. And when will I ever be able to relax?

A strange day. Started off by doing a lot of sewing, learned about darning and the hex stitch. Then Frau S. walked in and decided to transport me to her house to learn cooking and the Bible. For some reason I suddenly became sad, dissatisfied, self-pitying, couldn't stop crying. She started reading me some Witness article about the necessity of morality and Christian behavior being reflected by clothing. I've heard so much about clothing (mine in particular) from that family, and I got fed up and left, very upset. After a while, I went back to the tranquillity of darning with Frau Mehringer. And then was given some very nice baked rice pudding. . . .

I know that this is right because I feel cleaner and everything around me is purer than it has ever been.

Today in the late afternoon, after a nap, I went to Klaus's house, the tailor, the Witness of Jehovah. I was feeling tired and a little bit

213

shy and nauseated because this morning I bought a dirndl, a pocketbook, and a bakery bun, and as always when I deal with worldly
things, it drained me. . . .

I will write to my brother and tell him I have found The Truth.

What a wonderful thing it is to be able to really trust people because you know they're seeking after the truth. How can I describe
the atmosphere around these good, honest people? Brother O. spoke
so wisely while we were sitting there drinking a bit of schnapps and
eating a bit of garlic, bacon, cheese, and bread. He also spoke of his
six years in prison under Hitler. Oh, how brave! How I admire that
happiness of his, and I know it's good.
—from the diary of Vera Retsoff

Vera was 17 when she wrote this, having been converted by Jehovah's
Witnesses in a small village in Germany. Multilingual, from an affluent,
achieving family, Vera ran away from college and was a Jesus Freak for two
years before she became a Witness. She remained a Witness for three years,
until her marriage to her childhood sweetheart; and her growing doubts
together with her growing conviction that it was not "selfish" to use her
talents effectively divorced her from the Society.

Yeah, it's hard. It's hard to be a Jehovah's Witness. It's hard . . .
like the Witnesses can't . . . you don't supposed to like . . . you gotta
be good, you can't party, you gotta go to all the meetings, field service
and stuff. And like people on the street are saying, like lots of people
think we're crazy, so it's hard to cope with the people. But what else
is there? You be out on the streets, man, you be missin' a good thing.
'Cause there's *nothin'* out there. I mean, the majority of teen-agers is
bad. I'm gonna keep on tryin'. But it's hard. I mean, it's bad on the
street, but we *gotta* be out on the street. Now, me, I been president of
the Black Knights—there was thousands of us. I'm not talkin' about
killin' nobody, you understand; but I wanted to feel big, dig it? I'm
tryin' now, though, you know. To be good. 'Cause the Witnesses are
right: There's nobody out there gonna do *nothin'* about all the poverty
and shit and war and stuff. *Nobody.*
—Booker Smith, a 17-year-old black from Harlem who is an unbaptized Witness

You get used to the South Bronx; you don't see the suffering anymore. To the people who live there, it's not suffering, it's their life.
They are casualties of the Devil's system. And so are you. From
Adam all have sinned and all are victimized. You too. Jehovah's Witnesses are not hanging out on street corners or into immorality or
dope. We're not violent like the rest of the people. *Our* people in the
South Bronx are physically and spiritually clean. . . . As far as all
those programs to feed people and help people with dope problems,
and day-care centers and social work. . . some people think that's

doing good, but if they're not following the Bible, they're not doing good.

We're treated differently, given respect by fellow workers and employers. Worldly people know we are honest and faithful workers. They know we're not subversive. They know we're discreet, and they know we don't overindulge. Young ladies treat us with honor because they know we wouldn't engage in premarital sex. That would be like jumping off a building. Fornication can kill you. We keep clean.
—Thomas Bart, 21-year-old black Witness elder

I'm not like the rest of the kids in high school . . . the way how they dress and the way how they act and fool around and not listening to the teacher and talking like what they're not supposed to talk about, like obscene words and things that corrode your mind like sex.
—14-year-old black Witness (male)

All of a sudden there are so many questions and they're so heavy. Jehovah knows I want to serve him. But how can I do so out of a clean heart with no reservations or disagreements? How come there are so many questions when I really know all the answers? What about all the wickedness and suffering God has permitted on the earth? Why, if he has the power . . . why, if he loves? Why? I know the answer from the book: The issue is political—God's rule against Satan's. For the last 6,000 years, man has had the opportunity to rule, and he has proved incapable of doing so. And the suffering of the innocent is the result of man's choosing worldly governments instead of God's heavenly kingdom. The suffering is a result of man's choice, not God's doing. Also, because he hasn't ended the world yet, Jehovah is really merciful: He's giving more people the opportunity to serve him. . . . But way down deep, I don't really believe it. . . . The waiting seems so long. I wish the end would come now. This instant. Now. I'm tired of waiting. . . . But maybe God's taking his spirit away from me bacause I have sexual feelings toward S. . . . I never realized how important the words of the brothers are: how treacherous the heart is, how unclean. . . . I want everything, I really do. . . . I want the end to come now.
—from the diary of a 23-year-old Witness who left the Society soon after she wrote this

I was so desperately needy when I became a Witness, just barely functioning, just surviving. I didn't like anything about the present, I hated my past, and the Witnesses gave me a future, and I gave myself to it. I loved the idea of a New World . . . someday I'd be tall and beautiful, and everything evil and unfair would go away, and there'd be justice. It's odd; I really didn't like anything about being a Witness, but I gave myself to them fully and completely. I held nothing in reserve. I was looking to them for honesty and decency. I couldn't find it. But I couldn't allow myself to be critical. Then I had a ner-

vous breakdown. Maybe that was my way of getting out? The Witnesses felt betrayed by my breakdown. Their faces were so hard. No
help. After the breakdown, I couldn't go from door to door anymore.
I wanted God to tell me directly what to do. I couldn't get Him off
my back. . . . I was so conscientious. Wouldn't you think that the
more conscientious I was, the more rewards I should have gotten? But
the more I lent myself to the Witnesses, the more I suffered. Which
proves that sacrifice is awful. So now I follow Ayn Rand.
—a former Witness

They shrink from the intolerable fear that God does not care about men.
Perhaps the original impulse was one of love: can a God-hungry soul contemplate the thought of souls damned in hell? Charles Taze Russell gazed
into the fires of hell, averted his eyes from that vision of eternal suffering
and damnation, and substituted for the God of the Passion—the suffering
Christ of the gospel—a pragmatic, tribal God.

For some men, the stubborn, painful certainty that God does not exist
has (though suffused with nausea and dread) been gorgeously energizing:

Must not lanterns be lit in the morning? . . . God is dead. God
remains dead. And we have killed him. How shall we, the murderers
of all murders, comfort ourselves? What was holiest and most powerful of all that the world has yet owned has bled to death under our
knives. . . . Is not the greatness of this deed too great for us? Must
not we ourselves become gods simply to seem worthy of it? There has
never been a greater deed; and whoever will be born after us—for the
sake of this deed he will be part of a higher history than all history
hitherto.
—Nietzsche, *Thus Spake Zarathustra*

For other men, the absence of the sure knowledge of God has been a
thrilling and lucid invitation to act absolutely as if He did not exist, to be
fully human, to substitute duty and struggle and human love for the impulse to devotion and praise, to adore a flawed and wonderful world.

For Russell and his followers, who had a sense of premonition and foreboding, it was necessary to invent a personal, concrete, and immediate solution to the injustices of life. "The mean and the vulgar flourish, the righteous suffer," said the Psalmist, praising God in radiant despair. The mean
and the vulgar flourish, the righteous suffer, said Russell . . . and he made
charts and juggled dates and numbers in a frenzied attempt to reduce the
beauty and the terror of the world to manageable proportions. In the process—in his fear of the absurd, the unexplained, the incomprehensible, in
his flight from mystery, from the desert of God's uncertain grace—he was
obliged to renounce both the world and the divinity of Christ.

The Witnesses have modified their ideology through the years, but what
has never changed is that in order to accommodate a wholesome hatred for

injustice, the Witnesses have had to embrace an unhealthy hatred of the physical, material world. The world is evil, loathsome and abhorrent; man's nature is evil, loathsome, and abhorrent. They have never been able to reconcile love of God with love of the world.

Their religion is neither one of austere penance nor one of sublime contemplation. They move in our midst like disdainful strangers, waiting for Jehovah—a hard and irritable judge, not a living flame—to enter into wrath. They neither tremble at the abyss nor swoon at the altar of a magnificent God. They spit out the world as if it tasted of ashes; they reject the large idea of a mystical union with God, a communion of brothers and saints. Their God is querulous and small; their religion nourishes damaged deserters from the world, offering them a brittle certainty.

Because God will accomplish all things without the collaboration of man, they do not strive to accomplish the Kingdom of Heaven on earth.

Because they believe the world exists only to be despised, because they believe it is rotten, they are content to leave it to rot.

It is alien to their thinking that God and man can work together to perfect and transform the world—and just as alien to their thinking that man, unsupported by God, is made beautiful by struggle and human love. They do not rejoice in the salvation of man by God-made-man, or in the redemption of man by man. They are outside the tradition of the other Christian churches: they do not believe in the Trinity, the Incarnation, the Eucharist, the immortality of the soul. Their linear, eschatological religion is literalist. The consequences of not acting are, of course, as weighty as the consequences of acting. Absenting themselves from the conflicts of the world, they surrender the organization of the world to others.

It would be easy to conclude that they love neither God (if by God we mean the God of the gospel who died for men's sins), nor man; to judge them so lacking in idealism and compassion as to be monstrous in their indifference. Still, their religion allows them to believe that the world is terrible, but that life is not hopeless. Because it rigidly controls all aspects of their behavior, it gives them the illusion of moral superiority, and of safety. It delivers people who have no tolerance for ambiguity from having to make ethical choices. It allows self-loathers to project their hatred onto the world. It translates the allure of the world into Satanic temptation, so that those who fear its enticements are armed against seduction. It provides ego balm for the lowly, an identification with The Chosen. Because Jehovah's Witnesses believe as little in psychology as they do in philosophy, it tames or numbs the wilderness of the heart by closing the valves of inquiry. It exalts mediocrity, at the same time conferring status on and granting acceptance to the exploited and the oppressed. Moralistic rather than moral, it rescues its adherents from vice (drug addiction, criminality, dirty dishes) and from the demands of art. Obsession, which characterizes geniuses, children, madmen, saints, and artists, is seen as idolatrous.

Yet in the heart of every Witness is the felt knowledge that should he leave his spiritual home, he will die a social death at the hands of his brothers now, a spiritual death at the hands of his God later. And the messages received by the Witnesses from their leaders remind them always of the first Fall, the dangerous tightrope they walk between omnipotence and disinheritance. Repressing human needs, individual desires, they may seem smug—but never entirely, never joyously, sure.

To understand them, it is necessary to understand their doctrine, and particularly their views on evil and salvation, from which all their hopes and fears and their social attitudes (and their appeal—which seems to outsiders bloodless and legalistic) stem:

EVIL; THE FALL; IMMORTALITY

> By revealing an original fall, Christianity provides our intelligence with a reason for the disconcerting excess of sin and suffering. . . . Next, in order to win our love and secure our faith, it unveils to our eyes and hearts the moving and unfathomable reality of the historical Christ in whom the exemplary life of an individual man conceals this mysterious drama: The master of the world, leading, like an element of the world, not only an elemental life, but (in addition to this and because of it) leading the total life of the universe, which he has shouldered and assimilated by experiencing it himself. And finally by the crucifixion and death of this adored being, Christianity signifies to our thirst for happiness that the term of creation is not to be sought in the temporal zones of our visible world, but that the effort required of our fidelity must be consummated beyond a total transformation of ourselves and everything surrounding us.
> —Pierre Teilhard de Chardin, *The Divine Milieu* (pp. 102–103)

The existence of evil is the central problem for all religions. Jehovah's Witnesses explain it by legalisms:

> God, though able to bring an end to bad things, restrains himself for mankind's own benefit.—*TW*, June 1, 1974

> [God's] vindication is more important than the salvation of men.—*LGBT* (See pp. 29–36.)

> The fundamental issue between God and Satan . . . involves man's integrity to Jehovah as his Sovereign.—*All Scrip* (See pp. 7–8.)

They base their case on Job's great cry of despair, tidying his heart's pain into logic:

> Why does God permit evil? . . . From the book of Job we can see that Jehovah has permitted such because of a boast that his adversary,

Satan the Devil, made, namely, that he could turn all men away from God. Yes, Satan claimed that Jehovah God does not deserve to be feared and worshipped and that the only reason why men do obey him is to make selfish gain for themselves. Satan boasted that if God would let him get at Job, a very righteous man, Satan could cause Job to curse God. God accepted the challenge and let Satan bring all manner of hardship and suffering on Job. . . . But Satan failed to turn Job against God. Job thereby upheld Jehovah as the rightful Sovereign and the One deserving to be feared and worshipped.
—*TW*, April 15, 1976

It began, of course, in Eden 6,000 years ago: perfect Adam and Eve were created "free moral agents"; but Satan, in the form of the Serpent, caused the first human pair to eat of the forbidden fruit (a real tree, a real fruit, in the Witnesses' literal version):

> The Devil was originally a spirit son of God and, as such, he was perfect; but he allowed pride and greed for power to be like God to develop in his heart, and this led him to rebel and to get Adam and Eve to join him in his rebellion. He wanted to be a god and have creatures worship and serve him. [*This Good*]

Lucifer was "perfect," the Witnesses say, "till iniquity was found in him, when he conceived a rebellion against God."

Adam and Eve, "although they were perfect in body and mind, . . . were as yet untried, and God gave them the opportunity of proving their obedience to him under the test." [*Ibid.*]

God's prohibition is seen as an act of love, an opportunity for Adam and Eve. How perfect man might entertain imperfect desires is not, for the Witnesses, an interesting question, nor is why or how "selfish ambition" entered Lucifer's perfect breast. This is as close as the Witnesses come to a metaphysical explanation of the entrance of evil into the world:

> God gave to his human son and daughter the freedom of choice, free moral agency . . . because God cared about them and had feeling for them. He had shown love by bringing them to life and by his preparations for their earthly happiness. If God had created them so that they were automatically obedient and incapable of doing otherwise, then they could never show genuine love in return to their Creator. Their obedience would be mechanical. Real love requires a *wanting* to do things that please another or that are in his interests. . . . We get our greatest joy out of doing things for others when we sincerely want to do them because we care about them . . . spontaneously, freely. [*Awake!*, Oct. 8, 1974, p. 12]

Had Adam and Eve not been seduced by the Serpent's invitation to "become like Gods," they would have lived forever on a perfect earth. Instead, they were cast out of the Edenic paradise garden to the "unfinished" part of the earth, there to live out their days in toil and pain.

Thus, Adam and Eve sinned through disobedience to God, and their sin involved all men in death, depriving man of infinite bliss in Eden and of free access to the tree of life. But Christ, in obedience to Jehovah, sacrificed himself as the "lamb of God," and thereby caused the "river of life" to rush forth again for the benefit of the obedient among men.

God has permitted Satan (evil) to exist in order to "raise up his witnesses to declare and publish his fame or name throughout all the earth before all his enemies are destroyed." [*LGBT*]

Satan has, during the course of human history, set up an "organization" to rival God's. This organization—composed of religious, political, and commercial elements—perpetuates the Serpent's original lie to Adam and Eve: "Ye shall not surely die."

The immortality of the soul is a devilish lie:

> Satan . . . brought forth the religious idea that when man dies he just appears to die, that it is just the body that dies, but something inside him, a soul or spirit, lives on, either being born again to some other human or into an animal, or going off into some spirit realm. . . .
>
> [But, in fact] when a person dies his soul does not go straight to heaven, nor does his soul go to a place of torment called "hell," nor would that soul be able to come back as a "spirit" or "ghost" to haunt the dead person's relatives. All such teachings are based on Satan's religious lie that the soul of man does not die, and he has caused many to believe such teachings in order to hold them in fear and turn them from the true understanding of God's purposes. . . .
>
> The simple truth about the matter is that, when a person dies, he is dead, unconscious, and knows nothing. . . . Jehovah's most wonderful and merciful provision for the human race . . . is the Ransom. . . . Sin and death entered into the world when Adam rebelled against God. Adam lost for himself and for his offspring perfect human life in a paradise on earth. By means of the ransom Jesus Christ bought back for mankind this that was lost, namely, perfect human life with its rights and earthly prospects. . . . God . . . did this by transferring the life of his only-begotten son, who was with him in heaven, to the womb of Mary, a Jewish virgin. . . . Jesus was miraculously born *as a perfect human*. . . .
>
> The provision of the ransom . . . opened up a hope of everlasting life. Some believers would be granted life in the heavens, others on the earth. [*This Good;* see pp. 7–26]
>
> After [Armageddon] mankind . . . will be told to make preparations for the restoration of their beloved dead. What a happy thing it will be to prepare a room for Mother and Dad! Some day while working

about your lovely garden park home you will hear the familiar voice
of father or mother calling from the room you prepared for them. You
will run to their room and tell them about the new world and its joys
and all the things that happened on earth while they were asleep in
death. How happy they will be to have no more pain, for they will
come back without the sickness that caused their death, and they will
have before them the glorious hope of living forever on the perfected
earth! This process will go on until all in the memorial tombs are
brought forth. [*Faith*, p. 225]

The absorbing problem of whether God calls men to Him or if, on the
other hand, men choose God, the question of where grace and will join to
provide redemption and union is not directly addressed by the Witnesses.

The closest approach to the problem of grace and will or whether salvation depends on faith or works, is the distinction between "the heart" and
"the mind":

The mind must of necessity take in and digest information. It is the
seat of intellect, the knowledge-processing center. It assembles information and by process of reason and logic it reaches certain conclusions. And the Scriptures indicate that it is, in some amazing way,
directly related to the heart. The heart has a vital role, for with it are
associated the affections and motivation. The heart's direction of one's
whole course in life becomes evident to onlookers. They find out
eventually what the person really is on the inside. But Jehovah at all
times knows the "secret person of the heart." . . . At times the heart
may overrule the conclusions of the mind, giving motivation that favors and elevates emotions or desires over logical reasoning. Not only
does a person have to know with his mind what is right in Jehovah's
eyes, but he has to have the desire in his heart to follow that course.
[*TMSG*, Study 15: "Reaching the Heart of Your Listeners," p. 75]

This evades the question of how God's grace operates to save men. It
does allow the Witnesses to explain why men who are held in general to be
good or wise reject their message: Their "hearts" are "bad" . . . "It is much
more to Satan's liking to hold sway in a subtle way over intelligent, capable
persons who are highly respected." [*All Scrip*; see pp. 207–08]

THE DIVINITY OF CHRIST; THE TRINITY; THE RANSOM

But truly, Lord, if I wanted to cherish only a man, then I would
surely turn to those whom you have given me in the allurement of
their present flowering. Are there not, with our mothers, brothers,
friends and sisters, enough irresistibly lovable people around us? Why
should we turn to Judaea two thousand years ago? No, what I cry out
for, like every being, with my whole life and all my earthly passion, is

something very different from an equal to cherish: it is a God to
adore.—Teilhard, p. 127

I want no pallid humanitarianism—If Christ be not God, I want none
of him; I will hack my way through existence alone.—Romano Guardini

If God gave his life for a man, would that be a corresponding ransom?
Could a lion redeem a mouse?—Watchtower Society

In addition to denying the immortality of the soul, the Witnesses deny
the Incarnation.

Dorothy Sayers called the Incarnation and the crucifixion the terrifying
drama of which God is the victim and the hero. It is that ecstatic version of
God—the version that says that God bore the anguish of being human (by
virtue of which, as Teilhard says, "nothing is profane") that permits of the
idea that we may be sacramentally joined to Him. We are led back to God
through the humanity of Christ:

> [God] plunged [himself] into matter in order to redeem it. . . . The
> immense enchantment of the divine milieu owes all its value in the
> long run to the human–divine contact which was revealed at the
> Epiphany of Jesus. . . . As our humanity assimilates the material
> world, and as the Host assimilates our humanity, the eucharistic
> transformation goes beyond and completes the transubstantiation of
> the bread on the altar. Step by step it irresistibly invades the universe.
> [Teilhard, pp. 107, 117, 125]

Traditional Christianity teaches us that God became man to die for our
sins; and that the godhead is composed of God the Father, God the Son,
and God the Holy Spirit; that the Incarnation may be realized, for each
individual, through the Eucharist.

The Witnesses, perhaps out of aversion to mystery and a determination
to root everything in the concrete, deny the personality and the deity of the
Holy Spirit, which they define, instead, as "the active force of God" which
moves His servants to do His will. They argue that the Trinity is a pagan
doctrine that originated with the Egyptians, Hindus, and Babylonians.

The Witnesses say that Jesus was a perfect human creature, no more, no
less; and that God his father required the sacrifice of a perfect human life to
"buy back," or ransom, what the perfect Adam had forfeited—life forever
(for the faithful) on a perfect earth. Jesus is described as a "perfect parent"
who took the place of sinful Adam. Jesus was, they say, before he became
"a tiny bundle of live energy" who was "transferred from heaven to the egg-
cell in the womb of the unmarried girl Mary" [*FPL*, p. 127], a perfect spirit
creature, the archangel Michael. He divested himself of his spiritual nature
when he came to earth; and, when he died (on a stake—the cross is pre-

sumed to be "pagan" too), he was resurrected to spiritual life (a cut above the spiritual life he had enjoyed before, it would seem, since he was raised to rule over "all other parts of God's organization"):

> He was a spirit person, just as "God is a Spirit"; he was a mighty one, although not almighty as Jehovah God is; also he was before all others of God's creatures, for he was the first son that Jehovah God brought forth. . . . He was the first of Jehovah God's creations. . . . After God had created him as his firstborn Son, then God used him as his working Partner in the creating of all the rest of creation. . . . The life of the Son of God was transferred from his glorious position with God his father in heaven to the embryo of a human. On the third day of his being dead in the grave his immortal Father Jehovah God raised him from the dead, not as a human Son, but as a mighty immortal spirit Son, with all power in heaven and earth under the Most High God. . . . After he had sacrificed his perfect manhood, God raised him to deathless life as a glorious spirit creature. He exalted him above all angels and other parts of God's universal organization, to be next-highest to himself, the Most High God. [*LGBT*, see pp. 31–36, 115–16. See also *Aid*, pp. 917–32.]

So, in the Witness version of Christ, there would seem to be three Christs (none is God); and each is independent of the other. There is the spiritual archangel Michael (called also "the Word," or "Logos"); then there is the perfect human Jesus—born, according to the Witnesses, innocent of ("ignorant of") his prehuman life, who sacrificed his human nature on the stake; and finally there is the resurrected Christ, who enters a higher spiritual plane than the one he enjoyed in his prehuman existence.

The Witnesses say it was not Jesus' earthly body, but a kind of "suit of flesh" that manifested itself to his disciples upon his resurrection on the third day. (Rutherford, ever inventive, suggested that God might have preserved Jesus' human body somewhere to exhibit it during the Millennium. [*The Harp of God* (New York: WB&TS, 1928)]

The churches have consistently argued that to deny the divinity of Christ, the agony of God in the garden, is heresy: "For if, being a creature, He had become man, man had remained just what he was, not joined to God, for how had a work been joined to the Creator by a work?" [Athanasius: *Discourses Against the Arians*]

To deny the divinity of Christ is also to deny oneself the Eucharistic sacrament: When Jehovah's Witnesses "celebrate" the "Memorial" of Christ's death, a small number—those who expect a heavenly, rather than an earthly, reward—share unleavened bread and wine. The bread is merely "symbolic of [Christ's] own fleshly body, head and all"; the wine is "symbolic of his own blood"; and to partake of these emblems is a token that one "imitates Jesus," and "appreciate[s] the sanctification of his blood." (Compare this with Teilhard: "There are certain noble and cherished moments of the day—those when we pray or receive the sacraments. Were it not for these moments of more efficient or explicit commerce with God, the tide of divine omnipresence, and our perception of it, would weaken until all that was best in our human endeavor . . . would be for us emptied of God." [Teilhard, pp. 65–66] The Witnesses believe that human endeavor is, by its nature, devoid of God, and that God is not present in the evil world.) Nor is one baptized into the Church as an infant. Adult baptism is a "symbol of one's dedication to do God's will." [*LGBT*, pp. 296–98]

Charles Taze Russell's waspish attitudes toward the Mass, the sacraments, the Eucharist (those doctrines of union of God and man which thrill mystics and exert a magical pull even among unbelievers, for those especially whom Eliot called the "children at the Gate") set the tone for future Watchtower writings: "Papacy denies and sets aside the true Continual Sacrifice, and substitutes the 'abomination,' the Mass, in its stead . . . the very foundation of all the various schemes of the Church of Rome for wringing money from the people, for all her extravagancies and luxuries." [*SS*, Vol. III, *Thy Kingdom Come*, p. 102]

How splendid it must be, how exalting, to feel, to know:

> Ah, you know it yourself, Lord, through having borne the anguish of it as man: On certain days the world seems a terrifying thing: huge, blind, and brutal. . . . The things in our life which terrify us, the things that threw you yourself into agony in the garden, are, ultimately, only the species or appearance, the matter of one and the same sacrament. We have only to believe.

"We have only to believe." [Teilhard, pp. 136–37] Irresistible words; there is a tension amounting to glory even in resisting them.

But for Russell, everything not rooted in numbers and dates and legal analyses was anathema. The low churches did not escape the raspings of his sharp tongue, either:

"[The] year 1846 witnessed the organization of Protestant sects into one great system called the Evangelical Alliance . . . many of those . . . cleansed . . . thus became entangled with the yoke of bondage." [*SS*, Vol. III, pp. 119–20] The Papacy and the Protestants were both wiped out by Russell's heavy, whipping, sex-stained hand.

And how do the churches feel about what they are obliged to regard as apostasy?

Father Robert Kennedy (of the Brooklyn diocese) says, most charitably:

> Catholics are indeed dissatisfied with the institutional aspects of the Church, with its wealth and clericalism. They turn to Jehovah's Witnesses as an alternative. . . . In Latin America, for example, where the Witnesses make great gains, Catholic belief tends to be authoritar-

ian. We have, in the past, represented forces of oppression, and worship revolves around the saints and the Virgin. The Church's Christology—the Christ of the Trinity—is remote. Jehovah's Witnesses offer an immediate, vivid, living Christ—a man, even as other men—who, they think, has relevance to their lives. A carpenter. Not God. He is more real to them than the Christ of the Catechism. And just as the early church succeeded in slave cultures, like Corinth, the immediacy of the Second Coming appeals to the underprivileged. . . . And the simplicity and uniformity of belief among Jehovah's Witnesses, for people who feel that the Church is baroque and disengaged from daily life, is attractive. . . . Intellectual Catholics ask refined questions. Jehovah's Witnesses ask no questions.

The evangelical churches regard Jehovah's Witnesses as "people of the cults . . . unreached by the church." The Witnesses are equated with Reverend Ike, the Mormons, Christian Science, and Sun Myung Moon: "All of them turn away from the central doctrine of the Christian faith." And they are considered as pernicious as the occult—as "witches, Satanism, astrology, and tarot cards." Dr. Walter Martin, of the Christian Research Institute of Melodyland, California, says:

Satan manipulates the church. The Christians have been afraid of the cults. A JW comes to the door . . . a million times a day all over the world this happens. The Christian says, "Well, I belong to such-and-such a church; I'm a Christian." Then the JW zaps him with the Trinity: "Can you prove to me that it's in the Bible?" he asks. The Christian can't prove it; he's frustrated when he can't answer questions. So the scenario is that the Christian's blood pressure goes up to about 5000; he gives his testimony; he talks about how he's been filled with the Holy Spirit; the JW is entirely unmoved by it and says, "But you didn't answer my question from the Bible." The Christian says, "You're going to hell." Bang. And that ends it. . . .

What we should recognize is that JWs are lost souls for whom Christ has died. The Watchtower is a cult; it's a group gathered around somebody's interpretation of the Bible, and it ends up denying that Jesus Christ is literally God in human flesh. . . . The church has failed them for a hundred years: "Let the Lord convert them," we've said; "Don't have them in your homes, whatever you do; just be positive, preach Jesus and everything will work out fine."

Well, it hasn't. The ostrich approach has made things worse. What we have to do is evangelize by presenting them with answers. We need to go to them. We've got to go to their Kingdom Halls—their meeting places—to hand out tracts. We have organized a whole movement in Southern California which we call Operation Recovery. We have hundreds of young people volunteering to pass out tracts (designed to look like Watchtower literature) at their conventions. We have teams of people all over Southern California being trained to go to JW meeting places and pass out tracts to lead these people back to Christ. . . .

The Witnesses appear to be impenetrable, brainwashed. But it's an illusion. Their minds are blinded by Satan. The only way to communicate with them is by God the Holy Spirit. The Charismatic movement is the spearhead of the Holy Spirit to open their eyes. . . . The Witnesses don't dialogue—they have prerecorded answers, like eight-track tapes. . . . They love to talk about the Trinity, Armageddon.

We send out one tract—*100 Years of Divine Direction*—and quote from *The Watchtower*. We show how they predicted Armageddon seventeen times, and were wrong each time. They missed 1874, 1914, 1918, 1925, 1941—and most recently, October, 1975. . . . We have to wake up to the fact that this is a mission field. [Christian Broadcasting Network 700 Club broadcast, June 11, 1976]

To grasp the Witnesses' theology, it must be asked, For whom was Christ's ransom sacrifice made? For whose sins did he atone? Not, according to the Witnesses, for *all* men: Departing again from Christian tradition, the Witnesses say there are two "classes" of people who will benefit from his sacrifice: "a heavenly class," and "an earthly class." For a "great multitude" of "other sheep" the reward for faithful service to God will be everlasting life on an earth soon to be reclaimed from the wicked at Armageddon. A much smaller number, "the anointed," 144,000 spiritual brothers of Christ, will be "co-rulers" and "associate kings" with Christ in heaven. Since 1918, when "Christ came to his temple," these "anointed ones" have been "resurrected"—or raised, "in the twinkling of an eye." (They were joined by the apostles and the early church members.) The heavenly class has been being gathered since the First Coming of Christ; its ranks, according to the Witnesses, are rapidly closing. The invitation the Witnesses now extend by means of their proselytizing is to the "great multitude":

With the rebellion of Satan the Devil wicked heavenly rule gained control of mankind, and God purposed to set up later a new heavenly rulership over the earth. It would be called "the kingdom of the heavens." The heavenly kingdom would be made up of tried and tested creatures who would maintain their integrity on earth down till death in following faithfully the footsteps of Jesus Christ. . . . The number of these is limited to 144,000, . . . associated with him in this heavenly kingdom. . . . Today, after nineteen centuries of selecting, there is yet on earth a small remnant of the 144,000.

When the last members of the Kingdom class finish their earthly course faithful to death, then the heavenly kingdom of the 144,000 under Jesus Christ the king will be completed by their resurrection from the dead to life in heaven. It will rule over all other creatures in the heavens and those who gain life on earth. . . . It will destroy Satan and all his agents. . . . The call for heavenly inheritance is now closing. [*FPL*]

Charles Taze Russell distinguished between two classes of "spiritual-be-
gotten" people—a higher class, which (with his passion for numbers and
dates and concrete emblems which extended even to the alphabet) he called
Class *n*, who would sit with the resurrected Lord in heavenly glory; and
Class *m*, mortals who "shrank from the death of the human will" and as a
consequence would not reign with Christ in glory, but would become spirit
beings of a lower order within the divine nature. [*SS*, Vol. I, *The Divine
Plan of the Ages*] As the Witnesses had to accommodate more and more
converts, however, a new scenario was invented. *M* and *n* are no longer
operative.

THE SCENARIO:

> At Har-Magedon, . . . the kings and their armies and those having
> the marks of the "wild beast" will all be "killed off" in execution of the
> death sentence that proceeds out of the mouth of the victorious King
> of kings like a "long sword." Their corpses will not be buried with
> religious, military, or civil honors. All the scavenger birds will feast
> upon their dead bodies, and the eyes of God's protected remnant and
> their "great crowd" of godly companions will also feast. These will be
> satisfied at seeing this glorious vindication of the universal sovereignty
> of the Most High God, Jehovah. . . . They will be glad afterward to
> bury any bones remaining of the wicked ones and so cleanse the earth.
> . . . This will also serve as a health measure, to rid the earth of the
> foul smell of putrefying human corpses and to prevent water and air
> pollution and the spreading of diseases to the survivors of this war at
> "Har-Magedon." [*Babylon;* see p. 630]

Before Armageddon, this is what the Witnesses say will happen: "A scarlet-colored wild beast with seven heads and ten horns" will turn against
"the international religious harlot, Babylon the Great" [*TW*, Jan. 15, 1976],
who has been "riding the beast," and will destroy the "symbolical woman
that, figuratively speaking, has had immoral sexual relations with the
world."

Less vividly, all worldly rulers, acting through the United Nations, will
turn against organized religion and destroy all religions:

> They will make her appear shameful like a naked woman in public.
> [Like the] dogs that ate up . . . Jezebel . . . they will devour her body
> with which they once had liked to unite. They will destroy all her
> beauty of form and her religious capacity to give soothing pleasure to
> ungodly, worldly men. . . . They will feed on her, as long as there is
> anything to her. What is left of her frame they will burn with fire, as
> if she were, not a Babylonian temple prostitute, but the unchaste
> daughter of a priest in ancient Israel." [*Ibid.;* see pp. 599–604.]

The seven-headed scarlet-colored dragon spoken of in the 17th chapter of
Revelation is the eighth (and final) world power of Satan's organization set

up to rival God's: it is the United Nations, which God bends to His will to destroy "false religion." In the Old Testament book of Daniel, seven wild beasts are spoken of; for reasons impervious to logic, these beasts represent, to the Witnesses, seven successive world powers. The first six are Egypt, Assyria, Babylonia, Medo-Persia, Greece, and Rome, all of whom have ranged themselves against God. The seventh beast represents "the dual world power of Great Britain and the United States." (Other great civilizations, such as the Mayans and the Indus Valley, to say nothing of the Axis powers and China and the Communist countries, have no place in this collage.) Now, it follows that the eighth world power is necessarily the United Nations—because it springs from the previous seven world powers.

"Since these religious organizations claim to represent the true God, the desolator [the beast, or the UN] will act also in hatred against the One whom they pretend to serve. This vicious, beastly attitude against God [is] blaspheming his name." [*TW*, Dec. 15, 1975, p. 744] God is obliged to destroy the U.N.

Meanwhile, what about the Witnesses? One can hardly expect them not to assign themselves a leading role in this theater of the absurd:

> Should the [Watchtower] Society survive that violent destruction of Babylon . . . the Society will absolutely refuse to unite itself [with the UN]. Such a refusal would certainly move the [UN] to take drastic action against the Society and the Christian witnesses of Jehovah whom the Society represents and serves. . . . International action against these announcers of Jehovah's Kingdom . . . would be the way in which the UN "wild beast" fights against the "lamb," the Lord of Lords and King of kings. . . . Anti-religious political authorities of the earth will be able to dissolve religious corporations . . . but never will they be able to dissolve the worldwide brotherhood of Jehovah's Christian witnesses. [*TW*, Jan. 15, 1976]

> Jehovah's witnesses, sheltered within his Theocratic organization, will be under siege and will seem threatened with destruction by the overwhelming hosts of . . . Satan. . . . Yet be not anxious . . . Jehovah will fight the battle for his remnant and their companions. He will perform his "strange act" at Armageddon. [*TW*, April 1, 1945, pp. 108–09]

There will then follow, so the scenario goes, a period of anarchy. As Charles Taze Russell wrote, "The closing in of this night will evidently put a stop to any further labor to disseminate the truth, which, misunderstood by the public generally, will probably be accused of being the cause of much of the anarchy and confusion then prevailing." (The Watchtower Society is, and always has been, obsessed with anarchy—to the extent of imagining that it will be regarded as the cause of anarchy, as the source of all power failures.)

After all the survivors of Armageddon pile up dead bones and watch birds feast on the eyes of dead enemies, they will begin, under the direction of God, to prepare the earth for Paradise. The 1,000-year reign of Christ will have begun.

The Witnesses anticipate the charge that their zest for gore is unbecoming; as if to excuse their God's bloody excesses, they compare His war to the wars of men:

> "There will be a rotting away of one's flesh, while one is standing upon one's feet; and one's very eyes will rot away in their sockets, and one's very tongue will rot away in one's mouth." Frightful? Gruesome? Sadistic? Ghoulish? Fiendish? Bible readers in Christendom may express shock at that inspired battle account! . . . How can they sincerely be shocked, when the so-called "Christian" nations that they so patriotically support now stand prepared to fight the final war with . . . flaming napalm bombs . . . with liquid fire belched forth from guns, with corrosive chemical gases, with explosives that will blast away a person's face so that the surviving victim needs to wear a mask and be fed intravenously, with nuclear bombs of such enormous power as to make tens of thousands of human creatures disappear into thin air? How can the supporters of such wartime viciousness find fault with Jehovah of armies? [*Paradise Restored to Mankind by Theocracy!* (New York: WB & TS, 1972), pp. 389–90]

Satan, for the duration of the reign of Christ and his "144,000 royal associates," is "abyssed" before his ultimate annihilation. For a thousand years, a series of "resurrections" will take place: Brought forth to "a resurrection of life" will be "the other sheep" who died before Armageddon and "the faithful men of old"—pre-Christian "Witnesses." Brought forth to "a resurrection of judgment" will be people "whose hearts may have been wanting to do right, but who died without ever having had an opportunity to hear of God's purposes or to learn what he expects of men." [*FPL*, p. 229]

Not to be resurrected—but to sleep forever in uneventful death—are "those who deliberately and willfully did wrong," those who "died wicked beyond reform or correction," [*Aid*, pp. 1399–1400] such star sinners as Judas, Adam and Eve, those who perished in the Flood and at Armageddon, and the inhabitants of Sodom and Gomorrah.

Those who are "raised," or resurrected, will arrive in fallen, imperfect bodies, but not in the identical bodies they took with them to the grave. God will not collect their scattered atoms; He will "reactivate the life pattern of the creature" which He has stored in His memory.

The logistics of all these resurrections—which will be spaced over a period of 1,000 years—might give population experts a very large headache.

Other, less literal, religions might simply trust in God and hope for the good. But the Witnesses have worked it all out in advance, down to the closest half-acre:

> A very liberal estimate of the number of persons that have ever lived on earth is twenty billion. . . . Not *all* of these . . . will receive a resurrection, but even assuming that they did, there would be no problem as to living space and food for them. The land surface of the earth at present is about 57,000,000 square miles . . . or more than 36,000,000,000 acres. . . . Even allowing half of that to be set aside for other uses, there would be more than half an acre . . . for each person. . . . One-half acre . . . will actually provide much more than enough food for one person. . . .
>
> Let us assume that those who compose the "great crowd" of righteous persons who "come out of the great tribulation" on this system of things alive . . . number one million (about . . . one thirty-five hundreth of earth's present population). Then if, after allowing, say, one hundred years spent in their training and "subduing" a portion of the earth . . . God purposes to bring back three percent of this number, this would mean that each newly arrived person would be looked after by thirty-three trained ones. Since a yearly increase of three percent, compounded, doubles the number about every twenty-four years, the entire twenty billion could be resurrected before five hundred years of Christ's thousand-year reign had elapsed. [*Ibid.*]

Not all, after these resurrections, is yet perfect: After the Millennium (during which man will have achieved physical and mental perfection), God will schedule another test of man's integrity. Satan is "let loose out of his prison," and he and "his demons come again into the vicinity of the earth, where they can exert an invisible control over those of mankind who succumb to them." For reasons that are unclear, "Satan the Devil will be confident of himself, in spite of the mental, moral, spiritual, physical perfection of mankind." He will again "challenge God's sovereignty"; the issue will at last be settled in God's favor. [*God's Kingdom of 1000 Years Has Approached* (New York: WB & TS, 1973), p. 149] Anyone seduced by the Devil will be consigned to "the second death." (All of this, for anyone who's interested, is an odd reading of Ezekiel and Revelation.) With God's name "sanctified forever," Christ will be able to hand over to his Father a forever-perfect kingdom; and all shall be well, world without end.

He hath made everything beautiful in his time. —Ecclesiastes 3:11, KJV
Everything he has made pretty in its time. —Ecclesiastes 3:11, NWT
The Witnesses' translation of the Old and New Testaments (which they prefer to call the Hebrew and Greek Scriptures) both diminishes emotions and—by clever manipulation of words and punctuation unsupported by unbiased scholars—furthers their own doctrine. (For example, "Cross" is

translated "torturestake"; by a replacement of a comma, the meaning of Luke 23:43 is changed to destroy the idea that Jesus was offering the malefactor who died with him immortality: "Verily I say unto thee, Today shalt thou be with me in paradise."—KJV. "Truly I tell you today, You will be with me in Paradise."—NWT.)

The Watchtower Society published its translation of the New Testament (the "Greek Scriptures") in 1950—to something short of critical acclaim. The Old Testament (the "Hebrew Scriptures") was published in five volumes from 1953 to 1960, and the entire New World Translation of the Bible was published in 1961. Prior to 1961, the Society had relied chiefly on the American Standard Version (1901), primarily because this translation used the name *Jehovah* over 6,000 times in the Old Testament. In 1944, the Society purchased the use of the plates of the American Standard Version in order to print it on its own presses.

But the Society, while acknowledging its indebtedness to other versions of the Bible, found fault with them all—for their "inconsistencies or unsatisfactory renderings, infected with sectarian traditions or worldly philosophies." [*All Scrip*, p. 323]

Thus, a decision was made by the Society to bring out its own translation from the original languages. This New World Translation was intended to bring the Bible as close to present-day readers as were the original Scriptures to their audience. An announcement was made on September 3, 1949, at the Society's Brooklyn headquarters that a committee had completed such a translation and was presenting it to the Society for publication. The gift also gave the Society complete possession and control of the property, in recognition of its work in spreading knowledge of the Scriptures. The translation was accepted by the directors of the Society, who then proceeded to have it published.

This bland account implies that Knorr had stumbled upon a work by disinterested (anonymous) translators. The New World Translation of the Bible was, of course, an in-house version. The "Committee" labored with Knorr peering over their shoulders. All of us who worked at Watchtower headquarters knew it was in the works; Fred Franz, then the Society's vice-president and Knorr's confidant, was known to be the chief translator; I proofread portions of it when I worked at headquarters. (I sometimes think that the single thing that clinched my decision to leave the Watchtower Society was reading that *Job was scared*. I may not have known exactly what I was doing, but I knew life was larger than that.)

The New World Translation places ("restores" according to the Watchtower Society) the name *Jehovah* 6,962 times in the Old Testament and 237 times in the New Testament. The Society acknowledges that "the pronunciation *Yahweh* may be a more correct one, but the Latinized form *Jehovah* continues to be used because it is the most commonly accepted form of English translation of the tetragrammaton." [*Ibid.*, p. 326]

One of the aims of the translators was to achieve a high "degree of literalness":

> Many Bible translators have abandoned literalness for what they contend to be elegance of language and form. They argue that literal renderings are wooden, stiff and confining. However, their abandonment of literal translation has brought about many departures from the accurate, original statments of truth. They have in fact watered down the very thoughts of God. [*Ibid.*, p. 325]

This presupposes, of course, that the Watchtower Society alone knows what "the very thoughts of God" are. How well its translators succeeded in achieving "a high degree of literalness" may be seen from the following comparative readings:

> The Lord reigneth; let the people tremble; he sitteth between the cherubims; let the earth be moved.—Psalm 99:1, KJV
> Jehovah himself has become King. Let the peoples be agitated. He is sitting upon the cherubs.—Psalm 99:1, NWT

> But who may abide the day of his coming? and who shall stand when he appeareth? for he is like a refiner's fire.—Malachi 3:2, KJV
> Who will be the one standing when he appears? For he will be like the lye of laundrymen.—Malachi 3:2, NWT [Try setting that to Handel.]

> The Lord is my shepherd; I shall not want.—Psalm 23:1, KJV
> Jehovah is my shepherd, I shall lack nothing.—Psalm 23:1, NWT

> Vanity of vanities, saith the Preacher, vanity of vanities; all is vanity. What profit hath a man of all his labour which he taketh under the sun?—Ecclesiastes 1:2–3, KJV
> "The greatest vanity!" the Congregator has said, "The greatest vanity! Everything is vanity." What profit does a man have in all his hard work at which he works hard under the sun?—Ecclesiastes 1:2–3, NWT

> The flowers appear on the earth; the time of the singing of birds is come, and the voice of the turtle is heard in our land; The fig tree putteth forth her green figs, and the vines with the tender grape give a good smell. Arise, my love, my fair one, and come away.—Song of Solomon 2:12–13, KJV
> Blossoms themselves have appeared in the land, the very time of vine trimming has arrived, and the voice of the turtle dove itself has been heard in our land. As for the fig tree, it has gained a mature color for its early figs; and the vines are abloom, they have given their fragrance. Rise up, come, O girl companion of mine, my beautiful one, and come away.—Song of Solomon 2:12–13, NWT
> Lo, I am with you alway, even unto the end of the world. Amen.—Matthew 28:20, KJV

> Look, I am with you all the days until the conclusion of the system of
> things.—Matthew 28:20, NWT

Yes, one is obliged to admit that the New World Translation is inelegant,
not to say tin-eared, lacking "the perfect order of speech, and the beauty of
incantation." What the Committee says is "Ideas, once cloaked in archaic
English, now shine out with meaningful brilliance. Its everyday language
helps you to grasp information vital for eternal life." [*All Scrip.* See pp.
327–28]

In fact, the Watchtower Society despises "ideas." The Committee says:

> Since the Bible has been written in these down-to-earth, easily un-
> derstandable terms, it is possible to translate its symbols and actions
> clearly and accurately into most modern-day images. The original
> power and force of truth are preserved. . . . Simple everyday words,
> such as "horse," "war," "crown," "throne," "husband," "wife," and
> "children" communicate accurate thought clearly in every language.
> This is in contrast to human philosophical writings, which do not
> lend themselves to accurate translation. Their complicated expressions
> and up-in-the-air terminology often cannot be conveyed precisely in
> another tongue. [*Ibid.*, p. 9]

Well, it is easier to translate *horse* than it is to translate *existential*, as it's
easier to translate *war* than *goodness*. Still, is the Book of Revelation any
more accessible than "human philosophical writings"?

> The Bible's power of expression is far superior. Even when God
> communicated judgment messages to nonbelievers, he did not use
> philosophical language, but, rather, everyday symbols. This is shown
> at Daniel 4:10–21. Here the kingdom of the self-glorifying pagan king
> was described in some detail under the symbol of a tree, and then, by
> means of actions involving this tree, future happenings were clearly
> foretold. [*Ibid.*]

But who is to determine what the symbols *symbolize?* One gets the feeling
that when the Watchtower Society talks about "human philosophical writings" it means anything other than common nouns; the Society cherishes
the facts and it alone determines what the facts "mean." [*Ibid.*]

The point about the New World Translation is not just that it is inelegant and uncharming; it is hardly worth laboring the point that God ought
to be praised (or, for that matter, damned) in language that attempts to
approximate His magnificence (or His awfulness). Nor is it profitable to
point up a pious Philistinism of the Witnesses. What the New World
Translation reveals about the Watchtower Society is its fear of the terror,
beauty and wonder of the world, its fierce desire to make all that is awful
pallid, its determination to reduce the world to small, manageable proportions. Its lust for literalness is a desperation for certainty.

But one of the odd things about the Society (some people have experienced this as terrible) is that while it has provided its followers with a narrow certainty, there is something niggling about its dogma, something thin-voiced about its imperatives, that denies its followers the rapture of abandon. It is dogmatic rather than Absolute. The lure of certainty attracts different kinds of people. Some (most) of Jehovah's Witnesses choose their belief in order to be enhanced: It confers upon them a status, a feeling of being accepted, that they would otherwise never enjoy. Others choose the Witnesses out of a need to be reduced; some of these—particularly those who suffer from the guilt of affluence, combined with idealistic temperaments—wish to be delivered from the fullness of their personalities; they have a need to throw in their lot with the oppressed. Whatever the reason for the choice, however, many ultimately feel cheated—because the dry certitude they are given is not a substitute for Absolution.

Jesus please let there be much less of me . . . And Jesus, please, much more of you.—Vera Retsoff

Vera went looking for a large ecstasy, and found a shriveling pain instead. She found herself, as she was later to say, not "reduced to an atom of praise," but "diminished to a speck of suffering."

Vera was born to a large, rich, aristocratic White Russian family of artistic and cultivated exemplars. Her mother was a socialite. Multilingual, Vera spent part of her childhood in boarding schools in England and Switzerland. She was a stern and an ardent adolescent. Her early journals and diaries are full of sincere, albeit self-conscious, ennui, rage, self-loathing, self-adoration, necessity to fix the blame ("There's so much bad in me" . . . "Other people are so *little*"), and seesawing between narcissism and masochism ("I am separate and 'bumbled' and lonely and bad and silly"; "I feel a light burning within me—I am marked"). She disliked her mother, whom she regarded as narrow-minded and intolerant.

Vera spoke to me as she was on the verge of leaving the Witnesses. During the whole of our conversation she spoke of the Witnesses as "They" (not "We"). I think she was really out already, but didn't know it. It was one of the hungriest conversations I've ever been involved in. Vera's need to explain herself was so immense it was almost as if she wanted to be exposed and eaten and every part of her found good; she wanted my life (which was, while in some disarray, clearly a chosen life) to prove to her that one could leave "The Truth" and not only survive, but live with some grace and hope of joy. She searched my children's faces and found (to her mild astonishment, I think) that there was nothing to despise in them. She gazed and gazed at me, wondering, I think, if some visible stain could be found on me, some brand of the wickedness she had been told to expect. She even attempted to extract messages from tangible objects; I remember her running her fingers over the smooth surfaces of waxed tables, tentatively touching plants and *objets*, and taking surprised delight in each thing that was whole and fresh and thriving and clean and beautiful. She twisted a Venetian wine goblet in her hand, amazed (I thought for a moment) that the clear liquid did not turn into blood and the glass shatter in her hand.

(Six months after this conversation, Vera sent a formal letter of renunciation to the Watchtower Society—an act she said she felt was necessary because "they loom so large in my dream life . . . I don't want them relegated to my unconscious . . . I have to make a real break with them in the real world—and on my own terms.")

When Vera was 16, she had written in her diary, "I'm so rotten that the only person who could love me is God and He's not there—and I'm mad at Him; why doesn't He *make* me believe in Him?"

Because she didn't want to go to college, she ran away to Mexico.

I couldn't imagine what good art and poetry were. Everybody in my family was successful. But still, life is terrible: people get old and they're thrown out like garbage. I felt there had to be an answer to all the suffering . . . and a community of people who had the answer. And I felt that if I had any talent—like languages, or acting—I should use my talents to help humanity. What good was it to write a book? So many other people had—practically everybody in my family had. I wanted my cause to be *the* cause.

When I was in Mexico I met some Jesus Freaks. What I really wanted was to relate to people on a deep level—a deep intellectual level and a deep emotional level, and no artsy bullshit. I accepted Jesus. I thought I found what I'd wanted—a community; but there was no real sharing. I couldn't talk about my inner life. Praying and speaking in tongues seemed to me a good substitute for acid and protests, but it was all so simplistic. And I had this terrible feeling that it was too easy. Why would Jesus suddenly allow me to find Him? I wanted an intellectual exploration of religion, and that wasn't happening; so I lulled myself into thinking that I had at least found enthusiasm, love, and security.

I came back home to Long Island, determined to find other Jesus people there. And I went to work in a day-care center . . . my God, the deprivation of other people! My boyfriend, David, who had accepted Jesus with me, couldn't reconcile his desire to be an artist—which he equated with elitism—with the fact that people were starving. And I couldn't accept my family's ambitions for me when people all around me didn't have enough to feed their children. David's commitment to Jesus wavered, and he set off for New Orleans, where he got lost in the drug culture again. I went off to a small mountain village in Germany. I had my Bible. I imagined I'd be ascetic, I would fast, I'd get involved with simple crafts—and leave all my selfish, ugly ambitions behind. . . . I'd hitchhike, and preach in my primitive way.

I wanted fellowship. My landlady introduced me to the people

down the road. They were Jehovah's Witnesses. The first question
they asked me was Do you read the Bible? I wanted to embrace them!
They loved God too! I felt as if I were starving and they were offering
me food. They tried to turn me on to the name *Jehovah*, which I saw
as a denial of my personal attachment to Christ. I wanted to believe
that Jesus was God, and they were taking that away from me. But I
allowed myself to be convinced by their arguments. I loved them very
much. I was impressed, the first night, with their systematic study of
Revelation, which I'd found confusing. I felt I'd discovered what I'd
been looking for—*the people*, the real people. They weren't chattering
about art and politics—everything that seemed vain and petty and
quarrelsome to me; they didn't care about worldly success or failure;
and they weren't just saying Praise the Lord—they were approaching
the Bible (I thought) rationally. How beautiful!

When Vera was very young, she had written in her diary: "Is thinking
bad? Is feeling bad? Or both? Or neither? How can I just *be?*" What impressed her about O-Ma, the grandmotherly woman who converted her,
was her apparent homely simplicity:

> She never had to ask herself whether she had to forfeit her intelli-
> gence or her instincts. She just was. All she wanted out of life was to
> live in the New World on a little farm and raise pigs. That's all she
> asked of God. I felt as if I'd been bludgeoned all my life before into
> being special . . . with O-Ma and the Witnesses, everything seemed
> simple and good, like bread. She was the salt of the earth. I'd had
> Freud and dope and Radcliffe up to my ears. When I was hungry she
> gave me something to eat. When I cried, she gave me schnapps. . . .
> The Witnesses at the first meeting I went to were so warm and
> friendly. I remember singing a song: "Come here all you thirsty ones,
> come and drink—life's water is free" . . . and I said oh, I'm so thirsty.
> I felt as if I'd found the fountain of living waters.

But the idyll was wormy. It was not so simple and good after all. Vera
says:

> I loved feeling like a real woman, not an intellectual machine. I
> gardened and cooked and sewed—all the things I'd never done. In my
> aristocratic family, those were things servants had done. But pretty
> soon I understood that some of the Witnesses thought I was a prize—
> they used to point me out to people as an example of an educated,
> upper-class hippie who'd doped and slept around . . . they made me
> testify at conventions about my former life; and I felt I was being
> used. I used to wear long skirts, and they told me not to, it made me
> look as if I were still a hippie. But they wore nail polish—I thought
> that was silly and artificial. Still, my need was so great, I overlooked
> all their harangues. In the eight months I spent in Germany, I became
> a real Witness. I wrote to David that I could never sleep with him

again, although I still loved him, because intercourse was sinful. David, who was living on skid row in New Orleans, wrote that if the Witnesses were thrown in prison and persecuted he'd feel he'd have to go with them, because if there's a choice between the victims and the victimizers, you have to choose the victims (he'd been reading Camus); but he also said that I was narrowing my definition of love so much he couldn't recognize me anymore—and he asked me, If God is good, why doesn't He love all victims, not just Jehovah's Witnesses?

So I felt I had to choose between God and David, and of course I chose God. It was a terrible wrenching.

When Vera came back to New York, her parents wanted her to return to college; she wanted to become a missionary. They made a deal: "My father said he'd study the Bible with the Witnesses if I went to college. So I studied Russian at school. I had a fantasy that I'd go to Russia and help all the spiritually thirsty people there. And I fantasized about being thrown into prison camps. I loved the idea of going to prison, suffering for—maybe dying for—Jehovah."

While Vera was enjoying her persecution fantasies, she also derived pleasure from preaching in the poor, black part of town—to people whom she would otherwise never have known.

It really turned me on to go into the black part of town—think what my socialite mother would have said to that! I know there was an element of rebellion in what I was doing; but I did truly love feeling that I could be with different kinds of people and be accepted as an equal. I could go into a black house and feel that we could transcend our differences . . . there was a feeling of community; social reform and protest became irrelevant because you got this feeling that it had all happened already—that we were black and white and together and loved one another.

At the Witness assemblies, I felt just like everybody else, like part of a family. For me, the theological content of what the Witnesses had to say was never as important as that feeling I had when I taught at Bible studies that I was giving and receiving love. . . . That wonderful feeling that you can meet people and help them, provide them with easy answers to all their problems. I wanted to help. And I felt omnipotent. This is blasphemous: I felt like God; because I could say, "If only you believe in this, you'll be happy." I loved being special and different and inviting people to be special and different and happy like me; I've always felt unique. Preaching made me feel *full.*

While Vera was in this heightened state of consciousnesss, she met André, a French Jehovah's Witness whose Russian mother had been in a concentration camp in Germany. He seemed to be the fulfillment of her fantasies: they would marry, go to Russia together, and preach. But she describes him as a "paper person."

I wanted a mating of souls. He wanted to quote Scriptures. He told me that all my efforts to "understand" him were "Devilish psychology"—and he told me that all the fairy tales I grew up with and loved (I used to read them to him in Russian) were "demonism." He wanted to quote Scriptures—and he had a huge erection all the while he was talking about "demonism." I started dreaming about David; and I started masturbating. I tried to convince myself that God had provided me with André, a perfect mate. But I'd masturbate and think of David and love David and know that God would take His spirit away from me because I was masturbating. . . .

The guiltier I felt, the worse I behaved. I renewed a friendship with a nonbeliever, who was an actor: I was so jealous of that acting troupe—they had the freedom to do what they wanted, and I hadn't. But then I'd look at them and think, It's all ego and publicity, there is no pure art, there are no pure people. . . . But if I were pure, all things would be pure. And I was getting a lot of pressure from my local congregation elders to leave college and go into the full-time preaching work. . . . I went to see André in France—to marry him— and I felt as if I were falling down a deep well. He went, physically, as far as he could go without breaking the Watchtower rules—and I was sickened. There was no physical basis for our union, no spiritual basis, nothing but sloppy need—his, mine.

Out of all this conflict came Vera's decision to go back to the simplicity of the people who had converted her in Germany. She thought they would put her right, but:

> That whole congregation—the congregation I had thought was so pure and simple and sweet and wise—had split apart over the issue of whether women should wear pants or not! The male elders said it would "stumble" worldlings if the Witness women wore pants; the women said it was too cold to preach in the mountains wearing dresses. They finally fixed on a compromise: If it went below a certain temperature, the women could wear pants, but never to meetings. . . .
> I remembered thinking that they had seemed like the fountain of life to me, and now . . .

Vera came back to America. David agreed to study the Bible with the Witnesses . . . and the inevitable upshot was that Vera and David went to bed together. Vera had by this time been celibate for three years.

> Once I had sinned against Jehovah by sleeping with David—although in my heart I could never feel that my love for him, and my full expression of it, was a sin—my relationship with Him was broken. I couldn't pray anymore. Had there ever been a real connection between me and God? I felt totally abandoned. By God, by the Society—and of course my terrible fear was that David would abandon me too.

So after David and I got married, which we did almost immediately after we'd made love, I confessed to the elders. I was "put on public reproof." It was announced at the meeting in the Kingdom Hall that I'd committed fornication; and there was fifteen minutes of graphic description of what we'd done and how often we'd done it. I was, of course, humiliated. But relieved, too. I thought God's spirit would return to me.

What happened instead was that Vera's doubts about the Witnesses increased; and the Witnesses' coldness toward her increased. At the time I spoke with her, she still hadn't figured out which was cause and which was effect.

David is a totally honest person, and he stopped coming to meetings because, though he'd tried, he just couldn't believe. They were mean to him. An elder suggested that because he was an artist, and because both his father and then his stepfather had died when he was very young, he was "prone to homosexuality" and that he should overcompensate by being dominant in the home and doing manual labor. He said, Fuck that. And then *I* started to think about homosexuality. I realized that part of my attraction to the Witnesses was the opportunity it afforded me for intense relationships with other women. There is so much female bonding among the Witnesses, and in my opinion it's unconscious and unacknowledged homosexuality— not that I could ever have expressed that. If I said to them, "I like women's breasts"—and I do—they would probably deny ever having homosexual fantasies.

When David stopped coming to meetings, they asked me if he was "rebellious." They told me my appearance wasn't as "nice" and "clean" as it had been before I married David. They told me I was dirty. I told them that being married wasn't exactly the same as not being married, and that I loved David, and that he was good . . . but they obviously thought I was some kind of predator, a devourer of young boys; because once they talked to me about having evil sexual intentions because I gave a hippie boy a ride to a meeting in my car. They said it might give worldly people the wrong impression. . . .

All that emphasis on outward appearances, the ridiculousness of their sexual preoccupations. . . . It became harder and harder for me to go to meetings. I became obsessive: Was innocence, I wondered, the lack of sexual appetite? How could that be? Why did Adam and Eve suffer a revulsion against their genitals the minute they broke God's law? Why did He give them that prohibition in the first place? It's like telling a kid not to put beans in his nose—of course he'll put beans in his nose the minute you tell him not to. . . .

I began to lose something. I couldn't talk honestly to the Witnesses anymore. It was all just superficial jargon. . . . I couldn't preach. And I missed that terribly. I couldn't make my mouth say things I didn't fully believe—but I missed instructing people in Bible studies; I missed the exchange of closeness and love. That terrifying feeling that you're living a double life! . . . I realized I was getting so much more from the people I had been "instructing" than they were getting from me. I was getting love. I was instructing a woman from Haiti, a maid; I was practically her only friend. How she loved it when I told her that the bad people were going to get their lumps and someday she wouldn't be poor anymore. And she made me feel that it was all right that I'd been born rich because someday we'd all be equals.

I wanted to hold on to those feelings; but every time I went to a meeting, the Witnesses would give me the hairy eye. . . . They asked me if I practiced fellatio or cunnilingus with David. Why? What business was it of theirs? And at the last meeting I went to, an elder told me that Women's Libbers should be satisfied that God has lovingly provided for some women to be of the heavenly anointed class, and that that should make me rejoice in my submission to David. As if David had ever asked for submission. . . . They slander *everybody*! And it all began to feel empty.

But you see, how could I be sure that all my doubts weren't the result of God's taking His spirit away from me because I'd committed fornication? Or because I was ambitious? (They told me I was like Lucifer because I wanted to be an actress.) Or maybe it's because I'm a snob? I gave my grandmother a Watchtower publication in Russian, and she despised it because it was ungrammatical. I told her that Jesus and his disciples spoke the language of the uneducated masses; she said, Language is the way we communicate, and if it is inexact and sloppy, then the thought is bound to be inexact and sloppy.

Well, I am a snob. If that means having standards. Why are their publications illiterate? Why are their meetings so leaden and dull and oppressive, so boring? . . . Is it wicked of me to want surprises?

I think a large part of my attraction to the Witnesses was that I had a terrible fear of success—or of failure, which is the same thing, I suppose. Once I became a Witness, I didn't have to go to Juilliard, I didn't have to become an actress, I didn't have to prove anything. Except that I was good. Or bad? I can't sort it out. I was idealistic. I was narcissistic, too. Did I choose God, or did He choose me? Did I leave Him or did He leave me? And why me? Why not David? I'm no better than David. And probably not very much worse. They can't answer any of my questions. . . .

Like, I've been thinking: What if Voltaire and Diderot came back to the New World? Wouldn't they hate it? A suburban paradise? . . . Do you know they don't even know who Solzhenitsyn and Doestoevsky are? And if they did, they wouldn't care. . . . And yet they have a sense of foreboding. They feel they're at the verge of the end, and maybe we are; maybe they're instinctually right. . . .

I don't know if I can make a clean break. Sometimes I dream that I'll get back to being spiritually strong. And I'll find a congregation that won't be mean to me. (But they'd all be mean to me if I told them I loved Solzhenitsyn.) Sometimes I think God's spirit will come back. And then I think, But it'll be talking that horrible English they talk. . . .

I've been told by them so many times that if I left "The Truth" I'd have no friends. But I've been with acting troupes and with people who are good and kind and helpful. How awful that I should be surprised by the fact that people are kind! I was really beginning to believe that the whole world was composed of monsters. It isn't really all that cold on the outside. . . .

But suppose the error really is all in me. Suppose all my doubts are from Satan because I offended God and He took His spirit away from me. . . .

Several months after I met Vera, I got this letter from her:

Dear Barbara,

I went to an assembly at Ozone Park to test my feelings. There was this black woman there with a little baby on her back and her baby-pack was slipping off and she was having a hard time with it, and I was trying to help her. And she immediately told me she was disfellowshipped, as if she were warning me off her, as if she were a leper, not clean, not good enough to talk to. And I felt, out of all the people there, she was the only one who was really my sister. . . . As you are my sister. . . .

I will never go back again. I am trying to be good and happy. (Are they the same thing?)

Love,
Vera

Vera is now acting, and working with Soviet dissidents, and researching a biography of one of her ancestors—and living happily with David. She has survived her experiences remarkably unscathed—although, as is the case with many ex-Witnesses, her longing for a "perfect brotherhood," a communion or community, will probably never leave her. Unlike many ex-Witnesses, she is not shopping for a new certainty; her experience has taught her to tolerate ambiguity—and to tolerate herself.

The world already hates us, but Jehovah God and Jesus Christ do not.—The Watchtower, Jan. 15, 1976

When Vera was a Witness, one of her fantasies was that she would be "persecuted"—die, perhaps, for Jehovah in a Russian prison camp.

I have never known a Witness who did not have a similar notion. (According to a recent Watchtower publication, one of Jehovah's Witnesses in an unspecified country named her baby "Persecution"—and one must believe that that mother thought she was blessing, not cursing, her infant.)

I remember how the hot exploration of evil poisoned my childhood; how

Witness women sat around kitchen tables (those kitchens never seemed sunny) and spoke with lust of the evil in men's hearts—of doctors who maimed, teachers who corrupted, public figures whose dishonor was disclosed.

When my mother went shopping or to a restaurant, she handled everything that did not belong to her as if there were some hidden menace in it; she had repulsion and fear for everything she had not appropriated. Her look to all inanimate objects said, Stop; let whatever evil lies in you be obedient to my will. She touched skirts on hangers gingerly, with trepidation and fascination, as if they might leap off and enshroud her. Until she got them home. Then she cared for them so solicitously, as tenderly as if they were frail children who could have no independent existence without her. She fingered rolls in restaurants as if they were malignant objects that might attack or hiss at her or explode in her face. Then she conquered them, ate them up ravenously—and pronounced them good. Everything that was hers was good. Everything that was *other*—that existed apart from her—was bad. In order to love things, she had to make them *her* things.

The Witnesses have to make the world *theirs*. They love only what they appropriate.

One way to control the world is to formalize one's behavior in it. The Witnesses have the illusion of total control; they are instructed on what to do and how to feel on everything from grief to body odor to baseball statistics (an encyclopedic knowledge of the latter is criticized as "unbecoming passion") to music to fashion.

> A common reason why some have B.O. is that they are wearing underwear in which they have sweated profusely. . . . Change . . . underwear more often. . . . Some doctors believe that lack of personal cleanliness is the "common denominator" involved in the majority of B.O. problems. . . . If water is very limited, . . . a sponge bath can be taken. . . . One can get clean without using soap. [*Aw,* March 8, 1974, p. 25, "Banishing B.O."]

> True followers of Christ . . . evidence grief in their "hearts and not in their garments." . . . While we will deeply miss a deceased loved one, we should avoid feeling unduly sorry for ourselves. . . . The wonderful hope of the resurrection will prevent us from being overcome by sadness. . . . A Christian may indeed be sad. But he should not become hysterical and act as if everything were lost. Others should be able to see that he has a marvelous hope, a hope that truly strengthens him. The grief of true Christians should be balanced. . . . Also, weeping that reflects disagreement with God's judgments or is contrary to his express commands would likewise be wrong. [*Aw,* Dec. 8, 1974; March 22, 1976, pp. 26–28]

> There may be something that appears to be allowed. . . . It may be some aspect of your dress or grooming, what decorations you put up

in your home or what you do for recreation. But what if the conscience of many others around you leads them to feel that it is not
fitting for a Christian? Does your Christianity move you to conclude
happily, "If this makes my brother stumble, I will never do it"? . . .
Perhaps you have taken a liking to a certain modern fashion or mode
of grooming. Your conscience is not disturbed by it. But as a minor or
a married woman you must seek permission from your father or husband. Have you considered his conscience? [*TW*, April 1, 1975, p.
219, "Are You Guided by a Sensitive Christian Conscience?"]

Classical music . . . generally has a dignified, sometimes majestic
sound. But while much of it may have a rather noble effect on one's
thoughts, some of it deals with and even glorifies the sordid or selfish
side of life. . . . Many famous classical composers lived immoral, even
dissolute, lives. . . . It is almost unavoidable that some of their
warped outlook and warped emotions would filter into their music,
with or without words. So, if we want to guard the health of our
minds and hearts, even so-called "serious" music cannot be taken too
seriously or be accepted without question. [*TW*, May 15, 1974, p.
303, "The Music You Choose"]

How can Christian men and women determine what to wear or not
to wear? Naturally, they do not desire to stand out as being old-fashioned or out-of-style, but to go to the other extreme and let the old
world lead one along completely in clothing and grooming styles
would be to fall right into these alluring fad-traps of the Devil. . . .
When a sister bends over or tries to seat herself modestly on the platform, does she have difficulty because of her short dress? Do we . . .
mislead others into thinking that we have loose morals or have a
proud, militant attitude? . . . Extreme hair styles can easily lead one
into a trap of the Devil. [*TW*, Aug. 15, 1975, p. 500, "Do Not Let
Yourself Be Ensnared by Fads and Entertainment"]

But while this kind of mechanistic approach gives Jehovah's Witnesses
the illusion of control over their inner and outer environments, it is also
conducive to restless and sometimes immobilizing guilt.

How much grief is "too much" grief?

How does one know when classical music reflects its composer's "warped
outlook"?

How is one able to know when one's dress misleads others (*which* others?)
into thinking "we have loose morals"?

How can we know when the decorations in our house are "stumbling"
someone?

While everything is apparently centrally controlled and rigidly ordered,
this effort to avoid the twin evils of flexibility and mystery causes Witnesses
to fall victim to what Freud called "the narcissism of small distinctions."
Because they have the answers to all the large questions, the Witnesses fret

ceaselessly over nuances of behavior. (The Witnesses call this a search for "balance"):

> A self-respecting person does not want a reputation for being a thief. . . . But, on the other extreme, he does not care to be known, perhaps even among his own Christian brothers, as a fanatic. . . . Suppose a person is in a public phone booth; when he completes his call his coin . . . returns to him. Then what? . . . Balance is mandatory. [*Aw*, Dec. 8, 1974, pp. 5–6, "The Appeal of Honesty"]

(It should be apparent by now that the Witnesses' "morality" pushes them in the safe direction of traditional American middle-class ideals; it upholds a strong, male-dominated nuclear family, honesty, conventional good manners, and an honest day's work.)

There are an endless number of *Watchtower* and *Awake!* articles dealing with the role of conscience in one's employment. Is it right for a Witness to work in a blood bank? No; not in a case

> where everything was devoted to an end [the preparation of blood for transfusions] that [is] in violation of God's law. . . . [But] a Jew finding a carcass of an animal that died of itself could clear it away by selling it to a foreigner who was not under the Law's restrictions about animal flesh not drained of its blood. So the technician's conscience [might allow] him to run blood tests, including those of blood for transfusions to patients who did not care about God's law on blood. . . . But where does one "draw the line"? Here is where conscience comes into play. [*TW*, April 1, 1975, pp. 215–16]

Larger ethical or moral questions remain unexplored, or are dismissed.

I remember this awful discussion: A young woman, a Witness, grieved because she'd allowed her sister, a nonbeliever, to be sent to an orphanage rather than care for her herself. The Witness woman had recently been married when the sisters were orphaned, and she felt that she did not want the responsibility for her younger sibling's care. Her sister hanged herself in the orphanage. Now L., the Witness, was seeking absolution from an elder for having deserted her sister. The elder said: "Your conscience need not trouble you. You must only question whether you are doing God's will in matters of worship—and the impression you create on nonbelievers. What happened to your sister had nothing to do with worship." When I said "L., everybody does terrible things, and everybody has to learn to live with them," the elder said, "L. has done nothing terrible; and she has not 'stumbled' anybody because nobody blames her for what happened. She is a good member of the congregation, and her field-service record has not been affected." This is what is called having a "balanced view."

The Witnesses have, or seek to have, a "balanced view" even about suicide. While (predictably) deploring a suicide committed "while in possession of one's mental faculties," because it "shows one to be void of morality, lacking faith, having no fear of God . . . cowardly," *The Watchtower*, rhetorically asking, "What then should be the attitude of members of a Christian congregation as to attending funerals of reported suicides who may have been associated with the congregation?" requires Witnesses to answer these questions (as if the answers to them were as easy as the answer to how to stay clean when there isn't enough soap):

"Was there mental illness involved? Was the person in his right mind? Was he culpable or blameworthy?" If these questions cannot be satisfactorily answered, then "members of the congregation and elders may desire not to become involved in the funeral. . . . Arrangements would be left to the family itself for a private funeral where some member of the household might say a few words for the sake of the relatives. Furthermore, some may not desire to attend a funeral of one who is believed to have committed suicide." [*TW*, July 15, 1975, p. 447–48]

It is hard to imagine a colder, more loveless way of dealing with the outcome (and the relatives) of despair. The despair is in fact not dealt with at all—it is buried with the dead, by the Witnesses' dead rules. (And yet, for anyone who is truly lovingly involved with God, or with man, for anyone who believes that God wishes man to be happy, the suicide, because he has despaired of the love of God and therefore threatened the peace of the believer as well as mortified God, must be not just the object of the most intense fascination, but the source of greatest anguish.)

This motif—the reduction of everything terrible and large in order to make the world manageable and comprehensible (which, because it can never be fully successful, turns back on itself to produce spasms of guilt in all of Jehovah's Witnesses)—runs through everything the Watchtower Society publishes.

About dreams, for example, the Society, speaking as if Freud or Jung had never existed, says, "Natural dreams may be stimulated by certain thoughts or emotions, sensations or daily activities (anxiety, one's physical condition, his occupation, and so forth). These dreams are of no great significance." [*Aid*, p. 465] "What about gaining insight into one's own personality? No human can provide that through interpretation of dreams, no matter how skillful the analyst." [*Aw*, Jan. 22, 1975] But it isn't enough for the Watchtower Society to say that dreams are "insignificant," thus closing off the most direct path to the believer's inner life. The Society attempts to manipulate the unconscious (implicitly recognizing that dreams are significant) in a way that can lead to the most excruciating guilt: "But what if you are troubled by repetition of the same type of unpleasant dreams, perhaps ones that contain allusions to sexual immorality, egotism, aggression or similar things. Remember the close relationship between recent events and dreams. The cause of your bad dreams may be in the things you practice and dwell on mentally from day to day. The solution to bad dreams may call for an adjustment in your routine of life, especially in what you regularly feed your mind." [*Ibid.*] The Witnesses are cut off from their own feelings, censoring not just data from the outside world, but their own revealing fantasies.

(Psychiatrists have reported that under the Nazis, dissident Germans frequently censored their own dreams—a self-protective device. They automatically awakened whenever anything in their dreams began to signal to them disobedience to, or vengeance toward, Hitler, the SS, or the Gestapo. Sometimes their startled awakening was triggered by the appearance, in their dreams, of a uniformed Nazi hovering over their beds demanding that they cease such "unnatural" dream activity. To what extent this censoring of their own assertiveness and this internalizing of authoritarian imperatives contributed to the national psychosis is an interesting question.)

Of course Jehovah's Witnesses consider psychology and all allied disciplines a threat to their own control over the minds of their followers. As an elder once told me, "Superiority and inferiority complexes are all the same words for self-centeredness." Retrospection and introspection are considered evil; and Witnesses are told to abjure the "unprofitable study of philosophy, sociology and similar professions" and to get instead "the mind of God." [*Faith*]

No literature that threatens their system of belief may be included in the Witnesses' Kingdom Hall libraries:

> "Watchtower" and "Awake!," bound volumes from past years and older publications of the Society. . . . Encyclopedias, atlases, or books on grammar and history may be useful, but we do not recommend purchasing them.
>
> It is not necessary to include books on health, genetics, politics, science, mathematics, etc. . . . It is inadvisable to have books on spiritism, mysticism, higher criticism, evolution or fiction. [*Kingdom Ministry*, May, 1972, p. 4]

One must be constantly on guard. The Devil lurks in all the material zones of the world. One must, for example, abhor even the suggestion of "demonism" or witchcraft; one must even be vigilant about entertaining "strange talk" from fellow workers at one's secular place of employment. One may not accept gifts from "persons who practice some form of spiritism, astrology, who rely on charms":

> In modern times many persons have been seriously harassed by the demons because of taking these things into their homes. . . . A middle-aged woman in New York suddenly suffered occasional seizures of paralysis. She would lie in bed stiff, rigid and cold. She was able to speak but was very despondent, wishing that she would die. She was

. . . visited by two of the elders of the congregation. They recognized it as a possible case of demon harassment, and questioned the woman closely as to whether she had any association with any person connected with spiritism. She recalled having worked alongside such a person in a factory, finally quitting her job to get away from this person's constant "predictions" and strange talk. . . . The spiritistic woman had given her a pair of gloves and a string of beads. These were then hunted out and thrown into the incinerator. Immediately the woman recovered fully and has not had such an attack since. [*TW*, Dec. 1, 1974, pp. 715–16, "Is There Danger in Occult Charms?"]

The Watchtower concludes, from this bizarre account, that "one can see from this that [one] need not live in fear of the demons." But of course the result of all this misbegotten advice is to keep the Witnesses in constant fear of "demon harassment." Their demons are never exorcised.

But they believe—and this is surely the mark of the *ir*religious man (unless it's whistling past the graveyard)—that they *deserve* to be lucky. Watchtower publications are full of accounts of Witnesses who avoid disaster by adhering to simple Watchtower rules—like the Witness whose boss asked him to cancel plans to go to one of the Society's conventions:

Because he refused to give up his plans to go to the assembly, another person took his place [on a business trip, presumably], taking Eastern Airlines flight No. 66 to New York. The plane crashed in its approach to Kennedy airport, killing practically everyone aboard. [*Aw*, Oct. 22, 1975]

To struggle against evil and to reduce to a minimum even the ordinary physical evil which threatens us, is unquestionably the first act of our Father who is in heaven; it would be impossible to conceive him in any other way, and still more impossible to love him. . . . Providence . . . brood[s] across the ages over the world in ceaseless effort to spare that world its bitter wounds and to bind up its hurts.— Teilhard, p. 84

The Witnesses do not say, "Teach us to care/and not to care": their prayer is "Teach us not to care, so as not to hurt." Not only does their conviction that the world is evil and unredeemable save them from the pain and trouble of analysis ("the Devil did it" is sufficient explanation for all worldly ills); it saves them from having to act in the world to change it (thus protecting themselves from the inevitable disappointments of men and women of action); and it pushes them to an extreme form of blaming the victim for his own victimization (if victims would only listen to their advice, they would no longer be victims).

While conceding that "Most people are not poor because they are lazy or refuse to work," the thrust of Watchtower rhetoric is that the poor are poor because they like it that way, so reduced are their sensibilities. (The Society is able to say, without irony, "It cannot be denied that some people would be better off if they worked harder.") The poor are poor, they say (confusing cause with effect) because they "gamble, use tobacco and narcotics"; " 'They'll eat nothing but bread and onions all day, and will go into debt up to their ears in order to be able to boast ownership of a car.' . . . The poor, accustomed to living in slums, unless educated otherwise, will often make even a new home a slum." [*TW*, Feb. 1, 1975, p. 69, "Growing Poverty, a Threat to All"]

Self-help, and "getting the mind of the Lord" are suggested to ameliorate all problems, from mental illness to muggings. (The similarity between Witness teachings and such fad therapies as est is interesting: both the new therapies and Jehovah's Witnesses extend the overt message that one is entirely responsible for and in control of one's life, while promulgating the covert message that salvation from life's ills comes from a group-network support and that the group must be sustained by the will and imperatives of a central authority figure—in the case of est, Werner Erhard; in the case of the Witnesses, "the Society." Where one says, Get the mind of Werner, the other says, Get the mind of the Watchtower Society.)

This is called "getting the mind of God":

> Since excessive stress is frequently a [primary] factor in mental illness, do all that you can to remove or diminish the source of the stress that may be causing the problem. . . . Resolve the indecision, or else do all you can to put the matter out of your mind. . . . Basically, the mentally ill person needs help in getting control of his thinking. [*Aw*, April 22, 1975, p. 15]

The suggestion that mental health is a matter of willpower and of reading *The Watchtower* and *Awake!* does not strike the Witnesses as exaggerated.

> Victims themselves often provoke crimes. . . . The self-control that can protect you from such violence is a product of God's spirit, available to those who apply Bible counsel. [*Aw*, Nov. 22, 1975, p. 12, "How Can You Protect Yourself?"]

("Blaming the victim," according to psychiatrist Robert Jay Lifton, is one of the techniques applied by all authoritarian groups who attempt to change hearts and minds through "coercive persuasion.")

Blaming the victim leads the Watchtower Society inevitably—though it claims to be apolitical—to a position of social and political conservatism.

People on welfare are advised, in effect, to pull themselves up by their own bootstraps; drug addicts and alcoholics need only heed the Society's advice in order to kick their habits. (A methadone user "would certainly not be encouraged to go from house to house on his own or to represent himself at the homes as one of Jehovah's witnesses. Neither would a field service report be accepted from such a one. . . . The deciding factor is whether their accompanying us in our field ministry will be cause for stumbling [giving a bad impression to nonbelievers] or not." [*KM*, April, 1973] Methadone users are denied baptism.)

The Witnesses' position on all social issues is certainly somewhere to the right of Ayn Rand: *Awake!* magazine, for example [Jan 8, 1976] deplores the "money-giveaways" to big cities which "transfer the strain to the entire nation": "The remedy for big-city troubles is not more money and give-away programs." (No political or economic analyses accompany this rhetoric, nor does it occur to the Watchtower Society that it places itself firmly in the corner of big-money interests when it remarks blandly, "owners abandon thousands of [urban] dwelling units due to high taxes." [*op. cit.*] The effect on the displaced poor whose lives may be brutalized by derelict landlords is glossed over. The wretched are dismissed as "selfish, thought-less people [who] reduce fine housing projects to something resembling ghettoes and slums." [*TW*, Apr. 15, 1976]

Extolling the virtues of whatever is pastoral over whatever is civilized is not uncommon among the superficially religious; cities are, after all, where art as well as vice happens. Part of the Witnesses' animus toward the urban poor springs from an intense hatred for cities. Everything agrarian is good, godly, and clean, and "natural." Cities are "unnatural"; they are synony-mous with sin, dirt, and evil. Cities represent man's achievements, flying in the face of the God who tore down the Tower of Babel.

In the book *Children*, written by "Judge" Rutherford in 1941, a kind of country romance in which protagonists named John and Eunice vow to serve Jehovah together in a sexless idyll, at work in the fields of the Lord where "the air [is] filled with sweet perfume from the numerous wild roses . . . the sun [shines] brightly, and the songbirds [sing] to the glory of the Creator," John expresses his (and Rutherford's) hatred of big cities:

> The cities have no real attraction for me. What is generally called "society" appears to me to be entirely empty and means nothing. As to politics, that has become so involved that an honest man must shun it. The fact is, I love these broad fields and the things they contain. The great Creator put them here. They are the handiwork of the Almighty. . . . Here we breathe the pure air, eat pure food, indulge in purity of speech, and our friends are sincere. . . . I should be loath to leave. . . . What think you, my childhood companion? [*Children*, pp. 13–16]

Jehovah's paradisical New World will not accommodate skyscrapers. *Watchtower* illustrations of the New World run to ranch houses and barbe-cues—or a kind of theocratized *Our Town*: "God's viewpoint" demanded that "the nation of Israel had provisions that were not encouraging to big-city living." (Never mind that the Jews were a nomadic tribe.) "A more agricultural way of life will no doubt predominate over the soon-to-be realized 'new earth.' " [*Aw*, Jan. 8, 1976]

> Cooped up in cramped apartments and narrow city streeets, children, too, suffer. They lose much of the joy of openness, discovery, and interacting with nature found in more rural environments. Destroying, crushing and breaking things are often the way they satisfy the need for excitement and experience. The consequent vandalism and graffiti bring further deterioration to the cities, and more seeds of crime are planted. [*Op. cit.*]

In describing the problems (but never the joys) of the cities, the Watchtower Society, which charges the poor in underdeveloped countries with living in shantytowns "*of their own making*" [italics mine], again places the blame on the victim:

> The growth of black and other ethnic communities in American cities has created intractable housing problems. Deep-rooted prejudices and fears sped the exodus of whites to the suburbs, creating another big-city problem: *de facto* segregation. [*Ibid.*]

An ingrained conservatism which proceeds from the Witnesses' view of evil extends to hunger and food shortages too. One reality of life the Watchtower Society finds it convenient to ignore is agribusiness. It perpetuates the myth of the small farmer who has "difficulty in hiring honest and dependable labor. . . . 'Many farmers feel that their occupation brings them close to God.' . . . But they detest the oppressive worldwide system that will work honest men—farmers, packers, sellers, shippers, distributors—day and night, give them minimum returns for their labors and then somehow never get the food to the people that really need it." [*Aw*, June 22, 1975, pp. 10, 13]

The "oppressive worldwide system" is never identified; only one villain needs to be—the Devil. Class analysis has no place in Watchtower rhetoric. Given a choice between what the Watchtower Society terms "international communism" and "capitalistic democracy," the Witnesses choose the latter: "[Communism] is for the regimentation, the complete regulation, of the people in their private and public affairs. . . . The other side ["capitalist democracy"] allows for a measure of liberty in the personal lives and pursuits of the citizens." [*TW*, Nov. 1, 1975, p. 652]

The Society, protesting that it is "not of this world," makes oblique political statements. *Awake!*, February 8, 1975: "Africa! What is the first thing that comes into your mind when you read that word?" The first thing that pops into the mind of the *Awake!* correspondent in Rhodesia is wild flowers: "A Bouquet for Every Day."

As they fear chaos and mystery and love patterns, hate what is random or accidental, desire stability, insist upon a safety that "the demons" cannot

violate, the Witnesses support law-and-order; they support capital punishment: "The Supreme Law-Giver . . . authorized the exercise of human authority in executing murderers." What if there is a mistake? "Occasionally,
human authorities have executed persons unjustly." But the blood is not on
their hands: "Jehovah is not responsible for travesties of justice that result in
death by execution, for he is just. . . . Capital punishment for deliberate
murder was part of divine law that applies to all mankind." [*Aw*, July 22,
1974, pp. 27–28, "Capital Punishment—Is It God's Law?"]

(Think of Teilhard: "Religion which is judged to be inferior to our human ideal . . . is already *condemned.*")

An increase in crime is attributed to "this modern, permissive attitude,
where anything goes," and to an "anti-police attitude"; critics speak inap-
propriately when they "censure police for using their guns too quickly and
for unnecessary use of force." [*Aw*, Nov. 22, 1975, p. 7] One might guess
that as the "hunted and persecuted," the Witnesses would have sympathy
for other victims; but it doesn't follow:

> People in these areas [Bedford-Stuyvesant and Brownsville] become
> hardened, too. In [one] case, the husband had killed his wife. They
> had twelve children, and as the investigation was going on, a number
> of them were playing tag around the house, as though nothing had
> happened! [*Op. cit.*, p. 7]

And yet, in spite of their determination to blame the victims, the Witnesses' appeal to victims, to the marginal, the exploited, the disenfranchised, is inestimable. Millennarian movements, sociologists say, do not appeal to those who are integrated into cohesive existing frameworks. They
burgeon in times of social disorder and cultural conflict when social controls
are eroded, when the center does not hold—among those who feel themselves to be aliens and outsiders. (I often think that if my mother had been a
rich Florentine and not a poor Abruzzese, I'd never have been one of Jehovah's Witnesses.) What Nathan Adler says of people who are "in retreat
from rationality"—"a generation of university students [who give] credence
to astrology, the *I Ching*, the folklore of extrasensory perceptions, flying
saucers, space people"—might be relevant here:

> We live in a time that permits the psychotics' fanciful vision of
> world destruction to coincide with the actuality of atomic brinksman-
> ship, a time in which the apocalyptic vision finds reinforcement in the
> sudden recognition that we do in fact live within a limited biosphere,
> a shallow, fragile, delicately balanced ecological system that supports
> the only kind of life we can have. ["Ritual, Release and Orientation,"
> Z & L; see p. 286]

In 1940, after the Great Depression, the Catholic magazine *America*—
calling attention to the fact that many Witnesses came from "the poorer

classes of Southern farm tenants; . . . from the Okies who, dejected and rejected, wander about hopelessly; from the ignorant, superstitious, and illiterate of the city slums"—remarked astutely that Pastor Russell and "Judge" Rutherford "answered the anguish" of the chronically unemployed and victims of social injustice.

We are again living in a time of social dislocation and distress; it is no accident that blacks are now turning to the Witnesses in enormous numbers.

> The sect churches provide immediate gains in terms of social cohesion and support, a social outlet for repressed emotions, and a belief system that justifies God's ways to men. . . . The ideologies of these sects tend to promote the values of the culture at large, and consequently the sects are actually a socializing medium for converting lower-class values to dominant middle-class values . . . a social mechanism for integrating a subculture into the culture at large. . . . Sometimes explicitly and almost always implicitly these groups support the existing social structure. Rituals are clearly used in many of the churches to uplift daily life and to return the individual to his occupation. . . . They socialize people back into mainstream society.—E. Mansell Pattison [Z&L; p. 442, p. xxvi (Introduction)]

Jehovah's Witnesses are uniquely successful at changing the life-styles of converts.

Think what it must mean to be poor, black, and uneducated and to read and believe that "The wise men of this world are highly intelligent but they cannot understand the good news. . . . Let them know that you are . . . an instrument to bring things to their attention." [*TW*, June 1, 1974]

Fired by the conviction that their status derives not from their "secular work" (a janitor may be a congregational elder) or from their standing in the blind eyes of the world, but from their relationship to God and the Watchtower Society, Witnesses—including former convicts, addicts, and criminals—change their lives in matters big and small. Watchtower publications are full of testimonials, all no doubt true, of formerly "marginal" people who have begun to exercise middle-class virtues. ("The home that had been very dirty and disorderly was now neat and clean. The children were dressed presentably." [*Aw*, Oct. 8, 1975, p. 19, "Proof in the Lives of People"]

Jehovah's Witnesses are all desirable employees. A Witness has "a desire to perform work that excels in quality. He tries to be a cooperative, helpful and honest employee [and, while he pays union dues, he doesn't join union protests]. Working hours are used to the best advantage without needless waste of time or materials. He strives to earn a reputation for being reliable and true to his word." [*TW*, May 15, 1975]

> Get sufficient sleep so that you are rested, alert and friendly when appearing for an interview. Your clothing, too, is important. It should be neat and clean. A conservative style of dress is usually best, rather than one that may detract in some way. Be confident, yet, at the same time, avoid a superior know-it-all attitude. . . . Do not look down or mumble, and do not chew gum. . . . Be courteous and cooperative at all times. [*Aw*, May 8, 1975, p. 15, "Are You Looking for a Job?"]

Work in the world is viewed not as an inward renewal, but as a means to purchase time in which to serve God in prescribed fashion. Man's secular work enhances neither man nor God; the Witnesses lack what Teilhard called "faith in the heavenly value of human endeavor," "the loveable duty of growth." It does not occur to them that one's natural talents can bear fruit that will praise God and serve man. This enforced separation of the secular from the narrowly "religious"—the failure to see that there is an interrelation between matter (or labor, art) and soul and God—is of a piece with their theology; it comes from the same mind-set that separates the Godhead into three separate entities, Father, lesser son, and (impersonal) Holy Spirit. There is, in the Witnesses, a proclivity to fragment which leads, perhaps, to the lack of integration in their own personalities. And it also follows, from their view of work as an essentially meaningless means to a religious end (rather than as a collaboration with God to perfect the world), that business is much to be preferred to art as a means of making money: Art is a personal (and therefore a suspect) statement. One of Jehovah's Witnesses may be a storm-window-manufacturer millionaire and not be despised by his peers; if, on the other hand, he were to have a painting at the Whitney, he would immediately become the object of derision. Witnesses give up promising careers in the arts, and are given group recognition for so doing. Creative work has one's personal signature; it is far better to labor anonymously, without credit, in entrepreneurial fields. Only God may have a name: *Jehovah*. For an individual to have a "name" is seen as a diminishment of God.

There is a strongly Calvinistic flavor to Watchtower advice, which reinforces middle-class values: Honesty is good because honesty "pays": Jehovah's Witnesses don't steal, and as a consequence they are offered managerial jobs; living in accordance with Bible principles brings material reward.

But for those who do not manage to achieve material reward, in spite of "living by Bible principles," the Watchtower Society's attitude toward work exerts this appeal: It minimizes the effect of economic hardship and deprivation. It gives people with menial jobs compensatory status—one does not have to rely on one's work for ego gratification. And it gives the Witnesses the feeling that they are all in this together.

Here is some advice to the unemployed, written during a recesssion:

> If you are looking for a job, an adjustment in mental attitude to-
> ward employment may be what is needed. . . . You may need only to
> adjust your thinking.
> Work that you might do could range from picking up garbage to
> grooming poodles. You may need to readjust your thinking somewhat
> to collect garbage. But, then, someone has to do this work. . . . Jani-
> torial work . . . gives individuals considerable free time, and some
> full-time preachers of the Kingdom message find it desirable for that
> reason. . . . Domestic work [leaves time] for spiritual interests. . . .
> Women . . . might take in washing and ironing, do mending or cloth-
> ing alterations . . . raise rabbits, chinchillas or chickens. [*Aw*, Aug.
> 22, 1975, pp. 9–11, "Making a Job for Yourself"]

Advice is designed to help the Witnesses maintain optimism and hope in
times of distress—without their ever having to address themselves directly
to the sources of distress:

> True, times are difficult. But there is sound reason for optimism,
> even should unemployment grow much worse. For these critical times
> are evidence that soon now God will wipe out this unjust system and
> usher in his righteous new one. This hope can sustain us. [*Aw*, May
> 8, 1975, p. 15]

And one of the effects of all this advice is to mystify the sources of temporal power.

*We don't spearhead anything. We're not reformers. When the door opened for
colored and white brothers to meet together, we took advantage of it. We didn't sit-
in, we didn't protest, we didn't march. We didn't push. We don't push. We practiced strict segregation when local law dictated it. We give to Caesar what belongs to
him.*—Fountain Van Shriver

Fountain Van Shriver, a 50-year-old New York City subway worker
who is a congregational elder in Harlem, spent most of his life in Georgia,
under circumstances calculated, one would think, to leave any black man
with a bitter residue of anger. At the Watchtower convention at Aqueduct
Race Track at which I met Van Shriver, black Witnesses outnumbered
white Witnesses by roughly 3 to 1. (It was estimated in the early 1960s [Lee
Cooper, Z&L] that 20 to 30 percent of all Jehovah's Witnesses in the United
States were black. If these estimates are correct, there are almost twice as
many blacks among Witnesses as among the general population.) At Aqueduct, white and black Witnesses were baptized together and were together
generally in a way that seemed genuinely easy and friendly. But it interested me that there were no black administrators managing the Witnesses'
affairs at Aqueduct. (It interested the Witnesses not at all.) Every convention official I spoke with was white, male, and middle-aged. Young black
men, who might reasonably have been expected to deplore, or at least to

question, this state of affairs, smilingly assured me that they were "confident Jehovah [had] picked the right men. Convention overseers are usually chosen because they are of the 'heavenly class' who will reign with Christ, overseeing matters here on the cleansed earth."

"Is everybody in heaven going to be white, then?" I asked.

I was accused of racism: "You're seeing discrimination where none exists. Satan comes in *all* colors and sizes and shapes—and sexes."

Black liberation?

"We are like Jesus. We remain neutral in the struggles of this world. God will take care of that. All of Jehovah's servants are like flowers in His sight—different colors and shapes, but equal, and beautiful."

Black Witnesses reject strenuously the notion that, their leadership being white, their religion is racist. No voices are heard in protest. So great are the satisfactions they derive from being of the Chosen, it would do little good to remind them of Pastor Russell's implicit racism. In 1904, Russell wrote that

> The interests of the New Creation will, we believe, be generally conserved by the preservation of a measure of separation in the flesh, because the ideals, tastes, appetites, dispositions, etc., of one race necessarily are more or less in conflict with the ideals, etc., of another; hence the several races of humanity will probably find their spiritual interests as New Creatures best conserved by a measure of separateness. [*SS*, Vol. VI]

When I was at Bethel headquarters in the 1950s, there were only, as I recall, two (male) black Witnesses working there—both at menial tasks. The explanation given for this disproportionately low number of black Witnesses was that it might "stumble"—that is, distress, or give a bad impression to—the Witnesses' Brooklyn Heights neighbors, who were presumed not to want Negroes in their moneyed midst. In the late 1960s, when not to be overtly racist became chic (the Heights is a liberal neighborhood), the Watchtower Society pragmatically admitted many more blacks to its headquarters staff.

In any case, black Witnesses are likely to give offense only to the most obdurate racist. They, as they are fond of pointing out, stay out of trouble. That was clear at the convention at Aqueduct.

Beatific is not a word I thought I'd ever use to describe the countenance of a police officer; but the cops—two black, two white—who sat in the command post at the entrance to Aqueduct when Jehovah's Witnesses convened there were as close to being blissed out as makes no matter. ("Man, the next time one of them comes to my door on a Sunday morning, I'm going to listen to what they say, let me tell you.") They weren't wearing their hard-work, dirty-work faces. They looked the way cops look in kindergarten primers—relaxed, unguarded, smiling protectors of the good, the helpless, the maimed, and the true. They were loving their assignment; there was little for them to do. One white officer ventured two minor criticisms— "The women's skirts are longer than what people usually wear, and some of them ain't such hot drivers. I guess they got their minds on higher things"—but he added, fervently and ebulliently, "These are *good* people. Ever see such respectful coloreds?" That encomium came immediately after a 14-year-old black Witness popped his head in the door to ask a question: "Please, Mr. Policeman, Officer, Sir," he began. They drank it up, an offering sweeter than milk and honey. Those are words that could make a cop forget Serpico.

"Do you expect any trouble here?" I asked.

"Not unless you start it," the officer answered. "Jehovah's Witnesses don't *make* trouble."

When, at that convention, I came upon two black Witnesses who did not fit the standard mold (they were dressed vividly and, not having forgotten street language, they talked vividly, too, and their loose-limbed bodies made the other Witnesses look like stick figures), it became apparent immediately that we were under surveillance. Within minutes, eight or ten standard-product black Witnesses converged upon us and tried to put a wedge between me and "these two young men who are like two immature babies speaking on their own authority. [The two young man had confessed it was "hard as shit, man, to be a Witness . . . you gotta be good all the time."] They haven't dedicated their lives. Why are you talking to them? What you should do is tape the speeches at the convention—and then you won't ever have to talk to anyone."

It had, in fact, amazed me (but not the Witnesses, apparently) that at an earlier convention in Yankee Stadium, in the Witnesses' "demonstrations" (skits), white Witnesses role-played middle-class businessmen, while young black Witnesses role-played street kids who smoked what they anachronistically referred to as "reefers."

Sociologist Lee R. Cooper (Z&L) found himself perplexed by similar questions:

> Why are urban Negroes attracted to this millennial and authoritarian religious movement dominated by white American leadership? More specifically at the local community level, what do the Jehovah's Witnesses offer as a total life style for today's ghetto dweller that makes this sect movement attractive to growing numbers of Negroes? [See "Publish or Perish: Negro Jehovah's Witness Adaptation in the Ghetto," p. 700]

After spending eight months with a congregation of black Witnesses in a North Philadelphia ghetto, he concluded that

An analysis of Negro Jehovah's Witnesses as they interact in a hostile environment, including ghetto society and unsympathethic audiences of non-Witnesses, shows that their own shared definitions of reality and patterns of daily living, revealed in a "contract" of obligations and rewards, constitute a functionally adaptive way of life for certain segments of Negroes living in U.S. urban ghettos. [*Ibid.*, p. 701]

(Cooper had his work cut out for him: "What I did not understand until well into my study, when I thought some basis for friendship and trust had been established," he says, "was that my very presence as a social scientist constituted a spiritual and social threat to the families who opened their doors to me. The Society forbids any fellowship with outsiders that is not in the context of winning that person to become a Witness; if a 'publisher' persists in an 'outside' friendship, he is excommunicated from the Society. This restriction . . . meant that I was not able to be with them informally as much as I would have preferred and that conversations almost invariably returned to what I thought about 'the Truth.' ")

These are some of the satisfactions and rewards Cooper lists as accruing to black Witnesses:

The individual Witness believes that within his lifetime he and his family will live in the new earthly kingdom of Jehovah. . . . "You know" [one black Witness said], "I just can't wait to live with my family in that peace of Jehovah's Kingdom after the battle of Armageddon. Everything'll be so wonderful."

Each Witness . . . proves his membership in Jehovah's elect by his good works for the Society, activities which are tangible and weekly reminders that you belong to the one select group of people worth belonging to.

In their own congregational life Witnesses form a genuine community of trust and acceptance. The small in-group feeling . . . is facilitated by the Society rule that no local congregation can grow beyond 150 members; when that figure is reached the congregation splits into two new groups. Such a practice means that it is always possible to know group members by name.

Self-identity and respect . . . they are convinced they are Jehovah's chosen people. One is no longer identified as Bill Green, warehouse clerk or shoe salesman, lower middle or lower class, Negro. As a "publisher," he is Brother Green, . . . one of Jehovah's elect. It is an identity impervious to outside opinion. . . . Brother Green gains a sense of purity and superiority, factors of importance to an American Negro seeking . . . a new image of self-esteem to overwhelm feelings of self-hatred.

[Being a Witness] reinforces mainstream aspirations for a strong nuclear family headed by the male. In a conversation about the Witnesses' model for marriage a wife confirmed her description of his role as head of the family: "What's okay with him is okay with me; he makes the decisions in this family." . . . The Witnesses offer an alternative by giving the man the household leadership. The male Witness' status, then, comes from his membership in the New World Society and from his unquestioned position as family head. [*Ibid.*, pp. 709, 715, 718]

(It is interesting that Cooper does not analyze the appeal for *female* black Witnesses.)

The alternative way of life offered by the Witnesses . . . minimizes the hardship of living on a low income. . . . They are reminded that they do not depend upon new cars, expensive clothes, or lavish living for their status. At the same time a Witness is to give a just day's work to his employer, be scrupulously honest, and not engage in union activities, though he may pay dues. Such traits make even a man without many skills a useful employee, and some Witnesses in North Philadelphia have moved up to positions of considerable job responsibility.

Negro Witnesses can ignore the low status that mainstream America accords many of their jobs because they belong to an exclusive subcultural group that confers its own identity and status. [*Ibid.*, pp. 719–20]

The Jehovah's Witness life style is an adaptive strategy to cope with the racial prejudice experienced by American blacks. . . . By selectively withdrawing from both mainstream and ghetto culture into the movement of the Jehovah's Witnesses [they] have found psychic protection. As Negroes they are no longer dominated by the frustrating American socio-political scene. Now they are citizens of the one Society that assures them of an impending future earthly paradise, members of an international and interracial community. Racism does not exist in the New World Society, or if it does it is not recognized. . . . Racial injustices experienced in the secular world are reinterpreted as signs that point to the approaching end of this present evil system. [*Ibid.*, p. 720]

Cooper concludes that

[While] outsiders may object that Negro Witnesses pay a heavy price for such a way of life for in adopting it they lose most of any black cultural distinctiveness, . . . as long as the societal structures and cultural values of the United States make the black man a marginal man, the Jehovah's Witnesses offer him an alternative life strategy that gives its adherents a way to find identity and self-respect, a community of acceptance, and hope for the future. [*Ibid.*, p. 721]

An account by a black Witness [*TW*, Dec. 1, 1974] illuminates what blacks gain, and also what they lose, by becoming Jehovah's Witnesses.

The young man who writes this (anonymous) account was the child of sharecroppers. His story (up to the time he became a Witness) might, with minor variations, be the story of thousands of angry black men: "Why, I asked myself, did whites want to keep us down? What was wrong with being black?"

Threatened with lynching because he'd held a gun to the head of his landowner for his refusal to take a sick black child to a hospital, the young man's father fled to New York, where eventually his son joined him. The North—with the opportunity it provided him to study "singing, ballet, journalism . . . nursing and . . . modeling," and to go to college and become "a recording artist, working at one time with Paul Simon"—seemed, for a time, like heaven. "In time," however, he realized "that I was a victim . . . of self-deception. I was unrealistic to think that perhaps the color of one's skin did not matter. It was a lie that racism existed only in the South; it was bad, too, in the North, only neatly camouflaged."

His response to this delayed understanding—and to the deaths of Chaney, Schwerner, and Goodman—was to work for CORE and for SNCC. Another illusion crumbled when Martin Luther King was murdered. "I had to ask myself, . . . 'What did the non-violence he advocated accomplish?' " Then a personal tragedy: His father was brutally murdered. "I refused to cry. Instead, in my heart I made a vow. I was going to do something about the injustices I saw my people suffering."

So far, clearly, this young black man has feelings, but no ideology. He is completely unarmored.

He joins the Panthers. "By then I agreed with their ideology that it was time for blacks to arm themselves." In 1970, he joins a group of "radicals" (he doesn't say which group) to go to Cuba "for advanced training in revolutionary tactics. My goal was to initiate armed insurrection against the American system." By the end of his stay in Cuba, where, he says, he "worked side by side with hard-core Communist fighters from Vietnam, Africa, Korea, and Russia," he is "willing to fight and die to bring about the liberation of black people."

He is asked by "a revolutionary group" to "subvert the military, to use 'any means necessary' to find and bring over to the revolutionary side black military men who had technical skills that could be used."

(So far, what is remarkable, it seems to me, about this story is its studied absence of specificity: no names of individuals or groups or comrades are mentioned, nor is the author's own. What is also remarkable is the kind of unfocused quality of his life: he still has no developed ideology; he has only a history of pain around which to center. He is ripe for a religious withdrawal from worldly defeat.)

And disillusion piles upon disillusion (in all of which self-loathing plays its wormy part): "Soon . . . I became totally repelled by the way I was using myself. . . . The revolutionaries I knew did not live up to the moral idealism I had come to expect of the liberation movement. They became grossly promiscuous. One night, after a comrade had relations with his woman companion, he turned to me. I saw this . . . as revolting."

It is at this point in his life—when he has made the mistake of confusing the justice of a cause with the behavior of its adherents—that one of Jehovah's Witnesses knocks at his door. (It is also at this point in his account that it becomes clear that the past no longer has any reality or meaning to him—except to prove a point.)

His immediate capitulation to the simplicities the Witness offers can be explained only in terms of his weariness (how many black militants were *not* weary in 1970?), his ardent desire to achieve an eschatological finality. He is tired of having to renew the struggle every day; he reminds himself that even in socialist countries, people "still get sick, grow old, and die. Human rulers are unable to prevent this."

And so, when the Witness reads rhetorical questions to him from a Watchtower publication—"Do you want to live in peace and happiness? Do you desire good health and long life for yourself and your loved ones? Why is the world so filled with trouble? What does it all mean? Is there any sound reason to believe that things will get better in our lifetime?"—he says, with the innocent rapacity of a dying man who has been offered a quick pill cure for cancer, "I had never seen a book with such thought-provoking questions."

He is "staggered" to learn that "God does not like these governments either. And he is going to destroy them!" He then begins seriously to "consider the idea of God as having a heavenly government with earthly subjects. Could it be possible that these Witnesses are earthly subjects of God's government? And when God crushes all earthly governments to pieces, are these the people He will preserve to start a new earthly society?"

He learns that the Witnesses, as is he himself, are willing to die for their convictions; and he is convinced that the Watchtower Society, unlike charismatic ghetto churches, is not venal, not "milking people of their money and blinding them to the source of oppression."

He is won over. He will become part of the elect—and withdraw from the struggle. Everything that was difficult has become simple: The Devil is the source of all oppression; Jehovah will soon destroy the Devil and all worldly governments; Jehovah's Witnesses are His people.

He has found a teleological explanation, and a community, a completely unambiguous solution to everything in his life that oppressed him:

"I am not saying that Jehovah's witnesses are perfect," he writes.

> At times I detect among certain ones of them leftover attitudes of
> racial superiority, and I have sometimes seen a certain uncomfortable-
> ness of some of them when in close association with persons of an-
> other race. But really, what can you expect after centuries of this

world's carefully indoctrinated hatred? . . . However, because they live by the constitution of God's government, Jehovah's witnesses have, to a degree unmatched by any other people on earth, rid themselves of racial prejudice. They do strive to love one another regardless of race. . . . On occasion my heart has been warmed to the point of uncontrollable tears to experience the genuine love of white Witnesses, people whom shortly before I would have killed without hesitation to further the cause of a revolution.

It can't be underestimated, the appeal of this community. The appeal, and the need to belong, are so great it makes it impossible for black Witnesses to question the monolithically white nature of their leadership; it allows them to defend the fact that Jehovah's Witnesses were among the last of all religious groups to be integrated in the South. They waited until integration became law; they did not question the segregation laws that had kept them apart until then, nor did they protest them in the name of God. When nuns and priests and ministers and students marched to protest against what the Watchtower Society believed was Caesar's business, the Society called them "crazed mobs."

The need to belong to a community, and the appeal, to weary souls, of final solutions, lead otherwise rational people to take leave of their (vexing) senses.

I have a young black friend who, raised as a Witness in the South Bronx, left the Society when she was 22, when the world and its opportunities (and its sorrows) opened up for her. What had catapulted her out of the Society was her work in a drug-rehabilitation center (work the Society frowned upon), her deep involvement with hard-core addicts, and her feeling that the Watchtower Society was irrelevant to these lives. She could not make herself stop loving and caring for addicts who did not respond to "Scriptural" treatment and Watchtower self-help advice. For several years she led a busy and purposeful, sensual, exploring life. Then she was offered a scholarship to a small Northeastern college. After six months at school—having confronted not just racism, but the reality of class privilege (she was no happier among rich blacks than among rich whites), and having felt herself to be exploited by sexually demanding men, who asked her to violate her own conventional nature in the name of "liberation"—she was ready to become a Witness again. "How can you?" I asked. "You know you don't believe it." "I don't believe it," she said, "but what else is there? I can't stand the way nobody seems to care about anybody else at college, and I can't stand all the screwing around; and I want to be anchored again." "You know the Witnesses are really racist and sexist," I said; "what will you do about that?" "*Everybody's* racist and sexist," she said tearfully. "What I'll do about it is overlook it—and throw myself so hard into Witness activity I'll numb myself to it. . . . I want to be with people who all want the same thing and don't make me feel like a freak." "Do you think you'll be able to blunt your sexuality and numb your intelligence?" "My sexuality and my intelligence haven't gotten me much." "You won't be able to be my friend anymore; you'll have to think of me as evil. That makes me very sad. Doesn't it make you sad?" "Life is terrible," she said; "when I believed in the New World, I could stand it." (Six months later, again involved in a drug-rehabilitation program, and having found compatible people at school, she put her passing desire to rejoin the Witnesses down to a bout of mononucleosis—and guilt over a one-night stand.)

The former revolutionary who chose the simplicities and certainties and the community that my friend (not without a certain amount of sadness) put behind her concludes his account by saying that now "no government official need ever fear trouble at my hand."

He has a point.

Jehovah's Witnesses reject the idea that Christ's was a social gospel (even as they reject the idea that God died for man; they offer neither ecstatic union with God nor social reform on behalf of their brothers). Heaping disdain upon Vatican II, they charge the Catholic hierarchy with being the "darling of the wealthy classes"—and of "promoting Communism" by supporting revolutionaries and political activists. The Witnesses think that the Church is damned in either case, whether it consorts with kings or with beggars. They criticize not apartheid in South Africa, but clergymen who speak out against it, charging them with being derelict in their duty to be "not of this world." All this follows logically from a view of the world as evil. Protest is rendered irrelevant when it is accepted that "vicious spirit creatures are exploiting the sinful inclinations of imperfect humans who ignore God's law. What other reasons could there be for the horrors of the past and of those of the 20th century?" That there might be political or economic reasons does not occur to them, nor does it occur to them that man can help God do His work by bearing witness against evil:

> Sometimes social, racial and religious barriers and prejudices result in hardship and oppression for many. They often make the Christian race for life much more difficult. The tendency is to speak out, to fight back, to take things into one's own hands, to demand justice. . . . There is a need to maintain neutrality and avoid getting involved in the affairs of this world. Rest assured that Jehovah will settle accounts for any wrongs committed. . . . "Vengeance is mine; I will repay, says Jehovah." [*TW*, Aug. 15,1975]

I'll never forget the camaraderie that existed among Witnesses traveling to conventions. It was like a frontier spirit we had. I remember in '41 we drove in a caravan to a convention in St. Louis, and as we drove along, more and more cars with Watchtower posters would join us, and we'd sing . . . it really felt like making a joyful noise unto the Lord. . . . You have to remember that we were a small group then, in lots of trouble with the law; and that all-alone-in-the-cold-world feeling intensified our joy. We knew that every time we'd find another Witness, we'd find a brother. . . . Woodstock and the peace marches really knocked me out, because it was like a replay of those convention times—or I wanted it to be. . . . You miss that communal tenderness. I do.—Walter Szykitka, ex-Witness

Even if the Witnesses were inclined to protest, it's hard to see where they'd find the time. In addition to their obligatory preaching, they spend almost as many hours at weekly meetings and at semiannual conventions as a nun does at prayer. (It has been estimated that the average Witness spends a *minimum* of sixteen hours a week preaching and at congregational meetings.) [Lee Cooper, *op. cit.*, p. 707]

I agree with my friend Walter Szykitka that Watchtower conventions have a spirit of "communal tenderness." They are also extraordinarily well run. It's too bad the Witnesses don't organize protests and boycotts; they're good at logistics.

The spirit of communal tenderness Walter speaks of nostalgically is noticeably missing, however, at weekly congregation meetings, which tend, in my experience, to be repetitive, dull, infantilizing, leaden, and oppressive. But they are an important part of Witnesses' lives; and there are built-in rewards for attending them. The Witnesses are "schooled" at these meetings—and for people who lack formal education, they are an important means of acquiring status and self-respect. The Witnesses are continually assured, at these meetings, that they are indeed chosen and special and will receive the reward of eternal life (but only if they're letter-of-the-law good: the meetings inspire as much guilt as confidence); they are trained in public speaking and proselytizing; their behavior is modified (or, as Lee Cooper more delicately puts it, they receive "moral guidance by an unambiguous code"). [*Op. cit.*, p. 707]

All programs at all meetings are dictated by Watchtower headquarters, which provides a yearly schedule for each congregation.

Every Sunday, the Witnesses attend an hour-long "public speech," given by an elder or someone judged to be equally qualified to address nonbelievers from the podium; these speeches, which are advertised locally, are delivered from outlines prepared at Watchtower headquarters.

Also on Sunday, the Witnesses convene for an hour-long study of *The Watchtower* magazine. In preparing for this meeting, they will have read (and scrupulously underlined) *The Watchtower* in advance. The magazine is "studied" paragraph by paragraph; questions (printed at the bottom of each page) are asked, and members of the congregation are called on, or volunteer, to answer. All answers summarize or play back (sometimes word for word) the material in the paragraphs. No one is permitted to ask "individual questions," or to engage in "private speculation." The text is never departed from. (And since many *Watchtower* articles deal with the importance of reading *Watchtower* articles, what frequently happens is that the Witnesses spend a Sunday hour discussing the importance of discussing the importance of what they're discussing.)

Meetings are opened and closed with a song. (The Watchtower Society has its own hymnal, *Singing and Accompanying Yourselves with Music in Your Hearts* [1966]. This is a sample lyric: "Hail the good news of the Kingdom rule that Jesus Christ foretold! / This good news of the the Kingdom let us preach! And in preaching this good news let's be courageous, firm and bold. / This good news of the Kingdom let us preach! Preach the good news of the Kingdom on the streets, from door to door; / Preach this good news with the printed page all nations o'er. / Preach with skill and preach with kindness, with more zeal than e'er before. / This good news of the Kingdom let us preach!" [pp. 28–29]) There are no meetings devoted exclusively to song or prayer or praise, nor anything that resembles a liturgical year; there is, of course, no litany and no Mass.

On a midweek evening, small clusters of Witnesses from within the local congregation meet in private homes (these "cells" also work as proselytizing teams); they study, paragraph by paragraph, by means of a question-and-answer rote formula, the Society's latest handbook.

At the Kingdom Hall midweek, there is another two-hour meeting, during the course of which Witnesses are given speech training (in the "Theocratic Ministry School") and instructed on proselytizing techniques (at the "Service Meeting"). Just as a lot of *The Watchtower* consists of admonitions to read *The Watchtower*, a lot of the Service Meetings are devoted to the admonition to go to Service Meetings.

Recently, I went to a Ministry School/Service Meeting in an upper-middle-class neighborhood in Brooklyn. There were, for this brownstone-revival neighborhood, a number of blacks disproportionate to the general population; and everybody was dressed with 1940-ish lower-middle-class propriety and sobriety. (Toni home permanents and nylons with seams were very much in evidence. Not a single woman was wearing pants.) The Kingdom Hall, faultlessly clean, looked more like the rec room of a Levittown tract house than a place of worship. There were many children visible—but almost preternaturally inaudible. Women diapered and bottle-fed babies who never squawked; and toddlers were controlled apparently by invisible means, since they showed no inclination to act their age.

The Society exhorts parents not to permit small children to "occupy their time with material that is foreign to the program." [*TMSG*, p. 27] In typically Skinnerian fashion, it recommends that "As a stimulus to listening, [children] can be given to understand that when they get home they will be asked to repeat something they have learned. And they should be warmly commended if they do remember or make note of something said during the meeting." [*Ibid.*, p. 12] The Witnesses are also told that "concentration comes more easily if we have been careful to avoid eating a heavy meal just prior to meeting time, for this is sleep inducing. . . . With mental perception thus dulled, there is danger of simply listening sluggishly to what is said, without response or deep appreciation, or of dozing off altogether." [*Ibid.*] Actually, it's the meetings that are sleep-inducing; but the Witnesses are not permitted to acknowledge, even to themselves, that the meetings are boring. If they are bored, they have only themselves, they are told, to blame. No wonder they operate at a high level of anxiety. Inducing a high level of anxiety is a standard device for authoritarian groups that deal in persuasion.

The first audience-participation event at the Service Meeting I attended was a rehash of an article in *Kingdom Ministry* (a four-page tabloid newsletter received by each congregation but not distributed to outsiders): "How Elders Encourage Brothers to Come [to meetings] on Time." These are some of the questions asked and answered from the printed material:

Q: What questions might one ask about getting to the meeting on time?

A: Am I on time for all meetings? Do I come early enough to greet people warmly?

Q: When we're punctual for meetings, who is it we're really pleasing?

A: Jehovah.

Q: If we come late what do we miss?

A: The song.

Q: If we come even later, who is affected?

A: Brothers who come on time.

This was followed by a ten-minute speech on "Keeping in Touch with the Brothers During Times of Pressure," the theme of which was how, in spite of the fact that the wars and revolutions of worldlings discommoded the brothers and caused them to be "persecuted"—in Ireland, the speaker said, Witnesses had often as a result of the "Catholic-Protestant" war, to wait up to forty-five minutes for a bus to get to a meeting, and in China the Witnesses were required to read Chairman Mao's writings for four hours every day—they should remember that nothing was more important than coming to meetings on time.

Then there was a skit on family problems. Three men discussed how to be "good family heads":

"My wife is a bad cook, she burns things, she isn't thrifty."

"*My* wife is something *else*. She doesn't even *cook!*"

Elder: "Take the lead in loving her. . . . Even if she improves in small ways, compliment her. If a decision isn't important, let *her* make it."

The rest of the Service Meeting was given over to a detailed training course on how to present the Society's latest handbook to householders:

("One might ask: 'Do you think it is possible to establish a completely righteous government that will last for a thousand years?' Pause for reply.")

In the Theocratic Ministry School, which followed the Service Meeting,
a fifteen-minute "instruction speech" was given by an elder: "The Bible
Views on Sex." A middle-aged man who looked hand-pressed, deodorized,
and as if sex and he had been strangers for many years informed us that
"nudidity" [sic] was not "upbuilding" and that "all the perverts, pornography, homosexuality, and sex murders are because youth does not have a
proper understanding of sex. God approves of sex, but there are limits to
everything. Eating is good, but you don't eat for hours and hours. The
same with drinking and sleeping and the same with sex: too much is no
good. Proper use of your sexual organs will protect your happiness."

After this depressing exercise in guilt-producing obfuscation (how much
sex is "too much sex"?) there were two skits.

In one, two women demonstrated how to "preach to our neighbors on
our jobs during coffee breaks": "You might illustrate to your fellow worker
how Jehovah's Witnesses are blessed through being persecuted. For example, one Witness in Africa compromised his integrity under duress, and he
dropped dead six months later."

(When I became a Witness, women were not allowed to participate in the
Theocratic Ministry School. They may still not address the congregation
directly, but since the late 1950s they have been encouraged to accept
School assignments that allow them to engage in role playing. Their performance of these assignments is publicly criticized by the "School Servant.")

In the second of the skits, two women demonstrated how "talking to
one's fleshly [*i.e.*, natural, not spiritual] sister should be uplifting and encouraging": "During meals, we should talk about *Watchtower* articles and
field service, not about movies. Although there is nothing wrong with talking about something humorous or informative, Jehovah really blessed us by
providing us with a tongue; we should show our appreciation by talking
about spiritual things."

It was hard for me to believe, as I sat through these meetings, that (lacking anything resembling a sense of humor) I hadn't been bored out of my
skull all those years I attended them. Then I remembered what had kept
me from being bored. In later years, it was the prospect of meeting men, of
flirting with unattainable objects—which, in my case, meant trying desperately to prove that I was smart and good (and wondering why nobody loved
me, and guessing that it was because I was too smart and not good enough).
What had kept me from being bored into somnolence earlier, however, was
that at the Theocratic Ministry School my profound ignorance of life (and
learning) was papered over with what then seemed to me like exotic knowledge: What other 9-year-old knew about prepositions? Or got instructed on
"fluent, conversational, proper pronunciation"?

I was a child; but ill-educated adults must also feel enhanced by the kind of instruction they receive in the Ministry School. The School takes people with low self-esteem and prepares them to be public speakers. At the School, student speakers (any male Witness from the age of 8 is encouraged to enroll) are given public criticism of their five-minute talks. They are criticized for style as well as for ideological substance. In addition to the oral criticism administered by the School Servant, all speakers are given a "speech counsel" sheet; they are marked *W* ("work on this"), *I* ("improved"), or *G* ("good") on "accuracy of statement, articulation, bearing, choice of words, grammar, mannerisms, relevancy, teaching techniques, and voice quality."

Some of the specific areas of criticism mentioned on the counsel sheet (a couple of which defy analysis) are

> Pausing
> Gestures
> Enthusiasm
> Coherence Through Connectives
> Warmth
> Confidence and Poise
> Personal Appearance. [*TMSG*, pp. 104–05]

At some Ministry School meetings the Witnesses are instructed on how to approach "tenants who live in exclusive apartment buildings . . . by means of letters." ("It helps to have a fairly uniform margin. . . . Smudges do not give a good impression." [*TMSG*])

Granted, it sounds not unlike a Dale Carnegie Course, or something offered on the back of a match folder; but think how a high school dropout feels when he is invited to give a talk on—say—The New World Translation of the Bible, using the Society's material to discuss "the genitive and accusative cases in the Greek Scriptures," or "The Important [Hebrew] Verbal Form Called Today the Waw Consecutive." He may never have read *Hamlet;* he may know nothing about the "Catholic-Protestant" war in Ireland; but he feels terrific.

And he's fortified by passages such as this, from the *Theocratic Ministry School Guidebook:*

> Those who perhaps lack some school education should keep in mind that God foresaw that the message of the Kingdom would be heard without response by many who are wise in a fleshly way, of noble birth, highly educated from a worldly viewpoint. But he also foreknew that many who are despised from the world's point of view would heed it and willingly pass it on to other truth-hungry persons. By enrolling in this school and by faithfully following through with its lessons you will be guided to speak delightful words of truth to honest-hearted ones. [p. 8]

Many, as a result of Theocratic Ministry School training, have been
able to give a fine defense before courts and rulers, while others have
spoken to school or social groups. . . . Whether at a place of secular
employment, at a public school or elsewhere, our training as Jehovah's
witnesses becomes apparent to observers. [p. 12]

The negative part of all of this is that while their training does help some
Witnesses to feel good about themselves, it also makes them feel smugly
superior to everybody else. True, they may meet many people in their
ministry who've read Tolstoy and Blake (which they have not); but how
many will have heard of the "waw consecutive"? The Witnesses have the
illusion of wisdom, while in fact they have esoteric pieces of knowledge.
And they feel good about themselves only in relation to "worldlings"; their
relationship to God and to "his organization" is a constant source of guilt
and anxiety. It may not be calculated to have this effect, but even the
speech counsel the Witnesses receive keeps them off balance: Be confident,
but not overconfident. Increase your vocabulary, but don't use multisyl-
labic words to put on airs. Express warmth, but don't be overemotional.
Not only does advice like this encourage extreme and debilitating self-con-
sciousness; it increases the individual's dependence on the Society, which
alone can assure him whether he has passed its tests.

The guilt and the anxiety take their toll: One-third of American Witnesses have been members of the Society for less than five years. [*KM*,
April, 1974, p. 1] This figure reflects not only the rapid growth of the
movement, but the rapid turnover. The dropout rate, as several former
headquarters-staff members will testify, is high; for many, this escape from
the hardships and humiliations of life proves only temporary.

For those who remain Witnesses for ten, twenty, or thirty years—preoccupation with Armageddon growing with the passing time—each year provides at least one occasion for refreshment, one source of sweetness: the
communal tenderness that is so lacking in dreary local congregational meetings is at evidence at large conventions of Jehovah's Witnesses, and particularly at international conventions.

In 1958, for example, almost a quarter of a million Witnesses from 123
countries gathered at the "Divine Will International Assembly" held at
Yankee Stadium, with an overflow crowd filling New York's Polo Grounds,
to reaffirm their faith, and to rejoice in the samenesses that transcended
their national differences.

In 1955, for a series of thirteen conventions held in the United States and
Europe, the Society chartered planes and two ocean liners to carry American Witnesses to European cities in what was referred to as "probably the
biggest mass movement of Americans through Europe since the Allied invasion during World War II."

I went to a number of those European conventions (in a chartered converted Flying Tiger prop cargo plane), and my waning faith (soon to die a total death) was briefly, vividly, revived: I don't forget, even now, standing with 100,000 Witnesses at the convention grounds at the Zeppelinwiese in Nuremberg and thinking "Here is where Hitler—who sought to crush us—held his barbaric rallies; and now he is dead, and we survive." It seemed to me a glorious victory of good over evil; and because such transcendental moments are so rare in the ordered life of the Witnesses, they are the more thrilling when they come. And I remember the testimonies of Witnesses who had survived both Hitler's concentration camps and incarceration at the hands of the Communists in East Germany after the war; and thinking how small I was in comparison with them, what a novice I was in suffering, and how great was the cause to which we were commonly joined. And I remember—it was in Paris, I think—listening to the recorded voices of African Witnesses singing hymns, the unaccompanied vocal music almost like Gregorian plainsong, full of a lyrical sweetness, fervor, and intensity, and thinking that they were my brothers, and that my irritable doubts were nothing compared with the immensity of that shared love.

This is the kind of fervor, and nourishment, the Witnesses bring to and derive from these assemblies:

> At the missionary meeting in 1958 in New York, Brother Franz [then the Society's vice-president] commented on the assembly talk based on Isaiah 8:18, and said, "Well, now you can go back to your assignments and tell the brothers you have seen the remnant [of the heavenly class]. The remnant are for signs and wonders, as Isaiah's sons were in their time." At that time I thought: "How I wish all the brothers back in South America could see the remnant and feel how we feel on this historic occasion!
>
> Now this wish has become a reality at this marvelous assembly [in 1967]. When I was encouraging the publishers to attend this assembly, I referred to Brother Franz' words and told them: "You must not miss this assembly, for when the New Order comes you, too, will be able to tell the new generations that you have seen the most representative part of the remnant!" [*Yearbook*, 1972, p. 118]

All those smiling faces, smiling because they are together, united in a common cause! I remember how good and sweet it felt to suspend disbelief and feel, however fleetingly, that all around me were my brothers and sisters; and that nothing, oceans or persecution or the Devil's wrath, could separate us. And I remember too, how boring the speeches were: It was context, not content, that mattered.

Even when something is anticlimactic, at a large convention, it is made to feel, at least in retrospect, climactic—as, for example, at Yankee Stadium in August, 1950, where the Witnesses were reminded of the old belief that God's faithful—Abraham, Joseph, David—would rise from the dead before the end of the world. This aroused tremendous expectations, which were heightened by the speaker, F. W. Franz, when he suggested that among those gathered together were the "Princes of the New Earth."

The spectators were roused to tears by the prevailing excitement, expecting to see these biblical figures. Some stood up; others rushed to the entrance near the speakers' stand, where they would have a better view. The speaker quieted the crowd and then compared the new Jehovah's Witnesses to those of old. In effect, he assured them that they were the new princes, those who had turned their backs on a world slated for doom and who must persevere in going forward to build the New Jerusalem.

Forward, indeed. This was, in fact, a denial of a previously cherished and defended belief, couched so as to make conventioneers feel that something had been added unto, not taken away from, them. David didn't pop out of the dugout, and Solomon didn't surface on the speaking stand; but Franz had thrilled his audience nonetheless. (I myself was irritated—though I applauded as fervently as anyone else; I had a distinct sense of having been had, and I felt guilt as a consequence. And I wondered how many coronaries Franz had occasioned by his initial provocative remarks. And from some of the mutterings I heard as I left the Stadium that night, I deduced that others were irritated as well, though not, perhaps, as guilt-stricken as I was for allowing myself to feel vexed.)

It has been said that the U.S. Navy, the Civil Defense Administration, and the New York City Department of Health have sent observers to study crowd-handling and mass-feeding techniques at Watchtower conventions. (One has also heard unsubstantiated rumors that during World War II, when the Watchtower Society's official position was one of "absolute neutrality" and noncooperation with the U.S. Government, the Army Quartermaster Corps asked for, and got, the Society's advice on mass-feeding operations.)

During the late 1930s and early '40s, when the Witnesses were undergoing legal trials, the conventions were suffused with special joy. The Witnesses huddled together for warmth; infatuated with their pain, they took violent satisfaction in their suffering. The assemblies were a blessed relief from their tribulations. They were like sanctuaries. Today's assemblies have lost that encampment feeling; they are no longer a refuge, a benevolent enclosure. (But they receive a terrifically good press—the Witnesses *behave* so well at conventions; and that, perhaps, is almost as gratifying to the Witnesses as feeling threatened and besieged.)

In any case, whatever the circumstances, Watchtower conventions have been and are well-oiled machines, impressively run by an all-volunteer army of administrators, menial workers, and technicians.

The larger conventions are like mini-cities that have the appearance of having sprung up overnight. Actually, preparations begin months in advance: Reasonable accommodations for out-of-town delegates, who make exemplary houseguests, are found in the host city, in spare rooms of private homes, by means of a house-to-house search undertaken by the local "rooming department." At some conventions, tent-and-trailer cities are established near the convention grounds; volunteer Witnesses set up water and sanitation systems, in accordance with government health regulations, and traffic-control patterns. Thousands of conventioneers are fed, cafeteria style, in fast-moving lines, three times daily, at convention sites; they eat standing up at waist-high tables. (I have never observed a hassle at one of these lines, or a stoppage of traffic.)

Now that the Witnesses have grown in numbers, they are obliged to have fewer national, and more regional, conventions.

The assembly I attended at Aqueduct Race Track in Queens, in 1974, was one of eighty-five held around the world; in all, almost a million people attended. Each convention delegate—whether in Tahiti or Kansas City—heard the same program, designed at Brooklyn headquarters.

The New York Racing Association rented Aqueduct to the Witnesses for $32,000, plus expenses, which, according to Association attorney Heffernan, were "not insubstantial"; utilities, for example, ran over $1,000 a day. Confirmation of these financial statistics could not be pried loose from the assembly overseer, Michael Haraczaz (who is a buyer for a plastics firm when he is not engaged in "kingdom preaching" or assembly organizing); Haraczaz, and all the other administrative officers I spoke with, sought to give the impression that the Racing Association was loath to rent to other groups "because no one else is as clean and orderly as the Witnesses." No one else *is;* in fact, only one-third of the Pinkerton guards regularly assigned to duty at Aqueduct were required to be there for the Witnesses' assembly.

Over 4,700 volunteers, some as young as 10 years old, worked in the twenty highly organized convention departments set up at Watchtower headquarters.

Volunteer workers erected a California-contemporary simulated-slate-and-brick patio/stage; speakers were sheltered from the sun by a 20-x-70-foot "ornamental" shingled structure flanked by masses of plastic ferns, peonies, and giant mums. A jet-aircraft balancing agent nailed the shingles, and an optician and a refrigerator engineer stained them. (The Witnesses, miraculously, never seem to have any problems with the trade unions.) The stage, and the 8-x-12-foot Bible that adorned it, were made in movable parts at Watchtower headquarters in Brooklyn and trucked to Aqueduct for final assembly on the racetrack. One was forced to admit that the labor was prodigious and the laborers generous, even if one were not convinced that the final result justified the energy and enthusiasm brought to the task: I overheard one reporter compare the thing to an idealized suburban McDonald's hamburger stand. Another thought it was only slightly more lamentable than some of the quainter architecture at Forest Lawn; I agree that Evelyn Waugh would have found it something to write home about.

Volunteer cooks and butchers working in Aqueduct's kitchens fed 4,000 to 7,000 people noonday and evening meals in an impromptu cafeteria set up by volunteer carpenters. It was an operation the Salvation Army might well have envied. Substantial meals cost convention delegates only $1 each. Everything had been thought of: Witnesses had bought their meal tickets at local congregations in advance of the assembly. The order and discipline of hungry conventioneers—whose appetite for "spiritual food" had been appeased by a six-hour daily diet of sermons, discussions, and skits—were as impressive as the food was bland.

Volunteer janitors kept Aqueduct so litter-free that a racing fan, had he inadvertently wandered in, would surely have been the victim of culture shock. (There wasn't much to clean up: As an Association sanitation officer remarked to me, glancing balefully at my lit cigarette, "I haven't seen one smoker. The crowd is very interesting and very pleasant and they throw everything in baskets." There weren't any beer cans to clean up, either, because there wasn't any beer.)

Volunteer ushers kept track of attendance.

Volunteer plumbers installed the aboveground plastic pool in which 1,003 new converts were immersed to "symbolize their dedication to do God's will." In this pool, ringed with fuchsia plastic flowers, volunteers immersed the converts—among whom there were no bikinis, an 11-year-old boy with chicken pox, an 86-year-old woman, and a 350-pound woman totally immobilized in a wheelchair—with deft assembly-line dispatch.

According to the Pinkerton guards, and according to New York's 106th Precinct cops assigned to the assembly, and according to the drivers who drove the chartered buses that brought the Witnesses to Aqueduct, and according to the waitresses at the nearby Big A Restaurant on Rockaway Boulevard, the Witnesses were "the most courteous, orderly, law-abiding, decent, sincere, best bunchapeople we ever saw."

It was a young crowd.

Outside the gates of Aqueduct were a handful of ex-Witnesses, who, looking forlorn and exhausted of hope, attempted to distribute mimeographed anti-Witness literature, offering their own speculations about the date of Armageddon—and being pointedly ignored. Their presence was a reminder of the high dropout rate among Jehovah's Witnesses, and of their inability to sever ties with the Watchtower Society completely. They were still drawn to certainty, schismatically.

My mother raised me to believe that there were some very nice people who were not Jehovah's Witnesses and some stinkers who were; so I was prepared to discover that there were nice people who weren't really nice people . . . but I stuck at their being destroyed at Armageddon.—Walter Szykitka, ex-Witness

Some ex-Witnesses do make a final and complete break, though they frequently substitute one form of certainty for another. For those who remain with the Society, the sustaining conviction is that God will destroy their enemies in their time and restore them to a perfect life in the New World; that hope redeems them from the degradations of daily living. "This is good; this is what I want; what I've been looking for": that is what H.M. Macmillan, who was a member of the Society for over fifty years, says, of his conversion by a Watchtower representative, in his autobiography, *Faith on the March*. What he was saying was "This *ought* to be; therefore it is."

For others, it is not enough that it *ought* to be. Some begin to doubt the premises upon which their waiting is based; or they quail, ultimately revulsed, at the idea that their entry into the New World will be paved, as it were, with the bones and carcasses of "nice" (but insufficiently nice) unbelievers; or they doubt the good faith and goodwill of the Society which claims to be God's own.

All these factors were at work in the person of Walter Szykitka, who, having been raised a Witness, left the Society after eight years at Bethel headquarters (where his father, before he married, had also worked). Walter began to doubt the accuracy of the chronology upon which his expectations that Armageddon would come in his lifetime were based; he questioned the arbitrary nature of the decisions he saw made at Bethel and the mischief he saw practiced there; and he began to love "worldly people."

Walter says:

> When I first came to Bethel, if someone had said to me, "We have a lot of jobs here—why don't you tell us which one you don't want to do?" I would have said, "I don't want to do anything involved with buckets of water and scrubbing—I'll do anything but that." And as luck would have it, they gave me a job washing walls and stairwells. My first day at it, as I was washing on a scaffold (scared), some brother came by and said, "Oh, you must be doing my old job." I asked him how long he'd worked at it; he said, "Twenty-two years." So I pictured myself washing walls for the next twenty-two years.
>
> There was this whole mystique about the job you did there; everybody was aware of what everybody else did, and what that meant. While you were told that every job—no matter how menial—was "noble," you always felt—they always kept you feeling trapped and guilty—that if you were promoted to an office or administrative job, you had passed some test; but you never knew what the test was. They let you know, obliquely, that when you got a job of "greater responsibility"—that was code for a cushy job—it was because they'd been taking your spiritual temperature and you'd been found healthy. But you never knew what constituted health in the President's eyes.
>
> Like I remember one guy who was smart and zealous; but President Knorr heard him say in the dining room one day that the mashed

potatoes were lumpy—and they kept that guy waiting tables for *nine years*. I thought I'd be washing walls till I was seventy.

And another guy, equally bright and zealous, was working a hand press, and they'd say, "There's a reason why Tony, with all his intelligence, is doing manual work, and the Lord knows the reason."

But after a while you began to feel that President Knorr knew and determined the reasons, and that everything was arbitrary and capricious. After a while, you began to get Knorr and Jehovah mixed up. And you wondered if it was a coincidence that all the offices that had prestige, like the President's office, were staffed by tall, good-looking young men, like a palace guard.

And you had to wonder how disingenuous Knorr was being when he said, anticipating complaints about assembly-line work, "I get bored too, shuffling papers around my desk and making decisions; flying around the world is just as boring and repetitious as putting staples in a magazine." Was he kidding?

The thing was, you were always walking this fine line between being aggressive and "wanting to shine"—which was *bad*—and endearing yourself to Knorr, which worked out to be *good*. Why was it that certain people struck Knorr's fancy? People were always dropping into and out of his favor. You never knew what to do.

Walter washed walls for a year and a half. He worked on the top floors of the Bethel residence, where the presidential, legal, and administrative staff lived and worked.

On the first floor—where the factory workers were—it was pretty spartan; on the top floor it was private kitchens, eggnogs, and valets . . . and you couldn't reconcile that with their rhetoric (I tried). That kind of high living was what they denounced the *Church* for. It didn't jibe. . . .

After a year and a half, somehow they found out that I could type, so I was given an office job. A lot of the guys were jealous—as I would have been if the positions had been reversed. I must have behaved pretty well, or I wouldn't have gotten the job. But it increased my irritation with the way things were run to understand that I didn't know what I had done that had put me in the way of Knorr's favor. I didn't know what it meant to be good.

These are problems and disaffections common to all religious communities; and Walter used the rationale standardly employed by religious people who see abuse of temporal power at the hands of "sacred" authority: "I figured the Lord's servants were 'imperfect vessels,' and that however harshly or whimsically they behaved, that was nothing compared with the fact that they had The Truth."

That rationale works, however, only as long as one is absolutely convinced that the words of one's leaders spring from The Word; and Walter was beginning to have his doubts:

After a year or so at the Service Department, I started wondering whether they *did* have The Truth. I was one of the lucky ones: I had a good job. But I was beginnning to question basic doctrine. I was really interested, for example, in proof of whether man had free will. I was developing a very deterministic, mechanistic view of the universe, beginning to believe that everything was just a chain of cause and effect . . . that there was no room for free will; but if there was no free will, if everybody was preordained and predestined to his fate, then God's punishments and rewards were rendered meaningless. I wasn't satisfied with the Watchtower Society's analogies about God's foreknowledge—which were that an engineer could know a building was going to fall, but that didn't mean his *knowing* it *caused* the building to fall. I mean, yeah, but the building *is* going to fall, it has no choice in the matter. (You have to remember that if this sounds like nursery-school metaphysics, I'd never read a book in my life except for Watchtower literature—maybe a Jesuit could have answered me. I wanted everything to be *rational;* I should have known that was the end of faith.)

So I used to brainstorm these ideas with a few Witnesses I trusted. But I found that every time I opened up and expressed doubts with people I regarded as kindred souls, I was being "reported." . . . And you could go just so far with them. It was like a declension. They'd keep taking you another step backwards: Like, Do you believe that the Bible is infallible? Don't you believe that this is God's organization? Do you believe there is a God? They came to some point where they figured you had to agree with them.

So when I could see that the conversation was about to leave the argument itself and return to their basic frame of reference—which was that God's organization had all the answers and had the mind of God, and it wasn't for us to question—I began to edge off. I wasn't ready to declare myself a heretic. Though I started to have fantasies that I was another Martin Luther. In fact, I no longer believed that the Bible was infallible; but it took me a year after I had that realization before I left Bethel. Because, on the other hand, I'd tell myself, "If this is the Lord's organization, and you find a couple of things wrong with it, that's not enough to outweigh all the good." But all the doubts—and their faults—began to accumulate and tip the scales. And I left.

Even after Walter left Bethel, he could not tear himself away from the organization he had served for all his life. With his wife, Peggy, whom he'd met at Bethel, he continued to participate in local congregational activities, and to go from door to door, almost as if by reflex (and despairingly: if *he* didn't really believe, how could he convince anybody else?).

And he had an extraordinary correspondence with the Society on the subject of Biblical chronology.

My own instinct tells me that Walter's preoccupation with chronological accuracy had less to do with wanting to be certain that Armageddon would come, as predicted, in this generation than with his metamorphosis from a person who relished the notion of a newly ordered universe to a person who was no longer able to take the required delight and relish in a disaster for which he could find no justification and which could by no effort of his be ameliorated.

I have Walter's obsessional correspondence. I find it heartbreaking. Walter's letters run to nine pages (single-spaced) of rigorous questions designed to elicit proof from the Society that there is both Biblical and secular evidence to support 1914 as the date of Christ's Second (invisible) Coming. The Society's answers are niggardly and refer Walter back to internal sources—to the Watchtower publications which gave rise to the questions in the first place.

Walter, at the time he wrote these searching letters, had checked literally scores of scholarly and religious authorities in an attempt to substantiate one of the Society's key dates: 607 B.C.E.—the date the Society claims "Jerusalem fell under Nebuchadnezzar's hordes"; it is from this date, working with various unconnected Biblical texts, that they arrive at the date 1914 for the establishment of the "heavenly kingdom of Israel in heaven."

Historians ascribe no particular noteworthy event to the year 607 B.C. (It is to be remembered that Pastor Russell's chronology was arrived at in an entirely different way, using different dates; it was no less dogmatic.)

In answer to Walter's questions on chronology, the Society merely referred him to reference books on Babylonian, Egyptian, and Assyrian cultures, as well as several Watchtower publications—*The Truth Shall Make You Free, The Kingdom Is at Hand, New Heavens and a New Earth, Your Will Be Done on Earth*—and, of course, to *The Watchtower*. The suggestion was made that he do his own research.

Letter of February 9, 1959, Walter Szykitka to Watchtower Bible and Tract Society:

Dear Brothers:

. . .

You say you do not know why I desire material I requested, "but that it appears to have no relation to the reckoning of Biblical events." I am sorry that I did not explain my request a little more fully, but I did not want to burden you down with a lot of extraneous material. I thought you would naturally conclude that all my questions were related to the reckoning of Biblical events, otherwise I would not have bothered you with them.

As you say, the bulk of my questions "can be answered by reference to secular works on Babylonian, Egyptian and Assyrian cultures." But unfortunately secular works on these cultures do not agree with the Society's position on a number of points, and, in fact, oftentimes do not even agree with themselves. I thought the most logical thing to do would be to ask the Society's position regarding their chronological methods, and then endeavor to answer questions of detail on the basis of the Society's general principles.

You refer me to chronological material in four of the Society's books. . . . But unfortunately my questions are not answered by a study of this material. Rather, more questions are raised. For example, a tremendous shift is made in the method used from *The Truth Shall Make You Free* [1943] . . . to *The Kingdom Is at Hand* [1944]. . . .

I have been making an effort lately to make more than a superficial study of the Bible. And the more I study, the more I realize that there is a great deal I do not know. This study has taken me on several different avenues, but my interest in chronology was sparked by a comment to me in field service that chronology is not reliable. I had to confess to myself at the time that I was unaware that there was so much to be learned about [it]. But I was determined to learn it, and to study it down to the finest details. It was then that I became aware of some knotty chronology problems. As far as those of a minor nature are concerned, it was of minor concern, excepting where those persons took up the problems of chronology as being evidences of the Bible's lack of authority. And to study . . . some of these "minor" problems would have been rewarding.

But of more concern are chronological questions of a major nature. There are a number of doctrines of major importance that are based on chronology. I refer particularly to the fact that God's creative days were 7,000 years in length, as is his now-existing day of rest; the times of the gentiles; and the 70 weeks of years. . . .

I asked about the chronological figures in the Masoretic text as compared with those in the Septuagint version because there is a discrepancy between the two. . . .

I inquired about Ptolemy's Canon because of its position and standing in secular works. . . .

References do not agree on the year 607, but instead offer 586 as the year of Jerusalem's destruction, varying perhaps a year at the most. . . .

And the problem is further compounded by the fact that I have been unable to find a single reference work to use the date 607 B.C. as the time for Jerusalem's destruction. . . .

To underscore the widespread disagreement with the Society's reckoning, . . . I offer below some references on these . . . dates:

The new edition of *The Pulpit Commentary*, . . . *The Jewish Encyclopedia*, . . . *Lange's Commentary of the Holy Scriptures* . . . *The Preacher's Homiletic Commentary* by George Barlow . . . John D. Davis' *Dictionary of the Bible* . . . *A Standard Bible Dictionary* . . . *The Outline of History*, H. G. Wells . . . *The Mysterious Numbers of the Hebrew Kings*, by Edwin R. Thiele. . . .

He explained that his interest was only natural, for he felt his responsibility, as a preacher, not only to those who heard him but also to himself, to be fully informed on "major" as well as "minor" chronological matters. He was cognizant of the burden of their work, but was sure of their desire to assist one attempting to "leave the elementary doctrine," and he spoke of his desire that Jehovah's blessings enrich their work.

In reply, the Society pointed out its belief in the weakness and inaccuracies of all chronological authorities other than Scripture, and suggested that as a believer he should learn to accept and understand the chronological information contained therein, provided by God's "faithful and discreet slave."

Suppose the Watchtower Society had taken more pains to convince Walter that its chronological reckonings were based on solid historical fact. Would he have remained a Witness? My guess would be that he would have found another reason to leave. He has a sanguine temperament; and this is a religion that offers solace and certainty to souls in despair—to people who regard their past as refuse, have no appetite for the present, and need, with all their alienated hearts, a sure hope for the future.

Walter still believes in large solutions. During the 1960s, when Buckminster Fuller and Marshall McLuhan were his heroes, he substituted the counterculture for God; and he believes that everything that conduces to individual happiness and fulfillment produces "waves of goodness" that will eventually change society. He sees now "a movement toward an incredible expansion of human consciousness, awareness of our essential social nature. . . . This System is based on competition and evil and greed; but humanity will reach a point in evolution when suddenly it becomes more beneficial for human beings to cooperate with one another because competing for the survival of the fittest has gotten us nowhere. We're moving in that direction now. What's happening now is different from anything that has happened before."

He believes (as he once believed, but for different reasons) that we are living in a marked time. Whatever one might think of Walter's beliefs— regarding them as naive, or as the mirror image of the fantasies of dread apocalypse he lived with for so long—they spring from a mind that can no longer entertain visions of God-death and destruction; from a soul that joins its struggle with life; and from an ego sufficiently strong to dispense with the false comforts of the no-comforters. Walter's Yes may not suit everyone (it is not, for example, mine); but it is at work, and at play, in a larger world of human beings he had once been taught to despise.

Still, it is interesting that Walter, once obsessed with Biblical chronology, sees human evolution toward goodness as "a kind of *mathematical* progression" (or accumulation); he describes his perspective as "global."

> It colored my life, the idea that what was happening for me was
> happening all over the world. I used to belong to a group that had

missionaries all over the world, conventions all over the world. I've experienced the joy of knowing that you're part of a thing that encompasses the whole globe and it's growing. It's a hard high to come down from . . . and I've come full circle; I've come back to a global perspective again in another way, seeing the world change in other terms. I've been able once more to put myself in the position of believing that I'm part of a thing that's global and growing . . . it gives me a sense of continuity . . . I don't feel that one part of my life has been cut off and hasn't informed what I am now.

Walter is a lucky survivor, able to integrate his past with his present. Not all ex-Witnesses are so fortunate. And he is also proof that once one has been drawn to certainty, it is almost impossible not to seek it in other places.

(Walter says: "We could never have had this easy, good conversation while we were still Witnesses. Now you and I seem beautiful to each other against that shared past and background, against the pain we survived . . . but we had to leave it to find the joy we left behind.")

IX. The Heroic Opportunity and Adventure: Jehovah's Witnesses Overseas

All invasive moral states and passionate enthusiasms make one feeling-less to evil in some direction. The common penalties cease to deter the patriot; the usual prudences are flung by the lover to the winds. When the passion is extreme, suffering may actually be gloried in; provided it be for the ideal cause, death may lose its sting, the grave its victory. In these states, the ordinary contrast of good and ill seems to be swallowed up in a higher denomination, an omnipotent excitement which engulfs the evil, and which the human being welcomes as the crowning experience of his life. This, he says, is truly to live, and I exult in the heroic opportunity and adventure.—William James, *The Varieties of Religious Experience*

IN THE WITNESSES' solipsistic view of human history, World War II was a demon-inspired "global attack on Jehovah's Witnesses" executed by the "Nazi-Fascist-Catholic" coalition, "an international . . . conspiracy to 'get' Jehovah's witnesses." [*Yearbook*, 1974; *Faith*, pp. 171–72; *JWDP*, p. 153] This egocentric view may give rise to justifiable irritation. Nevertheless, the facts demonstrate amply that the Witnesses were persecuted during World War II, that their treatment at the hands of totalitarian or war-threatened governments was barbaric. They suffered, gloried in their suffering, and endured.

More recently, revolutionary governments (such as Dr. Banda's Malawi) have seen in them a threat to national unity; emerging nations have regarded their nonparticipation as a drain on the vital energy necessary to make political and economic policies cohere. In Europe and in Latin America, conservative elements of the Church have been happy to align themselves with conservative governments to paralyze or to place constraints upon the work of the Witnesses.

On the other hand, the Witnesses have sometimes lent support to conservative governments by refusing (as in South Africa) to protest against injustice; by not bearing witness, like many of us, they have helped in some totalitarian countries, to maintain the status quo.

As the Nazis overran Europe, the Witnesses were restrained and their work banned in France, Spain, Poland, Belgium, Greece, Bulgaria, Hungary, Italy, the Netherlands, Rumania, Yugoslavia, Estonia, Denmark, and Norway, as well as Northern Rhodesia, Southern Rhodesia, Nigeria, and the Gold Coast.

After 1941, their work was proscribed in Japan, the Philippines, Burma, Malaya, the East Indies, Fiji, New Zealand, and Ceylon.

Bans were imposed throughout the British Empire. There were 12,000 Witnesses living in the British Isles when war broke out. They were able to continue to preach and to gather together in spite of what they now refer to as "Catholic-inspired action." According to the Witnesses, the English authorities as well as the people among whom the Witnesses lived realized that they had no connection with pacifist groups and were not pacifists themselves. Only the "Catholic-controlled press" pointed them out as subversive.

The Witnesses claim to have received three threats from "those maniacs signing themselves as the I.R.A. in the course of four months." [*Yearbook*, 1940, pp. 81–82; *JWDP*, pp. 152–53]

Over 1,500 Witnesses were sentenced to prison in Britain for failure to join the armed services; 334 female Witnesses received prison terms for failure to perform war duties. Witnesses from Poland, Germany, Austria, Belgium, and France who had come to England before the war were interned in a camp on the Isle of Man for the duration. American and Swiss nationals were deported.

The Witnesses regarded their London headquarters as a Luftwaffe target (or a target of "demons"), offering as proof the bombings that took place near the Society's London office. One of the bombs exploded directly across the street from Bethel; another, only seventy yards to its rear. In all, twenty-nine bombs were dropped close to the office within a space of three months. Despite the heavy bombing, the Witnesses continued to preach and push their work forward.

An Australian Order-in-Council banning Jehovah's Witnesses in Australia was declared illegal by the High Court of Australia, which ruled in favor of the Witnesses and against the Commonwealth. The Court held that Jehovah's Witnesses were not a subversive organization prejudicial to the prosecution of the war. Chief Justice Latham, speaking for the Court, said:

> It should not be forgotten that such a provision [for free exercise of religion] is not required for the protection of the religion of a majority. The religion of the majority of the people can look after itself. Section 116 [relating to freedom of religion] is required to protect the religion

(or absence of religion) of minorities, and, in particular, of unpopular minorities.

It is sometimes suggested . . . that, though the civil government should not interfere with religious *opinions*, it nevertheless may deal as it pleases with any *acts* which are done in pursuance of religious belief without infringing the principle of freedom of religion. It appears to me to be difficult to maintain this distinction as relevant to the interpretation of s. 116. The section refers in express terms to the *exercise* of religion, and therefore it is intended to protect from the operation of any Commonwealth laws acts which are done in the exercise of religion. Thus the section goes far beyond protecting liberty of opinion. It protects also acts done in pursuance of religious belief as part of religion. [*Adelaide Company of Jehovah's Witnesses, Inc., v. The Commonwealth* (1943) 67 C.L.R. 116, 124]

GERMANY

Nowhere is the record of suffering by Witnesses more awful than in Nazi Germany. And nowhere is one of their paradoxes more marked: They refused to Heil Hitler (regarding the salute as idolatrous), and to bear arms; and they were assigned to death camps. But, on the other hand, some boast of having received special privileges at the hands of the SS for their docility in the camps; and some consented to work as domestics in the Lebensbornheime, the notorious Nazi breeding farms.

(The institution of Lebensfonborn [Fount of Life] was established in 1936, under the auspices of Himmler, in order "to foster fecundity among the SS, to protect all mothers of good blood, as well as to care for them and to look after pregnant mothers and children of good blood. From this endeavor there will arise an elite youth of equal worth both spiritually and physically, the nobility of the future." [*Wiener Library Bulletin*, XVI/3 (July 1962) pp. 52–53, quoted by J. S. Conway, *NPC*, p. 273] In effect, their very presence at the Lebensbornheime made Witness women the servants of "rank-and-file SS men, [who] were encouraged to enter into promiscuous or even adulterous relationships for selective breeding." Unmarried women of "racially pure stock" were "given comfort and attention in country welfare homes, many of them plundered from the Jews or opponents of Nazism." [*Ibid.*])

It would be ridiculous to seek to diminish the extent of the Witnesses' suffering, and of their commitment and zeal, but one remarks that they offered both their deaths and their "miraculous escapes from death" as proof that they are chosen by Jehovah; everything attested to their singularity.

Opposition to the Witnesses in Germany was most virulent during the mid-1930s; pressure on them abated somewhat at the height of the war, when the Reich tended to see them as valuable work units. (Himmler is said to have called them "good-natured lunatics.") Toward the end of the war, when Hitler's armies were everywhere in retreat, Himmler

> expressed admiration for the Witnesses, who, he suggested, once victory had been won, would be a useful group to settle in the vast plains of Russia where they would act as a barrier to Russian ambitions beyond the fringes of the German empire. If they converted the local population, so much the better, since their pacifism would prevent them from taking up arms against the Nazis, *and their hatred of both Roman Catholics and Jews would ensure their non-collaboration with those enemies of the Reich.* Moreover, they were sober, abstemious and hardworking people who kept their word; they were excellent farmers, and, with their minds set on eternity, they were not ambitious for worldly goods. Like the Mennonites, wrote Himmler, the dedicated Witnesses had characteristics which were to be envied. [Conway, *op. cit.*, pp. 198–99; from Himmler's personal files, quoted in F. Zipfel, *Kirchenkampf in Deutschland* (Berlin, 1965) p. 200; italics mine.]

At the very last, when the camps were about to be liberated by the Allies, the Witnesses were included in Himmler's directives that everyone within the camps should be exterminated.

Watchtower sources estimate that at any one time, 10,000 Witnesses (known in Germany as Bible Students) were incarcerated, "while equal thousands were free on the outside to maintain underground activity and energetic, though cautious, witness work." [*JWDP*, p. 163] Out of approximately 25,000 Bible Students then active in Germany, 6,019 received prison sentences; 203 of the 253 Witnesses sentenced to death were actually executed—shot or beheaded; and 635 died in prison, most of them of starvation. [*Aw*, Feb. 22, 1975, and *Yearbook*, 1974, p. 212] According to the same sources, 860 Witness children were forcibly taken from their parents by the Reich.

A historian sympathetic to the Witnesses (Conway, *op. cit.*) offers a different set of figures: He says that "a higher proportion (97%) suffered some form of persecution than any of the other churches" and that "No less than a third of the whole following were to lose their lives as a result of refusal to conform or compromise." (If Conway—who uses Zipfel [*op. cit.* pp. 175–203] as a source—is correct, over 8,000 Witnesses were killed in the camps; the Witnesses themselves claim only 838 deaths out of their total number, which they give as 25,000.)

Opposition to the Witnesses (or Bible Students) began in 1933. The German Witnesses were vociferously anti-Communist. That may have been one reason they were not viewed, until the ascension of Hitler to full power, as a threat to the Reich. A directive from the Ministry of the Interior, April 19, 1930, circulated among police officers, stated that "The

[Watchtower] association at present pursues solely religious objectives and is not politically active . . . in the future the introduction of criminal proceedings, especially as regards violations of the Reich's Peddling Laws, is to be avoided." [*Yearbook*, 1974, p. 105]

By 1933, however, conditions had changed dramatically. The Witnesses were listed first on the List of Proscribed Sects. [*NPC*, p. 371] In June of 1933, according to Watchtower sources, the American-held property of the Watch Tower Society in Magdeburg was seized; public meetings and literature distribution were banned. Following negotiations between the U.S. State Department and the German government, the property was returned to the American Society in October of 1933. In that same year, Hitler issued an edict to confiscate all Watch Tower literature. Bavaria was the first German state to impose a total ban on all gatherings of Witnesses, including singing and praying in private homes. By 1935, the ban had become national. And Gestapo searches of Witnesses' homes had become routine.

Within weeks of the Nazis' ascension to power, ruthless persecution had begun:

> The danger to the State from these Jehovah's Witnesses is not to be underestimated, since the members of this sect on the grounds of their unbelievably strong fanaticism are completely hostile to the law and order of the State. Not only do they refuse to use the German greeting, to participate in any National Socialist or State functions and to do military service, but they put out propaganda against joining the army, and attempt, despite prohibition, to distribute their publications. [*NPC*, p. 197; quoted in H. Buchheim, *Glaubenskrise Im Dritten Reich* (Stuttgart, 1953), p. 85; Bundesarchiv, Schumacher Akten, vol. 267/I/33]

This is Conway's explanation of the persecution of the Witnesses:

> It stemmed from the Nazi belief that this tiny sect presented a real political danger. In the first place, the international connections of the Witnesses and their reliance on Old Testament apocalyptic prophecies were together taken as "proof" of their being disciples of the Jew Karl Marx and "pacemakers of world Bolshevism." But even more significantly, in the Witnesses' "petit bourgeois" milieu, their messianic message, their fanaticism and readiness to make ultimate sacrifices, and their skilful manipulation of propaganda, the Nazis believed they saw a new form of their own Party organization. Since the Nazis could not credit the reality of the Witnesses' so-called theological beliefs, they believed that these must be only a subtle disguise for much more dangerous political purposes, designed to repeat their own astonishing success in achieving total control of the country within a matter of years. [*NPC*, p. 197; from a Nazi description of Jehovah's Witness theories titled "The Bible in Service of World Revolution: the

political background of the Jehovah's Witnesses," quoted in Zipfel, *op. cit.*, pp. 203 and 366–71]

And here are some further details of their persecution from Conway's sympathetic (and well-documented) account:

> When short periods of protective custody failed to deter the Witnesses, orders were issued that persistent offenders should be sent to concentration camps, though in the case of families both parents were not to be arrested at the same time, since the State could not be burdened with the care of the children. [Bundesarchiv, Schumacher Akten, vol. 267/I/35, quoted in Buchheim, *op. cit.*, p. 85] The Witnesses, still undeterred, continued their activities as best they could. When their supporters abroad broadcast the details of their widespread persecution in Germany, the Nazis redoubled their efforts against an intransigence which they feared might infect the public mind. Extended periods of incarceration were ordered by the courts. After 1937, whole families were imprisoned and the children were placed in State homes; when the wife of an official embraced the faith, her conversion became actionable as grounds for divorce. Those who had served a term of imprisonment found re-employment on release difficult or impossible to secure. As a condition for release some were called on to sign an undertaking to have no further association with the Sect on pain of continued incarceration. [Zipfel, *op. cit.*, pp. 193–94] By 1938, 700 members had been taken into protective custody for refusing to comply with such an undertaking. . . .
>
> Many in fact paid the [death] penalty; others were sentenced to enforced service with the troops, while others were consigned to lunatic asylums, and large numbers were transported to Dachau. [*NPC*, pp. 197–98]

In a White Paper (Germany No. 2, Treatment of German Nationals in Germany, issued October 30, 1939) based on a report compiled by Sir Neville Henderson, Britain's ambassador to Berlin until war was declared, it was noted that Bible Students were obliged to wear violet arm badges and that they were allowed no communication with the outside world, but that, on the other hand, their rations were not cut down. Sir Neville remarks that they "professed themselves ready to suffer to the uttermost what they felt God had ordained for them." [*JWDP*, p. 155]

What God had ordained for them they believed the Catholic Church had arranged for them. In American Watchtower publications during the late 1930s and '40s, representatives of the Vatican and the Nazis were pictured in lurid embrace; Fascists and Nazis and the Vatican were depicted as piling money into and out of one another's coffers. The Witnesses had no doubt that the Roman Catholic Hierarchy instigated all atrocities against them. In a recent publication (*JWDP*), which refers to the Hierarchy as "a bunch of hijackers," they quote a letter purportedly "written by a Catholic priest in Berlin and published in *The German Way* under date of May 29, 1938":

> There is now one country on earth where the so-called "Earnest Bible Students" [Jehovah's Witnesses] are forbidden. That is Germany! The dissolution of the sect which, at that time, had found a strong foothold in Germany, did not come to pass under Bruning [Chancellor of the German Reich before Hitler], although the Catholic Church in Bruning's time urged to have this done. However, the "most Catholic chancellor" Bruning answered that he had no law which authorized him to dissolve the sect of the "Earnest Bible Students."
>
> When Adolph Hitler had come to power and the German episcopate repeated their request, Hitler said: "These so-called 'Earnest Bible Students' are trouble-makers; they disturb the harmonious life among the Germans; I consider them quacks; I do not tolerate that the German Catholics be besmirched in such a manner by this American 'Judge' Rutherford; I dissolve the 'Earnest Bible Students' in Germany; their property I dedicate to the people's welfare; I will have all their literature confiscated." Bravo!
>
> However, the American Episcopate, even Cardinal Mundelein, is not able to have Rutherford's books, in which the Catholic Church is slandered, to be taken away from the book-market in the United States! [*JWDP*, Chapters 21 and 22]

The Witnesses presume that the Church used Hitler as its instrument to destroy the Witnesses, the Vatican is the archenemy that instigated their persecution in Nazi Germany, and the churches were apostate during the war:

Awake! (February 22, 1975) asks, "Why could not [the Catholic Church] with all the resources and well over a thousand years to train the consciences of the faithful produce evidence of *just one* German Catholic among *32 million* (.000003 percent) whose conscience would not allow him to fight for the Nazis?" [p. 22, "Pope Pius XII and the Nazis—A Fresh Viewpoint"]

The Witnesses' contention that not one German Catholic fought the Nazis deserves attention only as an indication of their state of mind. Very few church historians defend the role of the churches under Hitler. (As Dorothy Day once remarked, the Church—"our mother"—occasionally behaves "like a harlot"; and much of the German episcopate remained silent. Still, the churches, hesitant, irresolute, and passive, did have their martyrs. Voices were raised against the persecution of the Jews and against Nazi expansionism, though they were weak and few. The churches, both Catholic and Evangelical, lacked courage. Their history from 1933 to 1945 in

Germany was one of compromise and accommodation. The Pope did not speak out against Nazi aggression in Czechoslovakia or Poland (and in fact sent Hitler a letter of congratulation after a 1939 attempt to assassinate him failed). But Hitler in fact loathed "black Catholicism" and the "sly foxes at the Vatican" [*NPC*, p. 295] as much as the Witnesses did.

The churches were derelict; but, for that matter, the Witnesses did not raise their voices, though they maintained their integrity by refusing to fight.

I have quoted extensively from historian J. S. Conway precisely because he is sympathethic to the conduct of the Witnesses during the war ("No other sect," he writes, "displayed anything like the same determination in face of the full force of Gestapo terrorism." [*Ibid.*, p. 199]) So it seems appropriate to quote him to place the persecution of the Witnesses in context: Hitler used the Church as his instrument and for his purposes, though the Witnesses would have it the other way around.

> One group within the Nazi hierarchy advocated a flexible policy of persuasion and gradual assimilation, while another pressed for repression and persecution. As the war progressed . . . Hitler increasingly inclined towards the plans for forcible repression which Himmler, Bormann and their associates tried out in certain of the eastern territories. . . . In this process of "final settlement" three stages are discernible: first, the eradication of the Churches' resistance; second, the elimination of any outside interference, including that of the Vatican; and third, the establishment of a new era in Church-State relations, in which the Churches would be subordinated to the German "New Order," the priests stripped of their privileges, and Christianity left to suffer what Hitler called "a natural death." [*Ibid.*, pp. 291–92]

The evidence is that Hitler conducted a war of attrition against the churches, signing the Concordat with the Vatican in order to lull the Church into a false sense of security and in order not to alienate the large Catholic population. But, in 1942,

> Hitler announced that only "military reasons connected with the war" had deterred him from severing diplomatic relations with the Vatican and from abrogating the Reich Concordat. But, "once the war is over we will put a swift end to the Concordat. It will give me the greatest personal pleasure to point out to the Church all those occasions on which it has broken the terms of it." [*Ibid.*, p. 301, quoting from *Hitler's Table Talk*, July 4, 1942]

The facts prove also that Hitler did everything within his power to stir up anticlerical feeling among the Germans; that the Nazis exerted control over all aspects of church life; that his aim was to crush Christianity, and to substitute state religion. From historians like Conway and Guenter Lewy we learn that while the churches were indeed complicit in their own victim-ization, Hitler always considered both the Evangelical churches and the Catholic Church to be his rivals; he never considered his aims and theirs identical. The Catholic hierarchy welcomed the signing of the Concordat all too readily in 1933; and it cannot be denied that "By compromising them-selves in this way, the Catholic hierarchy was never able to lead the Catho-lic Church in wholehearted opposition to the Nazis, even after the hostile intentions of the latter were all too plainly revealed." [*Ibid.*, Introduction, pp. xxii–xxiii]

One need not deny that "there were churchmen—albeit very few—who had the courage to refuse submission to the Nazis' demands. Their stead-fastness was unavailing; but who can say that their sacrifice was in vain? While Pastor Niemöller was awaiting trial in a Berlin prison, he was visited by the prison chaplain, who asked him in astonishment, 'But Brother! What brings you here? Why are *you* in prison?' To which Niemöller replied, 'And, Brother, why are you *not* in prison?' " [*Ibid.*, pp. 332–33]

Guilty of political quietism, the Church, it has been argued, surrendered. And the churches have admitted their guilt and their shame: Meeting in the ruined city of Stuttgart in October, 1945, the German Evangelical church declared:

> . . . we know ourselves to be one with our people in a great company
> of suffering and in a great solidarity of guilt. With great pain do we
> say: Through us endless suffering has been brought to many people
> and countries. . . . We accuse ourselves for not witnessing more cou-
> rageously, for not praying more faithfully, for not believing more joy-
> ously, and for not loving more ardently. [*Ibid.*, p. 332; quoted in
> S. W. Herman, *The Rebirth of the German Church* (London, 1946),
> p. 137]

Too late, one might argue, to acknowledge guilt—after the terrible moral damage had been done. And yet, if we are playing a numbers game, more churchmen suffered and died for their Christian beliefs than did Witnesses—and the Witnesses refuse to honor their suffering. Without seeking to denigrate the Witnesses, it is necessary to point out that the churches, too, had their martyrs; and that churchmen praised God by nam-ing the monster:

> As early as 1931, Karl Barth, then Professor of Systematic Theol-
> ogy in Bonn, had attacked what he described as hyphenated Chris-
> tianity, in which the role of Christ himself was linked with nationalist
> feelings. [*NPC*, pp. 10–11]

In 1933, Protestant pastor Dietrich Bonhoeffer was arrested; he was hanged in Flossenburg Concentration Camp, April 9, 1945. [*Ibid.*, p. 400]

In the Catholic Church, a number of clearsighted theologians saw the incompatibility between Christian doctrine and the Nazi ideas of so-called "positive Christianity." In several parts of Germany [in 1930], Catholics were explicitly forbidden to become members of the Nazi party, and Nazi members were forbidden to take part in such Church ceremonies as funerals. The Bishop of Mainz refused to admit Nazi Party members to the sacraments. In his New Year's message on 1 January 1931, the Presiding Bishop in Germany, Cardinal Bertram of Breslau, issued a warning against false prophets and agitators, declaring that extreme nationalism, by overglorifying the Race, could lead only to a despisal of the revelation and commandments of God: "Away therefore with the vain imaginings of a national religious society, which is to be torn away from the Rock of Peter, and only guided by the racial theories of an Aryan-heathen teaching about salvation. This is no more than the foolish imaginings of false prophets." Despite such warnings, fear of "Marxist heresies" became a standard feature in the declarations of Catholic speakers. [*Ibid.*, pp. 6–7; from Hans Müller, *Katholische Kirche und Nationalsozialismus* (Munich, 1963), p. 17]

But there were other voices:

One was that of Niemöller himself, a pastor of the Evangelical Confessing Church. In his Sermon for the Fourth Sunday before Easter (1934), Niemöller identified Nazism as satanic:

> We have all of us—the whole Church and the whole community—been thrown into the Tempter's sieve, and he is shaking and the wind is blowing, and it must now become manifest whether we are wheat or chaff! Verily, a time of sifting has come upon us, and even the most indolent and peaceful person among us must see that the calm of a meditative Christianity is at an end. . . .
>
> It is now springtime for the hopeful and expectant Christian Church—it is now testing time, and God is giving Satan a free hand, so that he may shake us up and so that it may be seen what manner of men we are! . . .
>
> Satan swings his sieve and Christianity is thrown hither and thither; and he who is not ready to suffer, he who called himself a Christian only because he thereby hoped to gain something good for his race and his nation, is blown away like chaff by the wind of this time. [*NPC*, dedication page]

Niemöller was arrested by direct order of Hitler. By November, 1937, over 700 pastors of the Confessing Church had been arrested. One was Paul Schneider, pastor of a country parish in the southern Rhineland; he was arrested because he refused to leave his parish after the Gestapo had ordered him to do so. In November, 1937, he was sent to Buchenwald. He died there eighteen months later. [*Ibid.*, p. 209]

Bishop Galen of Westphalia also courageously defied Hitler. On August 3, 1941, he delivered a powerful attack against Hitler's euthanasia program, the secret transportation of patients to unknown destinations, the flouting of Catholic doctrine through cremation, and the issuance of false death certificates. For his stand, Bormann declared that Galen deserved the death sentence. It has been conjectured that it was Galen's rigorous defense of the sanctity of human life that aroused public opinion to such an extent that Hitler terminated his euthanasia program; Galen may have saved thousands of lives. [*Ibid.*, pp. 271, 280–81, 283]

Hitler could not afford to make martyrs of men like Galen. But Heydrich's hatred of the Catholic Church "bordered on the pathological." "He was obsessed with the idea that the Churches, led by the Vatican, were conspiring to destroy Germany." [*Ibid.*, p. 287] Men like Heydrich and Bormann were convinced that the Catholic clergy were traitorous partners of the intractable elements of the aristocracy. The Gestapo sought to prove that men like Father Alfred Delp (a Jesuit) and Pastor Eugen Gerstenmaier were involved in the plot to kill Hitler. Before his execution on January 11, 1945, Father Delp wrote:

> The actual reason for my sentence is that I am and remain a Jesuit. It was not possible to establish any connection with the event of 20 July. . . . The air was filled with hatred and animosity.
> The basic tenet is that a Jesuit is *a priori* an enemy and an adversary of the Reich. . . . This was not a trial: it was simply a functioning of the will to annihilate. [*Ibid.*, p. 290, from *Dying We Live*, Gollwitzer, Kuhn and Schneider, eds. (London, 1956), p. 121]

Alfred Delp and Dietrich Bonhoeffer went to their deaths because of their moral aversion to Nazism and their unfailing courage.

For tactical reasons, Hitler could not exercise his "will to annihilate" the clergy in Germany. But in the occupied countries, thousands of priests and nuns and pastors went to the camps, and to their deaths. In Poland, nuns were forced to discontinue their work of charity. Toward the middle of 1941 about 400 sisters were interned and employed in manual labor at a concentration camp established for them in Bojanowo. In West Prussia, out of 690 parish priests, at least two-thirds were arrested. No fewer than 214 were executed.

Almost all of the Evangelical clergymen in the Teschen area of Silesia were deported to concentration camps—Mauthausen, Buchenwald, Dachau, and Oranienburg. The Reverend Karol Kulisz, director of the largest Evangelical charitable institution, died in Buchenwald in November, 1939; and Professor Edmund Bursche, of the Evangelical Faculty of Theology in the University of Warsaw, died while working in the stone quarries of Mauthausen. [*Ibid.*, pp. 296–97; quoted in *The Nazi Kultur in Poland* (London, 1942), pp. 30–31]

Czech Orthodox Bishop Gorazd was executed.

> At the outbreak of war, 487 Catholic priests were among the thou-
> sands of Czech patriots arrested and sent to concentration camps as
> hostages. Venerable high ecclesiastical dignitaries were dragged to
> concentration camps in Germany. It was a common sight on the roads
> near the concentration camps to see a priest dressed in rags, ex-
> hausted, pulling a cart, and behind him a youth in SA uniform, whip
> in hand. [*Ibid.*, p. 297; from PS—998, International Military Tri-
> bunal, *Trial of the Major War Criminals* (Nuremberg, 1948), vol. XVI,
> p. 474]

"At least ninety priests from the diocese of Kulm (Chelm) lost their lives
in the concentration camps of Stutthof, Grenzdorf, Auschwitz, Sachsenhausen and Dachau." At least fifty priests are known to have died in Soldau
(Dzialdovo). [Quoted in M. Broszat, *Nationalsozialistische Polenpolitik* 1939–45
(Stuttgart, 1961), p. 162] "By 1942 there were no fewer than 1,773 Polish
priests in Dachau where they formed by far the largest single group of
prisoners." [*NPC*, p. 323; see R. Schnabel, *Die Frommen in der Hölle*. Berlin,
1966.]

> According to a recent collation of the available evidence, 2,771
> priests were imprisoned at Dachau alone, of whom at least 1,000 were
> estimated to have died in the camp from hunger, disease, or ill-treat-
> ment between 1942 and 1945. According to one source, no fewer than
> 4,000 Catholic priests were put to death during the same years, either
> as "political saboteurs" or, after incarceration in the concentration
> camps, by hanging, by starvation, by mishandling, from lack of medi-
> cal aid, or as the victims of medical experiments, including euthana-
> sia. [*Ibid.*, pp. 298–99; from B. M. Kempner, *Priester vor Hitlers Tri-
> bunalen* (Munich, 1966), p. 8]

"*We will protect the German priest who is the servant of God, we will wipe out
the priest who is a political enemy of the German Reich.*"—Adolph Hitler [*NPC*,
p. 219; quoted from M. Domarus, ed., *Hitler Reden und Proklamationen*,
1932–45, (Würzburg, 1963), Vol. II, pp. 1,058–61]
The Witnesses admit that "some churchmen [were] persecuted"; but they
enter the caveat that the persecution of the churches was a result of "anti-
Nazi *political* activity." [*Aw*, Feb. 22, 1975, pp. 20–21] This raises the question of how to divorce the political from the moral. Is it a political act to
speak out against genocide? against armed aggression? against euthanasia?
This dichotomy between the spiritual and the political is the same one advanced by Goebbels and Goering in order to clamp down on the churches:

> Whereas the Nazi Party, they claimed, had saved the Church from
> extinction at the hands of the Marxists and had established its status
> by means of the Reich Concordat, the Church had shown its gratitude
> by becoming a breeding-ground of political disaffection, creating, by

its doctrinal differences, a disunity among the people which was a
danger to the unity of the German Reich. The Churches, they maintained, would do far better to concentrate on charitable works than on
dogmatic squabbles. Politics must be wholly separate from the
Church, and the clergy would do well to remember the words "My
Kingdom is not of this world." [*NPC*, p. 78]

It may be argued that the moment a Christian ceases to apply spiritual
values to the events of the material world, and to protest against injustice,
he ceases to be a Christian and becomes apostate. This is, in fact, exactly
what the Barmen Synod declared in 1934: "We reject the false doctrine, as
though there were areas of our life in which we would not belong to Jesus
Christ, but to other Lords—areas in which we would not need justification
and sanctification through him." [*Ibid.*, p. 335]

The notion that politics does not concern the Church is the Manichaean
heresy; it says that the affairs of political and social life are irredeemable.
Intent upon maintaining its interior life, the Church in Germany fell into
this dangerous subjectivism. The truth is that the churches were not political enough. The churches and the Witnesses also shared the conviction that
left-wing programs for social and political activities and reform could not be
a vehicle for God's redemptive activity.

None of this is said to depreciate the Witnesses' heroic behavior in Germany; it is said merely to point out that the Nazis found the weakness in all
men, and exploited it. The Witnesses were silent, as the churches were
largely silent, about the sufferings of others. And the Witnesses refused,
and continue to refuse, to acknowledge that there were churchmen who
protested against Hitler's policies, and suffered: they draw a line between
politics and morality, and discount the persecution of the churches on the
ground that the churches invited it by their political activities, so that, in
their view, the sacrifices made by the few brave men of the Evangelical and
Catholic churches become useless sacrifices, of no value to God.

The canard that the Vatican used the Third Reich for its purposes is still
employed by the Witnesses to enlist nominal Catholics in their ranks. It is
an important part of their proselytizing work even now. That is one reason
it needs to be refuted.

As early as 1934, the activities of Catholic lay organizations in Germany
were restricted, in order to drive a wedge between the clergy and the people: "Church services were placed under regular surveillance"; "the activities of priests who were suspected of anti-Nazi sympathies were strictly
supervised." [*Ibid.*, pp. 67, 69; from D. Albrecht, *Der Notenwechsel zwischen
dem Heiligen Stuhl und der Deutschen Reichsregierung*, (Mainz, 1965), vol. I, p.
61] "Attempts of Catholic Action to consolidate the work of the Catholic
organizations was stigmatized by Goering as demonstrating the existence of
'a firm block within the Catholic clergy which continues to oppose the aims

and schemes of the State.' " [*Ibid.*, p. 79; from Bundesarchiv, Akten der Reichskanzlei, 43, II, 174]

In 1934, Himmler decreed that processions and pilgrimages could be held only under strict supervision. Jesuits were particularly feared, their activities reported on. In 1935, Goering issued directives against any kind of "political Catholics." [*Ibid.*, p. 113] Clearly, in spite of the compliance of most churchmen, the Nazis were prepared to tolerate the churches' activities only insofar as they related to the next world. Their aim was the total submission of the churches.

In 1935, a new campaign of vilification of the clergy began. Priests, monks, and nuns were accused of violating complicated currency regulations; they were accused of smuggling Jewish capital out of the country. Hitler Youth sang this song:

> Oh, the cloistered life is jolly
> Nowadays, instead of prayer,
> Smuggling money is their business;
> Forth on this sly sport they fare.
>
> Swift they say a Pater Noster
> Priest and monk and pious nun.
> Swifter then with zealous purpose
> Smuggling currency they run.
>
> Laden with the goodly specie
> Slinks the nun from place to place.
> No one would suspect the creature
> From her modest pious face.
>
> To monk she slips the packet . . .
>
> Priest and nun and holy friar—
> What a horror, they're in clink!
> From the labours of their smuggling
> To a well-earned rest they sink.
>
> To the priest the nun soft whispers,
> "Glorious was the task and grand,
> Backing up our Holy Father
> Smuggling Money through the land."

[*Ibid.*, p. 126; quoted from *The Persecution of the Catholic Church in the Third Reich: Facts and Documents Translated from the German* (London, 1940), p. 268.]

In official Nazi organs, in 1936 and 1937, sensational charges of priestly immorality were made. "Immorality trials" were staged in courts.

"For reasons of expediency, . . . the Nazis refrained from a head-on clash with the Catholic Church, relying instead on an intensified attack against all Church activities in order to limit its influence on the German people. The Gestapo were to be given free rein to isolate those of the clergy whose activities could be branded as 'hostile to the State.' One by one, the Church's bastions were to be breached until the possibility of resistance was broken forever." [*NPC*, p. 167] Informers, known as *V-Männer*, reported to the Gestapo from within the Church. (The Nazis—like the Witnesses—had a horror of the Jesuits in particular, whom they regarded as more sinister and cunning than other mortals.) "Church-sponsored courses on domestic science, marriage guidance and baby care were prohibited, since 'the Catholic attitudes to marriage guidance, racial nurture and biological hygiene differ in significant fashion from those of the National Socialist State.' " [*Ibid.*, pp. 173–74; from *Glaubenskrise im Dritten Reich*; Bundesarchiv, Schumacher Akten, vol. 243/2/I, quoted in Buchheim, *op. cit.*, p. 85]

In Austria, three months after Anschluss, all Catholic private schools were deprived of recognition and support. Denominational private schools were closed. Church property was confiscated. Priests were no longer permitted to conduct courses of religious instruction—an incredible deprivation to their flocks. [*NPC*, pp. 182–84; from *Persecution, op. cit.*, p. 137] Youth activities were curtailed; pastoral care in hospitals and in welfare institutions was restricted. In May, 1938, 60 Austrian Roman Catholic priests were arrested on charges of immoral conduct. Property of Catholic organizations was confiscated. [*Ibid.*, p. 225]

The Austrian Hitler Youth were led along the path of anticlericalism. The following are notes for a propaganda speech. It is deplorable how closely this Nazi harangue against Church history and doctrine resembles, on so many points, the Witnesses' harangues against the Church.

> . . . The Church always works by violence and terror. Where is the love of one's neighbour and the love of one's enemies? . . . In the Crusades German blood was shed uselessly. . . . The Catholic Church will come to an end. . . . Proof that Christ was not God; 'Woman, what have I to do with thee?' . . . How Christ dies (whimpering on the Cross). . . . The cult of the saints is ridiculous. When any one had his palm greased or was preeminently filthy he was pronounced a saint. . . . The Virgin Mary. The Immaculate Conception. . . . The Papacy is a swindle. The Pope claims to be God's representative on earth, but after Peter there was no Pope for 150 years. The Popes were always men of the baser sort. . . . The sale of indulgences . . . With the Jesuits all personality is suppressed. They become the blind instruments of the Pope. . . . The Catholic Church provoked the Thirty Years' War. . . . The strength of the Church and its inability to promote peace during the World War . . . The Catholic Church opposes the national movement of the German people. . . . If Germany no longer supports the Catholic Church, it is finished. . . . For us Germans the inactivity of eternal life is foolishness. . . . The "infallibility" of the Pope? . . . Predestination, rites of the Church,

the divine Trinity, original sin, etc.—what bosh! [*Ibid.*, pp. 226–27; from Micklem, Nathanial, *National Socialism and the Roman Catholic Church 1933–38*, (Oxford, 1939), pp. 227–29]

With the outbreak of war, and the necessity to mobilize the German people behind the war effort, Hitler declared that "no further action should be taken against the Evangelical and Catholic Churches for the duration of the war." [*Ibid.*, p. 232; quoted in a circular from the Chief of the Race and Settlement Headquarters, Sept. 8, 1939, unpublished Nuremberg Documents NG-1392 and NG-1755] Both the Evangelical and Catholic bishops called upon their followers to support the war—in spite of Nazi atrocities against Catholic priests and laypersons in Poland, details of which were broadcast by the Vatican radio. [*NPC*, p. 235; from Lewy, Guenter, *The Catholic Church and Nazi Germany* (Boston, 1964), p. 229]

However, in 1941, when the Nazis launched a series of new offenses against Eastern Europe, new and more stringent measures began to be taken against the churches: Himmler ordered the complete evacuation of all church properties without compensation. Monasteries and convents were emptied. In Luxembourg, 400 priests were evacuated on Hitler's personal orders. All Church hospitals were declared secular institutions. Catholic orphanages and kindergartens and welfare agencies were placed under the control of the state. The Catholic press was suppressed. Tolerating no rivalry, Heydrich ordered that immediate action be taken against all small sects, including Christian Scientists and the Salvation Army.

Hitler was forced to come to some degree of accommodation with the churches by virtue of their vast numbers. But it is manifestly clear from his words, as well as from the actions of the Reich, that he was intent upon a policy of deliberate repression. He loathed what he called the "satanic superstition" of the "hypocritical priests," who, he said, in language reminiscent of that of the Witnesses, were interested "in raking in the money" and "befuddling the minds of the gullible." [*Ibid.*, p. 3; from *Hitler's Table Talk*] Hitler fostered the illusion that he was pious; he never officially left the Church, and he continued to pay compulsory Church taxes. But his determination to avenge himself against the churches is left in no doubt. He combined "implacable hatred with practical flexibility" [*NPC*, p. 102], envy with respect:

> I promise you that, if I wished to, I could destroy the Church in a few years; it is hollow and rotten and false through and through. One push and the whole structure would collapse. We should trap the priests by their notorious greed and self-indulgence. We shall thus be able to settle everything with them in perfect peace and harmony. I shall give them a few years' reprieve. Why should we quarrel? They will swallow anything in order to keep their material advantages. Matters will never come to a head. They will recognize a firm will, and

we need only show them once or twice who is the master. Then they will know which way the wind blows. They are no fools. The Church was something really big. Now we are its heirs. We, too, are the Church. Its day has gone. [*Ibid.*, p. 103; from Hermann Rauschning, *Hitler Speaks* (London, 1939), p. 61]

> The evil that is gnawing at our vitals is our priests of both denominations. I cannot at present give them the answer they have been asking for, but it will cost them nothing to wait. It is all written down in my big book. The time will come when I shall settle my accounts with them and I shall go straight to the point. . . . I shall not let myself be hampered by juridical scruples. Only necessity has legal force. In less than ten years from now, things will have quite another look, I can promise them.—Adolf Hitler [*NPC*, p. 285; from *Hitler's Table Talk*, February 9, 1942; *The Goebbels Diaries 1942–3*, J. Lochner, ed. (New York, 1948), entries for March 20, 1942, and March 9, 1943]

Hitler's attitude toward the churches was governed by pragmatism; and the churches, in turn, evolved their own ill-conceived pragmatic response:

> It appeared likely that the mass appeal of the Nazi campaign might succeed in persuading thousands, even millions, to leave the Church. In the face of such promises, continued opposition could serve only to brand the bishops as the "black-reactionaries" which the anti-clericals had always considered them to be. . . . Opposition would drive the Catholic Church into a sort of ghetto. . . . The bishops believed [the Church] was incapable of surviving such a challenge. . . . Perhaps, they felt, Hitler could after all be trusted. Perhaps he could be persuaded of the value of Catholic support in a joint campaign against Communism and moral decadence. Perhaps he might be prevailed upon to accept the assistance of the Catholic Church and its many associated organs, in the reconstruction of an ordered unified society. [*NPC*, pp. 21–22]

Events proved the hierarchy wrong in its estimation of Hitler. But it was the threat to the spiritual and physical well-being of twenty million German Catholics that induced Eugenio Cardinal Pacelli (later Pope Pius XII) to sign the Concordat with Hitler. The signing of the Concordat effectively eliminated the Church as a potent political force.

> As Cardinal Pacelli himself acknowledged . . . "A pistol had been pointed at his head and he had no alternative. The German Government had offered him concessions . . . wider than any previous German Government would have agreed to, and he had to choose between an agreement on their lines and the virtual elimination of the Catholic Church in the Reich." [*Ibid.*, p. 30; from *Documents On British Foreign Policy, Series II*, Vol. 5, No. 342]

Hitler signed the Concordat because a subservient clergy was preferable to a host of noisy martyrs.

Among the Evangelical churches, which were "politically conservative, patriotic and paternalistic," [*NPC*, p. 9] there was a tendency to welcome the Nazi overthrow "as a first step towards the reintroduction of government by Christian authorities, affirming with St. Paul (Romans 13) that 'the powers that be are ordained of God.' " [*Ibid.*, p. 10] (That scripture, which the Witnesses too have time and again bent to their necessities, has perhaps created more political confusion—and mischief—than any other in the the Bible.)

How the churches must have felt when the Nazis gave birth to a new heathenism it is not difficult to imagine. Christian doctrines—the fall of man, redemption, salvation, Judgment—were transformed into an ersatz Nazi theology. [*Ibid.*, p. 145] The Nazis substituted their own liturgy, their own baptism and marriage and burial services for those of the Church. They parodied the Nicene Creed. The blood shed at the time of Hitler's unsuccessful Putsch of November 9, 1923, said Hitler, "is become the altar of baptism for our Reich." [*Ibid.*, p. 149] That blood was celebrated as a sacrament.

The Church, having signed the Concordat and lost its moral authority, was silent. It is even more amazing that while official anti-Nazi pronouncements were rare, and while both the Evangelical churches and the Catholic Church hierarchy maintained, for the most part, an official silence, some individuals did not fail. One such was Franz Jägerstätter. And the Witnesses have claimed him as their own.

Franz Jägerstätter was an Austrian peasant. He lived in St. Radegund, a small village in Upper Austria, where he was the sexton of the parish church. When Hitler's troops moved into Austria in 1938, Jägerstätter was the only man in his village to vote against Anschluss. When he was greeted with the Nazi salute—Heil Hitler!—he replied, "Pfui Hitler!" Acting on his Christian beliefs, he publicly declared that he would not fight in an unjust war. When he was reminded that other Catholics had found it possible to fight for Hitler—with the approval of their bishops—he replied, "They have not been given the grace" to do otherwise; he declared that this was a matter of individual conscience, between him and the God and the living Church he served. He was adamant that he would not serve the government that was persecuting his Church.

Jägerstätter was called to active duty, was imprisoned, and was sentenced to death. After his trial, he wrote his wife: "Only do not forget me in prayer, even as I will not forget you—and remember me especially at Mass. I can also give you the good news that I had a visit yesterday, and from a priest, no less! Next Tuesday he will come with the Holy of Holies. Even here, one is not abandoned by God." He went in the same spirit to his death, knowingly and heroically. He was beheaded after a military trial, on August 9, 1943. It is said that he walked to his death in a calm and composed manner. Before his execution, he had written, "I cannot . . . take an oath in favor of a government that is fighting an unjust war. . . . May God accept my life in reparation not only for my sins but for the sins of others as well." He left his wife and three daughters in the hands of God.

A Mother Superior of an Austrian convent remembers that Father Jochmann, the chaplain of Brandenberg prison, said to an audience of nuns, after Jägerstätter's death: "I can only congratulate you on this countryman of yours who lived as a saint and has now died a hero. I say with certainty that this simple man is the only saint that I have ever met in my lifetime." (The above information is taken from Gordon Zahn, *In Solitary Witness: The Life and Death of Franz Jägerstätter* [New York: Holt, Rinehart & Winston, 1964].)

The Witnesses call attention to the fact that "the courageous stand of [Austrian Bible Students] had some influence on the Catholic Franz Jägerstätter. Gordon Zahn reports that his village pastor noted that 'Franz had often spoken with admiration of their faithfulness,' and villagers who knew him made much of the fact that he 'spent hours discussing religion and studying the Bible' with his *Bibelforscher* cousin, the only non-Catholic in the village." [*Aw*, Feb. 22, 1975, p. 22]

Professor Zahn quite emphatically denies that Jägerstätter's refusal to serve in the army can in any way be attributed to his Bible Student cousin:

> Those closest to Franz at the time make it quite clear that this was not the case. One close friend introduced the surprising note that Franz had never really liked his cousin. Jägerstätter's wife insisted that his cousin had no influence at all upon her husband. Perhaps the most conclusive testimony on this point was provided by Fr. Furthauer and the woman who was married to the cousin at that time. The priest insisted that in all his discussions with Franz he had never brought up the theological position maintained by the sect. Fr. Furthauer was aware of the close relationship between his sexton and the local *Bibelforscher;* it is true, he admitted, that they spent a great deal of time together in religious discussions. The fact of the matter was that Jägerstätter was trying to bring his cousin into the Catholic fold. Moreover, he added, the cousin had already been inducted into the Home Guard before Jägerstätter was called into service in February, 1943. [Zahn, *op. cit.*, pp. 108–109]

The priest's claims might be dismissed as self-serving, but when "the cousin's former wife was interviewed," she reinforced them:

> When she was asked to indicate how much influence her husband and his religious beliefs had had upon Jägerstätter and his stand, she answered promptly and emphatically: "None at all." As she saw it,

Jägerstätter had studied the Bible on his own until he became "too one-sided" on the issue of the Fifth Commandment and its application—this led him to the independent conclusion that he could not fight in the war. Franz and her husband had discussed this issue at great length, but as for the question of influence, it was Jägerstätter who was always "working on" her husband. Her husband had taken the position that the individual believer should not permit himself to be trapped into a hopeless situation by taking the absolutist stand of refusing all military service; instead, he felt, one should try to get into some limited or noncombatant service. Jägerstätter, on the other hand, always insisted that nothing less than total refusal was required—and even after her husband had left for service—in the Signal Corps, she recalled—Franz continued to insist that his cousin had done the wrong thing. . . .

It is quite clear, then, that Jägerstätter's position cannot be traced to the influence of this fundamentalist sect. However, Pastor Karobath did introduce one reservation. He agreed that the sect's theology had no influence upon Franz's action, but he suggested that the *example* set by the members of that sect in holding fast to their beliefs no matter what sacrifice they were called upon to make might have strengthened his commitment. [*Ibid.*, pp. 108–110]

The Witnesses find it amazing that a man should bear solitary witness; it is essential to their belief that no one can do without a supportive organization (*their* organization). The Witnesses, from their fringe position, totally repudiated the world. Jägerstätter believed in the living Church of martyrs; and he believed that that Church—no matter what the hierarchy said—required open civil dissent when secular values threatened spiritual values. He did not divorce morality or religion from politics. And he believed in the communion of saints, even when his Church leaders urged him on to a different set of actions.

On October 7, 1934, the Watch Tower Bible and Tract Society sent this letter to "the officials of the German government":

> The Word of Jehovah God, as set out in the Holy Bible, is the Supreme Law, and to us it is our sole guide for the reason that we have devoted ourselves to God and are true and sincere followers of Christ Jesus.
> During the past year, and contrary to God's law and in violation of our rights, you have forbidden us as Jehovah's witnesses to meet together to study God's Word and worship and serve him. . . . There is a direct conflict between your law and God's law, and, following the lead of the faithful apostles, 'we ought to obey God rather than men,' and this we will do. . . . Therefore this is to advise you that at any cost we will obey God's commandments, will meet together for the

study of his Word, and will worship and serve him as he has commanded. If your government or officers do violence to us because we are obeying God, then our blood will be upon you and you will answer to Almighty God.

We have no interest in political affairs, but are wholly devoted to God's kingdom under Christ his King. We will do no injury or harm to anyone. We would delight to dwell in peace and do good to all men as we have opportunity, but, since your government and its officers continue in your attempt to force us to disobey the highest law of the universe, we are compelled to now give you notice that we will, by his grace, obey Jehovah God and fully trust Him to deliver us from all oppression and oppressors. [*Yearbook*, 1974, pp. 136–37]

It would be a mistake to underestimate the bravery this direct challenge to the Reich required; Watchtower publications indicate that among German Witnesses there was some attempt to vitiate the strength of this declaration; but the more resolute won the day.

In the United States a massive letter-writing campaign protesting the treatment of the Witnesses was initiated. According to the 1974 *Yearbook*, "The effect that the letters, and especially the telegrams, had upon Hitler can be seen by a report written by Karl R. Wittig [plenipotentiary of General Ludendorff], attested by a notary public in Frankfurt (Main) on November 13, 1947:

DECLARATION—On October 7, 1934, having been previously summoned, I visited Dr. Wilhelm Frick, at that time Minister of the Interior of the Reich and Prussia, in his home office of the Reich, located in Berlin. . . . I was to accept communications, contents of which were an attempt to persuade General Ludendorff to discontinuance of his objection to the Nazi regime. During my discussion with Dr. Frick, Hitler suddenly appeared and began taking part in the conversation. When our discussion obligatorily dealt with the action against the International Bible Students Association in Germany up until now, Dr. Frick showed Hitler a number of telegrams protesting against the Third Reich's persecution of the Bible Students, saying: "If the Bible Students do not immediately get in line we will act against them using the strongest means." After which Hitler jumped to his feet and with clenched fists hysterically screamed: "This brood will be exterminated in Germany!"

(The Witnesses add a picturesque detail: a vividly cursing Hitler, tossing an inkpot in an insane rage, screaming that he would wipe the Bible Student "vermin" from the Fatherland.)

Wittig continues:

Four years after this discussion I was able, by my own observations, to convince myself, during my seven years in protective custody in the hell of the Nazis' concentration camps at Sachsenhausen, Flossenburg and Mauthausen—I was in prison until released by the Allies—that Hitler's outburst of anger was not just an idle threat. No other group of prisoners of the named concentration camps was exposed to the sadism of the SS soldiery in such a fashion as the Bible Students were. It was a sadism marked by an unending chain of physical and mental tortures, the likes of which no language in the world can express. [*Ibid.*, pp. 138–39]

By their own account and those of others, the Bible Students were hypnotized, drugged, and tortured; some broke under torture, with the result that "the Gestapo was able to obtain information about how the work of Jehovah's witnesses was organized and carried out." [*Ibid.*, p. 126]

The year 1936 saw massive arrests of Bible Students in Germany. "There [were] numerous cases," the 1974 *Yearbook* reports, "when the Gestapo officials were apparently struck with blindness when they conducted their searches and where they were frequently outwitted by the lightning-quick actions of the brothers, clearly indicating Jehovah's protection and angelic help." [*Ibid.*, pp. 127–28; see also pp. 140–41]

Watchtower sources report infiltration of the movement by government spies—similar, no doubt, to the *V-Männer* who infiltrated the clergy and reported to the Gestapo. Watchtower sources also report that these infiltrators and betrayers frequently went "insane." [*Ibid.*, pp. 159–60]

The work of the Society having gone underground, Watch Tower publications were smuggled into Germany (one conveyor was a Bible Student's hollow wooden leg) by way of Switzerland.

In 1936, Witnesses worldwide adopted a resolution protesting their brothers' incarceration. Copies were sent to Hitler and his officials, and to Pope Pius XII. The resolution read, in part:

> We raise strong objections to the cruel treatment of Jehovah's witnesses by the Roman Catholic Hierarchy and their allies in Germany as well as in all other parts of the world, but we leave the outcome of the matter completely in the hands of the Lord, our God. [*Yearbook*, 1944, p. 155]

After 1937, the Gestapo ruled that the Witnesses might be incarcerated in concentration camps without judicial warrant, solely on grounds of suspicion.

By all accounts, the behavior of Witnesses held in Buchenwald, Ravensbrück, Sachsenhausen, Dachau, and Belsen was characterized by extraordinary bravery. The vast majority refused to sign a declaration disavowing their faith—a declaration that would have ensured their release from the camps. The Society contends that those Witnesses who succumbed to torture and threats received poisoned meats from God in return. They were, having "placed themselves outside of Jehovah's protection," imprisoned by the Soviets, starved, raped . . . Those who joined the German military, the Society says, for the most part "lost their lives." [*Yearbook*, 1974, p. 178]

So the Witnesses talk about their martyrs (those who died for their faith), and about those who died because their faith weakened—using both sets of circumstances as proof of divine dispensation. They need to see immediate rewards, immediate punishments, direct consequences to every act—as if faith must pay off promptly with tangible rewards.

There were, the Society acknowledges, Witnesses who did sign declarations disavowing their faith; later, before they were actually released from the camps, they had their signatures annulled. And there were others who were released as a result of their disavowal but who, "after the breakdown of Hitler's regime, spontaneously joined the [Witnesses'] ranks." (Commenting on this, the *Yearbook* reports charitably (and correctly): "Many were comforted by the experience of Peter, who had denied his Lord and Master too, but had been taken back into his favor." [*Ibid.*, p. 178] I find this remark from a Watchtower publication refreshing, because it treats tenderly of human frailty and acknowledges that human beings do sometimes act out of human motives and human circumstances—especially since so often what one reads suggests that everything that happens to Jehovah's Witnesses is a result of angelic or demonic intervention. It has the sweet taste of the merciful God of the Gospels: we did not need Christ to teach us ethics—we needed Him to understand mercy.)

Within the camps, the Witnesses were highly organized—although, according to the Watchtower Society, schisms flourished even under these unlikely conditions. Some Bible Students were rebuked for "having an exaggerated view [of their] own importance." One man with an eidetic memory was reproached by his fellow Witness inmates because he recited past issues of *The Watch Tower*; he was charged with the sin of pride. [*Yearbook*, 1974]

Whether humility is a virtue in a concentration camp is a good question; that pride should assert itself in a death camp might seem a victory of the human spirit over the forces of oppression. It may be sad, but it is hardly remarkable, that some Witnesses joined their oppressors in order to survive. Some, for example, collaborated with the SS as work-gang leaders. [*Ibid.*] (The Witnesses, by the way, seem never to have heard of Anne Frank. Her idealism and her egalitarian love would not endear her to them. And there is her Jewishness. I remember a Jewish woman with whom I studied the Bible when I was a child. Her family had been wiped out in the camps. When she came to meetings, she insisted, wildly struggling against the Witnesses' smugness, that the Jews too had suffered during the war. But the Witnesses insisted blandly that after all, the Jews had had no choice— they'd been born Jews, and so had not the virtue of choosing their suffering; and the Jews had not, they said, blindly ignoring her pain, suffered for *Christ's* name's sake. "The thing that made me want to look into Christianity," she said, "was the smallness of the Old Testament God that sent bears to tear children apart when they teased the Prophet Elijah for being bald. And your Christ seems even smaller than that." They had no idea what she was talking about.)

The cohesive ideology of the Witnesses—like the cohesive ideology of the Communists—and their communal life and faith in the camps (where they even managed to baptize new converts by total immersion in water) enabled them to survive their ordeals. It is significant that *after* their liberation from the camps many Witnesses fell away from their faith. It is almost as if their persecution had been the jell that united them to one another and to God, the adrenaline that charged and sustained them. They got through tragedy, with its harsh, sharp focus, together; like most of us, they found commonplace muddle harder to deal with.

In general, behavior of the Witnesses as a whole in the camps seems to be survival behavior, and Watchtower publications report not only stories of sadistic treatment at the hands of the SS, but the fact that the Witnesses were placed, even in Auschwitz, in "positions of trust":

> Those brothers and sisters who had been in Auschwitz for a time had positions of trust. Several sisters were allowed to walk to the city without a guard to make purchases for their mistresses. In this way the sisters could contact brothers outside. They cared for a special, hard and dangerous job. They copied whole *Watchtower* articles into blue paper-covered school notebooks and tried to circulate them. . . . [*Yearbook*, 1976, p. 40]

Again, both sets of treatment—the torture they received and the special treatment they received—are used as proof of God's providence.

What appears to have happened is that after 1942, when the Nazis were more concerned with winning the war than with eradicating one small dissident sect, many Witnesses were employed in "projects productive to the economy" and were therefore left alone, since all available manpower was being mobilized for production. This can be seen from a comment made by SS leader Pohl to Himmler vis-à-vis the camps:

> The war has brought about a visible change in the structure of the concentration camps and basically changed their function with regard to the use of prisoners.
> The incarceration of prisoners solely because of security, educational or preventative reasons no longer predominates. The emphasis has swung to the economic aspect of the matter. The mobilization of all prisoners, in the first place, for war-related jobs (increase of armament production) and, secondly, for peace-related matters becomes more and more the predominating factor.

The necessary measures being taken result from this realization, requiring a gradual transfer of the concentration camps from their previous one-sided political design to an organization meeting the economic needs. [*Yearbook*, 1974, p. 195]

Because of this new policy, prisoners, including Witnesses, were better fed. The officials were careful, too, not to force Witnesses to work in armament factories, but placed them in shops where the work was suitable to their abilities. For this, the Witnesses praised God in the belief that He had directed their enemies.

This is a variation of "God works in strange and wondrous ways": the implication is that the Witnesses' integrity aroused the ire of Satan and their docility and industriousness aroused the sympathy of Satan's agents. And, indeed, except when their faith was directly assaulted, the Witnesses appear to have been docile and cooperative in the camps (they have always prided themselves on being model prisoners); they were thus more valuable to the state alive than dead.

That they were not exterminated owes something to the fact that, as the war progressed, they were not high-priority state enemies—and something, perhaps, to Himmler's personal physician, the Finnish masseur Kersten, who sought to moderate Himmler's bloody fanaticism toward all concentration-camp inmates. Kersten secured work releases for several Witness women incarcerated in the camps in order for them to work as domestics at his home. He was impressed by their dutiful industry; he liked them. As an apparent result of Kersten's experience with the Bible Students and his intercession, Himmler wrote the following letter to SS leaders Pohl and Mueller:

Enclosed is a report about the ten Bible Students that are working on my doctor's farm. I had an opportunity to study the matter of the Earnest Bible Students from all angles. Mrs. Kersten made a very good suggestion. She said that she had never had such good, willing, faithful and obedient personnel as these ten women. These people do much out of love and kindness. . . . One of the women once received 5.00 RM as a tip from a guest. She accepted the money since she did not want to cast aspersions upon the home, and gave it to Mrs. Kersten, since it was prohibited to have money in the camp. The women voluntarily did any work required of them. Evenings they knitted, Sundays they were kept busy in some other way. During the summer they did not let the opportunity pass to get up two hours earlier and gather baskets full of mushrooms, even though they were required to work ten, eleven, and twelve hours a day. These facts complete my picture of the Bible Students. They are incredibly fanatical, willing people, ready to sacrifice. If we could put their fanaticism to work for Germany or instill such fanaticism into our people, then we would be stronger than we are today. Of course, since they reject the war, their teaching is so detrimental that we cannot permit it lest we do Germany the greatest damage. . . .

Nothing is accomplished by punishing them, since they only talk about it afterward with enthusiasm. . . . Each punishment serves as a merit for the other world. That is why every true Bible Student will let himself be executed without hesitation. . . . Every confinement in the dungeon, every pang of hunger, every period of freezing is a merit, every punishment, every blow is a merit with Jehovah.

Should problems develop in camp in the future involving the Bible Students, then I prohibit the camp commander from pronouncing any punishment. Such cases should be reported to me with a brief description of the circumstances. From now on I plan on doing the opposite and telling the respective individual: "You are forbidden to work. You are to be better fed than the others and you do not have to do anything."

For according to the belief of these good-natured lunatics merit ceases then, yes, to the contrary, previous merits will be deducted by Jehovah.

Now my suggestion is that all of the Bible Students be put to work—for example, farm work, which has nothing to do with war and all its madness. One can leave them unguarded if properly assigned; they will not run away. They can be given uncontrolled jobs, they will prove to be the best administrators and workers.

Another use for them as suggested by Mrs. Kersten: We can employ the Bible Students in our "Lebensbornheime," . . . not as nurses, but, rather, as cooks, housekeepers, or to do work in the laundry or similar jobs. In cases where we still have men serving as janitors we can use strong women Bible Students. I am convinced that, in most cases, we will have little difficulty with them.

I am also in agreement with suggestions that Bible Students be assigned to large families. Qualified Bible Students who have the necessary ability should be found and reported to me. I will then personally distribute them among large families. In such households they are not to wear prison garb, however, but civilian clothes. . . .

In all these cases where prisoners are partially free and have been assigned to such work we want to avoid written records or signatures and make such agreements with just a handshake. . . . [*Ibid.*, pp. 196–97]

Witness women were subsequently sent to work in SS households, in truck gardens, on estates, and in the *Lebensbornheime*.

The SS were willing, according to the Watchtower Society, to take the Witnesses into their homes because the Nazis had become wary of their servants, fearing death by poison or some other method. Two Witnesses, Max Schroer and Paul Wauer, were called upon to act as barbers because the SS knew Witnesses would not cut the throats of their enemies. Because of this trust, visits to and from relatives—even vacations of several weeks—were allowed to Society members working outside the camps.

They were chosen to supervise and direct workers on SS officers' private estates. One Witness reports that he was permitted to have his accordion sent from home, and that often in the evenings he and other Witnesses would go out onto Lake Wolfgang (Austria), where the songs and light music they played entertained not only their brethren but local residents, including the SS officials in whose charge they were.

The Witnesses were apparently able, in the words psychiatrist Rollo May uses to describe "constructive schizoid behavior," "to live and work with the machine without becoming machines." [Rollo May, *Love and Will* (New York: W. W. Norton, 1969), p. 32, "Our Schizoid World"] It would be fair to say of a German Witness that he found it "necessary to remain detached enough to get meaning from the experience, but in doing so to protect his own inner life from impoverishment." [*Ibid.*] They were not entirely indifferent to the suffering of others: The Yiddish New York daily *Der Tag* (July 2, 1939) reported that "when like an epidemic all kinds of food stores began to post the well-known signs 'Juden unerwunscht,' Witnesses frequently provided their Jewish neighbors or mere acquaintances with food or milk without asking any reward for it." [quoted in *Aw*, Feb. 22, 1975, p. 22] Their apathy arose from the fact that, inasmuch as they saw themselves as the only focus of all events, they were (in the words Rollo May applies to alienated personalities) basically "uninvolved, detached, unrelated to the significant events." [May, *op. cit.*] As individuals, they were able to extend humankindness to individual Jews; as a group, they were obliged to declare that the suffering they sought to alleviate as individuals had no value and no significance.

May describes the healthy person in whom love and will function creatively as being "in the process of reaching out, moving toward the world, seeking to affect others or the inanimate world, and opening himself to be affected; molding, forming, relating to the world, or requiring that it relate to him." [*Op. cit.*, Foreword, p. 9, p. 276] The Witnesses "reached out, or moved toward the world" insofar as their proselytizing was an outreach; but their full genuine embrace was extended only to converts. They did not "open themselves up to be affected"; they lived within their own constructs and their own community. Nevertheless, it is possible to conjecture that their behavior in the camps was characteristic of what May calls "the constructive schizoid personality"; it enabled them to survive.

"Dr. Bruno Bettelheim," May says, "finds the same supremacy of the aloof person—whom I would call schizoid—in his experiences in the concentration camps during World War II."

Bettelheim:

> According to psychoanalytic convictions then current . . . aloofness
> from other persons and emotional distance from the world were

viewed as weakness of character. My comments . . . on the admirable way in which a group of what I call "anointed persons" behaved in the concentration camps suggest how struck I was with these very aloof persons. They were very much out of contact with their unconscious but nevertheless retained their old personality structure, stuck to their values in the face of extreme hardships, and as persons were hardly touched by the camp experience. . . . These very persons who, according to existing psychoanalytic theory, should have had weak personalities apt to readily disintegrate, turned out to be heroic leaders, mainly because of the strength of their character. [Bruno Bettelheim, *The Informed Heart* (Glencoe, Ill.: The Free Press, 1960), pp. 20–21; quoted in May, *op. cit.*, pp. 32–33]

In the early 1900s, Pastor Russell pointed out that the Witnesses ought to reap their greatest rewards in Germany, for it was there that the Society had gone to its greatest expense to spread the word. He added the caveat, however, that the large numbers of the "consecrated" might have been diminished by immigration to the United States.

The work Russell started in Germany, a country for which he had a great affinity, has not fared badly. In 1975, there were, in West Germany, over 100,000 Witnesses—or one Witness in every 597 West Germans. [*Yearbook*, 1976] And the many Catholics in the councils of the West German government have not troubled to place any obstacles in their way.

AFRICA

Malawi:

They are not Jehovah's Witnesses, they are the Devil's Witnesses.—Dr. H. K. Banda, President of Malawi, 1972 [reported in *Newsweek*, May 10, 1976, p. 106]

The determination of Jehovah's Witnesses to remain aloof from politics has brought them into conflict with African nationalism—particularly in Malawi.

On October 23, 1967, Jehovah's Witnesses were officially listed, in *The Times* of Malawi, as an "unlawful society." In 1972, contending that the 30,000 Malawian Witnesses hindered the country's political and economic development, the Malawi Congress Party is reported to have adopted the following resolution:

. . . Resolved that all the members of these fanatical religious sects employed in commerce and industry should be dismissed forthwith, and that any commercial or industrial concern that does not comply with this resolution should have its license cancelled.

Resolved that all the members of these fanatical religious sects employed by the Government should be dismissed forthwith and that any member of these sects who is self-employed, either in business or farming, have his business or farming activities discouraged.

> Resolved that all the members of these sects who live in the villages
> should be chased away from there, and appealed to the Government
> [*sic*] to give maximum possible protection to members of the party
> who deal with the adherents to these sects. [*Aw*, Dec. 8, 1975, p. 6]

Newsweek reported:

> A series of pogrom-style persecutions has apparently decimated the
> sect [in Malawi]. Newsmen have been banned from Malawi, but nu-
> merous eyewitness reports of torture and murder have leaked out of
> the small southeastern African nation. Jehovah's Witnesses have re-
> portedly been hacked to death, gang-raped and forced to walk with
> nails through their feet. Thousands of Witnesses have fled to neigh-
> boring Zambia and Mozambique only to be deported back to Malawi.
> "There are still 12,000 to 15,000 of our members in Malawi," says
> Jehovah's Witness leader Keath Eaton in Salisbury, Rhodesia. "Most
> are being persecuted and about a third are in concentration camps."
> [*Op. cit.*, p. 106]

According to Amnesty International's *Report on Torture* (1973):

> Well-substantiated reports indicate that both in 1967 and in 1972
> the Young Pioneers [the youth wing of the Malawi Congress Party]
> and their supporters inflicted torture on the Jehovah's Witnesses in the
> form of rape, beatings, shaving with broken bottles and burning. In
> the autumn of 1972, these persecutions caused a number of deaths and
> the migration of some 21,000 Jehovah's Witnesses to Zambia, where
> several hundred died in an inadequate refugee camp.

The Witnesses were expelled from the Zambian camps in December,
1972; unable to practice their religion in Malawi, they fled to refugee camps
in neighboring Mozambique. From 1973 to August, 1975, 20,000 Witnesses
lived in the Mozambique camps. According to Amnesty International:

> In June 1975 the FRELIMO government took power in Mozam-
> bique, and shortly thereafter a number of highly placed officials in the
> FRELIMO government began to attack the Jehovah's Witnesses. . . .
> Probably as a result of this the refugee camps in the Vila Coutinho/
> Mlangeni area appear to have been closed during the month of Au-
> gust. From independent witnesses, Amnesty International knows that
> Jehovah's Witness refugees in large numbers were seen on the Malawi
> Mozambique border in late August [1975], apparently confused as to
> where to go next.

The Witnesses' offense in Malawi was to refuse to purchase a 25-cent
membership card in the Malawi Congress Party.

On May 31, 1976, Dr. Philip A. Potter, of the World Council of
Churches, appealed to Dr. Banda to release Witnesses detained in camps

and urged that they be sent back to their villages to lead a "normal life." In his letter to Dr. Banda, Dr. Potter wrote:

> We are not unaware of the difficulties that have existed during the last several years between the Jehovah's Witnesses in your country and the political authorities there. We also realize that their teachings on, and attitude to, the state have in part at least contributed to this tension. The World Council of Churches, as you are aware, has always encouraged participation by all Christians in the welfare of the countries in which they live.
>
> But the fundamental human right of such participation also involves the freedom to dissent as well as the freedom to refuse to join any particular political grouping or party. We, therefore, feel that your country's apparent policy of compulsory membership in the Malawi Congress Party is a curtailment of human rights and that punitive measures against those who do not take membership are unjustifiable. The WCC has attempted to uphold human rights everywhere and for all and we express our deep concern abut the Jehovah's Witnesses in Malawi, especially those who are reported to be in detention or under arrest for refusing to buy membership cards in the Congress Party. [quoted in *Aw*, Dec. 8, 1976]

A massive letter-writing campaign initiated by American Witnesses resulted in statements of concern from Senator Frank Church and from Representatives George Brown, Paul Tsongas, and Tom Hartkin.

When, in the summer of 1975, Portugal relinquished control of Mozambique to the Front for the Liberation of Mozambique (FRELIMO), the 7,000 Witnesses of that newly independent country became subject to mass arrests and, according to a story in *Awake!* of January 8, 1976, to harassment and torture. FRELIMO propaganda organs denounced them as "agents left behind by Portuguese colonialism," "former 'Pides' [Portuguese secret police] whose aim was to upset the social order." [*Noticias*, Oct. 9, 1975] *A Tribuna* [Oct. 22, 1975] accused them of "a religious fanaticism" that permitted them "not to show respect for the social order and to annihilate the mobilization and organization of the people."

"When we were tied and beaten by Portuguese colonialists, where were these Witnesses of Jehovah?" Mozambique President Samora Machel asked. [*Noticias, op. cit.*]

The Witnesses' response is that they too were imprisoned—by the Pides. This, as published in *Awake!* of January 8, 1976, is their account:

In 1935, when Antonio Salazar ruled Portugal and Mozambique with an iron fist, two white South African Witnesses entered Mozambique "to cooperate with the Mozambican Witnesses in their activity." They were deported, as were other foreign missionaries, in 1938 and 1939. Native Mozambicans who received *The Watchtower* magazine were also arrested, and some were deported to the penal colony of São Tome; others were assigned to work camps in the northern part of Mozambique.

When a British Witness was sent to Mozambique in the 1940s to seek official recognition of the work of the Society, the secret police accused him of being a Communist: "Though the interview convinced the official that Jehovah's witnesses are not Communists, he told [the Society's representative] John Cooke: 'Nevertheless, you people are against the Catholic Church and the Catholic Church is our church. She helped us to build up the Portuguese Empire!' Cooke was given forty-eight hours to leave the country."

The main charge leveled against the Witnesses by the Portuguese authorities and the secret police had been that they refused to take part in fighting against FRELIMO. But in 1973, when another wave of persecution hit the Witnesses, they were accused of having been *supporters* of FRELIMO. And when FRELIMO took full power, the revolutionary government accused them of "obscurantism." Radio and press dispatches repeated that "Mozambique is not Jehovah's country"; "these fanatical 'Jehovahs' must be reeducated." Beatings, torture, and mass arrests have followed; Witnesses have been separated from their children, and their property has been confiscated.

It is extremely difficult to get outside corroboration for this account. George Houser, Executive Director of the American Committee on Africa, visited Mozambique in October, 1975. He reports that Marcelinos Dos Santos, vice-president of FRELIMO, regarded Jehovah's Witnesses as a vexing problem: "What to do with them?" Dos Santos asked. "They are not cooperating. We have organized new productive communal villages—and they do not take part in the life of the community." According to Dos Santos, Mozambican Witnesses are being assigned to "re-education centers."

Willis Logan, of the Africa Office of the National Council of Churches, agrees that the treatment meted out to the Witnesses is harsh: "They refuse," he says,

> to work in any way to support struggling governments; they withhold their allegiance from countries that are struggling for survival; they do not participate in the civic or civil affairs of the country. Religious tolerance as we know it does not exist in many of the emerging nations. Governments like that of Mozambique can't be convinced that their refusal to vote and to become members of the party is not a result of foreign interference. Their leaders have always been white— and white South Africans, in particular. FRELIMO is bound to take a jaundiced view of this. And the priority of a country like Mozambique is its own development and survival; religious liberties become a casualty of the national will to survive. Jehovah's Witnesses pressure the Council of Churches to protest in their behalf, even though they

never show any ecumenical spirit in return, and in fact denounce the spirit of ecumenicism. We know they are harassed; we don't know to what extent they are harassed.

Meanwhile, Jehovah's Witnesses are buoyed by the belief that "they have the firm guarantee by God that they will be rewarded with the opportunity for eternal life in his new order. For this reason they rejoice, knowing that the 'tested quality' of their faith, 'of much greater value than gold that perishes despite its being proved by fire, may be found a cause for praise and glory and honor at the revelation of Jesus Christ.' " [1 Peter 1:7, NWT; *Aw*, Dec. 22, 1975]

They can also take pleasure in the fact that while Mozambique oppresses them, Portugal, the country that formerly oppressed Mozambique, now officially recognizes them. On December 18, 1974, Jehovah's Witnesses were legally recognized by Portugal's revolutionary government, which restored civil liberties after almost a decade of totalitarian rule. The same government that gave Mozambique independence gave Jehovah's Witnesses free reign. There were, as of September, 1976, 18,000 Jehovah's Witnesses in Portugal—which makes them the second-largest religion in that Catholic country.

And to all charges that they endanger the spirit of nationalism and the mobilization of energies necessary to emerging nations, the Witnesses reply that on the contrary, they are industrious, reliable, and honest; that they pay their taxes; and that they have helped hundreds of thousands to "overcome sexual immorality, alcoholism, drug addiction and similar degrading habits" [*Aw*, Jan. 8, 1976, p. 24]; that they have aided the cause of literacy. In Mozambique, they claim, 4,000 people achieved literacy through the Witnesses' efforts (and through their handbooks—the sole vehicle by which illiterate would-be converts are taught). Similar claims are made for the Witnesses' work in Mexico, where, according to the Watchtower Society, 48,000 persons learned to read and write through their efforts in the past twenty-eight years; and for Nigeria, where, the Witnesses say, they have taught 5,000 people to read and write in 1974 and 1975. [*Ibid.*] The Witnesses further argue that they "have helped the people to gain a progressive, practical approach to life and its problems, contributing to the forming of united families, responsible workers, and considerate peaceful neighbors" and have "helped Africans of all tribes to become free from all kinds of superstitious beliefs [including] the practice of witchcraft, enslaving rituals, fears, and tribal taboos." [*Ibid.*, p. 25]

It is true that African countries that have been colonized, whose fight for independence has been arduous and bitter, interpret the Witnesses' history of political "neutrality" as a kind of passive resistance to progressive change. The Witnesses themselves argue that they have been a "stabilizing element" in the native populations that were oppressed by imperialist regimes. What some newly independent African nations (whose use of force against the Witnesses is not, of course, justifiable, while it may be understandable) feel about Jehovah's Witnesses is not unlike what Jesus said to his erstwhile followers: If "you are not for me, you are against me; if you are neither hot nor cold, but lukewarm, I will spit you out of my mouth."

Zambia:

Kenneth Kaunda of Zambia, for example (himself a devout Christian and a believer in Gandhian nonviolence), must find it hard to love the Witnesses when he remembers that their role in preindependent Northern Rhodesia was, in effect, to be "good natives":

> One incident involving the brothers that took place in 1940 shows the good effect the truth was having on them. Mine workers at Rhokana Corporation's Nkana Mine went on strike, but the brothers employed at the mine continued to present themselves for work, since soldiers had been called in to prevent picketing. It began to be realized by employers that Jehovah's witnesses were in fact a stabilizing element in the population. [*Yearbook*, 1972, pp. 238–39]

Another edition of the *Yearbook* says blandly, speaking of a 1940 "riot" in the Copper Belt, that "the ringleaders were all Roman Catholic." [*Yearbook*, 1976, p. 155]

The Witnesses were not officially recognized in Northern Rhodesia until after 1946—although they were generally perceived to be "good natives." There were, in fact, no white Northern Rhodesians who were Witnesses until 1944, though the Society's branch depot and the administration of the local Witnesses were in the hands of a white South African, Llewelyn Phillips. During World War II, Phillips was arrested by government authorities for refusing to surrender Watchtower publications and for refusal to join the army. A ban was placed on Watchtower activity by the Solicitor General.

Still, as Watchtower publications point out, the services of black Witnesses were in great demand: "The Society's adherents have the best reputation of any in this [labor] Corps and it is well known that farmers and other employers specify that they specially want them." [*Yearbook*, 1944] "The official mind is one of nonrecognition still, but individually there are some encouraging instances of a definite respect for the cleanliness, decency and industry of Jehovah's witnesses." [*Yearbook*, 1946]

After World War II, when the Witnesses were no longer seen as a threat to national security, they were permitted to go about their work unmolested. They were, in fact, as agitation for independence accelerated, viewed by colonial administrators as a stabilizing influence. The Witnesses cite with pride a preindependence newspaper editorial that remarked that "those areas in which Jehovah's Witnesses are strongest among Africans are now . . . more trouble-free than the average. Certainly they have been active against agitators, witchcraft, drunkenness and violence of any kind." [*Yearbook*, 1972] The newspaper also eulogizes their middle-class propriety: "the Witness families [are] easily recognized in their meetings as little clusters of father, mother and children." [*Ibid.*] The political passivity that endeared them to colonialists made them the targets for attack by African political nationalists and activists; just prior to independence, African militants—seeing in their docility and cooperation with the state an implicit threat to independence and national freedom—harassed and persecuted them. Kenneth Kaunda—then head of the United National Independence Party—implored all regional party members to put a stop to the violence and terrorism directed against them. But with the coming of independence and the need to consolidate and unify the new nation—referred to by the Witnesses as "a patriotic hysteria" [*Ibid.*]—Witness children were expelled from school for not saluting the flag around which the new nation proudly rallied. Foreign Witnesses were deported. Violence against the Witnesses again broke out; rapes and beatings were reported. Kaunda's government spoke out against these atrocities; but President Kaunda felt constrained to ban the work of the Witnesses temporarily.

(I met Kenneth Kaunda in New York in the hard and heady days prior to independence. He struck me—as I think he strikes most observers—as a man of impressive dignity and scrupulous conscience. Many political observers think that Kaunda's influence alone may keep Africa from exploding into black–white violence. I can imagine that it grieved him deeply to see the fervor of his people translated into acts of brutality against the Witnesses and that his banning the work of the Witnesses was conceived as a way to defuse a situation which he deplored.)

When there is internal stability, the Witnesses are usually unmolested, their work placed under no restraints; according to the 1977 *Yearbook*, this is the case today with the more than 57,000 Witnesses now in Zambia. It is not surprising that a sect that does not practice a social gospel, and that has had white men as its leaders, has given rise, among black Africans who tend to view white missionaries as partners of white imperialists, to fear and suspicion.

Southern Africa:

To be a Christian in South Africa—if one understands Christianity to mean not only obeying the awesomely difficult injunction to "love one another" but performing the equally difficult task of "bearing witness"—is not easy.

The Witnesses have proselytized in the face of enormous difficulties in South Africa and maintained their neutrality in the face of bloody racial conflict; but their construction of "neutrality" precludes the kind of savage/

compassionate outrage against racial injustice that men like Father Huddleston and Alan Paton have found it their duty to express. As the Church hierarchy did not vehemently attack the treatment of the Jews in Hitler's Germany, the Witnesses do not attack and expose the treatment of black South Africans.

They carry no man's cross but their own. If they deplore, say, the massacre at Sharpville, their modest indignation is no different in tone from their derision of rock music; both, for them, are proofs that the Devil rules the world. Their anger does not burn hot; indeed, they reserve their scathing attacks for members of the clergy who *do* denounce racial atrocities—because, according to them, those churchmen have entered the secular arena, in which they themselves claim to have no part.

They do, however, love one another. When a drought in Lesotho in 1970 created a severe food shortage, South African Witnesses provided relief maize and cash; and acts of charity like this convince black Witnesses that their white brothers love them: "We reached the point where we had nothing in our house, not even ten cents to buy some mealie meal. Then the money for food arrived from our white brothers in South Africa. I could only cry and not say anything."—Report from a black Witness in Lesotho [*Yearbook*, 1976, p. 212]

The section dealing with South Africa and neighboring territories in the 1976 *Yearbook* reads more like a travel brochure written by a public relations firm than an account of the land of apartheid and bloody racial uprisings:

> Come with us to a land of intriguing contrasts—bustling cities and remote places in the bush, modern dwellings and humble African huts. Walk among people of many races. Listen and you will hear millions speak English or Afrikaans (derived from Old Dutch). Others of this land's 26,000,000 inhabitants are at home with such tongues as Xhosa and Zulu. . . . Many a modern African, though driving a late-model car, occasionally sacrifices a goat to appease the spirits of his dead ancestors. [pp. 67–69]

The Witnesses' own account of their history in South Africa is fascinating, particularly as it reveals the sect's antipathy to social reform and reformers, and its almost rabid wish to disassociate itself from "indigenous" nationalistic Watchtower movements.

The proselytizing work of the Witnesses in South Africa began at the turn of the century when, according to the 1976 *Yearbook*, "South Africa's population was smaller, the pace slower, and life more simple . . . [and] the time proved ripe for the good news to reach this fascinating field." [p. 69] Russellite literature was carried into the Transvaal in 1902 by a Dutch Reform missionary. In 1906, two Scottish Bible Students began to collect subscriptions for *Zion's Watch Tower* in Durban.

It is at this point—when there were forty subscribers to the *Watch Tower* in South Africa—that the man cast by the Witnesses as a villain enters the "simple" life of the country. In 1907, Joseph Booth, an Englishman who had been a sheep farmer in New Zealand and an entrepreneur in Australia before he found his vocation, "appeared on the stage of the Kingdom drama" [p. 70] in Southern Africa. In the last decade of the 19th century, Booth, who had allied himself with various adventist sects at different times, came to Nyasaland (now Malawi) as an independent missionary. (Booth moved around in adventist sects so much that he was described as a religious hitchhiker.) He was outspoken in his espousal of African equality; and his slogan—"Africa for the Africans"—put him in bad odor with government authorities, with whom he was soon *persona non grata*.

Knowing nothing of this, Pastor Russell interviewed Booth in 1906, and as a result the Society underwrote his missionary activities for a time, under the impression that he would open up wide new fields for the brethren. Unfortunately for the Society—and for Russell—Booth's activities merely increased its difficulties and brought its name into disrepute.

Booth took off for South Africa, where he acquired a fervent disciple, an African miner named Elliott Kamwana, who had been educated at the Livingstonia Mission on Lake Nyasa. Soon Kamwana was distributing Russellite tracts among Africans in Johannesburg and Pretoria. He claimed to have baptized over 9,000 Africans in Nyasaland in one year, 1909, alone.

But Booth and Kamwana, while they appear to have used Watch Tower literature to some extent, were at least as much interested in social justice and equality on earth as they were in preaching a heavenly reward. The 1976 *Yearbook* reports that while Bible Students in Durban sang "Free from the Law" (no doubt referring to the Mosaic Law), Booth stationed himself outside their meeting hall and sang, in protest, "Not free from the law" (meaning, no doubt, South Africa's discriminatory racial laws). [p. 73]

("Actually," says the *Yearbook*, "neither Booth nor Kamwana had really left Babylon the Great, or false religion; they never became Bible Students or Jehovah's Christian witnesses. Their relationship with the Watch Tower Society was short and superficial." [*Ibid.*])

When Kamwana got back to his native Nyasaland—carrying Booth's social gospel with him—he was deported to the Seychelles Islands. He was not permitted to return to his homeland until 1937. Upon his return, he became the leader of an indigenous "Watch Tower movement"—one of many that proliferated in the Rhodesias, the Congo, and South Africa; they sprang, it is likely, from seeds sown in Nyasaland by Booth and Kamwana; and the schismatic Watch Tower movement was carried from Nyasaland by Africans emigrating for work.

Kamwana, who called his sect "The Watchtower Mission," used some of

Russell's ideas and more of his own. He regarded the American Watch Tower Bible and Tract Society as a European organization.

Russell was nervous; in 1910, he sent European Bible Students in good standing with the Society to oversee the work in Southern Africa. But the indigenous Watchtower movements continued to flourish—and to cause grave concern to the American Society, which had no wish to be associated, in the public mind, with the indigenous religious/socialist/nationalist groups, many of which refused to pay taxes and engaged in other acts of civil disobedience.

So many groups were going around calling themselves "Watch Tower" people that there was understandable confusion about who was who. In January of 1915, there was an uprising—quickly crushed by African troops under European officers and European volunteers—in Nyasaland. It was led by one John Chilembwe.

"Subsequently," according to the 1976 *Yearbook*,

> accusations were made that the Watch Tower Society had something to do with the revolt. In fact, the official *History of the Great War* refers to Chilembwe as a "religious fanatic . . . of the so-called 'Watch Tower' sect." Careful investigation has since proved that those in Nyasaland who were interested in the truth, and even those of Kamwana's movement, a false 'Watchtower movement,' as such, had no direct connection with or responsibility for the rioting. The book *Independent African* examines the evidence on this very thoroughly and, on page 324, comes to this conclusion: "Chilembwe himself had no apparent connection with the American Watch Tower movement and attempts to link his insurrectionary projects with this organization in the United States seem misguided." Of course, since Chilembwe had been one of Booth's converts, and Booth once had some connection with the Society, enemies of the truth used these facts to make accusations and turn the Society into a scapegoat. In actual fact, Chilembwe and his lieutenants were members of the highly respected orthodox missions. These, too, came in for a lot of criticism from the government.
>
> The book *Independent African*, page 232, also has this interesting comment to make regarding the false accusation that the Watch Tower Society's publications influenced some Africans to take part in the uprisings: "But it must also be noted that nowhere in the Russell volumes was it suggested that the believers in his teachings should take active steps to hasten the overthrow of these institutions in preparation for the Millennial Age: rather they were recommended to wait patiently for divine intervention." [p. 81]

Religious historian and ethnologist Vittorio Lanternari takes the story of the indigenous Watchtower movements further:

Sometime after 1910, in the small South African village of Bullboek, near

Queenstown, "a prophet named Enoch Mgijima, whose gospel was similar to that preached in Rhodesia by John Chilembwe," had a vision in which he saw two great colonial powers, which he identified as the Netherlands and Britain, engaged in battle first with each other, "and then suddenly being both annihilated by an enormous monkey, which the prophet recognized as representing the African people, destined to destroy their white rulers." Inspired by his vision, Mgijima formed a new sect called the Israelites, proclaiming himself "bishop, prophet, and guardian." The Israelites rejected the New Testament "as a hoax perpetrated by the missionaries"; they "regarded themselves as the chosen people of Jehovah, who would not fail to come to their aid when the time was ripe for throwing off the foreign yoke." The South African government ordered the sect dispersed and the village of Bullboek razed to the ground. "A massacre ensued in which 117 villagers of the 500 who had resisted at Mgijima's side were killed. The incident . . . forced the government to retreat from its intransigent position against recognizing the native churches, and to appoint a Native Church Commission, which, in 1925, published norms for their official acceptance." [*The Religions of the Oppressed* (New York: New American Library, 1965), pp. 42–43]

In the 1920s, a native of Nyasaland named Tom Nyirenda, who called himself Mwana Lesa, or "Son of God," traveled from village to village in Northern Rhodesia, proclaiming himself a prophet of the "Watchtower movement" and declaring that Africa belonged to the Africans and the white man ought to be chased out.

According to the 1976 *Yearbook*, Nyirenda—taking a page from *Foxe's Book of Martyrs*—labeled his political enemies "witches," tied them to a dunking stool, and drowned them. The *Yearbook* quotes an account by Scott Lindberg in *The Sunday Times* of July 1, 1934:

> [Nyirenda] called the headmen together and told them that he had been sent by God to cleanse the tribe of witchcraft, and that every man, woman and child must be baptised in the river.
>
> The superstitious natives were decoyed to a place where a swift river forced its way through a winding ravine among the hills, and there, on top of a boulder in the middle of the river, stood Tom, dressed in long white robes.
>
> He told the people that God had sent him to separate the sheep from the goats. He then baptised each person by immersion in the river, with the help of [an ally and his supporters], who held their enemies under the water, with their heads upstream, until they were drowned.
>
> The people sang hymns as they stood gazing at each lifeless victim, and all night long the forest echoed the frenzied exhortations of Mwana Lesa.

Having drowned twenty-two natives that night, Tom decided to
cross the border and settle in the Katanga Province of the Belgian
Congo, where the Rhodesian authorities would not be able to get him.
[pp. 95–96]

Nyirenda was at last arrested by the Northern Rhodesian police, and
after trial and conviction, he was hanged in Broken Hill Prison Square in
the presence of native chiefs. He is reported to have been received into the
Roman Catholic Church and granted absolution while in prison.

The Watchtower Society's account is basically that of the colonial authorities. Lanternari's more sympathetic account of Nyirenda's activities under-
scores his contention that

> native Christian movements are never a "passive" imitation of their
> European models; . . . they are an active force, which stimulates the
> indigenous people to seek emancipation and to build religious organi-
> zations of their own, as substantial as the Christian missions them-
> selves. The label of "heretical" or "dissident" with which the missions
> tag the native churches is quite unrealistic. . . . The native churches
> testify to the successful penetration of Christian teaching, their divers-
> ities being proof of the universal character of Christianity. [*Op. cit.*,
> pp. 59–60]

Nyirenda, Lanternari says, introduced the Kitawala or Kitower sect into
the mining areas of Katanga, "where clashes between natives and whites
were frequent and bitter." [p. 37] (*Kitawala* and *Kitower* are corruptions of
the English word Watchtower.) Lanternari contends that Watchtower beliefs appealed to Africans because they were antimilitarist. Nyirenda and
other African leaders bent Watchtower teachings to their nationalist wills:

> Confronted with the possible disintegration of native culture at the
> hands of the white man, the preachers of Kitawala, traveling through
> Rhodesia, Kenya, Nyasa, and Uganda, publicly accused the mission-
> aries of distorting the Bible. . . . They maintained, for example, that
> since polygamy, a cornerstone of African society, had been regarded
> as a legitimate practice in the Old Testament, the missionaries had no
> right to insist that under the Christian dispensation it had to be wiped
> out. [*Ibid.*]
>
> Colonial authorities . . . accused [Nyirenda] of having killed "bap-
> tized people," by which they meant "white Christians." . . . His
> death infused the movement with an even greater determination to
> survive and caused it to spread into the Belgian colonies and into terri-
> tories under French and British rule, where it fomented uprisings and
> attacks upon foreigners. . . . Kitawala's preachers prophesied the im-
> minent end of all foreign religious and political bodies and dissemi-
> nated a Pan-African ideology based on the expectation of a day when
> justice would prevail in the name of Jesus Christ. [*Ibid.*, p. 38]

Seen in this light, the Kitawala was a response to cultural and spiritual crisis, "for which a solution was being sought through new religious movements." [*Ibid.*, p. 39] (One must also wonder if the dunking/drowning story, so eagerly taken up by the Witnesses, was a colonialist prevarication to dispose of a nationalist leader.) It

> point[s] to the fact that when native peoples strive to renovate their religion and their society in the midst of pressures from without and from within, their efforts often take them back to traditional forms and ancient myths. Although their actions are sometimes puerile and confused, they always reflect the instinctive reaction of the native people to the events and experiences caused by these pressures. [*Ibid.*]

Kitawala

> remains one of the most forceful nativistic religious bodies in Africa. When a group of Kitawala followers organized an anti-British revolt in Uganda in 1942, their cry was: "We are the children of God and therefore not bound by the laws of man. The times have changed; we shall no longer obey the secular laws, for to obey man means to obey Satan." [*Ibid.*]

The Watchtower Society is determined to imprint on the official mind its separateness from any indigenous African-run movements; the way in which it has done this is to insist, for the public record, that it represents no threat to the status quo.

Their being good natives does not ensure that Witnesses will be treated benevolently in times of national unrest or total mobilization. Before the outbreak of World War II, Watch Tower literature was impounded in Southern Rhodesia. The Supreme Court of South Africa (*The Magistrate, Bulawayo v. Kabungo*, 1938 S.A. Law Reports 304–316) held that Watch Tower publications did not violate the Sedition Act of Southern Rhodesia. The court ordered that the literature seized and retained be returned to the Witnesses. After the war, they were permitted to carry on their work without disturbance in South Africa and in fact were granted exemption from the draft up to 1972. But with increasing racial unrest, after 1972, the Witnesses who refused to undergo military training became subject to arrest. Any Witness who refuses to take military training is now sentenced to detention barracks for one year, after which he is exempt from service.

In 1975, there were almost 30,000 active Witnesses in South Africa. (No breakdown is available as to how many of these were "European," how many "Colored," how many "Black," and how many Indian. But from figures given of attendance at conventions of Witnesses in South Africa, it would appear that black South Africans outnumber white South Africans by approximately four to one. [*Yearbook*, 1976, p. 30]

In looking at the Witnesses in South Africa, we are again confronted with moral ambiguity and anomalies. Here is a small sect, brave, willing to suffer for its beliefs, nonviolent—but unwilling to bear witness to the suffering of others, to give powerful voice to that indignation which Simone Weil called "the fiercest form of love."

The Witnesses do not, as does the Catholic Church, actively challenge apartheid; it may be argued that their religion serves as an opiate to keep non-Europeans satisfied with their painful earthly lives. The Witnesses would counter that they do genuinely enjoy fellowship when, within the context of the law, it is possible.

Mass assemblies held in South Africa are, of necessity, held in separate auditoriums for Coloreds, Blacks, and Europeans. In stadiums where the government permits mixed groups to meet, each group is obliged to sit separately.

An exception to this arrangement occurred on January 6, 1974, at Rand Stadium in Johannesburg. (Convention delegates from outside the country were in many cases refused visas because the Department of Interior was exercised over the refusal of South African Witnesses to comply with draft laws.)

On that occasion segregation was not practiced. Regardless of color, all worshiped together, and many chose to sit with their brothers of other races. Those who spoke Portuguese could sit where they wished, as could Zulu-, Afrikaans-, Lesotho-, and English-speaking individuals. The group was happily integrated; they were so joyful that applause had to be held down, and for many of the company it was the most joyous occasion in their experience.

Luckily (according to the Witnesses, "under divine guidance and without realizing it"), the Witnesses had convened in the only Johannesburg stadium used for international, interracial meetings for which no permit was necessary for a single gathering.

The Witnesses point out that the European brethren do what is regarded as "native" work in South Africa: housekeeping, janitorial, and laundry duties; while the Africans take care of the office work and do the typing. Working together on a building project in South Africa brought all the races together—white, African, Colored, Indian—and achieved a unity they regard as unknown in the secular world.

The Witnesses do not pray that the world may achieve it. They long for the day when God will erase all outside noises; they yearn for Armageddon, when, in one bloody swoop, Jehovah will wipe away all the blood and all the anguish. It is an understandable, if ultimately dangerous, withdrawal from worldly defeat.*

* Here is a partial listing of the Witnesses' status in African countries as of September, 1976. (A table listing the activities of Witnesses in all countries where they are currently active appears on pages 336–38.)

Benin (formerly Dahomey): Banned; as of April 30, 1976. From the Benin newspaper *Ehuzu:*

QUEBEC

The history of Jehovah's Witnesses in Quebec is a raucous and colorful one. The Witnesses, on the one hand, secured civil liberties by their precedent-setting Supreme Court cases—a victory for all Canadians—and, on the other hand, surpassed themselves in clergy-baiting in this French-Canadian province, provoking hysteria, responding to abuse with more abuse. Their principal antagonist in Quebec was Maurice Duplessis, *grand seigneur*, petty tyrant, Premier of Quebec from 1936 until his death in 1959 with the exception of a one-term hiatus from 1939 to 1944. Duplessis' allies, during his long reign, were conservative elements of the Church, farmers, the reactionary English-speaking elite. The Witnesses' allies, in their long legal struggle, were the French and English liberal press and eventually the Supreme Court itself. In their accounts of their victories and defeats in Quebec, the Witnesses ignore the essential political reality that provided the context for their struggles: the tension between French and English Canadians, the drive for French separatism, the social turmoil and unrest, and the economic dissatisfactions of French Canadians.

Jehovah's Witnesses were incorporated as a charitable organization in Canada in 1925, under the name International Bible Students Association of Canada.

Their history, after a temporary ban was imposed on them during World War I, was uneventful until the 1940s. During the '40s and '50s,

"All real estate used in the past by the representatives and followers of the said sect will be inventoried by the local authorities and will be used for purposes of public benefit. . . . The representatives of the said sect, and more precisely the expatriates of whichever nationality they may be, have only a few hours to leave the country after the publication of the present measures." [*Aw.*, Sept. 8, 1976, p. 7] Minister of Interior Martin Dohou Azonhiho is reported to have said, in a speech on April 16, 1976: "If they do not change their attitude these expatriates will be expelled from our national territory. . . . If by the end of the month, Jehovah's Witnesses do not shout the revolutionary slogans, do not sing the national anthem, do not respect the flag, I am going to expel all the expatriate representatives of Jehovah's Witnesses, these licensed agents of the C.I.A." [*Ibid.*, p. 4]

Cameroon: Banned.

Ethiopia: An unspecified number of Witnesses imprisoned, "due to the hostile action of the Ethiopian Church." [*Yearbook*, 1975, p. 7]

Kenya: Short-term ban on Witness activity lifted in 1973.

Morocco: Banned.

Nigeria: There are more Jehovah's Witnesses active in Nigeria than in any other country save the United States—112,164.

Rhodesia: No impediments have been put in the way of their proselytizing. The most severe hardship endured by the 12,000 Witnesses in Ian Smith's Rhodesia is that they are obliged, by Watchtower edict, not to engage in any form of tobacco production and distribution.

Togo: Permitted to proselytize, but not to hold mass meetings.

Uganda: Idi Amin has placed no obstacles in the way of the 158 Witnesses in Uganda.

Zaïre: No outright persecution; but large assemblies are banned. The Society claims that schoolchildren have been expelled for failure to salute the flag.

> Jehovah's Witnesses were virtually outlawed in Quebec. Arrests and
> prosecutions took place by the hundreds—in fact, a total of 1,775
> prosecutions were instituted—the biggest volume of litigation on any
> one subject in the history of the British Empire! It was a reign of
> terror. Mobs, beatings, violence, discrimination, loss of jobs—the
> whole gamut of official and private harassment of a minority was
> brought to play. [*Aw*, March 8, 1975, p. 16]

The Church wielded great secular power over matters of state in French
Canada during the years of the Witnesses' persecution; and the Witnesses
compare their "confrontation" with "a powerful, rich and politically en-
trenched Catholic Church" to the confrontation of early Christians with
Nero. [*Ibid.*, pp. 21, 25]

By August, 1946, over 800 cases against the Witnesses were pending in
the courts—where Witnesses had been brought on charges of violating bylaws such as peddling without a license. The Witnesses complain of
"clergy-inspired" riots and mob violence in rural Quebec. They countered,
in 1946, with the publication and distribution of a tract called "Quebec's
Burning Hate for God and Christ and Freedom Is the Shame of All Canada." The pamphlet featured, on its cover, a map of Canada with the Province of Quebec represented by a black area on which was superimposed a
massive cathedral. One million copies were printed in English; 500,000 copies were printed in French, and 75,000 in Ukrainian. In addition, 110 missionaries who'd been given crash courses in French were dispatched from
New York to "priest-infested Quebec" to share in the distribution of the
tract. [*JWDP*, p. 241]

For sixteen days, the Witnesses distributed the pamphlet from one end of
the country to the other. They accuse the "Hierarchy" of counterattacking
with "lies, violence and the pressure of Quebec's corrupt political machine
upon the law enforcement bodies." [*Yearbook*, 1948; *JWDP*] In the vicinity
of Montreal 260 arrests took place. Maurice Duplessis, whom the Witnesses
characterized as "fascist-minded" and a "tool of the Church," went to the
extreme of destroying the flourishing business of one of their members because he put up bail for one of those jailed. This, however, brought adverse
publicity to Duplessis, and the press called him a "Sawdust Caesar," a
"minor-league Franco," and "the focal point of fascism." In addition, protest meetings were organized, resolutions were passed, and Canadians were
thoroughly aroused.

A new pamphlet, "Quebec, You Have Jailed Your People," was got up in
three languages and circulated nationally. Arrests continued, until by February more than thirteen hundred cases were awaiting hearings. Charges of
"sedition" and "seditious conspiracy" were leveled against sixty-four Witnesses. So inflammatory were the tracts that they had to be distributed in
this manner:

We flew around the countryside over the cold winter snows, often with the police in hot pursuit. In the middle of the night a carload of Witnesses would dash into a village with a supply of leaflets. Each of us would run to the assigned houses, deliver the leaflets, dash back to the car and away we went! While the police were searching that village, we would be on to another.—Janet MacDonald, Witness missionary [*Aw.*, March 8, 1975, p. 20]

This is what *Commonweal*, the American liberal Catholic magazine, had to say about these events:

The Witnesses within the last few years have really begun to make their weight felt in the Province of Quebec, which is a region nearly ninety percent Catholic. Here, also, they have invaded the privacy of people's houses and have been pretty much public nuisances. The unfortunate reaction has been a number of cases of mob violence as well as numerous arrests and fines and jail sentences. Then, a few weeks ago, the Witnesses published over a million and a half broadsides entitled "Quebec's Burning Hate for God and Christ and Freedom Is the Shame of All Canada." This production was issued in English, French, and Ukrainian. It is addressed to all people, and is not so much an appeal for conversions as it is an indictment of Quebec for its treatment of the Witnesses. In old-fashioned Orangeman style it speaks of "that benighted, priest-ridden province." It goes on: "Quebec, Jehovah's Witnesses are telling all Canada of the shame you have brought on the nation by your evil deeds. In English, French and Ukrainian languages this leaflet is broadcasting your delinquency to the nation. You claim to be for God; you claim to be for freedom. Yet [when] it is exercised by those who disagree with you, you crush freedom by mob rule and gestapo tactics. . . ."

It can be imagined what was the reaction of French Catholics to such a broadside. Had the Witnesses expressly wanted to stir up trouble, they could have used no more effective means. . . . The Province immediately started . . . wholesale arrests—of doubtful legality—and then capped the climax [by suspending] the liquor license of a Montreal restaurateur named Frank Roncarelli, who was using his private means to supply bail for the arrested Witnesses. The result is the most wonderful hullabaloo and more free publicity for the followers of the late Judge Rutherford than they have perhaps ever received in a single area. A few of the French Canadian papers approved, but a great many of them did not—especially those with Liberal political sentiments who loved a chance to get a dig at a politician not of their party. The English press came out strong for freedom. The Montreal English Catholic paper, professing to find diabolism in the "Watch Tower Movement," said, . . . "We cannot combat devilish forces by vituperation, violence, or hate, for these are all the Devil's own instruments, and the Bible has warned us against the folly of trying to cast out Beelzebub with Beelzebub." When Mr. Roncarelli was deprived of his license, the same *Canadian Register* said: "By forcing an arbitrary power of the Quebec Liquor Commission to subserve a frankly punitive purpose, the Provincial Government has rightly drawn upon itself a storm of protest from all sections of the community. Nothing could be more dangerous than unnecessarily to divorce punishment from trial, and to place power to inflict it in the hands of the executive authority. The cause of justice cannot be served by illegal means."

Harry Lorin Binsse, the author of this *Commonweal* article, adds a poignant final note, which reflects the torment of the Church during the war years:

> There are two sentences in the New York *Times*'s brief account of this whole fracas which stick in my mind: "Mr. Roncarelli is a convert from Catholicism, as a result, he says, of an experience in Italy. He had gone to Italy on a pleasure trip, and when he heard Benito Mussolini described from the pulpit as 'a man sent from God,' he says, he lost faith and apparently ran into difficulties by publicly denouncing Mussolini as anti-religious." [*Commonweal*, Jan. 10, 1947]

The *Commonweal* article implicitly disputes the Witnesses' contention that *all* of Catholic Quebec was monolithically opposed to them. Catholic liberals were, on the contrary, happy to have the opportunity to snipe at Duplessis. And it is illustrative of the fact that feelings about the Witnesses were very much colored and informed by nationalistic feelings: French-speaking Canadians were more inclined to oppose them than were English-speaking Canadians. And *Commonweal* also raises an interesting question, one that has been raised by civil-libertarians in the United States (and one that it is impossible to answer with any degree of authority): did the Witnesses contribute to their own oppression, or intensify it, to gain publicity?

It is useless to conjecture. We can only deplore—as *Commonweal* and the liberal Catholic Canadian press deplored—the fact that they were persecuted. And we must be grateful that the Witnesses' Supreme Court victories secured civil liberties for millions of Canadians, Catholic and Protestant, French- and English-speaking.

One of the ways in which the Witnesses served the cause of civil liberties in Quebec was to broaden the right of appeals to the Supreme Court. Prior to the publication of their tracts, they had been arrested and charged with violating bylaws, such as the one against peddling. The Supreme Court kept these cases under the jurisdiction of the provincial courts. After the publication and distribution of "Quebec's Burning Hate," Quebec authorities began to pile sedition and libel charges on them—and the gravity of these charges obliged the Supreme Court to hear arguments.

Time and again, the Witnesses, denied protection in the lower courts, had appealed to the Supreme Court, and their cases had been thrown back into Quebec's municipal Recorder's courts. Actions, appeals, writs, motions, and special remedies proved unavailing until, in 1949, the Supreme Court accepted jurisdiction in the case of Aimé Boucher, a Witness who had been arrested and tried for the distribution of "Quebec's Burning Hate." Boucher was charged with publishing seditious and defamatory libel, and convicted. Justices of Quebec's appellate courts condemned the conduct of the trial-court judge; and five judges of the Supreme Court in Ottawa heard arguments from May 31 to June 3, 1949. The decision, handed down on December 5, 1949, went against the Witnesses 3 to 2. An application asking for a reargument of the case before a full court of nine judges was granted.

The decision, handed down on December 18, was 5 to 4 for acquittal. The deciding vote was cast by a member of the original five-judge court who reversed himself; he was an Irish Catholic. One of the judges voting for acquittal said, in his opinion:

> The incidents as described, are of peaceable Canadians who seem not to be lacking in meekness, but who, for distributing, apparently without permits, Bibles and tracts on Christian doctrine; for conducting religious services in private homes or on private lands in Christian fellowship; for holding public lecture meetings to teach religious truth as they believe it of the Christian religion; who, for this exercise of what has been taken for granted to be the unchallengeable rights of Canadians, have been assaulted and beaten and their Bibles and publications torn up and destroyed, by individuals and by mobs. . . .
>
> The conduct of the accused appears to have been unexceptionable; so far as disclosed, he is an exemplary citizen who is at least sympathetic to doctrines of the Christian religion which are, evidently, different from either the Protestant or the Roman Catholic versions: but the foundation in all is the same, Christ and his relation to God and humanity. . . .
>
> . . . It is not challenged that, as they allege, whatever they did was done peaceably, and, as they saw it, in the way of bringing the light and peace of the Christian religion to the souls of men and women. To say that is to say that their acts were lawful. [*Boucher v. The King*, (1950) S.C.R. 265, 285, 291; *JWDP*, pp. 243–44]

The achievement of the Witnesses was to have written into law what had previously "been taken for granted." Canada had no Bill of Rights; religious freedoms were a matter of tolerance and sufferance and precedent. The *Boucher* case changed that.

In 1953, the Witnesses scored another victory for civil liberties. In 1933, Quebec City had passed a bylaw that forbade the distribution of any literature in Quebec without the written permission of the Chief of Police.

(Many Witnesses circumvented this law by preaching orally from house to house, using only the Catholic Douay Bible.) The Supreme Court, on December 9, 1952, heard arguments as to the legitimacy of this law. [*Saumur v. The King* (1953) 2 S.C.R. 299] Because Canada had no written Bill of Rights on which the Witnesses could rest their case, they enterprisingly unearthed and presented to the Court a Freedom of Worship Act that had been passed by the Canadian Parliament in 1852:

> WHEREAS the recognition of legal equality among all Religious Denominations is an admitted principle of Colonial Legislation; . . . be it therefore declared . . . That the free exercise and enjoyment of Religious Profession and Worship, without discrimination or preference, so as to the same be not made an excuse of acts of licentiousness, or a justification of practices inconsistent with the peace and safety of the Province, is by the constitution and laws of this Province allowed to all Her Majesty's subjects within the same.—Statute of 1852 of Old Province of Canada [*JWDP*, pp. 245–46]

This Freedom of Worship Act had not appeared on the statute books of Ontario for forty years. Ironically, the original intent of the Act was to protect French-speaking Canadians from religious persecution similar to that which they had experienced in England during the Seven Years War.

Now, while the Court had been asked to rule on a bylaw relating to the distribution of literature, the real issue before the Court was whether Jehovah's Witnesses were a religious denomination; prosecuting attorneys argued that they were not, and that their distribution of literature could not be considered an exercise of worship protected by law. (Quebec's attorneys also argued that the Witnesses had defamed the Catholic Church and were guilty of "acts of licentiousness" and that their refusal to honor the bylaw was "inconsistent with the protection and safety of the Province.")

The decision, handed down on October 6, 1953, went in favor of the Witnesses, the justices voting 5 to 4 in their favor. In Canada, as in the United States, unorthodox religious acts and the promulgation of religious doctrine by minority groups outside of the pulpit and the churches were deemed by law to be the right of all citizens.

(A personal footnote: I was living and working at Watchtower headquarters in Brooklyn when this test case was won after a six-year legal battle. I remember the jubilation when the victory was announced one morning at breakfast. I also remember an anecdote F. W. Franz, then the Society's vice-president, told us about the trial, at which he had given testimony: In the lower courts, Catholic, Protestant, and Jewish clergymen had been brought in as experts to define what was or what was not a religious organization. Franz was interrogated by prosecuting attorneys in an effort to prove that the Witnesses were not a religion in the normally accepted use of the term. One of the prosecuting attorneys, in an attempt to discredit Franz and the International Bible Students, asked Franz what *reincarnation* meant. Franz drew a blank: "Well, now," he said to us at breakfast, "I didn't *know!*" As I remember it, he confused the Eastern belief in reincarnation with the Christian doctrine of Incarnation. I don't know how he got himself out of that blunder, but it was not, in any case, sufficiently prejudicial to influence the Court's decision. He laughed a lot when he told us about this, and we laughed heartily with him.)

The English-speaking press was almost unanimous in its praise of the Court's decision:

A VERDICT FOR FREEDOM OF WORSHIP

In upholding the right of the Witnesses of Jehovah to distribute literature in the streets, without restriction, the Supreme Court of Canada has lifted a load from the conscience of this country. Liberal-minded citizens of all religious affiliations and both major language groups have long been uneasy about tendencies toward indirect persecution of opinion. In Quebec especially, this decision . . . should result in the dismissal of some 800 similar cases involving charges under municipal bylaws. It means that no community anywhere in Canada can require advocates of religious views to be licensed. The ruling is one of several court decisions in recent years by which civil liberty has been clarified within the provinces or throughout the country. . . . In a free country, the few must be allowed to try to change the opinions of the many, whatever the issue. Canadians can be proud that their courts are showing themselves vigilant against the intolerance that would whittle freedom away.—*Evening Citizen*, Ottawa, Ontario, Oct. 7, 1953 [*JWDP*, p. 246]

FREEDOM OF BELIEF

The Supreme Court of Canada, in a majority opinion of considerable significance, has established an important principle underlying civil liberties in Canada. . . . the judgment asserted that no inferior jurisdiction, such as province or municipality, may abridge the rights and liberties which constitutionally belong to every citizen of the country, regardless of residence. . . . A very important point was made by Mr. Justice Kellock when he said that the bylaw was so openly drawn that it might be applied in many different ways. . . . The same bylaw could be applied against political parties and newspapers. . . . To grant such broad powers to a single municipal official would be a gross infringement of elemental civil rights, whether or not the power was ever used.—*Globe and Mail*, Toronto, Ontario, Oct. 8, 1953. [*Ibid.*, pp. 246–47]

FREEDOM OF RELIGION

An important principle, that a man must be allowed to practice his religious beliefs, is upheld in the supreme court's close ruling in an-

> other case involving the Witnesses of Jehovah. . . . To interfere with
> a man's worship is evil. The fact that the sufferer may adhere to be-
> liefs not generally popular is beside the point.—*Herald*, Montreal,
> Quebec, Oct. 7, 1953. [*Ibid.*, p. 247]

The response in Canada to the Witnesses' civil-libertarian victories was similar to the way in which liberals in the United States had responded to the Witnesses' victories before the United States Supreme Court: They saw that it was to their own advantage. If the rights of one minority could be abrogated, so could the rights of another; and who knew whose turn would come next? And the press, in particular, understood that any abridgment of freedom of speech would ultimately damage a free press.

The Witnesses won a further substantial victory on January 7, 1959: the Supreme Court ruled that Duplessis had to pay Frank Roncarelli (the Witness bail-provider whose liquor license he had suspended) over $33,000 in damages, plus court costs, for a total of over $50,000 for what the Witnesses called Duplessis' "spiteful Catholic action." [*Ibid.*, p. 249] *Awake!* magazine comments laconically, "Three months after the judgment was paid, Duplessis was dead."

And, it adds: "Quebec of the 1960s really began to shed the old image of clergy domination and isolationism. It started to reach out for the North American life-style as it is found in the rest of Canada and the United States." [March 8, 1975, pp. 21–22]

It's true that with the death of Duplessis, Quebec—previously isolated and introverted—passed "from a state of virtual feudalism to a new stage of social transformation known as the Quiet Revolution. It also coincided with a new period of nationalist awakening, focused on the creation of an independent socialist Quebec state." [Ann Charney, *Ms.* magazine, March 1976, p. 27] A great many reforms were to take place. In 1940, for example, Quebec women won the right to vote in provincial elections, and in 1964 the oppressive Napoleonic Code—based on the principle that a married woman has no personal rights—began to be replaced by legislation that gave women legal protection.

In 1945, at the height of their troubles, there were only 356 Jehovah's Witnesses in Quebec. There are now over 7,000. [*Aw*, March 8, 1975, p. 27]

COMMUNIST COUNTRIES: CHINA, VIETNAM, SOVIET UNION, KOREA, EAST GERMANY

China:

Zion's Watch Tower magazine was first introduced to China in 1883. In 1898, a Baptist missionary resigned from his church and began to proselytize for the Bible Students in Protestant missions. In 1912, C. T. Russell paid a brief visit to Shanghai. Very brief; in an article headed " 'Pastor' Russell's Tour Exposed" in the *Brooklyn Eagle* (Oct. 14, 1912), an interviewer chats with Russell, who, among other things, thought Nippon was a city in Japan; Russell, who had been on what appears to have been a 107-day cruise around the world, seems quite eager to prove that he spent one full day on solid ground in Shanghai, where, by his own admission, he did not meet a single missionary. In any case, in 1939, two years after the Sino-Japanese War broke out, three German Witnesses were assigned to Shanghai by the Society's Swiss branch. "Since Japan became partners with Germany [the missionaries] had little trouble getting in" to China. [*Yearbook*, 1974, p. 44]

By 1956, although there was no official ban placed on Watchtower publications, supplies of literature had stopped reaching the country. Expediency had led the three German missionaries to leave; in 1958, two remaining European missionaries were, according to Watchtower sources, placed under arrest and labeled "reactionaries." One of them, the Society reports, served a seven-year prison sentence. No statistical reports of Watchtower activity have come out of China since 1958. The last available evidence is that there were, at that time, fewer than 150 Witnesses in all of China.

For several years after Mao's victory, the Witnesses were undisturbed. There were only 25 of them, which may have had something to do with the Communists not becoming too much exercised over their work. The Witnesses do complain, however: There was a spy in their midst, they say; they were "required to study 'the thoughts of Mao.' During and after working hours they would find the doors locked so that no one could leave. They must listen to the expounding of Communism for up to four hours at a time." [*Ibid.*, p. 54] But they were still permitted to go to meetings, and to go from door to door without molestation. They had to register—as all religions that were not Chinese-financed had to register.

Vietnam:

The Watchtower Society was officially recognized in South Vietnam in 1973. [*KM*, June, 1973, p. 4] After the Communist victory, the Vietnamese branch of the Society was placed under supervision of the Paris branch. Watchtower sources estimate that there are 100 Witnesses remaining in Saigon. Before what the *Yearbook* [1976] refers to as the Communist "takeover," Watchtower President N. H. Knorr visited Saigon to present "photographic slide shows of the work of God's people in different parts of the world." After what the *Yearbook* refers to as the "fall" of Saigon, all communications between Vietnamese Witnesses and Brooklyn headquarters ended. American Watchtower missionaries left the country. However, a mission-

ary couple continued their work in a refugee camp in California. There
they held regular meetings, finding Witnesses they had known in Vietnam
as they visited each tent to press scriptural readings on the refugees.

Soviet Union:

The Witnesses are not permitted to organize; relationships with the headquarters organization have been severed.

> It is interesting to learn . . . [from] an extended denunciation in
> *Pravda*, that the sect of Jehovah's Witnesses has become almost as
> much of a headache to the rulers of Communist Russia as it was to the
> rulers of Nazi Germany. It seems that the Witnesses have been mak-
> ing converts all over the Soviet Union, even in such distant places as
> Siberia and Kurgan, and that they now constitute a formidable move-
> ment of underground resistance to the regime.
>
> The editors of *Pravda* affect to believe that the whole movement is
> being subsidized by "the most reactionary elements of American capi-
> talism" and that its purpose is to infect the Soviet masses with a spirit
> of meekness and resignation that will frustrate or delay the world-
> wide triumph of the revolutionary proletariat. The organizers of the
> movement are described as "former war criminals, Fascist collabora-
> tors and Gestapo informers" who were indoctrinated and trained for
> the work in German concentration camps.
>
> The assertion that they were indoctrinated in concentration camps
> may not be without an element of truth. Nearly all survivors of those
> camps have testified to the courage and obduracy of the Witness pris-
> oners and to their ability to withstand intimidation and even torture.
> It would not be surprising, then, if many Russian prisoners, who had
> hardly less reason than the German Witnesses to identify the state
> with the reign of antichrist and no less reason to accept an apocalyptic
> view of history, were much impressed by this example.
>
> At any rate, the chiliastic doctrine of the Witnesses . . . has had an
> immense appeal to people who live under the more totalitarian and
> tyrannous forms of government. Thus one can readily accept the esti-
> mate of the Witnesses themselves that the number of their converts
> beyond the Iron Curtain is more than 100,000. One can also believe
> the complaint of *Pravda* that in the collective farms and factories of the
> Soviet Union the Witnesses are resisting the coercive influences of
> communism . . . with quite as much stubbornness as their brethren
> in the United States have shown in refusing military service and per-
> functory homage to the flag. [*The Washington Post*, March 21, 1959, p.
> A8; *JWDP*, pp. 280–81]

(Watchtower sources report that 300 Russians and Ukrainians were baptized, during World War II, in Ravensbrück concentration camp. Soviet
dissident Pavel Litvinov has the impression that "Russian intelligentsia in
the camps were drawn to an ecumenical Christianity, while nonprivileged
people were drawn to 'Jehovahists.' ")

In 1956, from reports that reached Watchtower headquarters, the Society estimated that there were 64,000 Witnesses active behind the "Iron Curtain"; the number had grown to over 123,000 by 1959. In 1975, the official yearly report of the Society estimated that one-seventh of all the Witnesses active in the world were "behind the Iron Curtain." ("The Society does not publish figures for the individual countries behind the Iron Curtain now, so that the respective governments will not know how many real Christians reside in their territory." [*JWDP*, p. 279])

In 1956, seven directors of the Watch Tower Society sent a petition, adopted at conventions by 462,936 Witnesses, to Soviet Premier Bulganin. The petition (which went unanswered) read, in part:

> There are or have been some 2000 of Jehovah's witnesses in the penal camp of Vorkuta; at the beginning of April of the year 1951 some 7000 of Jehovah's witnesses were arrested from the Baltic States down to Bessarabia and were then transported in freight trains to the distant region between Tomsk and Irkutsk and near Lake Baykal in Siberia; there are witnesses of Jehovah kept in more than fifty camps from European Russia into Siberia and northward to the Arctic Ocean, even on the Arctic island of Novaya Zemlya; and a number of these, especially of the 7000 mentioned above, died of malnutrition the first two years of their sojourn in Siberia. [*Ibid.*]

The petition requested

> that an objective government investigation be made and that the witnesses be freed and authorized to organize themselves according to the way they are in other lands. Also that the witnesses in Russia be permitted to establish regular relations with their governing body in the United States and be allowed to publish and import such Bible literature as they need for their ministry.

The directors of the Watch Tower Society further proposed

> a discussion between the representatives of the governing body of Jehovah's witnesses and those of the Russian [sic] government [and suggested that] a delegation of witnesses be permitted to proceed to Moscow for this purpose, as well as for the purpose of visiting the various camps where the witnesses of Jehovah are interned. [*Ibid.*]

There is no evidence that the petition was acknowledged by the Soviets.

Father Arkadei Tyschuk, representative of the Moscow Patriarchate in the United States, with whom I spoke at the suggestion of the Soviet Mission to the United Nations, confined his remarks about the Witnesses to his own experience. There were no Witnesses that he knew of in his home city of Vladimir (east of Moscow), he said. He professed not to know if the Witnesses were "outlawed." (An American-born Russian Orthodox priest, who did not want his name used, said that he knew they were outlawed in the Soviet Union, "because they are not loyal citizens anywhere.") The

Soviet Constitution (Statute 125) permits the churches to attract members—as Father Tyschuk said—"within the framework of the constitution, through church services. The Russian Orthodox Church, the Baptists, Muslims, and Old Believers [whose theology is similar to that of the Orthodox Church] are tolerated. . . . They are permitted to hold church services, but not to aggressively proselytize." (The American-born Russian Orthodox priest who worked in the office of the Moscow Patriarchate had a slightly divergent point of view: "No church," he said, "has the right, in the Soviet Union, to promote its own well-being.")

Korea:

During World War II, the work of the Witnesses was banned. In 1948, American-trained missionaries were sent to proselytize in what was essentially virgin territory. When war broke out, the missionaries were evacuated to Japan, and most Korean Witnesses fled to the cities of the South. (No figures are currently available for North Korea.) [*JWDP*, p. 277; *KM*, June, 1973, p. 4]

East Germany:

Many of the same Witnesses who had been incarcerated in Nazi Germany were imprisoned by East German authorities. The Society's sources report that over 1,000 men and women have been sentenced to prison terms averaging six years. Fourteen were reported killed as of 1953. Nevertheless, the Witnesses seem to have more than a little mobility in East Germany: thousands of East Germans were able to attend assemblies held in West Germany. [*Yearbook*, 1954, p. 161; 1959, p. 126; *JWDP*, p. 278] The number of Witnesses currently active in East Germany is not known (or, if known, not published by Watchtower sources).

No statistics are available for Poland, Czechoslovakia, Yugoslavia, Bulgaria, Hungary, and Rumania—all countries in which the Watchtower Society's work is banned.

LATIN AMERICA AND EUROPE: CHILE, DOMINICAN REPUBLIC, GREECE, SPAIN

Chile:

The Watchtower Society's accounts of its activities in Chile speak for themselves. This is how the Society describes the days of revolution, junta, and CIA activity (and, by omission, the death of Allende—which served the Witnesses well):

> When the 1974 service year began, paralyzing strikes, violence, and unrest were part of day-to-day living in Chile. In every city there

were long lines of people waiting to buy bread and other necessities; housewives spent an average of six hours a day in such lineups. Well, before the time for the "Divine Victory International Assembly" there was a change of government. . . . Although difficulties and trials of many sorts have pressed in on our Chilean brothers, they have felt secure because of their reliance on Jehovah. [*Yearbook*, 1975, pp. 22–23]

The tides of change have contributed to the spiritual catch.

For a long time, Chile enjoyed one of the most stable political atmospheres in all of South America. Suddenly this changed. In five years the Chilean people have seen three forms of government, each radically different from the others. The political turmoil has produced disillusionment. As a result, many people find the Bible's message about a perfect government in the hands of Jesus Christ both appealing and reasonable.

. . . When the arrest of Communist activists in factories and industries left critical vacancies, witness employees were often put in key positions. In one case, on the morning of the coup, soldiers arrived at the home of a witness and asked how long it would take him to put the local oil refinery into operation. No other qualified man could be trusted!

Spot searches for firearms and the like were made of neighborhoods at the break of dawn. Often, known witness homes were simply passed by. One soldier, taking the publication *The Truth That Leads to Eternal Life* out of a bookcase, commented: "If everyone read and practiced what is in this book, we would not have to make these searches."

. . . Jehovah's witnesses in Chile . . . are . . . determined to take advantage of these swarming "waters" to continue in catching men alive so that these may gain life everlasting. [*TW*, Oct. 1, 1976, p. 591]

There are now over 15,000 Witnesses active in Chile.

Dominican Republic:

The fortunes of Jehovah's Witnesses have undergone many changes in the Dominican Republic. They were banned for a time under Trujillo; and then, in the early 1960s, when the Church began to raise its voice against Trujillo—pastoral letters warning the government against excesses were read in all the churches—the ban was removed. Even when their proselytizing work was banned, the Witnesses were regarded as valuable workers on sugar estates. Imprisoned, they were model prisoners; they boast of having had "the respect and trust of prison guards . . . the witness prisoners were allowed to enter the communications center where Trujillo had equipment and recorders for monitoring other Latin-American radio stations. . . . [They were] trusted with jobs on which even soldiers were not used." [*Yearbook*, 1972, p. 153]

When the Witnesses were banned in the Dominican Republic, they managed to smuggle *Watchtower* magazines in. One missionary says that she never had any problem getting the magazines through customs, in spite of an aiport fluoroscope machine that checked all luggage: "I often wondered what the staples on the magazines looked like on the machine. But, over the years, no literature was ever discovered. . . . It appeared that Jehovah blinded them in the way the men of Sodom evidently were blinded." [*Ibid.*, p. 156]

This is the Witnesses' response to the popular revolution of 1965 and the arrival of U.S. Marines on Dominican soil:

> In the city lawlessness and disorder prevailed. Issues arose that put the Christian conscience to the test. Neutrality had to be maintained. Oppression and injustices could influence a person to lean one way or another. It was a time to remember that both sides were part of this system of things and that both had Jehovah's disapproval. American Marines occupied certain homes, or set up machine guns on roofs or balconies. At least one brother had to go to the American officials to request the removal of the Marines and their weapons from his premises. Taking advantage of the absence of law, poor people took possession of vacant lots and built on them. Would our Christian brothers do that? Partially burned warehouses were opened by the revolutionaries and people were permitted to loot them, even being invited to do so. The test was on. Would the brothers join the people in doing these things? How far would they be guided by Christian neutrality? [*Ibid.*, p. 167]

(That they were to be "guided by Christian neutrality" was a logical conclusion, since "Jehovah disapproved of both sides.")

One sees, in the Dominican Republic, a familiar pattern. During the years of external hardship, the organization flourished. When the situation stabilized, "immorality and materialism" [*Ibid.*, p. 170] cost the Witnesses many members: "When violent methods fail, Satan tries other methods. . . . Materialism and immorality continue to raise their ugly heads, each contributing to the fall of some of the brothers who stood so faithfully through times of persecution." [*Ibid.*] Many who had served time in prison were excommunicated for "immoral conduct" when they were free. Perhaps even more than other human beings, the Witnesses rise to tragic or extraordinary occasions, and are reduced by commonplace ones. They are the most secure when they are the most threatened.

There are now approximately 6,000 active Witnesses in the Dominican Republic.

Greece:

The Witnesses have, at various times, been accused of being Communists, anarchists—and most recently, when George Papadopoulos was premier, of being agents of "international Zionism." "Jews control nine-tenths of the riches of the world," Papadopoulos' government is reported to have said; so, according to government sources, it followed that only Jews could afford to finance the work of the Witnesses. [*The New York Times*, June 4, 1970]

On November 13, 1970, the Ministry of Interior ordered the country's Registrars not to register marriages of Witnesses, or the children of such marriages, "because the religion of Jehovah's Witnesses is an unknown one." [*Aw*, June 8, 1975, p. 25] In 1974, when Constantine Karamanlis took power and civil liberties and a constitutional government were restored in Greece, the Witnesses were permitted to convene publicly for the first time in seven years; and in July, 1975, marriages between Witnesses were pronounced legal, and the children of those unions pronounced legitimate.

The Witnesses continue to wrestle with the Greek Orthodox Church, however. In 1976, priests in Crete tried to stop a convention of Witnesses in Heraklion, because, they argued, the "Millennialists" were agents of "international Zionism." [*Aw*, Nov. 22, 1976, p. 23] The Witnesses received the full protection of the law and were permitted to assemble.

There are now 18,000 Witnesses in Greece.

They are subject to imprisonment for failure to join the military.

Spain:

In 1949, there were only 34 Witnesses active. [*Yearbook*, 1949] There are now 30,000. Legal recognition was granted to the "Association of Jehovah's Witnesses" in 1970. Observers in Spain have commented that the Church in Spain was for a long time obdurately opposed both to the Witnesses and to the Seventh-day Adventists, seeing in both sects a denial of true religion and a threat to patriotic values. The appointment of a liberal cardinal and the ascension of liberal bishops (even before the death of Franco) swung Spain in the direction of religious liberties. This is the Witnesses' version of these events:

> There has been an easing up of the grip of Roman Catholicism in Spain. The clergy themselves have caused many individuals to turn away from the Catholic Church. People notice, for example, that priests become involved in politics. Some have turned to the liberal "left" in a display of favor toward the working classes. However, this belated tactic has not fooled the majority of the people. A lady remarked to one of Jehovah's witnesses preaching near Nijar, Almeria: "The priests make us lose faith by their conduct. They show up with their sleeves rolled up, their shirts all open—and smoking. They themselves stop us from believing in them." [*TW*, Aug. 1, 1975, p. 458]

In the past, the perceived rigidity of the Church, and its material glory, turned many Catholics away—straight into the arms of the Witnesses, who were perceived as less remote, less magisterial, and more concerned and involved in the intimate details of their hard daily lives. Since Vatican II, the increasing openness of the Church, its commitment to the oppressed, and the consequent ferment in which it finds itself have turned many Catholics away—straight into the arms of the Witnesses, whose apparent simplicity and "neutrality" have represented a relief from the yeasty changes taking place in a living and evolving Church. The Church—the religion of slaves, which has too frequently oppressed the oppressed (while at the same time being a sanctuary for the oppressed)—has always been the victim of its own paradoxes.

In countries where the Witnesses are felt to be a threat to national security or stability, they are persecuted. In countries where the Church and the State are symbiotically joined, they are persecuted. Otherwise, they are tolerated. (Paradoxically, this is also true in Italy, where the Witnesses have prospered and increased—10,000 converts in 1975 alone. But then, it is difficult to imagine the Italians—those cynical and sanguine people who can juggle Catholicism and Communism with humor and grace—doing more than shrugging their shoulders tolerantly over this interesting phenomenon in their midst.)

Report of Activities of Jehovah's Witnesses Worldwide 1976 (adapted from the 1977 *Yearbook of Jehovah's Witnesses*):

COUNTRY OR TERRITORY	WITNESSES	COUNTRY OR TERRITORY	WITNESSES
Abu Dhabi	11	Bolivia	2,476
Afars & Issas Terr.	7	Bonaire	35
Afghanistan	9	Botswana	283
Alaska	1,268	Brazil	106,228
Algeria	23	British Isles	80,544
American Samoa	89	Brunei	2
Andorra	70	Burma	845
Angola	3,822	Burundi	151
Anguilla	16	Cameroon	12,269
Antigua	170	Canada	62,880
Argentina	33,503	Canary Islands	1,128
Aruba	357	Cape Verde Rep.	60
Australia	29,101	Carriacou	27
Austria	12,514	Cayman Islands	27
Azores	248	Central Afr. Rep.	1,289
Bahamas	519	Chad	156
Bangladesh	2	Chile	16,862
Barbados	1,231	Colombia	16,286
Belgium	19,745	Comoro Islands	2
Belize	584	Congo	1,802
Benin	2,372	Cook Islands	48
Bequia	25	Costa Rica	5,104
Bermuda	217	Curaçao	681

COUNTRY OR TERRITORY	WITNESSES	COUNTRY OR TERRITORY	WITNESSES
Cyprus	846	Lebanon	1,827
Denmark	14,611	Lesotho	672
Dominica	226	Liberia	1,060
Dominican Rep.	6,540	Libya	2
Dubai	24	Liechtenstein	21
Ecuador	5,995	Luxembourg	819
El Salvador	6,010	Macao	7
Ethiopia	1,903	Madagascar	805
Faroe Islands	82	Madeira	252
Fiji	640	Malawi	5,631
Finland	13,402	Malaysia	433
France	65,827	Mali	32
French Guiana	200	Malta	91
Gabon	344	Malvinas Islands	3
Gambia	9	Manus Island	9
Germany, West	102,044	Marshall Islands	182
Ghana	22,381	Martinique	1,105
Gibraltar	87	Mauritania	2
Gilbert Islands	2	Mauritius	380
Greece	18,711	Mexico	84,356
Greenland	94	Montserrat	29
Grenada	324	Morocco	188
Guadeloupe	2,580	Mozambique	15,692
Guam	136	Nepal	17
Guatemala	5,259	Netherlands	29,723
Guinea	255	Nevis	47
Guinea Bissau	5	New Britain	200
Guyana	1,415	New Caledonia	359
Haiti	3,569	Newfoundland	1,146
Hawaii	4,872	New Guinea	492
Honduras	3,226	New Hebrides	47
Hong Kong	576	New Ireland	51
Iceland	165	New Zealand	7,442
India	4,687	Nicaragua	3,246
Indonesia	4,264	Niger	61
Iran	38	Nigeria	114,029
Iraq	28	Niue	16
Ireland	1,891	North Solomons	49
Israel	276	Norway	7,543
Italy	60,156	Okinawa	921
Ivory Coast	1,156	Pakistan	192
Jamaica	6,765	Palau	32
Japan	38,367	Panama	3,028
Jordan	76	Papua	731
Kenya	1,973	Paraguay	1,414
Korea	32,561	Peru	12,103
Kuwait	18	Philippines	77,248

COUNTRY OR TERRITORY	WITNESSES	COUNTRY OR TERRITORY	WITNESSES
Ponape	196	Tahiti	385
Portugal	18,119	Taiwan	1,233
Puerto Rico	16,620	Tanzania	1,575
Réunion	514	Thailand	732
Rhodesia	12,951	Tobago	133
Rodrigues	13	Togo	2,668
Rwanda	46	Tokelau Isls.	4
St. Helena	107	Tonga	27
St. Kitts	147	Trinidad	2,935
St. Lucia	271	Truk	41
St. Martin	48	Tunisia	48
St. Pierre & Miquelon	2	Turks & Caicos Isls.	19
St. Vincent	159	Tuvalu Isls.	5
Saipan	26	Uganda	166
San Marino	56	U.S. of America	577,362
Saudi Arabia	4	Upper Volta	65
Senegal	337	Uruguay	4,771
Seychelles	49	Venezuela	13,749
Sierra Leone	1,217	Virgin Is. (Brit.)	83
Singapore	344	Virgin Is. (U.S.)	479
Solomon Islands	610	West Berlin	5,620
South Africa	29,098	Western Samoa	128
South-West Africa	349	Yap	39
Spain	34,954	Zaïre	19,327
Sri Lanka	545	Zambia	57,885
Sudan	101	196 Countries	2,058,241
Surinam	911	14 Other Countries	190,149
Swaziland	689		
Sweden	16,444	GRAND TOTAL	
Switzerland	10,193	(210 countries)	2,248,390
Syria	203		

Nathan Homer Knorr became the third president of the Watch Tower Bible and Tract Society in 1942. Unlike his flashy predecessors, he was a dull, rather plodding man, unfanciful—nothing like the lyrical con artist Russell, and nothing at all like the pugnacious, publicity-seeking "Judge" Rutherford. He had little flair, but a certain genius for organizing. Russell's sexual and monetary appetites were scandalous, and Rutherford's abrasiveness and litigious nature were legendary.

Knorr, the quiet president, had appetites of his own: "World-wide expansion was now the order of the day." By the end of World War II, there were three times as many Jehovah's Witnesses worldwide as there had been before the outbreak of war. Knorr saw to it that the varied parts of his empire became one united whole, under the tight control of Brooklyn headquarters. In order to do this, he set off on a world tour in 1947 to determine what was needed to strengthen and tie together the outposts of the Society. His personal observation of the varied activities of Witnesses in all branches gave him the insight and knowledge necessary to help them in whatever way was most useful, most especially in training those in the field.

In 1944, two years after Knorr became president, there were 128,976 Witnesses preaching worldwide. [*JWDP*, p. 312; Yearly Reports, 1928–1958] There are now 2,248,390 [*Yearbook*, 1977, p. 30]

While the 1976 figures represent a 3.7-percent increase over the number of proselytizers in 1975, there is this anomaly to consider: the number of hours spent preaching decreased, as did the number of full-time preachers. The Watchtower Society ascribes this to "economic pressures." I wonder if it might not have something to do with the fact that so many Witnesses expected Armageddon to come in 1975.

In 1976, the Watchtower Society had ninety-seven branch offices, where almost 4,000 workers produced and shipped literature, handled correspondence, maintained "Bethel" homes (or residences), and, in addition, preached. To maintain its special representatives abroad, the Society spent $11,519,454.32 in 1976. [*Yearbook*, 1977, pp. 10, 23]

Missionaries, trained at the Brooklyn missionary school called Gilead (literally, "heap of witness"), are provided with a place to live and a cost-of-living allowance: $40 a month to cover all meals and transportation, all necessities (and probably very few luxuries). They are expected to preach 1,200 hours a year. [Information received orally from William Arthur, Gilead spokesman]

They don't have much time for sight-seeing, and they have neither the time nor the inclination to soak up local culture. When they get to their assignments, they must study the native language eleven hours a day the first month and five hours a day the second month (in addition to preaching from house to house with the minimal language skills they have brought with them). I once knew a missionary who'd been in Rome for three months and had yet to see the Fountain of Trevi or the Pincian Gardens; and I knew an American missionary in Delhi who'd been in India for six months without finding the time to travel the short distance to Agra to see the Taj Mahal.

The phrase "culture shock" is not in the vocabulary of the Witnesses; but almost all the Watchtower missionaries I have known have suffered culture shock to some degree. (Maybe if they were told that culture shock was a common phenomenon, they'd be prepared for it, feel less guilt when they experienced it. Instead, in the pep talks given to Gilead graduates, the Holy Spirit is made to sound like a windy Midwesterner who'll keep them free of all jarring encounters.) Because of the restraints placed on their activities, the denial of opportunity to insinuate themselves gently and exploratively into foreign cultures (or to allow foreign cultures to color *their* perceptions), they remain, however long they stay in their overseas assignments, alien and *other*. They look lost and perpetually out of place. They become defensive and insular, surrounding themselves, in their missionary homes, with familiar artifacts, consuming familiar food, never absorbing—or being absorbed into—the life of the country, where their aim is not to understand, but to persuade. There must be something between coming to a foreign culture as a blank slate and coming armed with tablets of law written on stone; they haven't found that middle way. A Watchtower elder describes them as "respecting [native] customs, although in their own homes they are free to maintain American or European standards as much as is practicable." [*Faith*, p. 198]

Sometimes the unexpected happens—a child is born to a missionary couple, for example. I knew missionaries to whom this happened, in Guatemala, at a time when the Society made no provision for children of missionaries. They were—as are all missionaries to whom the unexpected happens—forced to fall back on their limited resources, and they lived in a wasteland of unhappiness and alienation. They had been obliged to leave the missionary home when their child was born. I met the wife one day. She was teaching at a private school run by an expatriate married to a Guatemalan. She was dancing—if such spiritless movements as she made could be called dancing—with little children in a circle: "Here we go 'round the mulberry bush/ . . . /This is the day we go to church/Go to church, go to church/This is the day we go to church/So early Sunday morning." For a woman who had come to Guatemala to tell people *not* to go to church, making a living this way must have been agony—and the agony was reflected in her listless, worn face. Her husband had a small jewelry-repair shop in their spartan house in one of Guatemala City's dreary downtown streets. It was sad. They must have come with very high hopes; and they were reduced to graceless lower-middle-class life in a strange country, doing things they did not love to do, among people they did not love and could not understand.

Sometimes desperation takes different forms. I knew another missionary, a Midwestern woman assigned with her husband to Rome, who rang a doorbell on the Piazza Navona one day and never came home again: a man answered, and she fell into his bed and into his life. The Witnesses said "the demons" had gotten her. (I think Italy, and perhaps happiness, had gotten her.)

When I lived in Bombay, Watchtower missionaries occasionally called on me—I was the only American living in an apartment building largely inhabited by Gujaratis. I offered them tea—which they accepted. They rejected my sympathy. They didn't like me very much, I could see, but I was the only person in the building who'd open the door to them. Their efforts were thankless: they wanted to give, and nobody received them. It didn't occur to them that someone—or India itself—might have had something to give *them*. Their missionary home, which I visited one day, was in a remote suburb of Bombay. It was starkly modern (except that, in Bombay, everything starkly modern begins to look mildewed and patinaed with green mold and age after the first monsoon), and inside it was a replica of Watchtower headquarters in Brooklyn—plastic aspidistras, and pastel paintings of flowers that had never grown on Indian soil. I used to wonder what it was like to venture forth from that sterile (but familiar) world into the life of the bazaars—to get up after a hearty American breakfast and a reading from Deuteronomy and be greeted (or assaulted) by a burnt-out leper or a naked holy man. It must have been like being plunged alternately into hot and cold baths. The extremes of India are hard enough to bear even if you've willed yourself to bear and experience them; a lot of Europeans survive by cauterizing their senses. But the Watchtower missionaries were there to *change* things they had never entered into or experienced, to alter people and cultures whose values they despised without understanding or feeling them. Hard work. Hard work to close yourself off from what you're obliged to influence: a kind of spiritual imperialism; they are spiritual colonialists.

(When the missionary women visited me in Bombay, I asked them what they thought of Mother Teresa, that extraordinary woman who sweeps the dying off the streets of Calcutta and gives them clean sheets, holds their hands, and comforts them and makes their dying a less brutally lonely thing. They had never heard of her.)

I'm not saying that many Watchtower missionaries do not feel fulfilled and happy to see their work flourish and to gain converts. I am only saying that a system that impels them to keep essentially aloof and remote from the people they proselytize is bound to produce casualties. There are casualties among missionaries of all denominations; but when Watchtower missionaries break down, it is, it seems to me, not because of any fatal flaw in their characters, but because it is the implicit *policy* of their governing elders to keep them estranged, detached, in no significant way related to the events that swirl around them. Their insularity sometimes works to protect them and preserve them; and it sometimes works the other way—their enforced alienation becomes anguish. They are always strangers in strange lands. I knew another missionary who spent six months in a prison in Aleppo, Syria, before the Society and the U.S. State Department had her released. I don't even want to think about what a Syrian jail must be like. When I asked her what it had been like, she said, in a drifty, dreamy kind of way, "Oh, it was all right. Pleasant." It was as if nothing that had happened to her had happened to her.

"Everywhere I go," wrote a Society director, "I find the family arrangement is always the same amongst those who are really a part of the New World society. . . . When they get up in the morning they always have the morning text read, then perhaps a brief discussion. . . ." [*Faith*, p. 212] There must be something very comforting in knowing that all over the world—from Brooklyn to Benares—your people are behaving in the same way; and something strangely disassociative, too.

The Church . . . in establishing [Christ's] kingdom takes nothing away from the temporal welfare of any people. Rather does it foster and adopt, insofar as they are good, the ability, riches and customs of each people. Taking them to itself, it purifies, strengthens, elevates and consecrates them.—Constitution on the Church, No. 13

I'm always suspicious of people who don't see the symbolic and ritualistic importance of food (a consequence, no doubt, of growing up among Italians and Jews, for whom food offerings were love offerings). I read in *Awake!* magazine (Nov. 22, 1976) that Witnesses were discouraged from celebrating Thanksgiving, not only because "Jesus commanded but one celebration . . . to memorialize his death" but also because "for a growing majority, having a special meal is the extent of 'celebrating' Thanksgiving." I thought how, once again, they'd missed the point. The point being that tangible and tactile, visible symbols are the flesh of the soul's belief. The same issue of *Awake!* asks rhetorically, "Is there a visible symbol of Christianity? Do you think of the cross? What about the figure of a fish, which appears on some ancient artifacts associated with Christians?" What the Witnesses think, of course, is Nothing doing. No cross in the Witnesses' worship (because the cross was introduced, they say, by Emperor Constantine in his sun-worshiping days); and the emblem of the fish (for which the Greek word is *ICHTHYS*, thought to be a cipher for *Iesous CHristos THeou Yios Sotir*, or "Jesus Christ, Son of God, Savior"), is despised by the Witnesses because it often appears "in ancient pagan symbolism, possibly to represent duty, power, and fecundity."

If the local customs have no narrowly defined "religious" significance, the natives are permitted by the Witnesses to hold on to them: "Becoming one of Jehovah's Witnesses," says *Awake!*, "does not require persons to abandon customs of their land that are not in conflict with the Holy Bible." [July 22, 1974] In that same issue, the first example of the latitude permitted converts—and I can't believe this is an accident—is one that demeans the dignity of half the human race: "Most Christian women in India, in harmony with local custom, will not eat their meals with their husbands. Only after the husband has eaten will the wife eat. Also, when men enter the presence of women, the women cover their heads with their saris." No crosses and no Thanksgiving gorging are allowed; but it's perfectly in harmony with "Christian principles" to treat women as if Christ had not come to redeem them as well as their mates. Easter bunnies are more to be deplored than the servitude of oppressed women.

Some missionary societies obtain converts by setting up establishments for feeding and clothing the natives, but . . . a full stomach doesn't make a man a Christian. . . . [Jehovah's Witnesses] have endeavored to teach these people how to live

*by God's standards, to clean up their lives and their homes. . . . This changed out-
look enables them to improve their own living standards, and they learn to stand on
their own feet and not depend on some foreign society for continued handouts.*—
Faith, p.198

*The work is more important than talking and writing about the work. It has
always been through the performance of the works of mercy that love is expressed, that
people are converted, that the masses are reached.*—Dorothy Day, *Meditations*
(New York: Newman Press), p. 21

*Come—inherit the kingdom. You have my father's blessing. For I was hungry and
you fed me. I was thirsty and you gave me a drink, a stranger and you welcomed me.
I was sick and you cared for me, naked and you clothed me, imprisoned and you came
to me.*—Matthew 25:34–36

Although their names appear on the lists of Amnesty International
among those tortured and wrongfully imprisoned, the Witnesses will not
join their efforts with those of Amnesty International to free other men and
women illegally arrested or tortured. Although they ask the National Council of Churches for help to protest the treatment they have received in Malawi, they denigrate ecumenicism as a tool of the Devil.

They are very very proud of producing "genuine Christians, . . . not
'rice' Christians, 'bought' with material things, as those are called who turn
their children over to be raised by Christendom's missionary establishments
in exchange for food. Those hearing the good news receive *spiritual* suste-
nance." [*Aw*, Nov. 8, 1974, p. 25]

One day the Watchtower missionaries in India called on me just after I'd
returned from a small village in Andhra Pradesh, where I'd met a priest
who'd spent the best part of twenty years curing infants of roundworms. (A
most unglamorous job; but roundworms are killers.) "Do you try to convert
these people?" I'd asked him. "I baptize them," he said, "and I try to keep
them alive, and I say Mass, and I pray for the grace of the Holy Spirit on
us all. . . . It's hard to love God on an empty stomach." That day, the
priest had another visitor—an Indian doctor (an atheist) who lived and
worked in a nearby leprosarium. When they met, they embraced.

I told the Watchtower missionaries this story, not knowing myself exactly what the point of telling them was; and they said, "But the priest isn't
preaching the good news of the kingdom. . . . And Jehovah will cure lepers
in his New World." Across the way from the veranda where we were sitting, a new luxury high-rise building was going up. Tribal people from
northern India had been brought in as construction workers. They lived—
ate, cooked, drank, made love—on the girders of the building. The week
before, a worker had fallen to his death before my horrified children's eyes.
His widow had been given 25 rupees in compensation—just enough to cre-
mate her husband. I told the missionaries that story too; and they said, "If
we knew her language, we would tell her the wonderful hope of the resurrection." They had a cup of tea and talked about God's loving-kindness.

X. Leaving: 1955

> To some, the world has disclosed itself as too vast: within such immensity, man is lost and no longer counts; and there is nothing left for him to do but shut his eyes and disappear. To others, on the contrary, the world is too beautiful; and it, and it alone, must be adored.—Teilhard, p. 45

> Everything possible to be believed is an image of truth.—William Blake

I HAVE AN UNCLE who created a scandal once by asking for three fried eggs for breakfast. He became a family legend. He was often offered to me as an object lesson in extravagance and selfishness. I come from a frugal family. In my childhood, everything was carefully measured out—love, food, words, approval (even toilet tissue: when I got married, my mother's advice to me was "Don't buy two-ply. People will use as much as if you'd bought one-ply; they won't be able to tell the difference"). Everything was carefully measured out—except tears. We are a family that cries a lot. The women in my family were not ascetic and not, after the Depression, poor; but they had a strong conviction that there were invisible boundaries you didn't step over unless you wanted to join the company of the wasteful (who were also slothful, bad), that everything had its appointed limits ("*decent* limits," they would have said); and goodness was equated with restraint. It was always too cold in the houses I grew up in, and too dark. Conservation was regarded not as deprivation or as dreary self-denial, but as a way to enrich oneself. Love didn't, in their view, multiply and expand; it curled in on itself, fed itself, was kept within "decent limits."

I once got a beating for telling "the Jews next door" what we were having for dinner. That was the kind of information you didn't give away: you hugged it to yourself; you didn't give anything away. And if that was meanness, it wasn't calculated meanness: it was like an Arab's not wanting to have his picture taken for fear that his soul would be stolen away. We hoarded everything, so that we could remain inviolate, so that nobody could steal our souls away, or know our souls; we kept everything locked and secret and hidden. Maybe it was the centuries of Moorish blood in our Southern Italian veins, and our second-generation fears that *they* ("the Americans") would find us out—find us wanting.

Frugal and insular and suspicious; the outside world was full of menace. And when I became a Witness, it was the same story all over again: frugality and insularity and suspicion; the outside world was full of menace, and a niggardly Jehovah kept us safe by keeping us from the light and the heat of the world. He was a chilly and genteel God who didn't like ardent or extravagant gestures (and I got Him and my mother all mixed up).

He was the kind of God who regarded both Oxford and the Cathedral at Chartres as extravagances, the adoration of the saints and the "pursuit of worldly knowledge" as vulgar excesses, show-offy and flamboyant, self-aggrandizing and uncircumspect, wicked. (I asked Him to forgive me for loving stained glass and incense; I kept a copy of *Letters to a Young Poet* hidden in my laundry bag.) Once someone gave me a kaleidoscope. It was my favorite present.

One Sunday summer morning, as I left Watchtower headquarters to go out preaching from door to door, a member of a tightly huddled-together little group of fellow Witnesses, I saw two young women and two young men piling into a yellow convertible. They were all laughing. They carried picnic hampers covered with red-and-white-checked cloths, very full. One of the young men turned on the car radio—a Mozart quintet. I wanted to be with them. I wanted to *be* them. I longed for their world of color and light and sound. My longing was so acute it was like a physical pain; and it was followed by an intolerable ennui: I didn't know what I was doing holding a satchel of *Watchtower* magazines, or why I was going to preach, or what I had to do with the Witnesses or they with me. I wanted to run away. I didn't, but I knew at that moment that someday I would.

The four young men and women had come out of a house on Pineapple Street, an old wooden house, white, with a forest-green door and forest-green shutters and dimity curtains and chandeliers that seemed to be lit even in the daytime. The garden of the house, with its cherry tree that had blossoms like crepe paper, was surrounded by a high white wooden fence, and set in the garden fence was a lime-green door with no doorknob on the outside. For days I imagined that if I knocked at that door, they would recognize me and let me in and we would sit in the garden under the cherry tree and I would never have to go back to the Watchtower Building again.

Later that same week, on an impulse, I went alone to Birdland. Basie was playing, and Joe Williams was singing the blues. I had two rye-and-gingers, and felt scared and exhilarated. I came back with my hair smelling of cigarette smoke: "Dirty," my roommate said. It was the first time I had trouble falling asleep.

On the Saturday of that week, a Witness I knew and loved died. And the circumstances surrounding his dying made me understand that when I left (as I knew I would), it wouldn't be because I preferred yellow sports cars and summer picnics and Mozart or jazz to God; it would be because God didn't live in my religion. If He lived at all, He lived somewhere else (not in my heart).

Mike died at a party at a Witness' house. Unlike most Witnesses, he never seemed to give a damn what impression he created on other people. He was funky and loving and flamboyant. He was an iceman; he drove an ice truck. When I was younger, I'd had a temporary job at the UN bank. Mike used to drive me up to the Secretariat building in his truck. We laughed at the incongruity of driving to the UN in a Sicilian-decorated ice truck, and he never used the occasion to preach about the evils of the "beastly United Nations" (which ranked second, in the Witnesses' chamber of Satanic horrors, only to the Vatican). He may have accepted the Witnesses' belief that the UN was the "desolation of desolations," but that didn't deter him from driving up gaily and irreverently to its portals. The fear and loathing such "devilish" places inspired in the Witnesses' hearts, and the repulsion and fascination, seemed entirely lacking in his.

But it was his heart that killed him. He'd had two heart attacks; on the morning of that party, he'd been out preaching for the first time since his convalescence. He was talking about his delight in being able to go from door to door again, talking with gusto about his pleasure in "sharing" (other Witnesses might "give the truth"; Mike shared), when he clutched his chest and began to gasp for air. He took the diamond ring he wore off his finger and gave it and his wallet to his wife (he knew he was dying; his last thoughts were for someone else). A few Witnesses went, spontaneously and generously and compassionately, to his wife to support her. A respected elder from Watchtower headquarters launched—as Mike's gasps began to sound, horribly, more like the final rattle of death—into an interminable story about the people he'd known who'd been taken unaware by death ("I knew someone else who died like that," he said, looking at Mike). Three-quarters of the Witnesses present set themselves to clean up the room in order to "give a good witness" to the police when they arrived. Mike was pronounced DOA. The cops were given a speech about our hope in the resurrection. Mike himself was ignored (except by the police, whose attempts to resuscitate him were heroic); grief was shelved (Mike's wife was sedated). The Witnesses congratulated themselves on the way the police had seemed to be impressed by their decorum and their calm; in their zeal to "give a witness," the actual fact of Mike's death seemed almost forgotten. I can't remember anyone crying out in love or horror—or praying.

The task of telling Mike's young daughter that he had died was delegated to me. As an elder drove me to her house, he recited all the Scriptures I might use to comfort her. He might have been reciting the *Guinness Book of World Records*. (The rest of the Witnesses stayed behind; when I left, Mike's heavily sedated wife lay on a couch while, around her, Witnesses talked about what a pleasant change it must make for the cops to come into a "decent" house, how much nicer than having to break up a drunken fight.) I looked at the elder in a vain attempt to find some trace of sorrow or anger on his face as he continued to offer memorized words of comfort. He had already buried Mike in some recess of his mind; his concern was how to keep Mike's daughter from "going overboard with immoderate grief" (his words—she was 12 years old). I have hated very few people as much as I hated that man, then. "See if you can take Mike's daughter out preaching with you tomorrow morning," he said. "It'll keep her mind from selfishness."

Nobody had cried. Mike's daughter cried, and I couldn't find it in my heart to read a single Scripture to her.

I came to live and work at Bethel—Watchtower headquarters—in 1953, when I was 19. I left early in 1956.

I had had over the years, since my baptism in 1944, little niggles of doubt (and a constant conviction of sin). My doubts terrified me.

Nobody ever told me that all believers doubt, or that the logical consequence of the possession of free will is to question, or that even mystics have at times felt abandoned by the God they adore; what a lot of misery it would have saved me if someone had told me. But the Witnesses couldn't tell me that, because they themselves didn't acknowledge that it was true. To them, faith is total, unquestioning, uncritical, unwavering, and undemanding.

I regarded my irritable intelligence as a kind of predatory animal which, if not firmly reined, would spring on me, attack me, and destroy me.

Since to doubt at all was intolerable, the only solution that seemed possible was to submerge my doubts (to submerge myself) completely. I wanted to be eaten alive, devoured by Jehovah, to spend so much time in his service that my peevish spirit, humbled and exhausted, would no longer have time for querulous doubts. Women are good at turning their desolation to their advantage (or to what they think is their advantage); and what I was doing by entering Bethel was making spiritual capital out of spiritual despair, quelling my restlessness by giving it a death in a new life.

And I had other (baser) motives too: There was, for a woman, great spiritual prestige in being admitted to Bethel. It was both glamorous and holy. Men outnumbered women 10 to 1 at Bethel (although, among rank-and-file Witnesses, women outnumbered men 3 to 1). I had nothing against being surrounded by men. Part of the inner circle, circled about by men; I thought that part would be nice.

And I wanted to please my mother, whose standards I knew I never lived up to (I was never sure what they were) and whose ambition for me was boundless, at the same time that her competition with me was fierce. Simone Weil's mother is reported to have said once, with a mixture of exasperation and tenderness, "Thank God you don't have a daughter who's a saint." I had a mother who was thought to be a kind of saint—the Bible Lady of Brooklyn, they called her. It was a foregone conclusion that all my boyfriends would be more charmed by her than they would by me, by her sacrificial gravity, her seductive saintly gaiety, which were all the more alluring because she was beautiful, with wide blue eyes, a mouth that turned down just slightly—just enough to suggest ineradicable sadness (which everybody tried to eradicate). Viewing me as a spiritual extension of herself, she would be pleased, I knew, if I went to Bethel; she would feel validated and enhanced by my choice. And I would be making up to her for having failed to make her happy. I believed, at that time, that I held the power to make her happy. It was not a good thing, I know better in retrospect, to feel. I wanted to make things good for her, to make up to her for all the things she didn't have, for whatever it was she wept for in my bedroom every night. I wanted to get away from that weeping, and from the acrimony that bound her and my unbelieving father together more closely than the most enduring affection.

I wanted to allay her pain, and I wanted her to stop passing her pain on to me. I really did believe that I was the agent of her happiness; I don't know through what subtle instruction or self-delusion I came to believe that. (But I do know that when, years later, I read, in one of the works of the saints, that God wants us, *obliges* us, to be happy, my first angry reaction was followed immediately by understanding: of course He does; because if you're unhappy, all you can do is make someone else responsible for your unhappiness and pass along your terrible pain. It makes perfect sense to me that God forbids us to despair.)

And I wanted to get away from my father, whose bewilderment took the form of rage, who wept for me (not for himself), and whose tears I rejected and despised. I was in an alliance with my mother against him—an unnatural alliance: my inclination, till my mother and I joined forces against him, was to find him irresistible. It was an unholy bonding; and while, at the time, I dismissed my father as negligible or feared him as a monstrous "Opposer of The Truth," there must, I think, have been part of my nature that recoiled against the pitiless, hard person I was when I was with him. I wanted to get away from all of it—the fights, the yelling, the tears, the recriminations, and the whispered secrets. I didn't want to hear my mother's whispered secrets; I didn't want to be her girlfriend, her "sister." (She signed her notes to me *Connie*. And when she was mad at me, she mailed her notes to me—though we shared not only the same apartment, but the same bedroom—and then handed them to me when the mailman came, with a hard suffering face that I feared more than I feared the judgment of God.) If my mother insisted on going out preaching Christmas

Eve, I didn't want to be around to entertain my father's rages and then to defend her when she returned. I didn't want to fight with my father with her holding my hand, urging me on; I knew there was something sick and unholy about what we were doing. (When she introduced herself to my friends, she said, "I am Barbara's relative." She never called herself my mother.)

I took the only escape route I knew. But if you had asked me then, I would have said, "I came to Bethel to serve the Lord." And I would have meant it. Many of my motives were obscure to me. But I did want to love God. (I didn't understand that the will to believe is not quite the same as belief itself.)

I thought I loved God. I loved the idea of loving Him. I *knew* I loved Arnold; I had loved him since I was 15, when he was my high school English teacher who had held my hand in school assembly when I didn't salute the flag. Being at Bethel prevented me from walking down his street every day, hoping for an "accidental" meeting. But it didn't prevent me from fantasizing about him—from dreaming that he would be converted and that we would live together happily ever after in the New World.

I told Nathan H. Knorr, then the Watchtower Society's president, about Arnold—which was pretty stupid, because I must have known what he'd tell me, and I must have guessed I'd disregard it. He told me never to see Arnold again. If he had told me that I could never see my mother or father again, I might have obeyed him; but Arnold was my mother and father, and I couldn't not see him.

There were three public telephone booths at Bethel, unventilated and airless and smelling of the sweat of 500 bodies; like all the doors at Bethel, these had no locks; and I'd call Arnold from one of the booths when my craving couldn't be denied, and we'd arrange to meet. Once I got to his living room and I heard his beloved Schubert *Trout Quintet* or one of the Beethoven quartets he always played for me, there was only joy. A guilt hangover the next day took the form of headaches, a steel vise around my head. (And the guilt had nothing to do with sex—there was no sex; I was guilty for loving him.)

So I carried all this baggage to Bethel with me—my love for Arnold and my doubts; but I went, nevertheless (I really believe this), in good faith. I meant to stay forever. Before I had been there two years, I knew I would have to leave.

One afternoon, as I sat working in the proofreading department of the Watchtower plant at 117 Adams Street, a sudden black storm blew up, and two of the men with whom I shared proofreading tasks raced to the plate-glass windows and said, "Oh, boy! Maybe it's Armageddon. Wouldn't it be wonderful if it was Armageddon? Do you think it's Armageddon? Wow!" I laughed and laughed and laughed, because they sounded so much more like Batman and Robin anticipating a caper with the Joker than like decently awed men awaiting God's final judgment. And of course, my laughter infuriated them. Their little-boy glee gave way to sententiousness and censoriousness, and they silenced my hysterical laughter with glares, demanding to know what, exactly, I found so funny. Perhaps my laughter had made them aware of their own foolishness; I doubt it, though, because they took both Armageddon and themselves very seriously (never for a moment doubting that the Storm of Storms would leave 117 Adams Street, and them, unscathed). I quailed—anything male and angry had the power to subdue me—and said in a voice I didn't recognize as my own (it sounded like the voice of a petulant 9-year-old), "I don't *want* Armageddon to come."

It was the first visible crack in my defenses.

I covered myself very quickly, and very transparently (that was the kind of remark, I knew from experience, that was not likely to go unreported to higher authorities): "I don't think enough people are saved yet," I said. It must have sounded as hollow to them as it did to me; and I felt hollow, as if the storm outside had blown through me, leaving my soul as dry as a whistle.

Then I began to cry.

Margarita, the Spanish translator who shared the room with us, gave me a grave and quizzical look. (Laughter is threatening, tears are frightening when you are supposed at all times to reflect the joy of the Lord and the modesty and the decorum of a woman. Grief and raucous laughter are forms of aggression; they are the companions of doubt, of "wrong thinking.") "I'm tired," I said. "Sometimes when I think I'm going to have to get up for work at six thirty six days a week for the rest of my life, I just don't think I can do it." "I do it one day at a time," Margarita said sternly. "I do it because it would kill my mother if I didn't," I said. Margarita thought that was a joke; but the moment I said it, I knew it was true.

I stayed at Watchtower headquarters—where I'd worked first as a housekeeper, then as a proofreader, for two and a half years—six months after that outburst. It had been temperate compared with what I was feeling; but it was the first time that I had revealed my spiritual duplicity nakedly, or heard myself say something unguarded.

I had been frightened enough before, for myself, when I felt that my faith, never entirely sure, was on the point of breaking; now that I had exposed my feelings to others, judgmental others, I was terrified.

(My diary for that day has one entry: *I am afraid, afraid, afraid.*)

At night I went out preaching, or to study classes in the Bethel residence. I smiled, talked, walked, sang hymns, conducted myself like a real person in a real world. But I didn't feel real. I felt as if everything were happening to someone else—as if I were both a character trapped in someone else's story and the person who "read" the character; I was both inside and outside of my own life (which was someone else's life). Nobody noticed. The most appalling thing of all was that I had perfected my own part so well that nobody noticed.

At night I tried (as usual) to pray, and (as usual) could not.

Somewhere I'd read of an order of contemplative sisters who prayed till 5:30 every morning, to lessen the violence done in those dark hours after midnight. I thought of them when I couldn't sleep, which was most of the time. (I had traveled a long way in my mind since I'd been taught that nuns were whorish, wicked representatives of the Vatican—but nothing in the way I behaved reflected the way I was beginning to think.) There was some comfort in believing that they were keeping vigil during those long nights, when, for some reason, I always fell asleep at exactly 4:10 A.M. (I never knew why). I lay in bed picturing my body floating above itself; and my skin felt thin and crusty, like something dangerous and tender stretched across the mouth of a volcano. I felt as if my body were rent with enormous fissures, and that my skin was inadequate armor, no armor at all.

(The best thing anyone could have done for me then would have been to tell me I was going crazy. I envied crazy people because they *acted* crazy, and because there were names for them. I could not assign a name to the pain I felt. I smiled a lot. At one of my meetings with Arnold, to whom I did not confide my troubles—I confided in no one—he told me of a group of disturbed kids he was working with who screamed and flailed around and blindly struck out at things. I cried. He thought I was crying for them. But I was crying for myself. I thought they were lucky. My screams never got screamed; my rage was neatly contained.)

When I fell asleep, I dreamed. It was always the same dream: I am a little girl in a walled garden, full of old-fashioned flowers—freesias, sweet William, climbing roses, bachelor's buttons, and (with no regard to seasons) white and purple lilacs. At the end of the garden stands a creature of indeterminate sex, resplendent, dressed in cloth of gold, who extends his/her arms to me in a gesture both maternal and elegant, nurturant and magisterial. Will-less, I am drawn to the creature, who calls to me in a voice that is at once supplicating and commanding. And as I enter into its embrace, the voice (which I yearn for and fear) becomes tactile—it exists inside of me and outside of me; it becomes like molten silver pouring through my veins. Paralyzed (bloodless), unable to resist, I am swept away by the creature, who assumes various guises, some malevolent, some benign. Held tight in that icy embrace, I am swept out and over the garden walls, hurled into an empty sky, where, a Humpty-Dumpty of scattered parts, I hurtle through the void—and nothing puts me back together again.

I do not know the meaning of the dream. The bells wake me at 6:30 A.M.

(they are like an extension of the dream), and, pregnant with the dream, cold and aching, I shower in the communal shower, while the voices around me intrude on my nightmare. I put on the face and the demeanor I hope will see me through the day, and I run down three flights of stairs to the artificial light of the yellow dining room, where I take my assigned place at a rectangular blue-metal table, waiting for the Bible discussion that precedes our breakfast to begin. I feel drugged; but even in this state— which is like sleepwalking through someone else's dream—I will myself to have control. I try to behave like other people—insofar as I can see other people: People lack definition at this time; faces blur. But objects are harshly, clearly defined, like objects in a hallucination. (I will never forget that dining room, its metal-topped surfaces, cold and slippery to the touch.) I prepare myself to spend a day among people who hate me.

New Yorker journalist Richard Harris spent some time at Bethel in 1955; he was later to write [June 16, 1956], after sitting through a breakfast service, a description of "the women, a number of whom resembled 4-H Club beauty queens, in simple cotton dresses. All in all, they seemed a sprightly, contented-looking group." I was one of those women. So far from being contented, I had to resist the temptation to go up to him and whisper (or shout), "Raise High the Roof Beam, Carpenters!" I wanted to exchange a signal with an emissary from the outside world.

I say that I spent my days among people who hated me. I don't think that's a crazy perception (though, God knows, I was not what could be called normal in those final six months). What *was* crazy was that they would in a flash have said (*did* say) that they loved me; and if asked why, they might have responded, "Because the Watchtower Society says we are a family and we must love one another." (Words all lost their meanings: *good, bad, crazy, love*—they meant different things in different mouths; and one was never sure whom to trust.)

Lara, the pretty girl who sat next to me at table, hated me. (The eight men who sat at the same table more or less ignored me, but I felt no ill will emanating from them;-the worst they could do was make me feel lonely, and I was lonely already.) The first day I sat at that table, one of the men said, "Pass the coffee cream." So later I asked Lara to "pass the coffee cream." She said, her fork moving without a pause to her disdainful mouth, "It isn't *coffee cream*, it's milk." Maybe she thought I was trying to endear myself to the brother whose remark I'd parroted (and maybe she was right: I was a great mimic, of necessity, in those days; I thought the way you invented a life for yourself was to copy bits and pieces from other people). She chose from that moment to dislike me. The only other sentence I can remember her saying directly to me in the three years we sat together was "Your perfume makes me sick."

We were 450 men and 45 women at that time, and only a handful of the women were under 35; so to be intensely disliked by one young woman (who was herself cool and pretty and popular) was no small thing. I never knew exactly what I had done, what I *was*, to have incurred her displeasure. I could not believe anyone could be so unbending. I almost admired the constancy of her aloof and critical disdain. My gratitude was always there, waiting, ready to spill over her if she ever once smiled at me. She never did. I could only imagine, from the way she looked at me, that she believed I was always on the point of committing some outrage (and perhaps her instincts were right). "Too smart for her own good," I learned later she had pronounced me; "too goody-good." What an irony! *I am so ignorant*, I wrote in my diary at night; and if she knew how bad I felt myself to be, I doubt if she'd have liked me any better. I did the worst possible thing anyone can do under these circumstances: I tried to model my personality on those of successful people—a most unprofitable and ridiculous undertaking.

I can't think of many things more awful and more corrupting than having to wake up each morning to the sure knowledge that you will be spending your time in intimate association with people who despise you. Every day was like the first day of nursery school, knowing you had some invisible deformity that would make everyone shun you. (When my own children went to school for the first time, and were immediate social successes, and casual successes at that, I said seventeen Hallellujahs; I'd seen, in my imagination, their schoolrooms populated with Laras. I felt triumphant—and also vindictive: I recited a vengeful litany. I hoped everybody hated Lara's kids; I hoped they picked on them; I hoped they were the most unpopular girls in school; I hoped their stomachs ached every day from 9 to 3; I wanted Lara to know what it felt like. It is corrupting to be hated; I didn't know I could bear so much malice for so many years.)

Lara; and Stan Russell and Tom Whiting, who both felt that I had usurped their place in the printing plant and never let me forget it. They snickered and gossiped with each other and came all over pompous when I tried to talk with them. I deferred and deferred and embarked on long windy paragraphs to justify my putting a comma into copy they had edited. Which did me no good at all; they just muttered about women who had unbecoming ambition, and laughed at me for trying. I always felt as if I were the object of obscene teasing.

Stan punished me according to the means he had at hand: he had me dismissed from the small preaching cell of which he was the elder, because, he said, I didn't spend enough hours preaching. It was a great humiliation to be dismissed from a preaching cell; and Stan saw to it that my shame was bruited about. Whiting contented himself with telling me how the "brothers" thought I was becoming sick with pride, that they preferred the housekeeping sisters who made beds to me; and once, when someone in the proofreading department left Bethel abruptly, with no explanation, he said it was because I had "unmanned" him by red-penciling his copy and that I might be responsible for his loss of faith. (Satan had used women before to undo good men.) The man who left had later, Whiting alleged, tried to hold up a bank. I was given to understand that if I hadn't told him he'd let a dangling participle go by, he might still be hale and hearty in the faith.

Actually, it strikes me as funny now: Could I really have prayed to Jehovah to forgive me for being presumptuous enough to undangle a brother's participle? I did. No wonder I'm superstitious about words: I spent two years thinking my eternal salvation depended on my approach to commas and split infinitives and dangling participles. It wasn't funny at the time.

The truth is, there were people who loved me, too. (Well, I say *love:* is it love if it can be—as it was, the moment I left—so easily aborted?) There were women who loved me. There were men who asked me to marry them. I never entertained the idea of marrying a Bethelite. I must always have known, on some unconscious level, that I was going to leave someday, that I would not stick it out. The men I was attracted to were not the men who cared for me; I denied physical attraction (if a man kissed me and it felt good, I immediately found reasons for not loving him). I chose men who hadn't the remotest inclination to choose me—which is not so uncommon; women do it all the time. My perversity, however, was extreme: the impossible object was always the adorable object. Some of the men who sought after me were sweet and kind. I think about them sometimes; I want to call them up in the middle of the night and ask them if they still remember me with affection (I remember them with affection). But I tried that once, and I felt as if I were being rejected by a computer printout; he quoted the Bible at me, with special emphasis on Gehenna, Judas, and dogs returning to their own vomit. He had run his hands up my thighs once, and introduced me to his mother, and confessed his own doubts; but he was still in, and I was out, and "What is there to talk about?" he said. "You've divorced yourself from Jehovah's organization; you blaspheme."

(My friend Peggy, an ex-Witness who has survived, keeps telling me, whenever I announce my decision—usually late at night and after several glasses of wine—to call someone who once said he loved me, that I might as well go on a rescue mission to the Snow Kingdom. They can't allow their hearts to thaw out, she says; and she's probably right. Peggy knows my secret—which is that in my heart of hearts I believe that anyone who was nice enough to love me then might be good enough to like me now. Having once been cherished, however meagerly, I entertain the illusion that I will be cherished still. It's hard to believe that everything is lost; it would be good to believe that people can still connect.)

I'm talking about my life at Bethel as if it were one of unrelieved gloom; and that isn't true. There were times when I felt absolutely high—stoned on God-talk (which, as it happens, can be a powerful aphrodisiac, among other things). Walking across the Brooklyn Bridge with my friend Walter, holding hands and talking about God; learning to dance the tango with Walter and Peggy and Walter's roommate, Norman; dancing all night on the Society's missionary yacht in New York harbor; picnicking under the George Washington Bridge—there were easy, good times. And the best times were when we were in other people's homes, teaching them the Bible, and they offered us the intimate details of their lives and we felt enhanced and enriched and part of a loving community serving a higher cause.

But in the end, none of that was enough. In the end, my decision to leave had very little to do with people who loved me and people who didn't, with good times and bad times. In the end, it had everything to do with my feelings about the world, which I had been taught was reserved for destruction and which I nevertheless obdurately loved, though my ignorance of it was profound. It had to do with my feeling cramped and lonely and frightened; leaving was survival.

All of this is in the diary I kept the last six months I was at Bethel. When I read these diary notes now, they seem to me grossly self-conscious, not to say narcissistic (but I was, after all, writing as if God were peering over my shoulder—and it's hard to know how to play to that Audience); and they are full of Nichols-and-May 1950s joke words, like "evolve" and "aware" (I was reading Camus, and I was feeling like Columbus, discovering new continents of thought and hoping against hope that the way West was the way East—and that I would blunder my way out to the riches of the world). They sound like the writings of arrested adolescence (I was an arrested adolescent).

When I read these diary notes now, they seem not only florid and naive, but coy as well: I was afraid of revealing myself even to myself; I played mind tricks. Words that were too heavily charged for me to commit to paper—words like *leaving religion*—I wrote in shorthand (under the assumption, I suppose, that neither my roommate nor Jehovah knew Pittman).

The diaries abound in sentences, I'm sorry to say, like "I believe"—or, "I don't believe"—"in happiness"; "I think I can love spring again." I'm leaving them out; as, for the sake of this record, I'm leaving out all sentences of the "I-feel-I-can-stand-on-tiptoe-and-embrace-the-sun" variety. They were, at the time, deeply felt—which is, unfortunately, no guarantee that they sound authentic twenty years later. (*Authentic* is another 1950s word; I suppose that if I had left the Witnesses in the '60s, I would have fallen in love with geodesic domes or used a political vocabulary in which to couch my despair. As it was, I borrowed from the existentialists—which may not have been a bad thing. I still love Camus, Salinger, Brando-the-wild-one, and the rakish skinny Sinatra who faced the world, or so it seemed, with showy grit more than I love Abby, Jerry, Tom, Rennie.)

I can barely decipher these notes, they are written in such a wild, erratic hand; and the urgency and pain that are missing from the words are in the handwriting. (There are, as a friend of mine says, no inanimate objects.) It looks like the handwriting of three different people; and I won't labor the reason for that.

> God can't kill Arnold. How can God kill Arnold? Arnold sends pepperoni to all the New Utrecht High School hoods in jail. The other day he bought three bikes for the kids of the Chinese laundry-man. He spends his evenings listening to Beethoven quartets. (I wish he would kiss me.) He used to excuse us from English homework if we went to see a Marx Brothers film. Also he brought us chocolate-covered ants when we wrote good compositions. (Does Jehovah have a sense of humor? Why doesn't God ever laugh?) Once Arnold read an Archibald MacLeish poem to me in class. To *me:*

Not with my hands' strength nor with difficult labor
Springing the obstinate words to the bones of your breast
And the stubborn line to your young stride and the breath to your
    breathing
And the beat to your haste
Shall I prevail on the hearts of unborn men to remember
(What is a dead girl but a shadowy ghost
Or a dead man's voice but a distant or vain affirmation
Like dream words most)
Therefore I will not speak of the undying glory of women
I will say you were young and straight and your skin fair
And you stood in the door and the sun was a shadow of leaves on
    your shoulder
And a leaf on your hair
I will not speak of the famous beauty of dead women
I will say the shape of a leaf lay once on your hair
Till the world ends and the eyes are out and the mouths broken
Look! It is there!

> And why, for that matter, should God kill Archibald MacLeish? How come all the people I love are going to be killed at Armageddon, and I'm going to have to live forever in the New World with Stan Russell and Tom Whiting and Lara—who are *mean?* Brother K. says I'm presumptuous because I'm making myself out to be more compassionate than Jehovah. Is it presumptuous to like people who like you? And to want them to be saved? If I were God I'd want everybody to be saved. (And if I were God I guess I could love Stan and Tom and Lara, but I don't—so maybe I am presumptuous, after all.) I don't have the energy to be an apologist for things it's difficult for me to

accept or understand: Why were the Israelites so merciless? Why did they stone sex-offenders and delinquent children? (Poor Onan.) Why—as my father keeps asking—did Jehovah send bears to rip apart the children who mocked Elijah's baldness?

I love going out on Bible studies and teaching people. It feels so good, I feel so elevated. But does this mean that this is the Truth? It may mean only that when people are not dignified by exclusive devotion to a cause that demands more than their normal natures can supply, they are not extraordinary. And I'm afraid of ordinariness. At Bible studies we meet on the highest plane—we see each other in the most sympathetic light, as humans admitting our frailty and striving for beauty and order (for good? for the Divine?). But the relationship deteriorates when the mutual search is ended and we resume our daily lives. Then everything becomes flat. And off I go to new relationships, drawing strength from them. I feel like a parasite, battening on other people's needs and living off their hunger (I love their hunger); and teaching what I don't even know to be true. I don't feel lonely when I'm preaching. This wonderful thing that sometimes happens between me and another person, this interchange of love, this empathy—like hands held out in the darkness of our common suffering . . . I wouldn't have it any more if I left. I have a terrible fear that I would go around begging people, asking them to share their suffering and their need, to let me *see* them. Is it because I love them? Or am I using them? to enrich myself? I don't know the difference between giving and taking any more. . . . I'm not a successful proselytizer. I can't credit myself with victories for the faith, or even, lately, with propagating the faith. If I have victories at all, they're personal and human victories. They don't have much to do with God, and they have less to do with Judgment. I'm successful in establishing beautiful relationships, not often in gaining converts. One time a companion brought to my attention that I'd remarked to a couple with whom we were concluding a study, "We have to feel free to talk, to share. We can't be afraid of offering our feelings. We can be friends. Our religion doesn't matter." This was heresy. I hadn't even been aware that I'd said it.

Their only reality is otherworldly reality. They deny the world, and that denial is contrary to my nature. I can love Christ, but not Jehovah, and not the end of the world. Is that possible?

I can't judge or condemn—or be God's agent for condemnation. I can't bear to belong to a group that considers itself favored. I can't accept the destruction of a child. I can't exclude from my love all the people who cannot believe. "He who loves the world is an enemy of God." I love the world. I will not allow my friends to be chosen for me: "We must love one another and die."

Brother K. came back from a round-the-world trip today. Told us about it at meeting. Said he was bored on airplane—not enough magazines to read. I'd be bored on airplane too. But I'm not a spiritual leader. Isn't God's spirit supposed to un-bore you? If you were really full of the Holy Spirit, would you be bored? Why couldn't he *think*? Or pray? Or meditate? Or contemplate? What would he do on a desert island? How can I trust a spiritual leader who would be bored on a desert island? . . . Why am I so harsh? . . . (Can a spiritual leader of limited intelligence and compassion be qualified to lead the starved and suffering to God and to shepherd the flock of God?) Also told us that he sat behind Brando on airplane. (I.e., Brother K. travels first-class. So how can he rant at priests' "living off the fat of the land"? I don't see him practicing poverty.) Said Brando "behaved well." Suppose he expected him to wear torn tee-shirt and scratch armpits. Said he mentioned Brando because he'd heard one of the sisters had a crush on him. He meant me. Nobody knew whether to laugh or not, because nobody knew whether I was being reprimanded for having a crush on Brando, or whether Brother K. thought it was funny. So there was an embarrassed silence. (Anyway, I was embarrassed—nobody looked at me.)

I can't give myself to a religion unless it is completely and without reservation. (I *may* not.) This religion demands complete dedication, submission, acceptance. I have reservations. I have always had.

Fromm says that the story of Jonah and the whale shows that Jonah had a strong sense of order and law, but no love. But *we* say Jonah did not do his duty, was not obedient to God, because he didn't go to Nineveh, where he was sent. We stress duty and obedience to authority rather than love for man. Fromm says the whale was a symbol of the isolation and imprisonment that results from lack of love and solidarity: the whale is hell, the hell of not being able to love. I don't want to live my life in the belly of the whale. . . . I don't want to be contemptuous of weakness (including my own).

I've been sneaking into guest rooms to read, late at night: Emerson, Thoreau. Dead men are my comfort.

Why should intellectual curiosity be condemned and feared, and intelligence be regarded as an obstacle to overcome?

This is what I want: To be able to follow my thoughts wherever they lead me. Not to accept ready-made answers, easy, all encompassing solutions, panaceas. To be able to make my own connections, to read my own significance into relationships, to make my own meanings . . . no fetters. Not somebody else's ideas of what God's will is for me.

We escape the anguish of making decisions. We don't have to feel guilty or responsible when we see people starving because we are part of a movement that tells them how to escape their condition. We discharge our responsibility by offering a road to salvation they may—

but probably won't—take advantage of. For those who turn our brand of salvation down, we have no pity. They reject the way of happiness; but we can tell ourselves we've done our part.

I can understand the nature of the Living Being without me only through the Living Being which is in me.

They despise everything they can't understand. I cannot comprehend their inability to feel for those in anguish and doubt, who are seeking to understand—through means other than theirs—man's condition. They are ignorant of that which they condemn: "Philosophy is of the Devil." They are so ignorant, and so repulsively arrogant in their assertion of superiority over the "worldly wise." They are proud of not knowing. How dare they?

I can't accept their rationalization for segregation: "It might offend people of good-will if we integrated." Cowardice. Is a loss of membership worth this wishy-washy approach? They can accept bigots, but condemn activists. Even JWs who are Negroes accept it because the whole religion denies the freedom of the individual, and stresses the submergence of the individual for the good of the glorious whole.

I can't love only those whom God loves.

Last night at meeting, talk about the symbolic meaning of Deborah's camels. More energy brought to bear on the symbolic meaning of Deborah's camels (I fell asleep) than on capital punishment. I can't accept capital punishment or their reasons for espousing it. Also: Refuse to be told what I must feel and believe about artificial insemination, intermarriage, etc., etc., etc. Can't follow a party line.

I could never marry someone who has never had a doubt. It would have to be someone who has not arrived at a fixed state of mind, someone without an attitude. I will never *be;* I will always be going toward. But it really isn't important whether I marry or not. I think—feel, which is more reliable—that I won't.

What scares me is how good I am at dissembling. I've learned to give back to others the view of themselves they ask for. I keep a central core of disbelief, but *I act as if I believe.* I don't know what to do, how to stop.

Sometimes I do love them. They transcend themselves. That's beautiful. But then they become rigid and dogmatic. The love they inherit from the teachings of Christ is narrowed and limited by their rejection of the world. Many of them were attracted by love and goodness to a life of giving. But their goodness is contradicted by their hatred of the world, their relegating all who will not listen to destruction—the "goats" who are against them. Their work satisfies the need to express themselves, and to give. It is better to give than to receive, and their need to give is fulfilled in their preaching work. But so stern and inflexible. (Why do I say *they*? If I say *they*, what am I doing here? They think I am one of them. *Them*.)

I'm here; I go to meetings; I preach—and a lot of it gratifies me. How can it gratify me if I reject all their (our?) premises? Find myself thinking almost constantly in alien patterns of thought. Do I do what I do because I am carried away by momentum (inertia)? terror? habit? Can't think. Very tired. Mind is paralyzed. Can't carry thoughts to their logical conclusion—afraid to. Escape in daydreams—dreams of a life completely different from mine, lovely lovely dreams. I can't accept any of the old answers. I seem unable to find new ones that satisfy me. I don't know what to think anymore. I don't know who I am anymore.

I don't remember where I copied this from (Nietzsche?): "The human being who does not wish to belong to the mass must merely cease being comfortable with himself; let him follow his conscience which shouts at him: 'Be yourself! What you are at present doing, opining, and desiring, that is not really you.'" My roommate found it written on an index card; handed it to me without a word.

This is what I think about good acts: They're like sandbags piled up on the shore against waves and waves of evil. And every time somebody does something good—even if it goes unnoticed, or seems futile—it's another sandbag added to the barricades that stop evil from overcoming us; so the evil never completely conquers the good. *Nothing* is futile. (Sandbags. Or beanbags? Tossing beanbags against the Monster, so the Monster is always bruised by one good act—which can be a *playful* act, play is good.) But the Witnesses think everything has to be measured in terms of its immediate success. (Prefer the mentality of people who went off to the Spanish Civil War, myself.) And it has to be a *total* success: Armageddon, the New World.

There are good, beautiful, anguished people out there; I know there are. I can't despair. I know they *are* there. Their strivings may be futile; but they are beautiful. . . . Anne Frank: "I know it's terrible trying to have any faith . . . when people are doing such horrible . . . But you know what I sometimes think? I think the world may be going through a phase. It'll pass, maybe not for hundreds of years, but some day . . . I still believe, in spite of everything, that people are really good at heart."

Everything must be questioned. No complacency, no repose.

I'd like to see things clearly, for what they are—like a child, or a poet. Yesterday, out preaching with C.H., passed a fruit-and-veg stand, which prompted a homily on God's abundant harvest in the New World, Israel's jubilee, on and on—he never even *looked* at a single peach. Saw nothing. Everything exists in the future, or exists as an object lesson; no delight in the present. . . . The other day, some visitors came to Bethel, made some remark about the harbor view and the skyline (Oh, I *love* it: What kind of King Kong God would want to gobble it up?). L.F., who was shepherding them around, said (with that smile that's supposed to be razzle-dazzle, actually it's more phony than the smiles on pink-plaster madonnas), "Oh, we keep our eyes firmly on God's New World; we just don't have time to admire worldly scenery." I was mortified. (Not supposed to be mortified.) Then L. pointed out all the furniture in the lounge that had been made in our carpentry shop, which, even I can see, is *ugly*. Something has to be done about the plastic flowers. Is good taste an attribute of the Devil? Is it a mistake to want God to have some class? I know that the people in Brooklyn Heights laugh at us, and I know I'm not supposed to care, but I do care. . . . Like when Arnold said *Awake!* mag. sounded as if it were written by reasonably intelligent junior high school students.

Self-denial without a self: If I am to deny myself, I must first have a self to deny.

Reading Fromm on the distinction between universal ethics and "socially immanent ethics." *Love thy neighbor* is a universal ethic and valid for society today and for us all. But Jehovah also commanded the Israelites to stone sex offenders and disobedient children without compassion. Maybe that was a social ethic necessary to perpetuate the society and cultural structure of that time. (Tho you'd think God could have found a better way.) So I don't have to accept that as good, or justify it. But the witnesses make no distinction—they accept both the loving and the stoning as equally valid, both issuing from God. I'm not sure I can love such a God. . . . I wish there were someone I could talk to. Someone who loves God.

Courage is the result of calm consideration of what I risk and what I am after.

Lord have mercy, Christ have mercy. We never pray for mercy, we always pray for justice. Perfect justice—what a horror. *In the name of the Father and the Son and the Holy Ghost, Amen.* I'm not supposed to say that. I can't hate the Catholic Church. Maybe my Catholic baptism "took." I don't know if I believe in God. I love Jesus. Nothing I say or feel makes sense.

When we go from door to door, we urge Catholics and Jews to "read for themselves" what JWs have to say, not to take someone's word for it. ("Investigation never hurt anyone. Read our literature.") Yet JWs are warned on threat of spiritual death not to read the "poisonous" literature of other religions, or secular literature that advances another point of view. Which stems from conviction that we have the only truth. (Or from fear?) Everything I know about other religions, I know from them. Everything I know of God I know from them.

Brother Knorr wears terrible suits. . . . Also ties. . . . I got my $60 yearly clothing allowance today. Spent it on books and plants. So now will have to darn stockings, or ask my mother for money for clothes. Stupid, stupid, stupid thing to do. (Don't regret it.) Also bought tickets to *Death of a Salesman*. Three. Don't know whom to take.

If "The Truth" is so overpowering, why should it not be able to withstand the attacks of higher education?

Took Esther and Mike to see *Salesman*. A mistake. They wanted to leave. . . . Bro. Franz says all "worldly entertainment" is equally bad—*My Fair Lady* just as "distracting" as *Death of a Salesman*, therefore just as "obscene." Told Arnold this; first time I've heard him curse: Said to tell Franz to get a copy of *Hamlet* and shove it up his ————. Which, he said, was already accommodating his (Franz's) head, and, speaking of heads, when was I going to start to use mine? Said a little brute force would do me good, unfortunately he wasn't the man to apply it.

Went for a walk in Greenwood Cemetery. Very comforting. The dead are very nice, like children, they can't do anybody any harm. Wouldn't mind being dead.

I believe that doubt is an indispensable part of the search for truth. I do not believe there is anything greater than I am; except, perhaps, *all men*. And I know how to serve all men only by respecting myself, fulfilling myself, being true to the truth within me. I am part of all men. . . . Is God more important than man? Is reason ridiculous? Logic may have its drawbacks, but it's still the best thing we have. Isn't it?

I can't be bent by laws that others have made.

My mother cowers before life—just as she turned her back and ran up the subway steps when my brother walked dangerously near the tracks. She draws life from this religion. Negative meets negative (= positive?). Life overcame her. This gives her power over life.

I may be mediocre all the rest of my life. My whole life may be mediocre. But that's the chance I take, and I think it's worth taking. I've been living a split-level existence. Can't. I've been telling people for over ten years what life means, but I don't know myself. (And what is the meaning of my own existence, and are those two separate questions?)

My favorite sentences in the Bible: "What is truth?" (Jesus never said.) And, "Jesus wept."

I am so ignorant. My father should have stopped me. He tried. Not hard enough. Arnold, too. The men I love never *force* me to do anything. I wish they would. I wouldn't thank them if they did. I want somebody to make this *stop*. Afraid.

Clearly, something had to give, break, bend: me. Inaction had become intolerable (I couldn't, in honor, stay). Action seemed impossible (I was as afraid to leave as I was afraid of the psychic consequences of not leaving)— *physically* impossible, as in those dreams where you try to escape and your legs refuse to carry out your commands; you are all motion and no movement, stuck. I couldn't tread water any more without eventually drowning in my own contradictions.

I was very, very lucky (what I mean to say is, Providence was divinely good. But that understanding came later; I'm anticipating): I shuddered and shook and cracked, but slowly and quietly, and not explosively; I broke down in stages, not all at once. And picked up the pieces as I went along. Everything that happened was terrible, but the terror went on for so long, I learned to live with it familiarly; I made pain my ally. Like an amusement-park horror-house ride: every time you turn a corner, you say, Well, that one wasn't so bad, and you steel yourself for the next one and think that maybe that one will be easier, and you know there's an end somewhere, if only you can hang on.

The first thing that went was my voice. Which probably got sick of itself: it had told so many lies; it was so many voices, all fighting for equal time. Toward the end, when I rang doorbells to preach, I opened my mouth and nothing came out. Nothing. As effective a paralysis as if God Himself had severed my vocal cords. Out of everything wrong and terrible and bad, something good: I stopped going from door to door. The decision had been made for me; I had been rendered mute. Long, lazy Sunday mornings in bed: for the first time in almost fifteen years, Sunday mornings in bed. Doing nothing. Looking out at the harbor. Waiting. The passivity that is supposed to be woman's greatest enemy, a boon: too passive even to feel guilt.

Then, next, the thing with the stairs. I was still going out in the evenings to Bible studies. Only I didn't talk to would-be converts about the Bible anymore. I don't remember what we talked about (everything here gets blurred); I remember being fed a lot, plates of food and cups of tea, and holding children on my lap. (How good people were! I wish I could remember who they were, to repay them. This is the part of the horror ride where the tunnel is dark; I remember only their kindnesses. I don't know what they made of me. Did they think I was sane?)

But that, too, ended. First, I couldn't walk down stairs. Every house had stairs; the stairs were always narrow. After the doors were shut and the voices and the warmth were over, I hugged the banisters and edged down sidewise like a crab. Sometimes it took me an hour to negotiate a flight of stairs. Stood paralyzed and nauseated at the top of the stairs—a void at the bottom of the stairs. Once, this is funny, I bumped my way down three flights on my ass; couldn't trust my legs. (No; *not* funny.) Then (this *is* funny), I couldn't walk *up* stairs. The paralysis was spreading. (I told Arnold, making light of it. He said, "Fear of going *down* stairs is a death wish. Fear of going up stairs must be a life wish. You're making progress.") I stopped going out at night to Bible studies. (I never said goodbye to any of those people. I forgive myself for this. I can't regret anything anymore.)

Meanwhile, during the day, nothing had changed. (Everything had changed.) Except that I kept falling asleep. Every time I sat down, alone in my room, my eyes closed, and I slept, for what seemed to be five or ten minutes. Small blackouts. I didn't resist them. Delicious little secret deaths.

Then, one night, I was in the subway. (I don't remember what I was doing there, where I was coming from. My diary doesn't tell me. I'd stopped making notes in my diary, too enervated to write.) It was late at night. There were tracks on either side of me that seemed to stretch into black infinity. Marooned. I remember the subway walls—blistery with ugly wet patches—and a dim, sick light. A train pulled in, and I couldn't walk to it. And then another, and another—and I couldn't make myself walk. Will didn't enter into it at all. If I thought of anything at all, it was rats. In the damp, underground, there are rats. Waves and waves of nausea. I began to think I was hallucinating this. But the sweet-sour smell of vomit, mine, was real. (As was the unlovely fact that I had wet my pants.) At 6 A.M., as if a spell had been broken, I walked to a train. I had been standing there for seven hours.

I got to Bethel in time to shower. Doused myself with perfume (Lily of the Valley). I remember the morning text for that day: "What are these wounds in thine hands . . . Those with which I was wounded in the house of my friends."

That night, I began to write in my diary again. I began to rehearse the speech I would give Brother Knorr when I told him I would leave:

> Dear Brother Knorr: I am not equal to demands, fatigued in mind and body. Can't think. Don't have proper motivation. No go-power. Need renewal, refreshment, need to overcome my own moods and sensitivities. Not fair to Jehovah, his organization, or myself if I stay. Feel close to breaking.
>
> They will think this is the easy way. To them it means no responsibility, no doorbells, not having to submit to authority. I know it is the hard way. To fight my way to my own truth, accepting nothing easily, to make my own decisions, to accept my aloneness and my loneliness and to have no one at night to thank for joy or to ask respite from pain, never to be really sure—always struggle and uncertainty.
>
> They'll say rest is the answer. I know it isn't. I know this instinctively, just as I know I must leave. I know if I am ever to become

whole again, it must be in my own way. They'll tell me to work at the Watchtower farm—they send cuckoos to the farm. But I know that if I'm going to find God again, it has to be myself—not fourteen hours of work a day and cows for two weeks and no time to think. Different fetters. I need a broad margin to my life now—room to think under circumstances that make thinking possible. Slowly. I can't afford to get lost in a world of rushing and whirling and falling exhausted into bed every night, waking up knowing that everything is dry and gone.

I must leave a spiritual vocation because I have lost my spirituality. I know that I must leave to find myself. If I do not, nothing will ever be right again. In destroying myself, crushing myself, submerging myself, I am destroying my faith. In finding myself, I may find God. If I can just have the courage to take one step at a time. I must not panic. If life is mean, then I must accept it on my own. No artifice, no illusions. What is there left to bear? Mediocrity, futility, the nothingness of life without God? If that has to be my daily bread, so be it.

And still I couldn't leave.

Now this is where the fairy Godmother (God/Father?) steps in. In the guise of a balding optometrist (charlatan or scientist or saint, he may have saved my life), in Greenwich Village, across the street from St. Joseph's Church (where now I sometimes go to Mass). Why did I go to Greenwich Village, to which I had never been, for eyeglasses? The Lord knows. (I assume, so much have I changed, that He does.) I don't remember the name of that eye doctor; his shop is no longer there.

He took an inordinately long time examining my eyes. He said: "I don't know your life or who you are or what you're doing. But whatever you're doing, you have to stop it. I've never seen anybody so rigidly controlled, and I've never seen so much strain. You're seeing things that aren't there, and you're not seeing things that are there. You may last six days or six weeks or six months, but you're headed for a breakdown, and it won't be pretty when it comes." Then he said, with a flash of insight that frightened me with its acuity, "I sometimes have to tell priests to take six months off. I'm telling you to take the rest of your life off, if that's what you have to do. If you want to live."

It was all I needed.

I ran down the subway steps. No terror. Somebody had finally told me I was crazy, or as close to it as made no difference. I told my roommate not to wake me up for breakfast, overriding her protests almost gaily (the release!): "The doctor says I'm killing myself." Also slyly (and merrily): "He thinks I'm cracked."

All I'd needed was someone to *tell* me. Another voice, a voice outside my own head.

I slept, on and off, for three days. The resident chiropractor stuck his head in once in a while and offered me cans of soup. (I was not particularly enchanted with the resident chiropractor: his main approach to all physical ailments was a vibrator, which he applied to body parts we weren't even supposed to know the names of.) He sat there with his lap full of Campbell's, urging me to get out of bed to receive it. I nodded my thanks. I didn't want to get out of bed. I didn't want soup or voices or vibrators or sympathy.

My roommate looked frightened and didn't ask any questions. She prayed ostentatiously. The only complete sentence I can remember saying in those three days is "Mary, for God's sake, stop *flopping!*" Margarita came in once to ask me if I wanted anything. "An apple turnover," I said.

When the three days were over, I made an appointment to see Brother Knorr. I was taking in great greedy drafts of air; I felt buoyant.

Brother Knorr thought I needed a rest. He suggested that I transfer to the Society's farm in upstate New York: manual work to bludgeon my brain cells into acquiescence. He addressed all his remarks to the Statue of Liberty. Or so it seemed: he sat with his broad back toward me, facing New York Harbor. His enormous desk between us. More than that between us. Worlds (the world) between us.

I said No, no rest. I didn't trust myself to say anything more.

He swiveled around in his chair (made to order in the carpentry shop).

"Weren't you high school valedictorian?"

"No."

"But you were smart."

"Yes."

"That's your trouble."

I was dismissed.

(I was glad he didn't offer to shake my sweaty hand. I thought, on the way down in the elevator, how long it had been since anybody had held me or touched me.)

I packed my suitcase. I called my mother. She came with a friend to collect me, my suitcase, and a driftwood lamp (my only possessions). I dropped off my key at the front desk. It was snowing. We drove back to Bensonhurst in silence. Back to the bedroom I shared with my mother, and to a silence that has remained unbroken between us: she has never asked me why I left.

I would like to be able to say that that was it—clean and finished and a final door slammed; courage exercised and rewarded. But I was back in the bedroom with my mother's weeping; and another charade began.

(I was 22; I had no money and no job. I could have gone to Arnold, perhaps, but I was afraid to ask. I didn't want to go to him as a waif and a stray; and suppose he refused to take me in? And I was in love with him. I always had been. I didn't want him to bring me chicken soup. I was beginning to think about sex, and about his sexuality, which was ambiguous, and I felt stubbornly that I had to do what I was going to do alone—and that in any case, my passion and my pain were beginning to frighten him. He would always be there to offer me his hand; he would never really take me on. I wanted him, however, to ask. He didn't.)

I went to local congregation meetings with my mother. I didn't know how to take the final step out. Three meetings a week. Was this what I had left for? I enrolled in a course at the New School. The course was on a Friday evening, a meeting night. Only two meetings to go to now. No explanations to my mother.

But I never said out loud: *I don't believe.*

I wrote in my diary.

> I am burdened with guilt. My mother acts as if I had robbed her of joy, and I have no way to replenish it. I am guilty of a terrible theft, and can't think how to atone, except by contradicting my own nature. There are constant irritants and daily humiliations, and I am compromising myself so much I can't find myself. I am sorry for her and sorry for myself, and don't see how this will end. I can't stand being the instrument of her pain. I grieve for her (and for myself). What can I do?

> She speaks in a voice of relentless weariness. Her sadness—the feeling that I'm responsible for it. She averts her eyes from me, silently reproachful. I frighten her. . . . Even to read of violence repels her. She runs away from suffering, and I'm a constant reminder to her that her religion is not the lifesaver she chose. She has never been able to contribute her energies to anything she didn't regard as a sure winner. She can't bear defeat. I am her failure.

> I am afraid.

> When will I find my voice?

> All I do is daydream.

> My mother listens to other people's troubles with her body. Her pores seem to absorb the words as she leans forward, drinking it all in, like a sponge, absorbing it into her being. Am I like that? She gives advice. But not to me.

> Priests always look so self-conscious.

> Having gained my freedom, what do I do with it? Was it just freedom from a *place?* Not enough. I'm just beginning to learn the world, to learn how to live. I wanted freedom from that authority so passionately; and yet I'm not freed. I'll never be free till I can think, not dream, until I have the courage to work my thoughts out, and act in accordance with them. The moments that are wasted, the days, the

time! And I'm so afraid. (I'm thinking of Arnold.) I can't think as they do, but I can't cut myself off from them. Why? What am I afraid of? God? Destruction at Armageddon? Loneliness? Alone, cut off, alienated. But I can't take the final step. So many people would be hurt. My mother. But my life is a lie; and I hurt. There is more than one kind of destruction. Not just Armageddon. I am diluting myself, compromising myself. *I don't believe anymore.* But all I know is what I don't know. I've been trained to believe in the wickedness of the world. But there is beauty in the world. I believe it. And I believe in freedom. I believe that no one—not God—can tell me how to live. I believe that if life is ugly I have to find its ugliness for myself. I believe that no one—not God—is greater than I am. . . . I can't say any of this out loud.

Is it right to be happy when others are unhappy?

I never noticed the obscenities on billboards and subway ads before. Now I do. (Why do they always look as if they were in my father's handwriting?)

No vitality. I'm afraid of being alone. And all the going to meetings, what nonsense. All the people I call my friends (*the friends,* they say, as if there could be no others) speak a language alien to my deepest and truest feelings. To keep their friendship I mouth things I no longer believe to be true. This is a great trouble.

Why can my mother accept my brother although he doesn't conform to her standards? She still smiles at him, never at me; he gives her pleasure. But I'm such a disappointment to her. Her religion has taught her that if I'm not religious, in the way she understands religion, and she interprets this to mean if I'm not an active JW, there is "selfishness present." (How they simplify and ignore!) This chills her love and saddens her. Her voice is flat and dull, only alive when it's peevish. I have to learn not to let it frighten me. I can't go on needing her approval. She knows how important it is to me; is that why she withholds it? But it's wrong to accuse her of this cruelty—which is only a reflection of her pain. She is hurting very much.

I'm just beginning to realize how real money is—as real as all the other things, like pain. She hands me a dollar with such a hard, immobile face. I've got to go to work—and she's been hinting. But I don't know what to do. . . . I'm getting bitter (how stupid not to have thought of money), and I'm ashamed of it. It would be easier if I had somewhere to go.

Went to meeting last night. Didn't listen to C.'s speech. Always the same. Also people look at me peculiarly—and look at my mother consolingly. Little Karen cuddled next to me during the *Watchtower* study. How can anyone have the courage to have a child? Only affirmative, deeply religious, happy people. What would I teach a child?

I feel as if I'll drift aimlessly always. I am so afraid. To live a purposeful life must be the greatest of blessings. . . . Wasn't that what I had?

Maybe the person I think A. is existed only in my mind. I'd like either to forget him or to define him and I know that neither is possible. Does he love me? Was he happy that night at his house when he was play-acting that I was his wife? I wish I knew. Sometimes I'm sure he loves me, and other times I feel I've made it all up.

How much of this am I doing for A.? Did he give my struggles meaning? And how much is reaction against my mother?

"Whoever loses his life for my sake will find it." I gave God my life when I was 9 years old. I was giving Him a gift I didn't know the value of. Not much of a sacrifice. If I didn't find fulfillment in religion, where will I find it?

Called A. He has retreated into light witticisms. He can be no refuge.

I began to withhold part of myself, until, little by little, I became two separate persons. And I didn't know which was real. . . . I'm doing it again.

If only they could be moral without condemning those who do not meet their standards of morality! If only I could translate idealism and values into deeds and actions. But I don't know what my values are. I am destroying myself by trying to accommodate one set of actions to another way of thinking. . . . What are other people like, I often wonder.

Masquerade. Two worlds. Play-acting. The face I wear for them to see has nothing to do with my inner reality. The only world in which I am at home. The other day on the subway suddenly realized I could see everybody's face but my own. Suddenly terrified to realize that they could see my face, but I couldn't. Also understood that this wasn't sane—*real*, but not sane. Also felt giddy, and—*superior*. Superior because I knew—absolutely knew—that someday I would die; and didn't think anybody else on subway knew it the way I knew it. Got off subway to find a mirror. Looked at myself for a long time, learned nothing. (Somebody, however, caught me making faces at myself; the next step is talking out loud, muttering to myself like the old ladies—like the colored lady who unbuttons her blouse and does a shimmy on the BMT. My God! . . . Remembered the man who exposed himself to me when I was 10, on subway; I couldn't believe he was playing with *it*, so convinced myself it was a rubber-toy substitute. Wondered why he would want to do such a silly thing. Now nothing surprises me; and I keep thinking of disgusting things.)

How pathetic the way they keep insisting on their happiness—"We're happy, aren't we? Happier than other people?"

Went to a concert at the New School with Cathy. Alexander Schneider—Bach, Haydn. Wondered why C. had agreed to go with me—or, for that matter, why I'd asked her. (I guess I still want the people I've called my friends to *be* my friends.) During the intermission, I said, "It's a pity R. gave up the violin. He shouldn't be operating a clothes press, he should be making music." C. spat out, "Yes, but he'll live in the New World, and you won't." So they are all talking after all, because I don't go out preaching. (We were overheard by woman sitting behind us who teaches my writing class at the New School, who also saw me crying, and was especially tender to me at next class—which had the odd effect of making me feel brittle and irritable. Don't think I know how to respond to kindness anymore.) On the way home, Cathy said, "You're breaking your mother's heart." What about *my* heart? (I know why that tenderness upset me—because I feel myself giving in to self-pity; and am afraid I'll never stop crying if I begin in earnest—my eyes are so dry I can hear a little clicking noise when I blink. I can hear my eyes not crying.)

At the meeting, talk about "filth" of the world: Excerpts from some sensational tabloid about rate of nervous breakdowns among UN members and clergy. So what? How about the rate of breakdowns at Bethel? Also quoted obscure Staten Island paper attacking Tennessee Williams and Arthur Miller for decadence. Brother who gave this talk has never read Tennessee Williams or Arthur Miller. They'll use any quote, any statistic, any crackpot crank to bolster their arguments. Went to bathroom during all this nonsense. Remembered once at convention, Witness in next stall making strange gurgling noises in her throat and sighing: she was masturbating (though I didn't realize it at the time) while they were talking about God and destruction. . . . I don't like masturbating—makes me feel lonely.

I "turn into" the people I'm with. Which is scary. I have a fantasy that twenty of my "friends" will come to my funeral, and they'll all think they're in the wrong place, talking about someone else. One corpse—and twenty different versions of me. . . . I am myself with Arnold.

I don't understand how I can have resigned myself to destruction at a battle I don't believe is coming, at the hands of a God I don't believe exists.

Somewhere Nietzsche says, *The greatness of the deed was too great.* I took this step . . . was not able to follow through . . . could not rise up to what I had done.

When they use words like *compassion, tenderness, gentleness, kindness* they always sound as if they're scolding.

Unhappiness is boring.

Spring came. "Breeding lilacs out of the dead land, mixing memory and desire," Arnold quoted—nourishing, indoors, old wounds and humiliations he would never share with me. But for me, a different alchemy: a thaw, and a release. The winter's hibernation was over (years of hibernation); there was an end to all the squirreling around in my own brain—and a beginning: I felt open to nothing but pure feeling. I felt happiness rising up irresistibly, fiercely; why? Is it too simple to say that I had indeed grown bored with unhappiness? That a basically sanguine temperament had at last asserted itself? Of course it's too simple; but I don't know why the change came, except that I had youth and its regenerative powers on my side, and a determination to choose happiness, to throw everything bleak and wintry away.

(Years later, when I visited a psychiatrist, briefly, he said that given my history, he would have predicted I would be catatonic by the time I was 30; he regarded me as an interesting "specimen." But there are many such specimens walking around; one either dies of bereavement or moves on to other things—and very few people die of bereavement.)

I wanted to run away from the past. And in fact, that April, that May, I did literally run all over the place. Through Prospect Park; the Botanic Gardens, where the cherry trees were in bloom; up and down city blocks, as if some great source of energy had been unleashed. I spent long afternoons in the Gardens; sunlight had never seemed so sweet—not since I was a little child, a happy little pagan (before Jehovah came), hiding inside the overhanging branches of my grandmother's mulberry tree, loving the aqueous light filtering through the leaves, hugging myself in joy. A single cluster of lilacs was enough to intoxicate me, to send me into private raptures—and to send me running. (Sex, Freud would say; and he would be wrong. The thing about that time—when my love for the world was justified by the beauty of the world—was that nothing was a *symbol;* everything, simply and clearly and sweetly, *was.* And it was good.)

In the mild, disturbing air of that spring, even pain was an ally, an exquisite plaything. It was *my* pain. It belonged to me. And it cruelly excluded everyone else's pain. I fell into bed limp and exhausted every night, drunk on the beauty I saw everywhere; and my mother's tears moved me less than spring rain. They were *her* tears, not mine. I hardened my heart against them. And slept well.

There was still Arnold:

> An afternoon at the Botanic Gardens. I lay down on pine needles and moss. Pink leaves from a cherry tree floated around me. . . . A rosy light. . . . Nothing is anchored. . . . The next time I see him I will tell him: *I love you.* Why should it be so hard to say! ("And would it have been worth it, after all, Would it have been worth while, To have bitten off the matter with a smile, To have squeezed the universe

into a ball, To roll it toward some overwhelming question, To say: 'I
am Lazarus, come from the dead,' . . . If one . . . should say: 'That is
not what I meant at all; That is not it, at all.' ") But it will have been
said. I must. I can make him mine—by magic. Even if he doesn't
know. I can become A. I can listen to the same music he listens to,
hang the same picture over my bed that he has hung, so that it will be
the first and the last thing I see each day as it is the first and the last
thing he sees. ("Each day I salute the sun, the ocean and the land for
your dear sake, my love.") The same Picasso print he has—not dishonest, I love the Picasso with the knowing, despairing, wise eyes.
And frame it in white with a blue mat, as he has. I'll buy the records
he loves, read the books he reads. If this is the only way I can have
him, I want him. To be part of his life. Not even loved. Some people
walk in and out of his living room casually—as if it were not enormous to be with him. Just ring the bell and sit near him; I envy them.
I'm not a filling part of his life; I have a walk-on role. I could look at
him forever. I don't require that he be in love with me. If only he
loved me and let me be an active part of his life, why not? I know I'm
not as smart as his friends are. But if I could only be with them. No
one could love him more than I do. I would like to hold him forever,
protect him, be a mother to him, a child, a wife. "You said you might
not want to see me again after your soul-searching," he said. So quietly. Why didn't I tell him then?

The words are fake; the feeling wasn't. One has to be a greater person
than I was not to make the truth sound like lies on paper.

The day I called him, to say the words, and hear the words (so foolhardy, also gallant), he didn't answer his phone.

I loved him till he died. I still do, and miss him very much. And frequently feel the irrational anger of the child abandoned by death, as if his
death were something done to me. And I have thought until recently that
all the passionate loves of my life were somehow grounded in my love for
him, that all the intensity I have brought to other relationships derived
from my unspoken love for him.

I feel now that my love for him was rooted in something greater (but that
is another story); and I learned from him that men are both attracted to and
frightened by the intense love of intense women, and that men do not require women to be passive so that they may be aggressive (it is not as
simple as that, foil, counterfoil). They require women to be passive because
passion/suffering frightens and alarms them. We see passionate, intense
women as freaks, marked. We can only bear to read about them in books; in
real life they make us uncomfortable.

Which is why, though it may not at first seem to follow logically, there is
nothing so tender and thrilling as seeing a man in the posture of prayer and
devotion; not at all because it gratifies women to see men humbling them-

selves, but because it offers us the sight of men who do not flee in manly false pride from passion and suffering, and because in houses of prayer (which are so often women's houses, places where women bring their passion), men in attitudes of devotion take the risk of belief and make themselves vulnerable—they share the climate of risk and vulnerability in which women live, and for which women are so seldom, in worldly terms, rewarded.

Knowing finally (I "knew" everything by instinct in those days) that Arnold would never be my lover—or never fully explain himself to me—saddened me. But not with a crushing sadness. With a dreamy bittersweet sorrow that cast only a faint shadow over my life, not an oppressive mass. (The truth was, I was in love with my sadness—with everything that belonged to me; I loved my mysteries.)

I have a snapshot taken at that time in my life: I am wearing a black leotard and a flared quilted skirt that ends mid-calf in delicious, provocative waves; my feet are shod in Capezio ballet slippers; my mouth is fixed in a Tangee (orange-in-the-tube, pink-on-your-lips) grin; my hair is tortured in an improbable arrangement that has even less to do with art than it has to do with nature; oversized five-and-dime gold hoop earrings graze my neck. It is my Greenwich Village uniform. But Greenwich Village is still largely a country of the mind; and my beauty-parlor perm and my Tangee Natural and my screw-on earrings mark me as ineffably Brooklyn. Everything, in fact, is hopelessly out of sync. (How Diane Arbus would have loved me!) I have created myself in the image of my fantasies, fantasies drawn from movies and novels of the Bohemian life; I look like a child's energetic drawing of something he has never seen—crude, imaginative, and unfinished. The look on my face, bewildered but insanely grinning, is the look I have seen on men's faces two seconds before they've fully understood that their flies are open in public.

Decisions began to make themselves. (They had been making themselves, darkly and mysteriously, in my soul; but when they happened, it was as if I were being acted upon, not acting. I did not understand that all decisions are made this way—a slow ripening.) I stopped going to meetings, with no explanation to God, my mother, or myself. I got a job in Greenwich Village, that finishing school for my generation of energetic, imaginative, bemused young women. And my eccentric upbringing was in many ways a perfect preparation and a passport for my being alive-and-aware (we used the word *aware* a lot) in the Village of the 1950s. I fitted as sweetly into that decade as a nut fits into its shell. Because the thing about the '50s was that everybody—everybody being the people one knew or emulated or loved—felt out of sync with his time, and glad of it. We all cherished our idiosyncrasies and our neuroses; we would have laughed est, AT, Esalen, and all the '60s/'70s psychic-smoosh therapies to scorn. In spite of the somewhat paradoxical fact that practically everyone one knew spent his or her time on the analyst's couch, we couldn't imagine where we'd be without our disfiguring—but *interesting*—neuroses.

Narcissists worshiping our own singularity, we seldom thought that there might be public or group solutions to private problems. We had been teen-agers during the McCarthy, HUAC horror; but neither that cruel nightmare nor the Cold War nor the Korean War—so unlike the children of the '60s were we—served to "radicalize" or politicize us. (In my case, of course, these events had passed over my Jehovah-filled head. I fitted right in with the crowd. And the most interesting problem for people of my age—people who grew up in the '50s—remains how to unite the personal and the political, how to be in the world and of it, but not to be bent out of shape by it.)

Occasionally, it's true, we went to meetings of the Young Socialist Party, and we heaved sighs over our country's racism or America's intervention in the affairs of the banana republics, but mostly we took refuge in the rich interior lives we all believed we had; we did not know, or think to figure out, how our personal lives could mesh with public concerns. It was In to be an Outsider. To be an Outsider was to be of the elect.

People were nice to me! I was constantly amazed by the goodness of people. I had repudiated everything I'd been taught: I had left Bethel and left the Witnesses precisely because I couldn't believe that "worldlings" were "wicked." But every time I saw evidence of kindness, it was with a kind of gratified amazement: I'd been right after all. In my need and innocence and egocentricity, I made the mistake of thinking that to be pleasant was the same as to be good—and I thought that everybody who was nice to me was "good." (I still, to some extent, do.)

After a day at work, and on the weekends, I sat around in coffeehouses and bars, talking about Salinger and Camus, talking about "anguished awareness"—conversations that might have been tailor-made for my own concerns, my own hungers: Camus said "a subclerk in the post office is the equal of a conqueror if consciousness is common to them" (comforting words for a fledgling secretary); Salinger said that the Fat Lady sitting on her porch in the unendurable heat, swatting flies, cancer eating at her insides, was Jesus Christ. Where one registered *God*, the other registered *human*; for both, everything was hallowed by one's awareness of it. They both inclined us to regard pain as a sacrament. Knowing, or feeling, that there were no victorious causes, both loved lost causes, causes that required "uncontaminated souls." Both conveyed the message that the discipline of awareness led, inevitably, to creation: poets and artists were the true seers, the only seers. Both seemed to be living on the dangerous edge of the world. And we said, Whoopee! We'll go live there too.

So we did. We went looking for terrible beauty and beautiful pain, in search of holy fools and noble absurd men.

And if, in our coffeehouses and bars and jazz clubs, we found not poets and artists, but dilettantes and poseurs, men who managed to be thoroughly absurd in the vulgar sense—that is, silly—without being at all noble, we did find plenty of lost causes. Women found men, that is, who spoke the language of despair and the language of ecstasy, and took them to their bosoms and to their beds.

What it amounted to was that we would accept any damned nonsense from a man, provided that it was haloed by poetic *feeling*. If our men were struggling and in pain—not to put too fine a point on it, if they were losers—we brought them cups of consecrated chicken soup.

What we extrapolated from both Salinger and Camus was the message, perhaps unintended, that we were meant to be handmaidens to the gods. To the god-in-men. Camus regarded Don Juan as a great wise man who lived bravely without illusions of eternal love, a man for whom loving and possessing, conquering and consuming, were ways of knowing, means of provoking a nonexistent God. What good and faithful pupils we were! We invested every fast-talking faithless womanizer we knew with noble qualities. We lived to be loved, possessed, conquered, consumed.

I had left a consuming God—and fallen right into my generational trap: I longed to be a long-legged, cool, innocent young woman with an undiscriminating heart—a Salinger/Camus woman, to set off an ideal man's saintliness or heroism, to mediate between him and the harsh world, to console—to provide a backdrop for the essential deeds of an inspired lunatic.

And was nevertheless still a virgin, my search for an inspired lunatic frustrated by the fact that I lived at home. I had scruples about offending my parents' sexual morality while living under their roof and enjoying their protection. Leaving religion, while it had caused my mother irreparable grief, was for me a matter of survival; but going to bed with a man for the sake of going to bed with a man seemed capricious and dishonorable. To say nothing of the fact that I didn't want to go to bed with anyone I wasn't in love with. My sexual scenario was all in my head. I talked about sex all the time, as did everyone I knew; and I waited.

My poor father: He had welcomed me home like a prodigal; and here I was confounding all his expectations all over again. Was I never to be a dutiful daughter? Head in his hands, he awaited my return every night (hymen intact; but how was he to know that?): "How can a pretty girl like you do these things?"

"I want to get my own apartment, Daddy."

"Don't say that—I'll faint."

"But Daddy, I really have to . . ."

He fainted. My father fainted the way other people sneezed: often, and at the slightest irritant. (I was his allergy.) As soon as I left the Witnesses, my father—his daughter returned to him—expected me to conform to his idea

of what good Italian girls did (which was very little of anything). Good
Italian girls didn't leave home, God forbid, except to get married.

Who was getting married? My mother, whose hatred for Arnold had
previously been as intense as her dedication to Jehovah, took it into her
head that I should marry Arnold. Even Arnold (now that I was a hopeless
apostate) was preferable to the fleshpots of Greenwich Village (in which she
had never set foot). But Arnold—whom I still loved, who took me to con-
certs and the theater and kissed me chastely on the lips when we parted—
was never going to marry me; or anyone.

Are our lives determined by a single throw of the dice? If I hadn't had
Arnold to teach me to doubt, would I have learned how to doubt? (I think
so.) If I hadn't gone to Mintons one night almost a year after I left Bethel,
would I have found a reason to leave my mother's house and find my own,
chosen life? (I think so.)

But that one night at Mintons determined the shape my life was to take
for years to come. And it got me out of Bensonhurst in a very quick hurry.

Mintons was a jazz club on 128th Street in Harlem. Charlie Parker had
played there; Billie Holliday still sometimes came in, after hours, with her
phalanx of young men, her gardenias and her poodles, and her broken,
heartbreaking voice. In 1956, it was still a place where two young white
women could go unaccompanied. The night I went with my friend Rosalie
from Queens, I fell in love with the sax player. In about the time it takes to
say, "Will you have a drink with me?"

Now, at that time, when all the girls from Brooklyn and Queens who
wore leotards and dreamed of moving to the East Village were in love with
(men's) suffering, jazz musicians—if they were black—were high in the hierarchy of sufferers. I'm not saying that it was my Florence Nightingale
temperament that made me fall in love with M.; but I'm not denying that
that was a contributing factor. Chemistry did the rest. I went to bed with
him in about the time it takes to say, "Yes, thank you, I'll have a drink with
you."

He was wonderfully appealing: witty, wry, selfish, bitter, self-mocking,
poor, married, a libertine who demanded total commitment from his
women, a good and generous lover (when he was there). A perfect person
with whom to break all the rules. And I was of course determined to break
all the rules. Black jazz musicians were the inner circle of the Outsiders.
Proximity to him guaranteed a place in that privileged circle. I joined a
world celebrated by Beat poets. Paris had its existential chanteuses; I (and
women like me) had the real thing: we lived next to the real cry of the
heart.

Those musicians: they used women to sustain them (both sexually and
financially); and we, I am afraid, played our part in this dicey game. We
objectified them by loving their suffering better than we loved them. The
truth was, most jazz musicians wanted with all their hearts to become safe

studio musicians and to live on Park Avenue with German maids. It was we, their romantic camp followers, who thought the secular equivalent of the Holy Grail could be found at the Five Spot or Mintons or Birdland, we who thought their poverty was a mark of their noble not-belonging. Told to drain life to its dregs, where better could we do it than in smoky clubs, illegal after-hours joints, with wounded men who had lovers in other towns? Everything in that world gratified my hunger for experience; it was like being plunged into pure feeling unsullied by thought. We were chained to men we regarded, not without reason, as rebels and martyrs. The fact that these rebels and martyrs burned us up in the furnace of their own needs made everything all the more dangerous, hence all the more exciting. (And I was used to furnaces.)

That world was full of joy—those men were, after all, true creators, and they laughed a lot. But it was never really happy. To live in and for the moment is deadly serious work, fun of the most exhausting sort.

In her younger days, M.'s mother had been madam of a brothel. "A home for young ladies," she'd told me it was, one morning when she was sipping her cognac (also telling me that I was the "bluesiest" white lady she'd ever met. She was hiding me, at the time, from M.'s wife, a much-put-upon woman given to sudden raids). All the "young ladies" wore red taffeta. This was my introduction to her: M. and I had been seeing each other for about six months when he took me to Dayton, Ohio, where she lived. When we arrived, she was out, running numbers. M. and I went to bed. Sometime in the middle of the night, I felt the covers being pulled off me, and I awoke to find an enormous woman, dressed like a mountain on fire, peering over her son's naked body to examine mine. "B plus," she pronounced coolly; and she patted me on the head and sailed majestically out of the room.

If I'd wanted a baptism of fire into the world (and I did!), I couldn't have made a better choice. (I've never regretted it.)

I had by that time been living in the East Village for four months. (I don't know what the actual geographical distance is from Bensonhurst to Dayton, but the psychological distance could have been measured in light-years.) I had moved, not only because there was a limit to how much I was willing to outrage my family's sensibilities, but because I talked in my sleep. The morning my mother said (in the voice she reserved for the most awful, i.e., sexual, offenses), "You said *terrible* things in your sleep last night" was the morning of the day I began apartment-hunting in earnest.

What amazes me most about the two years I spent with M. was the total absence of sexual guilt. I never for a moment thought what I was doing was bad. If I had any twinges of conscience at all, they had to do with M.'s faraway wife—and those twinges were few: love, I thought, created its own rules, transcended ordinary definitions of right and wrong.

The time I spent with M. burned (I thought) the past away. A year after

I left Bethel, it was as if all those years had never been. M. was my exorcist, well chosen. I compressed a lifetime of learning and feeling and sexually loving into one year.

And so the Jehovah-less 1950s went. When my affair ended (I got *tired*, really), I tried on other lives. Another man, another life: I became a devoted practitioner of serial monogamy (and gave God not a thought), seeking nurturance and a way to live. I did not think of myself as marked by my religious experience, or as singular, or different from any other women I knew. The past had died without funeral rites. (I sometimes exhibited the corpse at parties: "I used to be a Jehovah's Witness." Calculated to amuse. Like saying, "I used to be a Teen-age Werewolf.")

A lot has been made of women's masochism. The women I knew in the '50s suffered from another disorder: we all had multiple personalities. When I said good-bye to M., I said good-bye to the jazz world. And hello to the Cedar Bar, hangout of Pollock and Franz Kline, home of Abstract Expressionists. The next man, you will have guessed, was an Artist. A Poor, Struggling Artist. So I tried on that life. Saturdays outside McSorley's—a Lower East Side bar which did not then admit women to its sacred saw-dusty precincts—sitting on a camp chair, knitting argyle socks for the Artist (those *sensitive* watercolors!). And after that, it was a Writer. A Bold, Uncompromising, Anti-Establishment Writer who hurt a lot. Blood on the page, and *Would you please correct my proofs?* Sundays at literary salons.

And so on. I'm not saying it was altogether bad, that multiplicity of personalities. It was, if you didn't forget entirely who you were, exciting. If you did forget entirely who you were, you could have a '50s identity crisis—after which you usually got married.

I got married.

I had two children.

Dorothy Day has said that the birth of her daughter was so joyous it convinced her of the existence of God. My births were joyous too—orgasmic; I did not, however, as a consequence praise God.

And I thought of God only when my husband, in casual conversation, stated his beliefs; which were that he didn't know if there was a God, but if God existed, God had to be good. Which provoked me to rage: I thought it was stupid, sentimental rubbish and maddeningly devoid of logic, and somehow smug (I couldn't bear his taking the word *God* casually in his mouth, along with his martinis and his gin-and-limes). How could one infer from the fact of God's existence the fact of God's goodness? It didn't follow.

It particularly didn't follow in India, where my husband had gone to work and where we lived. Where was the evidence of God's goodness? In the poverty and degradation that forced one either to cauterize one's senses or to curse one's own impotence every day of one's life? In the rats that bit off the deadened fingers of lepers while they slept? In the deformed beggars who dogged our path every time we set foot in the bazaar with our fat American purses? In the bland carelessness of the very rich who pronounced blessings over quadruple amputees on their way to tea parties where they discussed endlessly whether it hurt a fish to be pierced by a hook? In the bloated bellies of children who stuffed their mouths with mud to satisfy their hunger? In the blind *saddhu* who died outside our kitchen door, naked and erect? Once, when my husband came back from an inspection tour of a leprosarium, I taunted him: Do you still believe that if God exists He is good?

This is the worst fight I ever had with my husband: My son (born in Libya, where evidence of God's goodness didn't seem too manifold either) had been diagnosed (incorrectly) as having leukemia. We were living in Bombay; we got the diagnosis on Christmas Eve (and lived with it for thirty-six hours); I was eight months pregnant with my second child, my daughter. My husband said that he would pray for our son. I flew into an earsplitting rage, wild, demented: he had never, in good times and in fair domestic weather, prayed; how dare he pray now? My husband, in his great grief over our son, hardly knew how to answer the fury I had become. He said, mildly, "Do you mean you're *not* going to pray for Josh?" "Never," I said. "I wouldn't ask a crumb of Him, that bully."

My rage should have taught me something. I persisted in believing that all my ties to God had been severed, that my feeling for God was as moribund as I believed Him to be. I didn't understand how fraught His absence was, how significant.

When I lived in Tripoli, I loved to hear the high sweet call of the *muezzin*, calling the faithful to prayer.

On frequent visits to Rome, I spent most of my time in churches, some of it on my knees.

When I lived in Guatemala, I surreptitiously made the sign of the cross when religious processions passed.

Once, in Warangal, in central India, I entered (as a sight-seer—Eastern religion had little appeal for me) a temple no longer used for worship, set in a wooded hollow in a dry plain. The cool, dry temple smelled of bat dung, a sick-sweetish odor, and of old flower offerings and of centuries of bodies and time. I approached the Shiva altar and immediately felt what I can only describe as a presence—like the rushing and reverberating of great wings. I fled to the Land-Rover outside, words of self-mockery already forming on my lips.

But what was all this but aesthetics, architecture, and aberration? It had nothing to do with God. I would have been outraged at any such presumptuous suggestion.

I was lonely, and purposeless. I was not in love with my husband. (I remember, just before I married him, thinking, "I will never love his body"—and marrying him nevertheless. I thought marriage would be restful; I thought he was good. I was tired. We wanted to love each other; I thought that would be enough.) My children, nourishment and joy, did not provide what I felt I lacked: a central core to my existence. But, I told myself, most overseas wives were purposeless—unless they were able to regard a series of distractions as a life; and most, uprooted, were lonely—unless they were very much in love with their husbands (and sometimes even then).

I remember sitting in the ruins of Leptis Magna, tracing my fingers over mosaics thousands of years old, sitting under a bougainvillea tree (thousands of glorious purple clusters), gazing at the blue-green-turquoise Mediterranean, everything fresh and clean, ancient and formal—and feeling that nothing could ever dazzle or surprise me again.

There is an amphitheater that rises out of the desert in Tunisia, larger than the Colosseum at Rome, and a traveler comes upon it unprepared. It is suddenly, breathtakingly there. Except that it didn't take my breath away. If I had read about it in a book, I would have been thrilled and enraptured. When I saw it, it seemed unremarkable. Everything seemed unremarkable.

When people ask me what I did in India for four years, I say lightly, "I arranged flowers in vases." But of course I did, and felt, much more in that vast, maternal landscape, which is not so much a country as a state of mind. I was loved by two men, and I loved a third—all loves ephemeral, but all forcing a wedge between me and my husband. A tangled but banal story (and a story for another time). I was busy. India defeats busy-ness, as it has defeated travelers, seekers, conquerors. I drifted into and out of experience (changed, in some deep emotional way, by India itself—in a way it will no doubt take me years to fully understand). I drifted. India is not a country to which one gives, or from which one wrests; one can only give *in*—and for the vulnerable, passivity seems a voluptuous form of action. India happens to you. But: "What did you do in India? Did you like it?" "I arranged flowers in vases." One doesn't *like* India; one either loves or hates it, and it is frequently hard to distinguish one emotion from the other and surprisingly easy to entertain both at the same time. So much happened there; but on my 30th birthday in Hyderabad, I thought, This is what they'll write on my tombstone: "She had lovely friends, she gave good parties, she arranged flowers in vases." Thirty; and I had no reason to suppose that I'd ever have more than I had; and it wasn't enough.

I wanted to go home, to America: Listening to Martin Luther King say, "We shall overcome" on the U.S.I.S. overseas radio wasn't quite the real, exciting thing; deploring the war at cocktail parties in Guatemala City (where the Embassy's First Secretary considered Senator Fulbright a traitor) was an exercise in shrill futility. I'd acquired a taste for political activism. I wanted to go home.

We came home. I kept up with the times: came to New York, bought a Brooklyn brownstone, got a divorce, sent my children to a progressive school. It was 1966: civil rights, protest marches, consciousness-raising.

My life was centered around my work, my children, my friends, and an occasional (but never enduring) lover.

What more could one ask for? I had gotten more than I had bargained for when I left religion. I no longer engaged in puerile discussions with myself about whether it was "right" to be happy; I had experienced highs and lows and struggles and uncertainties and joys. Enough joy, always, to redeem the muddle. I reminded myself, occasionally, to prize my sexual and intellectual freedom; it had been bought at very great price. I never ever regretted the decision to leave the Witnesses—which seemed to have been made, in any case, by a very different person from the one I had become. I knew that it had been an act of great courage (or necessity—they are frequently the same thing). I didn't know whether I'd ever be able to find that courage again; but then, I doubted whether I'd ever need it again.

I cherished the intensity I brought to and found in friendships. It sometimes vexed the patience of other people; but it also resulted in friendships that were lasting, sustaining, and sometimes sublime. My work gratified me. (I still haven't recovered from the surprise I felt when I first realized that other people wanted to read what I wanted to write, and I still feel like an impostor. Maybe all writers feel like this; certainly most of the women writers I know do.) My children rescued me from frivolity and tied me to the world in the most healthy and sanguine way. The lesson I learn and relearn from them is that while pessimism of the intellect may be here to stay, optimism of the spirit is still possible. They give the lie to a society that tends to regard children as impediments, devourers of psychic time and energy. They nourish, they replenish; complex human beings, they bring one back to a simplicity that is beyond sophistication. They ask the questions adults find embarrassing to ask, which are the only questions worth asking: *Why?* and *What is good?* (They're also fun.) I love their flesh, the words they speak.

Words: I once had an almost encyclopedic knowledge of the Bible. After I left the Witnesses, I could remember only two Scriptures by heart. One of them was the first verse of the Gospel according to Saint John: "In the beginning was the Word, and the Word was with God, and the Word was God." It seemed to me that no novelist could be capable of such a dense and thrilling sentence. (The Witnesses vitiated and removed the mystery from this text in their *New World Translation of the Bible:* "In the beginning the Word was, and the Word was with God, and the Word was a god.")

There is a Welsh hymn (I didn't for a long time know it was a hymn; I thought it was a love song, which of course it is) that I sang over and over in moments of elation:

> Morning has broken like the first morning
> Blackbird has spoken like the first bird.
>
> Praise for the singing, Praise for the morning
> Praise for them springing fresh from the Word.
> Sweet the rains new fall, sunlit from heaven
> Like the first dew fall on the first grass
> Praise for the sweetness of the wet garden
> Sprung in completeness, where His feet pass.
> Mine is the sunlight
> Mine is the morning
> Born of the one light Eden saw play
> Praise with elation
> Praise every morning
> God's re-creation of the new day.
> Morning has broken like the first morning
> Blackbird has spoken like the first bird.
> Praise for the singing
> Praise for the morning
> Praise for them springing fresh from the Word.

My life was a chosen one; I was luckier than most. It would be a betrayal of my children, of the men and women who have loved me, and a betrayal of self, not to say that it was a good life. But the impulse to praise when there is No One to praise makes the heart sore. I did not, could not, praise the Word.

My experience with the Witnesses—more accurately, the experience of *leaving* that stale, dry religion (which was a form of servitude)—had created a hunger for words unsatisfied by a secular society; unfashionable words: *good, evil, love.* As we progressed into the 1970s, *love* became a word one heard on soap operas or read in gothic romances—or in poetry, of course; but so many poets are more infatuated with death and madness than concerned with love (and every poem that had the word *vagina* or *tampon* or *uterus* in it automatically became a Brave New World "woman's" poem, boring). One could talk about any variety of sexual experience without fear of being thought uncouth; *love* became a closet word that seldom saw the intellectual light of day. So cool were we (and so intent upon having multiple orgasms), we confused love with sentimentality and eschewed them both. The 1960s, when everybody "loved" everybody indiscriminately (which was the same as loving nobody at all), and everybody was "beautiful," put a curse on that word; *love* became as California-tacky as *groovy*.

Freud didn't satisfy that hunger for words; *neurotic* and *healthy* were poor, weak substitutes for *good* and *evil*, reductive and shallow.

"I want what is good," I said to my analyst.

"What is good for *you*," he reproached me gently.

"Why do you join protest marches?" he asked.

"Because the war is evil," I said.

"Now let's talk about the *real* reason you march," he said.

"Why are you ten minutes late?"

"Because my baby-sitter was twenty minutes late, and I have a sick child."

"Now let's talk about the *real* reason you're late."

"Why do you work with poor people?"

"Because they're poor."

"Now let's talk about the *real* reason you work with poor people."

We spoke different languages. Our association was short-lived.

Marxism, with its tension between the idealistic and the pragmatic, came closer to satisfying my hungers, but it left unsatisfied the desire to praise.

(Falling in love, to which I was prone, helped: an elevation of consciousness, a temporary state of grace.)

The sloppy pseudo-spiritual panaceas of the '70s spoke to me not at all. They all seemed gaudy and ephemeral and banal and narcissistic as well as politically reactionary—Werner-wastelands of garbage-language and second-rate ideas, as gritty as processed cheese and about as nourishing. Who wants to jabber endlessly about "experiencing one's experience"? (that's est-talk); and who wants to pretend, as do all our spiritual/assertive-happy gurus, that economics and Hiroshima have nothing to do with the way we live now? I can gaze at my own navel without anybody's assistance.

(If I've not mentioned the Women's Movement, it is because I think it's implicit in everything I've written that I'm a feminist; I fail to understand how any responsible human being can *not* be a feminist. And I hope it goes without saying that I could not have begun to understand my past, or to live with any measure of honesty in the present, without the help of the Women's Movement, which, if it has taught us anything at all, has taught us the dangers of interpreting our experience through the distorting lens of conventional wisdom—although I must say I resisted the Women's Movement for a long time, my experience with the Witnesses having inclined me to the mischievous idea that there can never be a public solution to a private problem. I shied away from Marxism for the same, stubborn, prideful reason: *my* way, alone. Until I understood something very simple: everything is connected. It is helpful to me to understand that I was a victim of the Witnesses' institutionalized sexism and that, ironically, many of the women who choose now to be Witnesses do so because they are casualties of a sexist society seeking desperate remedies.)

There are certain words, as there are certain passages of music, that move us without our knowing why. I cannot tell you why *Let us sit upon the ground and tell sad tales of the death of kings* moves me to tears—any more than I can explain why I find solace in walking through graveyards, touching the tombstones of people long dead (or prove to you that there is more of tenderness and quietude than of morbidity in these wanderings).

I have always, however, understood the magic of one Scripture I carried in my heart when I left the Witnesses; this one, from Isaiah (32:2): "And a man shall be as an hiding place from the wind, and a covert from the tempest; as rivers of water in a dry place, as the shadow of a great rock in a weary land."

When I left the Witnesses, it was to discover the world, which I was prepared to find beautiful. I found what everybody finds: It's as good a place as any to work in, beautiful and ugly in equal measure; there are moments of transcendent joy, and times when the world (like one's heart) is dry and weary.

There are temporary refuges; there are (it seems to those who live without God's grace) no "covert from the tempest," no refreshing river in the dry places, no shadows in which to hide.

Sisyphus, rolling the stone up the mountain, knew the dryness and the weariness and the harshness of the world; poised at the top of the mountain, for one brief moment, before he took up his intolerable burden again, he experienced the joy and exaltation of the free man who carries his burden alone, loving not only the moment of respite, but the burden itself, because it was *his* burden. That moment of intense awareness made up for, justified, an unending struggle against an appointed fate:

> His scorn of the gods, his hatred of death, and his passion for life won him that unspeakable penalty in which the whole being is exerted toward accomplishing nothing. This is the price that must be paid for the passions of this earth. . . . One sees merely the whole effort of a body straining to raise the huge stone, to roll it and push it up a slope a hundred times over; one sees the face screwed up, the cheek tight against the stone, the shoulder bracing the clay-covered mass, the foot wedging it, the fresh start with arms outstretched, the wholly human security of two earth-clotted hands. At the very end of his long effort measured by skyless space and time without depth, the purpose is achieved. Then Sisyphus watches the stone rush down in a few moments toward that lower world whence he will have to push it up again toward the summit. He goes back down to the plain.
>
> It is during that return, that pause, that Sisyphus interests me. . . . I see that man going back down with a heavy yet measured step toward the torment of which he will never know the end. That hour like a breathing-space which returns as surely as his suffering, that is the hour of consciousness. At each of those moments when he leaves the heights and gradually sinks toward the lairs of the gods, he is superior to his fate. He is stronger than his rock. . . .

Sisyphus, . . . powerless and rebellious, knows the whole extent of his wretched condition: it is what he thinks of during his descent. The lucidity that was to constitute his torture at the same time crowns his victory. There is no fate that cannot be surmounted by scorn.

If the descent is thus sometimes performed in sorrow, it can also take place in joy. . . .

When the images of earth cling too tightly to memory, when the call of happiness becomes too insistent, it happens that melancholy rises in man's heart: This is the rock's victory, this is the rock itself. The boundless grief is too heavy to bear. These are our nights of Gethsemane. . . .

. . . The struggle itself toward the heights is enough to fill a man's heart. One must imagine Sisyphus happy.

"I conclude that all is well," says Oedipus, and that remark is sacred.—*The Myth of Sisyphus and Other Essays*, Albert Camus, (New York: Knopf, 1955), pp. 120–23

When I left the Witnesses, I told myself that if I had to spend the rest of my life alone (believing that in all the important things, I would always be alone), the leaving would still have been worth it. I could not foresee the consequences of leaving; but I knew that the act itself was necessary, that I must not try to anticipate the consequences, and that the consequences of not acting would be worse than anything that might happen to me afterward. In all the years that followed, I never found reason to regret my decision, even through all the inescapable desolations and humiliations, the hurts and wounds that life inflicts upon us all. I vowed to accept as truth only that which I knew to be true, and to live—"convinced of the wholly human origin of all that is human"—with only that which I knew to be true. I expected to live and die without certainty, without the absolute, and without absolution.

(Sometimes there was pure joy in remembering why I had left. Crossing the Brooklyn Bridge at night, seeing that skyline burning hot and icy, the skyline that defined and was a symbol for the world—"This is mine, all mine"—I rejoiced; I had chosen it; I loved it (I love it). And sometimes when making love. Or decorating the Christmas tree with my children—squabbling, hassling, but alive and juicy, in love with whatever was human and whatever was magic. At those moments, I remembered the years of deprivation, but only to exult in the riches of the present. The past was like a bad dream. The nights of Gethsemane were lived through; there was always a morning.)

I was (am) often false, frivolous, silly, negligent. I read, when I was 35, the diary of a 17-year-old girl who swore "never to compromise," and I loved her: I was that girl, and I had compromised, and had been compromised. But I had never expected it to be easy. And I could tell myself that I had performed one tremendous, courageous act: I had left a religion that was small and peevish and meretricious to take my lumps and my joys where I found them. Where *I* found them. Nothing further I might ever do would equal that one deed; but it had been done. It was the source of my pride, and of my self-love.

And there were lovers and friends and comrades, brothers and sisters, along the way.

I learned to live with periods of self-loathing, self-doubt. I understood that my nature was too passionate and too intense for comfort—my own, or other people's—and that I had nothing and nobody to bring that passion and intensity to. But that was the price of being fully human: I had learned to live without God. Cynical and charming (and hungering), luckier than most, I made my way.

And that is where the story ought to end.

I thought, in fact, when I began to write this book, that (barring pleasant, but not earthshaking, surprises) the story had ended.

I was wrong.

Some thaw, some release may take place, some bolt be shot back in the barrenest breast, and the . . . hard heart may soften and break into religious feeling.—William James, *Varieties of Religious Experience*

If God does not exist, why isn't the universe all dark brown?—Louise Bogan, *What the Woman Lived*, Jean Limmer, ed.

Batter my heart, three person'd God . . . for I except you entrall mee, never shall be free, Nor ever chast, except you ravish mee.—John Donne, *Holy Sonnets*, XIV

This is the hardest part to write. Perhaps the best way is just to set down the facts.

When I began this book, I was a theological illiterate.

Words like *redemptive* and *sacramental* crept into my vocabulary, nonplusing my friends and vaguely disturbing me. I couldn't find their secular equivalent. I loved saying them.

A magazine asked me to interview Dorothy Day. In the course of a phone conversation, she talked about the Hell's Angels outside one of her Houses of Hospitality and how they were raucously threatening her peace. She said she was going to pray for them at Vespers; and would I join her? I said I was afraid I was unable to pray. She said, "Well, then, dear, I'll pray for you and for the Hell's Angels at Vespers." It tickled me to be thrown in with the Hell's Angels; I thought, You wouldn't catch the Witnesses praying for Hell's Angels; and I loved the word Vespers.

Later that week, a friend sent me a crucifix—a tiny pewter Jesus, warm and soft with age. "Why did you do that? I'm not religious." "Guess again," she said. (I'm not claiming to have seen the hand of God in this; one of the things I despised about the Witnesses was their ability to make supernatural hullabaloo about every natural occurrence if they were involved in it; I am saying that I cherished both the call and the present; and I began to carry the crucifix with me.)

Halfway through writing this book, I had a bitter experience with a man, the long and short of it being that I grew to hate him with a hatred so corrosive I felt I could not survive its toxin.

I did not know what to do with these feelings. I did not feel I could live with them. No admixture of pity—just pure, venomous hatred. I couldn't bear myself. (I have spoken of my mother in terms that are less than endearing. But I want to say: I have always wanted to love her; I have always wanted her to love me. And in fact I do love the person she was before she became what it was perhaps impossible for her not to become. It grieves me that what I've written will grieve her, that my necessities overcame my scruples. Where he was concerned, I had no grief, no pity, no scruples.)

Obsessed, I wrote him letters every day for six months, calling him everything vile and hateful and loathsome. I didn't mail them. They did not act as a catharsis; they made me hate him all the more. (For what it's worth: When we were happy together, he frequently sang—at my request, in a clear Irish tenor—Gregorian chants. He recited the liturgy to me. Anglo-Irish, he'd gone to a Benedictine public school in England; he hated the Church; he—and I—loved to hear the Latin words roll off his tongue— ancient, calm, and formal.) "And she offered her pain up to God." I'd read that in a novel. (What one learns from characters in books!) In desperation, without calculation, I asked God—in Whom I did not believe—to take my hatred away, to exorcise it.

I do not believe in magic.

I woke up the next morning, and the hatred was gone. From which I drew no conclusions.

I was a theological illiterate. I was faced, some time after the incident I have just described, with the task of comparing the doctrines of the Witnesses with the teachings of traditional Christianity. Providentially, I read Teilhard de Chardin. And fell in love with Teilhard; and—even I could not escape drawing the conclusion this time—with God.

Not with the *idea* of God, and not with the little, punitive Jehovah of my youth. With the Triune God of love and mercy who calls us to Him in spite of our callused hearts, "unto whom all hearts are open, all desires known, and from whom no secrets are hid"; with that God Who is "the shadow of a great rock in a weary land," "Begotten of his Father before all worlds, God of light, Light of Light, Very God of very God; Begotten, not made"; with the God Who asks us not to desert the world, but to join our works in the world to His, to be co-creators of the Kingdom of Heaven on earth. I fell in love with the God Who, made flesh, bore the anguish of man (by virtue of which nothing is profane); with the God Whose love brings us back to the things of this world, Who, knowing that the world can be terrifying, blind, and brutal, nevertheless commands us to be happy; with the God Who invites us to believe in the communion of saints and to share in the mystical totality of Christ.

(And don't ask me about the origins of evil, or about rats and bloated bellies and earthquakes and why He permits them. I don't know. When I was a Witness, I had the answer to all those questions, or thought I did. What I did not have was faith in the ultimate goodness of God. Now I don't have answers; I have faith. "For now we see through a glass, darkly; but then face to face: now I know in part; but then shall I know even as also I am known." I only know that I will know. And I know that that leap into belief was not an escape into passivity or resignation or withdrawal from the world; it was the beginning of a truly human struggle to realize God in the world.)

Why not, then, secular humanism? Why Christianity? Theologian Hans Küng says:

> Christians are no less humanists than all humanists. But they see the human, the truly human, the humane; they see man and his God; see humanity, freedom, justice, life, love, peace, meaning: all these they see in the light of this Jesus who for them is the concrete criterion, the Christ. In his light they think they cannot support just any kind of humanism which simply affirms all that is true, good, beautiful and human. But they can support a truly radical humanism which is able to integrate and cope with what is untrue, not good, unlovely, inhuman: not only everything positive, but also—and here we discern what a humanism has to offer—everything negative, even suffering, sin, death, futility.
>
> Looking to the crucified and living Christ, . . . man is able not only to act but also to suffer, not only to live but also to die. And even when pure reason breaks down, even in pointless misery and sin, he perceives a meaning, because he knows that here too in both positive and negative experience he is sustained by God. Thus faith in Jesus the Christ gives peace with God and with oneself, but does not play down the problems of the world. It makes man truly human, because truly one with other men: open to the very end for the other person, the one who needs him here and now, his "neighbor."
>
> . . .
>
> By following Jesus Christ man in the world of today can truly humanly live, act, suffer and die: in happiness and unhappiness, life and death, sustained by God and helpful to men.—*On Being a Christian* (New York: Doubleday, 1976), p. 602

Fair enough; but more telling cases, it seems to me, have been made for secular humanism—Camus, for example, is more thrilling to read than Hans Küng. In the end, whether or not one is a Christian has almost nothing to do with persuasive intellectual argument: it has to do with whether one has experienced God; it has to do with the grace of God—a mystery. It has little to do with how "good" a person is:

> Some . . . seem more inclined to affirm man than to deny God. Again, some form for themselves such a fallacious idea of God that when they repudiate this figment, they are by no means rejecting the God of the Gospel . . . Moreover, atheism results not rarely from a violent protest against the evil in this world.—Vatican Council II, *The Church in the Modern World*, No. 19
>
> It is the believer's conviction that many seek God—and find him in the depths of their being—without realizing it: some through their unrelenting pursuit of truth, justice, the good of the community, or another humanitarian ideal—and many through their insatiable thirst for love. . . . Through their total commitment to a transcendent ideal, they are, to the believer, reaching the absolute we call God. . . .
>
> Sometimes, perceiving no end to their quest, they lapse into a seeming cynicism, take refuge in flippancy or strike out against the believer—but to the discerning believer their reaction is only the measure of their unknowing love, a love that might be far greater than his. The believer must always pray, "O God, some know and serve you as truth, honor, integrity, service . . . as well as I, and perhaps better . . ."
>
> God is truly inaccessible and incomprehensible; we are totally dependent on his revelation of himself and can never take for granted that we know much at all about him and his will for us.
>
> The committed believer and unbeliever then have much in common. Both are dedicated seekers of truth. Both seek in darkness—to both God is an absence, one who is not there, for he is not an object to be found. Yet he is there, for both believer and unbeliever have an objective in their lifelong striving—though called different names, conceptualized differently, by each. To both, then, God is a presence and an absence, one who is there, and one who is not there.—Anthony Wilhelm, *Christ Among Us* (New York: Paulist Press, 1975)

I could not believe in a Church, or in a God, that required me to believe that the goodness and the idealism of the believer surpassed the goodness and the idealism of the nonbeliever. When I left the Witnesses, I said, "God can't kill Arnold." I am not required now to believe that Arnold is damned. I am not obliged to believe that anyone is damned. Which is not to say that evil is not given the name of evil: Blake says, "To love thine enemies is to betray thy friends/That surely is not what Christ intends." That is something to think about: the Church demands that we think and that we listen to the imperatives of our conscience, even when, especially when, the imperatives of our conscience go against the authoritative teachings of the Church. The law is not written on stone; it is written on the heart; that is something the Witnesses—in their literalism—do not understand.

That summer, the summer I read Teilhard and fell in love with God, I had an absolute conviction that He was present, that He was adorable, and finally that His wish to be known was as great as my wish to know Him. That is what I mean by "experiencing" God. I was not, like Paul, blinded by a sudden light, nor, like Saint Teresa, pierced to the quick by the arrows of His love. I did not swoon. My conversion, if it can be called such, did not feel like a sudden fall or a sudden flight. It didn't feel "sudden" at all. It felt like a coalescing, a culmination, a unifying, a knitting together of everything that had ever happened to me; and most of all it felt like a sweetness, sweeter than anything I had ever experienced before. It also did not feel like the end of a road; it felt like the beginning of a walk out of a tunnel into light. It was rapturous. The tears I cried that summer were tears of release, as if something frozen had shattered into a pinwheel of kaleidoscopic light.

I was living at MacDowell, an artists' colony in New Hampshire. I am an urban person; when I think of "Nature," I think of it as something other people do, involving mosquitoes and unidentifiable objects and gibberish noises in the too-dark night. Given a postcard-pretty New England green, I register "lovely"—and feel homesick for a New York bag lady and a bopping Puerto Rican with a transistor radio. (When I was young, there was a ladder leading up to my loft room in my grandparents' country house; it had been built by Bruno Hauptmann, with whom my grandfather had worked. No one could convince me that the scrabbling noises I heard on the roof were chipmunks or field mice or whatever creatures are supposed to inhabit the Country: I waited, every night, for footsteps to ascend the stairs, the ladder, for someone or thing, foreign and malevolent, to come and get me.) Every time I'd spent a summer on the ocean, I'd felt obliged to stand on the shore at night before going to bed, to see if a tidal wave was coming. I never gave any thought to what I'd do if I saw a tidal wave on the horizon; I just needed to reassure myself that the ocean was behaving itself. And I'd never spent a night in the Country without all my clothes on, in case of emergency. As far as I was concerned, the Country was a permanent state of emergency, incompatible with the needs of civilized humans.

But that summer, for the first time, the Country held no fears for me. The physical world had lost its menace, its threatening and overwhelming other-ness; it had never looked so beautiful.

There was this paradox: I felt a heightening of all my excited senses; I felt a profound peace, I entered a deep rest—and I felt a quiet power. This is what I knew: that I would never feel abandoned again. I knew, too, that the rapture would not last, but that all the things that were healed and better would stay healed and better.

Unable to contain my feelings (blasting Bach's *B Minor Mass* on the library stereo, hearing Eliot's solemn dry voice intoning *And let our cry come unto thee* wasn't enough), I talked to my fellow colonists about God. An embarrassing topic of conversation. Responses ranging from "Explain earthquakes" to "All those years I didn't eat meat on Friday, what a waste". . . and one woman's voice saying, "But if you did it for the love of God, it wasn't a waste, was it? That's the point of God: nothing is lost." And another voice saying wryly, "Welcome to the struggle. I'll be glad to know how you manage to reconcile your feminism with your Catholicism. I'm having a rather hard time of it myself." Lectures, mostly from atonal composers, on the venality and the contradictions and the iniquities of the Church (by which they meant the hierarchy). A contrapuntal voice saying, "God's Church is a terrible Church. Nevertheless it is God's Church, God help us."

The response I encountered most often was that I was in the throes of a summer romance. Which wasn't far off the mark. I had surrendered, without a question or a qualm. The questions, the qualms, were to come later. (I do not understand this mystery: faith precedes understanding.) I was later to quarrel with my lover/God; but, having fallen in love/belief, I had established a loving relationship within which to quarrel. So different from the Witness days: my doubts did not terrify me. To try to pray was to pray. To surrender was to lose nothing, but to be immeasurably enhanced. This to me seems the greatest mystery of faith, and the mark of true religion: The believer is enriched; sacrifice is not self-effacement.

When I compare the Church with the Witnesses, I think: The Witnesses explained everything, and explained everything legalistically. The Church does not attempt to explain everything: triumphant, militant, glorious, it is humble enough to get on its august knees and say "We do not know"; "We have committed grave errors." (I do love the paradoxes of the Church. With all the great art and music of the world at its disposal, the church in Peterborough, New Hampshire, alarms the Sunday-morning air with recorded electronic bells—which drives the local good-taste Episcopalians wild, and which I think is funny.) The Church has room for everything, including, God knows, vulgarity. That is what I love about it—that it is catholic, universal.

I sometimes wish, with the nostalgia of all recent converts who revere what they have never known, that the Church would return to its ancient, formal aesthetic ways. The vernacular does not thrill me, nor do folk masses; and—while I know I am guilty of hopelessly objectifying them—I wish that contemplative nuns would go back to contemplating and praying for me instead of throwing pots (there are enough bad potters in the world, and there is not enough prayer); and when my son said to me recently after a nun had visited us, "Since when do priest-ladies look like California stewardesses?" I found myself agreeing. But I know that I am being silly. Because along with all the changes in the Church (some of which I can't help deploring) has come a great openness, an embracing. The Church is in ferment, yeasty and alive. To enter the Church now is to become part of a living organism; choices are required of us all—and to choose prayerfully is harder than to worship by rote.

Mostly when I compare the Witnesses with the Church, I think: To be a Witness meant not to give, but to give *up;* whereas the Church says that not to use one's talents to join one's efforts to God's is "a serious wrongdoing." The Church says that to be godly is to be fully human, and to be fully human is to be godly.

What I fell in love with was the Mass, the mystery of the Sacraments, the liturgy. What I love is God.

I alarmed people in New Hampshire by being religious in what they perceived to be an unreligious way: I tried to steal a Book of Common Prayer (the beauty of that language—*And let our cry come unto Thee!*) from the local Episcopal church (which was beautiful, and where I attended Communion). I didn't think God would mind; my fellow colonists thought the minister would. (It is interesting to me how people who profess not to be religious are always telling people who profess to be religious *how* to be religious.)

I alarmed my friends at home more seriously: When the passage of time had convinced them that this wasn't an aberration, they expressed fear, bewilderment, cynicism ("Are you looking for an ending to your book?")—and worst and most painful, betrayal. They thought my intellect would take a vacation. They thought all my moral values would change (they have not; they have just been given a context). I found it difficult to convince my friends that I was still a feminist, still politically radical, only something had been added: God. In which case, they invariably responded, if nothing has changed, why do you need God? The answer is, of course, that while nothing has changed, everything has changed. I know what the internal changes are; the external changes are still revealing themselves. And when one's conscience propels one in the direction of the Church, there is very little one can do about it; nor would I wish to do anything about it.

It is a source of great joy to me that praise and doubt are not mutually exclusive; that I can question the hierarchy and not be regarded as a reprobate or a bad child; that I can engage in loving arguments with members of the Church and still be part of a loving family, a living community whose voices frequently clash with one another's, but who are united in love of God, united at the Mass. (And at the same time, I do not want to fall into the trap of making things too easy for myself, of accepting only that which is palatable and rejecting out of hand all that is difficult. I have my confessor's help in this—dear, holy man, he got a handful when he got me; and I pray that I have God's.)

Some of my friends say that what all this is about is a return to ethnic origins, a desire—inspired by my association with the Witnesses—for community. They are, of course, partly right. And others, less kindly, ask me why I need a "crutch." (That question usually comes from people in analysis; tact prevents me from asking them the obvious question.)

I do not feel that I have given up intellectual or moral responsibility for my life. I have questions that have to be answered. But I think the answers are to be found within the framework of the Church, and the struggle has to be fought within the framework of the Church—which does not despise questions or questioners. My New Hampshire friend was right: to be a Catholic and a feminist and a leftist sometimes appears to be a fantastic juggling act. I think of the hierarchy's position on abortion, and the Church's statements about sexuality, and of the position of women in the Church—all vexing and painful issues. I am not concerned with the gender of the Deity—Who seems to me to be a living flame, and that takes care of that—and furthermore, if God had come to earth as a woman, no one would have listened to Him/Her. When I learn more about the historical context in which Paul, that maddening, saintly man, wrote, I will be able to come to terms with him, talking about female submission in one breath, saying "In Christ there is no slave, no freeman, no male, no female" in the next. That can come later. In the meantime, I am patient. I have never been so patient in my life. Which is not the same as *passive*. But the thing about this juggling act is that the balls seem to float gaily up to heaven, from where a smiling God, Whom I cannot help thinking of as tenderly amused by the antics of His children, floats them down gently into their noisy hands.

(The last time I went to St. Patrick's Cathedral, a child's red balloon had floated up to the very top of the altar's canopy and affixed itself there. It did not look at all out of place.)

My father says: "Oh, my God, you're doing God-talk again."

I say, "It's different this time, though, isn't it?"

"We're not enemies this time," he says; and, "you're happy." Then he says, "Explain to me why God sent the bears to rip the children who mocked Elijah."

"I can't."

"When you were nine years old, you knew all the answers. And the answers separated us. It's different now."

Everything is different now.

> FATHER, part of his double interest
> Unto thy kingdome, thy Sonne gives to mee,
> His joynture in the knottie Trinitie
> Hee keepes, and gives to me his deaths conquest.
> This Lambe, whose death, with life the world hath blest,

Was from the worlds beginning slaine, and he
Hath made two Wills, which with the Legacie
Of his and thy kingdome, doe thy Sonnes invest.
Yet such are thy laws, that men argue yet
Whether a man those statutes can fulfill;
None doth; but all-healing grace and spirit
Revive again what law and letter kill.
Thy lawes abridgement, and thy last command
Is all but love; Oh let this last Will stand!

Abbreviated Codes for Sources Frequently Cited

CODE	SOURCE
	BOOKS
Aid	*Aid to Bible Understanding* (New York: Watchtower Bible and Tract Society, 1969, 1971)
All Scrip	*All Scripture Is Inspired of God and Beneficial* (New York: WB&TS, 1963)
Babylon	*Babylon the Great Has Fallen!* (New York: WB&TS, 1963)
Children	Rutherford, J. F., *Children* (New York: WB&TS, 1941)
Cole	Cole, Marley, *Jehovah's Witnesses* (New York: Vantage Press, 1955)
Faith	Macmillan, A. H., *Faith on the March* (Englewood Cliffs, N.J.: Prentice-Hall, 1957)
FPL	*From Paradise Lost to Paradise Regained* (New York: WB&TS, 1958)
Hoekema	Hoekema, Anthony A., *Jehovah's Witnesses* (Grand Rapids, Mich.: Eerdmans, 1974)
JWDP	*Jehovah's Witnesses in the Divine Purpose* (New York: WB&TS, 1959)
LGBT	*Let God Be True* (New York: WB&TS, 1946, revised 1952)
Life	*Life Everlasting in Freedom of the Sons of God* (New York: WB&TS, 1966)
NPC	Conway, J. S., *The Nazi Persecution of the Churches* (London: Weidenfeld and Nicolson, 1968)
NWT	*New World Translation of the Holy Scriptures* (New York: WB&TS, 1961)
Qualified	*Qualified to Be Ministers* (New York: WB&TS, 1955, revised 1967)
SS, vol.	Russell, Charles T., *Studies in the Scriptures*, Volumes I–VI (New York: WB&TS, 1886–1904)
Teilhard	Teilhard de Chardin, Pierre, *The Divine Milieu* (New York: Harper & Row, 1960)
This Good	*This Good News of the Kingdom* (New York: WB&TS, 1954, revised 1965)
TMSG	*Theocratic Ministry School Guidebook* (New York: WB&TS, 1971)
Truth	*The Truth Shall Make You Free* (New York: WB&TS, 1943)
Yearbook, date	*Yearbook of Jehovah's Witnesses* (New York: WB&TS, 1927–)

Z&L   Zaretsky, Irving I., and Leone, Mark P., eds., *Religious Move-
                 ments in Contemporary America* (Princeton, N.J.: Princeton Uni-
                 versity Press, 1974)

PERIODICALS

Aw   *Awake!* (New York: WB&TS)
KM   *Kingdom Ministry* (New York: WB&TS)
TW; TWT; ZWT   *The Watchtower* (New York: WB&TS); previously *The Watch
                 Tower* and *Zion's Watch Tower*

Additional Sources

Beard, Charles A. and Mary R., *The Rise of American Civilization*, Vol. I (New York: Macmillan, 1927)

Camus, Albert, *The Myth of Sisyphus and Other Essays* (New York: Knopf, 1955)

Gaylin, Willard, *In the Service of Their Country: War Resisters in Prison* (New York: Viking, 1970)

Küng, Hans, *On Being a Christian* (Garden City, N.Y.: Doubleday, 1976)

Zahn, Gordon, *In Solitary Witness: The Life and Death of Franz Jägerstätter* (New York: Holt, Rinehart and Winston, 1964)

Index

France Amendment, 174
Franco, Francisco, 335
Frank, Anne, 302
Frankfurt am Main (Germany), 300
Frankfurter, Felix, 188, 190
Franz, Frederick W., 37–38, 126, 144, 362
  Bible translation and, 231
  biography of, 143
  at 1950 convention, 181, 269–70
  testimony in Quebec by, 326–27
Freedom of Worship Act (Canada), 326
Free-will Baptists, 42
FRELIMO (Front for the Liberation of
  Mozambique), 308–10
French Guiana, 337
French Revolution, 48–49
Freud, Sigmund, 95, 243, 245, 371, 382
Frick, Wilhelm, 300
Friedman, Leon, 185, 209, 212
From Paradise Lost to Paradise Regained, 222–
  223, 226, 229
Fromm, Erich, 152, 358, 361
Fulbright, J. William, 381

Gabon, 337
Galen, Bishop Clemens von, 290
Gambia, 337
Gandhi, Mohandas K., 19, 200
Garden of Eden, *see* Adam; Eve
Gaylin, Willard, 206–7
Gentile Times, 35–36, 41, 47, 164, 166–67
Germany
  Communists in, 283–84
  Jews of, 160
  See also East Germany; Nazis; West
    Germany
Gerstenmaier, Eugen, 290
Get Christie Love! (TV series), 88
Ghana (Gold Coast), 127, 281, 337
Gibraltar, 337
Gideon, 208
Gilbert Islands, 337
Gilead missionary school, 70, 95, 130, 339
Gobitis case, 189–90, 192, 195
God
  author's final love for, 388–93
  See also Jehovah
*God's Kingdom of a Thousand Years Has
  Approached*, 47, 230
Gorgeous George, 88
Gestapo, *see* Nazis

Goebbels, Joseph, 291, 296
Goering, Hermann, 291–93
Gold Coast, *see* Ghana
Gollwitzer, Helmut, 290
Gorazd, Bishop, 291
Government, Witnesses' attitude toward,
  177–78
Graves, Teresa, 88
Great Britain (England), 127, 130, 228
  aid to, 123n
  International Bible Students Association as
    corporation of, 67n
  Witnesses in, 50, 151, 183, 281, 336
  in World War II, 22, 281
Great Depression, 75
Great Pyramid of Egypt, 44, 45, 50–51
Greece, 123n, 334–35, 337
Greenland, 337
Gregory, Thomas W., 176
Grenada, 337
Grenzdorf concentration camp, 291
Guadeloupe, 337
Guam, 337
Guardini, Romano, 222
Guatemala, 123, 337
  author in, 154, 340, 379, 380
Guinea, 337
Guinea-Bissau, 337
Guru Maharaj-ji, 145
Guyana, 337

Haiti, 337
Hamilton (Canada), 163
Hare Krishnas, 31
Harkin, Tom, 309
Harp of God, The, 223
Haraczaz, Michael, 271
Harris, Richard, 352
Hartman, George, 131n
Hartman, Ray Robert, 202
Harvard University, 96
Hassan, Sophie, 69
Hauptmann, Bruno, 390
Hawaii, 337
Hay, Hope, 118
Heath, William J., 148
Heaven
  Christ's taking power in, 17, 35–36, 164–
    166
  number of places reserved in, 182, 226
Heffernan (attorney), 271

number of members of, 23, 52, 127, 338, 339
no paid persons in, 144, 145
number of magazines distributed by, 52
presidents of, *see* Franz, Frederick W.; Knorr, Nathan H.; Russell, Charles Taze; Rutherford, J. F.
printing operations of, 78, 126–29, 179
publications of, 26–27, 67–68n, 395–96; *see also specific publications*
publications smuggled by, 301, 334
radio station of, 179, 184
solicitations by, 115, 118, 141
Tabernacle of, 67, 115–16, 133
tax exemption of, 130, 133–34
turnover in, 268, 272
working farms of, 95, 129–30
Watch Tower Bible and Tract Society of Pennsylvania (Watch Tower Society), 52–54, 56, 67–68n, 133, 143, 163
structure of, 141, 142n, 168
Watchtower Bible Missionary School of Gilead, 70, 95, 130, 339
Watchtower Farm (Newburgh, N.Y.), 129–130
Watchtower Mission (South Africa), 315–16
Watch Tower Society, *see* Watch Tower Bible and Tract Society of Pennsylvania
Waterman, Sterry R., 212
Wauer, Paul, 305
WBBR (radio station), 179, 184
Weil, Simone, 320, 347–48
Western Samoa, 338
West Germany, 214
aid to, 123n
convention in, 269
number of members in, 127, 337
West View (Philadelphia, Pa.), 131n
Wheat, miracle, 115–20, 146
When Prophecy Fails (Festinger, Riecken, and Schachter), 38
Whiting, Tom, 353–54, 356
Whitman, Walt, *Leaves of Grass*, 70
Who Are Jehovah's Witnesses? (Henschel), 17
Wilfred of Whitby, St., 89
Wilhelm, Anthony, 389
Williams, Joe, 345
Williams, Tennessee, 370
Wirin, A. L., 196
Wittig, Karl R., 300–1

Wolfe, Thomas, 70
Women
appeal of Witnesses to, 28
Beards on historical changes in lives of, 41–42
at Bethel, 347, 352, 353
in India, 342
psychology of, in Witnesses, 87
in Quebec, 328
Russell and, 55–56
as Temptation, 32
in Theocratic Ministry School, 266
Witnesses' attitude toward, 72–88, 107, 162, 383
See also Marriage; Women's Movement; Women's rights
Women's Movement, 80, 89, 383
Catholic Church and, 392–93
Women's rights, Russell on, 58, 64
Woodhull, Victoria, 46, 47
Woodrow (Staten Island, N.Y.), 179, 184
Woodworth, C. J., 147
Work, Witnesses' attitude toward, 252–54
World War I, 35, 163, 164, 166, 171, 173–77
World War II, 19–23, 123n, 177
international persecution of Witnesses during, 280–307, 312, 319, 332
mob violence in, 190–91
Russians baptized during, 330
Witnesses' advice to government during, 270
Worldly success, Witnesses' attitude toward, 88–89
Writing Committee, 142

Yap, 338
Yugoslavia, 281, 332

Zahn, Gordon, *In Solitary Witness*, 298–99
Zaïre (*formerly* Belgian Congo), 315, 318, 338
Zambia (*formerly* Northern Rhodesia), 281, 308, 312–13, 315, 317–18, 338
Zaretsky, Irving I., *see: Religious Movements in Contemporary America*
Zion, Sydney, 190
Zion's Watch Tower, see: Watchtower, The
Zion's Watch Tower and Herald of Christ's Presence, 52
Zion's Watch Tower Tract Society, 52–55
Zulu language, 314, 320

ABOUT THE AUTHOR

BARBARA GRIZZUTI HARRISON is a writer whose articles have appeared in many major periodicals, including *The New York Times, Saturday Review, Ms., Esquire, New York, The Nation, More, McCall's,* and *The New Republic,* and is the author of *Unlearning the Lie: Sexism in School.* She lives in Brooklyn with her two children.